Reviews of Research in
Behavior Pathology

Reviews of Research in Behavior Pathology

DAVID S. HOLMES, *Editor*
University of Texas

JOHN WILEY & SONS, INC.

New York · London · Sydney

Preface

The aim in preparing this book was to bring together a series of papers that review, compare, and evaluate the large amount of empirical research that has been done on some of the important aspects of behavior pathology. Not all areas of behavior pathology are covered by the seventeen articles that are included, but their references to more than 1590 other articles suggest that the topics under consideration are covered rather thoroughly. In selecting articles an attempt was made to include those that present different theoretical positions, a variety of methodological approaches, and numerous research findings, thus providing a firm and broad base for understanding the problems of behavior pathology.

In recent years there has been an increasing interest in the careful scientific investigation of behavior pathology. Because the methods used in any research can affect the results and conclusions that stem from the research, students of behavior pathology have turned more and more to reading original reports of research findings rather than relying solely on the conclusions presented in standard textbooks. In reading the original reports the student can learn exactly how the results and conclusions were reached by the experimenters. Moreover, exposure to numerous examples gives the student considerable knowledge about research methodology, which he may someday apply in his own research.

A number of difficulties are likely to be encountered, however, when the student reads original reports. In terms of the student's interests, needs, background, and ability, original reports often go beyond the point of diminishing returns in describing the apparatus, procedure, and statistical treatment of the data. Although vital to researchers who want to replicate the experiment or to investigate further one aspect of the experiment, such detail is of little benefit to the general student, who may very well become lost in it. Since even professional psychologists with years of graduate training and experience often find it difficult to read research outside their own area, there is little doubt that students sometimes have difficulty in understanding and placing in proper perspective the various original research reports that they read.

The selection of reports to be read by a student may also pose a problem. The student's time will often limit him to only two or three reports in each of the numerous areas of behavior pathology. Because a few articles cannot adequately reflect the entire range of methodologies and results in any one area, the student may be left with a distorted idea of the conclusions that should be drawn about that area of research. Also, the articles that the student reads may have serious limitations or methodological problems that would not be apparent to a reader unfamiliar with other work in the area.

The present collection of readings grew from an attempt to offer to my students in behavior pathology a group of readings that would give them close contact with research methodologies and results and at the same time would expose them to as many different research projects in an area as possible. This was done by having the students read *reviews of research* rather than original research reports. These reviews were published in scientific journals. In articles of this type the authors try to review the methodologies and results of all of the published research available on a particular question or problem, but do not include the small details that are not essential for the readers' understanding. The authors do discuss, compare, and criticize the different methodologies used and also point out the limitations of the results and conclusions reported in the original articles. These discussions and criticisms help to put the various projects into perspective and to protect readers from drawing unjustified conclusions. Because each review deals with the results of many studies, presents necessary details, stays close to the methodology and results of the studies, and offers comments and criticisms to guide the readers' understanding and evaluation, this series of papers seemed to fulfill some of the needs of my students in their study of behavior pathology.

As to the nature and scope of the research reviewed in this book, it should be noted that for the most part only reviews of objective, empirical investigations are included. The book contains very little material from papers reporting uncontrolled case studies, because case studies, although they are often very interesting and provide hypotheses concerning pathology, have usually been inadequate for testing hypotheses, primarily because of the problems of subjectivity and unquantified descriptions. On the other hand, the empirical research reviewed in the papers in this book is not limited to what would be traditionally called experimental research, because some of the data are correlational in nature. In summary, the criteria for inclusion were objectivity and quantification rather than the methods of data collection and analysis. The reviews that met the requirements and were finally selected for inclusion deal with some of the broad, important questions in psychopathology. Most of the reviews were originally published within the last few years. Regardless of the publication date, however, it was felt that the papers dealt with important research on fundamental problems that are still with us. The papers which are included in this book do not, of course, represent a comprehensive coverage of the entire field of behavior pathology. Unfortunately, suitable reviews were not available in all areas. It is hoped, however, that a careful study of the reviews and critiques that are presented will provide the reader with a background and guide for reviewing and evaluating other areas on his own. That is, the study of the reviews should provide the reader not only with a considerable amount of content, but also with an orientation and model for reading other reports of psychological investigations.

The book is organized into four main sections. The three articles in the first section deal with important issues or problems that play a role in all research on behavior pathology: the defining of pathology, the classifying of different types of pathology, and the relationship between clinical and experimental findings. The four articles that constitute the second section deal with research on problems that are usually considered to be of a neurotic rather than psychotic nature. The eight papers in the third section are devoted primarily to considerations of the research on schizophrenia, the most prevalent of the psychotic disorders. Here the data on sociocultural, interpersonal, learning, and biological variables as potential causes of schizophrenia are examined. Although the emphasis is on schizophrenia, the investigations involve considerations of many of the other major disorders as well. In the last two articles therapy rather than pathology per se is the primary concern. More specifically, the research reviewed deals with the application of the principles of learning to the modification of pathological behavior. In terms of the aim of this book an important reason for including the articles on therapy is that investigations of the effectiveness of therapy provide tests of our models for understanding pathology.

A brief editor's introduction opens each article and introduces the reader to the problem area and, where necessary, to the concepts and terminology used in the review. In addition, the reader is alerted to questions and issues that might be kept in mind when reading the reviews and seeking applications of the results. Lastly, these introductions are intended to put the various reviews into a general perspective.

A word of warning should be given at this point. The reader

should not assume that because the articles review all of the research reported on a problem prior to the time of writing, the review will necessarily lead to *an answer* or *a definite conclusion*. Often in an individual research project a hypothesis is offered, the data support the hypothesis, and it appears that the problem has been solved. However, when the seemingly definitive results of an individual project are placed in a larger context with other results and criticisms, the light offered by the once seemingly definitive results often fades or may even be completely extinguished. After reading these reviews, some students have been disappointed or depressed by the lack of clear-cut answers. A comment by August Hollingshead is relevant to concerns about the extent of our knowledge and provides a good preface to the reading of the reviews. After reviewing the state of knowledge with regard to the epidemiology of schizophrenia, he said: "I hope I have not overstressed how little we know about schizophrenia. The question is relative. If our ideal is the precise knowledge to prevent this disease, then our achievement is zero. On the other hand, when we compare what we do know with zero, our achievement is infinite. Nevertheless, the problem is still before us: what gives rise to the phenomena we call schizophrenia? The answer can come only from theoretically oriented and methodologically-disciplined future research" (Hollingshead, Some issues in the epidemiology of schizophrenia. *American Sociological Review*, 1961, 26, 5-13, p. 13). I hope that the following reviews will provide an understanding of what we know as well as an appreciation of the gaps in our knowledge.

DAVID S. HOLMES

Austin, Texas
January 1968

Acknowledgments

I express my grateful appreciation to the authors who granted me permission to reprint their work. As a student of behavior, I give additional thanks to the authors of the reviews, as well as to the individuals who carried out the original research, for furthering and refining our understanding of behavior pathology. Lastly, I thank the publishers who allowed me to reprint the copyrighted material.

D.S.H.

Contents

Reviews of Research in
Behavior Pathology

1

Research Definitions of Mental Health and Mental Illness

INTRODUCTION

This article and the following one are reviews of two important *issues* in behavior pathology: *what behavior is psychopathological* and *how should the different pathological behavior patterns be grouped or classified.* It is the first problem, that is, the definition of psychopathological behavior, which is dealt with in the paper by William Scott. As the reader will see, this problem is considerably more difficult than it first appears. The difficulty of the question is equaled, however, by its importance, because the answer has numerous ramifications for both clinical practice and research. For example, the definition of pathology will determine not only whom clinicians treat and for what, but also whom researchers study and what about them will be studied. Consequently, the answer to this question could broaden, narrow, or completely change the focus of interest and work.

Attempts have been made to skirt the problem of defining *what* behavior is pathological by identifying instead *who* is pathological. One definition—those who are being treated—is used very widely in research, but it entails a number of conceptual problems which are discussed by Scott in his article. Some practical problems can also result from the use of this definition in research. When exposure to treatment per se is used to define the population in which pathology exists, complications arise because there are many variations in the criteria for receiving treatment. These differences can lead to the use of very different research populations in different institutions and therefore can cause confusing inconsistencies in the results of studies carried out in different settings. Alternatively, drawing subjects from sources using different criteria for receiving treatment can result in an unwieldly, heterogeneous research population.

These are only some of the problems that might be caused by the definition of mental health and illness. In reading and comparing the various research reports presented in this book, the reader should be aware of the explicit or implicit definitions of pathological behavior that the various researchers have employed, for these definitions play an important role in determining what will or can be studied and they influence the interpretation, generalization, and application of the results of the research. Some of the issues highlighted by Scott will help prepare the reader for this critical approach.

1

RESEARCH DEFINITIONS OF MENTAL HEALTH AND MENTAL ILLNESS

WILLIAM A. SCOTT

A serious obstacle to research in the area of mental illness lies in the lack of a clear definition of the phenomenon to be studied. The term "mental ill health" has been used by different researchers to refer to such diverse manifestations as schizophrenia, suicide, unhappiness, juvenile delinquency, and passive acceptance of an intolerable environment. Whether some or all of these various reactions should be included in a single category of "mental illness" is not clear from a survey of the current literature. Theories describing the nature and antecedents of one sort of disturbance rarely relate it to another, and there is a paucity of research evidence indicating the extent to which such manifestations are empirically intercorrelated.

In the face of such ambiguity it would appear useful to attempt an organized review of the various definitions of mental illness which are explicit or implicit in recent research, with a view toward highlighting their commonalities and discrepancies on both a theoretical and an empirical level. Such a presentation might help students concerned with causative factors to assess the comparability of previous research findings on correlates of "mental illness," and also point toward some next steps in research to discover the degree to which these diverse phenomena represent either unitary, or multifold, psychological processes.

The research criteria for mental illness to be reviewed here are subsumed under the following categories: (*a*) exposure to psychiatric treatment; (*b*) social maladjustment; (*c*) psychiatric diagnosis; (*d*) subjective unhappiness; (*e*) objective psychological symptoms; and (*f*) failure of positive adaptation. For each category we shall review studies which appear to have employed the definition, either explicitly or implicitly. This will be accompanied by a critical discussion of the adequacy of each definition, together

SOURCE. Reprinted with permission of the American Psychological Association and the author from the *Psychological Bulletin*, 1958, 55, 29-46.

with an assessment, based on empirical data where possible, of the relation between this and other definitions. Finally, we shall attempt to summarize the differences among the definitions, by indicating their divergent approaches to certain basic problems in the conceptualization of mental illness and health.

Mental Illness as Exposure to Psychiatric Treatment

The most frequently used operational definition of mental illness, at least in terms of the number of studies employing it, is simply the fact of a person's being under psychiatric treatment. And this definition is usually restricted to hospital treatment, rather than outpatient service. Nearly all the ecological studies (Belknap & Jaco, 1953; Faris & Dunham, 1939; Gruenberg, 1954; Jaco, 1954; Lemert, 1948; Schroeder, 1942) and most of the studies correlating mental illness with demographic characteristics (Clark, 1949; Frumkin, 1955; Hyde & Kingsley, 1944; Malzberg, 1940; Rose & Stub, 1955) use this as a criterion. They obtain their information from hospital records or, in unusual instances (Hollingshead & Redlich, 1953), from psychiatrists in the area who furnish information about persons treated on an outpatient basis.

Such a definition of mental illness is operational rather than conceptual, but its implicit meaning for the interpretation of research results is that anyone who is regarded by someone (hospital authorities, relatives, neighbors, or himself) as disturbed enough to require hospitalization or outpatient treatment is mentally ill, and people who do not fit into such diagnoses are mentally healthy. Use of hospital records, moreover, requires that the criterion of the nature of the mental illness be the diagnosis which appears on the record.

Shortcomings of such an operational definition are recognized by no one better than its users. The reliability of psychiatric diagnosis is of course open to question, and any attempt to determine correlates of particular kinds of mental disturbance must take into account the large error inherent in the measuring processes. [One study of the association between diagnosis at Boston Psychopathic Hospital and previous diagnoses of the patients at other hospitals showed only 51 per cent above-chance agreement between the two (Milbank Memorial Fund, 1955, pp. 42-43)].

If "under the care of a psychiatrist" is to be regarded as the criterion of mental illness, one must realize the automatic limitation on the size of the mentally ill population that such a definition imposes. Kramer (1953, p. 124) has estimated that the maximum possible number of mentally ill, under such a definition, would be less than 7,000,000 given the present number of available psychiatrists.

It has been suggested by both sociologists (Clausen & Kohn, 1954; Dunham, 1947) and physicians (Felix & Bowers, 1948) that different rates of hospital admissions for different geographical areas may indicate more than anything else about the areas the relative degree to which the communities tolerate or reject persons with deviant behavior (Dunham, 1947). Or as the Chief of the National Institute of Mental Health puts it: researchers using hospital records are dependent on the public's rather uneven willingness to give up its mentally ill members and to support them in institutions (Felix & Bowers, 1948); this in addition to the admittedly unstandardized and often substandard methods of record-keeping used by the various hospitals is likely to render incomparable prevalence and incidence data from various geographical areas.

The effects of such differential thresholds for admission in various communities are difficult to estimate, since they cannot be uniform from study to study. In 1938 a house-to-house survey in Williamson County, Tennessee, yielded nearly one person diagnosed as psychotic, but never having been in a mental hospital, for every hospitalized psychotic from the county (Roth & Luton, 1943). By contrast, Eaton found in his study of the Hutterites (Eaton & Weil, 1955) that more intensive canvassing by psychiatrists did not yield a larger number of persons deemed psychotic than did a more superficial count based on community reports.

Eaton's study did yield higher proportions of neurotic diagnoses the more intensive the case finding procedure became, and this observation relates to the finding in New Haven that neurotics under outpatient treatment came disproportionately from the upper socioeconomic strata (Hollingshead & Redlich, 1953). At first consideration, such differential rates seem readily attributable to the cost of psychiatric treatment, but Hollingshead and Redlich prefer to seek an explanation in the greater social distance between lower-class neurotics and the psychiatrists than in the case of middle- and upper-class neurotics. Whatever the source of rate differences, it is clear that such correlations as have been reported make one wary of the hospital admissions or outpatient figures as indicative of the "true" incidence of psychiatric disorders. Thus the criterion of exposure to psychiatric treatment is at best a rough indicator of any underlying conceptual definition of mental illness.

Maladjustment as Mental Illness

Adjustment is necessarily determined with reference to norms of the total society or of some more restricted community within the society. Accordingly, one may conceptually define adjustment as adherence to social norms. Such a definition of mental health has an advantage over the preceding in encompassing a range of more-or-less healthy, more-or-less ill behavior, rather than posing a forced dichotomy. The operation for assessing mental health by this criterion might ideally be a community (or other relevant group) consensus concerning a given subject's degree of adjustment. This has been approximated by at least one set of studies (Beilen, in press; Beilen, 1957).

Rather than assess consensus by pooling many divergent individual opinions, it is possible to assume that a law or other visible sign of social norms constitutes the criterion against which adjustment is determined. Such reference is employed in studies of suicide (Durkheim, 1951; Henry & Short, 1954) or juvenile delinquency (Hathaway & Monachesi, 1955) or divorce (Locke; Terman & Wallin, 1949) as indicants of maladjustment. While the operational criterion may become dichotomous in such cases (whether or not the person comes in contact with the law), this is not necessarily so. Gordon (Gordon et al., 1950) has suggested considering the "biologic gradient" of suicide, extending from contemplation of the act to its actual accomplishment.

Finally, it would be possible to assess degree of adjustment with reference to some externally defined set of requirements for a given social system. Thus a work situation might be seen as demanding a high level of productivity from all its members, and the degree of adherence to this standard becomes the criterion of adjustment, without reference to the individual opinions of the group members or to the manifest norms of the group. This criterion of conformity to the requirements of a given social structure has not been explicitly employed by any of the researchers covered in the present review, but it has been hinted at (Lindemann et al., 1950) and remains a possibility, provided that the structural requirements of a social system can be determined independently of the members' behaviors.

Theory of social structure suggests that these three criteria of adjustment would tend toward congruence: The demands of a particular social system lead to the development of social norms, which are expressed in laws or customs and also in the individual participants' notions of what is acceptable behavior. Lack of congruence may be taken as evidence of cultural lag, of poor correspondence between manifest and latent function within the social structure, or of defensive psychological processes within the participating individuals. Since all of these factors supporting discrepancy do occur within most social systems, the criteria may be expected to yield somewhat different results.

When maladjustment is assessed by community consensus, one finds considerable divergence of opinion among various segments of the public regarding what constitutes good and poor adjustment. The Minnesota Child Welfare studies (Beilen, 1958) showed differences in criteria for assessing adjustment among different occupational groups in the community. Teachers tended to emphasize standards different from those emphasized by ministers, who in turn displayed some differences from a more heterogeneous group of community adults. Beilen concludes that it is meaningless to discuss "adjustment" in the abstract or to contemplate the prediction of "adjustment" in general. One must specify *adjustment to what, adjustment to whose standards* (Beilen, 1957). Lindemann reflects this relativistic conception of mental health when he states: "We find it preferable not to talk about a 'case' in psychiatry—rather, we try to assess functional impairment in specific situations as viewed by different professional groups in the community. So a 'case' is really a relationship of possibly pathogenic situation and appropriate or inappropriate behavior to that situation. It is often a matter of arbitrary choice whether such a person becomes an object of psychiatric care" (Lindemann, 1953, p. 130).

Thus, though adjustment appears a more conceptually adequate criterion of mental health than does exposure to treatment, the necessity for considering different personal frames of reference and the demands of different social structures poses seemingly insurmountable obstacles to the establishment of mutually consistent operational definitions. All such difficulties which lie "hidden," as it were, under the psychiatric treatment criterion, come to the fore to plague the researcher trying to establish a criterion for adjustment which applies to the treated and nontreated alike.

Psychiatric Diagnoses as Criterion for Mental Illness

There have been a few studies in which entire communities or samples of them have been systematically screened, either by direct examination (Rennie, 1953; Roth & Luton, 1943) or by evidence from community records or hearsay (Eaton, 1955; Eaton &

Weil, 1955; Tietze et al., 1942). Here the criterion for mental illness or health need not be dichotomous, but can be divided into
several gradations. Such intensive case-finding can be expected to
increase the yield of persons classified as neurotic (Kramer, 1953,
p. 124) over that provided by the criterion of exposure to treatment, but whether the psychotic group is thereby increased will
depend on the community (Kramer, 1953, p. 124; Roth & Luton,
1943) and, of course, on the standards for diagnosis employed by
the particular investigator.

The lack of standardization of diagnostic procedures and criteria
contributes to the incomparability of mental illness rates derived
from such studies (Kramer, 1953, p. 139; Tietze et al., 1943). So
long as the criterion of assessment is largely dependent on the
psychiatrist's subjective integration of a different set of facts for
each subject, nonuniform results can be anticipated. Expensive and
unreliable though the method may be, it at least places the judgment regarding mental illness or health in the hands of professionals, which is not the case when adjustment is the criterion.
And though hospitalization is in part determined by the judgment
of professionals, *who* is sent to the hospitals for psychiatric diagnosis is, for the most part, out of the hands of the psychiatrists.
As Felix and Bowers (1948) have observed, it is the community
rather than the clinician that operates the case-finding process
today, and this will continue to be so until diagnostic examinations
are given regularly to all people.

Mental Illness Defined Subjectively

It has been maintained by some that a major indication of need
for psychotherapy is the person's own feeling of unhappiness or
inadequacy. Conversely, the degree of mental health may be assessed by manifestations of subjective happiness, self-confidence,
and morale. Lewis (1951) quotes Ernest Jones to the effect that
the main criterion for effect of therapy is the patient's subjective
sense of strength, confidence, and well-being. Terman (Terman,
1938; Terman & Wallin, 1949) has used a "marriage happiness"
test, composed largely of subjective items, and Pollak (1948) has
suggested that old-age adjustment be assessed in terms of the person's degree of happiness or well-being in various areas of his life.

That such criteria of mental health correlate somewhat with independent diagnosis by physicians has been indicated in two sorts
of studies. In the Baltimore Eastern Health District (Downes &
Simon, 1954), cases diagnosed psychoneurotic were found to ex-

press complaints about their own physical health; it is suggested that persons who report chronic nervousness can be classified as suffering from a psychiatric condition. Rogers has maintained that a marked discrepancy between one's "perceived self" and "ideal self" constitutes evidence of psychiatric disturbances (Rogers, 1951), and some empirical studies lend support to this position. When Q sorts of subjects' self concepts are compared with Q sorts of their ideal selves, it is possible to distinguish psychiatric groups from nonpsychiatric groups on the basis of the degree of discrepancy between these two measures (Chase, 1956). Furthermore, progress in therapy (as judged by the therapists) tends to be associated with increasing similarity between the patient's self concept and ideal self (Rogers & Dymond, 1954).

Though subjective well-being is an appealing criterion for mental health in ordinary daily living, it might be presumed that under some circumstances psychological defense mechanisms could operate to prevent the person's reporting, or becoming aware of, his own underlying unhappiness and disturbance. Jahoda (1953) has rejected happiness as a criterion for mental health on somewhat different grounds: Happiness, she says, is a function not only of the person's behavior patterns, but of the environment in which he moves. If one wants to relate mental health to characteristics of the environment, then one must not take as a criterion of mental health something that already presupposes a benign environment. "There are certain circumstances in which to be happy would make it necessary first to be completely sick" (Jahoda, 1953, p. 105).

Such objections to this criterion imply that it is possible to find persons who are mentally ill by some other criterion, yet who nevertheless report themselves as happy or self-satisfied. Empirical demonstration of this implication is not available at present. In fact, while one study predicted defensively high Q sorts for the self concept of paranoid psychotics, they were found to have a greater discrepancy between self- and ideal-sorts than normals, and no less discrepancy between these measures than psychoneurotics (Chase, 1956).

Mental Illness Defined by Objective Psychological Symptoms

It is generally accepted almost by definition that mental illness entails both a disordering of psychological processes and a deviation of behavior from social norms (Clausen, 1956). The latter aspect of disturbance may be assessed as maladjustment to one's social environment (discussed above) ; the former aspect can presumably be assessed by psychological inventories aimed at the assumedly critical processes. The distinction between the psychological inventory approach and the subjective assessment procedure discussed above is not really a clear one. Subjective well-being may be regarded as one of the psychological processes which becomes disordered. Yet more "objective" measures of psychological process, which do not require the subject's verbal report of his degree of happiness, are frequently preferred, both to guard against purposeful distortion and to tap areas of disorder which may not be accompanied by subjective counterparts.

Such "objective" psychological inventories may represent various degrees of manifest purpose. For some, the objective of assessment is transparent, and the only reason they are not classed as devices for subjective report is that they stop just short of requiring the subject to report his overall level of well-being. Such a manifest-level inventory is Halmos' questionnaire concerning the respondent's difficulties in social relations (Halmos, 1952).

At a somewhat less obvious level are such inventories as the MMPI, the War Department Neuropsychiatric Screening Battery, and the Cornell Medical Index, which require subjects to check the presence of various subjective and objective symptoms (e.g., "I smoke too much."). Once validated against an accepted criterion, such as psychiatric diagnosis, these are frequently used as criteria themselves. Rennie constructed a composite instrument of this type to assess his respondent's levels of mental health in the Yorkville study (Rennie, 1953); at the same time, a validity analysis of the index was undertaken, by correlating each item with independent psychiatric diagnosis on a subsample of the respondents. On the basis of their experience with such a composite instrument one of Rennie's colleagues (Langner, personal communication, August 1956) suggests caution in abstracting parts of previously validated batteries, since the item validities are sometimes not maintained when they are used out of context of the total instrument.

An adaptation of the psychiatric screening battery approach for use with children is suggested in the work of the St. Louis County Public Health Department (Glidewell et al., 1957). It involves obtaining information about symptoms from the children's mothers rather than from the children themselves. Naturally, the symptoms covered must be of the "objective" type ("Does Johnny wet the bed?") rather than of the "subjective" type ("Does Johnny worry a lot?"). As validated by an outside criterion (teachers' and psychiatric social workers' ratings of the child's level of adjustment), the number of symptoms reported by the mothers appears to be a promising index of the child's mental health.

A general characteristic of the types of psychological inventories reviewed so far is that each item in the battery is assumed, a priori, to involve a "directional" quality, such that one type of answer (e.g., "yes" to "Are you troubled with nightmares?") may be taken as indicative of psychological disorder, and the opposite answer as indicative of normal functioning. Thus the index of disturbance is computed by adding all the positive indicators, weighted equally. That alternative methods of test construction may yield equally, or more, valid indices of mental illness is indicated by the extensive investigations of McQuitty (1954).

McQuitty proposes several different methods of diagnostic test scoring, each based on explicit assumptions about the diagnostic procedure which the test is supposed to represent. One of the simplest assumptions, for example, is that an individual is mentally ill to the extent that his psychological processes deviate from the culturally modal processes. Thus, any type of multiple-alternative test may be administered to a group of subjects representing a "normal" population. Each alternative of each item is then scored for its "popularity." The score for a subject is then computed by adding the popularity scores of the items he checks (McQuitty calls this the T method of scoring); a high popularity score is taken as evidence of mental health (by this "typicality" criterion).

An alternative assumption proposed by McQuitty as underlying the diagnostic procedure might be that mental health is manifest to the degree that the subject's responses conform to any pattern of answers represented by a significant number of community people, regardless of whether that pattern is the most popular one. Such an assumption leads to a scoring procedure (H method) whereby a subject's index of "cultural harmony" is based on the degree to which his responses to different questions "go together" in the same manner as do the responses of all people in the sample who check the same alternatives he does.

Elaborations on these basic procedures provide for differential weighting of responses depending on their degree of deviance (WH method), and correction for "linkage" between successive pairs of items (WHc method).

The Bernreuter Personality Test and the Strong Vocational Interest Inventory were administered by McQuitty to a group of mental patients and to a group of university students; they were scored by different methods, the scores for the two tests were correlated, and the mean scores of the two groups compared. Results of the comparisons indicate that: (a) when appropriately scored, the Strong can discriminate mental patients from normals, though not so well as the Bernreuter; (b) better results are obtained if, instead of treating each answer as a separate, independent measure, it is evaluated in terms of the pattern of other answers with which it occurs (WHc scoring method); (c) within the Bernreuter, those items which correlated best with the total score (McQuitty's WHc method of scoring) and provided the best discrimination between patients and normals tended to be of the "subjective" type (i.e., they depended on the subject's introspection, as in "Do you often have disturbing thoughts?") rather than the "objective" (items which an observer could report, such as "Do you talk very much?"); (d) different scoring procedures appeared differentially appropriate for the "subjective" and "objective" items; (e) when the "subjective" items were scored by the method most appropriate to them (i.e., the method which best discriminated patients from normals), and the "objective" items by their most appropriate method, the correlation between the two scores on the same group of subjects was about zero, indicating that two independent dimensions of mental health were being tapped by these two sets of items.

A separate study reported by McQuitty (1954) indicated that the simple T method of scoring (based on the popularity of the subject's responses) both subjective and objective items significantly discriminated groups of school children classified on the basis of independent criteria of mental health. There is considerable evidence from these studies that, especially with respect to those traits measured by the "objective" items, the person may be regarded as mentally ill to the extent that he deviates from the dominant community pattern.

The foregoing studies provide a certain amount of evidence that measures of mental illness according to psychometric criteria relate to two of the criteria discussed earlier—maladjustment and psychiatric diagnosis. That such concurrent validation may yield somewhat different results from studies of predictive validity is indicated in Beilin's report of the Nobles County study (1957). Two indices of student adjustment predictors were constructed, one (the "pupil index") based on students' responses to five different instruments, and the other (the "teacher index") based on teacher ratings. Both were concurrently validated against teachers' descriptions of the youngsters. Four years later the mental health of the youth was assessed by a number of different criteria—community reputation, interviewers' ratings, self-assessment, and an adaptation of the Rundquist-Sletto morale scale. The predictors correlated significantly with only some of the subsequent criteria, and all of the correlations were at best moderate. The "pupil index" correlated better with the interviewer's rating than with the community reputation criterion; while the "teacher index" correlated better with the subject's subsequent community reputation than with the interviewer's rating. Or, stated more generally, the psychologist's predictor predicted better to a psychologist's criterion, and a community predictor predicted better to a community criterion. Though the time span (four years) between the predictor and criterion measures may have been such as to allow for considerable change in the subjects, one is nevertheless reminded by these results that various criteria for mental health are not necessarily highly correlated.

In summarizing the various studies of mental health and illness defined by psychological testing batteries, we may note that many of them lack an underlying conception of the nature of mental illness from which to derive items and scoring procedures (a notable exception being McQuitty's measures), that some of them challenge the notion of the unidimensional nature of mental health, and that their degree of correlation with other criteria, such as adjustment or psychiatric diagnosis, depends on the nature of the criterion.

Mental Health as Positive Striving

A radically different approach to the assessment of mental health is indicated in the definitions proposed by some writers with a mental hygiene orientation. Gruenberg suggests that, though failure to live up to the expectations of those around him may constitute mental illness, one should also consider the person's failure to live up to his own potentialities (Gruenberg, 1953, p. 131). Frank speaks of the "positive" aspect of mental health—healthy personalities are those who "continue to grow, develop, and mature through life, accepting responsibilities, finding fulfillments, without paying too high a cost personally or socially, as they participate in maintaining the social order and carrying on our culture" (Frank, 1953). In a less exhortative tone, Henry (1953) discusses successful adaptation of the person in the "normal stressful situation." He sees many normal situations as situations of inherent stress. Some individuals in them develop mental disease, while others may develop out of them a more complex, but more successful, personality. It is this successful coping with the "normal stressful situation" that Henry regards as indicative of mental health.

Jahoda has translated this kind of emphasis on the positive, striving, aspects of behavior into a set of criteria amenable to empirical research. She proposes three basic features of mental health (Jahoda, 1955): (a) The person displays active adjustment, or attempts at mastery of his environment, in contrast to lack of adjustment or indiscriminate adjustment through passive acceptance of social conditions. (b) The person manifests unity of personality—the maintenance of a stable integration which remains intact in spite of the flexibility of behavior which derives from active adjustment. (c) The person perceives the world and himself correctly, independent of his personal needs.

Active mastery of the environment, according to Jahoda, presupposes a deliberate choice of what one does and does not conform to, and consists of the deliberate modification of environmental conditions. "In a society in which regimentation prevails, active adjustment will hardly be possible; in a society where overt regimentation is replaced by the invisible compulsiveness of conformity pressures, active adjustment will be equally rare. Only where there exists social recognition of alternative forms of behavior is there a chance for the individual to master his surroundings and attain mental health" (Jahoda, 1955, p. 563).

Such an approach is quite at odds with the subjective criterion of personal happiness, and with the conformity criterion referred to above as "adjustment." Attempted adjustment does not necessarily result in success, for success is dependent on the environment. The best mode of adjustment only maximizes the chances of success. It is mentally healthy behavior even if the environment does not permit a solution of the problem (Jahoda, 1953). Jahoda proposes that the criterion of happiness be replaced with some more "objective" definition of mental health, based on an explicit set of values.

In an unpublished community study, Jahoda apparently attempted to assess only two of the aspects of mental health incorporated in her definition. Veridicality of perception (actually, of judgment) was determined by asking respondents to estimate certain characteristics of their communities concerning which objective data were available (e.g., proportion of people with only grade-school education), and at the same time inferring needs to distort reality from the respondent's evaluative statements about the problem (e.g., how important R believed education to be). This method of assessing need-free perception was regarded as something less than satisfactory (Jahoda, personal communication, August, 1956), since the need was so difficult to determine, and it was difficult to establish unambiguously that distortion of judgment was due to the operation of a need rather than simply to lack of valid information.

The degree of attempted active adjustment was assessed by first asking a respondent to mention a particular problem in the community, then determining what he had done, or tried to do, about it, and how he felt about the problem at the time of interview (Jahoda, 1953). Three aspects of respondents' reactions were coded from their replies (Jahoda, 1953); (a) the stage of problem solution—mere consideration of the problem, consideration of solutions, or actual implementation; (b) the feeling tone associated with the problem—continued worry or improvement in feeling (either through partial solution or through passive acceptance); (c) the directness or indirectness of the approach—i.e., whether R went to the heart of the problem in his attempted solution or merely dealt temporarily with recurrent nuisances.

In her analysis Jahoda relates her measures of problem-solving and need-free perception to various characteristics of the respondents and of the communities in which they live. The relationships are interesting (e.g., in one of the communities the level of problem-solving was related to the degree of community participation of the respondent), but they appear to leave unanswered a basic question about the appropriateness of the criteria. If one accepts Jahoda's definition of mental health as involving the two components assessed in the study, then the results can be interpreted as showing what patterns of social interaction are associated with mental health. But if one is skeptical about the meaningfulness of the definition, then he is impelled to search for correlations between her two measures and other, more commonly accepted, criteria of mental health. These are not reported, although it would appear to be a fair question to ask about the relation of her concepts to those employed by other researchers.

If one is wedded to the happiness criterion of mental health, for example, one may speculate about the possibility of a negative relation between it and those provided by Jahoda. Unhappiness could conceivably lead to excessive coping behavior (attempted adjustment), or excessive coping behavior might elicit negative reactions from others which, in turn, would increase one's unhappiness. In like fashion, it could be that need-free perception would lead to increased unhappiness, since psychological defenses are not available to bolster one's self image. Though Jahoda might reject the suggestion that happiness is even relevant to her criteria, it would appear useful to explore, both conceptually and empirically, the interrelations among other measures of mental health and the novel one proposed by her.

Clausen (1956) has maintained that researchers must ultimately face the task of relating mental health defined in positive terms to the individual's ability to resist mental illness under stress. At present it is not known whether they represent a common factor or are independent characteristics. Jahoda (personal communication, August, 1956) suspects that positive mental health, as she defines it, may indeed represent a dimension orthogonal to that represented by the conventional psychological symptoms of mental illness. Thus, from a different approach than that employed by McQuitty comes the suggestion that mental health and illness may be a multidimensional phenomenon.

In employing these particular criteria, especially that of active adaptation, Jahoda seems willing to defend the evaluative standards implicit in it. And it may well be that values relating to attempted mastery of problems are every bit as defensible as the values of conformity implied in the adjustment criteria discussed above. Nevertheless, the former appear to exemplify the application of the Protestant ethic to the mental health movement in a manner which might introduce culture and class biases into one's conclusions. Miller and Swanson (1953) have hypothesized that lower-class children will show more defeatism than middle-class children, as a result of different interpersonal and environmental experiences. Would they thereby be less mentally healthy by any standards besides those of the middle class? Truly, the problems posed in setting up absolute values from which to judge mental health and illness are perplexing.

Basic Problems in the Definition of Mental Health and Illness

Underlying the diversities in definition of mental illness one can discern certain basic differences of viewpoint concerning how the phenomena should be conceptualized. We may abstract certain foci of disagreement by posing the following four points of contention: (a) Does mental illness refer to a unitary concept or to an artificial grouping of basically different specific disorders? (*b*) Is mental illness an acute or chronic state of the organism? (*c*) Is maladjustment (or deviance from social norms) an essential concomitant of mental illness? (*d*) Should mental illness be explicitly defined according to values other than social conformity?

Each of the proposed definitions takes a stand, either explicitly or implicitly, on one or more of these issues. It is likely that resolution of disagreements will depend in part on the outcome of future empirical research. But at least some of the divergence inheres in the theoretical formulation of the problem, and is more a matter of conceptual predilection than of empirical fact. In either case, if one is to arrive at consistent theoretical and operational definitions of mental illness, it would be well to make explicit one's bias concerning each of these issues, and attempt to rationalize it in terms of his conception of the causes of disturbance.

The Unitary or Specific Nature of Mental Illness

The position that mental illness is manifest in some rather general form, regardless of the specific diagnostic category in which the patient is placed, would appear to be implicit in the subjective definition of the phenomenon. If the person's feeling of happiness or adequacy is regarded as the crucial indicator of his mental state, this would appear to imply that over-all health or illness can be assessed for a particular person, regardless of the area of functioning referred to. Likewise, the definition of mental health in terms of purposeful striving or active adjustment tends to ignore differences in the underlying bases for such striving or lack thereof. Such a position has been stated explicitly by Stieglitz: "The mensuration of health . . . closely parallels the measurement of biological age as contrasted to chronological age. . . . We are no longer seeking to discover specific disease entities, or even clinical syndromes, but attempting to measure biological effectiveness in adaptation" (Stieglitz, 1949, p. 79). And such a unitary view of the phenomenon is implied in Schneider's comment: "The major 'cause' of mental disease is seen as some form of disorientation between the personality and society (Schneider, 1953, p. 31).

By contrast, the specific view of mental illness is taken by Gordon: "What we choose to call mental disease is an artificial grouping of many morbid processes. The first essential, in my opinion, is to separate the various entities, and in the approach to an epidemiology of mental diseases, to center attention on some one condition, or a few selected conditions, which have functions in common with other mass diseases well understood in their group relationships" (Milbank Memorial Fund, 1950, p. 107). McQuitty offers empirical evidence in favor of a specific view, in his isolation of two quite independent measures of mental illness (by psychological testing), both of which correlate with external diagnostic criteria. And he further speculates that the number of areas in which the degree of personality integration varies rather independently is probably greater than the two which he has isolated. "One might expect that mental illness might develop within any one or more patterns. In order to understand the mental illness of a particular subject, we must isolate the pattern, or patterns, of characteristics to which his mental illness pertains" (McQuitty, 1954, p. 22).

While the weight of opinion and evidence appears to favor the multidimensional view, this may simply be a function of the operational definitions employed (e.g., mental health defined by responses to a battery of tests is bound to turn out multidimensional to the extent that intercorrelations among the test items are low). But there are yet insufficient empirical data collected from the unitary point of view to test whether its assumption is correct. Indeed, it seems quite plausible that both happiness and active adaptation may be partially a function of the situation, hence the concept of mental health implied by them must become multidimensional to the extent that they allow for intersituational variability.

The Acute or Chronic Nature or Mental Illness

The psychologist's testing approach to assessing mental illness inclines him toward a view of the condition as chronic. That is, the predisposing conditions within the organism are generally presumed to be relatively enduring, though perhaps triggered off into an actual psychotic break by excessively stressful situations. The epidemiological approach, on the other hand, is usually concerned with the counting of actual hospitalized cases, and this may incline one toward a view of mental illness as predominantly acute. Felix has espoused this position explicitly: "Unless the kinds of mental illness are specified, I can't conceive that mental illness is a chronic disease. More mental illnesses by far are acute and even short term than there are mental illnesses which are chronic and long term" (Milbank Memorial Fund, 1950, p. 163). Of course, the epidemiological approach traditionally considers characteristics of the host, as well as characteristics of the agent and the environment. But the predisposing factors within the organism seem to be regarded, like "low resistance," not as a subliminal state of the disease, but rather as a general susceptibility to any acute attack precipitated by external factors.

It is easier to regard a psychosis as acute than it is similarly to regard a neurosis, since in the former disorder the break with normal behavior appears more precipitate. However, such a judgment, based on easily observable external behaviors, may be unduly superficial. Even in the case of such a discrete disturbance as suicide, at least one writer (Gordon, et al., 1950) recommends considering the biologic gradient of the disorder. He distinguishes varying degrees of suicide, with successful accomplishment as merely a possible end product. Where such continuity between morbid and nonmorbid states can be discerned, the possibility of chronic disturbance might well be considered.

The Problem of Mental Health as Conformity to Social Norms

The criterion of mental health based on adjustment clearly implies that conformity to the social situation in which the individual is permanently imbedded is a healthy response. And such an assumption would appear to be lurking, in various shapes, behind nearly all of the other definitions considered (with the possible exception of some of the "positive striving" criteria, which stress conformity to a set of standards independent of the person's immediate social group). In fact, McQuitty's methods of scoring psychological inventories are all explicitly based on the assumption that conformity (either to the total community or to a significant subgroup) is healthy.

If the stability of the larger social system be regarded as the final good, or if human development be seen as demanding harmony in relation to that social system, then such an assumption would appear basic and defensible. But one is still impelled to consider the possibility that the social system, or even an entire society, may be sick, and conformity to its norms would constitute mental illness, in some more absolute sense. If any particular behavior pattern is considered both from the standpoint of its adaptability within the social structure to which the individual maintains primary allegiance and from the standpoint of its relation to certain external ideal standards imposed by the observer, perhaps a comparison of the two discrepancy measures would yield information about the degree to which the social system approaches the ideal. On the other hand, such a comparison might be interpreted as merely indicating the degree to which the researcher who sets the external standards is himself adapted to the social system which he is studying. The dilemma appears insoluble.

The Problem of Values in Criteria for Mental Health

The mental hygiene movement has traditionally been identified with one or another set of values—ideal standards by which behavior could be assessed as appropriate or inappropriate. The particular set of values adopted probably depends to a considerable degree on who is doing the judging. Such a diversity of evaluative judgments leads to chaos in the popular literature and to considerable confusion in the usage of the term "mental health" in scientific research. Kingsley Davis (1938) presented a rather strong case for the proposition that mental hygiene, being a social movement and source of advice concerning personal conduct, has inevitably been influenced by the Protestant ethic inherent in our culture. The main features of this Protestant ethic, as seen by him, are its democratic, worldly, ascetic, individualistic, rationalistic, and utilitarian orientations.

To the extent that research on mental health is based on criteria devolved from such an ideology, it is middle-class-Protestant biased. To the extent that it is based on some other set of "absolute" norms for behavior, it is probably biased toward some other cultural configuration. At least one researcher, Jahoda (1953), has clearly taken the position that mental health criteria must be based on an explicit set of values. There is some advantage in allowing the assumptions to come into full view, but in this case the resulting criteria appear to be rather specialized and not comparable with those used by other researchers. Perhaps the difficulty lies not so much in the existence of explicit assumptions as in their level of generality. If a more basic set of assumptions could be found, from which the diverse criteria for mental health and illness can be derived, then comparability among researches might better be achieved. One would be in a better position to state when mental illness, as defined by psychological tests or by absence of active adjustment, is likely to be displayed in mental illness defined by psychiatric diagnosis or deviance from community standards.

Summary

The various categories of definitions of mental illness discussed here have been distinguished primarily on the basis of their differing operational definitions; the dependent variables employed in empirical research on the phenomena are clearly different. Moreover the conceptualizations of mental illness explicit or implicit in the empirical criteria are often quite divergent—viz., the radically different viewpoints underlying the "maladjustment," "subjective unhappiness," and "lack of positive striving" definitions.

Certain conceptual and methodological difficulties in each of these types of definition have been noted: "Exposure to treatment" is deficient in that only a limited proportion of those diagnosable as mentally ill ever reach psychiatric treatment. "Social maladjustment" is open to question because of the varying requirements of different social systems and the diversity of criteria for adjustment employed by community members. "Psychiatric diagnosis" provides an expensive, and often unreliable, method of assessing the state of mental health. "Subjective unhappiness" can be criticized as a criterion since it may be a function of intolerable environmental conditions as well as the psychological state of the person, and is subject to distortion by defense mechanisms. The validity of "objective testing procedures" appears to depend considerably on the method by which they are scored, and there is strong evidence that a major component of their score may simply be the degree of conformity of the person to the community average. Finally, criteria included under the heading of "positive striving" are subject to question in that they are inevitably based on disputable value systems of their proponents.

While many of these difficulties would not be considered damaging from the point of view of certain of the definitions of mental illness, they run into conflict with others. Also they suggest certain basic incompatibility among the various approaches to conceptualization of mental illness. Whether these incompatibilities should be reconciled by further theoretical and empirical exploration, or whether they should be regarded as valid indicators that mental health and illness constitute multidimensional phenomena is still a moot question. We can only note that various studies employing two or more of these different categories of criteria have tended to yield moderate, but not impressive, interrelations.

The criterion of "exposure to psychiatric treatment" has been related to "maladjustment," "psychiatric diagnosis," "subjective unhappiness," and "objective psychometrics." Also "maladjustment" has been related to "psychiatric diagnosis" and to certain "objective" measures; and "psychiatric diagnosis" has been related to both "subjective" and "objective" measures of mental illness. The areas of interrelationship for which no empirical studies have been found are between "subjective" measures and both "maladjustment" and "objective" assessment; also between the "positive striving" criteria and all of the other types of measures.

Two directions for future theory and research are indicated by these results. First, more investigations are needed of the extent of relationship among the various criteria, and of the conditions under which the magnitudes of the intercorrelations vary. Second, assuming absence of high intercorrelations under many conditions, it would be worthwhile to explore the implications of poor congruence between one measure and another—implications both for the person and for the social system in which he lives.

REFERENCES

Beilen, H.   The prediction of adjustment over a four year interval. *Journal of Clinical Psychology*, 1957, **13**, 270-274.

Beilen, H.   The effects of social (occupational) role and age upon the criteria of mental health. *Journal of Social Psychology*, 1958, 48, 247-256.

Belknap, I. V., & Jaco, E. G.   The epidemiology of mental disorders in a political-type city, 1946-1952. In *Interrelations between the social environment and psychiatric disorders*. New York: Milbank Memorial Fund, 1953.

Chase, P.   Concepts of self and concepts of others in adjusted and maladjusted hospital patients. Unpublished doctoral dissertation, University of Colorado, 1956.

Clark, R. E.   Psychoses, income and occupational prestige. *American Journal of Sociology*, 1949, 54, 433-440.

Clausen, J. A.   *Sociology and the field of mental health.* New York: Russell Sage Foundation, 1956.

Clausen, J. A. & Kohn M. L.   The ecological approach in social psychiatry. *American Journal of Sociology*, 1954, **60**, 140-151.

Davis, K.   Mental hygiene and the class structure. *Psychiatry*, 1938, **1**, 55-65.

Downes, Jean, & Simon, Katherine.   Characteristics of psychoneurotic patients and their families as revealed in a general morbidity study. *Milbank Memorial Fund Quarterly*, 1954, **32**, 42-64.

Dunham, H. W.   Current status of ecological research in mental disorder. *Social Forces*, 1947, **25**, 321-326.

Dunham, H. W.   Some persistent problems in the epidemiology of mental disorders. *American Journal of Psychiatry*, 1953, **109**, 567-575.

Durkheim, E.   *Le suicide.* Paris: F. Alcan, 1897. (English translation, Glencoe, Ill.: Free Press, 1951).

Eaton, J. W.   *Culture and mental disorders.* Glencoe, Ill.: Free Press, 1955.

Eaton, J. W., & Weil, R. J.   The mental health of the Hutterites. In A. M. Rose (ed.), *Mental health and mental disorder.* New York: Norton, 1955.

Epidemiology of mental disorder. New York: Milbank Memorial Fund, 1950.

Faris, R. E. L., & Dunham, H. W. *Mental disorders in urban areas.* Chicago: Chicago University Press, 1939.

Felix, R. H., & Bowers, R. V. Mental hygiene and socio-environmental factors. *Milbank Memorial Fund Quarterly,* 1948, **26,** 125-147.

Frank, L. K. The promotion of mental health. *Annals of American Academy of Political and Social Science,* 1953, **286,** 167-174.

Frumkin, R. M. Occupation and major mental disorders. In A. M. Rose (ed.), *Mental health and mental disorder.* New York: Norton, 1955.

Glidewell, J. C., et al. Behavior symptoms in children and degree of sickness. *American Journal of Psychiatry,* 1957, **114,** 47-53.

Gordon, J. C., et al. An epidemiologic analysis of suicide. In *Epidemiology of mental disorder.* New York: Milbank Memorial Fund, 1950.

Gruenberg, E. M. Comment in *Interrelations between the social environment and psychiatric disorders.* New York: Milbank Memorial Fund, 1953.

Gruenberg, E. M. Community conditions and psychoses of the elderly. *American Journal of Psychiatry,* 1954, **110,** 888-896.

Halmos, P. *Solitude and privacy.* London: Routledge & Kegan Paul, 1952.

Hathaway, S. R., & Monachesi, E. D. The Minnesota Multiphasic Personality Inventory in the study of juvenile delinquents. In A. M. Rose (ed.), *Mental health and mental disorder.* New York: Norton, 1955.

Henry, A. F., & Short, J. *Suicide and homicide.* Glencoe, Ill.: Free Press, 1954.

Henry, W. E. Psychology. In *Interrelations between the social environment and psychiatric disorders.* New York: Milbank Memorial Fund, 1953.

Hollingshead, A. B., & Redlich, F. C. Social stratification and psychiatric disorders. *American Sociological Review,* 1953, **18,** 163-169.

Hyde, P. W., & Kingsley, L. V. Studies in medical sociology. I: The relation of mental disorders to the community socio-economic level. *New England Journal of Medicine,* 1944, **231,** 543-548.

Jaco, E. G. The social isolation hypothesis and schizophrenia. *American Sociological Review,* 1954, **19,** 567-577.

Jahoda, Marie. The meaning of psychological health. *Social Casework,* 1953, **34,** 349-354.

Jahoda, Marie. Social psychology. In *Interrelations between the social environment and psychiatric disorders.* New York: Milbank Memorial Fund, 1953.

Jahoda, Marie. Toward a social psychology of mental health. In A. M. Rose (Ed.), *Mental health and mental disorder.* New York: Norton, 1955.

Kramer, M. Comment in *Interrelations between the social environment and psychiatric disorders.* New York: Milbank Memorial Fund, 1953.

Lemert, E. M. An exploratory study of mental disorders in a rural problem area. *Rural Sociology,* 1948, **13,** 48-64.

Lewis, A. Social aspects of psychiatry. *Edinburgh Medical Journal,* 1951, **58,** 241-247.

Lindemann, E., et al.   Minor disorders. In *Epidemiology of mental disorders.* New York: Milbank Memorial Fund, 1950.

Lindemann, E.   Comment in *Interrelations between the social environment and psychiatric disorders.* New York: Milbank Memorial Fund, 1953.

Locke, H.   *Predicting adjustment in marriage: a comparison of a divorced and a happily married group.* New York: Holt, Rinehart and Winston. 1951.

McQuitty, L. L.   Theories and methods in some objective assessments of psychological well-being. *Psychological Monograms,* 1954, **68**, No. 14.

Malzberg, B.   *Social and biological aspects of mental disease.* Utica: State Hospital Press, 1940.

Miller, D. R., & Swanson, G. E.   A proposed study of the learning of techniques for resolving conflicts of impulses. In *Interrelations between the social environment and psychiatric disorders.* New York: Milbank Memorial Fund, 1953.

Pollak, O.   Social adjustment in old age. *Social Science Research Council Bulletin,* No. 59, 1948.

Rennie, T. A. C.   The Yorkville community mental health research study. In *Interrelations between the social environment and psychiatric disorders.* New York: Milbank Memorial Fund, 1953.

Rogers, C.   *Client-centered therapy.* Boston: Houghton Mifflin, 1951.

Rogers, C., & Dymond, Rosalind.   *Psychotherapy and personality change.* Chicago: University of Chicago Press, 1954.

Rose, A. M., & Stub, H. R.   Summary of studies on the incidence of mental disorders. In A. M. Rose (Ed.), *Mental health and mental disorders.* New York: Norton, 1955.

Roth, W. F., & Luton, F. H.   The mental health program in Tennessee. *American Journal of Psychiatry,* 1943, **99**, 662-675.

Schneider, E. V.   Sociological concepts and psychiatric research. In *Interrelations between the social environment and psychiatric disorders.* New York: Milbank Memorial Fund, 1953.

Schroeder, C. W.   Mental disorders in cities. *American Journal of Sociology,* 1942, **48**, 40-47.

Stieglitz, E. J.   The integration of clinical and social medicine. In J. Galdston (Ed.), *Social medicine—its derivations and objectives.* New York: New York Academy of Medicine, 1947. New York: Commonwealth Fund, 1949.

Terman, L. M., et al.   *Psychological factors in marital happiness.* New York: McGraw-Hill, 1938.

Terman, L. M., & Wallin, P.   The validity of marriage prediction and marital adjustment tests. *American Sociological Review,* 1949, **14**, 497-505.

Tietze, C., et al.   Personal disorder and spatial mobility. *American Journal of Sociology,* 1942, **48**, 29-39.

Tietze, C., et al.   A survey of statistical studies on the prevalence and incidence of mental disorders in sample populations. *Public Health Report,* 1943, **58**, 1909-1927.

2

Psychiatric Diagnosis:
A Critique

INTRODUCTION

The diagnostic system presently used in psychology and psychiatry has received a considerable amount of criticism. The critics have suggested that the system is neither reliable nor valid and that it is of little value in providing answers to the important questions that are asked about patients. Since to a very large extent research in behavior pathology relies on the classification of patients, the question of the quality of the diagnostic classificatory system is of the utmost methodological importance. Also, since the nature of the system may reflect an orientation with regard to the *nature of pathology,* it is important to understand the concept on which the system is based, because different orientations may lead to completely different approaches to the problems. It is some of the critical issues arising from the diagnostic system that Edward Zigler and Leslie Phillips discuss in the article that follows.

The present diagnostic system classifies patients mostly on the basis of their *symptoms* at the time of the diagnosis. This does not differ from the classification systems used in other sciences, such as botany where plants are classified according to their present structural characteristics. For the purpose of description or counting, this system is perfectly suitable. This system of classifying patients has been severely criticized, however, for it seems to be of little value when one asks such questions as *what caused the disorder, what should be done* for the patient, and *what is the patient's prognosis.* In reviewing these criticisms, Zigler and Phillips point out that the system was not designed to answer prognostic and etiological questions. These questions, which the authors suggest are inappropriate for the present system, are asked of the system because over the years etiological and prognostic correlates have erroneously been attributed to the *descriptive* classes. Although understanding the nature of the system may explain some of the difficulties with its use (or misuse), is this descriptive system of value in comparing different types of patients with each other or with normals in the search for etiological factors and preferred treatments? That is, the explanation of why the system does not work will not help us answer the questions that face us. It may well be that we need a number of classification systems in which each would take different factors into consideration in an attempt to accurately answer different questions.

The criticism that diagnoses (i.e., symptom patterns) are not related to etiological factors and the defense that the present diagnostic system was not designed to demonstrate these relationships both suggest the possibility that there may not be a consistent relationship between specific symptoms and specific etiological factors. That is, there may be no consistent one-to-one relationship between causes and symptoms. If in fact such a relationship did exist, the present system would be able to answer at least the questions related to etiology, hence there would be no need for that criticism. The idea that there is no consistent relationship between a cause and a symptom is of course a departure from the traditional medical model that is usually followed in psychology. In view of what currently seems to be a lack of support for a consistent cause-symptom relationship, one might consider abandoning the medical model as being an inappropriate means of conceptualizing the problem or one might assume that the research methodology has not yet been accurate enough to ferret out the relationship that in fact exists. This is an issue that psychologists are debating at the present time. Whether or not there is a consistent relationship between causes and symptoms has important implications for research strategy. If there is no direct relationship between specific causes and specific symptom patterns (i.e., diagnoses), then the diagnosing of patients as we now do it becomes useless as a way of classifying patients for research on etiological factors. Because of this and allied problems, the reader should keep in mind the issues discussed by Zigler and Phillips when reading the reviews of research that have relied on diagnostic classes.

2

PSYCHIATRIC DIAGNOSIS: A CRITIQUE

EDWARD ZIGLER AND LESLIE PHILLIPS

The inadequacies of conventional psychiatric diagnosis have frequently been noted (Ash, 1949; Cattell, 1957; Eysenck, 1952; Foulds, 1955; Harrower, 1950; Hoch & Zubin, 1953; Jellinek, 1939; King, 1954; Leary & Coffey, 1955; Mehlman, 1952; Menninger, 1955; Noyes, 1953; Phillips & Rabinovitch, 1958; Roe, 1949; Rogers, 1951; Rotter, 1954; Scott, 1958; Thorne, 1953; Wittenborn & Weiss, 1952; Wittman & Sheldon, 1948). The responses to this rather imposing body of criticism have ranged from the position that the present classificatory system is in need of further refinement (Caveny, Wittson, Hunt, & Herman, 1955; Foulds, 1955), through steps towards major revisions (Cattell, 1957; Eysenck, 1952; Leary & Coffey, 1955; Phillips & Rabinovitch, 1958; Thorne, 1953; Wittman & Sheldon, 1948), to a plea for the abolishment of all "labeling" (Menninger, 1955; Noyes, 1953; Rogers, 1951). As other investigators have noted (Caveny et al., 1955; Jellinek, 1939), this last position suggests that the classificatory enterprise is valueless. This reaction against classification has gained considerable popularity in clinical circles. The alacrity with which many clinicians have accepted this view seems to represent more than a disillusionment with the specific current form of psychiatric diagnosis. These negative attitudes appear to reflect a belief that diagnostic classification is inherently antithetical to such clinically favored concepts as "dynamic," "idiographic," etc. Thus, a question is raised as to whether any diagnostic schema can be of value. Let us initially direct our attention to this question.

On Classification

The growth among clinicians of sentiment against categorization has coincided with a period of critical reappraisal within the

SOURCE. Reprinted with permission of the American Psychological Association and the authors from the *Journal of Abnormal and Social Psychology*, 1961, 3, 607-618. This investigation was supported by the Dementia Praecox Research Project, Worcester State Hospital, and a research grant (M-896) from the National Institute of Mental Health, United States Public Health Service.

behavioral sciences generally (Beach, 1950; Brower, 1949; Cronbach, 1957; Guthrie, 1950; Harlow, 1953; Koch, 1951; MacKinnon, 1953; Marquis, 1948; Rapaport, 1947; Roby, 1959; Scott, 1955; Tolman, 1953; Tyler, 1959). This parallel development is more than coincidental. The reaction against "labeling" can be viewed as an extreme outgrowth of this critical self-evaluation, i.e., that psychology's conceptual schemata are artificial in their construction, sterile in terms of their practical predictions, and lead only to greater and greater precision about matters which are more and more irrelevant. It is little wonder that in this atmosphere, conceptualization has itself become suspect nor that Maslow's (1948) exposition of the possible dangers of labeling or naming has been extended (Rotter, 1954) as a blanket indictment of the categorizing process.

The error in this extension is the failure to realize that what has been criticized is not the conceptual process but only certain of its products. The criticisms mentioned above have not been in favor of the abolishment of conceptualization, but have rather been directed at the prematurity and rarifications of many of our conceptual schemata and our slavish adherence to them. Indeed, many of these criticisms have been accompanied by pleas for lower-order conceptualization based more firmly on observational data (Koch, 1951; MacKinnon, 1953; Tolman, 1953).

In the clinical area, the sentiment against classification has become sufficiently serious that several investigators (Cattell, 1957; Caveny et al., 1955; Eysenck, 1952; Jellinek, 1939) have felt the need to champion the merits of psychiatric categorization. They have pointed out that diagnosis is a basic scientific classificatory enterprise to be viewed as essentially the practice of taxonomy, which is characteristic of all science. Eysenck (1952) puts the matter quite succinctly in his statement, "Measurement is essential to science, but before we can measure, we must know what it is we want to measure. Qualitative or taxonomic discovery must precede quantitative measurement" (p. 34).

Reduced to its essentials, diagnostic classification involves the establishment of categories to which phenomena can be ordered. The number of class systems that potentially may be constructed is limited only by man's ability to abstract from his experience. The principles employed to construct such classes may be inductive, deductive, or a combination of both, and may vary on a continuum from the closely descriptive to the highly abstract.

Related to the nature of the classificatory principle are the implications to be derived from class membership. Class membership may involve nothing more than descriptive compartmentalization, its only utility being greater ease in the handling of data. Obversely, the attributes or correlates of class membership may be widespread and farreaching in their consequences. The originators of a classificatory schema may assert that specified behavioral correlates accompany class membership. This assertion is open to test. If the hypothesized correlates represent the full heuristic value of the diagnostic schema and class membership is found not to be related to these correlates, then revision or discard is in order. A somewhat different type of problem may also arise. With the passage of time, correlates not originally related to the schema may erroneously be attributed to class membership. Nevertheless, the original taxonomy may still possess a degree of relevance to current objectives in a discipline. In these circumstances, its maintenance may be the rational choice, although a clarification and purification of categories is called for. The relationship of the two problems outlined here to the criticism of contemporary psychiatric diagnosis will be discussed later. What should be noted at this point is that the solution to neither problem implies the abolishment of the attempt at classification.

Another aspect of taxonomy is in need of clarification. When a phenomenon is assigned to a class, certain individual characteristics of that phenomenon are forever lost. No two class members are completely identical. Indeed, a single class member may be viewed as continuously differing from itself over time. It is this loss of uniqueness and an implied unconcern with process that have led many clinicians to reject classification in principle. While classificatory schemata inevitably involve losses of this type, it must be noted that they potentially offer a more than compensatory gain. This gain is represented in the significance of the class attributes and correlates. Class membership conveys information ranging from the descriptive similarity of two phenomena to a knowledge of the common operative processes underlying the phenomena.

A conceptual system minimizes the aforementioned loss to the extent that only irrelevant aspects of a phenomenon are deleted in the classificatory process. The implicit assumption is made that what is not class relevant is inconsequential. The dilemma, of course, lies in our lacking divine revelation as to what constitutes inconsequentiality. It is this issue which lies at the heart of the idiographic versus nomothetic controversy (Allport, 1937, 1946;

Beck, 1953; Eysenck, 1954; Falk, 1956; Hunt, 1951a, 1951b; Skaggs, 1945, 1947). The supporters of the idiographic position (Allport, 1937; Beck, 1953) have criticized certain conceptual schemata for treating idiosyncratic aspects of behavior as inconsequential when they are in fact pertinent data which must be utilized if a comprehensive and adequate view of human behavior is to emerge. However, the idiographic position is not a movement toward the abolishment of classification, a fact emphasized by Allport (1937) and Falk (1956). Rather, it represents a plea for broader and more meaningful classificatory schemata.

A conceptually different type of argument against the use of any diagnostic classification has been made by the adherents of nondirective psychotherapy (Patterson, 1948; Rogers, 1946, 1951). This position has advanced the specific contention that differential diagnosis is unnecessary for, and perhaps detrimental to, successful psychotherapy. This attitude of the nondirectivists has been interpreted (Thorne, 1953) as an attack on the entire classificatory enterprise. To argue against diagnosis on the grounds that it affects therapeutic outcome is to confuse diagnosis as an act of scientific classification with the present clinical practice of diagnosis with its use of interviewing, psychological testing, etc. The error here lies in turning one's attention away from diagnosis as an act of classification, a basic scientific enterprise, and attending instead to the immediate and prognostic consequences of some specific diagnostic technique in a specific therapeutic situation, i.e., an applied aspect. To reject the former on the basis of the latter would appear to be an unsound decision.

Although the nondirectivists' opposition to diagnosis seems to be based on a confusion between the basic and applied aspects of classification, implicitly contained within their position is a more fundamental argument against the classificatory effort. Undoubtedly, diagnosis both articulates and restricts the range of assumptions which may be entertained about a client. However, the philosophy of the nondirectivist forces him to reject any theoretical position which violates a belief in the unlimited psychological growth of the client. It would appear that this position represents the rejection, in principle, of the view that any individual can be like another in his essential characteristics, or that any predictable relationship can be established between a client's current level of functioning and the ends which may be achieved. In the setting of this assumption, a transindividual classificatory schema is inappropriate. There is no appeal from such a judgment, but one should be cognizant that it rejects the essence of a scientific discipline. If one insists on operating within the context of a predictive psychology, one argues for the necessity of a classificatory system, even though particular diagnostic schemata may be rejected as irrelevant, futile, or obscure.

Let us now direct our discussion toward some of the specific criticisms of conventional psychiatric diagnosis—that the categories employed lack homogeneity, reliability, and validity.

Homogeneity

A criticism often leveled against the contemporary diagnostic system is that its categories encompass heterogeneous groups of individuals, i.e., individuals varying in respect to symptomatology, test scores, prognosis, etc. (King, 1954; Rotter, 1954; Wittenborn, 1952; Wittenborn & Bailey, 1952; Wittenborn & Weiss, 1952). Contrary to the view of one investigator (Rotter, 1954), a lack of homogeneity does not necessarily imply a lack of reliability. King (1954) has clearly noted the distinction between these two concepts. Reliability refers to the agreement in assigning individuals to different diagnostic categories, whereas homogeneity refers to the diversity of behavior subsumed within categories. While the two concepts may be related, it is not difficult to conceptualize categories which, though quite reliable, subsume diverse phenomena.

King (1954) has argued in favor of constructing a new diagnostic classification having more restrictive and homogeneous categories. He supports his argument by noting his own findings and those of Kantor, Wallner, and Winder (1953), which have indicated that within the schizophrenic group subcategories may be formed which differ in test performance. King found further support for the construction of new and more homogeneous diagnostic categories in a study by Windle and Hamwi (1953). This study indicated that two subgroups could be constructed within a psychotic population which was composed of patients with diverse psychiatric diagnoses. Though matched on the distribution of these diagnostic types, the subgroups differed in the relationship obtained between test performance and prognosis. On the basis of these studies, King suggests that the type of homogeneous categories he would favor involves such classificatory dichotomies as reactive versus process schizophrenics and chronic versus nonchronic psychotics.

An analysis of King's (1954) criticism of the present diagnostic system discloses certain difficulties. The first is that King's heterogeneity criticism does not fully take into consideration certain basic aspects of classification. A common feature of classificatory systems is that they utilize classes which contain subclasses. An example drawn from biology would be a genus embracing a number of species. If schizophrenia is conceptualized as a genus, it cannot be criticized on the grounds that all its members do not share a particular attribute. Such a criticism would involve a confusion between the more specific attributes of the species and the more general attributes of the genus. This is not to assert that schizophrenia does in fact possess the characteristics of a genus. It is, of course, possible that a careful analysis will reveal that it does not, and the class schizophrenia will have to be replaced by an aggregate of entities which does constitute a legitimate genus. However, when a genus is formulated, it cannot be attacked because of its heterogeneous nature since genera are characterized by such heterogeneity.

A more serious difficulty with King's (1954) heterogeneity criticism lies in the inherent ambiguity of a homogeneity-heterogeneity parameter. To criticize a classificatory system because its categories subsume heterogeneous phenomena is to make the error of assuming that homogeneity is a quality which inheres in phenomena when in actuality it is a construction of the observer or classifier. In order to make this point clear, let us return to King's argument. What does it mean to assert that chronic psychosis is an example of an homogeneous class, while schizophrenia is an example of an heterogeneous one? In terms of the descriptively diverse phenomena encompassed, the latter would appear to have the greater homogeneity. The statement only has meaning insofar as a particular correlate—for instance, the relationship of test score to prognosis—is shared by all members of one class but not so shared by the members of the other class. Thus, the meaningfulness of the homogeneity concept is ultimately dependent on the correlates or attributes of class membership or to the classificatory principle related to these correlates or attributes. The intimacy of the relationship between the attributes of classes and the classificatory principle can best be exemplified by the extreme case in which a class has but a single attribute, and that attribute is defined by the classificatory principle, e.g., the classification of plants on the basis of the number of stamens they possess. Therefore, the heterogeneity criticism of a classificatory system is nothing more than a plea for the utilization of a new classificatory principle so that attention may be focused on particular class correlates or attributes not considered in the original schema. While this plea may be a justifiable one, depending on the significance of the new attributes, it has little to do with the homogeneity, in an absolute sense, of phenomena. Indeed, following the formulation of a new classificatory schema, the heterogeneity criticism could well be leveled against it by the adherents of the old system, since the phenomena encompassed by the new categories would probably not be considered homogeneous when evaluated by the older classificatory principle.

Although differing in its formulation, the heterogeneity criticism of present psychiatric classification made by Wittenborn and his colleagues (Wittenborn, 1952; Wittenborn & Bailey, 1952; Wittenborn & Weiss, 1952) suffers from the same difficulties as does King's (1954) criticism. Wittenborn's findings indicated that individuals given a common diagnosis showed differences in their symptom cluster score profiles based on nine symptom clusters isolated earlier by means of factor analytic techniques (Wittenborn, 1951; Wittenborn & Holzberg, 1951). It is upon the existence of these different profiles within a diagnostic category that Wittenborn bases his heterogeneity criticism. Here again the homogeneity-hetorogeneity distinction is only meaningful in terms of an independent criterion, a particular symptom cluster score profile. Had it been discovered that all individuals placed into a particular diagnostic category shared a common symptom cluster score profile, then this category would be described as subsuming homogeneous phenomena. But the phenomena—the symptoms mirrored by the symptom profile—are not homogeneous in any absolute sense because the pattern of symptoms may involve the symptoms in descriptively diverse symptom clusters. Thus, the homogeneity ascribed to the category would refer only to the fact that individuals within the category homogeneously exhibited a particular pattern of descriptively diverse behaviors. However, the organization of symptoms mirrored by the symptom cluster profiles is not in any fundamental sense different from that observed in conventional diagnostic syndromes. Both methods of categorization systematize diverse behaviors because of an observed regularity in their concurrent appearance.

The difference between these two approaches, then, lies only in the pattern of deviant behaviors that define the categories. Indeed, Eysenck (1953) has noted that both the clinician and the factor analyst derive syndromes in essentially the same manner, i.e., in terms of the observed intercorrelations of various symptoms. It is the difference in method, purely observational versus statistical, that explains why the final symptom structure may differ. The assumption must not be made that the advantage lies entirely with the factor analytic method. The merit accruing through the greater rigor of factor analysis may be outweighed by the limitations imposed in employing a restricted group of symptoms and a particular sample of patients. Thus, the factor analyst cannot claim that the class-defining symptom pattern he has derived is a standard of homogeneity against which classes within another schema can be evaluated. The plea that symptom cluster scores, derived from factor analytic techniques, substitute for the present method of psychiatric classification has little relevance to the heterogeneity issue.

In the light of this discussion we may conclude that the concept of homogeneity has little utility in evaluating classificatory schemata. Since the heterogeneity criticism invariably involves an implicit preference for one classificatory principle over another, it would perhaps be more fruitful to dispense entirely with the homogeneity-heterogeneity distinction, thus, allowing us to direct our attention to the underlying problem of the relative merits of different classificatory principles.

Reliability and Validity

A matter of continuing concern has been the degree of reliability of the present diagnostic system. Considerable energy has been expended by both those who criticize the present system for its lack of reliability (Ash, 1949; Boisen, 1938; Eysenck, 1952; Mehlman, 1952; Roe, 1949; Rotter, 1954; Scott, 1958) and those who defend it against this criticism (Foulds, 1955; Hunt, Wittson, & Hunt, 1953; Schmidt & Fonda, 1956; Seeman, 1953). Certain investigators (Foulds, 1955; Schmidt & Fonda, 1956) who have offered evidence that the present system is reliable have also pointed out that the earlier studies emphasizing the unreliability of psychiatric diagnosis have suffered from serious conceptual and methodological difficulties.

In evaluating the body of studies concerned with the reliability of psychiatric diagnosis, one must conclude that so long as diagnosis is confined to broad diagnostic categories, it is reasonably reliable, but the reliability diminishes as one proceeds from broad, inclusive class categories to narrower, more specific ones. As finer discriminations are called for, accuracy in diagnosis becomes increasingly difficult. Since this latter characteristic appears to be common to the classificatory efforts in many areas of knowledge, it would appear to be inappropriate to criticize psychiatric diagnosis on the grounds that it is less than perfectly reliable. This should not lead to an underestimation of the importance of reliability. While certain extraclassificatory factors, e.g., proficiency of the clinicians, biases of the particular clinical settings, etc., may influence it, reliability is primarily related to the precision with which classes of a schema are defined. Since the defining characteristic of most classes in psychiatric diagnosis is the occurrence of symptoms in particular combinations, the reliability of the system mirrors the specificity with which the various combinations of symptoms (syndromes) have been spelled out. It is mandatory for a classificatory schema to be reliable since reliability refers to the definiteness with which phenomena can be ordered to classes. If a system does not allow for such a division of phenomena, it can make no pretense of being a classificatory schema.

While reliability is a prerequisite if the diagnostic system is to have any value, it must not be assumed that if human effort were to make the present system perfectly reliable, it could escape all the difficulties attributed to it. This perfect reliability would only mean that individuals within each class shared a particular commonality in relation to the classificatory principle of symptom manifestation. If one were interested in attributes unrelated or minimally related to the classificatory principle employed, the perfect reliability of the system would offer little cause for rejoicing. Perfect reliability of the present system can only be the goal of those who are interested in nothing more than the present classificatory principle and the particular attributes of the classes constructed on the basis of this principle.

When attention is shifted from characteristics which define a class to the correlates of class membership, this implies a shift in concern from the reliability of a system to its validity. The distinction between the reliability and validity of a classificatory system would appear to involve certain conceptual difficulties. It is perhaps this conceptual difficulty which explains why the rather imposing body of literature concerned with diagnosis has been virtually silent on the question of the validity of the present system of psychiatric diagnosis. Only one group of investigators (Hunt, 1951; Hunt, Wittson, & Barton, 1950a, 1950b; Hunt, Wittson, & Hunt, 1953; Wittson & Hunt, 1951) has specifically been concerned with the predictive efficacy of diagnoses and, thus, to the validity of psychiatric classifications; and even in this work, the distinction between validity and reliability is not clearly drawn.

In order to grasp the distinction between the reliability and the validity of a classificatory schema, one must differentiate the defining characteristics of the classes from the correlates of the classes. In the former case, we are interested in the principles upon which classes are formed; in the latter, in the predictions or valid statements that can be made about phenomena once they are classified. The difficulty lies in the overlap between the classifying principles and the class correlates. If a classificatory system is reliable, it is also valid to the extent that we can predict that the individuals within a class will exhibit certain characteristics, namely, those behaviors or attributes which serve to define the class.

It is the rare class, however, that does not connote correlates beyond its defining characteristics. The predictions associated with class membership may vary from simple extensions of the classificatory principles to correlates which would appear to have little connection with these principles. Let us examine a simple illustration and see what follows from categorizing an individual. Once an individual has been classified as manifesting a manic-depressive reaction, depressed type, on the basis of the symptoms of depression of mood, motor retardation, and stupor (American Psychiatric Association, 1952), the prediction may be made that the individual will spend a great deal of time in bed, which represents an obvious extension of the symptom pattern. One may also hypothesize that the patient will show improvement if electroshock therapy is employed. This is a correlate which has little direct connection with the symptoms themselves. These predictions are open to test, and evidence may or may not be found to support them. Thus, measures of validity may be obtained which are independent of the reliability of the system of classification.

The problem of validity lies at the heart of the confusion which surrounds psychiatric diagnosis. When the present diagnostic schema is assailed, the common complaint is that class membership conveys little information beyond the gross symptomatology of the patient and contributes little to the solution of the pressing problems of etiology, treatment procedures, prognosis, etc. The criticism that class membership does not predict these important aspects of a disorder appears to be a legitimate one. This does not mean the present system has no validity. It simply indicates that the system may be valid in respect to certain correlates but invalid in respect to others. Much confusion would be dispelled if as much care were taken in noting the existing correlates of classes as is taken in noting the classificatory principles. A great deal of effort has gone into the formalization of the defining characteristics of classes (American Psychiatric Association, 1952), but one looks in vain for a formal delineation of the extraclassificatory attributes and correlates of class membership. As a result, the various diagnostic categories have been burdened with correlates not systematically derived from a classificatory principle but which were attributed to the classes because they were the focal points of clinical interest. A major question is just what correlates can justifiably be attributed to the class categories. To answer this question we must turn our attention to the purposes and philosophy underlying contemporary psychiatric diagnosis.

Philosophy and Purpose of Conventional Diagnosis

The validity of the conventional diagnostic system is least ambiguous and most free from potential criticism as a descriptive schema, a taxonomy of mental disorders analogous to the work of Ray and Linnaeus in biology. In this sense, class membership confirms that the inclusion of an individual within a class guarantees only that he exhibit the defining characteristics of that class. Only a modest extension of this system, in terms of a very limited number of well established correlates, makes for a system of impressive heuristic value, even though it falls considerably short of what would now be considered an optimal classificatory schema. As has been noted (Caveny et al., 1955; Hunt et al., 1953), the present diagnostic system is quite useful when evaluated in terms of its administrative and, to a lesser extent, its preventive implications. Caveny et al. (1955) and Wittenborn, Holzberg, and Simon (1953) should be consulted for a comprehensive list of such uses, but examples would include legal determination of insanity, declaration of incompetence, type of ward required for custodial care, census figures and statistical data upon which considerable planning is based, screening devices for the military services or other agencies, etc. In view of the extensive criticism of contemporary diagnosis, the surprising fact is not that so few valid predictions can be derived from class membership, but that so many can.

The value of the present psychiatric classification system would be further enhanced by its explicit divorcement from its Kraepelinian heritage by an emphasis on its descriptive aspect and, through careful empirical investigation, the cataloging of the reliable correlates of its categories. That this catalog of correlates would be an impressive one is expressed in Hoch's (1953) view that the present system is superior to any system which has been evolved to replace it. It is an open question whether the system merits this amount of praise. In general, however, the defense of the present system—or, for that matter, diagnosis in general (Caveny et al., 1955; Eysenck, 1952; Hunt et al., 1953; Jellinek, 1939)—tends to rest on the merits of its descriptive, empirical, and nondynamic aspects.

The present classificatory system, even as a purely descriptive device, is still open to a certain degree of criticism. Its classificatory principle is organized primarily about symptom manifestation. This would be adequate for a descriptive system if this principle were consistently applied to all classes of the schema and if the symptoms associated with each diagnostic category were clearly specified. There is some question, however, whether the system meets these requirements (Phillips & Rabinovitch, 1958; Rotter, 1954). The criticism has been advanced that the present system is based on a number of diverse principles of classification. Most classes are indeed defined by symptom manifestation, but the organic disorders, for example, tend to be identified by etiology, while such other factors as prognosis, social conformity, etc. are also employed as classificatory principles. This does not appear, however, to be an insurmountable problem, for the system could be made a completely consistent one by explicitly defining each category by the symptoms encompassed. The system would appear to be eminently amenable to the unitary application of this descriptive classificatory principle, for there are actually few cases where classes are not so defined. Where reliable relations between the present categories and etiology and prognosis have been established, these also could be incorporated explicitly within the system. Etiology and prognosis would be treated not as inherent attributes of the various classifications, but rather as correlates of the particular classes to which their relationship is known. They would, thus, not be confounded with the classificatory principle of the system.

This course of action would satisfy the requirement of consistency in the application of the classificatory principle. A remaining area of ambiguity would be the lack of agreement in what constitutes a symptom. In physical medicine, a clear distinction has been made between a symptom, which is defined as a subjectively experienced abnormality, and a sign, which is considered an objective indication of abnormality (Holmes, 1946). This differentiation has not, however, been extended to the sphere of mental disorders. A source of difficulty may lie in the definition of what is psychologically abnormal. In psychiatric terminology, symptoms include a wide range of phenomena from the grossest type of behavior deviation, through the complaints of the patient, to events almost completely inferential in nature. One suggestion (Yates, 1958) has been to eliminate the term "symptom" and direct attention to the manifest responses of the individual. This suggestion appears to be embodied in the work of Wittenborn and his colleagues (Wittenborn, 1951, 1952; Wittenborn & Bailey, 1952; Wittenborn & Holzberg, 1951; Wittenborn et al., 1953; Wittenborn & Weiss, 1952). Wittenborn's diagnostic system, in which symptoms are defined as currently discernible behaviors, represents a standard of clarity for purely descriptive systems of psychiatric classification. This clarity was achieved by clearly noting and limiting the group of behaviors which would be employed in the system. But even here a certain amount of ambiguity remains. The number of responses or discernible behaviors which may be considered for inclusion within a diagnostic schema borders on the infinite. The question arises, then, as to how one goes about the selection of those behaviors to be incorporated in the classificatory system. Parsimony demands that only "meaningful" items of behavior be chosen for inclusion, and this selective principle has certainly been at work in the construction of all systems of diagnosis. In this sense, the present method of psychiatric classification is not a purely descriptive one, nor can any classification schema truly meet this criterion of purity. Meaning and utility inevitably appear among the determinants of classificatory systems.

Several investigators (Cameron, 1953; Jellinek, 1939; Magaret, 1952) have stressed the inappropriateness of discussing diagnosis in the abstract, pointing out that such a discussion should center around the question of "diagnosis for what?" Indeed, a diagnostic system cannot be described as "true" or "false," but only as being useful or not useful in attaining prescribed goals. Therefore, when a system is devised, its purposes should be explicitly stated so that the system can be evaluated in terms of its success or failure in attaining these objectives. Furthermore, these goals should be kept explicit throughout the period during which the system is being employed. The present diagnostic schema has not met this requirement. Instead, its goals have been carried along in an implicit manner and have been allowed to become vague. The result has been that some see the purpose of the schema as being an adequate description of mental disorders (Hunt et al., 1953), others view it as being concerned with prognosis (Hoch, 1953), and still others view the schemata goal as the discovery of etiology (Cameron, 1953).

Typically, the present schema has been conceptualized as descriptive in nature, but a brief glance at its history indicates that the original purposes and goals in the construction of this schema went far beyond the desire for a descriptive taxonomy. As Zilboorg and Henry (1941) clearly note, Kraepelin not only studied the individual while hospitalized, but also the patient's premorbid history and posthospital course. His hope was to make our understanding of all mental disorders as precise as our knowledge of the course of general paresis. He insisted on the classification of mental disorders according to regularities in symptoms and course of illness, believing this would lead to a clearer discrimination among the different disease entities. He hoped for the subsequent discovery of a specific somatic malfunction responsible for each disease. For Kraepelin, then, classification was related to etiology, treatment, and prognosis. Had the system worked as envisaged, these variables would have become the extraclassificatory attributes of the schema. When matched against this aspiration, the present system must be considered a failure since the common complaint against it is that a diagnostic label tells us very little about etiology, treatment, or prognosis (Miles, 1953). However, it would be erroneous to conclude that the present system is valueless because its classes are only minimally related to etiology and prognosis.

What should be noted is that etiology and prognosis, though important, are but two of a multitude of variables of interest. The importance of these variables should not obscure the fact that their relationship to a classificatory system is exactly the same as that of any other variables. This relationship may take one of two forms. Etiology and prognosis may be the correlates of the classes of a diagnostic system which employs an independent classificatory principle like symptom manifestation. Optimally, we should prefer a classificatory schema in which the indices of etiology and preferred modes of treatment would be incorporated (Hunt et al., 1953; Pepinsky, 1948). In essence, this was Kraepelin's approach, and it continues to underlie some promising work in the area of psychopathology. Although Kraepelin's disease concept is in disrepute (Hoch & Zubin, 1953; Marzoff, 1947; Rotter, 1954) it is the opinion of several investigators (Eysenck, 1953; Phillips & Rabinovitch, 1958; Wittenborn et al., 1953) that further work employing the descriptive symptomatic approach could well lead to a greater understanding of the etiology underlying abnormal "processes."

Another manner in which etiology, treatment, or prognosis could be related to a classificatory schema is by utilizing each of these variables as the classificatory principle for a new diagnostic system. For instance, we might organize patients into groups which respond differentially to particular forms of treatment like electroshock, drugs, psychotherapy, etc. The new schemata which might be proposed could be of considerable value in respect to certain goals but useless in regard to others. Since we do not possess a diagnostic system based on all the variables of clinical interest, we might have to be satisfied with the construction of a variety of diagnostic systems, each based on a different principle of classification. These classificatory techniques would exist side by side, their use being determined by the specific objectives of the diagnostician.

Etiology versus Description in Diagnosis

The classical Kraepelinian classification schema shows two major characteristics: a commitment to a detailed description of the manifest symptomatic behaviors of the individual and an underlying assumption that such a descriptive classification would be transitory, eventually leading to and being replaced by a system whose classificatory principle was the etiology of the various mental disorders. Major criticism of this classificatory effort has been directed at the first of these. The reservations are that, in practice, such a descriptive effort allows no place for a process interpretation of psychopathology and that it has not encouraged the development of prevention and treatment programs in the mental disorders.

The authors do not feel that the failure of the Kraepelinian system has demonstrated the futility of employing symptoms as the basis for classification. It does suggest that if one approaches the problem of description with an assumption as to the necessary correlates of such descriptions, then the diagnostic system may well be in error. Kraepelin's empiricism is contaminated in just this way. For example, he refused to accept as cases of dementia praecox those individuals who recovered from the disorder, since he assumed irreversibility as a necessary concomitant of its hypothesized neurophysiological base. Bleuler, on the other hand, who was much less committed to any particular form of causality in this illness, readily recognized the possibility of its favorable outcome. It is not, then, the descriptive approach itself which is open to criticism, but description contaminated by preconception. An unfettered description of those schizophrenics with good prognosis in contrast to those with poor prognosis reveals clear differences in the symptom configuration between these kinds of patients (Farina & Webb, 1956; Phillips, 1953).

Kraepelin's basic concern with the problem of etiology has remained a focus of efforts in the clinical area. Although his postulate of central nervous system disease as the basis of mental disorder is in disrepute, and his systematic classificatory efforts are assailed, one nevertheless finds a striking congruence between Kraepelin's preconceptions and certain current attempts at the solution of the problem of psychopathology. There is an unwavering belief that some simple categorical system will quickly solve the mysteries of etiology. The exponents of these newer classificatory schemata have merely replaced symptoms by other phenomena like test scores (King, 1954), particular patterns of interpersonal relations (Leary & Coffey, 1955), etc. It is the authors' conviction that these new efforts to find short-cut solutions to the question of etiology will similarly remain unsuccessful. The amount of descriptive effort required before etiological factors are likely to be discovered has been underestimated (Kety, 1959a, 1959b), and the pursuit of etiology should represent an end point rather than a beginning for classificatory systems. The process of moving from an empirical orientation to an etiological one is, of necessity, inferential and therefore susceptible to the myriad dangers of premature inference. We propose that the greatest safeguard against such prematurity is not to be found in the scrapping of an empirical descriptive approach, but in an accelerated program of empirical research. What is needed at this time is a systematic, empirical attack on the problem of mental disorders. Inherent in this program is the employment of symptoms, broadly defined as meaningful and discernible behaviors, as the basis of a classificatory system. Rather than an abstract search for etiologies, it would appear more currently fruitful to investigate such empirical correlates of symptomatology as reactions to specific forms of treatment, outcome in the disorders, case history phenomena, etc.

The pervasive concern with etiology may derive from a belief that if this were known, prevention would shortly be forthcoming, thus, making the present complex problems of treatment and prognosis inconsequential. Unfortunately, efforts to short-circuit the drudgery involved in establishing an empirically founded psychiatry has not resulted in any major breakthroughs. Etiology is typically the last characteristic of a disorder to be discovered. Consequently, we would suggest the search for etiology be put aside and attempted only when a greater number of the correlates of symptomatic behaviors have been established.

The authors are impressed by the amount of energy that has been expended in both attacking and defending various contemporary systems of classification. We believe that a classificatory system should include any behavior or phenomenon that appears promising in terms of its significant correlates. At this stage of our investigations, the system employed should be an open and expanding one, not one which is closed and defended on conceptual grounds. Systems of classification must be treated as tools for further discovery, not as bases for polemic disputation.

As stated above, it is possible that a number of systems of classification may be needed to encompass the behaviors presently of clinical interest. It may appear that the espousal of this position, in conjunction with a plea for empirical exploration of the correlates of these behaviors, runs headlong into a desire for conceptual neatness and parsimony. It may be feared that the use of a number of classificatory systems concurrently, each with its own correlates, may lead to the creation of a gigantic actuarial table of unrelated elements. However, the authors do not feel that such a fear is well founded because it assumes that the correlates of these systems have no eventual relation one to the other.

We believe that this latter view is unnecessarily pessimistic. While in principle a multiplicity of classificatory systems might be called for, results from the authors' own research program suggests that a single, relatively restricted and coherent classification system can be derived from an empirical study of the correlates of symptomatic behaviors (Phillips & Rabinovitch, 1958; Zigler & Phillips, 1960). Such a system might serve a number of psychiatrically significant functions, including the optimum selection of patients for specific treatment programs and the prediction of treatment outcomes. In conclusion, a descriptive classificatory system appears far from dead, and if properly employed, it can lead to a fuller as well as a more conceptually based understanding of the psychopathologies.

REFERENCES

Allport, G. *Personality: A psychological interpretation.* New York: Holt, 1937.

Allport, G. Personalistic psychology as science: A reply. *Psychological Review,* 1946, **53,** 132-135.

American Psychiatric Association, Mental Hospital Service, Committee on Nomenclature and Statistics of the American Psychiatric Association. *Diagnostic and statistical manual: Mental disorders.* Washington, D.C.: APA, 1952.

Ash, P. The reliability of psychiatric diagnosis. *Journal of Abnormal and Social Psychology,* 1949, **44,** 272-277.

Beach, F. The snark was a boojum. *American Psychologist,* 1950, **5,** 115-124.

Beck, S. The science of personality: Nomothetic or idiographic? *Psychological Review,* 1953, **60,** 353-359.

Boisen, A. Types of dementia praecox: A study in psychiatric classification. *Psychiatry,* 1938, **1,** 233-236.

Brower, D. The problem of quantification in psychological science. *Psychological Review,* 1949, **56,** 325-333.

Cameron, D. A theory of diagnosis. In P. Hoch & J. Zubin (Eds.), *Current problems in psychiatric diagnosis.* New York: Grune & Stratton, 1953. Pp. 33-45.

Cattell, R. *Personality and motivation structure and measurement.* New York: World Book, 1957.

Caveny, E., Wittson, C., Hunt, W., & Herman, R. Psychiatric diagnosis, its nature and function. *Journal of Nervous and Mental Disorders,* 1955, **121,** 367-380.

Cronbach, L. The two disciplines of scientific psychology. *American Psychologist,* 1957, **12,** 671-684.

Eysenck, H. *The scientific study of personality.* London: Routledge & Kegan Paul, 1952.

Eysenck, H. The logical basis of factor analysis. *American Psychologist,* 1953, **8,** 105-113.

Eysenck, H. The science of personality: Nomothetic. *Psychological Review,* 1954, **61,** 339-341.

Falk, J. Issues distinguishing idiographic from nomothetic approaches to personality theory. *Psychological Review,* 1956, **63,** 53-62.

Farina, A., & Webb, W. Premorbid adjustment and subsequent discharge. *Journal of Nervous and Mental Disorders,* 1956, **124,** 612-613.

Foulds, G. The reliability of psychiatric, and the validity of psychological diagnosis. *Journal of Mental Science,* 1955, **101,** 851-862.

Guthrie, E. The status of systematic psychology. *American Psychologist,* 1950, **5,** 97-101.

Harlow, H. Mice, monkeys, men, and motives. *Psychological Review,* 1953, **60,** 23-32.

Harrower, Molly (Ed.). *Diagnostic psychological testing*. Springfield, Ill.: Charles C. Thomas, 1950.

Hoch, P. Discussion. In P. Hoch & J. Zubin (Eds.), *Current problems in psychiatric diagnosis*. New York: Grune & Stratton, 1953. Pp. 46-50.

Hoch, P., & Zubin, J. (Eds.). *Current problems in psychiatric diagnosis*. New York: Grune & Stratton, 1953.

Holmes, G. *Introduction to clinical neurology*. Edinburgh: Livingstone, 1946.

Hunt, W. Clinical psychology—science or superstition. *American Psychologist*, 1951, 6, 683-687. (a)

Hunt, W. An investigation of naval neuropsychiatric screening procedures. In H. Gruetskaw (Ed.), *Groups, leadership, and men*. Pittsburgh, Pa.: Carnegie Press, 1951. Pp. 245-256. (b)

Hunt, W., Wittson, C., & Barton, H. A further validation of naval neuropsychiatric screening. *Journal of Consulting Psychology*, 1950, 14, 485-488. (a)

Hunt, W., Wittson, C., & Barton, H. A validation study of naval neuropsychiatric screening. *Journal of Consulting Psychology*, 1950, 14, 35-39. (b)

Hunt, W., Wittson, C., & Hunt, E. A theoretical and practical analysis of the diagnostic process. In P. Hoch & J. Zubin (Eds.), *Current problems in psychiatric diagnosis*. New York: Grune & Stratton, 1953. Pp. 53-65.

Jellinek, E. Some principles of psychiatric classification. *Psychiatry*, 1939, 2, 161-165.

Kantor, R., Wallner, J., & Winder, C. Process and reactive schizophrenia. *Journal of Consulting Psychology*, 1953, 17, 157-162.

Kety, S. Biochemical theories of schizophrenia. Part I. *Science*, 1959, 129, 1528-1532. (a)

Kety, S. Biochemical theories of schizophrenia. Part II. *Science*, 1959, 129, 1950-1956. (b)

King, G. Research with neuropsychiatric samples. *Journal of Psychology*, 1954, 38, 383-387.

Koch, S. The current status of motivational psychology. *Psychological Review*, 1951, 58, 147-154.

Leary, T., & Coffey, H. Interpersonal diagnosis: Some problems of methodology and validation. *Journal of Abnormal and Social Psychology*, 1955, 50, 110-126.

MacKinnon, D. Fact and fancy in personality research. *American Psychologist*, 1953, 8, 138-146.

Magaret, Ann. Clinical methods: Psychodiagnostics. *Annual Review of Psychology*, 1952, 3, 283-320.

Marquis, D. Research planning at the frontiers of science. *American Psychologist*, 1948, 3, 430-438.

Marzoff, S. S. The disease concept in psychology, *Psychological Review*, 1947, 54, 211-221.

Maslow, A. Cognition of the particular and of the generic. *Psychological Review*, 1948, 55, 22-40.

Mehlman, B. The reliability of psychiatric diagnosis. *Journal of Abnormal and Social Psychology*, 1952, **47**, 577-578.

Menninger, K. The practice of psychiatry. *Digest of Neurological Psychiatry*, 1955, **23**, 101.

Miles, H. Discussion. In P. Hoch & J. Zubin (Eds.), *Current problems in psychiatric diagnosis*. New York: Grune & Stratton, 1953. Pp. 107-111.

Noyes, A. *Modern clinical psychiatry*. Philadelphia: Saunders, 1953.

Patterson, C. Is psychotherapy dependent on diagnosis? *American Psychologist*, 1948, **3**, 155-159.

Pepinsky, H. B. Diagnostic categories in clinical counseling. *Applied Psychological Monographs*, 1948, No. 15.

Phillips, L. Case history data and prognosis in schizophrenia. *Journal of Nervous and Mental Disorders*, 1953, **117**, 515-525.

Phillips, L., & Rabinovitch, M. Social role and patterns of symptomatic behaviors. *Journal of Abnormal and Social Psychology*, 1958, **57**, 181-186.

Rapaport, D. The future of research in clinical psychology and psychiatry. *American Psychologist*, 1947, **2**, 167-172.

Roby, T. An opinion on the construction of behavior theory. *American Psychologist*, 1959, **14**, 129-134.

Roe, Anne. Integration of personality theory and clinical practice. *Journal of Abnormal and Social Psychology*, 1949, **44**, 36-41.

Rogers, C. Significant aspects of client-centered therapy. *American Psychologist*, 1946, **1**, 415-422.

Rogers, C. *Client-centered therapy*. Boston: Houghton Mifflin, 1951.

Rotter, J. *Social learning and clinical psychology*. New York: Prentice-Hall, 1954.

Schmidt, H., & Fonda, C. The reliability of psychiatric diagnosis: A new look. *Journal of Abnormal and Social Psychology*, 1956, **52**, 262-267.

Scott, J. The place of observation in biological and psychological science. *American Psychologist*, 1955, **10**, 61-63.

Scott, W. Research definitions of mental health and mental illness. *Psychological Bulletin*, 1958, **55**, 1-45.

Seeman, W. Psychiatric diagnosis: An investigation of interperson-reliability after didactic instruction. *Journal of Nervous and Mental Disorders*, 1953, **118**, 541-544.

Skaggs, E. Personalistic psychology as science. *Psychological Review*, 1945, **52**, 234-238.

Skaggs, E. Ten basic postulates of personalistic psychology. *Psychological Review*, 1947, 54, 255-262.

Thorne, F. Back to fundamentals. *Journal of Clinical Psychology*, 1953, **9**, 89-91.

Tolman, R. Virtue rewarded and vice punished. *American Psychologist*, 1953, **8**, 721-733.

Tyler, Leona. Toward a workable psychology of individuality. *American Psychologist*, 1959, **14**, 75-81.

Windle, C., & Hamwi, V. An exploratory study of the prognostic value of the complex reaction time tests in early and chronic psychotics. *Journal of Clinical Psychology*, 1951, **15**, 290-302.

Wittenborn, J. The behavioral symptoms for certain organic psychoses. *Journal of Consulting Psychology*, 1952, **16**, 104-106.

Wittenborn, J., & Bailey, C. The symptoms of involutional psychosis. *Journal of Consulting Psychology*, 1952, **16**, 13-17.

Wittenborn, J., & Holzberg, J. The generality of psychiatric syndromes. *Journal of Consulting Psychology*, 1951, **15**, 372-380.

Wittenborn, J., Holzberg, J., & Simon, B. Symptom correlates for descriptive diagnosis. *Genetic Psychology Monographs*, 1953, **47**, 237-301.

Wittenborn, J., & Weiss, W. Patients diagnosed manic-depressive psychosismanic state. *Journal of Consulting Psychology*, 1952, **16**, 193-198.

Wittman, P., & Sheldon, W. A proposed classification of psychotic behavior reactions. *American Journal of Psychiatry*, 1948, **105**, 124-128.

Wittson, C., & Hunt, W. The predictive value of the brief psychiatric interview. *American Journal of Psychiatry*, 1951, **107**, 582-585.

Yates, A. Symptoms and symptom substitution. *Psychological Review*, 1958, **65**, 371-374.

Zigler, E., & Phillips, L. Social effectiveness and symptomatic behaviors. *Journal of Abnormal and Social Psychology*, 1960, **61**, 231-238.

Zilboorg, G., & Henry, G. W. *History of medical psychology.* New York: Norton, 1941.

3

On Behavior Pathology

INTRODUCTION

In the article that follows, Ronald Wilson reviews some of the experimental research on *lower animals* that is relevant for understanding psychopathology. More specifically, Wilson illustrates how experimental animal research can refine and extend the understanding of pathology that was derived from clinical work with humans. From this review it is clear that psychologists interested in pathology need not confine themselves to human subjects. Experimentation with lower animals may also provide interesting and valuable data for understanding man's difficulties. Research on pathology using lower animals has been criticized by some who feel that psychopathology is unique to man because it is manifested in the higher mental processes, that is, those that have been found only in man. A brief inspection of the symptoms and problems in pathology will reveal, however, that a large share of these do not necessarily involve processes that are possessed only by man. For example, few of the neurotic disorders involve distortions of the higher mental processes, that is, thought disturbances. Rather, much of the pathology in the neuroses can be viewed as inappropriate responses stemming from conflict or inappropriate learning, neither of which necessarily involves the higher mental functions. Furthermore, as Wilson suggests, pathology seen in the higher mental functions may not be the *cause* of the pathology but instead may be the area in which the symptoms are expressed. If this were true, it might still be appropriate to look for the causes of pathology in animals, which express their pathology in areas other than higher mental functions.

The use of animals in basic research on behavior pathology has a number of advantages. Not only are animals easier to observe, but the experimenter can more completely control the animals' experience. Also, the limitations imposed by ethical questions that arise when working with humans are considerably reduced when working with animals. In animal research, isolation, deprivation, negative early experience, drugs, and so on, can all be employed more easily (though not with complete freedom) than in research with humans. This provides the opportunity for actual experimental work on problems that would otherwise be inaccessible. In addition, animal research often tends to tighten up our definitions of the phenomena and conditions being studied. Working with animals in the laboratory, the experimenter is usually very careful to *operationally define* the phenomena and conditions that are under study. This approach is, of course, not exclusive to animal research. However, because of the problems involved in the interpretation of animal research on behavior pathology, as well as the general tradition of animal research, experimenters in this area often give greater attention to definitional problems than do many individuals who work with humans. Lastly, there is at present a wealth of data available on lower animals. Although most of these data were not collected with behavior pathology in mind, the pathologist might well benefit from a review of them for possible insights. In view of the growing interest in the *learning of pathology,* more and more of these animal data may become relevant, for by far the vast majority of them are devoted to problems and issues in learning. In summary, profitable use may be made of lower animals in research on pathology.

Animal research on behavior pathology cannot stand alone; it must be incorporated as one of the important phases of a research cycle. After the problems to be researched are identified in humans, research on lower animals can be used in suggesting, refining, and exploring various hypotheses in a controlled laboratory situation. The clarification and principles that would hopefully be arrived at through animal research can then be tested and applied on the human level. Only with this interaction and exchange can we use all of our techniques and abilities to the best advantage.

3

ON BEHAVIOR PATHOLOGY

RONALD S. WILSON[1]

Investigation of behavior pathology has a long heritage, but perhaps two significant trends can be nominated as having substantially increased our understanding of functional disorders since the turn of the century. On the one hand, the advent of psychoanalysis laid the foundation for a dynamic theory of human pathology, and in a broader sense it recast the traditional conceptions of personality into a more kinetic form. Emotion, conflict, and anxiety received increasing emphasis as basic operators in human behavior, and disturbances in emotional relationships became the focal point for interpreting behavior disorders. The theory was fashioned from data secured in the therapeutic treatment room, but as child psychiatry and clinical psychology developed, the domain of data expanded markedly and broadened the empirical framework on which the theory rested.

The transition from an organic view of pathology to a dynamic functional view was of inestimable significance for treatment and diagnosis. Nevertheless, the concepts introduced to account for pathological phenomena were not always clearly defined or open to verification; and some pointed criticisms were raised about the subjective bias of both patient and analyst that might enter into the interpretation of data.

The second major trend is of somewhat more recent vintage, dating from Pavlov's investigation of conditioned reflexes, and it can be referred to as the experimental investigation of behavior pathology. It is represented by the work of Gantt and Liddell on experimental neurosis, by Masserman's work on conflict, Maier on frustration, and the work of Solomon and his colleagues on traumatic avoidance learning. Although the conceptual schemata differ, these experiments share common properties in terms of the be-

SOURCE. Reprinted with permission of the American Psychological Association and the author from the *Psychological Bulletin*, 1963, 60, 130-146.
[1] This paper has been substantially strengthened by the comments and criticisms of A. L. Benton and A. B. Heilbrun, and I am privileged to record my indebtedness to them.

havior disturbances produced, and within the limits of design differences they generally corroborate one another. As will subsequently become evident, the major features of pathology revealed in these studies also correspond to several important features of human pathology as seen in the clinic. Yet this body of research, which clearly satisfies the criteria of being objective and controlled, has not been embraced by clinicians, mainly because its significance for human pathology is somewhat obscure; and the experimentalists themselves have made only nominal efforts to integrate their results with clinical data.

The purpose of the present essay is to focus upon points of common agreement between the clinical and experimental areas, and to suggest that the same principles apply to both areas. To this end a selected group of clinical studies will be reviewed in an effort to establish some basic parameters that cut across the traditional categories of behavior pathology. Subsequently the experimental literature will be examined for concepts and empirical laws that will anchor our clinical concepts more securely. The final section will touch briefly on the implications of this review for the analysis of behavior pathology.

Clinical Studies of Human Pathology

Kubie on Neurosis

In an early paper Kubie (1941) analyzed the characteristics of neurotic behavior in search of a general principle that would unify the commonly recognized symptoms. He proposed the principle of *repetitiveness,* or more particularly, that distortions in the normal process of repetitiveness constituted the core of neurotic behavior. Kubie argued that the organization of the central nervous system provides for sustained impulses through the operation of open and closed circuits; consequently, the psychological development of the organism is rooted in repetition of experience. Motivated by diffuse tension, the infant responds with random efforts which gradually evolve into more economical forms until they finally become specifically goal directed. The acquisition of skills depends upon endless but flexible and spontaneous repetition of motor activity.

While these skills are developed primarily to relieve states of tension, they soon acquire secondary meaning as rewarding activities in their own right. Functions such as walking, talking, manipulating objects, exploring and mastering new situations are practiced time and again because the child is highly gratified by the exercise of these new functions. Great emotional significance attaches to these skills, either of delight and satisfaction in the case of uninterrupted practice, or of tension and rage where such activities are interfered with.

Kubie believes that frustration intervenes most markedly at this point, for the repetitive behavior of the child may stimulate inhibitory controls from his parents. When punishment or threats are applied to curtail such behavior, the child responds with rage and temper tantrums. If the parents vigorously suppress this outlet also, the stage is set for severe conflict.

It is at this point that the shift from normal flexible repetitiveness to rigid neurotic repetitiveness takes place. Successive expressions of the need are no longer modified by reward or punishment, but are cast rigidly as the only possible compromise solution of all the child feels in the conflict situation. Consequently, the repetitive act becomes irresistible to the child, and it displays a rigid intensity that eliminates flexible problem solving behavior.

In a later paper, Kubie (1954) sums up the basic distinction between normal and neurotic behavior:

> [Normal] patterns of behavior, no matter how varied they may be, will have one basic characteristic in common, namely that any repetitiveness which that behavior may exhibit with respect to impulse, thought, action or feeling, or any combination of these, will be flexible, modifiable, satiable. . . . [Neurotic behavior] will have precisely opposite characteristics; it will be repetitive, obligatory, insatiable, and stereotyped (pp. 202-203).

Alexander and French (1946) are also persuaded that repetitive behavior is a prominent feature of neurosis. Drawing on extensive therapeutic contacts with neurotic patients, they summarize the basic problem as follows:

> In normal development, patterns from the past undergo progressive modification. One learns from experience by correcting earlier patterns in the light of later events. When a problem becomes too disturbing to face, however, this learning process is interrupted and subsequent attempts to solve the problem must, therefore, assume the character of stereotyped repetitions of previous unsuccessful attempts to solve it. A neurosis may be defined as a series of such stereotyped reactions to problems that the patient has never solved in the past and is still unable to solve in the present (p. 76).

Frustration and Schizophrenia

In behavior disturbances more severe than neurosis, similar tendencies toward rigid repetition of certain acts, regardless of their consequences, have been noted.

Jenkins (1950, 1952) has proposed that frustration carried beyond the tolerance level of the individual stimulates disorganization, withdrawal, and stereotypy. Drawing on Maier's (1949) experimental work, Jenkins attributes the schizophrenic process to profound frustration that arises chiefly in the area of interpersonal relationships. After repeated rebuffs, the schizophrenic gradually withdraws from emotional contact with other people and dwells more and more in the realm of fantasy. Efforts to establish rewarding relationships are gradually replaced by regressive, stereotyped responses that further aggravate the problem.

Jenkins (1950) finds considerable support for his position in the published clinical literature, much of which assigns a prominent role to early frustrating experiences as a causal factor in schizophrenia. Studies of the schizophrenic's family often disclose an overpowering mother who is described by such adjectives as perfectionistic, dominating, aggressive, overanxious and overprotective—the type of mother who markedly interferes with the child's growth toward independent selfhood. The point is illustrated by a sample of statements chosen more frequently by mothers of male schizophrenics (Mark, 1953).

1. A mother should make it her business to know everything her children are thinking.

2. Children should not annoy parents with their unimportant problems.

3. A watchful mother can keep her child out of all accidents.

4. A devoted mother has no time for social life.

5. Playing with a child too much will spoil him.

6. A mother has to suffer much and say little.

7. Children who take part in sex play become sex criminals when they grow up.

8. Too much affection will make a child a "softee."

Jenkins (1952) reasons that pervasive control measures invade the day-to-day experience of the child throughout a wide range of situations and "make it more than usually difficult for a child to maintain a sense of his individuality, except in the autistic withdrawal of fantasy" (p. 740). Frustration at this stage interferes with the development of effective coping mechanisms and forces the child into regressive, stereotyped patterns of behavior.

A more phenomenological analysis of schizophrenia is offered by Guntrip (1952), who states that the primary danger for psychological development lies in early object-relationships that are frustrating for the child. When the mother is cross, impatient, and punitive with her child, or is emotionally detached and unresponsive, the child experiences such behavior as frustrating his most important needs. Consequently the mother becomes a bad object, and "an inner psychic world is set up . . . in which one is tied to bad objects and feeling, therefore, always frustrated, hungry, angry and guilty, and profoundly anxious" (p. 348).

Guntrip argues that a bad object cannot simply be dismissed. The most primitive reaction to early deprivation is to become pathologically attached to the object, and to continually rehearse these frustrating experiences in fantasy in an effort to make them turn out positively. They never do, though, and the schizophrenic remains fixated at a primitive level of emotional development, intensely preoccupied with problems of nurturance and support. He senses his own needs as being overwhelming and all-consuming, capable of exhausting the resources of anyone offering a supportive relationship. By the same token, the schizophrenic is acutely fearful of being rejected or exploited by a potentially gratifying object. He is therefore repetitively drawn into relationships offering support, but once established, the schizophrenic finds them too threatening to be maintained. He is terrorized by the prospect of a relationship which he perceives as mutually destructive, and his emotions are so poorly controlled that he is in constant danger of being overwhelmed by tension.

Set aside the mentalistic overtones of Guntrip's argument and it is evident that he is pointing in the same direction as Kubie and Jenkins. Frustration and deprivation in severe degree interfere with the normal course of development, and pathology is reflected in repetitive patterns of behavior and thought, in extreme tension levels, and in a freezing of emotional development, where needs of historical significance continue to plague the individual long beyond the stage they are appropriate. There is a loose consensus here about the important features of human pathology, a grouping that is amenable to further investigation. Since the foregoing studies have cast childhood frustration in a principal role, we turn now to a series of reports on behavior pathology in children, to see if disturbances at an early age are expressed in the same way.

Behavior Problems in Children

Erikson (1940, 1953) has observed that repetitive sequences in a child's play activities are often traceable to conflicts being expressed with the toys. He suggests that play serves for the anxious child the same function as talking over problems or vicariously rehearsing them does for adults: it provides a limited sphere somewhat removed from the conflict situation in which the central features of the problem can be replayed, examined, and alternatives evaluated. But even here anxiety may intercede if the play activities too closely parallel the real life conflict. When the problem is of central significance to the child yet he cannot resolve it, play activities assume a repetitive, intense nature, inevitably leading to some emotional dead end and consequent play disruption. The problem may be defensively adjusted through unconscious transformations to avoid outright recognition, but its repetitive expression in play testifies to the position of prominence it occupies in the life of the child.

More serious behavior disturbances in children have been investigated by Bettelheim (1950) and by Redl and Wineman (1951, 1952). Bettelheim's children are notable for their withdrawal, their autistic reconstruction of reality, for serious problems with such fundamental processes as eating, elimination, and sleep; and they exhibit a host of repetitive behaviors that are heavily colored with symbolic significance. The prelude to these difficulties is suggested by the social history of the children, where deprivation and rejection are recurrent themes.

Perhaps the most significant change during treatment is the gradual freeing of needs and impulses that heretofore had been drastically inhibited. In the supportive atmosphere of the treatment center, where no restrictions are placed on regressive behavior, the child may experiment with indulging his primitive needs. If the problem touches on nourishment and security, as it does for most of these children, regressive behavior with food occupies a prominent role. Socialized eating habits are dispensed with in favor of manually stuffing the mouth full of food. Demands to be spoon fed or nursed from a bottle are not uncommon.

Yet the reactivation of these needs brings about a serious anxiety reaction that the child cannot cope with. It is particularly disruptive because his history is notably deficient of experiences wherein some behavior on his part was successful in relieving tension. Having only a limited repertoire of coping mechanisms, the child is overwhelmed by the strength of his impulses and he fears losing control of himself. As insurance he may institute compulsive rituals to protect himself from anxiety.

Behavior gradually becomes more flexible and reality-oriented as the child avails himself of unrestricted gratification. His emotional reactions are updated to conform to present circumstances, rather than being dominated by past experiences of frustration. He can enlarge his sphere of interests and more importantly, he develops inner controls to initiate and modify behavior in adaptive fashion —a series of coping mechanisms to operate on the environment and regulate impulse expression. Instead of being passively overwhelmed, the child now participates actively in growth experiences that promote a sense of confidence in his ability to manage his life.

The emphasis here upon inner controls recalls the point made by Jenkins and Kubie about the development of mastery skills— how these play a fundamental role in adjustment. Where circumstances combine to interfere with their growth, the child is seriously handicapped in his transactions with the environment and in the management of his impulses. The Pioneers of Redl and Wineman, to whom we turn next, also illustrate the point but with the unique twist of having a few mastery skills, or ego functions, overworked in the service of defense.

The children chosen for treatment by Redl and Wineman (1951, 1952) were highly aggressive and destructive, characterized by serious deficiences in behavior control. These delinquents were unable to handle reasonable amounts of tension without becoming disorganized. Fear, excitement, guilt, recall of past memories— even in minor doses these events sufficed to overwhelm the control system and stimulate violent acting out. The ego functions of appraisal, control, and delay were quickly swamped by unmanageable tension and the child's behavior exhibited regressive, stereotyped characteristics.

But in sharp contrast to their helplessness in coping with internal tension, the Pioneers exhibited a set of shrewdly developed defenses that protected their gratification outlets and insulated them from the implications of their behavior. It is exemplified by the delinquent's attempt to provoke restrictive, punitive action from adults, thereby justifying his belief that he is persecuted and is entitled to express his hatred and aggression against the persecutors. Distrust of adults is strongly rooted in early experiences of frustration and rejection, and techniques to close off interference from that quarter, to minimize potential danger to impulse expression, have been sharpened through a long history of warfare with a hostile environment. Concurrently, self-protective mechanisms develop as an armor against recognizing personal responsibility for the behavior in question. Thus fortified, the delinquent shrewdly gears his behavior to maintain free license and justify his delusional belief that all adults are out to get him. But the defensive nature of these activities is disclosed by their rigid repetitiveness even in the benign atmosphere of the treatment home, and by the appearance of regressive demands for gratification once a positive relationship with an adult is established.

Natural Experiment in Adult Frustration

The discussion thus far has emphasized the effects of frustration during early development. However, the same mechanism is conceived to be operative under conditions of stress at all stages of maturity, although during adulthood the effects on well established behavior patterns may be less marked. In particular, stereotypy of behavior is expected as an outgrowth of extreme tension, as well as a progressive breakdown in the more highly refined behavior controls.

Hinkle and Wolff (1956) have impressively documented this process in their study of Communist indoctrination techniques. Analyzing the prisoner's experience in the hands of the Communist police, Hinkle and Wolff emphasize that he is confronted with a continuous series of frustrations. They compare the indoctrination procedure with experimental studies of frustration and observe that the reaction of the prisoner is basically similar to that of the experimental subject, with the exception that the prisoner's reaction is more all-embracing and devastating. The sequence of behavior following imprisonment runs as follows: purposeful exploratory activity; random exploration, with a general increase in motor activity; excitement, anxiety, hyperactivity; gradual subsidence of activity, with the exception of isolated repetitive acts. Such acts are endlessly repeated although they can never provide a solution. If pressure is continued long enough, the ultimate response is one of total inactivity, accompanied by strong feelings of dejection. The prisoner is unusually receptive to approval or human support (adapted from Hinkle & Wolff, 1956, p. 160).

The prison situation is unique in the degree to which it interferes with the biological and social routines of the prisoner's life. In addition, the prisoner is subjected to repeated interrogations that play upon his emotional weak points and constantly pressure him to compromise his position on an issue he may not clearly understand. Effective use is made of stress, although seldom in the form of outright torture, until the prisoner's resistance eventually decays. Behavior becomes more primitive and psychological withdrawal accompanies the development of stereotyped responses.

The entire process may be understood as a reaction to acute and unremitting tension.

Common Parameters

This brief survey of clinical research discloses three significant features that seem to cut across all classes of behavior pathology. There is on the one hand a rigid, intense manner of expressing symptomatic behavior, no matter what the content may be. Symptomatic behavior may be understood as a compromise activity that has been crystallized by its success in relieving tension, although it is demonstrably ineffective in securing need satisfaction. As an activity it pursues a stereotyped course and is relatively indifferent to control through reward or punishment. In form and function the symptoms may mirror a behavior pattern of historical significance, now no longer appropriate; they may express a conflict symbolically, or they may include postural and motor adjustments that bear no discernible relationship to the problem at hand.

In the second place, needs and emotions operative at the time of frustration seem to be fixated, and they furnish the individual with residual tensions that are chronologically out of step with his development in other areas. It is obvious that much surplus and subjective meaning attaches to the terms "need" and "emotion"; nevertheless, they are roughly descriptive of an internal state of affairs that exercises pressing control on the individual's behavior. The adult who is described as an oral character still maintains certain interests appropriate to an earlier phase of development, and the gratifications he seeks are thinly disguised holdovers from this period. The steady progression to mature, differentiated forms of emotional expression and impulse control is interrupted, and old problems of historical significance continue to bias all contemporary relationships. The individual cannot escape the past, and his techniques for coping with the environment likewise remain at a primitive, immature level.

The third important feature of behavior pathology is the presence of an intense anxiety reaction, and the manifold changes in behavior produced by anxiety. Due to its compelling drive properties, anxiety forces the individual into response patterns that ward off or alleviate anxiety, regardless of their adaptive value for other purposes. Precision and control give way to disorganization and panic. Flexible, goal directed adjustments are disrupted and behavior is crystallized into a stereotyped pattern. Subjectively, an anxiety reaction is accompanied by feelings of overwhelming dread and terror that are unpleasant in the extreme for the individual. His behavior is then dominated by primitive attempts to terminate the anxiety reaction and to ward off future attacks at all costs. These attempts will generally include internal defensive operations that process threatening thoughts or memories out of awareness, as well as the formation of stereotyped symptoms that forestall anxiety. Where anxiety is severe enough or is chronically sustained, it forces drastic changes in behavior of a pathological nature. From this viewpoint, anxiety appears to be the common denominator that underwrites the major features of behavior pathology.

These clinical phenomena serve as a basic point of reference for interpreting behavior pathology. But we are hindered at this stage by a certain looseness of terminology and concept, a vagueness about the exact nature and operation of these phenomena. The experimental literature on behavior pathology has made substantial inroads in this direction, and a survey of some of these studies may help to clarify the points in question.

Experimental Investigations of Behavior Pathology

The transition from the clinic to the laboratory reveals some abrupt changes in design and procedure, as well as a shift from human to animal subjects. We shall be principally concerned with three overlapping categories of research that offer powerful concepts for interpreting human pathology. They are: frustration, traumatic avoidance learning, and experimental neurosis. While the procedures differ markedly in each case, the results uniformly reveal serious disturbances in behavior. A brief review of these studies may serve to illustrate the basic conditions that give rise to behavior pathology.

Frustration and Response Fixation

The most extensive work on frustration has been carried out by Maier, whose theory and experiments were reported originally in his 1949 monograph, and the theory has been extended in a more recent publication (Maier, 1956). The basic apparatus Maier uses is the Lashley jumping stand and the problem on which the animal is trained is a discrimination between two visual patterns. Once a discrimination is established, frustration is introduced by locking the two doors randomly, so that neither a position response nor a discriminated pattern response leads to reward more than 50% of the time. Maier's definition of frustration flows directly from this procedure: forcing the animal by means of an air blast or electric shock to respond to a presently insoluble problem.

Under these conditions, the jump latency increases and the animal may interpolate several abortive jumps into his response pattern. The tension under which the animal operates is reflected by the number of seizures experienced on the jumping platform. One response, usually a position response, becomes increasingly stereotyped and is routinely performed on each trial. As the stereotyped response is established, less resistance to jumping is manifest and seizures decrease; apparently it provides an outlet for tension. Once established, the response continues indefinitely. Even where the problem is made soluble again the animal does not break the pattern, although he may give evidence of recognizing what the correct response is. Short of some specialized therapeutic measures, the animal's behavior is remarkably invariant.

Maier (1956) has introduced the concept of frustration threshold to handle these data, suggesting that extreme frustration precipitates a sharp transition to massive and uniquely patterned autonomic reactions that override voluntary control. Maier reasons that tension pitched at a very high level may remove cortical inhibition of primitive neural mechanisms and facilitate gross emotional discharge in the form of seizures, tantrums, and rage. Tension functionally reverses the processes of individuation and specificity in neural control and pushes behavior towards more primitive forms. While Maier has not yet clearly coordinated these superthreshold tensions with the behavioral characteristics of frustration—response stereotypy, abnormal fixations—the evidence is strongly in favor of some mechanism by which internal tension transforms normally variable, goal oriented behavior into an immutable response pattern.

Traumatic Avoidance Learning

We turn now to a series of studies that have focused explicitly upon the behavior changes effected under acute pain-fear conditions. Using electric shock of just subtetanizing intensity, Solomon and his colleagues (e.g., Solomon & Wynne, 1953, 1954) have traced the course of avoidance learning and explored the physiological correlatives of massive pain-fear reactions mobilized by shock.

The apparatus is a shuttle box with a gridded floor, separated into two compartments by an adjustable barrier and a drop gate. The dog is placed in one compartment, the conditioned stimulus

(CS) is presented, the drop gate removed, and 10 seconds later shock is administered. After a period of intense panic activity, the dog scrambles over the barrier and by so doing terminates both shock and the CS.

The basic datum is the latency of the animal's jump over the barrier, measured from the onset of the CS. The first few trials are escape trials, the animal failing to jump until shocked, but by the fifth trial the average dog has executed an avoidance response within the 10-second interval and therefore is not shocked. By definition the animal is now in the extinction phase, and the experiment is continued indefinitely to assess resistance to extinction.

These animals manifest an abrupt shift from escape to avoidance responses, and of greater significance, the jump latencies gradually *decrease* while the animal is executing successful avoidance responses. As trials cumulate, the animal jumps with increasing rapidity until a stable latency of about 1.6 seconds is reached. It should be emphasized that latencies stabilize long after the last shock is received, i.e., during the extinction phase. Solomon and Wynne (1954) conclude that fear has replaced shock as the drive, and escape from the fear producing CS serves to strengthen and move forward the jumping response.

The persistence of the jumping response is remarkable. Animals carried through 600 or more extinction trials showed no sign of extinction. But during this period when the avoidance response is being precisely executed each time, the overt signs of anxiety rapidly disappear as the dog becomes more and more stereotyped in his jumping activities. A rather casual attitude replaces the acute panic reaction manifested earlier. If, however, the dog is forcibly prevented from jumping by means of a barrier, an intense overt anxiety reaction develops immediately (Solomon, Kamin, & Wynne, 1953).

Solomon and Wynne (1954) advance a carefully reasoned argument to account for their results. Their argument is derived from two-process learning theory, but with two additional principles: anxiety conservation, and partial irreversibility of high intensity pain-fear reactions. These additions form a conceptual base from which protracted resistance to extinction and the apparent loss of overt anxiety can be derived. The theory offers a major inroad to problems of human pathology and will be briefly outlined here.

Anxiety conservation. This principle grows out of observations that animals appear more relaxed as the response latency decreases to some stable value around 1½ seconds. Moreover, if an animal delays appreciably on one trial before jumping, he appears quite upset following the jump and responds very rapidly for the next few trials. On the strength of these observations, Solomon and Wynne suggest that the animal gradually establishes a stable response latency which is short enough to prevent full arousal of the anxiety reaction. When the CS is presented, a finite time lag intercedes before all components of the anxiety reaction are mobilized, and by virtue of a speedy instrumental response the animal terminates the CS and thus prevents full arousal of the anxiety reaction. Solomon and Wynne (1954) carefully evaluate the literature on latency of autonomic functioning and conclude that at least 2 seconds, perhaps longer, must elapse before feedback from the peripheral autonomic nervous system can appreciably affect central motor processes. Moreover, variations in latency exist for the several autonomic responses that constitute the anxiety reaction. Consequently, the intensity and scope of the anxiety reaction activated by the CS is a direct function of the exposure period and many elements of the anxiety reaction are not aroused.

Based on these considerations, the substance of the anxiety conservation principle is:

> *if nonreinforced exercise of a CS-CR relationship is the necessary condition for extinction*, then the extinction of the associational linkage and at least this [the unaroused] portion of the anxiety reaction cannot take place. In one sense, the amplitude of the anxiety reaction is being *conserved* as a relatively intact potentiality, a latent functional entity (p. 359).

Put another way, the animal does not test reality by remaining with the CS long enough to find that it is no longer followed by shock. The instrumental response, established under extraordinary levels of pain-fear, now is sustained by its efficacy in preventing full scale arousal of anxiety. So long as the animal can perform the avoidance response rapidly, he can control anxiety; he has, at the behavioral level, the equivalent of a defense mechanism. But the very act that prevents anxiety also eliminates the conditions that must obtain for extinction to occur, namely, repeated arousal of anxiety within the CS situation but with the original reinforcement absent. So anxiety continues as a latent but nonetheless potent state, supporting all manner of avoidance activities in a situation that has long since ceased to have its former significance.

This treatment is roughly analogous to the clinical interpretation of defense mechanisms. When some event has been associated with severe anxiety, defense mechanisms are instituted to prevent subsequent arousal of anxiety. Defense mechanisms usually process out internal stimuli (thoughts, impulses), but they may also impose selective distortions upon the perception of external events that are threatening to the individual. Anxiety is thus the motivator of defense mechanisms, and at the same time it is the emotionally distressed state the individual avoids by dint of his defenses. By eliminating or disguising the internal stimuli that have become a signal for anxiety, the defense mechanisms successfully prevent an anxiety attack, just as withdrawal from the CS eliminated signs of anxiety in Solomon's dogs.

Partial irreversibility of intense pain-fear reactions. While anxiety may be conserved against extinction by a rapidly performed avoidance response, there are instances where the instrumental response either is not or cannot be executed quickly. A barrier may prevent jumping altogether, or on one trial the jump latency may lag below its usual stable value. On such occasions more anxiety should be aroused, and in the absence of pain as the unconditioned stimulus (UCS) the anxiety reaction should be fractionally reduced. Theoretically, a slow and gradual loss in the anxiety reaction would be expected. While extinction may be extended by the principle of anxiety conservation, it should not be permanently postponed.

On the strength of their data and related literature on avoidance learning, Solomon and Wynne (1954) believe that it is empirically possible to produce avoidance responses that will last for thousands of trials. They believe that ordinary extinction procedures will be ineffective for cases of severe trauma; anxiety will never be completely eliminated. They conclude, "Therefore, there must be a point at which the anxiety conservation phase is buttressed in some way; there must be some reason for such resistance to extinction . . ." (p. 361).

The second principle, *partial irreversibility,* constitutes the reason, and it means simply that when an intense pain-fear reaction of wide autonomic scope is classically conditioned to a CS, the stimulus is permanently invested with power to evoke a residual anxiety reaction. Repeated extinction trials may depress the anxiety reaction, but there is a fixed threshold value beyond which normal extinction procedures have no effect. Solomon thinks of partial irreversibility as a neurophysiological phenomenon, reflecting a relatively permanent reorganization within the central nervous system. The change is assumed to represent a decreased threshold of sensitivity, analogous to the partial reorganization of hormonal functioning that Selye (1950) incorporates in his concept of the adaptation syndrome.

With these two principles, Solomon and Wynne are able to interpret behavior that is functionally impervious to extinction. Clinicians have long since suspected that maladaptive behavior must be controlled by some such principles because it persists paradoxically even though causing distress and punishment. Of prime significance here is Solomon's observation that punishment may actually strengthen rather than weaken the instrumental avoidance response. Once the jumping response is firmly established, shocking the animal for performing the response seems to increase anxiety more than it inhibits jumping. This gives rise to the peculiar spectacle of an animal squealing vigorously as the CS is presented, yet inexorably jumping into shock. If our earlier equation of avoidance responses with human defensive activities is valid, it becomes increasingly clear why punishment does not eradicate anxiety-motivated behavior in clinical patients.

Experimental Neurosis

Behavior disturbances in animals have occupied a prominent research niche ever since Pavlov produced a "neurosis" in dogs who could no longer discriminate between positive and negative conditioned stimuli. Gantt (1944, 1953) and Liddell (1944, 1953) are among the principal American investigators using the conditioned reflex technique to study behavior disturbances, and their results are of considerable theoretical significance for the problem of anxiety.

Liddell on the Vigilance Reaction

Liddell has experimented extensively with sheep, goats, and pigs, using a feeble electric current applied to the foreleg to condition leg flexion. A metronome beat is introduced as the CS, and after a number of pairings the CR is firmly established. Subsequently, a second metronome beat is introduced but this beat is never followed by the UCS. After repeated trials a clear discrimination is established and the animal does not flex the leg to the negative stimulus. The animal does exhibit a sharp alerting reaction, just as for the positive stimulus, but in the negative instance he remains tense and vigilant although no response is performed. Paradoxically, the mild current applied following the positive stimulus produces relaxation and an abrupt decrease in tension.

By steadily converging the two metronome beats, the animal is required to make finer and finer discriminations until the threshold is passed. At this point the animal responds erratically, former discriminations are lost, and behavior disturbances appear. The animal may attack the apparatus, he may exhibit continuous tantrum behavior, or he may become cataleptic. Liddell has used several other procedures which are covered in detail in his 1944 article, but in all instances his conclusions are basically the same.

As a prelude to Liddell's basic thesis, we might note that the feeble electric current used here is in distinct contrast to the shock applied in traumatic avoidance learning. Liddell emphasizes that it is a startle stimulus rather than a pain stimulus; the current is set to be barely perceptible on the moistened fingers of the experimenter. Consequently, disruptions in behavior must be referred to the preliminary training procedures and the internal tension level of the animal, not to the traumatizing nature of the external stimulus.

Liddell (1953) proposes that the vigilance reaction is the emotional foundation out of which experimental neurosis develops. He documents his thesis by observing that a primordial function of the nervous system is vigilance, watchfulness, and generalized suspiciousness. This primitive sentinel activity is a behavioral equivalent of Cannon's emergency reaction. It is graded in intensity and reveals itself in qualitatively diverse behaviors, ranging from a startle reaction to panic. The vigilance reaction constitutes an emotional substrate for behavior, and when raised to disabling intensity it will disrupt prior habits and the flexible adjustments needed to insure adaptive behavior.

Conditioned reflex techniques lay the first stone by introducing the animal to an unfamiliar situation in which he is restrained by straps and has portions of the apparatus attached to his body. A long period of training is required for the animal to submit docilely to the conditioning regimen, during which impulsive behavior is gradually subordinated to habits of remaining alert yet selfcontained and quiet while employed in the apparatus. Such restraints inevitably create tension in the animal, revealed by periodic outbursts of tantrum behavior. Measures of respiration, heart rate, and gastrointestinal activity similarly testify to internal arousal at the time the animal appears to be quietly responding to the CS. If training is continued long enough, emotional arousal reaches a disabling intensity and disrupts organic processes as well as overt behavior.

Whatever the neurological basis, behavior disturbances produced by this method seem to be facilitated by an absence of patterned motor activity which would relieve the aroused state of the animal. One might argue that the animal's spontaneous behavior, consisting mainly of efforts to escape, is gradually inhibited because it is ineffective in securing release from the confines of the Pavlov frame. But overt habituation does not signify a decline in emotional arousal. Self-restraint is maintained at some expense, and even a thoroughly trained animal is easily disturbed by events that increase arousal or otherwise depart from the normal training schedule. It appears that the animal can inhibit only a limited amount of tension before more primitive mechanisms in the nervous system effect a gross discharge. As Judson Herrick observed, the mammal is constructed to be active and cannot tolerate restrictions in this sphere indefinitely without pathological consequences.

Gantt on Experimental Neurosis

For a period of some 12 years, Gantt (1944) intensively studied the behavior disturbances produced in one dog by conditioned reflex techniques. Basically, Gantt used a procedure identical to that of Liddell except salivation was conditioned rather than leg flexion. After the neurosis was established, Gantt made extensive autonomic recordings and systematically altered features of the conditioning situation, always observing whether the animal's symptoms improved or degenerated. His conclusions have been validated with numerous other subjects, but Nick serves as the best focal point for discussion.

Once a discrimination between positive and negative conditioned stimuli had been established, Gantt gradually converged the two stimuli and forced the limits of discrimination. Under these circumstances a widescale emotional reaction developed that might be termed anxiety. The animal was extremely upset during the conditioning session and actively resisted being placed in the apparatus. Autonomic changes appeared that surpassed in intensity the effects produced by such natural trauma as fighting, attack by another animal, or painful insult to the body. Respiratory difficulties, cardiac acceleration, increased blood sugar, and chronic pollakiuria are representative of the changes at this level. Coincidentally, these reactions became keyed to the CS; whenever the stimulus was presented a widescale and abrupt acceleration in autonomic processes immediately followed. And these dysfunctions were intractable; once elaborated in the form of a widespread anxiety reaction, they persisted erratically long after the more obvious signs of pathology had disappeared. At a more molar level, the behavior of the animal fell into a stereotyped format of overt symptoms. Gantt refers repeatedly to the "marked character, regular manifestation and stereotypy of pattern of the symptom complexes."

It is a matter of some consequence to understand how a situation that does not include pain can produce such an intense, chronic level of anxiety. Disturbed behavior is intuitively reasonable when considerable amounts of punishment have been absorbed; but what is responsible for breakdown in the artificial world of reflex conditioning, where the most innocuous of stimuli are used?

Gantt and Liddell agree that conditioning in the Pavlov apparatus is essentially emotional in nature, and the nominal CR is but an incidental feature that best serves as an index of the underlying emotional state. Stable responses testify to reasonable stability and integration in the animal's emotional reaction; unstable and fluctuating CRs are an indicator of widespread autonomic and behavioral disruptions that may develop precipitately. Even in the traditional salivary conditioning experiments where no instance of behavior disturbance is reported, the emotional undertone is clearly revealed during extinction. When meat powder is omitted, the animal exhibits increasing agitation following the CS, and at a later stage he may become extremely upset and attack the apparatus. While the salivary response drops out under these circumstances, a simple report of the number of unreinforced trials to extinction hardly does justice to the complex features of the animal's behavior.[2]

Experimental neurosis capitalizes upon this emotional substrate of behavior; in Liddell's terms, upon the innate vigilance reaction the animal brings to the conditioning situation. It plays upon processes endogenous to the organism; processes, in fact, that are at the heart of adaptation and survival. But in this instance the emotional processes are not keyed to the contingencies of the environment. They are aroused in situations of no biological significance to the animal, and they cumulate because spontaneous escape activity is inhibited. So they pervert their normal function, contributing to disintegration rather than adaptation.

---

[2] In quite a different context, O. R. Lindsley (1956) has applied operant conditioning techniques to a psychotic population and he reports that chronic schizophrenics often urinate or defecate during the extinction phase, again suggesting a strong emotional involvement.

An Overview

With all their diversity of emphasis and procedure, the experimental studies nevertheless are tied together by certain recurrent themes. Taking the studies as a group, two significant features stand out in all cases of behavior pathology. On the one hand, the foundation for pathology is laid by a progressive state of emotional arousal that finally reaches disastrous proportions. Acute anxiety is the common denominator of these studies, and at early stages it is expressed in autonomic fluctuations, in panic reactions, and in behavioral disorganization. Whether initiated by traumatically painful episodes or elaborated out of the vigilance reaction, anxiety is the basic operator in behavior pathology.

Secondly, the constant feature of the behavioral symptoms is their stereotypy and repetitiveness. Once established, the symptoms are remarkably intractable to control by external reward or punishment. They may qualify as instrumental avoidance responses or they may simply include primitive response patterns that were incidentally fixated, but in either cases the behavior is continued long after the task requirements have changed.

These two characteristics of behavior pathology, anchored as they are in careful experimental work, furnish substantial corroboration for the two similar features noted earlier in the clinical literature. We seem to be dealing here with principles of sufficient generality and power to produce consistent results even when a wide variety of species and procedures are sampled. The experimental studies do not provide any evidence on the third feature of clinical pathology, namely, the fixation of emotions and needs during early stages of development, but they were not designed to obtain data of this sort. Perhaps a group of experiments designed for this purpose, such as those of Hunt and his colleagues (1941, 1947), would produce the type of data desired.

If this be true, if in fact a set of principles can be established that apply to pathology in various species, then it would seem that we are in a more powerful position to isolate the basic conditions that underwrite pathology. Through animal studies the conditions that aggravate the emotional state of the organism can be explored, and nonverbal methods of therapeutic treatment can be systematically examined. There are enough striking parallels in symptoms between man and other mammals to suggest that valuable insights might be derived from such studies, insights that could be transposed and beneficially applied at the human level.

This is not to suggest that human pathology is devoid of any distinguishing characteristics. Human pathology has many unique features, to be sure, features that are interwoven with the advanced mental processes available to man. One cannot fail to be impressed with the florid ideation and rich detail of schizophrenic thinking. But if disturbances in behavior are keyed principally to emotional conditioning, perhaps the cognitive processes serve chiefly to express the problem more complexly, to extend through language and ideation the range of relevant experiences that are associated with the pathological state. In this sense the peculiarly symbolic quality that enters into human disturbances may be considered a secondary phenomenon, just as the ability to cast the problem in verbal terms and communicate it to a therapist is. They are adjuncts that testify to man's ability to symbolically represent his experience at several different levels. But the indispensable feature of pathology is the state of anxiety keyed to significant portions of the individual's experience, not the special verbal or mental images through which the experience is elaborated.

Summary

Two separate realms of discourse have contributed heavily to current conceptions of behavior pathology. The clinical realm, influenced largely by the theories of Freud, has offered dynamic interpretations of human disorders that are couched in a framework of drive, conflict, and defense. Its opposite number, experimental psychopathology, has been mainly occupied with animal studies in which behavior disturbances are methodically produced under carefully controlled conditions. There has been a noticeable lack of interchange between the two areas, yet a selective review of the literature suggests that behavior pathology in humans and animals may share some common principles.

In the clinical area there appear to be three general characteristics that apply to the functional behavioral disorders. The first of these is the presence of an intense anxiety reaction that disrupts goal directed behavior and mobilizes defensive processes aimed at warding off anxiety. Secondly, behavior relevant to the anxiety provoking situation becomes stereotyped and repetitive, furnishing the individual with a set of symptoms that are remarkably intractable to change. Finally, needs and emotions operative at the point of severe frustration seem to be fixated, and consequently the steady progression to mature forms of emotional expression and impulse control is disrupted. The individual is preoccupied with residual interests that are appropriate to an earlier phase of development, and current experiences are refracted to conform with these themes.

The experimental literature reveals that the presence of acute anxiety and the formation of stereotyped, repetitive symptoms are typical characteristics of this area as well, and these data provide a firm experimental foundation for the two similar characteristics observed in the clinical realm. The experimental studies yield no evidence about the fixation of emotions and needs because they were not designed to obtain data of this sort, but some suggestive results in this direction have been obtained by other experiments on infantile feeding frustration.

In combination, the clinical and experimental research raises the possibility that the same principles control behavior pathology in more than one species. The unique features of human pathology seem to be traceable to the complex cognitive processes through which the problem is expressed, rather than a fundamental difference in how the pathology originates. We would tentatively conclude that the indispensable feature of pathology is a strong anxiety reaction keyed to significant aspects of the individual's experience; and if this be valid, suggest further that animal research on nonverbal techniques of therapy might yield results that could be translated and beneficially applied at the human level.

REFERENCES

Alexander, F., & French, T. M. *Psychoanalytic therapy*. New York: Ronald, 1946.

Bettelheim, B. *Love is not enough*. Glencoe, Ill.: Free Press, 1950.

Erikson, E. H. Studies in the interpretation of play: I. Clinical observation of play disruption in young children. *Genetic Psychology Monographs*, 1950, **22**(4), 557-671.

Erikson, E. H. Growth and crises of the "healthy personality." In C. Kluckhohn, H. A. Murray, and D. M. Schneider (Eds.), *Personality in nature, society and culture*. (2nd ed.) New York: Knopf, 1953. Pp. 185-225.

Gantt, W. H. *Experimental basis for neurotic behavior*. New York: Hoever, 1944.

Gantt, W. H. Principles of nervous breakdown: Schizokinesis and autokinesis. *Annals of New York Academy of Science*, 1953, **56**, 143-163.

Guntrip, H. A study of Fairbairn's theory of schizoid reactions. *British Journal of Medical Psychology*, 1952, **25**, 86-103. [Reprinted in C. F. Reed, I. E. Alexander, and S. S. Tomkins (Eds.), *Psychopathology*. Cambridge: Harvard University Press, 1953. Pp. 344-369.]

Hinkle, L. E., Jr., & Wolff, H. G.   Communist interrogation and indoctrination of "enemies of the states." *Archives of Neurological Psychiatry*, 1956, **76**, 115-174.

Hunt, J. MvV.   The effects of infant feeding-frustration upon adult hoarding behavior. *Journal of Abnormal and Social Psychology*, 1941, **36**, 336-360.

Hunt, J. MvV., Schlosberg, H., Solomon, R. L., & Stellar, E.   Studies of the effects of infantile experience on adult behavior in rats: I. Effects of infantile feeding-frustration on adult hoarding. *Journal of Comparative and Physiological Psychology*, 1947, **40**, 291-304.

Jenkins, R. L.   Nature of the schizophrenic process. *Archives of Neurological Psychiatry*, 1950, **64**, 243-262.

Jenkins, R. L.   The schizophrenic sequence: Withdrawal, disorganization, psychotic reorganization. *American Journal of Orthopsychiatry*, 1952, **22**, 738-748.

Kubie, L. S.   The repetitive core of neurosis. *Psychoanalysis Quarterly*, 1941, **10**, 23-43.

Kubie, L. S.   The fundamental nature of the distinction between normality and neurosis. *Psychoanalysis Quarterly*, 1954, **23**, 167-204.

Liddell, H. S.   Conditioned reflex method and experimental neurosis. In J. McV. Hunt (Ed.), *Personality and the behavior disorders.* New York: Ronald, 1944. Pp. 389-412.

Liddell, H. S.   A comparative approach to the dynamics of experimental neuroses. *Annals of the New York Academy of Science*, 1953, **56**, 164-170.

Lindsley, O. R.   Operant conditioning methods applied to research in chronic schizophrenia. *Psychiatric Research Report*, 1956, **5**, 118-139.

Maier, N. R. F.   *Frustration: The study of behavior without a goal.* New York: McGraw-Hill, 1949.

Maier, N. R. F.   Frustration theory: Restatement and extension. *Psychological Review*, 1956, **63**, 370-388.

Mark, J. C.   The attitudes of the mothers of male schizophrenics toward child behavior. *Journal of Abnormal and Social Psychology*, 1953, **48**, 185-189.

Redl, F., & Wineman, D.   *Children who hate.* Glencoe, Ill.: Free Press, 1951.

Redl, F., & Wineman, D.   *Controls from within.* Glencoe, Ill.: Free Press, 1952.

Selye, H.   *The physiology and pathology of exposure to stress.* Montreal: Acta, 1950.

Solomon, R. L., Kamin, L. J., & Wynne, L. C.   Traumatic avoidance learning: The outcomes of several extinction procedures with dogs. *Journal of Abnormal and Social Psychology*, 1953, **48**, 291-302.

Solomon, R. L., & Wynne, L. C.   Traumatic avoidance learning: Acquisition in normal dogs. *Psychological Monograms*, 1953, **67** (4, Whole No. 354).

Solomon, R. L., & Wynne, L. C.   Traumatic avoidance learning: The principles of anxiety conservation and partial irreversibility. *Psychological Review*, 1954, **61**, 353-384.

4

Masochism: An Empirical Analysis

INTRODUCTION

The following article is in the same spirit and tradition as the preceding one, that is, it deals with the application of experimental research on lower animals to the understanding of pathology in humans. In the traditional Freudian usage, masochism refers to the obtaining of sexual gratification as a result of punishment or pain that has been inflicted upon oneself. More generally, however, masochism is used to refer to the deriving of pleasure from what appear to be unpleasant or painful experiences. That is, the individual consistently performs acts that he knows will result in punishment, rather than working to avoid these situations as a normal individual would be expected to do.

This review provides another excellent example of the use of animal research in the investigation of behavior pathology. The problem of the involvement of higher mental processes might be raised by the critics of this approach, especially because most of the theories that have been proposed to explain masochism involve processes beyond those possible in the laboratory rat. For example, it has been suggested that masochism is the result of (a) a reaction formation in which sadistic impulses are turned on the self, (b) the individual's attempt to relieve feelings of guilt by punishing himself, or (c) the manifestation of a general masochistic attitude toward life. If one accepted any of these explanations as the cause of masochism, it would be senseless to try to study masochism in animals. However, if one also accepts the possibility that masochism is a form of pathological behavior that is learned like any other behavior, then lower animals become appropriate subjects for basic studies of this behavior. That is, if one does not invoke mental processes for the explanation, the issues become researchable on animals. Wherever the use of animals is not appropriate, it will become apparent when the data are analyzed, or at least when an attempt is made to apply the animal results in humans. Lastly, it should be noted that when animals are used to carry out research on masochism, the behavior in the animals is called masochistic*like*. Since the observed behavior of the animals does meet the definitions set down by clinicians working with humans, the term *masochisticlike* may be unduly conservative. The use of this term may stem from the fact that in changing species we cannot be positive that the behavior is identical in all respects. That is, the same overt behavior *may* have different causes in men and animals, though in at least the present case this possibility is doubtful. When animals are used to study masochism, the research process is complete only after the principles developed in the simple animal situation are shown to apply to the complex human situation. The process could be shortened by beginning the research on humans. On the other hand, the complexity of the human situation and the problems of control may retard identification of the principles that underlie masochism, principles that can probably be more readily identified in animals and then tested in humans.

In the article by Jack Sandler the reader will find a careful review of research relevant to masochism, or masochisticlike behavior, in lower animals. It will immediately be apparent that higher mental processes need not be invoked to account for the masochisticlike behavior and that this behavior, like many other pathological behaviors, may be attributed instead to learning. The reader will also note, however, that this review encompasses only one of the stages necessary for the solution of the problem, that is, the investigation of the problem on the animal level. Unfortunately, this review does not contain data on the human level, but there is a high degree of similarity between the principles that govern animal and human learning, which makes it relatively safe to apply the results that Sandler reviews to humans. The *empirical* analysis offered by Sandler, well supported as it is with controlled experimental data, will probably carry us further in understanding masochism than some other forms of analysis.

In one sense, it might appear inappropriate in a book like this to devote an entire paper to the rather narrow topic of masochism. Sandler's paper has more to offer, however, than substantive material on masochism. While this paper does convey specific content relevant to masochism, it also presents and illustrates an important but often overlooked orientation to pathology. Therefore, it was included both to increase the reader's understanding of masochism and to provide the reader with another perspective from which to conceptualize and view pathology. This approach, and the more familiar dynamic approach, should be kept in mind while studying the problems and data presented in subsequent papers. In the last two articles in this book specific attention is again devoted to the experimental-learning approach.

4

MASOCHISM: AN EMPIRICAL ANALYSIS

JACK SANDLER[1]

The customarily held opinion that man seeks pleasure and avoids pain has been central to most attempts to predict and control human behavior. Recognizing, however, that few situations are either completely punishing or completely pleasurable, learning theorists (Guthrie, 1935; Mowrer, 1960; Skinner, 1953) have expanded this principle to encompass a wider range of human events. In this connection, one argument which has a high degree of consensual validity maintains that some degree of pain is involved in all behavior, even though this may be merely in the form of effort, apprehension, etc. (Brown, 1955). Restating the law of effect then, other things being equal, those situations which involve relatively great pleasure and relatively little punishment will lead to continued functioning, and those events where the reverse is true will result in decreased responding. As Mowrer (1960) states, "It is only when the pain is relatively great and the reward obscure that continued functioning gives rise to confusion" (p. 436). Behavior under these conditions might be termed masochistic.

The concept is no longer restricted to perverse erotic experiences (Reik, 1957) but is often used to describe any situation which encompasses continued functioning in the face of punishing consequences, where common sense dictates a contradiction to a simple punishment effect.

As is true with most clinical concepts, then, the application of the term masochism implies the aberrant, unusual, or bizarre. Most of the current information relating to the topic stems from an accumulation of clinical experiences often formulated within the psychoanalytic framework which emphasizes the importance of guilt, superego conflict, etc. The view advocated here, however, is that masochistic behavior represents an extension of learning

SOURCE. Reprinted with permission of the American Psychological Association and the author from the *Psychological Bulletin*, 1964, **62**, 197-204.
[1] The author wishes to gratefully acknowledge the assistance and cooperation of Herbert Kimmel and Judson S. Brown in the preparation of this paper.

principles and a systematic analysis of the phenomenon will reveal the variables which mediate such events. It is the purpose of this paper to provide an empirical definition of masochism which also reflects the predominant features of the clinical event, to review some of the relevant experimental findings which have reported the development of masochistic behavior in the laboratory situation, and to summarize the variables reflected in these investigations which seem to mediate the phenomenon in question.

A Definition of Masochism

The masochist seems to be the peculiar individual who continues functioning where the punishment is prepotent; that is, where common sense tells us the typical reaction to a given stimulus is avoidance. Any empirical definition must attempt to include this quality of the concept. The crux of the issue rests on demonstrating the typically noxious effects of a stimulus, on the one hand, and the absence or modification of this reaction in the masochistic situation, that is, a change in reaction to what is typically regarded as a punishing stimulus. For our purposes, then, masochism will be regarded as having been demonstrated in those instances where an empirically determined noxious stimulus, defined in terms of a pain response (avoidance, withdrawal, howling, leaping, etc.) does not reveal such effects in another intact member of the same species. Within this framework, masochism may take the form of simple desensitization at one extreme, to the actual performance of an act which produces the noxious stimulus, at the other extreme.

Relevant Research

There have been few attempts to investigate the phenomenon of masochism as such. However, a considerable number of studies have reported findings relevant to the above definition. In some cases, punishment was shown to have little influence on ongoing activities; in others punishment was shown to have facilitated performance and, in still others, punishment was shown to have actually maintained behavior. An arbitrary distinction of these investigations is made in terms of those revealing the above effects.

Punishment

No effect on behavior. Perhaps the earliest finding with regard to unusual reactions to punishment is reported by Pavlov (1960). In these instances, the expected response to severe, painful stimuli (intense electric shocks and skin lacerations) was not observed.

Pavlov (1960) described the finding in this fashion: "under the very closest scrutiny, not even the tiniest and most subtle objective phenomenon usually exhibited by animals under the influence of strong, injurious stimuli can be observed in these dogs" (p. 30).

Other investigators, working within the classical conditioning framework (Liddell, 1944; Slutskaya, 1928), reported similar findings in children and in a pig, respectively. In each of these instances the noxious event was introduced in typical conditioning stimulus fashion.

Still others, working within the framework of other methods, have confirmed these observations. For example, Mowrer and Viek (1948) were able to reduce the suppressive effects of shock on eating behavior in rats. In this case, rats trained to run a maze for food were shocked 10 seconds after eating. In one group, the shock was terminated by a vertical leap in the air. A second group of rats was administered a physically identical shock independent of any activity. Far greater eating inhibition took place in the group which had no "control" over shock termination. More recently, Miller (1960) was also able to reduce the typically noxious effects of shock on eating behavior in rats. Control subjects, trained to run a goal for food and suddenly exposed to strong shock at the goal revealed far greater eating inhibition than did rats exposed to gradually increasing shocks at the goal.

Facilitating behavior. The view that punishment can serve to facilitate behavior under certain conditions has received considerable support. Muenzinger demonstrated such effects in a series of investigations stretching back to the early thirties. The initial finding (Muenzinger, 1934), that a shock which was twice the threshold value for young rats (Muenzinger & Mize, 1933) would actually facilitate the learning of a light-dark discrimination beyond the influence of reward alone, was confirmed in a number of subsequent investigations (Muenzinger & Baxter, 1957; Muenzinger, Bernstone, & Richards, 1938; Muenzinger, Brown, Crow, & Powloski, 1952; Muenzinger & Powlowski, 1951; Muenzinger & Wood, 1935). Likewise, Drew (1938) and Freeburne and Taylor (1952) found that shock enhanced discrimination learning in rats beyond the effect of reward alone.

Rosenblum and Harlow (1963) report a similar effect in connection with a different species operating in a different procedure. They provided six infant rhesus monkeys with free access to a cloth surrogate mother. Two of the monkeys were exposed to 45 seconds of an air blast while on the surrogate, delivered at irregular periods of time. Preliminary observations had demonstrated such a stimulus to have strong aversive qualities for infant rhesus monkeys (p. 83). The results revealed that the punished monkeys spent a significantly longer period of time with the surrogate than did the nonpunished subjects. The authors (Rosenblum & Harlow, 1963) concluded that "an aversive stimulus can augment responsiveness to the surrogate even though the aversive stimulus is coincident spatially and temporally with surrogate contact" (p. 84).

Maintaining behavior. Perhaps most convincing are those studies which reveal behavior being maintained by noxious stimuli. These efforts are characterized by resistance to extinction as a consequence of punishment occurring during acquisition as well as during extinction.

Several observations are reported by Masserman (1946) which reveal the development of this form of masochistic behavior. Here, cats were trained to press a switch for food reward. Air blasts of gradually increasing intensity were then added as a second contingency to the switch press response. Previously, the air blast was shown to have aversive qualities (p. 75). Finally the food was withdrawn and the cats continued to work the switch for air blasts alone, thus exposing themselves to punishment.

Brown and his associates have conducted a series of studies clearly demonstrating the manner in which behavior can actually be maintained through punishment in a shock escape situation. The assumption here is that electric shock may be regarded as a primary drive source (Brown, 1961). In the first of these attempts, an unpublished observation cited in Mowrer (1950), a rat was trained to run an alley to escape shock. After training, the shock was administered only in a small area just prior to the escape box. The results indicated that the inclusion of this stimulus led to increased resistance to extinction despite the fact that merely remaining in the starting box would have led to shock avoidance. In a similar procedure, Gwinn (1949) found that rats trained in this fashion would run the alley faster and resist extinction longer (thus also receiving more extinction shocks) than did control rats that were not shocked during extinction. Interestingly enough, during extinction, some of the experimental subjects were exposed to twice the initial shock used in training but this seemed to have little effect in reducing running rates.

More recently, Brown, Martin, and Morrow (1964) have shown that these effects can be even further enhanced by modifying the procedure. In two experiments, rats were trained to escape shocks in a starting box by running down a 6-foot alley into an uncharged goal box. During "extinction" shock was withdrawn from the starting box, but some groups were exposed to shock in part or all of the alley. Control rats received no shock, providing evidence of the usual extinction process. In the first study, the introduction of alley shock had no effect on interfering with running rates. This procedure was then slightly modified (reducing extinction shock, reducing the number of escape trials, and providing for a more gradual transition from acquisition to extinction) in an attempt to enhance resistance to extinction in the alley-shock groups. The results clearly revealed that rats shocked during extinction under these conditions ran more rapidly and over a longer period of time (thus needlessly exposing themselves to painful experiences) than did the control rats. The authors concluded that the repeated approaches toward noxious stimuli developed by these procedures justify describing the behavior as "masochisticlike."

Azrin and his associates (Azrin, 1959, 1960; Azrin & Holz, 1961; Holz & Azrin, 1961) provide further evidence of the extent to which punishing contingencies can contribute to resistance to extinction. The importance of these efforts for the present analysis rests in the fact that the administration of the noxious stimulus is generated by a specific response under the organism's own control. Furthermore, the procedure involves positive reinforcement rather than two extensities of punishment as in the Brown situation. Although the investigations were primarily designed to determine the effects of punishment on operant respondent under various reinforcement schedules, the findings are directly relevant to the topic at hand. Their method involves the pigeon pecking response in the typical Skinner box situation. Various schedules of food reinforcement are delivered during which time the pigeon's behavior is shaped up. Following this, shock of varying intensities and duration is introduced as a second contingency to the pecking response. Included in their results (Azrin, 1960) are data which indicate that pigeons will shock themselves literally hundreds of times in order to receive food on an intermittent basis. The extent to which this behavior is maintained is apparently a function of a number of variables including shock intensity and reinforcement schedule. In general, however, they offer strong evidence of an animal's continued responding for stimulation which it would ordinarily avoid, with little interference of typical reinforcement-schedule effects. In the most definitive study of these events (Holz & Azrin, 1961) evidence is offered which reveals that pigeons increase their response rates as a function of punishment alone. In this study, subjects were run under two different daily conditions, one in which the response contingency was variable-interval food reinforcement and continuous, 60-volt shock; and a second, independent, daily extinction session without the reinforcement-shock contingency. The sessions were randomly arranged to eliminate the possibility of the subjects establishing a procedural discrimination. The results indicated that responding for shock and food was always greater than in the alternate sessions. Furthermore, this behavior was maintained even when the reinforcement was withdrawn, revealing that response rate was a function of shock alone. Finally, the introduction of shock alone into the extinction sessions resulted in immediate increases in response rate. Holz and Azrin (1961) summarized their findings in this fashion:

> These experiments demonstrate that a relatively severe punishment can increase responding. . . . This procedure of selectively pairing a stimulus with a reinforcer is the usual procedure for establishing a discrimination. This discriminative property that the punishment acquired produced the apparent anomaly. Indeed, the discriminative property came to exert an even greater effect on responding than did the aversive property (p. 231).

Discussion

The experimental findings cited in the preceding section are offered as experimental analogues to various clinical forms of masochistic behavior. In each case, the action of punishment has revealed a change in the expected response to noxious stimuli. In the most dramatic examples, organisms have been found actually working for punishing results. That such effects can be demonstrated has been suggested by several authorities. Guthrie (1935) asserted that aversive stimuli will lose their power to evoke avoidance responses if they are repeatedly presented when responses incompatible with punishment are prepotent. Skinner (1953) proposes two forms of masochism. In discussing how self-injury may be arranged, he states that individuals might expose themselves to aversive stimulation if, by doing so, they avoid even more aversive consequences. In another instance, aversive stimuli might be paired with the reinforcer which follows a given activity. The end result may be that "the aversive stimulus becomes positively reinforcing in the same process" (Skinner, 1953, p. 367).

Surprisingly, this view is in accord with analytical thinking. Thus, Fenichel (1945) states several conditions under which masochism might occur:

Certain experiences may have so firmly established the conviction that sexual pleasure must be associated with pain that suffering has become the prerequisite for sexual pleasure (p. 357).

He further adds:

Masochistic activities may follow the mechanism of "sacrifice"; the price beforehand is made to appease the gods and to make them contented at a relatively small cost. Masochistic activities of this kind are a "lesser evil" (p. 358).

Stripped of his analytical terminology, Fenichel seems to be describing the same arrangement as Skinner. More recently, Kelleher and Gollub (1962) have likewise indicated that

under appropriate experimental conditions, a positively or negatively reinforcing stimulus can be established as a positive conditioned reinforcer (p. 590).

The factors governing such events have not been explicitly formulated but some clues are offered by the literature. First, in order for the phenomenon to appear, it seems clear that the punishing event must be introduced only after a response has been established in the usual reinforcing paradigm. Secondly, the punishment must be introduced in such a way that the response is not completely inhibited during acquisition. This is precisely the view offered by Martin (1963) wherein he suggests that such an arrangement will lead to greater resistance to extinction than is the case with reward alone. To the extent that Martin is describing the facilitative or maintenance effects of punishment, he is also discussing the masochistic event as herein defined. The number of studies cited revealing masochistic findings suggests that the phenomenon is genuine and reproducible. The conditions necessary for a punishing stimulus to lose its noxious effects, or to facilitate learning, or to elicit behavior have been explicated by the various investigators as well as summarized by Kelleher and Gollub (1962) and Martin (1963). Obviously, in any given instance certain limiting factors (frequency of association between reward and punishment, strength of punisher, degree of deprivation, etc.) may serve to enhance these effects. The exact nature of these limiting conditions, however, are amenable to experimental analysis.

Such a view offers a general approach to an experimental attack on masochistic behavior. One other condition deserves to be mentioned which may be particularly crucial in the current analysis. For example, some attempt must be made to provide for the maintenance of punished, nonreinforced behavior over longer periods of time than has currently been demonstrated since this would provide even more convincing data to support the argument. One possibility here stems from research investigating the effect of partial reinforcement schedules. There is little doubt that the appropriate scheduling of events has a powerful influence on response durability (Ferster & Skinner, 1957). Thus, behavior can be maintained over long periods of time in the absence of reinforcement through the use of training under intermittent schedules. This factor, together with the establishment of shock as a discriminative stimulus, seems to be responsible for the high rates of self-aversive stimulation which Azrin and his associates report. The author (Sandler, 1962) has confirmed these findings in five marmoset monkeys. Organisms operating under these conditions reveal continued responding in the face of repeated punishment. If observations of these subjects are limited to those periods of responding during which no reinforcement occurs (often as high as 95% of the time) one might even conclude that these are truly masochistic creatures.

Manipulating reward and punishment schedules during acquisition and extinction might provide further data of an even more convincing nature.

Conclusions

There seems to be little doubt that characteristic reactions to painful stimuli can be modified by experimental techniques. Even more to the point, organisms can actually be made to work for punishment. Further efforts to analyze the variables underlying such phenomena within a learning framework will, no doubt, provide additional knowledge regarding the prediction and control of such forms of behavior. Aside from the clinical implications, the view espoused here has bearing on conceptual issues. The typical use of the term masochism carries with it certain unfortunate consequences. Primarily, it focuses on current activities, emphasizing the bizarre qualities of the behavior, to the neglect of other factors which may be even more important determinants (e.g., the reinforcement, the association between the reinforcement and the punishment, etc.). Furthermore, there is an implied assumption regarding the absolute nature of stimuli; that is, certain stimuli always have certain effects and any deviation constitutes an anomaly. Yet common sense observation recognizes the existence of an infinite number of circumstances in which people readily expose themselves to painful experiences. Even presumed, irreversible patterns of avoidance behavior in relatively simple organisms can be modified quite readily (Schneirla, 1959). Finally, the search for clues underlying masochistic behavior usually involves such terms as guilt feelings, superego conflicts, etc.; none of which have proven very fruitful in providing basic insights into the general phenomenon. Current experimental evidence offers, at least, a promising suggestion that such events can be subsumed within a framework of learning principles without recourse to such concepts. Perhaps, then, psychology would be better served if the term masochism was completely eliminated from our vocabulary. When faced with a situation which represents an inconsistency in expected forms of behavior, extensions of the laws of learning might supply some of the answers, and a comprehensive analysis of an individual's reinforcement history might better serve treatment purposes.

REFERENCES

Azrin, N. H. Punishment and recovery during fixed-ratio performance. *Journal of Experimental Analysis of Behavior*, 1959, **2**, 301-305.

Azrin, N. H. Effects of punishment intensity during variable-interval reinforcement. *Journal of Experimental Analysis of Behavior*, 1960, **3**, 123-142.

Azrin, N. H., & Holz, W. C. Punishment during fixed-interval reinforcement. *Journal of Experimental Analysis of Behavior*, 1961, **4**, 343-347.

Brown, J. S. Pleasure-seeking behavior and the drive-reduction hypothesis. *Psychological Review*, 1955, **62**, 169-179.

Brown, J. S. *The motivation of behavior.* New York: McGraw-Hill, 1961.

Brown, J. S., Martin, R. C., & Marrow, M. W. Self-punitive behavior in the rat: Facilitative effects of punishment on resistance to extinction. *Journal of Comparative and Physiological Psychology*, 1964, 57, 127-133.

Drew, G. C. The function of punishment in learning. *Journal of Genetic Psychology*, 1938, **52**, 257-267.

Fenichel, O. *The psychoanalytic theory of neurosis.* New York: Norton, 1945.

Ferster, C. B., & Skinner, B. F. *Schedules of reinforcement.* New York: Appleton-Century-Crofts, 1957.

Freeburne, C. M., & Taylor, J. E. Discrimination learning with shock for right and wrong responses in the same subjects. *Journal of Comparative and Physiological Psychology*, 1952, 45, 264-268.

Guthrie, E. R. *The psychology of learning.* New York: Harper, 1935.

Gwinn, G. T. The effects of punishment on acts motivated by fear. *Journal of Experimental Psychology*, 1949, 39, 260-269.

Holz, W. C., & Azrin, N. H.   Discriminative properties of punishment. *Journal of Experimental Analysis of Behavior*, 1961, 4, 225-232.

Kelleher, R. T., & Gollub, L. R.   A review of positive conditioned reinforcement. *Journal of Experimental Analysis of Behavior*, 1962, 5 (4, Suppl.), 543-597.

Liddell, H. S.   Animal behavior studies bearing on the problem of pain. *Psychosomatic Medicine*, 1944, 6, 261-263.

Martin, B.   Reward and punishment associated with the same goal response: A factor in the learning of motives. *Psychological Bulletin*, 1963, 60, 441-451.

Masserman, J. H.   *Principles of dynamic psychiatry*. Philadelphia, Pa.: Saunders, 1946.

Miller, N. E.   Learning resistance to pain and fear: Effects of overlearning, exposure, and rewarded exposure in context. *Journal of Experimental Psychology*, 1960, 60, 137-145.

Mowrer, O. H.   *Learning theory and personality dynamics*. New York: Ronald Press, 1950.

Mowrer, O. H.   *Learning theory and behavior*. New York: Wiley, 1960.

Mowrer, O. H., & Viek, P.   An experimental analogue of fear from a sense of helplessness. *Journal of Abnormal and Social Psychology*, 1948, 43, 193-200.

Muenzinger, K. F.   Motivation in learning: I. Electric shock for correct response in the visual discrimination habit. *Journal of Comparative Psychology*, 1934, 17, 267-277.

Muenzinger, K. F., & Baxter, L. F.   The effect of training to approach versus training to escape from electric shock upon subsequent discrimination learning. *Journal of Comparative Psychology*, 1957, 50, 252-257.

Muenzinger, K. F., Bernstone, A. H., & Richards, L.   Motivation in learning: VIII. Equivalent amounts of electric shock for right and wrong responses in a visual discrimination habit. *Journal of Comparative Psychology*, 1938, 26, 177-186.

Muenzinger, K. F., Brown, W. O., Crow, W. J., & Powloski, R. F.   Motivation in learning: XI. An analysis of electric shock for correct responses into its avoidance and accelerating components. *Journal of Experimental Psychology* 1952, 43, 115-119.

Muenzinger, K. F., & Mize, R. H.   The sensitivity of the white rat to electric shock. *Journal of Comparative Psychology*, 1933, 15, 139-148.

Muenzinger, K. F., & Powloski, A. F.   Motivation in learning: X. Comparison of electric shock for correct turns in a corrective and noncorrective situation. *Journal of Experimental Psychology*, 1951, 42, 118-124.

Muenzinger, K. F., & Wood, Alda.   Motivation in learning: IV. The function of punishment as determined by its temporal relation to the act of choice in the visual discrimination habit. *Journal of Comparative Psychology*, 1935, 20, 95-106.

Pavlov, I. P.   *Conditioned reflexes*. New York: Dover, 1960.

Reik, T.   *Of love and lust.* New York: Farrar, Strauss, & Cudahy, 1957.

Rosenblum, L. A., & Harlow, H. F.   Approach-avoidance conflict in the mother-surrogate situation. *Psychological Report,* 1963, **12,** 83-85.

Sandler, J.   Reinforcement combinations and masochistic behavior: A preliminary report. *Psychological Report,* 1962, **11,** 110.

Schneirla, T. C.   An evolutionary and developmental theory of biphasic processes underlying approach and withdrawal. In M. R. Jones (Ed.), *Nebraska symposium on motivation,* 1959. Lincoln, Nebr.: Nebraska University Press, 1959.

Skinner, B. F.   *Science and human behavior.* New York: Macmillan, 1953.

Slutskaya, M. M.   Converting defensive into food reflexes in oligophrenics and in normal children. *Zhurnal Neuropatological,* 1928, **21,** 195-210. Reviewed in G. H. S. Razran, Conditioned reflexes in children. *Archives of Psychology,* New York, 1933, **23** (148).

5

Psychological Variables in Allergic Disorders: A Review

INTRODUCTION

In seeking to understand psychopathology, it is important to maintain vigilance over a wide range of variables because both the causes and the manifestations of psychopathology may appear in any one of a number of areas. For example, within an individual there may be important interactions between the psychological and physiological variables, and either or both of these can affect or be affected by sociological variables outside the individual. Therefore, to develop a thorough knowledge of psychopathology it is essential to study the interactions among areas. In their article, Freeman, Feingold, Schlesinger, and Gorman review the research that has attempted to determine the relationships between psychological ·factors and allergic (physiological) disorders. They place primary emphasis on the asthmatic response, one of the important disorders in the general category of "psychosomatic" medicine.

There are numerous methodological problems that make research on psychosomatic disorders difficult. First of all it is important that the reaction in the patients selected for study be known to be triggered by a psychological factor. In allergic disorders, for example, one must be certain that the allergy is a consequence of a psychological problem rather than a response to a physiological allergen. The inclusion of patients in the experimental population who are actually responding to an allergen will, of course, make the discovery of psychological causes difficult or impossible. The exclusion of nonpsychosomatic patients from the population is a difficult task, but it is of crucial importance.

Finding personality or background differences between individuals with and without psychosomatic reactions does not necessarily mean that causative factors have been identified. Both the physiological response and the personality factor, for example, may stem from still another variable. Alternatively, the personality differences may have been caused by the physiological response. For example, a prolonged illness may have profound effects on personality, and, therefore, personality differences between psychosomatically ill persons and normal control subjects cannot necessarily be considered to be the cause of the illness. This possibility suggests that an appropriate control group for studying psychosomatics would be a group of individuals who had physiological responses similar to those of the experimental subjects but whose responses were known to be physiologically determined. Another control group that would contribute to a refined understanding of the psychological correlates of any one psychosomatic disorder would be a group of patients who were suffering from a different psychosomatic disorder. A comparison of the two psychosomatic groups would indicate whether there was any specificity in the relationships between various psychological factors and specific psychosomatic disorders or whether numerous types of disorders can stem from any one psychological factor. As the reader will see in later articles in this book, such problems in determining cause are not unique to psychosomatics. To a large extent these are the problems of *correlational* research, and they are not found as often in the more definitive *experimental* research.

An extremely wide variety of hypotheses have been offered to explain psychosomatic disorders. These range from hypotheses that suggest that the physiological *symptom is a symbol* of an underlying conflict (i.e., the individual had unresolved dependency needs, and the inability to breathe was symbolic of a suppressed cry for mother) to hypotheses that suggest that the symptom is an inappropriate attempt at *problem solving* (i.e., the child solves the problem of how to keep his mother close to him by being unable to breathe). Some of the hypotheses are very psychoanalytic in nature (i.e., failure to adequately sublimate sexual curiosity resulted in a conflict over the primitive olfactory curiosity that caused respiratory problems), whereas others are based on learning (i.e., after an allergen that causes an asthma attack has been paired a number of times with a previously neutral stimulus, through the proceess of classical conditioning, the neutral stimulus alone will be sufficient to elicit the asthmatic response). Just as there are great differences in the hypotheses that have been suggested, the reader will find that there are great differences in the quality of research that has been carried out to test the hypotheses. There are many excellent, experimentally sound investigations, and there are also a large number of experiments that yielded very provocative results, but which need to be replicated with methodological improvements. The methodological problems of most of the studies have been pointed out by the authors of this review article, and therefore the article provides a lesson in methodology in addition to reviewing the results in an important area of psychosomatic medicine.

5

PSYCHOLOGICAL VARIABLES IN
ALLERGIC DISORDERS: A REVIEW

EDITH H. FREEMAN, BEN F. FEINGOLD
KURT SCHLESINGER, AND FRANK J. GORMAN

Psychological variables, viewed as etiological factors or as concomitant processes in allergic disease, have long been of speculative interest. Since 1950, the body of research and clinical reports relating psychological variables and allergic illness has grown rapidly. This paper will summarize and critically review this body of literature with the aim of integrating findings from diverse sources and methods. Special emphasis will be placed on methodological aspects in order to provide a focus for evaluating the current status of the area and to suggest profitable areas for future work.

Mainly, papers in English dealing with psychological factors in respiratory allergy, published since 1950, are reviewed. Previous work has been comprehensively reviewed by Dunbar and Leigh (1954) ; however, certain influential earlier papers are included in the present review as points of orientation. A few papers from other languages also are discussed and are conceptually linked to investigations in English-speaking countries. The great size of this body of research dictates these limitations and the focus on respiratory allergy.

Psychological Characteristics of Allergic Patients

Several investigators have dealt with the role of psychological factors in allergic disorders from an exploratory point of view, simply asking whether any psychological characteristics distinguish allergic and nonallergic individuals. This question has been approached from two directions; first, some authors have described the personalities of allergic individuals and then made comparisons, either directly or indirectly, with nonallergic individuals.

SOURCE. Reprinted with permission of the American Psychosomatic Association and the author from *Psychosomatic Medicine*, 1964, **26**, 543-576.

Another approach has used psychological treatment of allergy patients, with the assumption that, if a cure or improvement in symptoms was effected, psychological factors must have been important in the disease entity. Descriptive personality studies will be discussed first, and a review of psychological treatment techniques will follow.

Descriptive studies are customarily without explicit prior theoretical formulations or hypotheses. The aim has been to discover whether important differences exist on psychological dimensions between allergic and nonallergic individuals. Authors usually have avoided assigning a direction of causation, i.e., whether psychological problems lead to allergic illness or vice versa.

Many kinds of problems arise in such comparative studies. Two frequent sampling difficulties are of special interest. First, it is extremely important that the criteria for classifying subjects as allergic individuals be carefully specified. Only when this has been done is it possible to know whether various investigators are describing the same kind of patient. Secondly, if the allergic group is composed of patients referred for psychiatric evaluation or treatment, serious restrictions need to be placed on conclusions drawn about allergy patients in general. There are also wide differences in the objectivity of the methods used; these range from standardized psychological tests to interviews and impressions from medical histories. The use of interviews and historical material as the source of data requires specific description about what was done and how conclusions were drawn; rather frequently such description has been lacking.

Personality Inventories

Dekker et al. (1961) compared 79 adult female asthma outpatients with 30 female normal subjects and 100 women patients at a psychoanalytic institute by use of the Heron Two-Part Personality Inventory, a relatively new paper-and-pencil inventory. The authors reported no differences between asthmatics and neurotics on this test, but they did find significant differences between asthmatics and normals; these findings seemed to support the hypothesis that asthmatics are neurotic. These authors are among the few to report careful classification of their sample, in this case by the use of the specific procedures of skin and inhalation tests.

Smith (1962a) compared 36 people with various allergic symptoms and 36 nonallergic individuals on the Minnesota Multiphasic Personality Inventory, a widely used paper-and-pencil inventory.

On five scales he reported that the allergic group had significantly elevated, i.e., more disturbed, scores. In a second study (1962b) with 76 allergic and 76 nonallergic adults, Smith performed an item analysis of the MMPI. The allergic subjects admitted to a variety of conflicts more often than did nonallergics; these included conflicts over dissatisfaction with parents, and such manifestations of conflict as alienation and cynicism, feelings of inadequacy, and depression. In both studies, subjects were classified as allergic or nonallergic from a questionnaire dealing with history of elimination diets, positive skin tests, or symptoms typical of allergy. No corroborative medical information was reported. Additionally, Smith did not indicate whether the findings of the second study replicated those of the first.

Leigh and Marley (1956) administered the Cornell Medical Index, an inventory of medical complaints including neurotic symptoms, to four groups: 65 outpatient asthmatics, 77 hospitalized asthmatics, 118 neurotics in psychiatric treatment, and 118 department store workers. Comparing the frequency of admission of psychiatric symptoms, they found that asthmatics and neurotics in psychiatric treatment had similar scores; asthmatics in medical treatment mentioned fewer neurotic symptoms than the former groups but significantly more than the normal controls. The authors did not report any procedures to indicate whether the asthmatic subjects were in fact allergic.

Franks and Leigh (1959) gave the Maudsley Personality Inventory and conditioned the eye blink response to 20 outpatient asthmatics, 40 neurotics, and 20 normal adults. They found no differences in speed of conditioning or introversion-extraversion, but the neuroticism scores of asthmatics were between the neurotic and normal groups on the personality inventory. Again, it is not known whether these asthmatic subjects were demonstrably allergic.

Projective Techniques

A few studies have contrasted projective test responses of asthmatics and nonasthmatics. Israel (1954) compared Rorschach records of 30 adult asthmatics referred to a psychiatrist with those of 30 matched neurotics, and with Beck's normal sample. Compared with both groups, asthmatics had a lower response total, largely because they seldom produced very long records. She related this finding to the clinical assumption of constriction and inhibition in asthmatics.

Neuhaus (1958) contrasted 34 asthmatic children and 25 of their siblings with three other groups: 34 children with cardiac illness and 24 siblings, and 68 matched normal controls. Tests used were the Rorschach, Brown Personality Inventory, and Despert Fables. Based on test interpretations, the asthmatics were reported to be more neurotic, insecure, and dependent than the normal children, but they did not differ from children with cardiac illness or their siblings. The author concluded that there was no distinctive personality pattern for asthmatics; many previously reported psychological findings might be attributable to the experience of chronic illness.

Other Methods of Personality Description

Interviews, medical histories, and behavior ratings have also been used. Rees (1956a), for example, contrasted the histories of 441 asthmatic outpatients with 321 appendectomy, herniotomy, and accident cases of matched sex and age. Ratings indicated that 50–60% of asthma attacks were precipitated at least partially by emotional crises and that asthmatics displayed more neurotic symptoms than did the controls. Using similar methods (1956b), he found a somewhat higher percentage of emotional precipitation among elderly asthmatics. He contrasted hay fever patients (1959) with controls on a personality trait rating scale, and did not find differences between groups; however, hay fever patients with high neurotic trait scores were more often rated as having emotional precipitants for their symptoms.

Harris and Shure (1956) used teachers' subjective judgments of adjustment to compare asthmatic and nonasthmatic school children. They reported that the 2% of the sample with asthma did not have greater disturbances of adjustment or distinctive personality patterns.

Indirectly related studies by Leigh and Pond (1956) and Holmgren and Kraepelin (1953) found a substantial percentage of abnormal EEG's in asthmatics. Both papers, the former dealing with adults, the latter with children, reported that between 30–40% of the cases showed an excess of intermediate slow activity. The Leigh and Pond study, however, used asthmatics referred to a psychiatrist, and the dysrrthmias observed were similar to those found in a psychiatric sample.

Studies without Control Groups

A few studies have explored relationships between psychological disturbances and asthma without using comparison groups. Forty asthmatic adults in psychotherapy were rated from interview material by Knapp and Nemetz (1957a); only three approached a rating of psychological normality. Internists graded asthma for severity, and the authors reported a correlation of +0.813 between severity and degree of conflict about maturity.

Creak and Stephen (1958) reported that among 15 "routine referrals" of allergic children to a psychological clinic many exhibited maternal overprotection and fears of hostile expression. Gunnarson (1950) said that, with routine psychiatric examination, 53% of a sample of 58 asthmatic children seemed to exhibit "psychic disease," especially repressed aggression and pathological fixation to the mother. Strauss (1956) reported a similar proportion of "psychic participation" in a sample of 30 asthmatics he interviewed. Mansmann (1952) reported that the Rorschachs of 12 severe asthmatics suggested dependency, striving for recognition, and poor identification.

Comments. In summary, most of these studies seem to indicate greater psychological disturbance among asthmatics than among nonasthmatics, and there is some similar evidence for groups with other allergic symptoms. Before this conclusion can be accepted, however, certain crucial methodological improvements seem necessary. Of all these studies, only the paper by Dekker et al. (1961) reports a careful basis for classifying subjects as allergic and nonallergic. Until it is known to what extent investigators are actually dealing with allergic patients, and further with what kinds of allergic patients, conclusions about their psychological status will have little meaning. Furthermore, the Leigh and Marley study (1956) found that asthmatic patients in psychiatric therapy admitted to more neurotic symptoms than did an unselected sample of asthmatics. These results should make it quite clear that one cannot generalize from a psychiatric sample to other samples with allergic symptoms.

The work of Neuhaus (1958) indicated that some of the obtained personality differences may result from the experience of chronic illness; asthmatic children, those with another chronic illness, and siblings—all responded similarly to psychological tests and differed from a matched group of normal children. This would seem to be an important finding for further investigation.

Finally, these studies use a wide variety of measurement techniques—several personality inventories, projective techniques, and subjective ratings from medical history or observation. Rating of personality characteristics from medical histories poses many problems—the availability of pertinent information, accuracy of the original recording, the amount of inference used by the raters, and the different aspects of the material responded to by different raters. Studies using such techniques, therefore, should report the degree of agreement between raters and should use appropriate control groups. The same difficulties obtain in observational studies, unless rigorous criteria for rating behavior are set forth at the outset.

Psychological Treatment of Allergic Individuals

Over the years a very large number of authors have advocated formal psychological treatment or psychologically oriented management of allergic patients. Such authors differ in the importance they assign to psychological forms of treatment; some have viewed emotional support and counseling as helpful adjuncts, while others consider intensive psychotherapy as the necessary treatment for the patient's allergy. Implicit or explicit in all these workers' thinking has been the assignment of *some* degree of importance to psychological factors in the etiology of allergic symptoms.

With few exceptions, papers considered in this section are impressionistic accounts of cases handled with reported success by a variety of psychological techniques. There have been very few attempts to compare groups receiving only traditional allergy treatment. For the most part, explicit criteria of improvement have also been lacking.

Psychologically Oriented Medical Management

Certain writers have advocated what they termed "psychosomatic management" of allergic patients; by this they meant that the allergist should combine desensitization treatment or other allergy treatment of choice with permissive and nonthreatening discussions of difficulties in the patient's life. Brown (1951a) and Rackemann (1950) noted that allergists who functioned in a supportive, encouraging way with patients seemed to have good results. Unger and Unger (1952) and Sirmay (1953) considered reassurance an important part of treatment, but felt that psychological factors would be less significant when important allergens were discovered and eliminated. Ziwar (1954) and Stevenson (1950) stressed the importance of treating "the whole person." Abramson (1956) pointed out that all allergists do some "automatic psychotherapy" through their history taking and physical procedures, and estimated that 5% of allergy patients are suited for psychoanalysis. Kraft (1963) advocated treatment leading to awareness of the role of anxieties in producing symptoms, especially with intractable asthma. Miller and Baruch (1953, 1956, 1951, 1958) cited examples from their practice to show how an allergist might behave psychotherapeutically.

Tranquilizing Drugs and Hypnosis

Papers by Miller (1960), Taub (1961), and Eisenberg (1957) reported that symptoms such as anxiety, tension, and depression in allergy patients could sometimes be handled successfully with tranquilizing drugs. In these studies clinical judgments were used as standards of improvement.

Some workers have claimed great effectiveness for hypnosis in treating allergies, but without substantiating evidence. Aston (1959) reported that after one session of suggestion a patient was symptom-free 2 years later. Raginsky (1962) used a combination of hypnosis, clay modeling, and free association; he reported subsequent improvement in symptoms. Mayer-Laughman et al. (1962) compared the use of hypnosis on adult asthmatics with a bronchodilator drug over a 6-month period, the index of improvement being patients' diary recordings. Patients in hypnosis reported more improvement than those on the drug.

Two studies attempted objective evaluation of the usefulness of hypnosis. Edwards (1960) studied improvement with post-hypnotic suggestion in 6 hospitalized asthmatics via serial ventilatory function tests and found that the forced expiratory volume increased over several days. White (1961) conducted a careful study of hypnosis with 10 asthmatic patients, but his findings conflict with Edwards'. In seven to ten hypnotic sessions with each patient over a period of several months, posthypnotic suggestions of easier breathing, lessened bronchospasm, and increased confidence were used. Patients were asked after each session for subjective assessments of change, and tests of respiratory function before and after hypnosis were recorded. No differences were found with the respiratory function tests, but subjectively the patients reported improvement. The author attributes these findings—and the improvement in patients' general life situations—to the effects of posthypnotic suggestion without physiological change. This study underscores the need for careful evaluation of improvements reported by patients, and it deserves to be followed by similar work.

Environmental Manipulation

Manipulation of the environment has been another method of treating personality problems presumed to be important among allergic individuals. Murray and Bierer (1951) reported that a boy with continuous sneezing lost his symptoms after removal from a competitive school situation, though previous medical treatment had failed. A series of papers by Peshkin (1956, 1959, 1960), Peshkin and Abramson (1958), Tuft (1957), Hallowitz (1950), and Nitzberg (1952), have described success of a residential treatment center in rehabilitating chronic intractably asthmatic children. Their sample was composed of children with severe perennial symptoms requiring frequent hospitalizations and not responding to treatment in their communities. With separation from their homes for 18-24 months, 99% of a group of 150 children recovered substantially, and 95% had maintained this improvement after 3 years. Peshkin and his coworkers attributed the improvement mainly to the "parentectomy," which transferred the child to a more favorable environment for medical management and psychotherapy. Some efforts are currently being made to study systematically the various factors contributing to this success (see under *Subgroups within the Allergic Population*).

Individual Psychotherapy

Papers by Abramson (1948, 1956, 1961) have detailed his use of psychotherapy with asthmatic patients. Recorded excerpts from therapy hours illustrate changes he finds occurring in successful psychotherapy, e.g., marked decreases in references to somatic symptoms for patients "cured" of asthma and eczema. Elsewhere Abramson (1959) described types of allergic patients he feels need psychotherapy; one such group he called "pseudoallergic schizophrenics," i.e., those whose allergic symptomatology serves as a means to avoid dealing with psychotic processes.

Miller and Baruch (1953) have described psychotherapy in acute asthma attacks as "feeding the patient's affect hunger" and lessening fear of rejection; a later phase was release of anger. Gaudet (1950) traced the psychotherapy process with a severely asthmatic child and his parents over a one year period and considered the therapeutic relationship more important than insight development.

Group Psychotherapy

A few writers have commented on the use of group psychotherapy with allergic patients. Both Miller and Baruch (1958) and

Peshkin (1959) and Abramson (1960) described group therapy with parents of allergic children; they felt treatment of the parents enabled the child to express feelings more readily.

Miller and Baruch (1950, 1956) also described successful group therapy with adult allergic patients. Clapham and Sclare (1958) reported on group therapy with 6 asthmatics. After one year, 5 of the six were independently judged as "alleviated or much improved," while only 13 of 28 who had refused group therapy were so rated. Sclare and Crockett (1957) used group therapy with 16 asthmatics assessed as having "dominant psychological factors" in the etiology of their asthma. Six control groups of varying etiology received medical treatment for the same period. Clinical ratings of change did not show greater improvement in allergic symptoms for the therapy group, but anxiety and tension were reduced.

Groen and Pelser (1960) conducted group therapy with 18 men and 15 women asthma patients over several years. These patients also received symptomatic treatment; they were compared with asthmatics receiving symptomatic treatment only and were found to show a significantly larger amount of clinically rated improvement than the controls. Barendregt (1957) further compared those receiving group therapy and medical treatment. Testing and retesting with the Rorschach after a 19-month interval indicated that asthmatics in therapy gave fewer responses with themes of oppression and somewhat fewer "damage" responses.

Comments. To summarize, nearly all treatment methods used with neurotic patients have been tried with allergics, too. The accounts of success have usually been subjective statements that "this treatment seems to work." Few indeed are the attempts to test this assumption. Some users of group psychotherapy are exceptions; they seem to be aware of the need for controlled studies and have begun to take initial steps in this direction. Several workers have contrasted the usefulness of combining group psychotherapy and allergy treatment versus allergy treatment alone. Future investigators, however, need to specify criteria for assigning patients to psychotherapy or allergy management. The results from studies where psychotherapy was given to the most neurotic patients cannot be compared with those where psychotherapy was assigned in a random fashion. Assumptions about the role of psychological factors in allergy and the generalizability of results are obviously quite different for the two approaches.

There are enough accounts of successful psychological treatment with allergic patients to conclude that at least sometimes it proves to be of benefit in controlling allergic symptoms. These are, however, isolated clinical reports of success; one must wonder how many failures go unreported. Even more germane, however, is the question of what kind of patients benefit from psychological treatment. Are they all, in fact, allergic, or are many called allergic because of current symptoms rather than immunological patterns? If researchers took care to design studies aimed at answering these questions, treatment studies could begin to contribute to an overall understanding of the field.

Specific Hypotheses

In this section we consider the work that has been done to test a variety of specific hypotheses relating psychological factors to allergies. Some of these studies relate to allergies in general and some to asthma alone; but most assign major importance to psychological variables in the etiology of allergic symptoms. This assumption is less explicit, however, in the first hypothesis to be discussed.

Asthma and Psychosis

There is a widely shared belief that asthma seldom occurs among psychotic patients. Many writers have expressed the conviction that psychosomatic illness in general and asthma particularly cannot coexist with a functional psychosis. In any individual, it is expected that periods of psychosomatic illness will alternate with periods of psychosis; for the population as a whole, significantly fewer psychotics will have psychosomatic disturbances.

The basis for this assumption is somewhat difficult to determine. To a large degree it has simply been an observation of workers in mental hospitals that asthma is not reported among their patients. There is also an underlying assumption, seldom stated explicitly, that asthma functions as a psychological defense against psychosis and can be a substitute for psychosis. Whatever its origins, this assumed relationship has become accepted among many practitioners, and recently investigators have begun to look for evidence of its empirical validity.

Ross et al. (1950) surveyed medical data on 1600 hospitalized psychotics and found an asthma incidence of .8%, compared to the general U.S. incidence of 1.5–2.0%. Swartz and Semrad (1951) compared incidences of psychosomatic disorders among 578 hospitalized psychotic patients versus 264 nonpsychotics in the same hospital. On a questionnaire 4.5% of the nonpsychotics admitted to a psychosomatic complaint whereas only 3.5% of the psychotics did so. In interviews, half of the psychotics indicated that physical symptoms remained constant during psychosis and half said that symptoms improved.

Leigh and Doust (1953) examined histories and records of 28 psychotics with asthma, but could find no relationships between the two disorders. They then surveyed a mental hospital and found an asthma incidence of .64% which they compared to the estimated 1.5–2.0% in the general population. Sabbath and Luce (1952), from a study of 32 hospitalized psychotics, concluded that whether a patient retained or lost asthma symptoms was inversely related to the degree of psychotic organization; well-systematized paranoid patients tended to retain their asthma, while very disorganized patients stopped having attacks.

A few studies deal with this issue experimentally. Funkenstein (1950a, b) reported that in two small samples asthma and psychosis alternated, and there were concomitant shifts in autonomic functioning in response to mecholyl injections. When the patient was actively psychotic, mecholyl led to transient systolic blood pressure change and minor wheezing; when temporarily not psychotic, blood pressure reaction to mecholyl was marked, and asthma attacks occurred. Freedman et al. (1956) skin-tested 22 chronic hospitalized schizophrenics and 22 medical students with allergens, histamine, and cantharides, testing the hypothesis that psychosis involves diminished ability to react allergically. The patients did not show a diminished reaction to allergens as compared to control subjects, but did have smaller wheal responses to histamine.

Other writers have reached conclusions from clinical study of a few cases. Mandell and Younger (1962) noted that in 4 cases asthma symptoms stopped with increased psychiatric disturbance and vice versa; Prout (1951), however, reported 5 cases where this alternation did not occur. Appel and Rosen (1950) studied 4 psychotics with various psychosomatic illnesses and found alternation between exacerbation of one and the other in 3 cases; the exception was the patient with asthma.

Two studies have suggested relationships between asthma and addiction. Chessick et al. (1960) reported very high incidence of asthma history in institutionalized narcotics addicts, 5–6% of new admissions, 12.5% of those staying in the institution over two months. Eighty per cent of these patients reported that their asthmatic episodes stopped or became less frequent after physical dependence on heroin had developed. Hawkins (1958) studied the medical records of 100 alcoholic and 100 nonalcoholic discharged tuberculosis patients and found that the alcoholic patients had more nasal and respiratory complaints.

Comments. Whether the hypothesized negative relationship between asthma and psychosis actually exists remains unanswered. The evidence is contradictory, and much of the contradiction here again appears to be attributable to methodological shortcomings. In addition to the kinds of difficulties cited above, some special problems have handicapped this area of research. One difficulty has been dependence for allergy diagnosis on self reports of hospitalized psychotics. Earlier, Zeller and Eolin (1942) found allergy incidence in hospitalized psychotics to be equal to that of the general population; their methods involved scratch testing a large random sample of patients and sending a questionnaire about symptoms to relatives. Such methods would seem somewhat more objective, but even this alone is insufficient evidence for allergy in the absence of careful history and examination. Secondly, general population incidence statistics gathered in 1928 on various allergic disorders are still being used as the basis for comparison; some revision of these figures is very likely in order.

There appear to be substantial differences in the use of the term "psychotic" from one study to another and these discrepancies may have a great deal to do with the conflicting results. The work of Sabbath and Luce (1952) indicates that the severity of personality disorganization in psychosis may be an important differentiating variable in studies of asthma-psychosis relationships. Description of the patients in a sample with respect to extent of personality disturbance therefore becomes extremely important. Finally, further pursuit of the experimental approaches of Funkenstein (1950a, b) and Freedman et al. (1956)—i.e., the Funkenstein test using mecholyl injections and Freedman's experimental use of skin tests, histamine, and cantharide injections—would seem worth while. If relationships between asthma and psychosis are found in future studies using improved methods, such experimental investigations would help to explain underlying mechanisms.

Psychoanalytic Theories

Probably the most familiar hypotheses of psychological etiology in respiratory allergies are those propounded by Alexander and

French and their colleagues. We review briefly below their formulations and the work developing out of them.

The Theoretical Position

French and Alexander hypothesized (1941, 1950a, b) that conflict around excessive unresolved dependence on the mother was such that a threat of separation from her could precipitate an asthmatic attack. An attack represented a suppressed cry for the mother, and crying in the child or confession in the adult were dynamically linked; viz., either could relieve guilt and re-establish the dependent bond. French and Alexander observed no characteristic personality patterns in their patients other than preoccupation with themes of maternal rejection and wishes to be protected and loved; they believed that a combination of allergen sensitivity and conflict activation produced symptoms and that treatment of either problem would bring relief. Weiss (1950, p. 27) concurred in viewing asthma as a vegetative organ neurosis "representing early and profound deviations of personality development." The symptoms, then, are the physiological accompaniment of a constantly recurring emotional state. Saul and Lyons (1951) suggested that asthma develops when a child's longing for the mother is linked to the respiratory tract from its earliest crying and help-seeking. French (1950) noted that these hypotheses were developed from the study of asthmatics in severe enough emotional distress to undertake psychoanalysis, but he also felt that the *kinds* of conflicts associated with the illness should generalize to less disturbed groups.

A number of writers, e.g., Miller (1950), Edgell (1952), Alcock (1960), and Schatia (1950), reviewed these formulations favorably and stressed various facets of the hypothesized conflicts in asthma: emotional insecurity, repressed aggression, sadomasochistic trends, etc. Stovkis (1959), in his review of the literature, suggested that neither personality structure nor areas of conflict are unique to allergic patients, but that all allergic individuals share an ambivalent attitude toward the mother; further, asthmatics, considered separately from other types of allergic patients, seem to be hypersensitive to separation or loss of dependency.

A few writers, however, have been critical of these formulations. Ibor (1956), for instance, doubts psychogenic explanations for asthma, believing regressive wishes and other commonly attributed characteristics so ubiquitous as to lack explanatory value. Harris (1955) has also made critical statements, and Abramson (1954)

stressed the complexity and mutuality of relevant family interaction.

Case Reports

Many authors have presented case material illustrating these
viewpoints, beginning with the descriptions by French and Alexander (1941), and Gerard (1948). Gerard saw five children in
therapy who continued to react strongly to allergens but were
symptom free after psychotherapy. Alexander and Visotsky (1955)
detailed the onset of asthma in an elderly woman, relating her
symptoms to loss of dependence on the last of a life-long series of
mother substitutes. Hurst, Henkin, and Lustig (1950) described
focusing of conflict around the respiratory tract in patients with
various respiratory illnesses. Chessick et al. (1960) (see under
Relationship Between Asthma and Psychosis) reporting the very
high incidence of asthma among institutionalized narcotics addicts, pointed out the similarity of personality theories for manic-
depressive psychosis, addiction, and asthma, i.e., the centrality
accorded to loss of dependent gratification.

There is anecdotal evidence about the role of crying in asthma.
Selinsky (1960) described the therapy of several hypermasculine
asthma patients whose symptoms improved when they wept over
feelings of loneliness. Doust and Leigh (1953) noted from study
of 30 asthmatics that emotional tension could be relieved by motor
expression such as weeping, laughing, acting out, confession, or an
asthmatic attack. Scheflen (1953) described a schizophrenic patient
who screamed like an infant when she felt rejected; this typically
led into an asthma attack which stopped with sobbing and shedding
tears.

Psychiatric studies of groups of cases. Coolidge (1956) described
three asthmatic children with asthmatic mothers whom he felt
demonstrated mother-child relationships typical of 49 other asthmatic children he studied. He characterized the relationship as
symbiotic, with the mother participating in the dependent gratification of the illness. Both focused on the child's breathing, and when
the child's asthma and adjustment improved, the mother's often
worsened.

Mitchell et al. (1953) used psychological tests and interviewing
with 22 allergic children and their mothers. They characterized
the mothers as strong and active compared to the fathers. Allergic
children came early or late in the mother's child-bearing period,

identified more closely with the mothers, and exhibited strong dependency needs. The mother's marital frustration led to searching for satisfaction from the child, with ensuing rejection, illness, and overprotection. Bostock (1956), from a study of 38 asthmatic children, stressed the early genesis of the symptoms and the frequency of maternal rejection.

Jessner et al. (1955) studied 28 severely asthmatic children during hospitalization. The asthmatic child usually had an allergic family history and respiratory illness occurred early in life, so that critical conflicts were linked with respiratory symptoms. As in McDermott and Cobb's study (1939), their asthmatics were frequently the oldest child and occupied a special place for the mother who was in conflict about closeness or separation. The conflict was intensified when the child was with the mother and lessened, for the child, when he was away.

Research Reports

Discussion of more formal research work bearing on the French and Alexander (1941) hypotheses will begin with the series of papers by Miller and Baruch, who believed that maternal rejection is etiologically important in the development of allergic symptoms. They saw every child coming to an allergy clinic in play sessions or interviews; mothers were interviewed and often the father. These children were contrasted with nonallergic children referred to the psychologist during the same period. In a study with 63 allergic children and 37 nonallergics (1948), 24% of the mothers of the nonallergics were rated as rejecting, whereas 98% of the mothers of allergic children were rejecting. With 90 allergic and 53 nonallergic children (1950), they rated allergic children as less overtly hostile in their daily lives and in play sessions. One function of allergic symptoms was thus thought to be the expression of otherwise blocked hostility toward the mother. In later papers (1951, 1956, 1957) Miller and Baruch reported similar findings with larger samples; disturbances in the mother's psychosexual development were suggested and they believed that rejection antedated allergic symptoms. In a child with an allergic predisposition, symptoms expressed both anger and attempts to regain closeness through illness.

Because Miller and Baruch's work has had such impact in this field, it is important to study their research methods and try to evaluate their strongly positive results in this light. The biggest single difficulty in their work is lack of explicitness about how they arrived at their findings. They have not described their criteria for ratings of maternal rejection or hostility expression. It is difficult to know whether other workers would make similar interpretations from the data because the bases for judgments are not specified. Safeguards to ensure that gathering of information and performing ratings were done independently and without awareness of a subject's group membership (allergic or nonallergic) are not reported. Using a control group of children with a variety of behavior deviations does not solve these problems.

Harris et al. (1950) contrasted 22 asthmatic children with 17 children having allergic rhinitis on interviews, school reports, Rorschach, TAT, and Stanford-Binet tests. Asthmatic children, according to teachers' reports, had more fear of maternal separation, were more fearful generally, and less aggressive. Some asthmatics had difficulty crying and confiding, and the mothers of these children were rigidly angry over misbehavior. These interpretations from interviews and teachers' reports appeared to support French and Alexander, but findings from the battery of psychological tests were not reported.

Fine (1963) studied 30 asthmatic children and 30 nonasthmatic siblings on the Rorschach, Despert Fables, Thematic Apperception Test, Make-A-Picture-Story Test, drawings, and interviews. He reported greater dependency among asthmatics than their siblings, cycloid temperament, and low frustration tolerance.

Using 79 hospitalized intractably asthmatic children, Long et al. (1958) sprayed their rooms with dust from their homes after the children became symptom-free. There was no evidence of respiratory change despite the high concentration. Patients and their mothers were then interviewed and given psychological tests, and their performance was contrasted with 19 children hospitalized for nonpsychosomatic illnesses. In telling stories to pictures, asthmatics more often produced what were considered intrauterine themes—achievement was in the service of dependency rather than for its own sake and story heroes were ill at home and improved away from home.

A novel approach to the study of mother-child interactions in asthmatic children was developed by Owen (1963). Two hospitalized groups, asthmatics and other chronically ill children, participated in two experimental sessions. In the first half of each an unfamiliar voice read a recorded story; then each child listened to his mother's voice finishing the story. Patterns of respiratory function were recorded; measurements on control subjects were relatively constant during the two conditions, but there was substantial amplitude variability for asthmatic subjects between the two conditions.

In several studies predictions about behavior in an experimental setting were derived from the general ideas of French and Alexander. Greenfield (1958) reasoned that maternal rejection and unsatisfied longing for love among allergics should lead to greater need for recognition. He gave 35 college students in allergy treatment a test requiring recall of a series of pictures, each depicting a psychological need. Allergic subjects recalled need for recognition pictures sooner than did matched controls.

Epstein (1963) attempted verbal conditioning of neutral and hostile verbs among 100 asthmatic boys. Those with a high need for approval were more readily conditioned to hostile words, while nonapproval motivated children were more readily conditioned to neutral words. His evidence suggested that approval-oriented asthmatic children were intensely concerned with hostility and so were sensitized to the reinforcement of hostile words.

Little and Cohen (1951) predicted that maternal overprotection and overambition, and the child's consequent immaturity would be reflected in goal-setting. Thirty asthmatic children and their mothers were compared with nonasthmatics and their mothers on a game requiring that mother and child separately estimate the child's score before trials. Asthmatics set higher goals than did controls, and there was a larger discrepancy between goal and achievement for their mothers. Morris (1959) predicted that asthmatic children and their mothers would set more similar goals for the child than would nonasthmatic pairs, and the asthmatic child's aspiration level would rise with his mother participating. Both predictions were confirmed in an experiment where 20 asthmatic and 20 control children estimated their success at a game, part of the time alone and part of the time with the mother. Morris concluded that the asthmatic child depends on his mother for help in assessing his abilities, and she consistently revises the estimate upward.

Several investigators have tested hypotheses about the maternal role in asthma by psychological study of the mothers. Fitzelle (1959) contrasted 100 mothers of asthmatics and 100 mothers of nonasthmatic children in a pediatric clinic. Using interviews, MMPI, and a parent attitudes survey, he found no characteristic personality traits or child-rearing attitudes among mothers of asthmatics. Cutter (1955) developed a questionnaire dealing with parent-child warmth, freedom, and control. He found no differences between the 33 mothers of asthmatic children, the 24 mothers of children with eczema, and the 41 mothers of children with other medical problems.

Margolis (1961) used the Parent Attitude Research Inventory and Blacky Pictures, a projective technique designed to study ego defenses and characteristics of psychosexual development, with mothers of asthmatic, rheumatic heart disease, and surgical out-patients (Total $N = 75$). With the Blacky Pictures he found more psychosexual conflicts among mothers of asthmatics, but the PARI did not yield differences between groups.

Fitzelle (1959) also reported that among mothers of asthmatics, no differences were observed between mothers of children with mild and those with very severe symptoms. Similarly, Dubo et al. (1961) found no relationships between severity of a child's asthma and the level of disturbance in the family situation, as rated from psychiatric interviews. When the best and most poorly adjusted families were compared there was no evident relationship with asthma severity or response to treatment.

Comments. To sum up this complex body of theory, case reports, and research involves both methodological and theoretical issues. Many of the case studies and reports provide a variety of rich clinical insights and seem to be cogent illustrations of French and Alexander's observations. Similarly, Owen's work (1963) with tape recordings seems to be tapping important, although as yet unspeci-fied, variables related to mother-child interaction.

Too many research papers, however, continue a number of serious deficiencies enumerated earlier. These include failure to de-scribe samples carefully, both in terms of immunological and so-cial characteristics; not reporting the specific procedures by which raters' judgments of psychological characteristics were made and the extent to which raters were able to agree about such character-istics. Another frequent shortcoming has been the use of a large battery of psychological tests and interviews followed by a report dealing with only a few items yielding positive findings.

The group of studies by Fitzelle (1959), Cutter (1955), Margolis (1961), and Dubo et al. (1961) represents important methodologi-cal improvements over many others cited, in specification of samples and selection of control groups. These are also notable for a paucity of findings; Margolis noted that his positive findings were meager compared to the claims of many clinicians, and some of the variance in his study was due, he believed, to the effects of chronic illness.

Some authors have applied Alexander and French's formulations about bronchial asthma to other kinds of allergic symptoms. These workers seem to have assumed that psychological hypotheses pertaining to asthma should be relevant for other disease entities too. This is quite a logical jump, and there is little basis in evidence for making it as yet.

Another problem concerns the testing of psychoanalytically derived hypotheses. Margolis (1961) aptly suggested that a psychoanalytic hypothesis about unconscious conflict derived from the data of analytic sessions cannot usually be tested adequately with paper and pencil inventories. Thus, while Fitzelle and Cutter are to be commended for using objective measurement methods, the instruments chosen may not have provided adequate tests of the hypothesis. A good deal of care in design is needed to make the levels of behavior tapped in an experiment congruent with, or logically derived from, the behavioral level described in the hypothesis.

The studies by Greenfield (1958), Epstein (1963), Morris (1959), and Little and Cohen (1951), dealing experimentally with need for recognition, hostility expression, and aspiration level are notable for attempting to derive hypotheses amenable to experimental verification from analytic formulations. A larger amount of research efforts in such an area could be very fruitful. Probably many ideas put forward in clinical case descriptions can lend themselves to experimental validation, either directly or by logical derivation of testable hypotheses.

Thus, many years after the original writings of French and Alexander (1941), a definitive statement about the general usefulness or applicability of their views cannot be made. In surveying the literature, one gets the impression that lack of skepticism has been largely responsible for this state of affairs; investigators have often used their data to confirm or *illustrate* analytic formulations rather than to *test* their validity. It is to be hoped that a much larger number of future studies will be carefully designed and finally permit conclusions about the validity of Alexander and French's ideas.

Other Psychoanalytic Hypotheses

In this section we consider psychoanalytic hypotheses relating to allergic syndromes other than asthma and alternative psychoanalytic hypotheses in asthma. Wilson (1948) saw 5 hay fever patients in psychoanalysis; he felt that the salient conflict was failure to sublimate sexual curiosity along visual, intellectual lines, so that primitive olfactory curiosity remained a source of conflict and a constant irritant to the nose.

Fenichel (1954) spoke of respiratory introjection as an important phenomenon in early development, and believed that conflicts could occur around it just as around oral introjection. He classified asthma as a pregenital conversion neurosis representing conflict between the self and the lungs rather than between the self and others as in a classical conversion symptom.

Deutsch (1951) considered breathing an ego function similar to posture or gait. The asthmatic patient's ego cannot resolve intrapsychic conflict around moving toward others for gratification (inspiration) or moving away and inhibiting the impulse (expiration). The result is a disorganized breathing pattern.

Bell (1958) speculated that some asthmatic disturbances might have had their origins in very early respiratory experiences revived through memory traces on a muscular level during toilet training difficulties. Monsour (1960) emphasized the phobic fear of death a mother communicates to a child by her very anxious management when he cries. The child's primitive anxiety is thus intensified, and respiratory functioning is taxed beyond its physiological limits.

Bacon (1956), from the analysis of 6 cases, regarded conflicts around toilet training and compliance as the origin of asthma; she believed that excretory fantasies and stimulation could stimulate the respiratory tract reflexively.

Knapp and Nemetz (1957a) reported an attempt to compare varying psychogenic hypotheses about asthma. They did so in a *post hoc* fashion from intensive case studies of 40 severe asthmatics. Original position in the family was not different from a comparable group of neurotics, whereas McDermott and Cobb (1939) reported higher incidence of oldest and only children among asthmatics. The following hypotheses all seemed to have some relevance for a few patients: asthmatics show an intense clinging dependence (Dunbar, 1954); have chronically unsatisfied oral needs leading to shame and depression (Saul and Lyons, 1951); have nasal and olfactory preoccupations (Dunbar, 1954, and Fenichel, 1954); show concern over crying, concealment, confession (Weiss, 1950, and French and Alexander, 1941); were exposed to respiratory illness in important persons (Wittkower, 1952). No hypothesis had universal significance, but within their sample of severe asthmatics in intensive psychotherapy, each of these ideas was sometimes applicable.

Comments. While all these authors have provided a few case descriptions, little other substantiating evidence is available. Relying as they do on extremely inferential material from psychoanalytic sessions, it is difficult to see how these views could be tested adequately with any kind of research approach.

Other Psychological Hypotheses

A few other hypotheses have also been explored. These are considered separately from the previous section which dealt solely with psychoanalytically derived hypotheses.

The general view of Wolff and colleagues (1950), based on studies of patients with a variety of bodily diseases, is that under stress many physiological changes occur. If these protective physiological alterations, used originally as emeregncy measures, become standard ways of coping with continuous daily stresses, then permanent tissue damage may result, with a concomitant clinical pattern of asthma, rhinitis, hay fever, hypertension, etc. Different kinds of stresses can combine with each other to produce symptoms, when only one of these might be below the response threshold. Thus (Holmes, et al., 1950, 1951) exposure of pollen-sensitive and pollen-insensitive subjects to a ragweed pollen room was well tolerated when the mucous membranes were functioning well, but very poorly tolerated when there was previous hyperfunction due to allergy or infection. Further, when pollen sensitive subjects were exposed to high pollen concentration in a setting of conflict and anxiety, hay fever symptoms were exacerbated. When sensitive subjects who were reacting only mildly to pollen discussed conflictual material, their hay fever symptoms became more extreme.

Wolf et al. (1950) found that subjecting pollen-sensitive individuals to a nonspecific physical threat led to nasal symptoms. When a chronic rhinitis patient with temporarily normal nasal function was reminded of anger-provoking material, nasal hyperfunction, and almost complete obstruction resulted.

A chronic bronchitis patient made daily records for Stevenson (1950) of his experiences, barometric pressure, temperature, and amount of sputum removed. Quantity of sputum appeared to be related to his emotional state. An asthmatic patient during an interview was found to have dyspnea, sneezing, and increased mucus while discussing conflict; with reassurance, symptoms abated. In an attempt to understand these effects, Holmes et al. (1951) blocked one stellate ganglion with procaine with resulting hay fever symptoms in the involved nasal chamber; they postulated parasympathetic nervous system mediation.

This group of studies is notable for its explicit theoretical basis, some ingenious experimental techniques, and for attempting to tie physiology and behavior together concretely. It is unfortunate that the frequency of their observations is not reported. At least in some patients, the kinds of summative effects they report can indeed be demonstrated, but without some idea of how often they were able —or unable—to obtain these results, it is difficult to generalize beyond the cases they have described.

An extremely divergent viewpoint is that of Clarke (1950, 1952), who believes that allergy frequently causes behavior problems in children. He conducted an opinion poll among all the allergists in the U. S. and Canada; of 171 replies out of an unstated total number of requests, 92 agreed with him. He speculated that personality changes result from sudden increases of intracranial pressure, and many children with psychological problems are undiagnosed allergies. This work illustrates the point that opinion gathering is of little use in validating hypotheses.

Psychosomatic Specificity

A number of hypotheses, advanced originally by psychoanalytic writers—French and Alexander (1941), Dunbar (1954), Weiss (1950)—posit different constellations of psychological conflict in different psychosomatic disease syndromes. The assumption is that a particular psychosomatic illness eventuates out of the physiological accompaniments to particular psychological stresses. Most writers believe that these relationships pertain only to psychological conflict, and not to superficial traits of personality.

Groen (1951), however, favored a hypothesis of psychosomatic specificity in traits of personality and in areas of conflict. He presented the following formulations: colitis patients are mild, fussy, and insecure; attacks are precipitated by harsh treatment and loss of love. Ulcer patients are tense, self-assertive, live up to ideals, and symptoms are brought on by occupational or social frustration. Asthmatics are inclined to be impatient, tyrannical, egocentric, with attacks precipitated by submission to authority or frustration in dominating a loved person. Surface attitudes distinguish the groups from each other and from other neurotics. Many improved in concentration camps because only specific precipitants lead to the specific illness.

Barendregt (1957) tested these ideas by comparing 20 male hospitalized asthmatics with a like group of ulcer patients on the Rorschach. Hypotheses that asthmatics would have more themes of oppression, hostility, and impulsive behavior than ulcer patients were confirmed. When repeated on a second sample, he obtained the same results.

Seward et al. (1950) compared bronchial asthma, spastic colitis, and ulcer patients on the Rorschach and Rosensweig Picture Frustration Test. Each group was rated as immature and incapable of adequate relating to people, but asthma and ulcer groups were more extreme.

Stovkis (1959) compared 100 allergics with 125 unselected psychosomatic patients. There were no differences on the Wechsler-Bellevue Intelligence Test or the Rorschach psychogram; in Rorschach content, allergics gave more themes of oppression, confirming Barendregt's finding (1957). On the Szondi test, allergics showed more dependence on their mothers. These few differences out of the vast number of possible comparisons did not suggest important personality differences between allergics and patients with other illnesses.

Ross et al. (1950) looked for associations between types of psychosomatic illness and types of psychoses. They surveyed 1600 hospitalized psychotics for evidence of ulcer, asthma, diabetes, rheumatoid arthritis, or hypertension; they found no associations between psychotic diagnosis and asthma, diabetes, or arthritis, but did find associations for ulcer and hypertension.

Kepecs et al. (1958) gave asthma, neurodermatitis, arthritis, and hypertension patients cutaneous, muscular, and olfactory stimulation. After each modality, subjects were asked to draw freely and to associate. Associations were judged, and stimulation of the involved sensory modality aroused the most affect. Thus 8 of the 10 asthmatics were judged as reacting with most affect to odors, gave more anal associations, and exhibited more cleanliness conflicts than other groups.

Ring (1957) reasoned that if personality patterns and specific illnesses were associated, patients with one illness should be distinguished from those with another by personality study alone. He briefly interviewed 134 patients with colleagues present and classified each as having 1 of 14 illnesses. Clues to illnesses had been disguised, but Ring made 88 correct first choices, 27 correct second choices, and only 12 misses. He categorized subjects' responses to standard leading questions: e.g., how they reacted to and expressed anger or fear, and how active they were generally. He classified some illness groups as excessive reactors emotionally and others as deficient reactors; asthmatics were "restrained reactors."

Graham et al. (1962) proposed that attitudes predicted to be associated with certain illnesses should be more applicable to patients with that illness than with another. Thirty-six patients with 10 diseases were interviewed about general life attitudes, and judges rated the interview transcriptions. Judges selected attitudes predicted for a patient's disease more often than they attributed these attitudes to patients with other diseases, despite absence of diagnostic clues. Attitudes associated with bronchial asthma were feeling unloved, disapproved of, and rejected.

Comments. At this point hypotheses differ considerably from one study to the next so that it is difficult to arrive at substantive conclusions from this body of work as a whole. The postulated psychological characteristics differentiating people with a particular illness from those with another have varied greatly. Many of the studies have used poorly defined psychological terms and have separated groups of patients on a *post hoc* basis. Investigators have simply taken groups with different physical illnesses, and looked for whatever psychological differences they could find. Any study proceeding on this basis absolutely requires crossvalidation, and yet it is almost never performed. Two projects, however, those by Ring (1957) and Graham et al. (1962), deserve special notice for they have been very carefully executed, and both have reported identifiable psychological differences accompanying different illnesses. The particular value of these studies lies in their successful use of a *predictive* measure; i.e., raters made physical diagnoses on the basis of psychological characteristics. The success of these two investigators should serve to stimulate more careful work in this area; obviously it is premature to form conclusions about hypotheses of psychosomatic specificity until this small amount of dependable information is supplemented.

Subgroups within the Allergic Population

A promising hypothesis which has raised recent interest is that important psychological differences may exist within the population of patients with allergic symptoms. Since it is known that some patients with such symptoms demonstrate clearly an allergic constitution while others do so less clearly or not at all, a search for psychological differences between these groups may yield important results. It may be that the relevance of emotional factors for the etiology and course of allergic symptoms may be quite different for these groups.

There were a few early investigations, most of which lacked careful definition of samples, did not use objective methods, and drew overly broad generalizations from their findings. Mitchell et al. (1947) differentiated 100 patients with hay fever or perennial extrinsic asthma and positive skin tests from 147 patients with perennial vasomotor rhinitis, intrinsic asthma, or chronic urticaria. The latter group frequently had negative skin tests and did not respond to treatment. They were older and more often female, with many physical complaints and adjustment difficulties.

Rees (1956a, b) tried to assess the relative dominance of allergic, infective, and emotional factors in asthma from interviews and case histories. Fifty to 60% of asthmatics were rated as having emotional factors in the etiology, usually along with allergic or infective factors. The proportion increased in patients over 60 years old.

Fennell (1963) distinguished between nasal allergy and vasomotor rhinitis on the basis of negative skin tests, nasal secretions, and blood eosinophil study. He gave Librium to 45 patients in a doubleblind framework, reasoning that if psychogenic, rhinitis symptoms should improve with such a drug. Rhinitis patients did not report more improvement with the drug than the placebo, so he concluded that rhinitis was not a psychosomatic disorder.

Kraft et al. (1959) contrasted the Bell Adjustment Inventory performance of 5 adults who died in asthmatic attacks with 10 severe but nonfatal asthmatics; the former group appeared to deny all emotional conflicts and interpersonal tensions.

Notable improvements are seen in the next groups of studies. Purcell et al. (1960) studied two groups of children sent to a residential treatment center for chronic, intractable asthma. With one group of 54, symptoms remitted rapidly after admission, while a second group of 59 required continuous steroid medication. Parents of the rapidly remitting group ascribed to their children more symptoms of tension than did parents of the steroid dependent group and dated asthma onset later. Mothers of rapidly remitting children scored higher in authoritarian control and hostility-rejection on the Parent Attitude Research Inventory than did mothers of steroid-dependent children. The fathers of the former group also had higher scores on "psychologically unhealthy" scales.

In a second study by Purcell and Metz (1962) there were no significant differences in age of onset for the rapidly remitting and steroid dependent groups. For the rapidly remitting group, however, relatively late onset was positively associated with autocratic maternal attitudes. Purcell (1963) also found that the rapidly remitting children perceived emotional events as "triggers" of asthma attacks more often than did the steroid dependent group.

In another study, Purcell et al. (1962) reported no differences in neurotic characteristics between the two groups, as measured by Porteus Mazes, Children's Manifest Anxiety Scale, behavior ratings, and Cattell's Personality Questionnaire. The authors posed a dual explanation for these findings within the context of intractable asthma; For the steroid dependent group, physical and allergic factors were of primary importance even though they exhibited as many neurotic symptoms and behavior deviations as the other group. For the rapidly remitting group, asthma played a dominant role in dealing with psychological stress and may have been acquired to some extent as a means of reducing tension and conflict.

Dekker et al. (1961) stated that classifying asthmatics according to etiological factors depends on a negative correlation between allergic and psychological factors. They classified 79 adult female asthmatics as having "manifest allergy" or "no manifest allergy" on the basis of skin and inhalation tests. On the Heron Two-Part Personality Inventory they found no differences in neuroticism between groups and concluded that there was no evidence for differential etiology.

Feingold et al. (1962) on the other hand, found significant differences in personality pattern in a sample of allergic women related to severity of reaction to skin testing. On the Minnesota Multiphasic Personal Inventory, women who reacted slightly or not at all to allergy testing admitted to significantly more psychological disturbance than did women who reacted strongly to skin testing. Differences between diagnostic groups of asthma, rhinitis, and hay fever were not significant.

Block (1963) developed a 15-item scale along which asthmatic children were rated for "allergic potential;" it included such factors as family history of allergy, skin sensitivity, total number of allergies. The 31 children above the mean and the 31 below were contrasted on testing, interviews, and behavior ratings. Interactions of parents with children and with each other were observed, and parents evaluated their children. Children scoring low on the Allergic Potential Scale manifested more psychopathology than high scorers, and parents more often described them as inadequate and anxious. Mothers of low-scorers were less secure and less well integrated; interactions with their children were more negative, and with their spouses they were demanding and dependent. Thus asthmatic children with low "allergy potential" and their parents scored more frequently in psychopathological directions than did children for whom the allergic factor was high.

Comments. Here, then, is an area with several recent studies which have been well designed and which have had promising results. Three out of 4 groups of recent investigations have demonstrated psychological differences between groups differing in the extent of "manifest allergy" or response to treatment. Differences between the Dekker et al. (1961), Block (1963), and Feingold et al. (1962) studies may be attributable to different psychological techniques; Dekker pointed out that the Heron Inventory was in the early stages of validation. Purcell's work also cannot be compared completely because of the much greater severity of illness in his samples; thus, finding no differences in degree of psychological disturbance between rapidly remitting and steroid dependent children may be related to the effects of serious and prolonged illness.

There is, thus, important evidence that the allergic population is far from homogeneous psychologically, and the role of psychological variables varies along subgroups of patients with allergic symptoms. If borne out by further investigations, this view would suggest an important reason for the contradictions in so much of the work performed to date. It may well be fruitless to look at allergy patients as a single group, all sharing the same degree of psychological contribution to their symptoms. If samples of allergic patients are classified into groups for whom the allergic factor is high and those for whom it is low, psychological differences of importance are located. These studies underscore the need for very precise description of the allergic characteristics of samples being studied psychologically. Indeed, they may be pointing to a more precise rethinking of the status of allergy as a "psychosomatic" disorder.

Emotional Precipitation of Allergy Symptoms

Some workers have reasoned that if emotional factors are important in producing asthma or hay fever it should be possible to demonstrate a specific role for such stresses in the precipitation of individual attacks. The work of Wolff and Wolf et al. (1950) (see above), although oriented toward a general theory of psychosomatic illness, involved experimental production of hay fever symptoms through presentation of emotional and physical stresses. Their work can be considered some evidence for the precipitation of respiratory symptoms by means of psychological stimuli.

Dekker and Groen (1956) attempted to induce asthma attacks experimentally; they were able to elicit from 12 out of 31 patients a description of an environmental situation that could produce asthma for them. For one patient the stress was riding in an elevator; for another, knitting; for a third, seeing goldfish in a bowl. Six of these patients did in fact have respiratory symptoms when the situation they described was produced experimentally.

Stein and Ottenberg (1958) hypothesized that odors might be emotional as well as physical precipitants of asthma. Twenty-two out of 25 asthmatics interviewed said that odors could precipitate attacks. Having grouped these as oral (food), anal (cleanliness-uncleanliness), or genital (sex, romance), 74% of the odors were considered anal derivatives. (Although many were perfumes and cleaning substances, their allergenic properties were not discussed.) Next they asked 20 asthmatics and 20 nonasthmatics for associations to odorous substances. Asthmatics more often blocked out the odors perceptually although their associations did not differ from those of nonasthmatics.

In another study Ottenberg and Stein (1958) noted that completely enclosing a patient in a large plethysmograph for measurement purposes constituted a stress which in some patients produced an asthma attack.

Knapp and Nemetz (1960) studied 406 asthma attacks in 9 severe asthmatics in intensive psychotherapy. The main prodromal feature was anxious or angry excitement; after the attack was established depression was common. Two prominent categories of environmental changes during the 48 hours before an attack were loss of a person and closeness to a person. Knapp (1960) also described asthma episodes of a patient in psychoanalysis as being dominated by primitive fantasies and emotions.

Fink and Schneer (1963) evaluated 18 hospitalized asthmatic adolescents, half of whom had psychotic diagnoses. For 7 patients asthma onset seemed related to major life events such as separations or birth of siblings. Both parents and the child reported intense emotion, usually hostile, as an important precipitant of attacks.

From other theorists, Leigh (1953) classified seven groups of emotional precipitants; the category "sudden intense emotion—

usually rage" seemed important among asthmatics referred to him for psychiatric evaluation. Crying, sexual conflicts, and disturbance of a dependent relationship also had importance.

Sanger (1960) believed that no single psychological expla. ation was sufficient to explain asthma, and he cited cases with various precipitating stresses: aggression by others against oneself, envy, resentment, guilt over sexuality.

Miller and Baruch (1950), from their interviews with mothers of 90 allergic children, described traumas preceding the first symptoms: the largest category was loss or threatened loss of a parent. Also important were marital conflict, witnessing sexual intercourse, birth of a sibling, over-severe habit training, and physical violence to the child. The authors felt that any of these incidents could confirm fears of maternal rejection.

Comments. There have been few research reports in this particular area. Only the studies by Wolff et al. (1950) and Dekker and Groen (1956) attempted any kind of experimental manipulation, while other workers have relied on patients' reports. There are serious difficulties in both approaches; the experimental approach requires isolating quite specifically the various kinds of stresses that might be important, assigning at least grossly some relative degree of importance to each, and then duplicating them under controlled conditions. The use of patients' reports involves many problems around awareness of emotional factors, the effect of the interviewer's theoretical biases on what a patient reports, time lag between symptoms and interviewing, and rapport between patient and interviewer. A neglected but possibly very fruitful approach would be close observation of patients in an institutional setting, with an attempt to delineate in vitro the important precipitants.

Asthma and Conditioning

A number of studies, largely with animals, have shown that symptoms with varying degrees of clinical similarity to asthma can be produced by means of conditioning procedures. Some of these observations have emerged as by-products of the experimental setting or of the conditioning of other responses. These perhaps have less utility for the purposes of this paper than studies in "conditioned asthma" per se and so will be considered fairly briefly.

Non-Respiratory Unconditioned Stimulus: Animal Studies

Investigators have observed experimentally induced respiratory changes primarily as a byproduct of other conditioning procedures.

Thus Gantt (1941) described "loud and raucous breathing with quick inspiration and labored expiration . . . accompanied by a loud wheezing" in his experimentally neurotic dog, Nick, as he approached the experimental room. Masserman and Pechtel (1953) described asthma-like responses in their neurotic monkeys when they were brought to the experimental situation.

An earlier study by Walker and Kellogg (1939) compared respiratory conditioning with leg flexion conditioning. Leg flexion was conditioned to the sound of a buzzer with electric shock to the foreleg as the unconditioned stimulus. Respiratory changes were conditioned to the buzzer long before leg flexion, and were not extinguished in twice the number of trials necessary to extinguish the leg flexion. Eldridge (1955) found that removing an animal from the place where he could make the appropriate avoidance response to an aversive stimulus led to increased respiration rate. Freedman (1951) reported that conditioned enhancement of respiration (inspiratory gasps with or without hyperpnea or polypnea) accompanied leg flexion conditioning. It could occur with the auditory stimulus, with flexion, between them, or after flexion. It was sometimes established before flexion and often outlasted it. Freedman felt that the respiratory response was a byproduct of avoidance conditioning, and thought of it as an anxiety signal.

Allergens as Unconditioned Stimuli

Animal Studies

The term "experimental asthma" as used in the literature has generally referred to laboratory induction of sensitivity to an allergen such as egg white. The study by Ottenberg et al. (1958) illustrates one experimental method that has been used frequently in the development of "learned asthma;" guinea pigs were injected three times with undiluted egg white; this was followed by a two-week time lapse for sensitization, and then they inhaled a dilute egg-white spray. The animals responded to the spray with asthma attacks as judged by trained observers, but the number of animals responding decreased over trials. After a period of exposure to the spray in the chamber, the animals had asthma-like attacks in the chamber in the absence of the egg-white spray. This learned response failed to appear after repeated trials. The authors noted that the response may not have been analogous to human bronchial asthma, that they may have been autonomic manifestations of severe emotional response, and that not all the animals showed the learned asthma. But within these limits, these manipulations seemed to produce asthma-like responses to a conditioned stimulus.

Noelpp and Noelpp-Eschenhagen (1951) also sensitized guinea pigs to egg white, then paired the exposure of egg-white spray with an auditory signal. Many animals showed respiratory reactions (heightening of frequency and amplitude of respiration and phase shifts in favor of expiration) to the tone alone after repeated pairing with the egg-white spray. When these workers systematically subjected animals to stressful sensory stimuli (1952) before and during the experimentally induced asthma, the frequency and duration of learned asthma responses increased.

Various studies indicate that these responses vary with individuals. Ratner (1951, 1953) noted that animals differ in their readiness to become sensitized as well as in the extent to which asthma responses can be conditioned to previously neutral stimuli. Class differences may well be genetic since some strains of guinea pigs can develop sensitivity to allergens and some cannot.

Feinberg et al. (1953) found that a variety of drugs and physiological stresses as pretreatment could have a protective effect. Cortison, ACTH, Pyribenzamine, localized chemical inflammation, and various physical stresses reduced the asthmatic response to egg-white inhalation. Freedman and Fenichel (1958) placed bilaterally symmetrical lesions in the midbrain reticulum of guinea pigs after sensitization and inhibited anaphylaxis which their intracardiac dose of albumin would otherwise have produced. These studies suggest that experimental asthma is subject to individual differences and can be experimentally modified; the same might hold true for learned or conditioned asthma.

Studies Using Human Subjects

Dekker et al. (1957) report obtaining a learned asthma response in human subjects. They used an allergen known to be effective with each subject and paired it with a neutral solvent. After repeated pairings, inhalation of pure oxygen was sufficient to cause respiratory changes, as measured by clinical signs, and respiratory distress. After additional trials the mouthpiece alone was sufficient to bring on symptoms.

Interpretations. Schiavi et al. (1961) noted in a critical paper that many studies with the conditioned asthma response failed to demonstrate bronchiolar obstruction. They administered electric shock to 10 guinea pigs, and measured ventilatory variables and mechanical properties of the lungs. These records were compared with a group of animals given experimental asthma by sensitization and later exposure to egg white. The animals in the shock condition showed a pain-fear reaction of generalized body activity and screeching, and a respiratory pattern of shortened inspiration and lengthened expiration, but bronchiolar obstruction did not occur, as it did in experimental asthma. After eliminating the animals' vocalizing and no longer getting a changed breathing pattern with shock, they concluded that the asthma-like breathing pattern was related to the animals' screeching.

Turnbull (1962) noted that in some studies an allergic unconditioned stimulus paired with a conditioned stimulus leads to an asthma-like breathing pattern, but rapid extinction occurs. Conversely, response to an emotion eliciting stimulus (shock avoidance) shows much greater resistance to extinction, but the breathing pattern resembles asthma less closely. He therefore proposed that the asthma response is learned initially through conditioning and maintained through anxiety reduction as reinforcement in a setting where asthma produces solicitude from an otherwise unresponding mother.

Seitz's work has some similar implications (1959). He observed three groups of kittens: one group was weaned very early and observed to vocalize or "cry" during feeding for a brief period after this; the second group was appropriately weaned at 6 weeks; the third group was forced to suckle twice as long. When exposed to a feeding conflict as adults, the first group developed chronic respiratory wheezing with each exposure; neither of the other groups showed such behavior.

It should be noted that several different procedures have been described here. First, there is the experimental asthma of Ratner (1953) and others in which allergen sensitization is produced in the laboratory. Second, when this response is established it can be conditioned to a previously neutral stimulus—a tone, a bell, the chamber itself; this was demonstrated by Ottenberg et al. (1958), Noelpp and Noelpp-Eschenhagen (1952), and others. Third, there are the respiratory accompaniments of the conditioning situation —namely, the respiratory changes of Gantt's (1941) and Masserman and Pechtel's (1953) neurotic animals, and the observations of Walker and Kellogg (1939), Freedman (1951), and Schiavi et al. (1961). In the latter studies, respiratory enhancement was an unconditioned response to unspecific noxious stimuli. These changes in breathing pattern appear to be but one of many physiological accompaniments of the conditioning situation. Probably they have little explanatory value for the development of asthma. The more relevant studies are those where asthmatic breathing has been established to an allergic stimulus and conditioned to an extraneous stimulus.

An Overview: Comments by Others

Many writers have presented the logic favoring an important role for psychological factors in the etiology of allergic illness. Both Baldwin (1963) and Wittkower (1952) cited the inadequacy of the immunological model in explaining such allergic conditions as asthma; Wittkower noted the seeming precipitation or exacerbation of symptoms by emotional crises in some patients. Brown (1951b) noted that the nose, like other organs, can, through learning, come to have associations with important conflicts for the individual, and he cited a variety of folklore describing such associations. Sontag (1950) argued that a psychosomatic view of allergy in no way minimizes immunological findings, and he presented some ideas as to how psychological stresses, by altering autonomic functioning, can be important in the allergic reaction of cells. Reed (1962) advanced a position like that of Wolff (1950), namely, that asthma represents a symptom of an unsuccessful attempt to deal with life stress, with the disease involving an interaction of etiological factors.

While the logic of these viewpoints and many others cited in the course of this paper often seems adequate, the confirmation or negation of any of them is not nearly so clear-cut. Although this condition may often be due to inadequacy or overgenerality of theory, a frequent difficulty is inadequate methodology for testing hypotheses. When Leigh (1953) critically reviewed the literature on psychological factors in asthma in 1953, he made the following suggestions for needed improvements in research: (1) Comparison groups of asthmatics not in psychiatric treatment are needed to evaluate the effects of psychiatric treatment on asthma; (2) standardized methods of allergy treatment and psychiatric treatment should be used and explicitly stated in reports; (3) a sufficiently long follow-up period—at least 5 years—is necessary in treatment studies to allow for the naturally phasic character of asthma; (4) statistical analyses should be undertaken.

Similarly, Pearson (1956) noted the great number of descriptive psychiatric reports and the lack of measurable criteria; he called for long-term studies by interdisciplinary teams to replace the reports of "solitary biased observers" based on experiences of brief duration. Both emphasize that asthma is an illness of natural variability, requiring observation over a period.

Summary and Evaluation

After this brief examination of the nearly 200 papers that have been written since 1950, the necessary question arises as to what general statements can be made of the knowledge acquired about the role of psychological factors in allergic diseases. In general the yield from all the effort expended to date is small indeed. The catalog of critical methodological shortcomings is lengthy and the number of well-established findings meager. A brief summary of findings and comments in each of the areas reviewed demonstrates the basis for this statement.

Several investigations have found that asthmatics appear more neurotic than nonasthmatics on a variety of psychological tests, interviews, and behavior rating scales. However, such findings are questionable because of critical problems in methodology. One of these is the often repeated and obvious error of using asthmatic patients in psychiatric treatment as representative of asthmatic —or allergic—populations in general. Another was the failure to specify whether the patients with allergic symptoms who were being studied psychologically were in fact demonstrably allergic. Further, attempts to use control groups have been fairly unsystematic. To use a control group adequately requires that one be able to specify and measure one or a very few crucial variables on which the experimental and control groups are to differ. In this new area of research, however, specifying the important variables to be controlled is an extremely difficult matter. Control groups in allergy research have been: children with various behavioral problems, unselected psychosomatic patients, nonpsychosomatic surgical patients, unspecified outpatients, and "normals," to name a few representative categories.

Because there have been scarcely any attempts to cross-validate findings, inconsistencies and contradictions between studies remain unresolved. If a number of the more promising studies in the field were replicated, this would constitute a major improvement.

Psychological treatment studies to date have been, with few exceptions, testimonials for various procedures previously used with psychiatric patients. There are frequent reports of success, but many cautions apply. In particular, patients chosen for psychotherapy are probably those for whom emotional problems seemed important at the outset, though this is seldom specified in reports. One must ask what relevance these studies have for understanding the allergic populations. Perhaps it is presumed that all allergy patients have some degree of emotional precipitation for their symptoms, and therefore their symptoms will improve with psychotherapy. Or perhaps it is presumed that there are etiological differences between allergy patients and that, for some with important psychological factors, psychotherapy is a useful treatment method. Whichever view an investigator espouses, implicitly or explicitly, will determine the sample he selects and the conclusions he draws.

Some methodological improvements frequently mentioned in this paper are needed in treatment studies: specifying whether patients are demonstrably allergic; reporting whether allergy symptoms, not neurotic characteristics, improved; developing more adequate criteria of improvement than patients' reports; and reporting failures with psychological treatment.

Studies of asthma-psychosis relationships have been so contradictory that no conclusions are in order. Some experimental approaches which have been reported (Freeman, 1951; Funkenstein, 1950a, b) may help to resolve the contradictions, as will use of objective indices of asthma or allergy and greater specificity about the types of psychotic patients studied.

The French and Alexander monograph (1941) developed the most detailed hypotheses yet published about the psychogenic contribution to bronchial asthma. Although there is a wealth of suggestive clinical material in the literature, there has been no adequate test of their hypotheses. Obviously the testing of hypotheses derived from psychoanalytic interviews of unconscious conflict is no simple matter. One does not gather evidence about the occurrence of maternal rejection, for instance, simply by asking mothers whether they have rejected their children, yet such approaches have been attempted. Just criticisms have been leveled at the simplistic use of personality inventories to test psychoanalytic hypotheses. A good deal of care is needed to ensure that the level of behavior tapped in experimental tests of a hypothesis be congruent with the level at which the original observations were made. One solution to this problem has been used in several studies: a prediction about overt behavior has been derived from psychoanalytic hypotheses and tested in a laboratory setting. Thus, there have been predictions that the mother-child interaction in asthma would lead to greater need for recognition in the asthmatic (Greenfield, 1958) and a higher level of aspiration (Little & Cohen, 1951; Morris, 1959). An accumulation of studies of this kind which attempt to integrate clinical findings and experimental methods would help to appraise the relevance of the French and Alexander hypotheses and contribute a good deal of basic information.

Recent studies have explored the possibility that the allergic population is both psychologically and immunologically heterogeneous, and these are among the most promising investigations to date. It may well be that one major source of inconsistencies between studies has to do with the confounding of allergic and non-allergic patients, all of whom suffer from similar symptoms. Thus it becomes extremely important for all workers to report precisely the basis for classifying their samples as allergic. The findings thus far suggest that a greater degree of psychopathology is to be found among patients with a lesser degree of immunological evidence for allergy. If findings from subsequent studies concur, theories about the role of psychological factors in allergy can become considerably more precise.

Relatively little attention has been given to hypotheses of psychosomatic specificity in recent years, and most of the work has been poorly designed and executed. Two well-designed studies (Graham, Lundy, Benjamin, Kalber, Lewis, Kunish, and Graham, 1962; Ring, 1957), however, have yielded positive findings, indicating that there may be specific emotional attitudes associated with the experiences of different illnesses. The direction of causation is quite uncertain, but findings are of sufficient interest to commend future research attention.

The role of psychological factors in allergy has occasionally been studied by attempting to isolate specific emotional precipitants of symptoms. Apart from the ingenious laboratory studies of Wolff and his colleagues (1950) most work in this area has suffered from major methodological problems in obtaining pertinent and reliable information about life circumstances at the time of onset of symptoms.

Lastly, findings from the study of conditioning of the asthma response would seem to have great potential usefulness. In animal studies it has been possible to develop a conditioned asthma response to a chamber in which an allergen was administered or to an auditory signal previously paired with the introduction of the allergen. Only one study (Dekker, Pelser, and Groen, 1957) of conditioning in humans has been reported but many more are needed. Conditioning studies may be very useful in explaining how asthma in the human is developed and maintained through a combination of allergenic and emotional stimulation.

Thus, few substantive statements can be made about knowledge in the field because of the many critical weaknesses in the vast bulk of research performed. Yet, promising directions of research for the future can be identified with some certainty. If these directions are followed, the next decade should see a decrease in the unsystematic explorations that have characterized the past. The number of formal research reports, in comparison to the number of case reports, appears to be growing. It needs to be emphasized that this is a very complex research area where many of the methodological problems discussed do not lend themselves to easy solutions. Awareness of these problems, however, and a closer liaison between investigators from the fields of allergy and the behavioral sciences should permit the formulation of more precise theory and more sophisticated research methods.

REFERENCES

Abramson, H. A.   Evaluation of maternal rejection theory in allergy. *Ann. Allergy* **12**:129, 1954.

Abramson, H. A.   Psychic factors in allergy and their treatment. *Ann. Allergy* **14**:145, 1956.

Abramson, H. A.   Pseudoallergic schizophrenia: A new clinical entity. *Ann. Allergy* **17**:576, 1959.

Abramson, H. A.   *The Patient Speaks.* Vantage Press, New York, 1956.

Abramson, H. A.   *Psychodynamics and the Allergic Patient.* Bruce, Saint Paul, 1948.

Abramson, H. A., Gettner, H. H., and Sklarofsky, B.   Content analysis of somatic symptoms in 314 verbatim psychotherapeutic interviews in an allergic patient. *J. Child. Asthma Res. Inst. Hosp.* **1**:165, 1961.

Abramson, H. A., and Peshkin, M. M.   Psychosomatic group therapy with parents of children with intractable asthma. II. Adaptation mechanisms. *Ann. Allergy* **18**:87, 1960.

Alcock, T.   Some personality characteristics of asthmatic children. *Brit. J. Med. Psychol.* **33**:133, 1960.

Alexander, F.   "Emotional factors in respiratory disturbance." In *Psychosomatic Medicine.* Norton, New York, 1950(a), pp. 132-141.

Alexander, F.   *Psychosomatic Medicine, Its Principles and Application.* Norton, New York, 1950(b).

Alexander, F., and Visotsky, H.   Psychosomatic study of a case of asthma. *Psychosom. Med.* **17**:470, 1955.

Appel, J., and Rosen S. R.   Psychotic factors in psychosomatic illness. *Psychosom. Med.* **12**:236, 1950.

Aston, E. E.   Treatment of allergy by suggestion: An experiment. *Amer. J. Clin. Hypnosis* **1**:163, 1959.

Bacon, C. L. The role of aggression in the asthmatic attack. *Psychoanal. Quart.* **25**:309, 1956.

Baldwin, H. S. Constitutional factors in asthma. *Ann. Allergy* **21**:637, 1963.

Barendregt, J. T. A cross-validation study of the hypothesis of psychosomatic specificity, with special reference to bronchial asthma. *J. Psychosom. Res.* **2**:109, 1957.

Barendregt, J. T. A psychological investigation of the effects of group psychotherapy in patients with bronchial asthma. *J. Psychosom. Res.* **2**:115, 1957.

Bell, A. I. Some thoughts on postpartum respiratory experiences and their relationship to pregenital mastery, particularly in asthmatics. *Int. J. Psychoanal.* **39**:159, 1958.

Block, J. Are psychosomatic syndromes homogeneous? Evidence supporting a differentiated approach. Paper read at the Society for Research in Child Development, Berkeley, April, 1963.

Bostock, J. Asthma: A synthesis involving primitive speech, organism, and insecurity. *J. Ment. Sci.* **102**:559, 1956.

Brown, E. A. Combined allergic and psychosomatic treatment of bronchial asthma. *Ann. Allergy* **9**:324, 1951(a).

Brown, E. A. Nasal function and nasal neurosis. *Ann. Allergy* **9**:563, 1951(b).

Chessick, R. D., Kurland, M. L., Husted, R. M., and Diamond, M. A. The asthmatic narcotic addict. *Psychosomatics* **1**:346, 1960.

Clapham, H. I., and Sclare, A. B. Group psychotherapy with asthmatic patients. *Int. J. Group Psychotherapy* **8**:44, 1958.

Clarke, T. W. The relation of allergy to character problems in children. *Ann. Allergy* **8**:175, 1950.

Clarke, T. W. Allergy and the "problem child." *Nerv. Child* **9**:278, 1952.

Clausen, J. Respiration movement in normal, neurotic, and psychotic subjects. *Acta Psychiat. Scand.* suppl. **68**, 1951.

Coolidge, J. C. Asthma in mother and child as a special type of intercommunication. *Amer. J. Orthopsychiat.* **26**:165, 1956.

Creak, M., and Stephen, J. M. The psychological aspects of asthma in children. *Pediat. Clin. N. Amer.* **5**:731, 1958.

Cutter, F. *Maternal Behavior and Childhood Allergy.* Catholic University of America Press, Washington, 1955.

Dekker, E., Barendregt, J. T., and de Vries, K. Allergy and neurosis in asthma. *J. Psychosom. Res.* **5**:83, 1961.

Dekker, E., and Groen, J. Reproducible psychogenic attacks of asthma. *J. Psychosom. Res.* **1**:58, 1956.

Dekker, E., Pelser, H. E., and Groen, J. Conditioning as a cause of asthma attacks. *J. Psychosom. Res.* **2**:97, 1957.

Deutsch, F. Thus speaks the body. Some psychosomatic aspects of the respiratory disorder: Asthma. *Acta Med. Orient.* **10**:67, 1951.

Doust, J. W. L., and Leigh, D. Studies on the physiology of awareness; the interrelationships of emotions, life situations, and anoxemia in patients with bronchial asthma. *Psychosom. Med.* **15**:292, 1953.

Dubo, S., McLean, J. A., Chine, A. Y. T., Wright, H. L., Kauffman, P. E., and Sheldon, J. M. A study of relationships between family situation, bronchial asthma, and personal adjustment in children. *J. Pediat.* 59:402, 1961.

Dunbar, F. *Emotions and Bodily Changes, a Survey of Literature on Psychosomatic Interrelationships 1910-1953.* (ed. 4). Columbia University Press, New York, 1954.

Edgell, P. G. The psychology of asthma. *Canad. Med. Ass. J.* 67:121, 1952.

Edwards, G. Hypnotic treatment of asthma. *Brit. Med. J.* 5197:492, 1960.

Eisenberg, B. C. Role of tranquilizing drugs in allergy. *J.A.M.A* 163:934, 1957

Eldridge, L. Respiration rate change and its relation to avoidance behavior. *Dissertation Abstr.* 15/2:290, 1955.

Epstein, R. Need for approval and the conditioning of verbal hostility in asthmatic children. Paper read at American Psychological Association Convention, Philadelphia, September, 1963.

Fagerberg, E. The importance of psychologic factors in bronchial asthma. *Acta Allerg.* 6:61, 1953.

Feinberg, S. M., Malkiel, S., and McIntire, F. C. The effect of stress factors of asthma induced in guinea pigs by aerosolized antigens. *J. Allergy* 24:302, 1953.

Feingold, B. F., Gorman, F. J., Singer, M. T., and Schlesinger, K. Psychological studies of allergic women. *Psychosom. Med.* 24:195, 1962.

Fenichel, O. "Respiratory Introjection." In *The Collected Papers of Otto Fenichel.* First series. Macmillan, London, 1954, pp. 221-240.

Fennell, G. Psychogenic factors in vasomotor rhinorrhea. *Brit. J. Psychiat.* 108:447, 1963.

Fine, R. The personality of the asthmatic child. In *The Asthmatic Child. Psychosomatic Approach to Problems and Treatment.* Schneer, H. I. Hoeber, New York, 1963, pp. 39-57.

Fink, G., and Schneer, H. Psychiatric evaluation of adolescent asthmatics. In *The Asthmatic Child. Psychosomatic Approach to Problems and Treatment.* Schneer, H. I. Hoeber, New York, 1963, pp. 205-223.

Fitzelle, G. T. Personality factors and certain attitudes toward child rearing among parents of asthmatic children. *Psychosom. Med.* 21:208, 1959.

Franks, C. M., and Leigh, D. The theoretical and experimental application of a conditioning model to a consideration of bronchial asthma in man. *J. Psychosom. Res.* 4:88, 1959.

Freedman, B. Conditioning of respiration and its psychosomatic implications. *J. Nerv. Ment. Dis.* 113:1, 1951.

Freedman, D. X., and Fenichel, G. Effect of midbrain lesion on experimental allergy. *AMA Arch. Neurol.* 79:164, 1958.

Freedman, D. X., Redlich, F. C., and Igersheimer, W. W. Psychosis and allergy. Experimental approach. *Amer. J. Psychiat.* 112:873, 1956.

French, T. M. Emotional conflict and allergy. *Int. Arch. Allergy* 1:28, 1950.

French, T. M., and Alexander, F. Psychogenic factors in bronchial asthma.

Psychosom. Med. Monographs 4, National Research Council, Washington, D. C., 1941.

Funkenstein, D. H.   Psychophysiological relationship of asthma and urticaria to mental illness. *Psychosom. Med.* **12**:377, 1950(a).

Funkenstein, D. H.   Variations in response to standard amounts of chemical agents during alterations in feeling states in relation to occurrence of asthma. In *Res. Publ. Ass. Res. Nerv. Ment. Dis.* **29**, 1950(b).

Gantt, W. H.   Experimental basis for neurotic behavior *Psychosom. Med. Monograph 3*, nos. 3 & 4. National Research Council, Washington, D. C., 1941, p. 59.

Gaudet, E. L.   Dynamic interpretation and treatment of asthma in a child. *Amer. J. Orthopsychiat.* **20**:328, 1950.

Gerard, M. W.   Bronchial asthma in children. In *Studies in Psychosomatic Medicine*, Alexander, F. G., and French, T. M. Ronald Press, New York, 1948, pp. 243-248.

Glasser, A. J.   Personality attributes related to bronchial asthma in the adult male. Unpublished doctoral dissertation, Boston University, Boston, 1953.

Goldensohn, E. S.   Role of the respiratory mechanism. *Psychosom. Med.* **17**: 377, 1955.

Graham, D. T., Lundy, R. M., Benjamin, L. S., Kabler, J. D., Lewis, W. C., Kunish, N. O., and Graham, F. K.   Specific attitudes in initial interviews with patients having different "psychosomatic" diseases. *Psychosom. Med.* **24**:257, 1962.

Greenfield, N. S.   Allergy and the need for recognition. *J. Consult. Psychol.* **22**:230, 1958.

Groen, J.   Emotional factors in the etiology of internal diseases. *J. Mount Sinai Hosp. N. Y.* **18**:71, 1951-52.

Groen, J. J., and Pelser, H. E.   Experiences with, and results of, group psychotherapy in patients with bronchial asthma. *J. Psychosom. Res.* **4**: 191, 1960.

Gunnarson, S.   Asthma in children as a psychosomatic disease. *Int. Arch. Allergy* **1**:103, 1950.

Hallowitz, D.   Residential treatment of chronic asthmatic children. *Amer. J. Orthopsychiat.* **20**:490, 1950.

Harms, E.   *Somatic and Psychiatric Aspects of Childhood Allergies.* Macmillan, New York, 1963.

Harris, I. D., Rapaport, L., Rynerson, M. A., and Samter, M.   Observations on asthmatic children. *Amer. J. Orthopsychiat.* **20**:490, 1950.

Harris, M. C.   Is there a specific emotional pattern in allergic disease? *Ann. Allergy* **13**:654, 1955.

Harris, M. C., and Shure, N.   A study of behavior patterns in asthmatic children. *J. Allergy* **27**:312, 1956.

Hawkins, N. G.   Breathing deficit, allergy, and alcoholism. *Amer. J. Psychiat.* **114**:707, 1958.

Holmes, T. H., Treuting, T., and Wolff, H.   Life situations, emotions, and nasal diseases: Evidence on summative effects exhibited in patients with hay-fever. In Wolff, H. G., *Life Stress and Bodily Disease. Res. Publ. Ass. Nerv. Ment. Dis.* **29**:545, 1950.

Holmes, T H., Treuting, T., and Wolff, H. G.   Life situations, emotions, and nasal diseases: Evidence on summative effects exhibited in patients with hay-fever. *Psychosom. Med.* **13**:71, 1951.

Holmgren, B., and Kraepelin, S.   Electroencephalographic studies of asthmatic children. *Acta Paediat. (Upps)* **42**:432, 1953.

Hurst, A., Henkin, R., and Lustig, G. J.   Some psychosomatic aspects of respiratory disease. *Amer. Practit.* **1**:486, 1950.

Ibor, J. J. L.   Problems presented by asthma as a psychosomatic illness. *J. Psychosom. Res.* **1**:115, 1956.

Israel, M.   Rorschach responses of a group of adult asthmatics. *J. Ment. Sci.* **100**:753, 1954.

Jessner, L., Lamont, J., Long, R., Rollins, N., Whipple, B., and Prentice, N.   Emotional impact of nearness and separation for the asthmatic child and his mother. *Psychoanal. Study Child.* **10**:353, 1955.

Kepecs, J. G., Robin, M., and Munro, C.   Responses to sensory stimulation in certain psychosomatic disorders. *Psychosom. Med.* **20**:351, 1958.

Kerman, E. F.   Bronchial asthma and affective psychoses: Report of two cases treated with electric shock. *Psychosom. Med.* **8**:53, 1946.

Knapp, P. H., and Nemetz, S. J.   Personality variations in bronchial asthma. *Psychosom. Med.* **19**:443, 1957(a).

Knapp, P. H., and Nemetz, S. J.   Sources of tension in bronchial asthma. *Psychosom. Med.* **19**:466, 1957(b).

Knapp, P. H., and Nemetz, S. J.   Acute bronchial asthma: I. Concomitant depression and excitement, and varied antecedent patterns in 406 attacks. *Psychosom. Med.* **22**:42, 1960.

Knapp, P. H.   Acute bronchial asthma: II. Psychoanalytic observations on fantasy, emotional arousal, and partial discharge. *Psychosom. Med.* **22**:88, 1960.

Koupernik, C.   Epileptic paroxysms of a vegetational and anxious nature in children: Two case histories. *J. Child. Psychol. Psychiat.* **1**:146, 1960.

Kraft, B.   The role of emotions in intractable asthma. *Geriatrics* **18**:361, 1963.

Kraft, B., Countryman, F. W., and Blumenthal, D. L.   Suicide by asthma. *Ann. Allergy* **17**:394, 1959.

Leigh, D.   Asthma and the psychiatrist: A critical review. *Int. Arch. Allergy* **4**:227, 1953.

Leigh, D.   Some psychiatric aspects of asthma. *Practitioner* **170**:381, 1953.

Leigh, D., and Doust, J. W. L.   Asthma and psychosis. *J. Ment. Sci.* **99**:489, 1953.

Leigh, D., and Marley, E.   A psychiatric assessment of adult asthmatics: A statistical study. *J. Psychosom. Res.* **1**:128, 1956.

Leigh, D., and Pond, D. A.   The electroencephalogram in cases of bronchial asthma. *J. Psychosom. Res.* **1**:120, 1956.

Liddell, H.   The influence of experimental neuroses on respiratory function. In *Somatic and Psychiatric Treatment of Asthma.* Abramson, H. A. (Ed.). Williams & Wilkins, Baltimore, 1951.

Little, S. W., and Cohen, L. D.   Goal-setting behavior of asthmatic children and of their mothers for them. *J. Personality* 19:376, 1951.

Long, R. T., Lamont, J. H., Whipple, B., Bandler, L., Blom, G., Burgin, L., and Jessner, L.   A psychosomatic study of allergic and emotional factors in children with asthma. *Am. J. Psychiat.* 114:890, 1958.

Mandell, A. J., and Younger, C. B.   Asthma alternating with psychiatric symptomatology. *Calif. Med.* 96:251, 1962.

Mansmann, J. A.   Projective psychological tests applied to the study of bronchial asthma. *Ann. Allergy* 10:583, 1952.

Margolis, M.   The mother-child relationship in bronchial asthma. *J. Abnorm. Soc. Psychol.* 63:360, 1961.

Masserman, J. H., and Pechtel, C.   Neurosis in monkeys: A preliminary report of experimental observations. *Ann. N. Y. Acad. Sci.* 56:253, 1953.

Mayer-Loughman, G. P., Mason, A. A., Macdonald, N., and Fry, L.   Controlled trial of hypnosis in the symptomatic treatment of asthma. *Brit. Med. J.* 2:371, 1962.

McDermott, N., and Cobb, S.   A psychiatric survey of 50 cases of bronchial asthma. *Psychosom. Med.* 1:203, 1939.

Miller, H., and Baruch, D. W.   A study of hostility in allergic children. *Amer. J. Orthopsychiat.* 20:506, 1950.

Miller, H., and Baruch, D. W.   The emotional problems of childhood and their relation to asthma. *AMA J. Dis. Child.* 93:242, 1957.

Miller, H., and Baruch, D.   Emotional traumata preceding the onset of allergy symptoms in a group of children. *Ann. Allergy* 8:100, 1950.

Miller, H., and Baruch, D. W.   Marital adjustments in the parents of allergic children. *Ann. Allergy* 8:754, 1950.

Miller, H., and Baruch, D. W.   Psychotherapy in acute attacks of bronchial asthma. *Ann. Allergy* 11:438, 1953.

Miller, H., and Baruch, D.   Psychotherapy of parents of allergic children. *Ann. Allergy* 18:990, 1958.

Miller, H., and Baruch, D. W.   "Allergies." In Slavson, S. R., *The Fields of Group Psychotherapy.* McGraw, New York, 1956.

Miller, H., and Baruch, D. W.   The patient, the allergist, and emotions. *First Int. Congress for All.* Basil: S. Kargcr, 1951.

Miller, H., and Baruch, D. W.   Some paintings by allergic patients in group psychotherapy and their dynamic implications in the practice of allergy. *Int. Arch. Allergy* 1:60, 1950.

Miller, H., and Baruch, D. W.   The psychosomatic aspects of the management of asthmatic children. *Int. Arch. Allergy* 13:102, 1958.

Miller, H., and Baruch, D.   *The Practice of Psychosomatic Medicine as Illustrated in Allergy.* McGraw-Hill, New York, 1956.

Miller, H., and Baruch, D. W.   Psychosomatic studies of children with allergic manifestations. I. Maternal rejection: A study of 63 cases. *Psychosom. Med.* 10:275, 1948.

Miller, J.   Treatment of emotional problems in allergic disorders: A double-blind placebo-controlled study. *Psychosom.* 1:338, 1960.

Miller, M. L.   Emotional conflicts in asthma. *Dis. Nerv. Syst.* 13:10, 1952.

Miller, M. M.   Allergy and emotions: A review. *Int. Arch. Allergy* 1:40, 1950.

Mitchell, A. J., Frost, L., and Marx, J. R.   Emotional aspects of pediatric allergy—the role of the mother-child relationship. *Ann. Allergy* 11:744, 1953.

Mitchell, J. H., Curran, C. A., Myers, Ruth N.   Some psychosomatic aspects of allergic diseases. *Psychosom. Med.* 9:184, 1947.

Mohr, G. J., Tansend, H., Selenick, S., and Augenbraun, B.   Studies of asthma and eczema in the pre-school child. Paper read at the meeting of the American Psychiatric Association, May, 1961. In press.

Monsour, K. J.   Asthma and the fear of death. *Psychoanal. Quart.* 29:56, 1960.

Morris, R. P.   Effect of the mother on goal setting behavior of the asthmatic child. *Dissertation Abst.* 20:1440, 1959.

Murray, N., and Bierer, J.   Prolonged Sneezing: A case report. *Psychosom. Med.* 13:56, 1951.

Neuhaus, E. C.   A personality study of asthmatic and cardiac children. *Psychosom. Med.* 20:181, 1958.

Nitzberg, H.   The social worker in an institution for asthmatic children. *Social Casework* 33:111, 1952.

Noelpp, B., and Noelpp-Eschenhagen, I.   Das experimentelle asthma bronchiale des meerschweinhens. II. Mitterlung die ralle ludingter reflexes in der pathogenese des asthma bronchialle. *Int. Arch. Allergy* 2:321, 1951.

Noelpp, B., and Noelpp-Eschenhagen, I.   Das experimentelle asthma bronchiale des meerschweinchens. III. Mitterlung. Studien zur beduntung bedingter reflexe. Bahnung-slureitschaft und hastfahigkeit inter "Stress." *Int. Arch. Allergy* 3:108, 1952.

Ottenberg, P., and Stein, M.   Psychological determinants in asthma. *Trans. Acad. Psychosom. Med.* 122:63, 1958.

Ottenberg, P., Stein, M., Lewis, J., and Hamilton, C.   Learned asthma in the guinea pig. *Psychosom. Med.* 20:395, 1958.

Owen, F. W.   Psychosomatic behavior—a theoretical position. Paper read at Society for Research in Childhood Development, Berkeley, April, 1963.

Pearson, R. S. B.   Conf. Maudsley Hospital, London, April, 1955. *J. Psychosom. Res.* 1:169, 1956.

Peshkin, M. M.   The treatment of institutionalized children with intractable asthma. *Conn. Med.* 24:166, 1960.

Peshkin, M. M.   Intractable asthma of childhood: Rehabilitation at the institutional level with a follow-up of 150 cases. *Int. Arch. Allergy* 15:91, 1959.

Peshkin, M. M.   Rehabilitation of the intractable asthmatic child by the institutional approach. *Quart. Rev. Pediat.* 11:7, 1956.

Peshkin, M. M., and Abramson, H. A.   First National Seminar of Regional Medical Consultants. *Ann. Allergy* 16:473, 1958.

Peshkin, M. M., and Abramson, H. A.   Psychosomatic group therapy with parents of children having intractable asthma. *Ann. Allergy* 17:344, 1959.

Prout, C.   Psychiatric aspects of asthma. *Psychiat. Quart.* 25:237, 1951.

Pshonic, A. T. Corticovisceral theory and some problems in higher nervous activity in pathological subjects. *Zh. Vyssh. Nerv. Deiat. Pavlov.* 10:355, 1960.

Purcell, K. Distinctions between subgroups of asthmatic children: Children's perceptions of events associated with asthma. *Pediatrics.* 1963, 31, 486-494.

Purcell, K., Bernstein, L., and Bukantz, S. C. A preliminary comparison of rapidly remitting and persistently "steroid-dependent" asthmatic children. *Psychosom. Med.* 23:305, 1960.

Purcell, K., and Metz, J. R. Distinctions between subgroups of asthmatic children: Some parent attitude variables related to age of onset of asthma. *J. Psychosom. Res.* 6:251, 1962.

Purcell, K., Turnbull, J. W., and Bernstein, L. Distinctions between subgroups of asthmatic children: Psychological tests and behavior rating comparisons. *J. Psychosom. Res.* 6:283, 1962.

Rackemann, F. M. Other factors besides allergy in asthma. *J.A.M.A.* 142:534, 1950.

Raginsky, B. B. The investigation of allergy through hypnotic techniques. *Psychosomatics* 3:137, 1962.

Ratner, B. Temporal and quantitative influencing the development of experimental asthma in the guinea pig. *J. Allergy* 24:316, 1953.

Ratner, B. Experimental asthma. In Abramson, H. A., *Somatic and Psychiatric Treatment of Asthma.* Williams & Wilkins, Baltimore, 1951, pp. 62-92.

Reed, J. W. Emotional factors in bronchial asthma. *Psychosomatics* 3:57, 1962.

Rees, L. Physical and emotional factors in bronchial asthma. *J. Psychosom. Res.* 1:98, 1956(a).

Rees, L. Psychosomatic aspects of asthma in elderly patients. *J. Psychosom. Res.* 1:212, 1956(b).

Rees, L. The role of emotional and allergic factors in hay fever. *J. Psychosomatic Res.* 3:234, 1959.

Ring, F. O. Testing the validity of personality profiles in psychosomatic illnesses. *Amer. J. Psychiat.* 113:1075, 1957.

Ross, W. D., Hay, J., and McDowall, M. F. The association of certain vegetative disturbances with various psychoses. *Psychosom. Med.* 12:170, 1950.

Ross, W. D., Hay, J., and McDowall, M. F. The incidence of certain vegetative disturbances in relation to psychosis. *Psychosom. Med.* 12:179, 1950.

Sabbath, J. C., and Luce, R. A. Psychosis and bronchial asthma. *Psychiat. Quart.* 26:562, 1952.

Sanger, M. D. Emotional factors in respiratory and dermatological allergy. *Psychosomatics* 1:81, 1960.

Saul, L. J., and Lyons, J. W. The psychodynamics of respiration. In Abramson, H. A., *Somatic and Psychiatric Treatment of Asthma.* Williams & Wilkins, Baltimore, 1951, pp. 93-103.

Schatia, V. The role of emotions in allergic diseases. *Int. Arch. Allergy* 1:93, 1950.

Scheflen, A. E.   On bronchial asthma: a case report. *Psychiat. Quart.* 27:650, 1953.

Scheibel, A. B.   Treatment of bronchial asthma with psychotherapy. Report of a case. *U.S. Armed Forces Med. J.* 1:557, 1950.

Schiavi, R. C., Stein, M., and Sethi, B. B.   Respiratory variables in response to a pain-fear stimulus and an experimental asthma. *Psychosom. Med.* 23:485, 1961.

Schneer, H. I.   *The Asthmatic Child. Psychosomatic Approach to Problems and Treatment.* Harper & Row, New York, 1963.

Sclare, A. B., and Crockett, J. A.   Group psychotherapy in bronchial asthma. *J. Psychosom. Res.* 2:157, 1957.

Seitz, P. D. F.   Infantile experience and adult behavior in animal subjects: II. Age of separation from the mother and adult behavior in the cat. *Psychosom. Med.* 21:353, 1959.

Selinsky, H.   Emotional factors relating to perennial allergy. *Ann. Allergy* 18:886, 1960.

Seward, G. H., Goodwin, P., Prince, S., and Morrison, L. M.   A personality study of spastic colitis in relation to peptic ulcer and bronchial asthma. *Amer. Psychologist.* 5:471, 1950.

Sirmay, E. A.   The role of psychotherapy in allergy. Credits and debits. *Calif. Med.* 78:456, 1953.

Skands, M. C.   A case of asthma treated with psychotherapy. *Amer. J. Med.* 9:117, 1951.

Smith, R. E.   A Minnesota Multiphasic Personality Inventory profile of allergy. *Psychosom. Med.* 24:203, 1962(a).

Smith, R. E.   A Minnesota Multiphasic Personality Inventory profile of allergy. II. Conscious conflict. *Psychosom. Med.* 24:543, 1962(b).

Sontag, L. W.   A psychiatrist's view of allergy. *Int. Arch. Allergy* 1:50, 1950.

Stein, M., and Ottenberg, P.   Role of odors in asthma. *Psychosom. Med.* 20:60, 1958.

Stevenson, I.   Variations in the Secretion of Bronchial Mucus During Periods of Life Stress." In *Life Stress & Bodily Diseases,* Wolff, H. G. (Ed.). *Res. Publ. Ass. Nerv. Ment. Dis.* 29:596, 1950.

Stevenson, S. S.   The management of the allergic child. *Ann. Allergy* 2:770, 1952.

Strauss, E. B.   Conf. Maudsley Hospital, London, April, 1955. *J. Psychosom. Res.* 1:167, 1956.

Stovkis, B.   Psychosomatic aspects and psychotherapy in allergic diseases. In Jamar, J. M., *International Textbook of Allergy.* Munksgaard, Copenhagen, 1959, pp. 353-412.

Swartz, J., and Semrad, E. V.   Psychosomatic disorders in psychoses. *Psychosom. Med.* 13:314, 1951.

Taub, S. J.   The management of anxiety in allergic disorders—a new approach. *Psychosomatics* 2:349, 1961.

Tuft, H. S.   The development and management of intractable asthma of childhood. *Am. J. Dis. Child.* 93:251, 1957.

Turnbull, J. W.   Asthma conceived as a learned response. *J. Psychosom. Res.* 6:59, 1962.

Unger, L., and Unger, A. H.   Treatment of bronchial asthma. *J.A.M.A.* 150: 562, 1952.

Walker, E. J., and Kellogg, W. W.   Conditioned respiration and the conditioned flexion response in dogs. *J. Comp. Physiol. Psychol.* 27:393, 1939.

Weiss, E.   Psychosomatic aspects of certain allergic disorders. *Int. Arch. Allergy* 1:4, 1950.

Weiss, E., and English, O. S.   The respiratory system. In *Psychosomatic Medicine.* Saunders, Philadelphia, 1957, pp. 415-428.

White, H. C.   Hypnosis in bronchial asthma. *J. Psychosom. Res.* 5:272, 1961.

Willard, H., Swan, R., and Wolf, G.   "Life Situations, Emotions, and Dyspnea." In *Life Stress and Bodily Diseases,* Wolff, H. G. (Ed.). *Res. Publ. Ass. Nerv. Ment. Dis.* 39:583, 1950.

Wilson, G. W.   "A Study of Structural and Instinctual Conflicts in Cases of Hay Fever." In *Studies in Psychosomatic Medicine,* Alexander and French. Ronald, New York, 1948, pp. 266-286.

Wittkower, E.   Psyche and allergy. *J. Allergy* 23:76, 1952.

Wittkower, E. D., and White, K. L.   "Psychophysiologic Aspects of Respiratory Disorders. In *American Handbook of Psychiatry.* Areiti, S. (Ed.). Basic Books, New York, 1959, pp. 693-694.

Wolf, S.   Causes and mechanisms in rhinitis. *Laryngoscope* 6:601, 1952.

Wolf, S., Holmes, T. H., Treuting, T., Goodell, Helen, and Wolff, H. G.   An experimental approach to psychosomatic phenomena in rhinitis and asthma. *J. Allergy* 21:1, 1950.

Wolff, H. G.   "Life Stress and Bodily Disease—a Formulation." In *Life Stress and Bodily Diseases,* Wolff, H. G., (Ed.). *Res. Publ. Ass. Nerv. Ment. Dis.* 29:1059, 1950.

Zeller, M., and Eolin, J. V.   Allergy in the insane. *J. Allergy* 14:564, 1942.

Ziwar, M.   Allergy and psyche, a psychosomatic study. *Egypt. Yearb. Psychol.* 1:7, 1954.

6

The Personality of Epileptics: A Discussion of the Evidence

INTRODUCTION

In the preceding article the major emphasis was on the possible psychological causes of organic pathology. In the following article the emphasis is reversed and an attempt is made to relate organic pathology, specifically the neural dysfunctions that are known to cause epilepsy, to personality differences. Although the personalities of individuals who have neurological problems may be found to differ from those who do not have them, one must be very cautious in suggesting a direct causal relationship between the dysfunction and the personality. That is, if a particular personality type is found in a person with a neurological dysfunction that causes epilepsy, the dysfunction may have caused the personality or, for example, the personality type may have resulted from the adjustment to the problems of being epileptic. This particular methodological difficulty is not unique to this area. As is pointed out later, some of the symptoms found in schizophrenics are probably due to their hospitalization rather than to the disorder itself.

The accurate identification of appropriate subjects provides another problem in the study of epilepsy and personality. One of the difficulties in solving this problem was stated by Strauss (1959) when he pointed out that "A truly satisfactory definition of 'epilepsy' on the basis of clinical characteristics is nonexistent." Without a generally agreed-upon definition, it is doubtful whether results found by one investigator can be generalized to individuals identified as epileptics by another investigator, since differences in the definitions used by the two investigators may result in very different populations for study. In fact, it may not even be accurate

137

to consider epilepsy as *one* disorder, for neurological research indicates that the disorder can stem from a *variety of causes,* that is, different types of neurological malfunctions in different areas of the brain. If different types of neurological malfunctions result in different types of personalities, a considerable amount of variance will be introduced into any study that lumps all individuals suffering from different seizure-causing neurological problems into one class (i.e., "epileptics") for a study of personality. In addition to being a problem of definition, the identification of epileptics is also a problem of diagnosis. Many of the clinical tests used to diagnose organic pathology have low reliabilities and, therefore, may misclassify subjects. It should also be noted that there are some known cases of epilepsy (e.g., those identified by the presence of seizures) for which the presently available tests have been unsuccessful in finding a neurological etiology. These cases are said to be suffering from idopathic or cryptogenic epilepsy. Their existence clearly illustrates the gaps in our knowledge and the medical problems involved in identifying individuals for study.

In evaluating the research in this area, it quickly becomes apparent that not all of the problems are related to the assessment of the independent variable. Unfortunately, serious questions can also be raised with regard to the measurement of the dependent variable, that is, personality. As the reader will find in reading the following article, most of the personality assessments have been carried out through the use of the Rorschach test. At the present time there are growing concerns and doubts in psychology about the reliability and validity of this technique for assessing personality.

It may very well be that because of methodological and measurement problems no definitive answer can yet be given with regard to the relationship between epilepsy and personality. Since the possibility of an epileptic personality is central to the controversial question of neurological determinants of personality functioning, it is important for the student of behavior pathology to be aware of the data on both sides of the issue and of the problems and limitations of these data.

Strauss, H. Epileptic disorders. In S. Arieti (ed.), *American Handbook of Psychiatry.* New York: Basic Books, 1959. Pp. 1109-1143.

6

THE PERSONALITY OF EPILEPTICS:
A DISCUSSION OF THE EVIDENCE

BARBARA TIZARD

The aim of this article is to assess the extent to which the various theories about the personality of epileptics have been affirmed or refuted, and to discuss some of the more important variables which should in the future be investigated by those working in this field. The complexity of the theoretical and methodological problems involved is also pointed out.

Theories

The theories discussed here are for the most part generalizations of particular clinicians' experiences, with little attempt to relate them to a wider body of knowledge. Five basic theories may be distinguished as follows:

1. That all or most epileptics share a characteristic personality. This was the original theory advanced in the nineteenth century by Falret and Féré, and extensively held on the Continent. It still has advocates, especially in Germany. The personality traits considered characteristic of epileptics have been variously described by different authors. There is some agreement on a basic syndrome of perseveration and viscosity in both the intellectual and affective spheres. Emotional explosiveness has also been named as a central trait by most authors, either co-existing with viscosity (Minkowska, 1946) or replacing it (Clark, 1918; Stauder, 1938). Traits such as suspiciousness, religiosity, meticulousness, and selfishness have been emphasized by others. According to these writers, the epileptic personality and the predisposition to convulsions are constitutionally determined. American writers who have recognized a characteristic if not universal epileptic personality have usually attributed it to the frustrating environment and the social stigma to which the epileptic is exposed, or to the effect of brain dysfunc-

SOURCE. Reprinted with permission of the American Psychological Association and the author from the *Psychological Bulletin*, 1962, 59, 196-210.

tion on the personality, or to both these factors (Notkin, 1928; Revitch, 1955).

2. That there is no characteristic epileptic personality, and the same range and combination of personality traits may be found among epileptics and nonepileptics (Lennox, 1944). This theory was widely held in America during the "thirties" and "forties," particularly by clinicians whose main experience was with private patients.

3. That there is no characteristic epileptic personality or personality disturbance, but a higher proportion of neurotic disturbance is found among epileptics than among nonepileptics (Bridge, 1949).

4. That there is no characteristic epileptic personality, but epileptics tend to have a personality resembling that of patients with organic lesions, which differ from that of normal persons. This theory has been particularly favored by clinicians working with epileptic children (Bradley, 1951).

Each of these theories has been advanced largely on the basis of clinical observation, but in each case has been supported by evidence from more objective studies, which will be considered in the sections on Rorschach Studies and Studies Other than Rorschach Studies.

5. That there is no characteristic personality common to all or most epileptics, but different types of personality are associated with different types of epilepsy. This is not a new theory—as far back as 1938 German authors were describing two distinct personality types, associated with idiopathic and symptomatic epilepsy. Since about 1950, however, with the delineation of, and growing interest in temporal lobe epilepsy, it has assumed a new importance. Temporal lobe epilepsy is now generally held to be associated with personality disturbance, and many of the unpleasant traits formerly attributed to epileptics in general are now said to characterize temporal lobe epileptics. In some neurosurgical centers temporal lobectomy is performed primarily in order to alleviate the personality disturbance of these epileptics. Some writers also describe a characteristic personality pattern found in children with petit mal epilepsy, and Gastaut and his colleagues have recently delineated an idiopathic epileptic personality type.

The theory that differences in personality among epileptics are related to differences in type of epilepsy has, in the case of temporal lobe epilepsy in turn been related to the results of experimental work with animals and to the results of surgery. Its advocates point out that bilateral ablation of the rhinencephalon in monkeys results in increased activity and docility (Kluver & Bucy, 1939) hence, the hypoactivity and aggressive outbursts of the patient with temporal lobe epilepsy may be considered to represent a state of excitation of the rhinencephalon. Moreover, some neurosurgical centers report a specific decrease in aggressive behavior after temporal lobectomy for epilepsy (Alajouanine, Nehlil, & Houdart, 1958; James, 1960). This theory is thus more than a clinical generalization, and has a rather different status from those outlined above. For this reason, as well as for its therapeutic implications, and because it has received little attention in psychological journals, the clinical evidence on which it is based will be briefly described. The evidence from psychological tests will be discussed in the sections on Rorschach Studies and Studies Other than Rorschach Studies.

The clinical evidence includes incidental observation, systematic studies of series of patients, and observations of the large proportion of patients with temporal lobe epilepsy amongst epileptics in mental hospitals. Typical of the incidental observations is Robertiello's (1953) description of the child with psychomotor epilepsy as usually cooperative, good, quiet and overcontrolled, but with episodes of impulsive and often violent and destructive behavior." Peterman (1953) describes him as a child with "an abnormal personality, with recurring episodes of behaviour disorder," in contrast to the child with petit mal epilepsy, who is usually "mentally precocious, alert, sensitive and temperamental." Pond's contrast is between the aggressive child with temporal lobe epilepsy, and the timid passive child with petit mal epilepsy (Pond, 1952, 1961).

More systematic studies have reported the incidence of personality disturbance among temporal lobe epileptics. Hill (1957) reported that 50% suffer from personality disorders, and of these 25% have psychotic episodes. Gibbs (1958) stated that about 40% of the patients with psychomotor epilepsy have severe personality disorders, and of these about one third are classifiable as psychotic. Gastaut and Gastaut (1951 unpublished) found that 52% of psychomotor epileptics attending outpatient clinics have psychiatric disorders and Bingley (1958) identified personality changes in 52% of epileptics with temporal lobe foci. Vislie and Henriksen (1958), reviewing the psychiatric symptoms of 162 epileptics, excluding psychotics, found a tendency for a higher incidence of neurotic symptoms when the localization signs pointed to the temporal region. The only comparable study with children, separating personality disturbance from intellectual defect, is that of Glaser and Dixon (1956). They found that 19 out of 25 children with psychomotor seizures had interictal personality disturbance.

Two recent studies have reported a large proportion of patients with temporal lobe epilepsy among epileptics in mental hospitals. Liddell (1953) reported an incidence of 50% and Roger and Dongier (1950) 64%, as compared with 30% in a series of outpatient epileptics (Gastaut, 1950).

The nature of the personality disturbance has been variously described. Gibbs (1958) found no specific symptoms, but Mulder and Daly (1952) stressed the frequency of anxiety and depression. Falconer, Hill, Meyer, and Wilson (1958) found explosive or persistent aggressiveness the commonest symptoms, as did Liddell (1953) and Roger and Dongier (1950) in their surveys of epileptics with temporal foci in mental hospitals. Paillas (1958) particularly noted the frequency of slowness, adhesiveness, and perseveration as well as aggressiveness, and Bingley (1958) found the commonest syndrome was "adhesiveness in the intellectual emotional and volitional spheres." Vislie and Henriksen (1958) however found these traits were associated with evidence of diffuse lesions and organic dementia rather than temporal localization.

There are two main difficulties in evaluating these studies. In the first place, there appear to be important differences between the epileptic populations studied. In some studies, mainly patients with pronounced psychiatric symptoms were included (Falconer et al., 1958; Liddell, 1953; Mulder & Daly, 1952; Roger & Dongier, 1950). In some studies the criterion for selection was purely clinical (Glaser & Dixon, 1956); in others, electrophysiological (Bingley, 1958; Vislie & Henriksen, 1958); whilst in still others a combination of clinical and electrophysiological criteria was used (Mulder & Daly, 1952; Gastaut et al., 1955). Since electroclinical correlations are far from perfect, different populations may have been sampled. This point is discussed further in Section 4.

Secondly, no study shows an adequate appreciation of the problems of bias and reliability in the judgments made. Precautions are not reported to prevent contamination of EEG interpretation by clinical data and the reliability of the EEG and clinical diagnoses is not assessed. Bingley's is the only study which describes reassessment of the EEG records by another judge, without knowledge of the previous interpretation of the patient's clinical symptoms.

The position is worse in respect of the assessment of the presence or type of psychiatric disturbance. This is left undefined in all studies and is never made without knowledge of clinical status. Nor is the reliability of the judgments assessed.

One study of greater methodological sophistication than the others is that of Nuffield (1961). The EEG records of 233 epileptic children who had attended the Maudsley Hospital during the previous 10 years were classified into 7 electrophysiological groups. Each child was rated for aggressiveness and neurotic manifestations on the basis of the answers which had been recorded on the standardized psychiatric case history to such questions as "Is he irritable, a bully, timid, sensitive?" The mean "aggressive" score derived from these ratings of the children with a temporal lobe EEG focus was higher than that of any other EEG group, while their mean "neurotic" score was the lowest. Conversely, the mean aggressive score of the 3/sec SW group was the lowest, and their mean neurotic score was the highest. The correlations between fit patterns and behavioral ratings were much lower than those between EEG classifications and behavioral ratings. In this study contamination between EEG data and behavioral ratings was avoided, but the reliability of the judgments was not assessed.

Rorschach Studies

The great majority of psychologists who have studied the personality of epileptics have used the Rorschach test, and the evidence from these studies will be considered first. A specific epileptic Rorschach protocol common to all or many epileptics has been described by some authors (Minkowska, 1946; Rorschach, 1942; Stauder, 1938). More cautiously, others have concluded that while there is no specific epileptic personality, epileptics share many traits and can be identified by the use of the Rorschach test (Altable, 1947; Bovet, 1936; Kelly & Marquilies, 1940; Piotrowski, 1947; Zehrer, 1951). Other authors, however, have found no statistically significant difference between the Rorschach scores and patterns of epileptic and nonepileptic groups (Kogan, 1947; Lisansky, 1948; Shaw & Cruikshank, 1957). The theory that the personality of epileptics resembles that of brain injured patients is supported by a number of Rorschach studies (Piotrowski, 1947; Ross, 1941; Zimmerman, Burgemeister, & Putnam, 1951). Other studies, however, report evidence of neurosis but no signs characteristic of brain injury (Arluck, 1941; Kaye, 1951; Richards, 1952; Zehrer, 1951). The belief that temporal lobe epileptics share a characteristic personality is supported by three Rorschach studies (Delay, Pichot, Lemperiere, & Perse, 1955; Gastaut, Morin, & Lesevre, 1955; Paillas & Subirana, 1950). The Rorschach pattern identified as characteristic is, however, quite different in each of these studies.

There is thus evidence from Rorschach studies for and against each theory about the personality of epileptics which has been advanced. In attempting to account for the contradictory nature of these findings, one is struck by two rather crude methodological errors that invalidate the great majority of the studies.

1. Many of the earlier studies used institutionalized epileptics, a very small and uncharacteristic sample of the epileptic population. These patients are mentally disturbed and may also be of low intelligence. All the descriptions of a specific epileptic Rorschach protocol derive from studies of such patients.

2. The great majority of studies have not controlled for IQ. They have compared the Rorschach protocols of epileptics with the Rorschach norms, assuming either that intellectual level was not an important factor, or that the epileptic group and the Rorschach normal group were of similar intelligence. However, evidence has recently accumulated which shows that intellectual level affects a great range of Rorschach responses in all-pervasive ways. Neff and Lidz (1951) in a study of army personnel divided into three subgroups according to intelligence showed that only the group with superior intelligence gave Rorschach responses usually considered typical of normal persons. Men with average and below average intelligence gave responses that by the usual Rorschach norms would be considered indicative of emotional disturbance. Similar findings are reported by Wedemeyer (1954). Later, Neff and Glaser (1954) showed that in Beck's normal group, used to furnish control data for many Rorschach studies, the percentage of those with high school education was two and a half times greater than in the general population. The epileptic protocols have thus been assessed and found in various ways abnormal by comparison with those of a group of above average intelligence.

The same kind of evidence invalidates most of the Rorschach studies of children. Control groups have rarely been used, and the epileptic protocols have been compared with published Rorschach child norms, such as the Ames norms. Fielder and Stone (1956) have shown, however, that three quarters of the children in the Ames Rorschach normal group came from professional and managerial classes. The responses from their own group of predominantly lower class normal children departed very considerably from the Ames' criteria of normality.

It thus appears that the conclusions of the great majority of Rorschach studies are unacceptable. In fact, the Rorschach scores of the epileptic groups resemble, and compare rather favorably with, those reported by Neff and Lidz and Wedemeyer for normal service groups of equivalent IQ. Even if, however, one considers only those studies which compare epileptics living in the community with nonepileptics, matched for age and IQ, the results appear no less conflicting than before.

There are only five such studies published. In addition, two studies have compared the Rorschach protocols of temporal lobe epileptics with other epileptics. Lisansky (1948) compared the Rorschach protocols of 10 adult noninstitutionalized epileptics and 10 diabetics, matched for age, education, and duration of illness. Both groups were of average intelligence. She found that the only significant difference between them was the slower response time of the epileptic group. The Rorschach "epileptic signs" did not differentiate the two groups.

Piotrowski (1947) compared the records of 25 epileptic adults, "none psychotic, hospitalized, or conspicuously deteriorated" and 25 hysterics of similar age and IQ. He found 14 "epileptic signs." Six of these had previously been included in his scale for differentiating patients with organic lesions. Most of the other signs can be found in various scales for differentiating neurotic or other disturbed patients. He also found that the presence of seven or more of these signs in a protocol identified 80% of his epileptic group, while none of the hysterics' records had more than four signs.

Arluck (1941) compared the Rorschach records of 16 idiopathic epileptics without an EEG focus, aged 10-21, with control groups of their sibs, of cardiac patients, and of the sibs of cardiac patients. The groups were equated for sex, age, IQ, and socioeconomic status. He found several statistically significant differences in the Rorschach scores. The epileptic group showed more signs of color shock, had fewer Ws in their records, and their mean time for responses was greater.[1] All three of these signs are included among

---

[1] *Editor's note.* Definition of Rorschach terminology may be helpful at this point. Although most Rorschach inkblots are only black and white, some contain colors. If, when presented with a colored card, an individual fails to give a response or gives a response that is of a poorer quality than his previous

Piotrowski's epileptic signs, and the first two occur in most Rorschach scales that claim to differentiate normals from any other groups.

Shaw and Cruikshank (1951), however, obtained negative results when they compared the Rorschach protocols of 25 institutionalized idiopathic epileptic children and 25 institutionalized nonepileptic children matched for age, sex, and IQ. The only significant differences found were in FV and number of different types of content, both being larger for the epileptic group.

Kogan (1947) compared the Rorschach protocols of 10 idiopathic epileptic children with behavior problems and 10 nonepileptic children attending the same child guidance clinic, matched for age, IQ, and severity of emotional disturbance. She found no statistically significant differences between the two groups on any Rorschach variable. Clinically, both groups contained shy, quiet, anxious children and aggressive, antisocial children.

Delay et al. (1955) studied the Rorschach protocols of 50 epileptics of average intelligence classified according to presumed etiology and also site of EEG focus, if any. They found that 48% of the whole group gave seven or more of Piotrowski's epileptic signs, and 68% gave five or more of his organic signs. Patients with "psychomotor temporal epilepsy" had significantly more extratensive Rorschach protocols than the rest. Gastaut et al. (1955) compared the Rorschach protocols of 60 noninstitutionalized psychomotor epileptics of average intelligence and a group of idiopathic epileptics. Only general impressions of the results were given. They reported that 72% of the psychomotor epileptics showed a syndrome of hypoactivity and emotional indifference or depression. It was the idiopathic group whose protocols were predominantly extratensive.

There is thus on the one hand Piotrowski's evidence that the Rorschach protocols of epileptics resemble each other but differ from those of hysterics by the presence of certain characteristic signs. This is partially supported by Arluck's study, and by Delay's finding that the Rorschach protocols of 48% of an epileptic group

responses, he is said to be showing "color shock." Since the way a person uses color on the Rorschach is supposedly revealing of the way he handles affect or emotion, it has been hypothesized that color shock is indicative of problems or conflicts over emotions and their expression. A W score indicates that in making a response to a blot the individual used the whole blot rather than just a part of it. This type of responding is interpreted as evidence that the individual tends to organize and see relationships between various aspects of a situation rather than treating them separately.

of average intelligence contain a large number of these signs. On the other hand three further studies have been unable to differentiate the Rorschach protocols of epileptics and normal children, disturbed epileptic children and disturbed nonepileptic children, and epileptic adults and diabetic adults. Two studies of the Rorschach protocols of patients of average intelligence with temporal lobe epilepsy reached opposite conclusions.

The extent to which the clinical status of the patients in these studies is comparable will be discussed below. The question must be raised, however, whether there are any inadequacies in the Rorschach test which make it an unsuitable tool with which to investigate the personality of epileptics. The primary concern of Piotrowski (1947) and many workers in this field was differential diagnosis. Yet the Rorschach test has repeatedly been shown to be an unsatisfactory diagnostic instrument. When the items originally found to differentiate two groups are put into the form of a scale and a cross-validation study is made by a different worker on a fresh sample, the differentiating power of the scale invariably drops considerably (Yates, 1954). Subjective scoring systems and test unreliability no doubt contribute to this finding. The consistency of the subject, subject reliability, scoring reliability, interpretation reliability, and enquiry reliability have proved disappointingly low (Baughman, 1951; Campbell & Fiddleman, 1959; Fiske, 1959). Moreover, where real differences in personality are known to exist between groups the Rorschach test cannot be relied upon to detect them. Studies in the last decade which have taken care to avoid contamination of Rorschach interpretations with clinical data have found slight or no significant differences between the Rorschach scores of hospitalized schizophrenics and normals (Friedman, 1952), between different psychiatric groups (Wittenborn & Holzberg, 1951), or between neurotics and schizophrenics (Reiman, 1953). Too much confidence cannot therefore be placed in the Rorschach test as an instrument for determining whether epileptics as a group resemble or differ from neurotics, normals, or brain injured groups.

Some studies have used the Rorschach test as a tool not only to differentiate between epileptic and other groups, but to describe the characteristics of the epileptic personality. Thus Arluck (1941) deduced from the protocols of his group that they suffered emotional strain, had much conflict within their basic personality configuration, and tended to adjust by withdrawing from the external world.

Such a use of the test depends on the assumption that different modes of response to the blots are determined, in a manner that is known, by dominant and enduring personality traits. Thus an extratensive Rorschach experience balance (i.e., a record with overemphasis on color) is said to be characteristic of an egocentric emotionally explosive personality. However, as Pruyser points out (1953), Rorschach, in common with most of his contemporaries, believed that epileptics are by constitution predisposed to these traits. When he found an unusually large number of color responses, especially CF and C, in the protocols of deteriorated epileptics, he concluded that such responses were determined by emotional explosiveness. Alternative explanations were not considered or inevstigated. Recent experimental work, however, strongly suggests that there is no relationship between number and type of color responses and emotional lability (Baughman, 1954; Keehn, 1954; Lazarus & Oldfield, 1955).

Attempts to validate the alleged relationship between Rorschach signs and such traits as constriction and impulsiveness have been no more successful (Carp, 1950; Holtzman, 1950). Very few such studies have been made. There is no adequate evidence for most of the Rorschach sign-trait correlations, and interpretations such as Arluck's have to be accepted on faith. Hence, even if consistent findings had emerged from the Rorschach studies, their significance in terms of behavioral correlates would have been a matter for further experimental investigation.

Studies Other than Rorschach Studies

There have been very few studies by psychologists of the personality of epileptics which have not used the Rorschach test. Meyers and Brecher (1941), using the Kent-Rosanoff Word Association Test, found no significant differences between a group of idiopathic epileptics and normal persons, matched for age, sex, IQ, and socioeconomic status. Arluck (1941) found no significant differences between the scores of his epileptic and control groups on a level of aspiration test and a personality questionnaire. These results are difficult to evaluate in the absence of evidence that the tests can differentiate significantly between any diagnostic groups whatsoever.

Davies-Eysenck (1950) assessed 38 adults suffering from idiopathic epilepsy, using three tests of neuroticism, which had been shown to discriminate very significantly between normals and neurotics. Even though she selected only those patients who were not mental defectives, were capable of paid employment, and fairly regular in clinic attendance, she found the mean score of the group one standard deviation towards the neurotic end of the scale. There was no correlation between length of illness and degree of neuroticism.

Halstead (1957) compared 28 epileptic children attending ordinary schools, 12 epileptic children attending a physically handicapped school, and 28 attending a special epileptic residential school, with 54 normal children. The investigation was primarily concerned with cognitive abilities and educational attainments, but behavior was assessed from information supplied by parents and schools. Thirty-seven percent of the epileptic group were considered to have good behavior, 35% to have bad behavior (aggressive, destructive, etc.), and 28% to have negative behavior (sullen, timid, oversensitive, etc.). The only variable analyzed which showed a significant correlation with bad behavior was attendance at the special epileptic school. This was, of course, one of the main reasons for referral. Positive but not significant correlations with bad behavior included brain injury, symptomatic epilepsy, frequent seizures, and longer duration of epilepsy. There were no statistically significant correlations between negative or good behavior and other variables, although correlations between good behavior, normal milestones, short duration of epilepsy, having major seizures, and attendance at normal school were all positive. There were no known cases of brain injury among the group with good behavior.

This study is of particular interest because of its representative sample of epileptic children. Unfortunately, the method of making the behavioral ratings is not recorded, and the reliability is not recorded, and the reliability of the ratings was not assessed.

Gastaut et al. (1955) compared the performance of 60 adult psychomotor epileptics of average intelligence and an unspecified group of idiopathic epileptics on a variety of psychological tests. They described 72% of the psychomotor epileptics as slow and adhesive, with a flat depressed affect which was reflected in their TAT stories. The idiopathic epileptics on the other hand were found to be quick, hyperactive, and emotionally labile. The test results on which these conclusions were based were not reported, and the EEG and clinical criteria by which the epileptic groups were selected were not defined.

Grunberg and Pond (1957) compared from case history records the family background of three groups of children who had attended the Maudsley Hospital: 53 epileptics with conduct disorders, 53 epileptics without conduct disorders, and 33 nonepileptics with conduct disorders. They found very similar adverse factors (disturbed parental attitudes, marital disharmony, breaks and changes in the environment) were present in the families of both groups of children with conduct disorder, but absent from the background of welladjusted epileptic children. The method by which the adverse factors were assessed is not described, and the reliability of the judgments was not assessed. This study confirms the earlier finding of Sullivan and Gahagen (1935) that epileptic children with serious personality or conduct disorders "had almost without exception a poor home environment."

Discussion

The work surveyed above gives no support to the theory that all or most epileptics share a characteristic personality. It is, however, hardly adequate to affirm or refute the other theories that have been advanced. There is some evidence that the incidence of personality disturbance may be high among epileptics, or among some groups of epileptics, and that different types of personality disturbance are associated with different types of epilepsy. From Grunberg and Pond's and Nuffield's studies cited above one may infer that these personality differences result from a complex interaction of environmental and pathophysiological factors. The contribution of heredity has not been studied, although Harvald (1954) has shown that psychosis, psychopathy, suicide, and criminality do not occur more frequently among the relatives of epileptics than in the general population.

Little progress is likely to be made unless future studies define much more precisely than before the characteristics of the epileptic group on whom observations are made. Most of the studies reviewed above have described their patients only in terms of age, sex, and IQ, and classified their epilepsy either as idiopathic or symptomatic, or as involving major or minor seizures. Neither method of classification has proved illuminating, and both obscure factors that there is reason to believe may be important.

Patients showing no signs of brain lesion are said to have idiopathic epilepsy, a condition believed to result from an inherited instability of cerebral function (Lennox, Gibbs, & Gibbs, 1940), and differing markedly from symptomatic epilepsy, which is associated with demonstrable cerebral lesions. However, there is evidence of a multiple etiology in all epilepsies. Heredity has been shown to be an important factor in symptomatic epilepsy (Williams, 1950), while a high incidence of twin births and breech births has been found in the history of patients with petit mal seizures and 3 per second WS EEGs, the classical form of idiopathic epilepsy (Churchill, 1959). The diagnosis of idiopathic epilepsy depends mainly on negative evidence—the lack of evidence of a focal lesion or of a history of brain injury. But as our understanding of epilepsy grows, more precise diagnoses can be made. Many patients, for example, who were classified as idiopathic epileptics in the studies reported above would now be diagnosed as cases of temporal lobe epilepsy, with presumed focal lesions.

One might predict that classification of patients into those having major or minor seizures, or both, would have significance at least in terms of the different psychological effects of these types of seizure on the patient and on society. In fact, however, this prediction is not supported by Halstead's (1957) study. He found a correlation, not significant, between good behavior and having major seizures. Nor has this method of classification neurophysiological significance. Any type of minor seizure may develop into a major one, and both clinical forms may be associated with focal, diffuse, or no known lesions of cortical or subcortical origin. Hence, in the supposedly homogeneous groups of idiopathic or symptomatic epileptics, or epileptics suffering from major or minor seizures, investigated in the studies reviewed above, it is likely that the most varied range of brain dysfunction and lesion occurred. If personality differences between epileptics are related to neurophysiological factors, these studies could not have revealed them. Unfortunately, the current method of clinical classification of epilepsy is hardly more adequate for research purposes. This can be illustrated with reference to the concepts of temporal lobe epilepsy and petit mal epilepsy. The former term is generally used to denote clinically defined psychomotor seizures occurring in patients with a temporal lobe EEG focus. It has been shown, however, that such a focus can be associated with all kinds of clinical manifestations. Only 46% of one series of epileptics with EEG ictal discharges in the temporal region had clinical psychomotor seizures (Jasper, Pertuiset, & Flanigin, 1951). Moreover, Hill (1949) found that in 110 cases with clinical psychomotor seizures, only 32 had temporal lobe EEG foci. Electroclinical correlations are even lower in children (Glaser & Golub, 1955). Glaser and Dixon (1956) were unable to find any relationship between response to a particular drug, clinical form of seizure, or type of

EEG abnormality. Postmorten studies have revealed a great variation in the extent, type, and location of lesions in such patients (Gastaut, 1953).

Thus, while the term temporal lobe epilepsy implies the existence of a condition in which clinical symptoms, EEG findings, pathology and response to drugs are highly correlated, in fact the only common feature among patients so diagnosed might be their common site of discharge in the region of the temporal lobe. Symonds (1954) has suggested substituting the term "the temporal lobe epilepsies" to emphasize the variety of conditions found. For research purposes, it is desirable to select patients by well defined EEG and/or clinical criteria, rather than by diagnostic labels.

The term petit mal epilepsy is also inadequate for research purposes. Originally a clinical term for any minor attack, it took on a more precise meaning when Gibbs, Davis, and Lennox (1935) observed that momentary seizures, with or without falling, are often accompanied by a 3 per second SW EEG pattern. This electroclinical association is often called "true" petit mal, and appears to respond specifically to the dione drugs. Clinically identical momentary seizures may, however, be accompanied by bursts of spikes or by complex wave forms, and at least one third of epileptics with 3 per second SW have no petit mal attacks (Clarke & Knott, 1955; Lundervold, Henriksen, & Fegersten, 1959; Silverman, 1954). Unless both EEG and clinical data are given, the type of minor attack cannot be identified.

A satisfactory classification of the epilepsies awaits greater understanding of their mode of action. Meanwhile, in any attempt to establish the behavioral characteristics of particular groups of epileptics, it is important to select the patients according to a criterion whose reliability is known, and which there is some evidence to consider significant. Nuffield's study has shown the importance of EEG criteria. The reliability of such criteria has not yet been adequately studied, and the improvement of reliability probably awaits adequate quantification of certain EEG phenomena.

An important variable which has been neglected is the type and amount of medication taken. This is not specified in any study. However, the drugs used to control seizures have important effects on the nervous system, some excitatory, some inhibitory. One might reasonably postulate that personality differences between different groups of epileptics are primarily a function of the differential long term effects of different types of drugs. Loveland,

Smith, and Forster (1957) tackled this problem, but their study covered a period of 3 months only, and the numbers in each group were very small.

While it has often been suggested that personality disturbance in epileptics occurs only in the presence of cerebral lesions, this factor has been inadequately studied. Halstead (1957) found a positive but not significant correlation between bad behavior in epileptic children and a history of brain injury, and Vislie and Henricksen (1958) found a tendency for the severity of personality disturbances in epileptic adults to be related to the extent of brain lesion, as evaluated by neurological symptoms, pneumoencephalography, and EEG findings.

Without autopsy it is, however, often difficult to assess the presence, extent, and site of brain damage. A good history of birth injury in sometimes available, but there is no simple relationship between birth trauma and brain injury. In a series of 406 stillbirths and neonatal births, only 24% which had shown signs of cerebral irritation gave postmortem evidence of intracranial trauma (Bound, Butler, & Spector, 1956). Moreover, numerous cases are described in which serious lesions of the brain have been found at postmortem which were not suspected at birth.

Neurological signs may provide positive evidence of brain damage, but large sections of the brain may be damaged without giving rise to neurological signs. Pneumoencephalographic findings are rarely available and can only be regarded as valid criteria of brain damage when the lesion is gross. EEG abnormalities are not in themselves evidence of brain damage, nor do they necessarily represent accurately the locus and extent of brain damage. The EEG focus may be remote from the lesion, and the lesion may be more or less extensive than the focus. This is particularly true of temporal lobe foci, which because of the low convulsive threshold of the temporo-orbital regions may be secondary to a primary lesion elsewhere. Hence, estimates of the extent and locus of brain damage can with the techniques at present available be at best approximate. However, Meyer, Falconer, and Beck (1954) have found temporal lobe lesions in the brains of all epileptics with temporal lobe EEG foci who have come to autopsy, and according to Gastaut (1953) such lesions are more diffuse than those found in patients with any other focal epilepsy. The question arises, therefore, whether the relationship between personality disturbance and temporal lobe EEG foci is a function of the diffuse nature of the lesions rather than their location. An investigation of the relationship between these factors would seem to involve correlating behavioral studies and EEG studies with autopsy findings.

The contribution of social class differences to personality differences between epileptics has not been studied, and the social class distribution of different forms of epilepsy is not known. It is often held, however, that temporal lobe epilepsy is more frequent in the lower social classes, and there is some evidence that aggressive conduct disorders are more frequent in children of lower social class (O'Neal & Robins, 1958). It would therefore seem worthwhile to determine what contribution, if any, social class makes to the association between temporal lobe epilepsy and aggressive personality disorders. What has to be studied, in fact, is the behavior of individuals with malfunctioning nervous systems, damaged in different areas at different stages of development, controlled to a greater or lesser extent by different drugs, acting on and responding to different kinds of environment. It is clear that the methodological problems involved are very complex and hardly touched by the usual studies that control age and IQ. While most of the variables cannot be experimentally controlled, some of their interrelationships are open to study.

An additional problem which has received inadequate attention is that of sampling. Epileptics attending a neurological or psychiatric institute, especially over a long period are likely to differ in important respects, including psychological characteristics, from epileptics attending a general hospital. Pond's survey of epilepsy in general practice has shown that many epileptics are attended only by general practitioners, and that those seen as outpatients at hospitals tend to be more often psychologically disturbed (Pond & Bidwell, 1960).

A final problem, not specific to this field, lies in the selection of dimensions of personality and the development of reliable and valid instruments with which to measure them. For many years the only psychological tool used was the Rorschach test, the inadequacies of which have been discussed above. So far the main alternative has been the clinical assessment of behavior. The reliability of this method is generally undetermined, and indeed the development of criteria to assess such behavioral manifestations as hyperkinesis or distractibility is one of the more neglected problems in psychology.

To the present writer, however, the most fruitful approach appears to be one which relates personality to more elementary forms of psychological functioning. In epilepsy it is known that we are studying the behavior of a nervous system which is certainly malfunctioning, often more or less diffusely damaged. The intelligence test scores of epileptics with known or suspected brain lesion tend to be below average (Collins, 1951), but there has not yet been any study of the nature of the psychological functions impaired in these patients. It would seem worthwhile to investigate the relationship between the emotional and behavioral disturbances reported and more general defects, e.g., impairment in discriminative functions, or slowness to condition.

Summary

Five basic theories about the personality of epileptics are outlined, and the extent to which they have been affirmed or refuted by clinical and psychological investigations is considered. The findings of studies which have used the Rorschach test are shown to be contradictory, and the inadequacies of this test for research purposes are pointed out. It is argued that progress in this field depends on a recognition and study of the complex environmental and pathophysiological factors involved, and on the development of reliable criteria with which to classify epileptics.

REFERENCES

Alajounaine, T., Nehlil, J., & Boudart, R. Influence de la lobectomie temporelle sur l'état mental des épileptiques psychomoteurs. *Review of Neurology*, 1958, 98, 165-171.

Altable, J. P. Rorschach diagnosis in a group of epileptic children. *Nervous Child*, 1947, 6, 22-23.

Arluck, E. W. A study of some personality characteristics of epileptics. *Archives of Psychology*, New York, 1941, 37, No. 263.

Baughman, E. E. Rorschach scores as a function of examiner difference. *Journal of Projective Techniques*, 1951, 15, 243-249.

Baughman, E. E. A comparative analysis of Rorschach forms with altered stimulus characteristics. *Journal of Projective Techniques*, 1954, 18, 151-164.

Bingley, T. Mental symptoms in temporal lobe epilepsy and temporal gliomas. *Acta Psychiatrica et neurologica Scandinavica, Kbh.*, 1958, 33, Suppl. No. 120.

Bound, J. P., Butler, N. R., & Spector, W. G. Classification and causes of perinatal mortality. Part II. *British Medical Journal*, 1956, 2, 1260-1264.

Bovet, T. Der Rorschachversuch bei verschiedenen Formen von Epilepsie. *Schweiz. Archives of Psychiatry and Neurology*, 1936, 37, 156-157.

Bradley, C.   Behaviour disturbances in epileptic children. *Journal of the American Medical Association*, 1951, **146**, 436-441.

Bridge, E. M.   *Epilepsy and convulsive disorders in children*. New York: McGraw-Hill, 1949.

Campbell, F. A., & Fiddleman, P. B.   The effect of examiner status upon Rorschach performance. *Journal of Projective Techniques*, 1959, **23**, 303-306.

Carp, F. M.   Psychological constriction in several projective tests. *Journal of Consulting Psychology*, 1950, **14**, 268-275.

Churchill, J. A.   The relationship of epilepsy to breech delivery. *EEG in Clinical Neurophysiology*, 1959, **11**, 1-12.

Clarke, E. C., & Knott, J. R.   Paroxysmal wave and spike activity and diagnostic sub-classification. *EEG in Clinical Neurophysiology*, 1955, **7**, 161-164.

Clarke, L. P.   Treatment of the epileptic, based on a study of the fundamental makeup. *Journal of the American Medical Association*, 1918, **70**, 357-362.

Collins, A. L.   Epileptic intelligence. *Journal of Consulting Psychology*, 1951, **15**, 392-309.

Davies-Eysenck, M.   Neurotic tendencies in epilepsy. *Journal of Neurology, Neurosurgery and Psychiatry*, 1950, **13**, 237-240.

Delay, J., Pichot, P., Lemperiere, T., & Perse, J.   Le test de Rorschach dans l'épilepsie. Part III. *Encéphale*, 1955, **44**, 46-56.

Falconer, M. A., Hill, D. N., Meyer, A., & Wilson, J. L.   Clinical, radiological and EEG correlations with pathological changes in temporal lobe epilepsy. In M. Baldwin and P. Bailey (Eds.), *Temporal lobe epilepsy*. Springfield, Ill.: Charles C. Thomas, 1958. Pp. 396-411.

Fielder, M. F., & Stone, I. J.   The Rorschach of selected groups of children in comparison with the published norms. Part II. *Journal of Projective Techniques*, 1956, **20**, 276-279.

Fiske, D. W.   Variability of responses and the stability of scores and interpretations of projective protocols. *Journal of Projective Techniques*, 1959, **23**, 263-267.

Friedman, H. F.   Comparisons of a group of hebephrenic and catatonic schizophrenics with two groups of normal adults. *Journal of Projective Techniques*, 1952, **16**, 352-360.

Gastaut, H.   Étude électro-éncephalographique. *Revista Oto-Noro-Oftalmoloji*, 1950, **22**, 301-320.

Gastaut, H.   So-called psychomotor and temporal epilepsy. *Epilepsia*, 1953, **3**, 59-96.

Gastaut, H., Morin, G., & Lesevre, N.   Étude du comportement des épileptiques psychomoteurs dans l'intervalle de leurs crises. *Annual of Medical Psychology*, 1955, **113**, 1-27.

Gibbs, F. A.   Abnormal electrical activity in the temporal region. In *The brain and human behaviour*. Baltimore: Williams & Wilkins, 1958. Pp. 278-295.

Gibbs, F. A., Davis, H., & Lennox, W. G. The electro-encephalogram in epilepsy and in conditions of impaired consciousness. *Archives of Neurology and Psychiatry*, 1935, **34**, 1133-1148.

Glaser, G. H., & Dixon, M. A. Psychomotor seizures in childhood. *Neurology*, 1958, **6**, 646-655.

Glaser, G. H., & Golub, L. M. The E.E.G. of psychomotor seizures in childhood. *EEG in Clinical Neurophysiology*, 1955, **7**, 329-339.

Grunberg, F., & Pond, D. A. Conduct disorders in epileptic children. *Journal of Neurology, Neurosurgery and Psychiatry*, 1957, **20**, 65-68.

Halstead, H. Abilities and behaviour of epileptic children. *Journal of Mental Science*, 1957, **103**, 28-47.

Harrower-Erikson, M. R. Rorschach studies of patients with focal epilepsy. *Archives of Neurology and Psychiatry*, 1940, **43**, 1081-1107.

Harvald, B. *Heredity in epilepsy.* Copenhagen: Ejnar Munksgaard, 1954.

Hill, D. N. The EEG concept of psychomotor epilepsy. In *Fourth Congrès Neurologique Internationale*, 1949.

Hill, D. N. Epilepsy. In Lord Cohen (Ed.), *The British encyclopaedia of medical practice: Medical progress.* London: Butterworth, 1957. Pp. 86-99.

Holtzman, W. H. Validation studies of the Rorschach test. *Journal of Clinical Psychology*, 1950, **6**, 343-351.

James, I. P. Temporal lobectomy for psychomotor epilepsy. *Journal of Mental Science*, 1960, **106**, 543-557.

Jasper, M., Pertuiset, B., & Flanigin, H. EEG and cortical electrograms in patients with temporal lobe seizures. *Archives of Neurology and Psychiatry*, 1951, **65**, 272-290.

Kaye, I. What are the evidences of social and psychological maladjustment revealed in a study of seventeen children who have idiopathic petit mal epilepsy? *Journal of Child Psychiatry*, 1951, **2**, 115-159.

Keehn, J. D. A reinterpretation of the role played by color in the Rorschach test. *British Journal of Medical Psychology*, 1954, **27**, 89-93.

Kelley, D. M., & Marguiles, H. Rorschach case studies in the convulsive states. *Rorschach Research Exchange*, 1940, 4, 157-190.

Kluver, H., & Bucy, P. C. Preliminary analysis of functions of the temporal lobes in monkeys. *Archives of Neurology and Psychiatry*, 1939, **42**, 979-1000.

Kogan, K. L. The personality reaction pattern of children with epilepsy with special reference to the Rorschach method in epilepsy. *Association for Research in Nervous and Mental Diseases*, 1947, **26**, 616-630.

Lazarus, R. S., & Oldfield, M. Rorschach responses and the influence of color. *Journal of Personality*, 1955, **23**, 356-372.

Lennox, W. Seizure states. In J. McV. Hunt (Ed.), *Personality and the behaviour disorders*, Vol 2. New York: Ronald, 1944, Ch. 31.

Lennox, W., & Gibbs, F. Inheritance of cerebral dysrhythmia and epilepsy. *Archives of Neurology and Psychiatry*, 1940, **44**, 1155-1183.

Liddell, D. W. Observations on epileptic automatism in a mental hospital population. *Journal of Mental Science*, 1953, **99**, 732-748.

Lisansky, E. S. Convulsive disorders and personality. *Journal of Abnormal and Social Psychology*, 1948, **43**, 29-37.

Loveland, N., Smith, B., & Forster, F. M. Mental and emotional changes in epileptic patients on continuous anticonvulsant medication. *Neurology*, 1957, **7**, 856-865.

Lundervold, A., Henriksen, G. F., & Fegersten, L. The spike and ware complex: A clinical correlation. *EEG in Clinical Neurophysiology*, 1959, **11**, 13-22.

Meyer, A., Falconer, M. A., & Beck, E. Pathological findings in temporal lobe epilepsy. *Journal of Neurology, Neurosurgery and Psychiatry*, 1954, **17**, 276-285.

Meyers, R., & Brecher, S. The so-called epileptic personality as investigated by the Kent-Rosanoff test. *Journal of Abnormal and Social Psychology*, 1941, **36**, 413-422.

Minkowska, F. L'épilepsie essentielle, sa psychopathologie et le test de Rorschach. *Annual of Medical Psychology*, 1946, **104**, 321-355.

Mulder, D. W., & Daly, D. Psychiatric symptoms associated with lesions of the temporal lobs. *Journal of the American Medical Association*, 1952, **150**, 173-176.

Neff, W. S., & Glaser, N. M. Normative data on the Rorschach. *Journal of Psychology*, 1954, **37**, 95-104.

Neff, W. S., & Lidz, T. Rorschach patterns of normal subjects of graded intelligence. *Journal of Projective Techniques*, 1951, **15**, 45-57.

Notkin, J. Is there an epileptic personality makeup? *Archives of Neurology and Psychiatry*, 1928, **20**, 799-803.

Nuffield, E. J. A. Neurophysiology and behaviour disorders in epileptic children. *Journal of Mental Science*, 1961, **107**, 438-457.

O'Neal, P., & Robins, L. N. The relation of childhood behavior problems to adult psychiatric status. *American Journal of Psychiatry*, 1958, **114**, 961-969.

Paillas, J. E. Aspects cliniques de l'épilepsie temporale. In M. Baldwin and P. Bailey (Eds.), *Temporal lobe epilepsy*. Springfield, Ill.: Charles C. Thomas, 1958. Pp. 411-440.

Paillas, J., & Subirana, A. Séméiologie neuropsychique: Le lobe temporal. *Revista Oto-Noro-Oftalmoloji*, 1950, **20**, 123-218.

Peterman, M. G. Behavior in epileptic children. *Journal of Pediatrics*, 1953, **42**, 758-769.

Piotrowski, Z. A. The personality of the epileptic. In P. H. Hoch and R. P. Knight (Eds.), *Epilepsy*. New York: Grune & Stratton, 1947. Pp. 89-109.

Pond, D. A. Psychiatric aspects of epilepsy in children. *Journal of Mental Science*, 1952, **98**, 404-410.

Pond, D. A. Psychiatric aspects of epileptic and brain-damaged children. *British Medical Journal*, 1961, **2**, 1377-1382.

Pond, D. A., & Bidwell, B. M. A survey of epilepsy in fourteen general practices: II. Social and psychological aspects. *Epilepsia*, 1960, **1**, 285-299.

Pruyser, P. W. Psychological testing in epilepsy: II. Personality. *Epilepsia*, 1953, **2**, 23-35.

Reiman, G. R. The effectiveness of Rorschach elements in the discrimination between neurotic and ambulatory schizophrenic subjects. *Journal of Consulting Psychology*, 1953, **17**, 25-31.

Revitch, E. Psychiatric aspects of epilepsy. *Journal of the Medical Society of New Jersey*, 1955, **52**, 634-640.

Richards, T. W. The personality of the convulsive patient in military service. *Psychological Monographs*, 1952, **66** (14, Whole No. 346).

Robertiello, M. Psychomotor epilepsy in children. *Diseases of the Nervous System*, 1953, **14**, 337-339.

Roger, A., & Dongier, M. Correlations électrocliniques chez 50 épileptiques internes. *Review of Neurology*, 1950, **83**, 593-596.

Rorschach, H. *Psychodiagnostics*. (3rd ed.) Bern: Huber, 1942.

Ross, W. D. The Rorschach method and clinical diagnosis. *Journal of Mental Science*, 1941, **87**, 331-348.

Shaw, M. C., & Cruikshank, W. M. The Rorschach performance of epileptic children. *Journal of Consulting Psychology*, 1957, **21**, 422-424.

Silverman, D. Clinical correlates of the spike-wave complex. *EEG of Clinical Neurophysiology*, 1954, **6**, 663-669.

Stauder, K. H. *Konstitution und Wesensänderung der Epileptiker*. Leipzig: Thieme, 1938.

Sullivan, E. B., & Gahagan, L. On the intelligence of epileptic children. *Genetic Psychology Monographs*, 1935, **17**, 309.

Symonds, C. Classification of the epilepsies with particular refernce to psychomotor seizures. *Archives of Neurology and Psychiatry*, 1954, **72**, 631-637.

Vislie, H., & Henriksen, G. F. Psychic disturbances in epileptics. In A. M. Lorentz de Haas (Ed.), *Lectures on epilepsy*. Elsevier: Van Nostrand, 1958.

Wedemeyer, B. Rorschach statistics on a group of 136 normal men. *Journal of Psychology*, 1954, **37**, 51-58.

Williams, D. New orientations in epilepsy. *British Medical Journal*, 1950, **1**, 685-692.

Wittenborn, J. R., & Holzberg, J. D. The Rorschach and descriptive diagnosis. *Journal of Consulting Psychology*, 1951, **15**, 460-463.

Yates, A. J. The validity of some psychological tests of brain damage. *Psychological Bulletin*, 1954, **51**, 359-379.

Zehrer, F. A. Investigation of Rorschach factors in children who have convulsive disorders and in those who present problems of adjustment. *American Journal of Orthopsychiatry*, 1951, **21**, 292-300.

Zimmerman, F. T., Burgemeister, B. B., & Putnam, T. J. The intellectual and emotional makeup of the epileptic. *Archives of Neurology and Psychiatry*, 1951, **65**, 545-556.

7

Maternal Deprivation: Toward an Empirical and Conceptual Reevaluation

INTRODUCTION

Research on the effects of maternal deprivation is complicated by a number of problems. Although in contrast to other variables maternal deprivation would seem to be a relatively clear cut variable, this is not the case. In the following article by Leon Yarrow the "major objective is to clarify the concept of maternal deprivation." As the reader will find, this concept actually has a number of different components. Once the specific components of maternal deprivation are identified and refined, Yarrow attempts to relate them to the effects that have been attributed to maternal deprivation in general. This increase in specificity is an important step forward in our understanding of the *concept* of maternal deprivation as well as the *effects* of deprivation.

It might be expected that the majority of the studies on maternal deprivation would be follow-up studies. That is, since in most cases deprivation is relatively easily and objectively observable (institutionalization, e.g.), the best design would seem to be to identify a deprived group and a nondeprived (control) group and follow the subjects to determine the effects of the deprivation. Unfortunately, this has not often been done. The majority of the studies involve the *retrospective* comparison of the maternal care given to a group of individuals who have been identified as having a problem (usually a clinic population) and a control group. That is, they begin with the effect and check to see whether in fact the "cause" in which they are interested was related to the effect. With the proper controls this approach will answer some questions, but unfortunately it will not give us an indication of how many children subjected to maternal deprivation were *not* affected by it. This is an important question. As the reader will learn, some studies have indicated that the incidence of the negative effects of maternal deprivation may be lower than what might be expected. A further methodological problem that should be noted is that in most cases one does not know if a selective factor was operating in the determination of who was subjected to maternal deprivation. For example, a factor that led to institutionalization may have played a large role in the pathology. If this were true, it would be incorrect to attribute the resulting pathology to the deprivation per se. One way of avoiding criticism on this count is to eliminate the deprivation, once the pathology has been identified in the deprived child, and to determine the effect that this has on the pathology. Regrettably, this type of study is very rare.

Refinement of our understanding of the concept of maternal deprivation as it relates to resulting pathology must follow a number of avenues. First, one must separate the different *types of deprivation,* that is, loss of mothering, multiple mothering, and so on. Then one must be aware of the various *aspects of deprivation* that might occur within any type of deprivation. These include such things as differences in social stimulation, physical stimulation, and intellectual stimulation. In addition to these factors, however, one must account for the *context in which deprivation takes place* or the way in which it takes place. Variables in this category include the type of mothering that preceded the deprivation, the age at which deprivation occurred, the length of deprivation, and others. Parametric laboratory studies cannot easily be carried out on these variables because of the ethical problems in the manipulations of maternal deprivation in humans. Instead, research must await the natural occurrence of deprivation in its various types, aspects, and contexts. Since the problems and variables cannot be systematically studied, when reading the research the reader should try to piece together the results within the framework of the questions and variables that have been identified. All of the data for this task are not yet available, but the following review is an important step in formulating the problem and answering *some* of the questions.

MATERNAL DEPRIVATION:
TOWARD AN EMPIRICAL AND CONCEPTUAL
REEVALUATION

LEON J. YARROW

The significance of early infantile experience for later development has been reiterated so frequently and so persistently that
the general validity of this assertion is now almost unchallenged.
An extensive literature on deviating patterns of maternal care,
loosely labeled "maternal deprivation," adds up with an impressive
consistency in its *general* conclusions: deviating conditions of maternal care in early life tend to be associated with later disturbances in intellectual and personal-social functioning. It has been
difficult to build on this general premise in formulating more precise research hypotheses relating specific variables of early maternal care to later developmental characteristics. If one attempts
to order the empirical data from the many studies and the varied
contexts, it becomes apparent that the concept of maternal deprivation is a rather muddied one. Maternal deprivation has been
used as a broad descriptive term as well as an overall explanatory
concept. As a descriptive term it encompasses a variety of conditions of infant care which are phenotypically as well as dynamically very different. In this review of the research and theoretical
literature, our major objective is to clarify the concept of maternal
deprivation by identifying the basic variables and concepts which
have been indiscriminately combined under this term.

Previous reviews have dealt primarily with the findings
(Bowlby, 1951; Glaser & Eisenberg, 1956), or with the methodology of a few studies (Pinneau, 1950, 1955). The chief effort of
this review will be directed towards sorting out on an empirical

SOURCE. Reprinted with permission of the American Psychological Association
and the author from the *Psychological Bulletin*, 1961, 58, 459-490. This paper
was prepared in conjunction with a research project on The Effects of a
Change in Mother-Figure during Infancy on Personality Development, conducted under Research Grant 3M-9077 from the National Institute of Mental
Health, United States Public Health Service.

level the varied antecedent conditions of maternal care described in the literature, and relating these empirical conditions to some major theoretical concepts. Through this kind of analysis, it is hoped to facilitate the formulation of more explicit hypotheses on the relationship between specific aspects of early life experiences and later development.

Empirical Analysis of the Research on "Maternal Deprivation"

In the literature on maternal deprivation, four different kinds of deviations from a hypothetical mode of maternal care have been included: institutionalization; separation from a mother or mother-substitute; multiple mothering, in which there is no one continuous person performing the major mothering functions; distortions in the quality of mothering, e.g., rejection, overprotection, ambivalence. In very few studies do we find these "pure conditions." Most often several conditions occur concomitantly or sequentially in complex interaction, e.g., separation is followed by institutionalization, multiple mothering occurs in an institutional setting.

Tables 1 to 4 present the chief research studies organized in terms of the major conditions of early care: institutionalization, separation, multiple mothering. Studies on distortions in the mother-child relationship, e.g., rejection, overprotection, ambivalence, on which there are many clinical reports, but few research reports, have not been included. The studies presented in the tables are grouped according to their general research designs: retrospective, direct, or contemporaneous. The tables point out the major characteristics of the samples: the population from which the subjects were chosen, the ages at the time of study, and the ages at the time of the experience. Also presented are the major techniques used in data collection or the kinds of data obtained. For the retrospective studies, the presence or absence of data on earlier conditions of maternal care is noted. Finally, overlapping or contaminating conditions are noted where they have been reported.

It is clear from the tables that the major share of studies has been on institutional care. There are many fewer published reports on separation and multiple mothering. In the following section, in considering each of these types of studies, our focus will be on the analysis of the environmental conditions and the impact of these events and conditions on development. Throughout we will attempt to integrate the empirical data in terms of some basic psychological concepts, and to point up some hypotheses amenable to research.

Institutionalization

Most of the generalizations about the effects of "maternal deprivation" are based on retrospective research in which institutionalization has been a major background condition. The general research designs of the many retrospective studies reported between 1937 and 1955 are basically similar and tend to suffer from similar methodological deficiencies. In all but a few studies there is a sampling bias due to the method of selection of cases; subjects are chosen from clinic populations of cases under treatment for emotional or personality disturbances. (In delving back into the history of these patients, it was discovered that many had spent some part of their earlier life in an institutional setting.) Perhaps the most significant deficiency in many of these studies is the lack of specific data on early conditions of maternal care. The characteristics of the institutional environment are unknown or not described, and no data, or, at the best, very meager data are given about the circumstances associated with institutionalization. Such significant information as age at time of placement, duration of institutional care, traumatic conditions preceding or concomitant with institutional placement is rarely given. Frequently information about experiences following institutional care is scant and of uncertain validity. The data on the personality characteristics of the subjects also vary greatly in depth and adequacy; much data are derived from psychiatric diagnoses based on an unspecified number of interviews or consist of case history material from unspecified sources; in a few instances, projective or other kinds of personality tests have been used.

The Institutional Environment

In much of the research on institutions the environment has been dealt with so grossly that "institutionalization" has often referred to a setting as broad in many respects as "the home." Only a few contemporaneous studies of infants and young children give sufficiently detailed descriptions of the institutional setting to enable one to isolate discrete variables. Only one study, comparing the institutional and home environments of a small group of infants, makes a serious attempt to give an objective description of an institution (Rheingold, 1960).

The institutional environments in the direct studies can be or-

TABLE 1

RESEARCH ON INSTITUTIONALIZATION: DIRECT STUDIES OF CHILDREN IN INSTITUTIONS

Investigator	Subjects	Age at time of study	Age when institutionalized	Techniques or type of data	Description of environment
Brodbeck & Irwin (1946)	Institutional: 94 Controls: 217	Birth to 6 months	Birth to 6 months	Analysis of speech sounds	General—social, emotional
Brown (1937)	Institutional: 200 Controls: 200 from "poor" home environments	9–14 years	Broad range: birth to adolescence	Brown Personality Inventory	No data
Dennis & Najarian (1957)	Institutional: 49 infants; 30 preschool age Controls: 41	2–12 months 4½–6 years	Birth	Infant tests Goodenough Draw-A-Man Test	Detailed—physical, social, learning conditions
DuPan & Roth (1955)	Institutional: 14	4–30 months	Birth to 3 months	Gesell test	Detailed—physical, social, learning conditions
Fischer (1952)	Institutional: 62	6–7 months	Birth to 3 months	Cattell test Observation	Detailed—physical, social
Flint (1957)	Institutional: 16	2–20 months	Birth to 6 months	Infant security scale Observation	Detailed—physical, social, learning conditions
Freud & Burlingham (1944)	Institutional: approximately 90	Birth to 2 years Longitudinal	Early infancy—no specific data	Clinical observation	General—physical, social

TABLE 1 (*Continued*)

Investigator	Subjects	Age at time of study	Age when institutionalized	Techniques or type of data	Description of environment
Gesell & Amatruda (1941)	Institutional: unspecified number	Birth to 2 years	No data	Gesell test	No data
Goldfarb (1945a)	Institutional: 15 Controls: 15	First test mean: 34 months Follow-up mean: 43 months	Early infancy: mean—4½ months	Intelligence tests Language test Test of motor coordination Social maturity scale Rorschach Behavior ratings	General—physical, social
Levy (1947)	Institutional: 101 Foster home controls: 129	122 under 6 months, 34: 6 to 12 months, 74 over 12 months	Early infancy	Gesell test Stanford-Binet and other preschool intelligence tests Vineland Social Maturity Scale	Detailed—physical, social
Rheingold (1956)	Institutional: 16 8 controls, 8 experimental given special mothering	6–8 months	Early infancy	Cattell test Social responsiveness test	Detailed—physical, social, emotional

TABLE 1 (*Continued*)

Investigator	Subjects	Age at time of study	Age when institutionalized	Techniques or type of data	Description of environment
Skeels, Updegraff, Wellman & Williams (1938) Wellman & Pegram (1944)	Institutional: varying numbers of cases, main group 53 controls; 35 experimental, given preschool experience	1½ to 5½ years	Birth to 2 years	Intelligence test Language test Motor tests General information test Vineland Social Maturity Scale Behavior observations	Detailed—physical, social, emotional
Skeels & Dye (1938) Skeels (1942)	Institutional: 25 12 controls; 13 experimental given special stimulation	First test: controls—12 to 22 months experimental— 7 to 36 months Last test: controls—5 to 9 years experimental— 4½ to 9½ years	Birth to 2 years	Intelligence tests 4 follow-up tests	Detailed—physical, social, emotional

TABLE 1 (*Continued*)

Investigator	Subjects	Age at time of study	Age when institutionalized	Techniques or type of data	Description of environment
Spitz (1946)	61 infants in foundling home; 69 infants with own mothers in prison; 34 infants in own homes	Early infancy to 2½ years	Birth	Hetzer-Wolf Infant Test Clinical observation	Detailed—physical, social
Spitz & Wolf (1949)	170 infants with own mothers in prison; 61 infants in foundling home; 17 infants in own homes	Birth to 15 months	Birth	Observation Interview Hetzer-Wolf Infant Test Rorschach (mothers)	General—physical, social; detailed personality of mothers

169

TABLE 2

RESEARCH ON INSTITUTIONALIZATION: RETROSPECTIVE STUDIES

Investigator	Subjects	Age at time of study	Age when institutionalized	Duration of institutionalization	Techniques or type of data	Data on early experiences	Contaminating conditions
Bender (1947)	5000 clinic cases	Preadolescence	Birth to middle childhood	Range; not specified	Case history Psychiatric diagnosis	General retrospective	Repeated separations Rejection
Bender & Yarnell (1941)	250 clinic cases	1–6 years	Birth to 6 years	Range; not specified	Intelligence tests Psychiatric diagnosis Case history	General retrospective	
Beres & Obers (1950)	37 clinic cases with institutional background	Adolescence and adulthood	Birth to 12 months	Varying periods up to 4 years Average: 3 years	Case history Psychiatric diagnosis Intelligence tests	Detailed case history	Separation and rejection
Bodman et al. (1950)	51 cases with institutional background 52 controls	Early adolescence	16 cases under 2 years Average: 4.4 years	Range from 3 to 15 years Average: 9.6 years	Vineland Social Maturity Scale Case history	General data on variety of institutions	High incidence of mentally defective or disturbed parents Several changes in institutions

TABLE 2 (*Continued*)

Investigator	Subjects	Age at time of study	Age when institutionalized	Duration of institutionalization	Techniques or type of data	Data on early experiences	Contaminating conditions
Goldfarb (1943b)	20 children with institutional background 20 foster home controls	6–10 years Follow-up	1 to 24 months	3 years	Baruch Preschool Checklist Newell Problem Checklist	General retrospective data	Repeated separations from foster mothers
Goldfarb (1945b)	15 children with institutional background 15 foster home controls	Mean: 12 years	Early infancy	2½ to 3 years	Intelligence tests Concept formation tests—Weigl, Goldstein-Scheerer Clinical assessment of personal-social functioning	Some retrospective data	Repeated separations from foster mothers
Goldfarb (1944)	40 children with institutional background 40 foster home controls	Mean: 7½ years Follow-up	Early infancy	Average: 34 months	Analysis of problems and reasons for replacement	Some retrospective data	Repeated separations from foster mothers Maternal rejection

TABLE 2 (*Continued*)

Investigator	Subjects	Age at time of study	Age when institutionalized	Duration of institutionalization	Techniques or type of data	Data on early experiences	Contaminating conditions
Goldfarb (1947)	15 well-adjusted and 15 poorly adjusted children with institutional background	Mean: 14½ years	Poorly adjusted mean: 5.8 months / Well-adjusted mean: 10.9 months	Poorly adjusted: 34 months / Well-adjusted: 25 months	Caseworker's ratings on adjustment	Detailed retrospective data	Repeated separations
Goldfarb (1949)	15 institutional / 15 schizophrenic / 15 foster home	Mean: 12 years	Early infancy mean: 4½ months	Group average: 39 months	Rorschach test / Intelligence test	No data	Not reported
Haggerty (1959)	100 social agency cases with institutional background	Mean age: 12.7 years	"First few years of life"	Average: 3½ years	Analysis of language samples	No data	Separation
Lowrey (1940)	28 psychiatric clinic cases with institutional background	Range from 3 to 6 years	Range from 2 weeks to 34 months	Range from 6 to 42 months	Case history / Intelligence tests	Variable retrospective history	Repeated separations

dered in terms of several theoretically meaningful categories which can be further reduced to specific research variables.

The physical environment—quality and amount of sensory stimulation. The importance of sensory stimulation for development has recently been emphasized by a number of animal experiments. In most of the research, institutional settings are characterized in the extreme as lacking in sensory stimulation; they are described as colorless and drab with little visual or auditory stimulation and with few objects for the child to manipulate.

The emotional environment—affective stimulation. For research, the emotional environment can be defined in a restricted sense in terms of formal, measurable aspects of affective stimulation, i.e., intensity and variability. Institutions tend to be characterized by an emotional blandness and a lack of variation in feeling tone with the result that the infant is not exposed to strongly negative or strongly positive affective stimulation.

The social environment—social stimulation. The amount of mothering, the quality and consistency of mothering, and the amount and quality of general social stimulation are major aspects of the animate environment in terms of which institutional care is defined. Most of the studies describe a low adult-child ratio, averaging about one adult to 10 infants in institutional settings. There are usually many different caretakers, with the result that the infant has little opportunity to relate to one person as a consistent source of gratification. Compared with an infant in his own home, the research indicates that in institutions there is much less mothering contact, less total social stimulation, and less stability in mother-figures.

Learning conditions. Learning conditions which deviate from those in a "normal" home environment are reported characteristic of institutions: deviations in opportunities for acquiring or practicing new skills, deviations in motivational conditions, and in scheduling. Often infants are confined to the crib or playpen during most of the day, with very limited opportunity to practice emerging motor skills or to make perceptual discriminations. There tends to be little recognition by adults for positive achievements, with no or inconsistent reinforcement for positive learnings or socially desirable responses. Daily routines are sometimes characterized by an element of unpredictability, but more often routines are rigidly scheduled with little variation from day to day, and with little adaptation to individual differences.

It is clear that institutionalization is not a simple variable, and

TABLE 3
RESEARCH ON MATERNAL SEPARATION

Investigator	Subjects	Age at time of study	Age at time of experience	Techniques or type of data	Data on early experiences	Contaminating conditions
Ainsworth & Boston (1952)	One case	Observation: 3 years Follow-up tests: 5 to 6½ years	13 months	Rorschach CAT Stanford-Binet Weigl-Goldstein Sorting Test Goldstein-Scheerer Cube Test	Retrospective report	Hospitalization for tuberculosis
Berg & Cohen (1959)	40 schizophrenic women in mental hospital 40 neurotic women	20–40 years	Birth to adulthood	Case history	Limited retrospective data	Rejection
Bowlby (1944)	44 juvenile thieves	5.7 to 17 years	Birth to adolescence	Case history Psychiatric diagnosis	Variable retrospective data	Institutionalization Rejection
Bowlby (1953b)	49 children in residential nurseries or hospitals	12–48 months	12–24 months	Clinical observation	Direct observation	Institutionalization Rejection Hospitalization for illness
Bowlby, Ainsworth, Boston, & Rosenbluth (1956)	60 children with previous sanitarium experience 57 controls	6–14 years	Range: Birth to 4 years	Intelligence test Clinical evaluation by teacher, psychologist, psychiatrist, social worker	General retrospective data	Rejection Hospitalization for tuberculosis

174

TABLE 3 *(Continued)*

Investigator	Subjects	Age at time of study	Age at time of experience	Techniques or type of data	Data on early experiences	Contaminating conditions
Edelston (1943)	42 children hospitalized for illness	2½–15 years	Range from early infancy	Clinical observation	Limited retrospective data	Illness Rejection
Heinicke (1956)	Children in residential and day nurseries	15–31 months	12–30 months	Standardized observation and doll play	Direct observation	None reported
Lewis (1954)	500 children in reception center	Under 5 to over 15 years	Birth to adolescence	Clinical assessment	Variable retrospective data	Institutionalization Rejection
Robertson & Bowlby (1952)	Unspecified number of children in hospitals	18–24 months	18–24 months	Clinical observation	Direct observation	Hospitalization
Roundinesco, David, & Nicolas (1952)	20 children placed in institution	12–17 months	12–17 months	Clinical observation	Direct observation	Institutionalization
Schaffer (1958)	76 infants in hospital for illness	3–51 weeks	3–51 weeks	Cattell Infant Test Standardized observation Home follow-up	Direct observation	Illness Hospitalization
Spitz & Wolf (1946)	123 children in a nursery	14 days to 18 months	5–7 months	Clinical observation	Direct observation	None reported

TABLE 4
RESEARCH ON MULTIPLE MOTHERING

Investigators	Subjects	Techniques	Age at time of experience	Age at study	Data on early experiences
Rabin (1957)	38 children from kibbutz and 34 controls from neighboring villages	Rorschach	Birth to time of study	9–11 years	General description of environment
Rabin (1958a)	24 infants and 40 children in kibbutz	Rorschach	Birth to time of study	9–17 months	General description of environment
	20 control infants and 40 control children	Vineland Social Maturity Goodenough Draw-A-Man Griffiths Infant Scale		9–11 years	

cannot be used as a simple research variable or explanatory concept. Even in the limited sample of institutions found in the direct studies, the environments are not identical. Qualitative as well as quantitative variations are apparent among institutions in the amount of sensory stimulation, in the consistency of mothering, in the consistency of rewards, etc.

Intellectual, Personality, and Social Characteristics Associated with Institutionalization

Despite the methodological inadequacies and the great range of antecedent conditions in the research, there is a core of consistency in the findings on the characteristics of children, adolescents, and adults with institutional backgrounds. The major characteristics associated with institutional care are: general intellectual retardation, retardation in language functions, and social and "personality" disturbances, chiefly disturbances centering around the capacity to establish and maintain close personal relationships. Within the overall consistency, however, there is significant variation. Not all children with institutional experience give evidence of intellectual or personality damage, and there is a range in the extent of injury. These variations can sometimes be related to the characteristics of the environment; sometimes significant modifying or interacting variables can be identified.

Intellectual defects. General intellectual retardation is commonly found in older children and adolescents with a history of institutionalization (Bender, 1947; Goldfarb, 1945a; Levy, 1947; Lowrey, 1940) as well as in infants and young children growing up in institutional environments (Dennis & Najarian, 1957; Fischer, 1952, 1953; Gesell & Amatruda, 1941; Skeels, Updegraff, Wellman, & Williams, 1938; Spitz, 1945, 1946). The data do not, however, permit the simple conclusion that gross intellectual deficiency is a necessary consequence of institutional experience. The incidence and degree of retardation vary considerably from one study to another. In only *some* of the studies do *some* children show severe retardation (Dennis & Najarian, 1957; Gesell & Amatruda, 1941; Goldfarb, 1945a, 1945b; Skeels et al., 1938; Spitz, 1945, 1946). In others there is only relative retardation; they are functioning on a dull-normal level (DuPan & Roth, 1955; Fischer, 1952, 1953; Freud & Burlingham, 1944; Klackenburg, 1956; Rheingold, 1956). Several factors seem to be related to the varied outcomes in intellectual functioning:

1. The amount of individualized stimulation provided in these

environments seems to be significantly related to the degree of retardation. In the institutions in which attempts were made to provide individualized stimulation, and to foster a relationship between a single caretaker and infant, severe retardation was not found (DuPan & Roth, 1955; Fischer, 1952, 1953; Freud & Burlingham, 1944; Klackenburg, 1956; Rheingold, 1956).

2. The age of the child at the time of institutionalization varies greatly among the studies; several investigators have concluded that the younger the child at the time of institutionalization, the more likely is subsequent retardation (Bender, 1945, 1947; Beres & Obers, 1950; Goldfarb, 1947). The evidence is meager, consisting of data from two studies. In Goldfarb's research in which a large percentage of cases showed evidence of retardation, the mean age of admission to the institution was 4.5 months, with only three cases over 1 year of age. Of a group of 37 adolescents and young adults studied by Beres and Obers (1950) only four were mentally retarded; all four had entered the institution under 6 months.

3. Constitutional factors. There are no direct data, but the findings that, in seemingly identical environments, some children show retardation and others do not, have been interpreted as evidence of constitutional differences in vulnerability to institutional deprivation.

4. The duration of institutionalization. The data point to a cumulative impact of the institutional environment on intellectual functioning. In most studies, with continued institutional residence, infants show a progressive drop in developmental test quotients (Dennis & Najarian, 1957; Fischer, 1952, 1953; Freud & Burlingham, 1944, no test data; Skeels, 1942; Skeels & Dye, 1939; Spitz, 1945, 1946). A few studies (DuPan & Roth, 1955; Rheingold, 1956; Rheingold & Bayley, 1959) report no significant cumulative loss in intellectual functioning. Although Dennis and Najarian (1957) found a decrease in Cattell test scores in institutionalized infants between 3 and 12 months they discovered no significant retardation on the Goodenough Draw-A-Man Test among a group of older children, 4.5 to 6 years of age, who had been in the same institution for several years. They raise the interesting question as to whether an environment which fails to offer adequate intellectual stimulation to infants is necessarily retarding for preschool children.

The direct association between intellectual retardation and environmental impoverishment is dramatically emphasized by Skeels and Dye's study (1939). Retarded institutional children made significant gains in intellectual functions after special environmental stimulation. In another study (Skeels et al., 1938), the intellectual stimulation provided by an experimental nursery school in an institution was found effective in preventing deterioration in intellectual functioning. Whereas a control group showed cumulative losses in IQ scores, children given nursery school experience maintained their IQ level.

Two other studies suggest that intellectual retardation need not be attributed to some elusive, unknown aspect of the institutional environment, but can be directly related to lack of adequate stimulation. Rheingold (1943) studying infants in boarding homes found that children who shared the home with several other babies had significantly lower developmental test scores than infants who were "only children" in the boarding homes. Coleman and Provence (1957) observed retardation similar to the institutional pattern in children living in very unstimulating home environments.

Analysis of the separate aspects of intellectual functioning indicates that all functions are not equally affected by institutional living. Consistent evidence of retardation is found in language, in time and space concepts, and in capacity for abstract conceptualization.

Language is one function in which severe retardation has been found repeatedly in institutionalized infants and young children (Brodbeck & Irwin, 1946; DuPan & Roth, 1955; Fischer, 1952, 1953; Freud & Burlingham, 1944; Gesell & Amatruda, 1941; Skeels et al., 1938; Rheingold & Bayley, 1959) as well as in older children and adults with an institutional history (Bender, 1945, 1947; Goldfarb, 1945a; Haggerty, 1959; Lowery, 1940). There is disagreement in the literature on institutionalization only in the age at which language functions first seem to be affected. Brodbeck and Irwin (1946) found evidence of retardation in institutionalized infants in the first few months of life, whereas Freud and Burlingham (1944) report no indications of language retardation before 12 months. Brodbeck and Irwin's data were based on careful phonetic analysis of speech sounds, whereas Freud and Burlingham had no systematic language data on infants.

With regard to the etiology of language retardation, Fischer (1952, 1953) notes that in many institutions there is little reinforcement by adults of the infant's vocalizations, and consequently reduced opportunity for the child to acquire the signal functions and expressive functions of language. Recent data on the conditioning of vocalizations in infants (Rheingold, Gewirtz, & Ross,

1959) give evidence of the role of reinforcement in young infant's vocalizations. Early studies of language development (Day, 1932; Van Alstyne, 1929) pointed to a direct relationship between amount of environmental stimulation (e.g., number of hours the child was read to, "extensions of the environment") and vocabulary and sentence length in preschool children. On the simplest level, language retardation, like general intellectual retardation, can be related to inadequate language stimulation. Lack of motivation for imitative behavior may interact with inadequate reinforcement of speech sounds in determining language retardation.

Serious *defects in time and spatial concepts* in older children have been reported in clinical descriptions by Goldfarb (1945a, 1949) and Bender (1945, 1947). Poor memory for past events is linked by Bender with such character defects as inability to benefit from past mistakes, lack of future goals, and weak motivation to control behavior for future gains. Goldfarb relates social maladjustment to difficulties in time and spatial concepts. As a result of these conceptual difficulties, disregard of school and family rules occurs.

Disturbances in abstract thinking were also found by Bender (1947) and Goldfarb (1943b) in school aged children and in adolescents with an institutional background. Goldfarb (1945b) describes as characteristic of these children "an unusually defective level of conceptualization . . . manifested in difficulty in organizing a variety of stimuli meaningfully and in abstracting relationships" (p. 251). On the Rorschach test, adolescents with an institutional background showed "an unusual adherence to a concrete attitude and inadequate conceptualization" (1943a, p. 222).

Motor functions. Motor development seems to be less significantly affected than any other aspect of development, although there are markedly discrepant reports. DuPan and Roth (1955) and Fischer (1953) conclude that there is no significant retardation in motor development during the first year among institutionalized children, Freud and Burlingham (1944) report accelerated development during the early part of the second year, while Spitz (1946) notes marked retardation in motor functions during the first and second years. Differing opportunities for the exercise of developing motor functions in different institutional settings may be involved (Skeels et al., 1938).

Both extremes in *activity level* are found in institutionalized infants. Hyperactivity is sometimes noted (Fischer, 1952) but more common is a lowered activity level, associated with the general passivity noted as part of the pattern of intellectual retardation. There are only vague indications in the data of some factors which may account for these different findings: constitutional differences among infants, the age or developmental level at the time of institutionalization, and the length of institutionalization. For instance, in the initial stages of institutionalization, hyperactivity is often found, with lowered activity level more common after prolonged institutional residence.

Motor disturbances in the form of bizarre stereotyped motor patterns suggestive of neurological damage have been reported by Spitz (1946) in infants after a long period of institutional residence; similar but less extreme motor disturbances were noted by Fischer (1952, 1953). In older children, Bender (1947) and Goldfarb (1943a, 1945b, 1947) found hyperkinetic behavior, a pattern considered part of a syndrome of impulsivity, with psychogenic rather than neurogenic bases.

The findings on deviant motor patterns and the data on defects in conceptual thinking suggest the possibility of central nervous system damage as a result of institutionalization. The evidence is not very strong, however, nor are there clear bases in these data for hypothesizing the conditions under which irreversible neurological damage might occur.

Social and personality disturbances. Although the institutional syndrome has most frequently been described in terms of social and personality disturbances, in many respects the data are less clear than are the findings on intellectual development. Personality data are based primarily on clinical impressions, and the characteristics described are usually at the extreme end of the scale, reflecting exaggerated pathology or a complete lack of capacity, rather than a relative deficiency.

Interpersonal relationships. The major deviations reported in the literature are in the area of interpersonal relationship. Two overtly dissimilar, but dynamically related, types of interpersonal disturbance have been described: social apathy manifested by indifference to social attachments, and "affect hunger" characterized by incessant and insatiable seeking of affection. Several retrospective studies report a syndrome in older children and adolescents described as an inability to establish close, warm personal relationships (Bender, 1947; Bender & Yarnell, 1941, Goldfarb, 1943a, 1945b, 1949; Lowrey, 1940), a personality pattern labeled the "affectionless character" by Bowlby (1944), and one which Bender (1947) identifies as a psychopathic behavior disorder.

In the contemporaneous studies of infants in institutions, social apathy is described in terms of several specific response patterns:

1. Inadequate social, responsiveness, as evidenced by a complete lack of social initiative, by withdrawn or apathetic response to social approaches (Bakwin, 1949; Fischer, 1952, 1953; Freud & Burlingham, 1944), or in depressed scores on the social sector of developmental tests (DuPan & Roth, 1955; Fischer, 1952, 1953)

2. An indifference to social attachments, manifested by lack of any significant attachments or meaningful relationships with caretakers in the institution (Freud & Burlingham, 1944; Rheingold, 1956)

3. Inadequate social discrimination as evidenced by failure to give differentiated responses to strangers and familiar caretakers (Freud & Burlingham, 1944)

4. A lack of normal social sensitivity, indicated by inability to respond discriminatively to different kinds of emotional expression (Freud & Burlingham, 1944)

The specificity of the relationship between social stimulation and social responsiveness in infancy is pointed up by Rheingold's data (1956). Infants in an institution who were given intensive social stimulation by one mother-figure, from the sixth to the eighth month of life, showed significantly greater social responsiveness than control subjects cared for by the more usual institutional routine. General developmental progress was not affected, however, by this special type of stimulation. In a follow-up of these children in adoptive homes at 19 months of age, Rheingold and Bayley (1959) found no evidence of any lasting impact of this special experience.

The syndrome of "affect hunger" characterized by indiscriminate and insatiable demands for attention and affection is less common than social apathy. It is reported in several retrospective studies (Bender, 1945, 1947; Goldfarb, 1945b; Lowrey, 1940), but in only one contemporaneous study (Freud & Burlingham, 1944), in which children in an institution are described as "exacting, demanding, apparently passionate, but always disappointed in new attachments" (p. 58). A similar, but less intense pattern of indiscriminate sociability among 6–8 month old infants was observed by Rheingold (1956). Freud and Burlingham also noted in infants an associated pattern of exhibitionism, involving indiscriminate display of themselves before strangers.

Behavioral deviations considered symptomatic of disturbances in ego and superego development have been reported in older children (Bender, 1945, 1947; Beres & Obers, 1950; Goldfarb, 1943a, 1949; Lowrey, 1940). Frequently noted is a pattern of diffuse and impulsive behavior suggesting a lack of normal inhibitory controls. In these children overt antisocial and aggressive behavior is often found. Bender and Goldfarb both note a lack of normal anxiety or guilt about aggression, a low frustration tolerance, a lack of goal-directedness, and low achievement motivation. Goldfarb (1943a) summarizes the personality pattern as impoverished, meager, and undifferentiated, deficient in inhibition and control. Even as late as adolescence, the institution children show the simple, unrefined, undifferentiated kind of behavior typical of preschool children.

Beres and Obers (1950) is the one psychiatrically oriented study which raises some question as to the extent of personality damage resulting from institutionalization. They note a similar underlying pathology in all cases—a distortion in psychic structure, an immature ego, and deficient superego development—but conclude that by late adolescence about half of their 37 cases were making a favorable overt adjustment. They were

functioning well, whether in work situation or at school . . . and presented no evidence of overt disturbance in their behavior or in their relationships within their families or among friends (p. 228).

This study points up the problem for research of making a valid distinction between mental health and pathology. These conclusions illustrate sharply the conflict between a definition of mental health based on overt behavior and a definition derived from a psychodynamic assessment of strengths and liabilities.

In looking to the direct studies for clues to the antecedents of personality deviations in older children, one is disappointed by the limited data on the personality characteristics of infants in institutions. The meager data on infants suggest some precursors of defective ego and superego development such as failure to show imitative behavior at the appropriate developmental period (Freud & Burlingham, 1944; Fischer, 1953). The conflicting findings on autoerotic activity emphasize the lack of agreement as to what constitutes normal behavior in infancy. Freud and Burlingham (1944) as well as Fischer (1952, 1953) describe a high incidence of thumbsucking, rocking, head-banging in young infants, and masturbation in older children. Spitz and Wolf (1949), on the other hand, found "practically no autoerotic activities" among the infants in the foundling home. They hypothesize that an emotional relationship between the child and a mother-figure is a prerequisite for the appearance of autoerotic activities.

Few direct studies give information on the age at which personality disturbances first become evident. In most of this research, the youngest children are over 6 months at the time of study. Where younger children have been studied, frequently no data are given on social or personality characteristics. Only two studies offer data on the age at which personality disturbances are first noted. Freud and Burlingham (1944) note that infants in their institution did not show signs of social retardation before 5 months. Gesell and Amatruda (1941) report first signs of "social ineptness" evident at 24 weeks.

The one experimental study on human infants (Dennis, 1941) is often cited as evidence that early sensory and social deprivation need have no impact on development. Dennis found no significant retardation in a pair of twins who were given "minimum" social and sensory stimulation during the first 7 months of life. Stone (1954) on the basis of a careful analysis of a later report (Dennis & Dennis, 1951) suggests that minimum stimulation probably represented minimal adequate stimulation, much more than that provided in many institutional environments. In Dennis' study the infants were handled for the normal routines, and there was a consistent mother person. The fact that these conditions did not continue much beyond the first half year may also be significant.

Many ad hoc theories have been offered to account for the intellectual and language retardation, the specific defects in abstract thinking, and the varied social and personality disturbances associated with institutionalization. The explanations which offer "maternal deprivation" as the basic etiological entity tend, on the whole, to be vague and generalized, and offer little basis for systematic research. With regard to abstract thought, Bender (1946) states:

> The earliest identification with the mother and her continuous affectional care is necessary during the period of habit training and the rapid development of language and the formation of concepts within the family unit. Otherwise the higher semantic and social development and the expansion of the educational capacities does not take place (p. 76). (Quoted by permission of Child Study Association of America.)

Regarding time concepts, she speculates, "It appears that we develop a concept of time in the passage of time in our early love relationships with our mother" (p. 96). Kardiner (1954) suggests that the sense of time develops in relation to the child's activities in looking forward to gratification. Goldfarb (1955) hypothesizes that lack of an adult identification model (in institutions) inhibits the development of functions such as language, which are dependent on social forms of imitation and communication. Impairment in abstract thinking is interpreted (Goldfarb, 1955) in terms of Stern's theory (1938) which postulates that the development of conceptual thinking is dependent on the growth of a sense of continuity of the self. According to Stern, the grasp of identity, as well as judgments of equality, similarity, and difference are all derived from the sense of continuity of self. At first these judgments are related to concrete personal events; eventually, they are separated from them and become abstract. Without continuity of mothering in an institution, Goldfarb contends the normal development of the self-concept is impaired, with resulting defects in abstract thought processes. Social and personality disturbances are linked directly to lack of opportunity for close human relationships in infancy in institutional environments. Goldfarb attributes defective ego and superego development to inadequate opportunity for the child to identify with parental figures and to internalize the parental image. Bender (1946) describes the etiology of personality disturbances in similar terms:

There is a primary defect in ability to identify in their relationships with other people . . . due to the fact that they never experienced a continuous identification during the infantile period from the early weeks through the period when language and social concepts of right and wrong are normally built up and when psychosexual and personality development are proceeding (p. 76). (Quoted by permission of Child Study Association of America).

She hypothesizes that anxiety and guilt arise in reaction to "threats to object relationship or identification processes" (p. 76). Lack of anxiety and inability to feel guilt are related to the lack of capacity to identify or form object relationships.

Analysis of environmental variables in the research literature points to some more discrete factors than maternal deprivation in the institutional setting. This elusive variable, maternal deprivation, can be analyzed in terms of variables more amenable to research, e.g., amount and quality of tactile, auditory, or visual stimulation; reinforcement schedules; etc. Harlow's (1958) research on infant primates has demonstrated the efficacy for research of analyzing mothering in terms of simple stimulus conditions, such as contact stimulation. The discrepancies in the findings of the research on institutionalization suggest the need to consider interacting variables, such as constitutional differences in vulnerability, varying sensitivities at different developmental stages, etc., in formulating hypotheses for more critical research testing.

Maternal Separation

Maternal separation has never been studied under pure conditions. Most often separation has been associated with other traumatic events such as illness and hospitalization or operative procedures, and often with parental rejection or death or disability of a parent. Frequently separation from the parents has been followed by institutional placement with the result that the impact of institutional influences is superimposed on the loss of parental figures. In the literature on separation, the role of such contaminating variables has not been distinguished from the effects of a break in continuity of relationship with the mother. Spitz and Wolf's (1946) is the only study in which the physical environment remained unchanged following separation; it is one of the few studies in which the quality of the mother-child relationship prior to separation had been studied.

Most of the research is contemporaneous, reporting on the reactions of children at the time of separation. The long-term effects are almost unknown. Follow-up data more than a year later are given in a few studies (Bowlby, Ainsworth, Boston, & Rosenbluth, 1956; Lewis, 1954; Spitz, 1954a, 1954b; Spitz & Wolf, 1946), but in these studies there are many contaminating conditions, e.g., severely disturbed parental relationships, repeated separations, intermittent institutionalization.

Immediate Reactions to Separation

Despite the many different conditions associated with the separation experience, there is some degree of consistency in the findings reported on immediate and short-term reactions of infants and preschool children to separation. In each of the studies some children develop apparently severe reactions, and the behavior sequences in these extreme cases appear to be dynamically similar (Bowlby, 1953b; Robertson & Bowlby, 1952; Roundinesco, David, & Nicolas, 1952; Spitz & Wolf, 1946). The characteristic sequence of responses begins with active protest and violent emotional reactions, such as intense and prolonged crying and active reaching out to people, in apparent attempts to bring back the mother or to find a substitute. In time this behavior is followed by active rejection of adults, and finally by apathy and withdrawal of interest in people, accompanied by a decrease in general activity level. Robertson and Bowlby characterize this latter phase as "mourning"; Spitz and Wolf label it "anaclitic depression." Feeding disturbances —refusal of food, sometimes pathological appetite—and regression in motor and other functions are also reported. When the mother is not restored, Spitz found symptoms of progressive deterioration in infants, a complete withdrawal from social interaction, a sharp drop in developmental level on infant tests, and extreme physical debilitation, with loss of weight and increased susceptibility to infections. In older children (over 12 months) marked physical and intellectual deterioration have not been reported, but severe disturbances in interpersonal relationships have been noted (Bowlby, 1953b; Robertson & Bowlby, 1952). The "mourning phase" in infants and young children is followed by behavior described as a "denial of the need for his own mother," which Robertson and Bowlby interpret as an indication of a repression of the mother image. The child shows no apparent recognition of his own mother, but may transfer his attachment to a substitute mother. (There has been some controversy as to whether such behavior can be interpreted as evidence of repression or whether it should be considered more simply as a denial mechanism— Bowlby, 1953a; Heinicke, 1956.) If no substitute mother is available, the child may show promiscuously friendly behavior, using adults in an instrumental way, but without establishing meaningful attachments. Such behavior Bowlby considers indicative of a repression of all need for mothering, the prelude to a psychopathic character development. If, however, the child is reunited with his mother before the need for mothering is completely repressed (after some unstated critical time interval) the behavior pattern is believed to be reversible. The child is able on return to his mother to reestablish a relationship with her, although there may be several months of difficult adjustment, with irritability, impulsive expression of feelings, and an exaggeratedly intense attachment.

These descriptions of the reactions of young children to conditions involving loss of a mother-figure have provided the basis for most of the generalizations about the severe effects of maternal separation. The dramatic character of these changes has overshadowed the significant fact that a substantial portion of the children in each study did not show severe reactions to separation. In Spitz's study of 123 infants separated from their mothers between

6 and 8 months of age, severe reactions occurred in only 19 cases. Although in Robertson and Bowlby's (1952) research on 45 children ranging in age from 4 months to 4 years, all but three are reported to have shown some reaction; the intensity and duration of the reactions are not clearly specified. Less than half, 20 cases, are reported as showing "acute fretting," a behavior pattern which is not well-defined. The reported duration of the reaction varied from 1 to 17 days. There are no data on the number of children who showed prolonged reactions.

In a careful study of the reactions to hospitalization of 76 infants under 1 year of age (ranging from 3 to 51 weeks) Schaffer (1958) found that reactions varied with age. Infants over 7 months of age showed overt social and emotional reactions, such as excessive crying, fear of strangers, clinging and overdependence on the mother. Infants under 7 months evidenced more global disturbances, i.e., somatic upsets, blank facial expression, extreme preoccupation with the environment. Schaffer relates the global disturbances to sensory deprivation, whereas the social disturbance at the later age, an age at which more differentiated relationship with the mother exists, are interpreted as reactions to separation from the mother.

Heinicke's research (1956) points to less severe effects of simpler, less complicated separation situations. He found no extreme behavioral disturbances in two groups of children, 15 to 30 months of age, with different separation experiences, one group in a residential nursery, the other in a day nursery. The children in the residential nursery did show more overt and more intense aggression, greater frequency of autoerotic activities, and more frequent lapses in sphincter control. These findings are interpreted as indicating an imbalance between the child's impulses and his power to control and organize these impulses in relation to the external world.

Long-Term Effects of Separation

Conclusions about the long-term effects of separation are very tenuous. They are based on a few studies in which the information about the early history is not well-documented.

In an earlier study of 44 juvenile thieves, Bowlby (1944) concluded that separation experiences in childhood resulted in a character disorder distinguished by a "lack of affection or feeling for anyone." The conclusions are based on clinical findings that 12 out of 14 cases diagnosed as "affectionless characters" had been separated from their mothers in infancy or early childhood. Some of these children had been hospitalized for illness without any contact with their mothers over a long period of time, others had experienced frequent changes in foster mothers, and some had been institutionalized for long periods during infancy.

In a follow-up study of 60 children between 6 and 13 years of age, who had been in a sanitarium for tuberculosis for varying periods of time before their fourth birthday, Bowlby et al. (1956) found less serious long-term effects than in the earlier studies. No statistically significant difference in intelligence was found between the control and the sanitarium group. In personality characteristics, the sanitarium children were judged as showing tendencies towards withdrawal and apathy, as well as greater aggressiveness. On the basis of the psychiatric social worker's interview with the parents, 63% of the children were rated as maladjusted, 13% were considered well-adjusted, and 21% adjusted but with minor problems. Bowlby et al. conclude that "outcome is immensely varied, and of those who are damaged, only a small minority develop those very serious disabilities of personality which first drew attention to the pathogenic nature of the experience" (p. 240). They suggest that the potentially damaging effects of separation should not be minimized, but concede that "some of the workers who first drew attention to the dangers of maternal deprivation resulting from separation have tended on occasion to overstate their case" (p. 242).

The findings of Lewis (1954) are sometimes cited as evidence that early separation need not necessarily have lasting harmful effects. Among a group of 500 children who were studied in a reception center shortly after being separated from their parents, only 19 showed "morbid lack of affective responsiveness" (p. 41). Follow-up data were obtained on 240 of these children, 2–3.5 years later. Only 100 had a personal follow-up by a psychiatric social worker and a psychiatrist; information on the others was obtained through letters from social workers who had some contact with the children. Of the 100 more intensively studied children, only three were diagnosed as having marked personality disorders, 22 were having some difficulties in relationships, and 36 were showing mild neurotic symptoms or mild delinquent behavior. With reference to the timing of separation, Lewis concludes that "separation from the mother before the age of five years was a prognostically adverse feature" (p. 122). Apparently this is a clinically based conclusion, since the data presented in the tables show no significant differences between the children separated before 5 years of age and those separated after 5.

Data from several studies indicate that the impact of separation is modified by the character of the mother-child relationship preceding the separation experience and the adequacy of the substitute mothering following separation. Spitz and Wolf (1946) noted that the infants who did not develop severe depressive reactions were those separated from "poor mothers," and conclude that the better the mother-child relationship preceding separation, the more severe the immediate reactions. Lewis (1954), on the other hand, found a higher proportion of children who had been separated from normally affectionate mothers in "good" or "fair" condition than those who had not received "adequate" affection. It might be hypothesized that a close relationship with a mother-figure preceding separation will be followed by more severe immediate reaction but will be ultimately more favorable than a poor antecedent relationship. Children who have experienced a close relationship in infancy may be better prepared to form new attachments in later life than children without any experience of close relationships.

The amount, the quality, and the consistency of substitute mothering will presumably influence the intensity of immediate reactions as well as the long-term personality consequences. Spitz and Wolf (1946) concluded that infants who were provided with a satisfactory substitute mother did not develop the depressive syndrome. (There were no independent criteria of the adequacy of substitute mothering. The substitute relationship was considered satisfactory in those cases which did not develop depressive symptoms.) Robertson and Bowlby (1952) also note that where an adequate substitute mother was provided, there was not a complete withdrawal from social contact.

Multiple Mothering

Serious personality difficulties in later life have been postulated as a consequence of multiple mothering in infancy and early childhood. There has been little research, and in most of the clinical observations multiple mothering has been associated with impersonal or rejecting maternal care. The underlying assumption in much of the literature is that inadequate maternal care is a necessary concomitant of situations in which there is more than one mother-figure. Multiple mothering has never been very precisely defined. In its most general sense, it refers to an environmental setting in which a number of different persons perform the maternal functions for the child, with varying degrees of adequacy and with varying degrees of consistency. From the child's viewpoint, it may mean that there is no single person to whom he can relate as a major source of gratification and on whom his dependency needs can be focused. In some situations the biological mother may share the mothering functions with other chosen women; in other circumstances no biological tie exists between the child and the several mothers. Some current studies in home management houses, a few reports on the Israeli kibbutzim, and a very few anthropological reports provide all the available data on the effects of multiple mothering.

In the anthropological accounts of multiple mothering in different cultural contexts (DuBois, 1944; Eggan, 1945; Mead, 1935; Roscoe, 1953) there are variations in the number of people who share mothering functions as well as variations in the role of the natural mother. In cultures in which the extended family is the traditional pattern, the mothering functions may be shared by the mother, grandmother, aunts, and other female relatives of the child; in some groups, male relatives may take over some maternal functions. The biological mother may be clearly identified as the central, most significant person in some cultures; in others she may be assigned a very secondary role.

In Western cultures, grandmothers frequently assume some of the mothering functions, and in some social groups, child nurses play an important role. In the pre-Civil War Southern plantation class group, many mothering functions were taken over by the Negro nurse. The line of demarcation between supplemental maternal care and multiple mothering has never been very clear.

In none of these situations are disturbances in infant functioning associated with multiple mothering practices, nor are later personality characteristics or deviations attributed to this aspect of early maternal care.

The Israeli kibbutzim provide an unique set of conditions of multiple mothering. In this setting, there are two mother-figures, the natural mother and the metapelet, the children's caretaker, each of whom has very distinctive functions. The major share of the daily routine care as well as major training functions, such as toileting and impulse control, are assumed by the caretaker in the communal nurseries. The mother's contacts with the child tend to be limited to scheduled periods during the day, which are free periods and do not involve traditional family routines. The mother seems to function solely as an agent to provide affectional gratification, although obviously the extent of the mother's influence, as well as the specific areas of influence on the child's development, will vary with her concept of her role and with her personality characteristics.

There are several impressionistic reports (Golan, 1958; Irvine, 1952; Rapaport, 1958) and a few systematic studies (Rabin, 1957, 1958a) of the development of infants and children in the Israeli kibbutzim. Rabin (1958a), using the Griffiths Infant Developmental Scale, found slight developmental retardation in infants between 9 and 17 months of age living in a communal nursery. In only one sector of development—the personal-social area—were these infants significantly retarded. Rabin attributes this retardation to less individual stimulation in the kibbutzim as compared to a normal home environment. This study represents the only reported research in a setting in which there may be deprivation in the amount of stimulation without concomitant lack of affectional interchange with the mother.

In an attempt to assess the long-term effects of living under these special conditions of maternal care in the kibbutz, Rabin (1958a) studied a group of children, between 9 and 11 years of age, who had lived in this environment from infancy. He found no evidences of retardation (using the Goodenough Draw-A-Man Test), nor were there any indications of personality distortions. On the contrary, Rorschach data are interpreted as indicating that the children from the communal settlements showed "better emotional control and greater overall maturity." In ego-strength (using Beck's index) they were judged superior to the control group of children living with their parents. Rabin interprets these findings as evidence of the important role of later experiences in personality development.

In another study, Rabin (1958b) compared the psychosexual development of 10-year-old kibbutzim reared boys with boys from patriarchal type families. Using the Blacky test, he found significant differences, consistent with theoretical expectations. The kibbutz boys showed less "oedipal intensity," more diffuse positive identification with their fathers, and less intense sibling rivalry. This study also points up the fact that multiple mothering is only one of the significant factors which differentiate the kibbutz from the "normal" family setting. As in the case with other conditions associated with maternal deprivation the kibbutz is atypical in regard to the absence of the father.

Home management houses provide a setting in which multiple mothering occurs without associated deprivation of social stimulation. These houses are set up in university home economics departments to provide practical experience in child care for the students. The infant is separated from his foster mother or removed from a familiar institutional environment and placed in the home management house for a period of several weeks to several months. He is cared for by a number of young women, each of whom assumes primary responsibility for mothering activities for a limited period of time, usually about one week. There is one continuous figure— the instructor in the house—with whom the infant can maintain a relationship; she assumes some of the ordinary child care functions. In the course of his residence in the home management house, the infant may have 15 to 20 different "mothers." In this setting he receives much attention and stimulation from many different "mother-figures." Following his residence in the home management house, the infant is usually placed in a foster or adoptive home. The follow-up studies and the several direct studies of children in home management houses (Gardner, Pease, & Hawkes, 1959; Gardner & Swiger, 1958) are in agreement in finding no evidence of intellectual retardation and no gross personality disturbances. The long-term effects have not yet been evaluated.

These three settings—the home management house, the kibbutz, and the extended family—are comparable in only one respect; the mothering functions are distributed among several different persons. They differ in regard to the continuity of the mother-figure, in the role played by the substitute mothers, and in the amount of social stimulation given to the infant. In some situations, because of the high adult-child ratio, it is likely that the infant will receive more sensory as well as more social stimulation than the child in an average family home. For infants, the kibbutz may be similar to an institutional setting in terms of the amount of individual social stimulation provided. It is clear that none of these conditions necessarily involves severe deprivation of mothering, but the mothering experience of children in these settings may differ significantly from that of children in homes with one mother-figure.

None of these studies provides a crucial test of the prevalent hypothesis that multiple mothering results in a diffusion of the mother-image. This theory, developed in the context of institutional care, holds that the child who is cared for by a number of different persons cannot develop a focused image of one significant mother-person in infancy, and consequently, will have difficulties in relationships in later life. On the whole, the few relevant pieces of research suggest that multiple mothering per se is not necessarily damaging to the child.

Distortions in the Mother-Child Relationship

Although distortions in the mother-child relationship have frequently been included in the concept of maternal deprivation, in this report we shall not attempt any comprehensive review of this vast clinical literature. Institutionalization, separation, and multiple mothering represent deviations from a cultural norm of "mothering" primarily on the dimension of amount or consistency of contact with the mother. Under the category of distortions in the mother-child relationship are subsumed all the deviations in maternal relationships which usually have as their antecedents disturbances in the character or personality of the mother. These disturbances in maternal relationships are manifested in overtly or covertly hostile or rejecting behavior, sometimes more subtly in overprotective behavior, and often in unpredictable swings from affection to rejection or in ambivalent behavior. As distinguished from a lack of social stimulation, a lack of responsiveness, and the lack of a mother-figure, this type of deviation in maternal care tends to be characterized by either very strong emotional stimulation, or by stimulation with a preponderance of negative affect. In contrast to institutional care, there may even be very intense intellectual stimulation.

The literature on distorted maternal relationships suggests a somewhat different kind of personality outcome from the psychopathic or affectionless character. The personality distortions tend to be in the schizophrenic, depressive, and neurotic categories. Again there may be rather specific antecedent conditions and organismic vulnerabilities associated with these types of personality deviations (Spitz, 1951). A critical review pointed towards a clarification of the variables and an analysis of the many ad hoc theories concerning distorted mother-child relationships is very much needed.

Some Theoretical Issues and Research Implications

The data from the research on institutionalization, maternal separation, and multiple mothering have relevance for a number of fundamental issues in developmental theory: questions concerning the kinds of environmental conditions which facilitate, inhibit, or distort normal developmental progress; the conditions which influence the reversibility of effects of events in infancy and early childhood; and the extent to which the timing of an experience, i.e., the developmental stage at which it occurs, determines its specific impact.

In theories of the effects of early infantile experiences on later development, two concepts have been prominent: deprivation and stress. Although all the intricacies of the mother-child relationship cannot be conceptualized adequately in terms of these concepts, some of the environmental conditions and events found in the research on maternal deprivation can be ordered meaningfully in these terms. Deprivation is a key concept in the analysis of institutional environments. Many of the circumstances associated with maternal separation and multiple mothering can be ordered in terms of the concept of stress.

Deprivation

In institutional settings several types of deprivation, each with potentially different developmental implications, can be distinguished: sensory deprivation, social deprivation, and emotional deprivation. In many settings all three types of deprivation occur and are complexly interrelated, but they do not necessarily vary concomitantly, and they can be independently manipulated in research.

The studies on sensory deprivation in animals indicate that complete restriction of perceptual experience in early life results in permanent impairment in the functions in which deprivation occurs. In the most extreme institutional environments the degree of sensory deprivation is less severe than in the animal studies. Nevertheless, developmental retardation is found, with the extent of retardation corresponding to the degree of sensory deprivation.

Social deprivation probably acts in a similar way as deprivation of sensory stimulation, leading to disturbances in social functioning, such as, social apathy and social hyperresponsiveness. The simplest hypothesis relates social apathy to inadequate social stimulation during a developmental period which is critical for the acquisition of social responsiveness. If social deprivation occurs after appropriate social responses have been learned, affect hunger or intensified seeking of social response may occur. Although social deprivation is less amenable to experimental manipulation than is sensory deprivation, in natural situations, some simple indices can be used, such as the number of persons with whom the infant has contact during a 24-hour period, the amount of time during which he receives stimulation.

Emotional deprivation has been used popularly and in clinical writings as a catchall term to include deprivation of social, sensory, and affectional stimulation. For research, a more precise usage in terms of deprivation of affective stimulation may be useful. The term, emotional deprivation, can be restricted to characterize an environment with neutral feeling tone or without variation in feeling tone, an environment similar in some respects to the monotonous, bland environment described under sensory deprivation. Emotional apathy, withdrawn behavior, lack of differentiation of affect, and insensitivity to feelings or emotional nuances in others are characteristics which might be related to early emotional deprivation. Within this concept of emotional deprivation, simple objective measures are also possible, e.g., ratings of intensity of positive or negative affect, amount of time during a 24-hour period in which different types and intensities of affective stimulation are provided.

In addition to independent manipulation of each of these types of stimulation—sensory, social, and emotional—in more focused research there might be systematic variation in several dimensions of stimulation: quality of stimulation, e.g., monotonous, varied; intensity; frequency; regularity; cumulative duration of deprivation; sensory modalities in which deprivation occurs.

Stress Consequent to Change

Critical research on maternal separation requires a distinction between the event of separation and later conditions often associated with separation which may be similar to those described under deprivation. The event of separation is associated with significant changes in the physical, and social environments, changes which may be stressful for the young child. In the physical environment, the changes involve the disappearance of familiar objects, sounds, smells, and tactile stimuli; in the social environment, there may be changes in the amount and quality of social stimulation. The new environment may provide more tactile stimulation and less verbal stimulation. There may be modifications in the speed as well as kind of response to the child, e.g., the new caretaker may ignore the child's crying, or she may reward it by tactile stimulation rather than by oral gratification. For the infant or young child, these changes result in a loss of environmental predictability. The degree of stress experienced is likely to vary with the degree of unpredictability.

Change and novelty as stress inducing agents can be studied through research designs providing for careful measurement or systematic variation in the physical and human environments, i.e., the degree of carryover of familiar objects from the old to the new environment, the degree of similarity between the old and new caretakers in physical and psychological characteristics, variations among the old and new mothers in the modalities in which stimulation is given. The impact of change in the physical environment might be evaluated by holding constant the human environment while systematically varying the physical environment, and conversely, the human environment might be varied, with the physical environment constant. The amount of change necessary to produce a discriminable difference to the child may vary with developmental factors. The significance of a change in the human environment will almost certainly depend on whether a meaningful relationship has developed with the mother-figure. If separation occurs after this point, the stress of change is reinforced by the loss of a significant person.

In the research on multiple mothering the one consistent characteristic of the varied contexts of multiple mothering is environmental unpredictability associated with changing agents of gratification. Unpredictability may be based on differences in technique among the different mother-figures, on variations in speed of response to the child's expression of needs, on inconsistency in the kinds of behavior which are rewarded, punished, or ignored. Unlike separation conditions in which new predictable patterns may soon be established, in multiple mothering unpredictability remains the most characteristic aspect of the environment.

There is not strong research evidence nor very firm theoretical grounds to support the assumption that the presence of several concurrent mother-figures in early life results in a diffusion of the mother-image and later inability to establish meaningful relationships. The variable conditions of reinforcement which characterize some multiple mothering situations provide a special kind of learning situation which may lead to the development of atypical patterns of relationships, but not necessarily shallow ones. It is likely that the presence of several mother-figures will vary in significance at different developmental periods. The lack of a consistent role model is probably more serious during the early preschool period than in early infancy. In further research, attempts should be made to vary systematically the degree of stress associated with environmental unpredictability, while controlling other variables such as degree of role differentiation among the multiple mothers.

Although deprivation and trauma can be treated as independent concepts, there are conditions under which deprivation can be considered a traumatic stimulus. It is recognized that trauma may result from excessive stimulation, but the conditions under which inadequate stimulation may be traumatic are more obscure. Recent research indicates that extreme sensory deprivation may be stressful for adults (Wexler, Mendelson, Leiderman, & Solomon, 1959). We might assume that deprivation becomes a traumatic stimulus after the appropriate motivational conditions have developed. Thus Hebb (1955) suggests:

> The observed results seem to mean, not that the stimulus of another attentive organism (the mother) is necessary from the first, but that it may become necessary only as psychological dependence on the mother develops (p. 828).

Research Implications

Analysis of the research on institutionalization, separation, and multiple mothering highlights some theoretically significant questions and points to some specific variables which can be experimentally manipulated or controlled through the opportunistic utilization of natural situations.

Duration of deprivation or stress. In much of the research, the subjects have experienced a cumulative series of deprivations or stressful experiences, beginning in infancy and continuing through childhood. Few studies give specific data on the length of time the child has been exposed to these conditions. Goldfarb (1945b, 1947, 1955), Bender (1945, 1947), and Bowlby (1944) conclude from retrospective studies that the longer the period of institutional care, the more severe the ultimate damage. These conclusions are based largely on individual case findings. Those cases which did not show the same irreversible patterns as the rest of the population had been in institutions for a shorter period of time. Spitz and Wolf (1946) suggest that there may be a critical time interval after which the effects of maternal separation are irreversible. If the infant is reunited with his mother within 3 months, the process of physical, social, and intellectual deterioration may be arrested, but if the mother-child relationship is not restored within 5 months, irreparable damage occurs. There are no comparable data on children beyond infancy. One might hypothesize that the critical time interval might be longer with older children.

Research on older children attest to the damaging effects of repeated separations (Bowlby, 1944; Lewis, 1954). On the whole, no distinction has been made among several different separation experiences: a single instance of separation with reunion, a single separation without reunion, repeated small doses of separation with consistent reunion with the same mother, and cumulative separations with repeated changes in mothers. It can be assumed that each of these experiences provides different learning conditions for the development of meaningful relationships. The most extreme outcome, the "affectionless character," may be the result of the most extreme conditions, i.e., repeated traumatic separations.

Time or developmental stage at which deprivation or stress occurs. Psychoanalytic theories regarding the significance of early experience for later development have often been interpreted as postulating that the younger the organism, the more severe and fixed the effects of an environmental impact. Only limited data are available on human subjects. Ribble (1943) tends to interpret her data on maternal rejection as supporting this point of view. Bender's and Goldfarb's (1947) retrospective studies suggest that the younger the child, the more damaging the effects of deprivation and stress. Some animal research supports this hypothesis; other studies do not (Beach & Jaynes, 1954; King, 1958).

The findings on institutionalized infants that intellectual retardation is not apparent before 3 months of age and that personality disturbances are not evident before 5 or 6 months suggest that this type of deprivation has no significant impact in the early weeks of infancy. (Because of the known unreliability of infant tests, and the lack of sensitive measures of personality and intellectual functions in early infancy, some degree of caution is necessary in interpreting these findings.)

A more refined hypothesis regarding the significance of the timing of experiences is the critical phase hypothesis which holds that there are points in the developmental cycle during which the organism may be particularly sensitive to certain kinds of events or most vulnerable to specific types of deprivation or stress. Several animal studies (Moltz, 1960; Scott, Fredericson, & Fuller, 1951; Tinbergen, 1954) support the general outlines of the critical phase hypothesis. From the assorted data on the intellectual functioning of institutionalized children a testable hypothesis emerges regarding a critical period for institutional deprivation: vulnerability to intellectual damage is greatest during the 3–12 month period. Beres and Obers (1950) suggest that institutional deprivation will differ in its impact at different developmental periods. The data on which this conclusion is based are limited. Of their four cases showing mental retardation, all were admitted to the institution under 6 months of age; the four cases developing schizophrenia entered the institution at a later age (specific age not reported).

Although the general consensus in the literature is that maternal separation which occurs before the child is 5 years of age is likely to be most damaging, the findings are not sufficiently clear to pinpoint any one age as being most vulnerable. Bowlby (1944) notes among the affectionless thieves:

> In practically all these cases, the separation which appears to have been pathogenic occurred after the age of six months, and in a majority after twelve months. This suggests that there is a lower age limit, before which separations, whilst perhaps having undesirable effects, do not produce the particular results we are concerned with here—the affectionless and delinquent character (p. 41). (Quoted by permission of the *International Journal of Psycho-Analysis*.)

On the basis of our knowledge of the developmental characteristics of children, one might postulate differing vulnerabilities at different periods of development. The developmental level of the child is likely to influence the significance of deprivation or the meaning of a separation experience for him. With regard to separation, the period during which the child is in the process of consolidating a relationship with his mother may be an especially vulnerable one. Also significant may be the developmental stage with regard to memory functions. After the point in development at which the child can sustain an image of the mother in her absence and can anticipate her return, the meaning of a brief separation may be less severe than at an earlier developmental period. The degree of autonomy the child has achieved may also affect the extent of trauma experienced. The loss of the mother may represent a greater threat to the completely dependent infant than to the young child who has achieved some locomotion and some manipulatory control over his environment. The advent of language which symbolizes even a greater degree of environmental mastery may mitigate further the severity of trauma.

Similarly, the effects of institutional deprivation may be more severe for the young infant who is completely dependent on outside sources of stimulation than for the older child who is capable of seeking out stimulation. There may also be age linked effects of different types of deprivation. Some animal studies suggest that a minimal level of stimulation may be necessary to produce the biochemical changes necessary for the development of the underlying structures. Deprivation in certain sensory modalities may be more significant at one age than at another. For example, deprivation of tactile stimulation may be most significant during the first weeks of infancy, whereas auditory or visual deprivation may become more significant later. Social deprivation may be most damaging during the earliest period of the development of social responsiveness.

Constitutional factors. Although the role of constitutional factors in influencing the long-term effects of early trauma has been increasingly stressed, the meager data in support of the significance of constitutional factors have been indirect. Several retrospective studies have found similar deprivation experiences in the history of individuals who in later life made satisfactory life adjustments as in those who made poor adjustments. The different outcomes are accounted for in terms of constitutional factors. In considering the role of constitutional factors a distinction might be made between organismic differences in general vulnerability to deprivation or stress and vulnerabilities in specific sensory modalities. Data from a number of studies attest to individual differences in sensitivities in specific modalities. With regard to research design, it may be important, too, to distinguish between organismic differences which are constitutionally determined and differences in vulnerability which vary with developmental stage. While organismic sensitivities cannot be manipulated experimentally, it may be possible to study constitutional factors by developing research designs in which subjects with known differences in sensitivities are subjected to the same experimental conditions.

The Long-Term Effects: The Issue of Reversibility

It does not seem fruitful to state the question of reversibility in terms of an either-or hypothesis, i.e., whether or not early experiences produce irreversible effects. Rather the question might be: what are the conditions under which an earlier traumatic or depriving experience is likely to produce irreversible effects? The concept of irreversibility implies that an adverse experience results in permanent structural changes in the nervous system such that at some later developmental period a given response sequence is either facilitated or inhibited. A further implication is that subsequent experience plays no role in changing response potentialities or in developing responses which are incompatible with earlier established behavior patterns. Several studies suggest that permanent damage to the central nervous system may result from early sensory deprivation. Increasingly the research points to the resiliency of the organism. Beres and Obers' is one of the few investigations from the psychoanalytic orientation which makes a strong case for the modifiability of the effects of earlier infantile experience. They cite in support a conclusion by Hartmann, Kris, and Lowenstein (1946) that

the basic structure of the personality and the basic functional interrelationship of the systems of the ego and superego are fixed to some extent by the age of six, but after this age, the child does not stop growing and developing, and growth and development modify existing structure (p. 34). (Quoted by permission of International Universities Press, Inc.)

Many factors in complex interaction undoubtedly determine the extent to which recovery is possible from early intellectual or personality damage. More pointed research is needed to identify the specific conditions under which irreversible damage to the central nervous system occurs. Also needed are specific research designs on reversibility, designs aimed at reversing intellectual or personality damage.

Toward a Concept of Maternal Deprivation

In focusing on the isolation of simple variables for formulating testable hypotheses on the relationship between early environmental conditions and later development, we have avoided complex concepts centering around the emotional interchange between mother and infant, concepts which have been focal in psychodynamic theories. The mother as a social stimulus provides sensory stimulation to the infant through tactile, visual, and auditory media, i.e., through handling, cuddling, talking and playing with the child, as well as by simply being visually present. The mother also acts as a mediator of environmental stimuli, bringing the infant in contact with the environment and buffering or heightening the intensity of stimuli. The meaning of these mothering activities to the child and the impact of the mother's absence varies with the child's perceptual, cognitive, and motor capacities at different developmental levels. On the simplest level, if the mother is not present, the infant may be deprived of tactile, auditory, and visual stimuli from a social source, as well as of the environmental stimuli which the mother ordinarily makes available to him. At this point, the mother's absence may be experienced by the young infant only as a deprivation of distinctive stimuli offered by a social being. The impact on the infant may be more severe if the mother's absence is accompanied by deviations in need-gratification sequences, such as, failure to have needs anticipated or long delay before gratification is provided, by marked inconsistencies in patterns of gratification, or inadequate gratification. The significance of these kinds of frustration experiences will be modified by the length of time during which they operate, the developmental level of the child, e.g., the degree of autonomy he has achieved.

The usefulness of this reduction of maternal deprivation has been demonstrated in ordering the reported research findings and in suggesting more refined hypotheses for further research. It is likely, however, that not all aspects of the mother-child relationship can be meaningfully reduced to such simple variables. We can only speculate on the process through which the mother comes to acquire special meaning to the child. We assume that the mother-image gradually evolves as a distinctive perceptual entity out of a welter of tactile, visual, auditory, and kinesthetic cues. (There has been some speculation, without definitive data, that in early infancy before these sensory cues are organized into a percept of an object existing outside of himself, the infant may still "recognize" the mother as an assortment of familiar stimuli.) In time through repeated contact these cues become "familiar" or distinctive to the infant, and finally there is a fixation of positive feelings on this perceptual complex. After the point of fixation of positive feelings on the mother, new elements enter into the child's reactions to a loss or a change in mothers. At this point, sensory deprivation and environmental change may be secondary, the loss of a significant person becomes of primary significance. This experience cannot occur until the infant reaches a developmental point at which he is able to conceptualize the existence of an "object" outside of himself. As a matter of conceptual clarity, it might be desirable to limit the concept of maternal deprivation to the conditions associated with the loss of a specific, cathected person, a person who has acquired distinctive significance for the child, one on whom positive feelings have been fixated.

Conclusions

The wide range of circumstances included under the concept of maternal deprivation stand out when the research is carefully scrutinized. Included are studies of children who have been separated from their parents and placed in institutional settings, other studies deal with children who have been grossly maltreated or rejected by their families, others are concerned with children temporarily separated from their parents because of illness, and in others the maternal functions are assumed by several different persons. These experiences have occurred at different developmental stages in the children's life histories, and there has been considerable variation in the length of exposure to these conditions, and in the circumstances preceding and following the deviating conditions.

It is apparent that the data on maternal deprivation are based on research of varying degrees of methodological rigor. Most of the data consist of descriptive clinical findings arrived at fortuitously rather than through planned research, and frequently the findings are based on retrospective analyses which have been narrowly directed toward verification of clinical hunches.

The areas of knowledge and the areas of uncertainty become more sharply delimited when we break down the complex concept of maternal deprivation into some discrete variables. For instance, in the studies on institutional care in which sensory deprivation emerges as a major variable, we can conclude that severe sensory deprivation before one year of age, if it continues for a sufficiently long period of time, is likely to be associated with severe intellectual damage. Direct observation of children undergoing the experience of maternal separation shows a variety of immediate disturbances in behavior, permitting the simple conclusion that this is a stressful experience for children. There is no clear evidence that multiple mothering, without associated deprivation of stress, results in personality damage.

With regard to the long-term effects of early deprivation or stress associated with institutionalization or maternal separation, no simple conclusions can be drawn. In the retrospective studies, significant interacting variables are usually unknown. Longitudinal studies currently underway may offer data on the reinforcing or attenuating influence of later experiences. We might hope for more pointed longitudinal studies on questions of reversibility, such as, studies of human or animal subjects who have been subjected to experimental deprivation or trauma, or longitudinal studies of special populations chosen because of some known deviation from a cultural norm of mothering, e.g., infants who have experienced separation for adoption (Yarrow, 1955, 1956) and infants in multiple mothering situations (Pease & Gardner, 1958).

The analysis of the literature points up the need for more definitive research on the role of many "nonmaternal" variables, variables relating to the characteristics of environmental stimulation and variables dealing with organismic sensitivities. After clarification of the influence of such variables, then perhaps systematic research can come to grips with some of the more elusive aspects of the emotional interchange in the intimate dyadic relationship of mother and infant.

REFERENCES[1]

Ainsworth, Mary D., & Boston, Mary. Psychodiagnostic assessment of a child after prolonged separation in early childhood. *British Journal of Medical Psychology*, 1952, 25, 169-205.

Ainsworth, Mary D., & Bowlby, J. Research strategy in the study of mother-child separation. *Courrier du Centre Internationale de l'Enfance*, 1954, 4, 1-47.

Bakwin, H. Emotional deprivation in infants. *Journal of Pediatrics*, 1949, 35, 512-521.

Beach, F. A., & Jaynes, J. Effects of early experience upon the behavior of animals. *Psychological Bulletin*, 1954, 51, 239-263.

Bender, Lauretta. Infants reared in institutions: Permanently handicapped. *Bulletin of the Child Welfare League of America*, 1945, 24, 1-4.

Bender, Lauretta. There's no substitute for family life. *Child Studies*, 1946, 23, 74-76, 96.

Bender, Lauretta. Psychopathic behavior disorders in children. In R. M. Linder (Ed.), *Handbook of correctional psychology*. New York: New York Philosophical Library, 1947, Pp. 360-377.

Bender, Lauretta, & Yarnell, H. An observation nursery: A study of 250 children in the psychiatric division of Bellevue Hospital. *American Journal of Psychiatry*, 1941, 97, 1158-1174.

Beres, D., & Obers, S. J. The effects of extreme deprivation in infancy on psychic structure in adolescence. *Psychoanalytic Studies of Children*, 1950, 5, 121-140.

Berg, M., & Cohen, B. B. Early separation from mother in schizophrenia. *Journal of Nervous and Mental Disorders*, 1959, 128, 365-369.

Bodman, F., et al. The social adaptation of institution children. *Lancet*, 1950, 258, 173-176.

Bowlby, J. Forty-four juvenile thieves. *International Journal of Psychoanalysis*, 1944, 25, 1-57.

Bowlby, J. Maternal care and mental health. *WHO Monograms*, 1951, No. 2.

---

[1] Because of space limitations, many relevant references have not been cited. An extensive bibliography of earlier studies can be found in Bowlby (1951).

Bowlby, J. Some pathological processes engendered by early mother-child separation. In M. J. Senn (Ed.), *Infancy and childhood*. New York: Josiah Macy, Jr., Foundation, 1953. Pp. 38-87. (a)

Bowlby, J. Some pathological processes set in train by early mother-child separation. *Journal of Mental Science*, 1953, **99**, 265-272. (b)

Bowlby, J. An ethological approach to research in child development. *British Journal of Medical Psychology*, 1957, **30**, 230-240.

Bowlby, J. The nature of the child's tie to the mother. *International Journal of Psychoanalysis*, 1958, **39**, 1-24.

Bowlby, J., Ainsworth, Mary, Boston, Mary, & Rosenbluth, Dina. The effects of mother-child separation: A follow-up study. *British Journal of Medical Psychology*, 1956, **29**, 211-247.

Brodbeck, A. J., & Irwin, O. C. The speech behavior of infants without families. *Child Development*, 1946, **17**, 145-156.

Brown, F. Neuroticism of institution vs. non-institution children. *Journal of Applied Psychology*, 1937, **21**, 379-383.

Coleman, Ruth W., & Provence, Sally. Environmental retardation (hospitalism) in infants living in families. *Pediatrics*, 1957, **19**, 285-292.

Day, Ella J. The development of language in twins: I. A comparison of twins and single children. *Child Development*, 1932, **3**, 179-199.

Dennis, W. Infant development under conditions of restricted practice and of minimum social stimulation. *Genetic Psychology Monographs*, 1941, **23**, 143-190.

Dennis, W., & Dennis, Marsena G. Development under controlled environmental conditions. In W. Dennis (Ed.), *Readings in child psychology*. New York: Prentice-Hall, 1951. Pp. 104-131.

Dennis, W., & Najarian, P. Infant development under environmental handicap. *Psychological Monograms*, 1957, **71** (7, Whole No. 436).

DuBois, Cora. *The people of Alor*. Minneapolis: University of Minnesota Press, 1944.

DuPan, R. M., & Roth, S. The psychologic development of a group of children brought up in a hospital type residential nursery. *Journal of Pediatrics*, 1955, **47**, 124-129.

Edelston, H. Separation anxiety in young children: A study of hospital cases. *Genetic Psychology Monograms*, 1943, **28**, 3-95.

Eggan, D. The general problem of Hopi adjustment. *American Anthropologist*, 1945, **47**, 516-539.

Fischer, Liselotte. Hospitalism in six month old infants. *American Journal of Orthopsychiatry*, 1952, **22**, 522-533.

Fischer, Liselotte. Psychological appraisal of the unattached preschool child. *American Journal of Orthopsychiatry*, 1953, **23**, 803-814.

Flint, Betty. Babies who live in institutions. *Bulletin of the Institute of Child Studies, Toronto*, 1957, **19**, 1-5.

Freud, Anna, & Burlingham, Dorothy, T. *Infants without families*. New York: International University Press, 1944.

Gardner, D. B., Pease, Damaris, & Hawkes, G. R. Responses of two-year-old adopted children to controlled stress situations. Paper read at Society for Research in Child Development, Washington, D.C., March, 1959.

Gardner, D. B., & Swiger, M. K. Developmental status of two groups of infants released for adoption. *Child Development*, 1958, **29**, 521-530.

Gesell, A., & Amatruda, Catherine. *Developmental diagnosis*. New York: Hoeber, 1941.

Gewirtz, J. L. Social deprivation and dependency: A learning analysis. Paper read in symposium on Dependency in personality development. American Psychological Association, New York, August, 1957.

Glaser, K., & Eisenberg, L. Maternal deprivation. *Pediatrics*, 1956, **18**, 626-642.

Golan, S. Behavior research in collective settlements in Israel: Collective education in the kibbutz. *American Journal of Orthopsychiatry*, 1958, **28**, 549-556.

Goldfarb, W. Effects of early institutional care on adolescent personality (graphic Rorschach data). *Child Development*, 1943, **14**, 213-223. (a)

Goldfarb, W. Infant rearing and problem behavior. *American Journal of Orthopsychiatry*, 1943, **13**, 249-265. (b)

Goldfarb, W. Effects of early institutional care on adolescent personality: Rorschach data. *American Journal of Orthopsychiatry*, 1944, **14**, 441-447. (a)

Goldfarb, W. Infant rearing as a factor in foster home replacement. *American Journal of Orthopsychiatry*, 1944, **14**, 162-173. (b)

Goldfarb, W. Effects of psychological deprivation in infancy and subsequent stimulation. *American Journal of Psychiatry*, 1945, **102**, 18-33. (a)

Goldfarb, W. Psychological privation in infancy and subsequent adjustment. *American Journal of Orthopsychiatry*, 1945, **15**, 247-255. (b)

Goldfarb, W. Variations in adolescent adjustment of institutionally reared children. *American Journal of Orthopsychiatry*, 1947, **17**, 449-457.

Goldfarb, W. Rorschach test differences between family-reared, institution-reared, and schizophrenic children. *American Journal of Orthopsychiatry*, 1949, **19**, 625-633.

Goldfarb, W. Emotional and intellectual consequences of psychologic deprivation in infancy: A re-evaluation. In P. H. Hoch & J. Zubin (Eds.), *Psychopathology of childhood*. New York: Grune & Stratton, 1955. Pp. 105-119.

Haggerty, A. D. The effects of long-term hospitalization upon the language development of children. *Journal of Genetic Psychology*, 1959, **94**, 205-209.

Harlow, H. The nature of love. *American Psychologist*, 1958, **15**, 673-685.

Hartmann, H., Kris, E., Lowenstein, R. M. Comments on the formation of psychic structure. *Psychoanalytic Studies of Children*, 1946, **2**, 11-38.

Hebb, D. O. *The organization of behavior: A neuropsychological theory*. New York: Wiley, 1949.

Hebb, D. O. The mammal and his environment. *American Journal of Psychiatry*, 1955, **3**, 826-831.

Heinicke, C. Some effects of separating two-year-old children from their parents: A comparative study. *Human Relations*, 1956, **9**, 105-176.

Irvine, Elizabeth. Observations on aims and methods of child rearing in communal settlements in Israel. *Human Relations*, 1952, **5**, 247-275.

Kardiner, A. Social stress and deprivation. In I. Galdston (Ed.), *Beyond the germ theory*. New York: New York Health Education Council, 1954. Pp. 147-170.

King, J. A. Parameters relevant to determining the effect of early experience upon the adult behavior of animals. *Psychological Bulletin*, 1958, **55**, 46-58.

Klackenburg, G. Studies in maternal deprivation in infant homes. *Acta paediatrica Stockholm*, 1956, **45**, 1-12.

Levy, D. Primary affect hunger. *American Journal of Psychiatry*, 1937, **94**, 643-652.

Levy, Ruth. Institutional vs. boarding-home care. *Journal of Personality*, 1947, **15**, 233-241.

Lewis, Hilda. *Deprived children*. Toronto: Oxford University Press, 1954.

Lowrey, L. G. Personality distortion and early institutional care. *American Journal of Orthopsychiatry*, 1940, **10**, 576-585.

Mead, Margaret. *Sex and temperament in three primitive societies*. New York: Mentor, 1935.

Moltz, H. Imprinting: Empirical basis and theoretical significance. *Psychological Bulletin*, 1960, **57**, 291-314.

Pease, Damaris, & Gardner, D. B. Research on the effects of non-continuous mothering. *Child Development*, 1958, **29**, 141-148.

Pinneau, S. R. A critique on the articles by Margaret Ribble. *Child Development*, 1950, **21**, 203-228.

Pinneau, S. R. The infantiles disorders of hospitalism and anaclitic depression. *Psychological Bulletin*, 1955, **52**, 429-462.

Rabin, A. I. Personality maturity of kibbutz (Israeli collective settlement) and non-kibbutz children as reflected in Rorschach findings. *Journal of Projective Technology*, 1957, **31**, 148-153.

Rabin, A. I. Behavior research in collective settlements in Israel: Infants and children under conditions of "intermittent" mothering in the kibbutz. *American Journal of Orthopsychiatry*, 1958, **28**, 577-586. (a).

Rabin, A. I. Some psychosexual differences between kibbutz and non-kibbutz Israeli boys. *Journal of Projective Technology*, 1958, **22**, 328-332. (b)

Rapaport, D. Behavior research in collective settlements in Israel: The study of Kibbutz education and its bearing on the theory of development. *American Journal of Orthopsychiatry*, 1958, **28**, 587-597.

Rheingold, Harriet L. Mental and social development of infants in relation to the number of other infants in the boarding home. *American Journal of Orthopsychiatry*, 1943, **13**, 41-44.

Rheingold, Harriet L. The modification of social responsiveness in institutional babies. *Monographs of Social Research in Child Development*, 1956, **21**, No. 63.

Rheingold, Harriet L. The measurement of maternal care. *Child Development*, 1960, **31**, 565-573.

Rheingold, Harriet L., & Bayley, N. The later effects of an experimental modification of mothering. *Child Development*, 1959, **30**, 363-372.

Rheingold, Harriet L., Gewirtz, J., & Ross, Helen. Social conditioning of vocalizations in the infant. *Journal of Comparative and Physiological Psychology*, 1959, **52**, 58-73.

Ribble, Margaret. *Rights of infants.* New York: Columbia University Press, 1943.

Robertson, J., & Bowlby, J. Responses of young children to separation from their mothers: II. Observation of sequences of response of children aged 18-24 months during course of separation. *Courrier du Centre Internationale de l'Enfance*, 1952, **2**, 131-139.

Roscoe, J. Baganda: An account of their native customs and beliefs. In I. T. Sanders (Ed.), *Societies around the world.* New York: Dryden, 1953. Pp. 412-420.

Roundinesco, Jenny, David, Miriam, & Nicolas, J. Responses of young children to separation from their mothers: I. Observation of children 12 to 17 months recently separated from their families and living in an institution. *Courrier du Centre Internationale de l'Enfance*, 1952, **2**, 66-78.

Schaffer, H. R. Objective observations of personality development in early infancy. *British Journal of Medical Psychology*, 1958, **31**, 174-183.

Scott, J. P., Fredericson, E., & Fuller, J. L. Experimental exploration of the critical period hypothesis. *Personality*, 1951, **1**, 162-183.

Skeels, H. M. A study of the effects of differential stimulation on mentally retarded children: Follow-up report. *American Journal of Mental Deficiency*, 1942, **66**, 340-350.

Skeels, H. M., & Dye, H. A study of the effects of differential stimulation on mentally retarded children. *Proceedings of the American Association on Mental Deficiency*, 1939, **44**, 114-136.

Skeels, H. M., Updegraff, Ruth, Wellman, Beth L., & Williams, H. M. A study of environmental stimulation: An orphanage preschool project. *University of Iowa Studies on Child Welfare*, 1938, **15**, 7-191.

Spitz, R. A. Hospitalism: An inquiry into the genesis of psychiatric conditions in early childhood. *Psychoanalytic Studies of Children*, 1945, **1**, 53-74; 1946, **2**, 113-117.

Spitz, R. A. The psychogenic diseases in infancy: An attempt at their etiologic classification. *Psychoanalytic Studies of Children*, 1951, **6**, 255-275.

Spitz, R. A. Infantile depression and the general adaptation syndrome. In P. H. Hoch & J. Zubin (Eds.), *Depression.* New York: Grune & Stratton, 1954. Pp. 93-108. (a)

Spitz, R. A. Unhappy and fatal outcomes of emotional deprivation and stress in infancy. In I. Galdston (Ed.), *Beyond the germ theory.* New York: New York Health Education Council, 1954. Pp. 120-131. (b)

Spitz, R. A. Reply to Pinneau. *Psychological Bulletin,* 1955, **52,** 453-459.

Spitz, R. A., & Wolf, Katherine. Anaclitic depression. *Psychoanalytic Studies of Children,* 1946, **2,** 313-342.

Spitz, R. A., & Wolf, Katherine. Autoerotism. *Psychoanalytic Studies of Children,* 1949, **3-4,** 85-120.

Stern, W. *General psychology from the personalistic standpoint.* New York: Macmillan, 1938.

Stone, L. J. A critique of studies of infant isolation. *Child Development,* 1954, **25,** 9-20.

Tinbergen, N. Psychology and ethology as supplementary parts of a science of behavior. In B. Schaffner (Ed.), *Group processes.* New York: Josiah Macy, Jr., Foundation, 1954.

Van Alstyne, D. The environment of three-year-old children: Factors related to intelligence and vocabulary tests. *Teach. Coll. Contr. Educ.,* 1929, No. 366.

Wellman, Beth, & Pegram, E. L. Binet IQ changes of orphanage preschool children: A re-analysis. *Journal of Genetic Psychology,* 1944, **65,** 239-263.

Wexler, D., Mendelson, J., Liederman, P. H., & Solomon, P. Sensory deprivation. *American Medical Association Archives of Neurological Psychiatry,* 1958, **79,** 225-233.

Yarrow, L. J. Research on maternal deprivation. Paper read at symposium on Maternal deprivation, American Association for the Advancement of Science, Section 1, Atlanta, Georgia, December, 1955.

Yarrow, L. J. The development of object relationships during infancy, and the effects of a disruption of early mother-child relationships. *American Psychologist,* 1956, **11,** 423. (Abstract)

8

Psychological Differentiation
and Forms of Pathology

INTRODUCTION

One theme that comes up frequently in behavior pathology is the need for a new means of conceptualizing symptomology or classifying patients. A new approach might shed more light on the etiology of symptoms and might be more helpful in selecting the treatment for a particular syndrome. In the article that follows, Herman Witkin reviews the research on a new and interesting way of looking at differences in personality functioning and pathology. Essentially, the data that Witkin reviews suggest that a potentially fruitful attitude toward differences in personality functioning is to identify types of *cognitive styles*. Witkin focuses his attention on two styles—the *articulated* style and the *global* style.

The concepts of articulated and global cognitive styles correspond to the concepts of field-independence and field-dependence, which were identified some time ago by experimental psychologists. The individual with an articulated (field-independent) cognitive style clearly discriminates between the different aspects of his environment (field) and can respond differentially to the various aspects. His global (field-dependent) counterpart responds to the environment (field) as though it were a united whole. Recent work with these types has, however, broadened the range of areas in which individuals with these cognitive styles are known to differ from each other. It seems that in addition to one's field-independence-dependence, cognitive style affects the way one perceives himself in relation to the environment.

The effects of field-dependence also extend to psychological identity, for the global or field-dependent individual seems less able to establish an identity and direction that is separate from those around him. That is, individuals with a global cognitive style rely more heavily on external sources for self-definition and direction. Since the way one sees the environment and the degree to which one feels separate from the environment would have pervasive effects on behavior, understanding personality functioning in terms of cognitive styles has important implications for understanding behavior, both normal and pathological.

A number of things should be pointed out about the differences in cognitive styles that have been suggested. First, the global and articulated types actually represent *end points on a continuum* rather than two distinct classes. Second, there is a *developmental* aspect to the global-articulated dimension. The infant or young child tends to be global in his orientation. With time and experience, however, the individual achieves greater differentiation in his perception of the environment and in his response to the environment. It can be suggested therefore, that an individual with a global orientation might be more immature in his style than an individual with an articulated style. It is important to note, however, that although the global orientation may imply less maturity in cognitive style, it does *not imply greater pathology* than the articulated style. Witkin's point is not that one orientation is pathological whereas the other is not, but that *different orientations lead to different types of pathology*. Lastly, the reader should be aware that the different cognitive styles do not imply a distortion of the *content* of reality per se, but rather differences in the way the perceiver relates different aspects of reality to each other and to himself.

Interestingly enough, many of the measures that are used to determine a person's cognitive style are not those that have been developed by psychologists interested in pathology. Tests such as the tilted room test, rod and frame test, and embedded figure test have been borrowed from the more traditional experimental psychologist. Although these tests do not have a history of clinical use, they do have a long history of careful experimental use and refinement. This wealth of previous experimental data may offer dimensions to research on clinical problems that might otherwise have been ignored.

8

PSYCHOLOGICAL DIFFERENTIATION AND FORMS OF PATHOLOGY

HERMAN A. WITKIN

Recent research has demonstrated that people show characteristic, self-consistent ways of functioning in their perceptual and intellectual activities. These cognitive styles, as they have come to be called, appear to be manifestations, in the cognitive sphere, of still broader dimensions of personal functioning which cut across diverse psychological areas. The fact that these broader dimensions may be "picked up" in the person's cognitive activities, in the form of cognitive styles, has an important methodological advantage. Cognitive styles may be evaluated by controlled laboratory procedures, thereby providing an experimental, objective approach to personality study and assessment.

It is of interest, too, that the dimensions of personal functioning that have been identified through the cognitive-style work represent different ways of cutting the personality "pie" from those traditionally used. New ways of looking at personality organization are thus being suggested. Even if the personality dimensions that are now being explored, as outgrowths of the cognitive-style work, prove, in time, to be congruent with our more traditional dimensions, the outcome will be to deepen and enrich our understanding of these traditional dimensions.

The approach to cognitive activity followed in the research on cognitive styles has been a functional one. A primary concern has been with the adaptive function of cognitive processes in the psychological economy of the individual. This has led to a search for connections and consistencies across psychological areas. An outcome for this research enterprise has been to demonstrate further that the conventional categories often used in describing man's psychological life are not as separate as once believed. A by-

SOURCE. Reprinted with permission of the American Psychological Association and the author from the *Journal of Abnormal Psychology*, 1965, 70, 317-336. The work described in this paper was supported in part by a grant (M-628) from the United States Public Health Service, National Institutes of Health.

product of the cognitive-style research has thus been its contribution to a more integrated, holistic view of personality.

In these and other ways the recent extensive research on cognitive style has significant implications for personality theory, for the methodology of personality research, and for some of the practical problems encountered by the clinician in his work on diagnosis and therapy. Some of these implications may be demonstrated by considering, as illustrative, the particular cognitive style with which we have been concerned in our laboratory, (Witkin, Dyk, Faterson, Goodenough & Karp, 1962; Witkin, Lewis, Hertzman, Machover, Meissner & Wapner, 1954).

Indicators of Extent of Differentiation

Articulated versus Global Dimension of Cognitive Functioning

We first identified this cognitive style, and the dimension of personal functioning of which it is a part, in perception, where we called it "field-dependence-independence." In a field-dependent mode of perceiving, perception is strongly dominated by the overall organization of the field, and parts of the field are experienced as "fused." In a field-independent mode of perceiving, parts of the field are experienced as discrete from organized background. There is now considerable evidence that a tendency toward one or the other ways of perceiving is a consistent, pervasive characteristic of an individual's perception.

From our studies of the field-dependence-independence dimension there has emerged a variety of perceptual tests for evaluating individual differences along this dimension. In all of these tests the issue is whether or not the person is able to keep an object separate from organized field in perception. In one test, the "object" is the person's own body; in another, it is a stick; in still another, it is a simple geometric design. A brief account of these tests will make clearer the nature of the perceptual dimension they assess.

One test, the body-adjustment test, is concerned with perception of the position of the body in space. The test evaluates the person's ability to perceive his body apart from the surrounding visual field, through reference to sensations of body position. The apparatus for this test consists of a small room, which can be tilted left or right, within which is a chair, which can also be tilted left or right. The subject's task is to make his body straight while the room around him is tilted. Some persons, in carrying out this task, move their bodies into alignment with the tilted room, and in that position report that they are straight, though objectively tilted as much as 35 degrees, or even more. In this kind of performance, which we call "field dependent," perception of body position is dictated by the relation between the body and surrounding world. There seems to be a fusion between body and field in experience. At the other extreme of the performance range, we find subjects who, regardless of the position of the surrounding room, are able to bring their bodies close to the true upright. Persons who perform in this fashion—we call it a "field-independent" performance—seem to have an immediate sense of the separateness of their bodies from the surrounding world.

Another of our tests of field dependence again involves perception of the upright, but the object of perception is a neutral external object, a stick, instead of the body. The apparatus for this test consists of a luminous rod and frame, the only objects visible to the subject in the completely darkened room. With the frame tilted, the subject is required to adjust the rod to the upright. Some subjects perceive the rod as straight only when it is fully aligned with the tilted frame around it. For these field-dependent persons perception of rod position is dictated by the context provided by the axes of the surrounding frame. They cannot keep rod separate from frame; in this sense their perception is global. Other subjects, at the opposite extreme, are able to adjust the rod more or less to the true upright, independently of frame position. These field-independent persons are able to perceive a part of the field as discrete from the field; in this sense, their perception is analytical.

Still another test of field dependence, the embedded-figures test, requires the subject to locate a simple figure in a complex design which is so organized as to conceal the simple figure. For some persons the simple figure almost "pops out" of the complex design. Their perception is field independent. Others are not able to find the simple figure within the 5 minutes allowed. Their perception is field dependent.

People tend to perform in a consistent fashion in these three tests. The individual who cannot separate the simple figure from the complex embedding design also cannot keep his body apart from the surrounding tilted room or the rod apart from the surrounding frame. Going beyond the particular tests I have described, this same individual is unable to keep item apart from context in a wide variety of other perceptual situations (including such classical ones as the constancies, illusions, reversible perspective) and in situations involving other sense modalities, as touch (Axelrod & Cohen, 1961). Such consistency is indicative of a stylistic tendency in perception.

The particular stylistic tendencies we have been considering are not limited to a person's perception; they manifest themselves, in congruent form, in his intellectual activities as well. Thus, persons whose perception is field dependent do less well at solving problems which require isolating essential elements from the context in which they are presented and using them in different contexts, as, for example, the tasks employed by Duncker in his studies of functional fixity.

It is because these stylistic tendencies extend across both perception, where we are dealing with an immediately present stimulus configuration, and intellectual functioning, where we are dealing with symbolic representations, that we refer to them as *cognitive* styles. The particular cognitive style we have been considering may be described as follows: At one extreme there is a consistent tendency for experience to be global and diffuse; the organization of the field as a whole dictates the manner in which its parts are experienced. At the other extreme there is a tendency for experience to be delineated and structured; parts of a field are experienced as discrete and the field as a whole organized. To these opposite poles of the cognitive style we may apply the labels "global" and "articulated." As with the dimension of perceptual field dependence, there is no implication here that the world is peopled by two kinds of human beings. Scores for any large group on tests of this cognitive style show a continuous distribution.

I may add that a more global or more articulated quality is a stable characteristic of an individual's cognitive functioning over time. There are also consistent sex differences in the articulation-global cognitive dimension. Boys and men show greater articulation than girls and women. Small but consistent sex differences in tests of field dependence have been found with groups in the United States, in a number of western European countries (see, e.g., Andrieux, 1955; Bennet, 1956; Chateau, 1959; Franks, 1956; Wit, 1955), and in Hong Kong,[1] Israel,[2] and Sierra Leone, Africa (Dawson, 1963) as well.

Evidence that the global-articulated style of cognitive function-

---

[1] Personal communication from Robert Goodnow.
[2] Personal communication from Martin Rothman and Joel H. Kaplan.

ing is part of a still broader dimension of personal functioning has come from studies of the relation of this cognitive style to nature of the body concept, of the self and of controls and defenses.

Articulation of Body Concept

Let me consider first our studies of the body concept—that is to say, the systematic impression an individual has of his body, cognitive and affective, conscious and unconscious. Our concern has been with the cognitive, rather than the libidinal aspects of the body concept, and with the articulated-global dimension in particular. In turning to the body concept, we are in effect shifting the spotlight from experience which has its primary source "out there," our main concern to this point, to experience which has its primary source "within." There is now considerable evidence that children and adults who show an articulated cognitive style in their performance in perceptual and intellectual tasks of the kind we have been considering are also likely to have an articulated body concept—that is to say, they experience their bodies as having definite limits or boundaries and the parts within as discrete yet interrelated and formed into a definite structure.

Performance in the body-adjustment test, itself, permits some inference about articulation of the body concept. Take, for example, the person who, in order to perceive his body as upright, aligns it with the titled room, and in that position reports no experience of tilt. Such a fusion of body and field in experience, or inability to keep body and field separate, suggests a lack of clear body boundaries.

In another, more familiar approach to study of the body concept, we have used the figure-drawing technique. To evaluate extent of articulation of drawings of human figures, made in response to the request to draw a person and then to draw a person of the opposite sex, a 5-point sophistication-of-body-concept scale was devised. This scale does not follow the usual projective uses of the figure-drawing technique but rather considers directly characteristics of the figures drawn. Three areas of the drawings are considered in making ratings: form level, identity or role and sex differentiation, and level of detailing. In a number of studies, scores for the figure-drawing test have been shown to relate significantly to measures of cognitive style. In the drawings of field-dependent children, we find very little detail and unrealistic representation of proportioning and of body parts. Sexual characteristics are shown minimally or not at all, so that in some pairs of drawings it is difficult to tell which is male and which is female. In most cases, there is no attempt at role representation. On the other hand, in the drawings of children whose perceptual performance is at the field-independent extreme we find the body drawn in realistic proportion. Parts of the body are presented in some detail and fairly realistically. There is clear representations of sex and sex differences. Aside from indication of sex through body characteristics, the sex of the figure is also indicated by such externals as clothing. We also find attempts at role representation, suggesting a sense of the uses to which the body may be put. These differences among children in the way in which they represent the body on paper are significantly related to how they perform in the cognitive tests in the laboratory.

It may appear from the description of the kinds of drawings they make that field-dependent children, who tend to make relatively unarticulated drawings, are just not as bright as field-independent children, who tend to make highly articulated drawings. Significant correlations are in fact found between figure-drawing articulation scores and total IQ. Several studies have shown, however, that this relation is carried mainly by particular subtests of standard intelligence tests which, like the cognitive tests we use, have the task requirement of separating item from context. These subtests are block design, picture completion, and object assembly which in past factor analytic studies of the Wechsler were shown to load what we would designate an "analytical factor" (Cohen, 1957, 1959). There are only low, nonsignificant relations between figure-drawing articulation scores and scores for the Wechsler vocabulary, information, and comprehension subtests which have been shown to define a "verbal-comprehension factor." I should mention that scores for tests of field dependence, similarly, relate very highly to scores for the triumvirate of block design, picture completion, and object assembly; and they do not relate to scores for the triumvirate of vocabulary, information, and comprehension (Goodenough & Karp, 1961; Karp, 1963).

The sophistication-of-body-concept scale is easily learned and applied, even by persons without experience in the figure-drawing technique. Checks on interjudge agreement in a number of studies have shown good reliability. And, as we have just seen, scores based on the scale relate well to scores of tests of the articulated-global cognitive dimension. These characteristics of the scale, together with the ease of obtaining figure drawings from subjects, make the scale a useful assessment technique.

Let me interpolate that other studies, using more experimental means to evaluate articulation, have confirmed the relation between articulation of body concept and cognitive style (Epstein, 1957; Silverman, Cohen, Shmavonian, & Greenberg, 1961).

Sense of Separate Identity

To continue, persons with a more articulated or more global mode of cognitive functioning also differ in an important aspect of the self, namely, sense of separate identity. Persons with an articulated cognitive style give evidence of a developed sense of separate identity—that is to say, they have an awareness of needs, feelings, attributes which they recognize as their own and which they identify as distinct from those of others. Sense of separate identity implies experience of the self as segregated. It also implies experience of the self as structured; internal frames of reference have been formed and are available as guides for definition of the self. The less developed sense of separate identity of persons with a global cognitive style manifests itself in reliance on external sources for definition of their attitudes, judgments, sentiments, and of their views of themselves.

The nature of this relation may be made clearer by considering a few studies from among the many that have been done in this area.

Konstadt and Forman (1965) observed that children with a global cognitive style, when taking a test under stress and so concerned about their performance, looked up at the *face* of the adult examiner about as twice as often as children with an articulated cognitive style. Similarly, Crutchfield, Woodworth, and Albrecht (1958) found that persons with a global cognitive style were relatively better at recognizing and recalling faces of people they had been with earlier. Messick and Damarin (1964) observed that field-dependent subjects showed greater incidental learning than field-independent subjects when the incidental material consisted of human faces; the relation is in the opposite direction with non-human incidental material (Witkin et al., 1962). These studies suggest that persons with a global style are particularly attentive to faces, the major source of cues as to what others are feeling and thinking. The reliance of persons with a global cognitive style on external sources for self-definition was demonstrated in quite a different way by Linton (1955). She found that in an autokinetic situation, such persons more often changed their judgment about movement of the point of light in conformance with the suggestion of a planted confederate. The results of these and numerous other studies may be summarized by saying that the person for whom the frame around the rod, or the room around his body, strongly influence the manner in which rod and body are experienced, is, similarly, strongly influenced by the immediate social context in his experience of himself.

I would like to mention here a recently completed study by Winestine (1964) on the "twinning reaction" of boy twins because of the particularly direct way in which sense of separate identity was evaluated. The twinning reaction, assessed by interview, was rated as strong for a given twin if in his specific attitudes, feelings, and actions he showed that he experienced himself as an integral part of the twinship rather than as individuated. Twins rated high on the twinning reaction were strikingly more field dependent and their representation of the body in their figure drawings much more global. In fact, so specific a characteristic as whether the twins dressed alike or differently proved to be significantly dis-.criminating with regard to both perceptual field dependence and nature of body concept in figure drawings. It would be of interest to study the parents of twins in relation to strength of the twinning reaction. We might expect that mothers of twins who show a weak twinning reaction and who are field independent to perceive their twins as separate individuals, rather than as a unit; to have a distinct relation with each child; and to foster the separation of the twins. These expectations are based on an earlier finding that mothers of more field-independent children, in their interactions with them, give their children greater opportunity for separation (Witkin et al., 1962).

Differences between field-dependent and field-independent persons, as a function of differences in sense of separate identity, have even been observed in characteristics of their dreams. In an experimental study of dreaming, using rapid eye movements and Stage-1 EEG sleep as indicators of the dream state,[3] observed that field-dependent subjects more often dreamed overtly about the laboratory situation. Moreover, in a recent analysis of the data from that study we found a difference between field-dependent and field-independent subjects in the kinds of incorporation they made. Field-dependent subjects more often had dreams concerned with their relation to the experimenter. Apparently these subjects get

---

[3] Unpublished manuscript from Helen B. Lewis, D. R. Goodenough, A. Shapiro, and I. Sleser, 1965.

"caught up" more with another person in the laboratory situation, as we have found they do in general, and these feelings are carried over into the dream.

Specialization of Defenses

Finally, let me comment on the relation between cognitive style and nature of defenses. Studies have shown that persons who experience in articulated fashion tend to use specialized defenses, as isolation. In contrast, persons with a global cognitive style tend to use such defenses as massive repression and primitive denial. These latter defenses involve an indiscriminate, total blotting out of memory for past experiences and of perception of stimuli. Compared to such mechanisms as isolation, they represent relatively nonspecific ways of functioning.

The contrasting kinds of defenses used by persons with a more global or more articulated cognitive style may be conceived in terms similar to those we used earlier in characterizing their cognitive functioning. In the last analysis, defenses help determine the content of a person's experience—what enters into consciousness and what is put aside. They do this, in part, through regulating the interrelation between affect, on the one hand, and ideation and perception on the other. It seems true of persons with a global cognitive style that feelings strongly influence thought and perception, in other words, that feelings are not kept sufficiently discrete from thoughts and percepts. This is congruent with what we saw happen within their perception, where again they are unable to "keep things separate"—as body separate from field, rod separate from frame, or simple figure separate from organized ground. Persons with an articulated cognitive style, in their use of isolation, maintain the discreteness of feelings and ideas, although the feeling component may be "split off."

This view of communality in mode of functioning in the areas of cognition and of defenses may be made more evident by considering a few representative studies.

Bertini (1961) carried out a study of the relation between cognitive style and defenses, following this view. He considered that the "capacity" to separate and isolate an idea from its emotional content, involved in the mechanism of isolation, parallels the capacity in field-independent perception to "separate several elements from the phenomenal field in isolating them from a context." To assess the use of isolation as a defense, Bertini relied on the Rorschach, basing his analysis on the work of Schafer (1954). The expectation that the tendency to use isolation would go with field-independent perception was confirmed.

A recent study by Minard[4] on perceptual defense effectively complements Bertini's study. Words matched in structure, and previously found in a free-association test to be neutral or charged for the particular subject, were presented tachistoscopically. Persons who were field dependent showed a considerable perceptual-defense effect; their speed of perception of words was markedly affected by whether or not the word carried an emotional connotation for them. Percept and feeling were, in other words, not kept separate. Field-independent persons showed no difference in speed of perception of neutral and charged words, suggesting discreteness of percept and feeling. In their use of denial and repression as characteristic defenses, persons with a global cognitive style are in effect showing a particularly extreme influence of feeling on percepts and memories. In these instances the total experience, including both its cognitive and affective components, is "split off."

A particularly striking example of this kind of complete blotting out of experience by field-dependent persons is found in their tendency to forget their dreams, presumably because of their use of repression as a characteristic defense. A connection between field dependence and dream recall has been found by Eagle[5] in one study of 10-year-olds and in another study of 17-year-olds. It has been observed by Linton[6] and Schonbar (1964) with groups of college students. More recently it was found again in an analysis we made of data from the study of Lewis et al. (see Footnote 6). Eight subjects at each extreme of the field-dependence dimension were picked from their total group of 46 college students. Considering frequency of dream reports in a home dream diary these subjects kept, seven of the eight most field-dependent subjects and only one of the eight most field-independent subjects were found to be "non-reporters"—that is, failed to recall dreams. Recent evidence from studies using rapid eye movement and Stage-1 EEG sleep as indicators of dreaming makes it entirely clear that everyone dreams a number of times each night (Aserinsky & Kleitman, 1953; Dement & Kleitman, 1957). A lack of dream reports is therefore indicative of a failure to recall dreams rather than a failure to dream.

The hypothesis that the failure of field-dependent persons to

[4] Personal communication from James Minard.
[5] Personal communication from Carol Eagle.
[6] Personal communication from Harriet Linton.

remember their dreams is, in part at least, a function of repression, is being tested in a study Donald Goodenough, Helen Lewis, Arthur Shapiro and I are carrying out. This study is making use of a technique Helen Lewis and I developed in an earlier preliminary study (Witkin & Lewis, in press). The technique consists of creating an important psychological event for the person just before he goes to sleep and obtaining his subsequent dreams by awakening him during each period of rapid eye movement and Stage-1 EEG. The presleep event we use consists, on some occasions, of viewing an emotionally charged film; on other occasions, viewing a neutral film; and on still other occasions, an encounter with another person through the medium of suggestion. The results of the preliminary study showed, first of all, that the presleep event often found expression in the subject's subsequent dreams in a clearly identifiable way. Further, reports from subjects that they had been dreaming, but could not remember the dream, occurred more often on awakenings following the exciting presleep event than on awakenings following the neutral presleep event. We anticipated this outcome on the premise that the exciting presleep event, by "charging" subsequent dreams, would make these dreams better "candidates for repression" and so reduce dream recall. In the study Goodenough, Lewis, Shapiro, and I are now doing we are following this same procedure of presleep stimulation, using field-dependent and field-independent persons as our subjects. It is our expectation that field-dependent persons will be more likely to "lose" dreams charged by an exciting presleep experience. Such an outcome would lend further support to the view that field-dependent persons tend to use repression as a typical mode of defense.

Summary of Indicators of Differentiation

Reviewing the evidence considered to this point, a tendency toward a more global or more articulated cognitive style has been shown to be associated with differences in body concept, in sense of separate identity, and in nature of defenses. It is now our view that the characteristics which make up the contrasting constellations described may be conceived as diverse manifestations of more developed or less developd psychological differentiation. Thus, we consider it more differentiated if, in his perception of the world, the person perceives parts of the field as discrete and the field as structured. We consider it more differentiated if, in his concept of his body, the person has a definite sense of the boundaries of the body and of the interrelation among its parts. We consider it more differentiated if the person has a feeling of himself as an individual distinct from others and has internalized, developed standards to guide his view of the world and of himself. We consider it more differentiated if the defenses the person uses are specialized. It is our view that these various characteristics, which we have found to cluster together, are not the end-products of development in separate channels, but are diverse expressions of an underlying process of development toward greater psychological complexity. "Level of differentiation" is a concept which encourages us to look across psychological areas and provides a basis for thinking about self-consistency in individual psychological make-up.

The level of differentiation at which a person functions may be assessed in different areas. For clinical evaluation one or several areas may be considered. It is perhaps best assessed through the person's cognitive style, where, as noted earlier, objective, experimental means of evaluation may be used. In this sense a person's cognitive style, in the articulated-global dimension, may be considered a "tracer element." Certainly, assessment of psychological differentiation need not be limited to the cognitive sphere. It may also be assessed effectively, for example, in the area of the body concept, by means of the figure-drawing sophistication-of-body-concept scale which I described earlier. In our own work, when we want to make a rapid assessment with regard to differentiation we use the embedded-figures test and figure-drawing test, both of which are easily administered and scored, but time permitting, we like to use the rod-and-frame test as well. If the Wechsler has been given, we use the score for the block-design subtest, which, as we saw, is very similar in its requirements to the tests of field dependence and is in fact a good test of field dependence.

Differentiation and Problems of Pathology

The concept of differentiation and the techniques devised to evaluate level of differentiation appear useful in both the conceptualization and the assessment of normal personality functioning. They have relevance to pathological functioning as well.

To make this clear, we need to consider the relation between differentiation and integration. Differentiation refers to the complexity of structure of a psychological system. One of the main characteristics of greater differentiation is specialization of function; another is clear separation of self from nonself. Integration refers particularly to the form of the functional relations among parts of a psychological system and between the system and its surroundings. At any level of differentiation varied modes of integration are possible, although more complex integrations may be expected with more developed differentiation. Adjustment is mainly a function of effectiveness of integration—that is, a more or less harmonious working together of parts of the system with each other and of the system as a whole with its environment.[7] Adequate adjustment is to be found at any level of differentiation, resulting from integrations effective for that level, although the nature of adjustment that may be considered adequate varies from level to level. Moreover, impaired integration, with resulting pathology, may also occur at all levels of differentiation. However, and this is of particular importance, impairment is likely to take different forms in relatively more differentiated and less differentiated personalities.

The evidence now clearly indicates that pathology occurs at both extremes of the differentiation dimension. In fact, there is some suggestion of greater frequency of pathology at the extremes than in the middle of the range. Further, pathology takes quite different forms at the two extremes. And the kinds of pathology that have been found at each extreme may be conceived as having the form which impaired integration is likely to take when more differentiated or less differentiated personalities break down. Let me illustrate this.

When personality disturbances occur among persons with a global cognitive style, and with other characteristics of limited differentiation associated with it, we are likely to find severe identity problems, with little struggle for maintenance of identity; symptoms often considered suggestive of deep-seated problems of dependence; inadequately developed controls, resulting in chaotic functioning; and passivity and helplessness. Several studies have demonstrated marked field dependence in clinical groups with symptoms commonly regarded as rooted in severe dependency problems, or in what we earlier called a lack of developed sense of separate identity. Alcoholics have been found to present a consistent picture of marked field dependence (Bailey, Hustmyer, & Kristofferson, 1961; Karp & Konstadt[8]; Karp, Poster, & Goodman, 1963; Karp, Witkin, & Goodenough, 1965a; Karp, Witkin, & Goodenough, 1965b; Witkin, Karp, & Goodenough, 1959). This picture

[7] Poorly developed differentiation may sometimes be a main source of psychopathology, as, for example, when the nervous system is inadequately formed. Such impairment hampers the development of the kinds of integration needed for adjustment to many life situations.
[8] Personal communication from Stephen A. Karp.

has been found among alcoholic men and alcoholic women; among current drinkers and among abstaining former drinkers; among alcoholics who are under the influence of alcohol and among alcoholics who are sober; among long-term drinkers and among relatively new drinkers. As another indicator of their limited differentiation, alcoholics also show a relatively global body concept in their figure drawings.

In addition to alcoholics, other clinical groups commonly conceived to suffer severe dependency problems, which also show marked field dependence, are ulcer patients (Gordon, 1953), obese people (Pardes & Karp, in press), and asthmatic children (Fishbein, 1958).

Other kinds of clinical groups observed to show a global cognitive style have included patients with an hysterical character structure (Zukmann, 1957) ; patients with character disorders—that is, generally inadequate personalities unable to manage the ordinary problems of living, patients who somatize their complaints and deny any psychological problems, patients whose primary symptom is affective discharge, rather than defensive symptom organization (Korchin[9]) ; patients with functional cardiac disorders (Soll, 1963) ; and catatonics (Janucci, 1964).

Taylor (1956) has shown that psychotics who hallucinate are more likely to be field dependent, as compared to delusional psychotics, who tend to be field independent. He predicted this outcome on the ground that hallucinatory states imply dissolution of ego boundaries, whereas delusional states represent attempts to maintain separate identity and ego integrity. Compared to hallucinations, delusions have a more logical structure and they do not represent as gross a fusion between self and nonself. In hallucinations, inner states often become indistinguishable from reality, reflecting reduction of ego-integrity and of sense of individuality to an infantile stage. Taylor's finding has recently been confirmed by Powell (1964).

A recent experimental study (Bertini, Lewis, & Witkin, 1964) in which we sought to induce a hypnagogic reverie state in normal subjects yielded results consistent with Taylor's. White noise was fed into the subject's ears and halves of ping-pong balls were placed over his open eyes creating a homogeneous visual field. Under these circumstances the subject was asked, while lying down, to keep on talking continuously, describing any thoughts, feelings, or images he might have. White noise, which creates a

[9] Personal communication from Sheldon Korchin.

continuous monotonous sound, has been generally known to facilitate drowsiness. It also reduces feedback from the subject's own voice and distorts the quality of the voice. A homogeneous field facilitates imagery and makes the images more plausible. Our subjects were college students, selected as being extremely field dependent or extremely field independent. Each subject was tested first under the conditions described and on another occasion immediately after viewing an exciting film. Preliminary observations suggest, as predicted, that field-dependent and field-independent subjects react quite differently to this experimental-hypnagogic procedure. Particularly relevant to the Taylor finding is the observation that field-dependent subjects more often reported vivid imagery. However bizarre the imagery, it had the quality of "actually being there," rather than of "being imagined." The reports of these field-dependent subjects suggest that the experience was one of being caught up in an ongoing scene. Of course, in contrast to Taylor's hallucinating patients, our subjects who had this imagery experience were able to tell it was not "real" even when it appeared very vivid to them. Another observation was that the hypnagogic reverie of field-dependent subjects, after viewing the exciting film, tended to be flooded with symbolic references to the film. The field-dependent subjects were also made more uneasy and even frightened by the experimental situation. Silverman, Cohen, Shmavonian and Greenberg (1961) have also reported greater "ego weakening" in field-dependent subjects under conditions of sensory isolation; and they report, as do Holt and Goldberger (1959), that field-dependent subjects more often experience imagery which appears to have an "outside" source. The indication that hallucinatorylike experiences are more readily induced in field-dependent persons, with accompanying feelings of severe discomfort, reflects on their weak ego boundaries.

Turning to the kinds of pathology encountered among differentiated persons, when they break down, we find that they tend to show delusions, expansive and euphoric ideas of grandeur, outward direction of aggression, overideation, and continuing struggle for the maintenance of identity, however bizarre the attempt. An articulated cognitive style has been found among paranoids (Janucci, 1964; Powell, 1964; Witkin et al., 1954), obsessive-compulsive characters (Zukmann, 1957), neurotics with organized symptom pictures, and those ambulatory schizophrenics who have a well-developed defensive structure (Korchin[10]).

[10] Personal communication from Sheldon Korchin.

It is not easy to work out precisely the linkages between extent of differentiation and forms of pathology. For one thing, the pathways by which particular kinds of pathology may emerge in a given personality setting are inordinately complex and difficult to trace; for another, level of differentiation is only one determinant, though an important one, of the course that pathological development may take. Moreover, present knowledge of the dynamics of various kinds of pathology is uncertain. Even with these difficulties, it seems possible to see, for at least some of the pathological states listed, why they may be expected in a setting of relatively developed differentiation, on the one hand, or limited differentiation, on the other.

As one illustration, we may speculate about some of the ways in which the characteristics of limitedly differentiated persons may make the development of obesity more likely among them. Their inadequately developed sense of separate identity makes it plausible that under stress they would seek comfort in oral activities that had been an important source of satisfaction in the period of close unity with mother. As a technique of defense for dealing with anxiety, eating is a nonspecialized defense. It is applied indiscriminately in a wide range of stressful situations, and it does not act in a specific, directed fashion upon the source of stress. In particular kinds of persons, it may suffuse the organism with an animal pleasure which blurs anxiety.

We may think along similar lines about alcoholism, a condition which, in its dynamic aspects, is often considered equivalent to obesity. The nonspecialized character of the defense which the use of alcohol represents is particularly clear. Alcohol is resorted to when stress becomes too great, regardless of the source of the stress, and it seems to affect experience in general, not only the part responsible for the anxiety. If the drinking is carried far enough, the self, which to begin with is limitedly differentiated, may be temporarily obliterated.

Obviously, a symptom like alcoholism is only one of many possible "choices" of pathology open to the relatively undifferentiated person when integration is impaired. Reflecting the possibility that the same symptom may be achieved by different dynamic routes, we must note that alcoholism may also sometimes, though rarely, be the choice of relatively differentiated persons. Although we have found that alcoholics who perform in a field-independent fashion are quite uncommon, their very existence points to the need for seeking other routes to the development of alcoholism than the one considered. Cognitive style may be a means of differential diagnosis of these different kinds of alcoholics. And it is possible that through the cognitive style approach other presumably homogeneous diagnostic categories may be broken down and diagnostic classification thereby refined.

A final illustration may be found in patients in whom paranoid reactions are central in the symptom picture. In this patient group, an articulated cognitive style is frequently found. Projection, a characteristic defense of the paranoid, is quite specialized, in comparison to such generalized tension-reducing techniques as eating and drinking. The paranoid projects his own system of ideas upon the world, and does so in a highly selective fashion—particular people, particular situations may be especially implicated. Such selectivity requires that experience of the world be articulated. In this connection, the paranoid is noted for his detailed, articulated system of ideas. As an attempt at preservation of the self, projection contrasts with the alcoholic's preferred way of dealing with stress, which in extreme cases results in the dissolution of the self in drink. The use of projection as a device for self-preservation, however bizarre, presupposes a self that has achieved some degree of differentiation.

These illustrations, though sketchy, suggest some of the ways in which level of differentiation may help determine form of pathology.

Although cognitive style, and associated characteristics of more developed and less developed differentiation, relate to particular symptoms and symptom pictures, they do not relate to major conventional nosological categories, as neuroses and schizophrenia (Bound, 1951; Franks, 1956). Among hospitalized psychiatric patients we found cases diagnosed "schizophrenic" scattered throughout the distribution of measures of perceptual field dependence (Witkin et al., 1954). Bennett (1956) and Bailey et al. (1961) have reported similar results.[11] There is no contradiction in the finding that cognitive style relates to symptoms but not to conventional nosological categories. Nosological categories are, in varying degree, based on symptoms, dynamics, and etiology. There is further a lack of consistency with which nosological categories are

---

[11] Cognitive style does, however, seem to relate to kind of schizophrenia. As noted, paranoids tend to be field independent (Janucci, 1964; Witkin et al., 1954). On the other hand, catatonics tend to be field dependent (Janucci, 1964). Bryant (1961) has found process schizophrenics to be significantly more field dependent than reactive schizophrenics, although this finding was not confirmed by Cancro (1962).

applied in assessment. On the other hand, to the extent that a given symptom is the end-product of particular dynamic processes, it may serve to identify these processes. Classification in terms of particular symptom pictures is therefore likely to bring together persons with common underlying dynamic processes. Although symptoms are the main basis of classification in some diagnostic categories, in many instances classification on the basis of symptoms may transcend common diagnostic categories. For example, depression may be a major symptom regardless of whether the overall diagnosis is neurosis, schizophrenia, reactive depression, etc.

The finding that cognitive style, which mirrors a deep aspect of psychological makeup, cuts across some of the conventional nosological categories is consistent with the growing shift in clinical classification from an emphasis on behavior to an emphasis on dynamic characterization. Cognitive style may thus offer one potentially useful basis for clarifying nosological problems.

That cognitive style may relate to deeper levels of functioning, and so go beyond manifest behavior, is indicated in an interesting way in a study by Gordon (1953). Gordon found ulcer patients to be markedly field dependent; and he also found significant agreement between their field-dependence scores and ratings made of them by their physicians on a specially devised dependency scale. However, ratings of dependence by the patients themselves, using the same scale, did *not* relate to their field-dependence scores. (Let me interpolate here that, for a comparison group of neurotics, field-dependence measures, physician's ratings of dependence and self-ratings of dependence were all significantly interrelated.)

In interpreting these findings for the ulcer patients, it is of special interest that on the dependency scale they rated themselves as more independent than did their physicians. The direction of the discrepancy between self-ratings of dependency, on the one hand, and physician's ratings and field-dependence measures, on the other hand, seems to suggest that, although tending to be very dependent, these patients viewed themselves as relatively independent. A common clinical view of the ulcer patient is of an overstriving person who, through his striving, is seeking to compensate for deep-seated passivity and persistent dependency needs (see for example, Alexander, 1950). He seeks to make himself appear, both to himself and to others, as more active than he is, and as capable of functioning independently of external support. Such an interpretation would be consistent with Gordon's results. It is thus possible that an individual's cognitive style may "penetrate" his apparent assertiveness and reflect the strong underlying passivity and need for external support.

Findings such as these suggest again that assessment of cognitive style may, in particular instances, be of aid in differential diagnosis.

The differentiation concept seems to provide a useful approach to the study of differences among people in directions of pathological development and in choice of symptoms. At the present time, however, it is more useful in understanding the basis of differences in general classes of pathology and symptom formation than in understanding of "choices" within a general class. For example, as we saw, both alcoholics and obese people tend to be extremely field dependent. The question remains as to why some limitedly differentiated people choose drinking as their main symptom while others choose overeating. To answer this question, intensive study of individual cases, showing such symptoms, is required, with attention given to specific patterns of integration, to particular content aspects of personality, and to nature of life circumstances. As an illustration of how these may be important, the suggestion has been made that an individual's personal values, derived from his cultural group, may place a taboo on drinking and so make overeating a more likely symptom choice.

I have tried in this discussion of pathology to suggest that the characteristics of relatively greater or more limited differentiation may play a role in channeling pathological development. It follows from this view that the techniques devised to evaluate level of differentiation in various areas—and particularly in the area of cognitive functioning—may contribute to a more discriminating assessment of psychopathology.

The cognitive style approach has promise for the study of another kind of pathology—mental retardation. Its value is demonstrated by the results of a study we recently completed with two groups of high grade retarded boys (Witkin, Faterson, Goodenough, & Birnbaum, in press). One group consisted of "teachable" institutionalized retarded boys in the 60-80 IQ range; the other group consisted of boys in the same IQ range but living at home and attending public school classes for the mentally retarded. All the boys were given the Wechsler, tests of perceptual field dependence and the figure-drawing test. We found, first of all, that the pattern of relation among test measures in both retarded groups was similar to that previously observed in normals. Thus, measures of perceptual field dependence for the retarded boys were related to pro-rated "analytical IQs" (based, it will be recalled, on the Wechsler block design, picture completion, and object assembly subtests) ; they did not relate to pro-rated "verbal-comprehension IQs" (based on the vocabulary, information, and comprehension subtests). Again paralleling previous findings for normals, measures of analytical competence both from tests of field dependence and from the Wechsler scales were related to figure-drawing measures of articulation of body concept.

A second finding of interest was a marked and pervasive discrepancy in level of functioning between the analytical and verbal-comprehension clusters. Thus, on the Wechsler scales, almost all the retarded boys showed a pattern of extremely poor performance on the triumvirate of verbal-comprehension subtests and relatively much better performance on the triumvirate of analytical subtests. The discrepancy in cognitive functioning that seems to exist in these retarded boys is much sharper when the verbal-comprehension and analytical pro-rated IQs are compared than when the usual Verbal and Performance IQs are compared. Thus, in the group of institutionalized retarded boys the pro-rated verbal-comprehension and analytical IQs were 61.2 and 80.8, respectively, whereas the Verbal and Performance IQs were 71.1 and 76.3.

The frequency of occurrence of cases with relatively high analytical ability and relatively low verbal-comprehension ability in groups now identified as retarded may be the result of "routing" of children on the basis of particular emphasis upon verbal skills. If we consider children as nature made them, rather than as they are defined by Wechsler performance, we may expect to find a great many different kinds of cognitive patterns among them, with the possibility as well of deficits in one or more cognitive areas. Children with a deficit in verbal skills, whatever other cognitive strengths they may have, are especially likely to come to attention in the family, in society and in school; and on standard intelligence tests they are likely to earn a low IQ because of the emphasis on subtests involving verbal skills in the total IQ. On the other hand, we may speculate, children with other kinds of cognitive deficit than a verbal one, and who function at an overall level similar to those now commonly classified as retarded, do not come to attention as readily. Though not classified as retarded by the standards currently used in our society, such children may be as handicapped in their cognitive and personality functioning as those now labelled "retarded," but in different ways.

A cognitive-style approach to the understanding and assessment of the retarded has clear advantages over an IQ approach. In particular the cognitive-style approach offers a more comprehensive and complex view of cognitive functioning than does the IQ. It has a more developed conceptual rationale, it encompasses broader segments of cognitive functioning, and it recognizes the rooting of intellectual characteristics in personality.[12]

Differentiation and Problems of Therapy

Problems of assessment arise in a particularly complex and interesting way in the area of therapy. Persons functioning at a more differentiated or less differentiated level may be expected to differ predictably with regard to their attitudes toward psychotherapy, and their performance in the psychotherapy situation, in ways that are likely to affect the course of therapy. I would like to consider several of the specific areas in which differences may be anticipated. In some of these areas, studies are under way that I can tell you about; for other areas I can only specify the issues involved.

One important area is the nature of presenting symptoms. Our earlier discussion of forms of pathology in relation to extent of differentiation is of course relevant here.

A second area is suitability for psychological forms of therapy. Several studies have shown that therapists are not likely to accept

---

[12] Another illustration of the usefulness of the cognitive-style approach in understanding and evaluating groups with developmental deficits is found in a study we made of blind children (Witkin, 1965). Using nonvisual tests of perceptual field dependence and of analytical functioning in problem solving we were able to demonstrate that blind children, like normals, show a wide range of individual differences along the global-articulated cognitive dimension. It is of special significance for the problem of assessment that children of the same level on the verbal components of the Wechsler, to which testing of the blind is necessarily limited, differed in the extent to which their performance on our cognitive test battery showed a more global or articulated style. Assessment of the blind has, understandably, placed great emphasis on verbal kinds of performance, resulting, in some cases, in an unrepresentative and even misleading picture of their cognitive make-up. The possibility of adding tests of cognitive style to existing test procedures offers the promise of a more comprehensive cognitive evaluation of the blind. Thus, the demonstration that measures of perceptual field dependence relate highly to Wechsler analytical subtest scores, which cannot be obtained from the blind, means that through nonvisual tests of field dependence, measures of this area of Wechsler performance may be obtained. Moreover, to the extent that an individual's cognitive style carries a message about his personality functioning, opportunities for assessing personality, which are again severely limited in the blind, may be opened up.

field-dependent patients for psychotherapy; they are more apt to recommend them for somatic forms of therapy. There thus seems to be considerable agreement between the performance of a particular patient on the rod-and-frame test and the judgment independently made by the therapist about that patient. The significance of this finding needs to be explored further; its pursuit may help us in identifying more precisely the criteria used in decisions about suitability for therapy, and in determining the validity of these criteria.

A judgment that needs to be made as a prelude to deciding whether a given patient is suitable for psychotherapy is the nature of the problems he is likely to present in the course of therapy. There can be little doubt, from the characterizations given earlier, that more differentiated and less differentiated patients are likely to differ in the difficulties encountered with them. But it is hard to accept the idea that the one kind of patient is amenable to psychotherapy and the other not. Even if there is some difference between them in this respect, it may very well be that each will benefit from quite different treatment procedures. Perhaps the core issue is not suitability for psychotherapy, but which form of psychotherapy for which kind of patient. Focusing on the kinds of therapy that may help persons who show the characteristics associated with field dependence may aid us in finding ways of treating at least some of the field-dependent patients who now seem to be rejected en masse.

As a related point, we have the impression—and it is only an impression at this point—that field-dependent persons are less likely to present themselves as candidates for psychotherapy. I am sure that this relation, if substantiated, will turn out to have quite a complex basis. One factor that may be involved is the tendency of field-dependent persons, noted earlier, to somatize their difficulties. On this basis, we would be more likely to pick up psychologically disturbed field-dependent patients at medical than at psychiatric clinics. Another factor may be that relatively undifferentiated persons are not as active in seeking help of an out-patient kind.

A third aspect of psychotherapy in which more differentiated and less differentiated patients may differ is in the nature of their relation to the therapist—that is, in the transference. Freedman (1962) has observed that field-dependent patients are likely to "feel better" earlier than field-independent patients, although the improvement is not maintained. We are now doing a study to check the idea that this difference is a function of differences in manner of relating to the therapist. We may speculate that the easier "fusion" of the less differentiated patient with another person, dictated by his limited sense of separate identity, manifests itself in his relation to the therapist as we know it does in his everyday relations with people. This fusion represents, in salient ways, a return to an earlier state—that of unity with mother—which, as our studies of family background suggest, such persons may not have outgrown. The reestablishment of this state may itself make such persons feel better without any real problems having been worked through. In addition to this transference effect, it may be expected that less differentiated patients are likely to be more accepting of the therapist's suggestions and interpretations, again with the consequence that they would feel better. On the other side, relatively differentiated patients are apt to be more cautious in the development of their relation to the therapist, and to filter the therapist's suggestions through their own structured systems of feelings and values.

In a study Helen Lewis, Edmund Weil, and I are now doing we are examining the development of the patient-therapist relation, in a small group of patients, in the course of the first 20 sessions of therapy. Our patients were at the extremes of the differentiation dimension, selected from a large outpatient clinic population who received our tests as part of the initial clinic screening. Each participating therapist was assigned one highly differentiated and one relatively undifferentiated patient. The therapist knew nothing of our findings on his patients. All therapy sessions were tape-recorded.

The data-gathering phase of this study has been completed, but the microscopic analysis of the records, required to check out hypotheses about differences in patient-therapist relations at the two extremes, is still under way. The kinds of specific issues we are examining in our study of the transcripts of the therapy sessions, bearing on these hypotheses, include the patient's expectations of the therapist—for example, "you will make me better" versus "you will help me figure things out so I can think straight"; the patient's reaction to the therapist's suggestions—for example, whether readily accepting or circumspect; the speed with which the patient establishes an overt bond with the therapist; the patient's ability to keep separate the transference and the reality of the doctor-patient relationship.

Though the focus in this study is on the patient's contribution to the patient-therapist relation, inevitably we are dealing with an interaction to which both participants contribute. That characteristics of the therapist himself are important and need to be considered is demonstrated in an interesting way in a study by Pollack and Kiev (1963). This study showed that psychiatrists who tested extremely field independent on our perceptual tests tended to favor either a directive and instructional or a passive observational approach to their patients in therapy, whereas relatively more (though not extremely) field-dependent therapists favored personal and mutual relations with their patients. The importance of considering the patient-therapist relation in interaction terms is indicated by an observation we made of frequency of comments by the therapist in the course of a therapy session. Therapists made strikingly more comments with limitedly differentiated patients than with highly differentiated patients (in the first session, for example, about three times as many) ; but at the same time therapists seemed to differ among themselves in frequency of making comments, whatever kind of patient they were treating.

Obviously, for each comment by the therapist, made at his initiative, there is a patient comment in reaction, and vice-versa. Accordingly, another way of stating the finding on frequency of comments is that there are many more patient-therapist interactions per session on the side of relatively undifferentiated patients than on the side of differentiated patients. An analysis we made of transcripts of the first therapy session indicates a variety of reasons for this difference, reflecting differences in interaction that might be expected from already known differences between more differentiated and less differentiated persons. Thus, among undifferentiated patients we find some of whom the therapist had to ask many specific questions in order to obtain the information he wanted, and the patient's responses were typically very brief. The outcome, of course, was a large number of interactions per session. Other undifferentiated patients showed a state of diffuse excitement, spurting out in a pressured way accounts of their pervasive difficulties, troubled feelings, and inadequacies.[13] Though in contrast to the

---

13 This behavior reflects strong open feelings of shame; such feelings seem prevalent among undifferentiated patients and less common (at least in open form) among differentiated ones. It may very well be that the "teeth pulling" in the first kind of undifferentiated patient may also have strong feelings of shame as one of its bases.

14 The rod-and-frame test is the only one of our tests of field dependence which seems to show no practice effect. It is therefore our best test for studies which require repeated testing, as this longitudinal study. The correlations are

first kind of undifferentiated patients these patients "pour out" a great deal, what they tell often comes in eruptive spurts, involves a great deal of repetition, and requires "containment" by the therapist. To obtain the information he wants, the therapist may still need to ask many questions, again making for many interactions.

Obviously, with both the "teeth-pulling" behavior and the "spilling" behavior observed on the undifferentiated side, considerable participation by the therapist is required for the therapist to obtain the information he wants about the patient's difficulties. In contrast, differentiated patients typically came to the first session with an articulated account of their problems and their ideas about the sources of these problems, whether dynamically correct or not. Sometimes their "opening presentation" gave the impression of a prepared statement. One of these patients actually brought with him a letter he had written to his wife about himself, which he proceeded to read to the therapist. Because such presentations may go on at great length sometimes even bypassing the therapist's occasional attempts at intervention, the result is a small number of total interactions per session.

Another characteristic of some undifferentiated patients which contributes to a large frequency of interactions is their ready acceptance of the therapist's suggestions, sometimes in a single phrase of agreement ("You're right, doctor.") or a repetition of part of the therapist's statement. The tendency among more differentiated patients to qualify their agreement with the therapist's proposals or to disagree with them, sometimes at great length, of course makes for a smaller total number of interactions in the session. Another feature of the behavior of some undifferentiated patients contributing to a greater frequency of interactions is their attempt to prolong the hour out of feelings of separation anxiety; this has even been observed in the very first hour. An occasional differentiated patient may also resist the ending of the session, but where this has been found it was because the patient was interrupted in the midst of a developed account he was presenting and which he was intent on completing. Still another phenomenon observed in some undifferentiated patients, which again increases number of interactions, is their repeated solicitation of support from the therapist. ("Do you think I'm mentally ill, doctor, from the way I'm talking?" "Is this normal with a person?" "Did you

based on scores for the body-erect condition of the test, a shortened version of the test we now use.

come across anybody who had this, doctor? (Yes) Have you helped them?") Such solicitation was not evident in the first-session transcripts of differentiated patients.

We are now devising ways of pursuing these observations systematically. First, we are attempting to establish criteria for identifying meaningful units of patient-therapist interaction. Second, we are working out methods of evaluating such units with regard to the variables I outlined.

A final aspect of psychotherapy we may consider is the achievement of change. The issue of change in therapy arises in two ways. First, will the characteristics of more developed or less developed differentiation themselves change in the course of therapy? Second, is the potential for change related to initial level of differentiation?

As for the first question, we are inclined to expect that the cluster of characteristics subsumed under differentiation, and the cognitive-style component in particular, are not likely to change with therapy. We expect this mainly because formal features of an individual's psychological make-up, of the kind represented by differentiation, are likely to show considerable stability as compared to content features.

There are already several lines of evidence from areas other than therapy, which support the expectation of marked relative stability of level of differentiation. Stability has been found even over long periods of time and in the face of strenuous attempts to bring about change.

First, longitudinal studies we have done demonstrate considerable relative stability during the growth years in characteristics of differentiation we have thus far examined. In one study we followed a group of boys for 14 years, testing them at ages 10, 14, 17, and 24. Of the 30 boys first seen at age 10, we were still able to obtain 28 for testing at age 24. Considering group means, there was a change in the group as a whole, over the 14-year span, toward greater field independence and a more articulated body concept. At the same time, test-retest correlations were high, indicating that children who show more developed differentiation in the areas considered at one age, compared to their group, tend to have the same relative standing at other ages as well. Test-retest correlations for the rod-and-frame test[14] for various age combinations were: 10 versus 14, .75; 10 versus 17, .80; 10 versus 24, .66; 14 versus 17, .93; 14 versus 24, .86; and 17 versus 24, .93 (all significant). Test-retest correlations for figure-drawing sophistication-of-body-concept scores were equally high: 10 versus 14, .84; 10

versus 17, .79; 10 versus 24, .64; 14 versus 17, .67; 14 versus 24, .67; 17 versus 24, .68 (all significant). This evidence of stability is particularly impressive since a 14-year period was covered, and, moreover, a period when the child enters many new areas of life, when important new needs within himself are emerging, and when ways of coping with these new life circumstances and needs are being developed.

Comparable longitudinal data for adults (Bauman, 1951) again show striking stability in characteristics of differentiation over time. The test-retest correlations after a 3-year interval, for Bauman's group of young men, were .84 for rod-and-frame test scores and .86 for figure-drawing sophistication-of-body-concept scores (both significant).

Another kind of evidence of stability comes from studies which showed that the articulated-global cognitive style could not be changed by experimental intervention. The methods used in an attempt to bring about change have included drug administration (Karp, Witkin & Goodenough, 1965b; Pollack, Kahn, Karp & Fink, 1960), electro-convulsive shock (Pollack et al., 1960), stress due to anticipated heart surgery (Kraidman, 1959), special training (Gruen, 1955, Witkin, 1948), hypnosis.[15] Consistent with these results, Bauman (1951) found no difference in test-retest stability, over a 3-year period, between subjects who underwent important changes in life circumstances (as marriage, divorce, psychotherapy) and subjects who did not.[16]

---

[15] Personal communication from Rochelle M. Wexler.

[16] There is another kind of evidence, less direct in nature, which suggests that perceptual field dependence may be under some degree of genetic control. With the ultimate aim of studying neurophysiological correlates of this perceptual dimension, and the effect of radical variations in early sensory and social experience upon its development, we have undertaken studies of field dependence in monkeys. Preliminary results with an embedded-figures type of task devised for monkeys show that at least some of these animals are quite adept at even difficult perceptual disembedding tasks (Rosenblum, Witkin, Kaufman, & Brosgole, 1965). This finding is perhaps not surprising when we consider that disembedding may be a perceptual function of great adaptive significance. Under feral conditions survival may depend on the ability to separate quickly from the complex visual and auditory fields in which the animal lives those sights and sounds which signify danger, food, etc. Functions which have such survival value, and which may therefore have been selected for, may well be under at least partial genetic control. In biological time man is not so very far away from his feral existence so that such genetic control may still exist in him. Stafford (1963) has recently presented some evidence which suggests that the capacity to perform tasks similar to those used to evaluate perceptual field dependence is under the influence of a recessive gene on the X chromosome (one of the sex chromosomes). Also

The nature of differentiation as a structural aspect of personality, and the stability of relative level of differentiation over time and with experimental intervention, lead us to think that the characteristics of differentiation may not change with psychotherapy. A check on this expectation remains to be carried out. It would be of particular interest to examine change with the most probing form of therapy now in use—psychoanalysis.

Let me turn now to the second question I raised about change in therapy—namely, whether more differentiated and less differentiated patients may differ in their potential for change. Even if it turns out that cognitive style and associated characteristics of differentiation themselves remain more or less stable during therapy, we may of course expect other important features of personality to change. A variety of modes of integration is possible at any level of differentiation. Reintegrations, leading to salient alterations in personality, may take place with a given level of differentiation fundamentally maintained. In this connection the children in our longitudinal studies, though presenting a stable picture with regard to relative level of differentiation, showed many important personality changes during the time we studied them. To answer the question of whether potential for change during therapy, of whatever kind, is at all a function of level of differentiation we must consider the dimension of "fixity-mobility" which relates to differentiation in a very complex way, and may actually cut across the differentiation dimension.

Our clinical observations strongly suggest that some persons who are field independent and show other characteristics of developed differentiation function consistently at a highly differentiated level, whereas, others vary more according to circumstances and inner state. The first kind of subject shows "fixity" of functioning, the second shows "mobility." The perceptual tasks we devised to assess cognitive style, by design, press the subject to perform analytically if he possibly can.[17] They therefore do not

---

relevant here is the observation that Turner women, who lack one of the two X chromosomes of normal women, are consistently and extremely field dependent as indicated by their very poor performance on the analytical triumvirate of Wechsler subtests (Shafer, 1962). These observations, if substantiated, are of particular interest in view of the repeated finding of significant sex differences in field dependence under a wide range of cultural conditions.

[17] For example, in the embedded-figures test the subject, on each trial, is told if this choice of the simple figure is incorrect, and he is required to continue his search for 5 minutes if he does not find it before then.

permit us to distinguish between these two kinds of subjects. Cognitive tests may of course be devised which leave it to the option of the subject to function at his maximum analytical capacity or not. Results of a study by Perez (1955), using a brightness constancy situation, suggest that with instructions which pushed them toward an analytical attitude subjects identified as field independent tended to perform in a consistently field-independent fashion; with instructions which encouraged a global attitude they varied more with respect to extent of field independence.

We may venture the prediction that patients who are relatively differentiated (and in this sense have developed resources available to them), and who at the same time show "mobility," would be the best candidates for change. On the other hand, undifferentiated personalities, whose resources are limited and who patently cannot have great "mobility," would be the least likely candidates for change. It is further possible that patients who are intermediate in the range of measures of differentiation are in general more amenable to change than highly differentiated patients. This view, which remains to be checked, is based on the clinical impression that the latter group is likely to include relatively more patients with limited "mobility."[18]

Obviously, differentiation is only part of what must be considered in evaluating change in therapy. Should it turn out that cognitive style, for example, does not change, it would be of considerable interest. For a comprehensive view of the accomplishments of therapy we need to know what changes as well as what does not change. Changes in given characteristics may have a different meaning when occurring in the context of presence or absence of change in other characteristics.

I hope this account has helped suggest some of the ways in which the concept of differentiation, and the technique we have devised for the assessment of differentiation, may prove useful to the clinician in the problems he faces in his work in diagnosis and therapy.

[18] Numerous studies have shown that greater authoritarianism (as measured by the F scale) goes with greater field dependence (see, for example, Jackson, 1955; Linton, 1952; Pollack et al., 1960; Rudin & Stagner, 1958). An unpublished study by Mednick suggests, however, that the relation may be nonlinear; both field-dependent and field-independent persons seem to score higher for authoritarianism than intermediates. In view of the personal characteristics associated with F scale scores, it seems reasonable to consider these scores as rough indicators of "fixity" or "mobility."

REFERENCES

Alexander, F. *Psychosomatic medicine*. New York: Norton, 1950.

Andrieux, C. Contribution a l'étude des differences entre hommes et femmes dans la perception spatiale. *L'annee Psychologique*, 1955, 55, 41-60.

Aserinsky, E., & Kleitman, N. Regularly occurring periods of eye motility and concomitant phenomena during sleep. *Science*, 1953, 118, 273.

Axelrod, S., & Cohen, L. D. Senescence and embedded-figures performance in vision and touch. *Perceptual & Motor Skills*, 1961, 12, 283-288.

Bailey, W., Hustmyer, F., & Kristofferson, A. Alcoholism, brain damage and perceptual dependence. *Quarterly Journal of Studies on Alcohol*, 1961, 22, 387-393.

Bauman, G. The stability of the individual's mode of perception, and of perception-personality relationships. Unpublished doctoral dissertation, New York University, 1951.

Bennett, D. H. Perception of the upright in relation to body image. *Journal of Mental Science*, 1956, 102, 487-506.

Bertini, M. Il tratto difensivo dell'isolamento nella sua determinazione dinamica et strutturale. *Contributi dell' Istituto di Psicologica*, 1961, Serie XXV. (Milano: Univer. Cattolica)

Bertini, M., Lewis, Helen B., & Witkin, H. A. Some preliminary observations with an experimental procedure for the study of hypnagogic and related phenomena. *Archivio di psicologia, neurologia e psichiatria*, 1964, xxv(6), 495-534.

Bound, Mae M. A study of the relationship between Witkin's indices of field dependency and Eysenck's indices of neuroticism. Unpublished doctoral dissertation, Purdue University, 1951.

Bryant, A. R. An investigation of process-reactive schizophrenia with relation to perception of visual space. Unpublished doctoral dissertation, University of Utah, 1961.

Cancro, R. A comparison of process and reactive schizophrenia. Unpublished doctoral dissertation, State University of New York Downstate Medical Center, 1962.

Chateau, J. Le test de structuration spatiale TIB. I. S. *Le travail humain*, 1959, 22, 281-297.

Cohen, J. The factorial structure of the WAIS between early adulthood and old age. *Journal of Consulting Psychology*, 1957, 21, 283-290.

Cohen, J. The factorial structure of the WISC at ages 7-6, 10-6, and 13-6. *Journal of Consulting Psychology*, 1959, 23, 285-299.

Crutchfield, R. S., Woodworth, D. G., & Albrecht, Ruth E. Perceptual performance and the effective person. Lackland AFB, Texas, *USAF WADC tech. Note*, 1958, No. 58-60.

Dawson, J. L. M. Psychological effects of social change in a West African community. Unpublished doctoral dissertation, University of Oxford, 1963.

Dement, W., & Kleitmen, N. The relation of eye movements during sleep to dream activity: An objective method for the study of dreaming. *Journal of Experimental Psychology*, 1957, **53**, 339-346.

Epstein, L. The relationship of certain aspects of the body image to the perception of the upright. Unpublished doctoral dissertation, New York University, 1957.

Fishbein, G. M. Perceptual modes and asthmatic symptoms: An application of Witkin's hypothesis. *Journal of Consulting Psychology*, 1963, **27**, 54-58.

Franks, C. M. Differences déterminées par le personalité dans la perception visuelle de la verticalité. *Revue de Psychologique Appliques*, 1956, **6**, 235-246.

Freedman, N. The process of symptom modification in psychopharmacological therapy. Paper presented at Department of Psychiatry meeting, State University of New York Downstate Medical Center, Brooklyn, New York, 1962.

Goodenough, D. R., & Karp, S. A. Field dependence and intellectual functioning. *Journal of Abnormal and Social Psychology*, 1961, **63**, 241-246.

Gordon, B. An experimental study of dependence-independence in a social and a laboratory setting. Unpublished doctoral dissertation, University of Southern California, 1953.

Gruen, A. The relation of dancing experience and personality to perception. *Psychological Monographs*, 1955, **69** (14, Whole No. 399).

Holt, R. R., & Goldberger, L. Personological correlates of reactions to perceptual isolation. *WADC tech. Rep.*, 1959, No. 59-735.

Jackson, D. N. Stability in resistance to field forces. Unpublished doctoral dissertation, Purdue University, 1955.

Jannucci, Gloria I. Size constancy in schizophrenia: A study of subgroup differences. Unpublished doctoral dissertation, Rutgers State University, 1964.

Karp, S. A. Field dependence and overcoming embeddedness. *Journal of Consulting Psychology*, 1963, **27**, 294-302.

Karp, S. A., Poster, Dorothy, & Goodman, A. Differentiation in alcoholic women. *Journal of Personality*, 1963, **31**(3), 386-393.

Karp, S. A., Witkin, H. A., & Goodenough, D. R. Alcoholism and psychological differentiation: Effect of achievement of sobriety on field dependence. *Quarterly Journal of Studies on Alcohol*, 1965, in press. (a)

Karp, S. A., Witkin, H. A., & Goodenough, D. R. Alcoholism and psychological differentiation: The effect of alcohol on field dependence. *Journal of Abnormal Psychology*, 1965, **70**, 262-265.

Konstadt, Norma, & Forman, Elaine. Field dependence and external directedness. *Journal of Personality & Social Psychology*, 1965, **1**, 490-493.

Kraidman, Emma.   Developmental analysis of conceptual and perceptual functioning under stress and non-stress conditions. Unpublished doctoral
dissertation, Clark University, 1959.

Linton, Harriet B.   Relations between mode of perception and tendency to
conform. Unpublished doctoral dissertation, Yale University, 1952.

Linton, Harriet B.   Dependence on external influence: Correlates in perception, attitudes, and judgement. *Journal of Abnormal & Social Psychology*,
1955, **51**, 502-507.

Messick, S., & Damarin, F.   Cognitive styles and memory for faces. *Journal
of Abnormal & Social Psychology*, 1964, **69**, 313-318.

Pardes, H., & Karp, S. A.   Field dependence in obese women. *Psychosomatic
Medicine*, 1965, **27**, 238-244.

Perez, P.   Experimental instructions and stimulus content as variables in the
size constancy perception of schizophrenics and normals. Unpublished
doctoral dissertation, New York University, 1955.

Pollack, M., Kahn, R. L., Karp, E., & Fink, M.   Individual differences in the
perception of the upright in hospitalized psychiatric patients. Paper
read at Eastern Psychological Association, New York, 1960.

Pollack, I. W., & Kiev, A.   Spatial orientation and psychotherapy: An experimental study of perception. *Journal of Nervous & Mental Disease*, 1963,
137(1), 93-97.

Powell, B. J.   A study of the perceptual field approach of normal subjects
and schizophrenic patients under conditions of an oversize stimulus.
Unpublished doctoral dissertation, Washington University, 1964.

Rosenblum, L. A., Witkin, H. A., Kaufman, I. C., & Brosgole, L.   Perceptual
disembedding in monkeys: A note on method and preliminary findings.
Perceptual & Motor Skills, 1965, **20**, 729-736.

Rudin, S. A., & Stagner, R.   Figure-ground phenomena in the perception of
physical and social stimuli. *Journal of Psychology*, 1958, 45, 213-225.

Schafer, R.   *Psychoanalytic interpretation in Rorschach testing*. New York:
Grune & Stratton, 1954.

Sohonbar, Rosalea, A.   Some dimensions of sensitivity of recallers and non-
recallers of dreams. In (Chm.), Dream research and theory. Symposium
presented at the Postgraduate Center for Mental Health, March 14, 1964.

Shafer, J. W.   A specific cognitive deficit observed in gonadal aplasia
(Turner's Syndrome). *Journal of Clinical Psychology*, 1962, **18**(4), 403-
406.

Silverman, A. J., Cohen, S. I., Shmavonian, B. M., & Greenberg, G.   Psycho-
physical investigations in sensory deprivation: The body-field dimension.
Psychosomatic Medicine, 1961, **23**, 48-61.

Soll, J.   The effect of frustration on functional cardiac disorder as related to
field orientation. Unpublished doctoral dissertation, Adelphi University,
1963.

Stafford, A. E.   An investigation in parent-child test scores for evidence of
hereditary components. Unpublished doctoral dissertation, Princeton
University, 1963.

Taylor, J. M. A comparison of delusional and hallucinatory individuals using field dependency as a measure. Unpublished doctoral dissertation, Purdue University, 1956.

Winestine, Muriel C. Twinship and psychological differentiation. Unpublished doctoral dissertation, New York University, 1964.

Wit, O. C. Sex differences in perception. Unpublished master's thesis, University of Utrecht, 1955.

Witkin, H. A. The effect of training of structural aids on performance in three tests of space orientation. *CAA Div. Res. Rep.* 1948, No. 80.

Witkin, H. A. Cognitive patterning in congenitally blind children. Presented at a symposium on "Cognitive Structure and Personality," American Psychological Association, Chicago, Ill., 1965.

Witkin, H. A., Dyk, Ruth B., Faterson, Hanna F., Goodenough, D. R., & Karp, S. A. *Psychological Differentiation*, New York: Wiley, 1962.

Witkin, H. A., Faterson, Hanna F., Goodenough, D. R., & Birnbaum, Judith. Cognitive patterning in high grade mentally retarded boys. *Child Development*, in press.

Witkin, H. A., Karp, S. A., & Goodenough, D. R. Dependence in alcoholics. *Quarterly Journal of Studies on Alcohol*, 1959, **20**, 493-504.

Witkin, H. A., & Lewis, Helen, B. The relation of experimentally induced pre-sleep experiences to dreams: A report on method and preliminary findings. *Journal of the American Psychoanalytic Association*, in press.

Witkin, H. A., Lewis, Helen B., Hertzman, M. Machover, Karen, Meissner, Pearl B., & Wapner, S. *Personality through perception*, New York: Harper, 1954.

Zukmann, L. Hysteric compulsive factors in perceptual organization. Unpublished doctoral dissertation, New School for Social Research, 1957.

9

Sociocultural Factors in the Epidemiology of Schizophrenia

INTRODUCTION

The epidemiological approach is one of a number of approaches available to the researcher studying behavior pathology. In the following paper Elliot Mishler and Norman Scotch discuss the methodological difficulties and review the findings of epidemiological research on schizophrenia.

It might be helpful at this point to discuss the nature and scope of epidemiological research. Essentially, in epidemiological research the aim is to identify variables that are related to the health and sickness of *groups* of people. To a large extent, epidemiology is the study of epidemics broadly defined. With regard to the nature of the variables studied, Hollingshead (1961) has pointed out that "Attributes and variables pertinent to epidemiological study include such things as sex, race, age, occupation, education, diet, family composition, group customs, and personal habits. In addition, it encompasses genetic composition, biochemistry, other forms of plant and animal life, and geographic environment. In brief, epidemiology is the application of ecological principles to the study of health, as well as disease, in a society" (p. 6).

The nature of the variables investigated by the epidemiologist determine the strategy used in the research. That is, since the epidemiologist studies variables that for the most part cannot be experimentally manipulated, his research usually involves searching for naturally occurring relationships between specific variables and health or disease. Thus, epidemiological research is primarily correlational in nature and in this way it differs from the laboratory-experimental research, which is reviewed in many of the papers in this book.

In the present paper the authors limit themselves to considering only sociocultural variables and the relationships of these variables to behavior pathology. While much of the data in this research may seem sociological or anthropological in nature, the psychologist should not disregard such data. The individual does live within a culture, is a member of numerous groups, and must constantly interact with his environment. All of these factors, of course, have an effect on the individual and therefore must be studied.

A knowledge of epidemiological data is important to psychology because some of the hypotheses regarding the etiology of schizophrenia that have been developed by psychologists for understanding the *individual* may in fact be tested within the epidemiological framework. Moreover, since the epidemiologist studies healthy as well as disordered populations, an understanding of this research may broaden the view of the psychologist–behavior pathologist who too frequently is limited in his observation to disordered individuals. This broadening of our knowledge will be of considerable value in view of psychology's move in the direction of community psychology or "community mental health."

Hollingshead, A. B. Some issues in the epidemiology of schizophrenia. *American Sociological Review*, 1961, 26, 5-13.

9

SOCIOCULTURAL FACTORS IN
THE EPIDEMIOLOGY OF SCHIZOPHRENIA

ELLIOT G. MISHLER AND NORMAN A. SCOTCH

In much the same way that the schizophrenic patient is the despair of his therapist in his imperviousness to treatment, the disease entity of schizophrenia is the despair of investigators in its stubborn resistance to their efforts to understand it. Each year innumerable research reports, reviews, and conceptual analyses appear. They represent a variety of points of view and present diverse types of data, reflecting a wide range of authors that includes psychiatrists, epidemiologists, psychologists, sociologists, anthropologists, and biological scientists. Despite this intensive effort and an increasing amount of interest in recent years, schizophrenia remains an illness about which there is little definite or reliable knowledge. Like both clinical and experimental investigations, the epidemiological study of schizophrenia has had to face serious methodological and conceptual problems that have interfered with the steady growth of empirical information and also of theoretical understanding. While these problems manifest themselves in a particularly striking way in the study of schizophrenia, they are also present in other epidemiological inquiries. We believe, therefore, that a review of the issues involved may have significance not for schizophrenia alone but for the study of other diseases as well.

In general, the social epidemiology of mental disorders is a field with a particularly high ratio of review papers to original studies. Several recent reviews are available (Clausen, 1959; Dunham, 1959; Leacook, 1957). In addition, five volumes that have appeared during the last few years include extended discussions of important methodological and conceptual issues in this area of research, with a number of these analyses focused specifically on schizophrenia (Hoch & Zubin, 1961; Milbank, 1959; Pasamanick, 1959; Plunkett & Gordon, 1960; Zubin, 1961).

SOURCE. Reprinted with permission of the authors and the William Alanson White Psychiatric Foundation from *Psychiatry*, 1963, **26**, 315-343.

The surfeit of summaries, analyses, and commentaries on schizophrenia contrasts sharply with the situation described in the earlier papers in this series, which reviewed the literature on social factors in the epidemiology of essential hypertension and rheumatoid arthritis (Scotch & Geiger, 1962; Geiger & Scotch, 1963; Scotch & Geiger, 1963). Another review of materials on social factors and schizophrenia is not to be undertaken lightly. This review has a three-fold objective: To summarize and evaluate findings on the relationship of schizophrenia to selected social and cultural variables; to note and compare alternative hypotheses proposed to account for these findings; and to suggest guidelines for future research. We have drawn upon other reviews whenever possible, but in comparison with them, the present review is more restricted in focus and objectives. These restrictions, deriving from certain methodological and clinical concerns that are outlined below, have permitted a more selective and systematic coverage of studies.

In many of the general articles on the role of sociocultural factors in the occurrence of mental disorders there is a broad concern with all such disorders or with all psychoses. This paper focuses solely on schizophrenia. In some instances studies not specifically concerned with schizophrenia are used as points of reference for discussion, but the interest remains in their implications for schizophrenia. The rationale for this restriction is that we do not expect the same variables necessarily to be associated with different mental disorders. While we do not hold sacred the traditional diagnostic categories of psychiatry, it seems to be most in accord with current knowledge to view schizophrenia as a clinical entity that has different characteristics from other mental illnesses.

Existing reviews tend to be neither systematic nor comprehensive in coverage. A few well-known studies are discussed by all commentators; other studies are sometimes ignored and sometimes selected for emphasis. In examining a large number of investigations we attempted to set up criteria for adequacy and relevance; we found relatively few that met these criteria.

Our particular methodological viewpoint and concerns will become clear in the following sections. On the whole, we have tried to differentiate among studies in terms of the methods and procedures used for case findings and for calculating moribidity rates. We believe that this permits a comparison of different studies with each other in a meaningful and systematic way, and results in a more rigorous and precise statement of current knowledge on the relationship of particular factors to schizophrenia.

Finally, we believe that clinical considerations have not received adequate attention in studies and analyses of the epidemiology of schizophrenia. Problems of nosology and diagnosis appear to be viewed by epidemiologists primarily as sources of error. Their solutions to these problems are aimed narrowly at increasing the reliability of diagnoses. In contrast, we see them as reflecting critical and unsolved questions about the nature of the illness. These are clinical problems to whose solutions epidemiological findings might contribute, but only if there is an awareness of the nature of the issues so that relevant information may be gathered. We have endeavored to suggest how an understanding of clinical issues could play a more important role in the design and interpretation of studies in this area.

Characteristics of Schizophrenia

Extent of the Problem

It is not easy to pick a starting point for a discussion of the epidemiology of schizophrenia. If, for example, we begin by trying to estimate the frequency of its occurrence, then we must make assumptions with regard to the conceptual agreement on and diagnostic reliability of the classification among different investigators; however, as will be seen later, available evidence argues against placing much confidence in these assumptions. If we start instead with an analysis of conceptual issues or with problems in the interpretation of social differentials in rates of schizophrenia, then in the absence of information on over-all rates of occurrence the reader does not have a context in which to evaluate the potential significance of the issues raised. Recognizing that there are difficulties with any scheme of organization, we will follow the pattern set in earlier papers in this series—that is, beginning with the more descriptive material, namely, information on the over-all extent of the problem, before proceeding to conceptual and analytic issues.

In an instructive article focused on the problem of estimating the over-all rate of schizophrenia, Lemkau and Crocetti (1958) make explicit a number of assumptions that underlie such estimates. They point out that in order to establish

. . . the true incidence of any disease, three basic conditions must be met. First, the identification of the entity in question should be highly reliable and objective for the investigators, i.e., susceptible of replication. Second, all cases should be known, or the ratio between known and unknown cases clearly established. Third, the population from which the cases are drawn should be clearly defined and carefully enumerated (Lemkau & Crocetti, 1958, p. 68).

These are ideal conditions not met in practice with regard to other illnesses, but perhaps even less closely approximated with regard to schizophrenia.

Where there is a high degree of "variability" in diagnosis and measurement, Lemkau and Crocetti (1958, p. 70) suggest that the

. . . most reliable technique open to the medical statistician is to establish a basic minimal figure on the narrowest basis possible, and a theoretical maximum on the broadest possible basis, and to attempt to establish, by a series of inferences, that estimate of incidence least likely to be in error.

They follow their own suggestion, and by making a number of inferences, particularly with regard to the likely numbers of unhospitalized and unknown cases of schizophrenia in the community, they arrive at the following estimates:

In summary, it would appear that the true incidence of schizophrenia in a Western European-type society can hardly be leses than 50 per 100,000, and within all reasonable probability should not exceed 250 per 100,000 per annum . . . the incidence range most likely to contain the least error in its general application to various communities in Western European-type societies is in the vicinity of 150 cases per 100,000 population per year. That is to say that the true rate for various communities in these societies can be expected to fall above as well as below this figure with equal frequency (Lemkau & Crocetti, 1958, pp. 71-72).

While one might quarrel with some of the details, the estimates arrived at by Lemkau and Crocetti reflect inferences that are reasonable and justifiable in view of what is known about schizophrenia. Their figures may be considered, therefore, as useful approximations to the true rate of occurrence of the illness. Further, as they note, considering the high level of chronicity, even the minimum estimate would entitle schizophrenia to rate as one of the major diseases of mankind.

Lemkau and Crocetti's figures include all cases of schizophrenia whether in treatment or not, hospitalized or not. Hospital admission rates for schizophrenia are not only lower but also much more variable over time and from state to state. A report of the Biometrics Branch of the National Institute of Mental Health on first admissions to state mental hospitals shows that between 1940 and 1950 ". . . the schizophrenic rate rose from 15.9 to 21.0, an increase of 32 percent with 37 states experiencing an increase in rate and only 10 a decrease" (Kramer, Pollack & Rednick, 1961). Their figures also show marked variability among states, with New York and Rhode Island in 1950 having age-adjusted first admission rates for schizophrenia of more than 35 per 100,000, while Virginia, New Mexico, Kansas, and Wyoming had rates of less than 10 per 100,000.

Prevalence and expectancy rates are other measures of morbidity that help to fill in the picture on the extent of the problem. The prevalence of schizophrenia—that is, the proportion of the population that would be diagnosed as schizophrenic at any one point in time—is estimated by Lemkau and Crocetti (1958) as 290 per 100,000. The several studies of admissions to mental hospitals reviewed by Norris (1959), including estimates derived from her own investigations, suggest that the minimum "expectancy rate" —that is, the proportion of an age cohort that may be expected to be hospitalized for schizophrenia between birth and age 75—lies between 8 and 12 per 1,000.

In summary, the proportion of the population likely to develop schizophrenia during the course of a year is about .15 percent; those hospitalized for schizophrenia for the first time during a year constitute about .02 percent of the population; approximately .30 percent suffer from the illness at any one time; about 1.00 percent of each age cohort may be expected to fall ill at some point during their lifetime.

There was a time when schizophrenia was considered to be almost entirely a disease of the young, as its early label of dementia praecox indicated. While there is a somewhat broader age range among those who develop schizophrenia than was first suspected, the view that it is primarily a disease of the younger age groups is borne out essentially in all reports. Locke and his co-workers, in a recent systematic and detailed investigation of first admissions to state mental hospitals, state:

> Among white and non-white for either sex, admission rates for schizophrenia are concentrated in the ages 20-40, with the peak occurring in the 25-34 age group. This finding is consistent with findings in earlier studies as well as recent national census data. Many of these studies showed the peak age of hospitalization to occur earlier among males than females (Locke, 1958, p. 175).

Lemkau and Crocetti also emphasize the relation of morbidity to age, pointing out that age differentials are among the most striking and consistent findings and stating that ". . . it is definitely a disease, as the older nomenclature would imply, of the younger age groups. Many more than half of the hospitalized cases—about 59% —are under 35 years of age. Less than 1% are over 65 years of age" (Lemkau & Crocetti, 1958, p. 78).

Findings with regard to sex differentials are more ambiguous. There seems to be general agreement about a somewhat later age of onset for women than men; Norris' (1959, p. 117) comment that her data "confirm the well-known finding that the exhibition of the disease is delayed in women" reaffirms the previous quotation from Locke and his colleagues. However, there is some question as to over-all rate differentials. Lemkau and Crocetti (1958, p. 78), for example, assert: "The morbidity of the schizophrenic disorder is about equally distributed between males and females." However, in both Norris' English study and Locke's study of Ohio mental hospitals there is evidence of a higher rate for females. The former reports annual first admission rates of 17.7 and 19.4 per 100,000 for males and females respectively for the years 1947-49; she also reports expectancy rates of 9 per 1,000 for males and 12 per 1,000 for females through their lifetime period of risk. Locke finds: "Adjustment for age does not alter the observation that the first admission rate is higher for females than for males. Indeed the ratio of age-specific male rates to female rates is usually higher only in the 15-24 group" (Locke, 1958, p. 177). These authors point out that pre-World War II studies had tended to show that males had higher rates than females, and speculate that the changes in ratios may reflect changes over time in patterns of hospitalization and the social role of women in society.

We have not been able to find information on the relative mortality of persons with schizophrenia vis-à-vis other populations; studies of death rates among hospitalized patients are not useful for this purpose. There appears, however, to be a widespread assumption that schizophrenics have a shorter life expectancy than the average.

The marked chronicity of the illness bears mention in concluding this section on the extent of the problem. Schizophrenics constitute about 25 percent of all hospital admissions, but about 50 percent of the patients in mental hospitals at any one time have this diagnosis. The median duration of hospitalization among schizophrenic patients currently in the hospital is found to be 10.8 years in the data provided by 17 Model Reporting Area States, with duration increasing markedly with age (Kramer, Pollack and Redick, 1961).

Sociocultural Factors

While the immediate objective of epidemiological inquiry is to determine the distribution of disease in various social and cultural groups, the ultimate aim is to increase understanding of the factors that influence the onset and course of different illnesses. An examination of the complex ideas of causation and the ways in which various types of epidemiological investigation are related to clinical and experimental studies may be found in other sources (Mac-Mahon, Pugh & Ipsen, 1960), and these issues need not be reviewed here. However, it seems useful to discuss briefly some alternative "frames of reference" (Clausen & Kohn, 1954) that have been proposed for interpreting associations between social and cultural variables and schizophrenia. The following discussion has benefited in particular from the analyses of the same problem by Clausen and Kohn (1954), Leighton and Hughes (1959), and Jackson (1960).

The studies discussed are concerned with the social and cultural characteristics of persons clinically diagnosed as schizophrenic. These analyses typically involve a comparison of the morbidity rates between two or more different social or cultural groups. It has been the convention to ignore similarities among groups for the purpose of theoretical interpretation and to focus on differences. Thus, the finding that many occupations have roughly equal morbidity rates for schizophrenia has not been seen as a valuable or interesting theoretical problem, while particularly high rates for one group of occupations relative to the others has been the object of considerable speculation.

In approaching the studies, one must first consider the question of artifacts—that is, the possibility that the relationship found between the social variable and the rate of schizophrenia does not reflect the "true" relationship but has arisen from errors or biases in the procedures. The main source of such artifacts lies in the diagnostic and case-finding procedures, and in the ways of computing morbidity indexes. Some concrete illustrations of these possibilities will be presented in our discussion of social class.

Another but different type of artifact is the concomitant variation between two variables that are both functions of a third. This kind of artifact is the idea underlying the two familiar hypotheses used to account for different rates of schizophrenia in different ecological areas of the city, namely, genetic or social draft. These hypotheses suggest that the association between ecological area and schizophrenia results not from the action of the social environment but from the selective migration or drift of such persons into this area.

If an empirical association is accepted as more than an artifact, then the question arises of how the social environment enters into the disease process—that is, some theoretical mechanism must be postulated. A division between indirect and direct mechanisms seems to be involved in a number of formulations. Indirect mechanisms refer to the ways in which the social environment acts to produce individuals who are particularly vulnerable to schizophrenia; direct mechanism refer to the types of situations the culture provides that may be more or less directly "schizophrenogenic." Child-rearing practices and styles of family life are often looked upon as being particularly important in creating high vulnerability. Role transitions, severe economic deprivation, and the disruption of primary group relationships have been regarded as among the stresses that might act directly to induce illness.

Finally, the most complex question is why some individuals develop schizophrenia while others exposed to the same social environment as children and adults do not. For many writers, the answer includes some reference to biological determinants either genetically given or resulting from organic defect or damage. Often these determinants are viewed as interacting with stressful features in the social environment, so that the interpretation is framed in terms of necessary and sufficient conditions rather than in terms of a single etiological agent.

This discussion of alternative approaches to interpretation has been purposefully brief. Some of them will be discussed in more detail in our discussion of specific findings. We hope that this introduction has been sufficient to convey to the reader our belief that the process of understanding the role played by sociocultural factors in schizophrenia depends not only upon empirical study, but upon theory and interpretation as well.

Conceptual and Methodological Issues

General discussions of schizophrenia often emphasize the high level of disagreement and confusion that exists. A typical comment is that of Cameron (1944, p. 886) in his review of almost 20 years ago: "Nowhere else in the field of psychopathology . . . is there less agreement on so many important points than in schizophrenia." The relative lack of change over time is underscored by a more recent paper which notes that approximately 500 papers on the etiology of schizophrenia have appeared since 1940 and ". . . these papers disagree widely with one another and reflect the fact that schizophrenia is a singularly difficult disorder to investigate" (Jackson, 1960, p. 4). Although these quotations refer to the clinical problems of nosology, diagnosis, and etiology, ignorance is equally pervasive with regard to the natural history of the illness and its response to various forms of treatment.

Thus, one could not expect a high level of consistency among the findings of different epidemiological studies. While it may not be necessary for social investigators to resolve all or most of the major clinical and theoretical issues before undertaking research, the design of their studies would benefit from an understanding of these issues and an appreciation of their relationship to methodological decisions and to the interpretation of resulting data.

The *Diagnostic and Statistical Manual of the American Psychiatric Association* (1952, p. 26) describes schizophrenic reactions as follows:

. . . a group of psychotic reactions characterized by fundamental disturbances in reality relationships and concept formation with affective, behavioral, and intellectual disturbances in varying degrees and mixtures . . . marked by strong tendency to retreat from reality, by emotional disharmony, unpredictable disturbances in stream of thought, regressive behavior, and in some by a tendency to "deterioration."

In Bleuler's (1950) classic monograph we find:

I call dementia praecox "schizophrenia" because (as I hope to show) the "splitting" of the different psychic functions is one of its most important characteristics . . . a group of psychoses . . . characterized by a specific type of alteration of thinking, feeling, and relation to the external world which appears nowhere else in this particular fashion (p. 8-a).

. . . The fundamental symptoms consist of disturbances of association and affectivity, the predilection for fantasy as against reality and the inclination to divorce oneself from reality (autism). Furthermore, we can add the absence of those very symptoms which play such a great role in certain other diseases such as primary disturbances of perception, orientation, memory, etc. (p. 14).

Although there is variation in emphasis and detail, writers since Bleuler tend to agree on certain symptoms as essential criteria of the schizophrenic process. These are the "blunting" or flattening of emotional responsiveness and the inappropriateness of associations, often accompanied by the use of language with private, symbolic meaning; and an inward orientation with marked indifference to, and uninvolvement with, the social environment. Persons diagnosed as schizophrenic may exhibit any or all of these symptoms to a marked, moderate, or mild degree. The general impression created in the observer of a severely ill patient is of strange, unpredictable, and unintelligible behavior. "It is as bewildering to come unprepared and untrained into the presence of a disturbed schizophrenic patient as it would be suddenly to happen on a disturbed disorganized community whose history one does not know or cannot understand" (Cameron, 1947, p. 451). However, many diagnosed schizophrenic patients may be actively psychotic only intermittently, and most of the time may display little bizarre behavior.

This brief excursion into the problem of describing the essential and critical features of schizophrenia makes it easy to understand why there is a high level of confusion and disagreement as soon as one moves to more complex issues. A disease that is defined with reference to varying degrees of impairment in any one of several major and different psychological functions—impairment which must be shown to be not attributable primarily to organic causes —is certain to create difficulties for diagnosis, theory, and research.

One would expect the reliability of diagnoses to be relatively poor. There are surprisingly few systematic studies of this problem, but this expectation appears to be borne out by the reports that are available. One recent review notes:

It would appear from the few papers dealing with the reliability of diagnoses that variation between even experienced clinicians is so great that comparisons between groups used by different investigators are subject to large error. In one study, three psychiatrists agreed in only 20 per cent of their cases and had a majority agreement in only 48 per cent. Another study revealed that the widest disagreement occurred among the most experienced clinicians (Jackson, 1960, p. 11).

Anecdotal reports of clinical and hospital practice indicate that changes over time in administrative practices within the same institution, and differences between institutions have a marked influence on the rates of diagnosed schizophrenia (Zubin, 1961, pp. 118-119). Similarly, a significant proportion of patients diagnosed as schizophrenic at one time or in one treatment institution may have their diagnoses changed either when readmitted to the same hospital or when transferred to another hospital. One report notes that while there is higher consistency in the rediagnoses of schizophrenia than in other mental illnesses, only 50 percent of a sample of patients diagnosed as having any "functional psychosis" on first admission received diagnoses on later admission to a different hospital that were in this same general category (Clausen & Kohn, 1959, pp. 69-86).

Conceptual agreement on the nature of schizophrenia is even more difficult to achieve than agreement at the empirical level. For many investigators, schizophrenia is a specific disease or class of diseases with specific symptoms and a specific etiological agent. There is, of course, great variety in the specific agent hypothesized. For others, it is not a specific disease but a "syndrome" in which the manifestations of ego disorganization may be quite variable from one patient to another and the responsible or predisposing factors may also be any of a multitude of stressful or traumatic disturbances (Bellak, 1958). In addition to the traditional sub-types of schizophrenia, many authors have suggested the possibility of two distinct illnesses with different etiologies, onsets, symptom pictures, and prognoses—with one group having an unfavorable and the other a favorable outcome (Vaillant, 1962).

Problems of nosology and case definition have received some discussion in the context of epidemiological research (Zubin, 1961). However, an examination of existing epidemiological studies suggests that investigators have, on the whole, been content to use as their study populations those cases diagnosed as schizophrenic in whatever institution was accessible to them as if such a diagnosis had a clear and unambiguous meaning. There has also been a general assumption that one set of findings about schizophrenia could be compared with another without examining carefully the source and meaning of the diagnosis in the different situations. There are, of course, exceptions to this optimistic tendency. For example, Eric Stromgren remarks: "In some cases we are suspicious from the beginning. When, for example, the word schizophrenia is used, everybody knows that the word is practically meaningless unless a detailed description is given of the sense in which the author wants to use the word" (Stromgren, 1961, p. 173).

It is one thing to point to these problems and quite another to derive from them some useful guidelines and principles for reviewing past work and for suggesting future research directions. Given the nature and level of disagreement on the basic features of schizophrenia and the unreliability of diagnosis, is there a meaningful way to compare findings from different studies? Given the great variety in conceptualizations and theories, how may research be oriented so as to have more direct and systematic relevance for the understanding of social factors in the etiology of schizophrenia?

We have adopted what may be termed a "fine-grained" approach to both of these questions—that is, we believe it is extremely important to specify the diagnostic and case-finding procedures in each study, as well as the other methodological procedures, in order to compare the findings of different studies with each other in a valid and meaningful way. Explicit attention to different methods may make it possible to clarify and to understand the significance of both the similarities and differences in the findings.

The specific implications of this fine-grained view will become evident in the following sections. We would like here merely to contrast it with two other approaches, one "coarse-grained" and the other involving a norm of arbitrariness. By a coarse-grained approach we refer to the collation of findings on schizophrenia regardless of the differences in methods and definitions among the studies. Here a reviewer attempts to search for an emerging consistency or pattern in the findings in spite of variance in procedures. A good example is a recent review paper where findings from community, hospital admission, and army rejection studies are used to arrive at generalizations about social variables and psychoses (Leacook, 1957). We have taken an alternate approach of restricting our comparisons to certain kinds of studies because we believe that there is already too much ambiguity involved in what is being studied.

The other alternative to the approach adopted here is a view associated with social statisticians and research epidemiologists. It begins with the standard scientific premise that all definitions are arbitrary and therefore urges that "some" definition be accepted so that investigators may get on with their work. There is an attractive simplicity to this approach, but, like Alexander's clean cut through the Gordian knot, it may destroy the phenomenon altogether. We believe that current disagreements about the nature of schizophrenia reflect basic and real issues in the attempt to understand this phenomenon. These issues should not be solved by arbitrary fiat. We believe the aim of investigations should be to clarify the nature and implications of the differences in definition and conceptualization so as to increase the understanding of schizophrenia. The critical need at the present time is not that everyone agree on "some" definition of schizophrenia, but that the several definitions be made explicit and operational.

Review of Studies

Our review of studies is divided into two major sections. The first examines investigations concerned with incidence differentials in the United States among persons with different social characteristics. We will discuss separately studies that focus on the variables of social class, social mobility, and migration. The second major section takes up comparative cross-cultural and total community studies. While no review in this field can claim to be exhaustive, we believe that the studies examined and used constitute a fairly comprehensive and representative sample of what is available.

The criteria for inclusion of studies in the review vary from section to section. The criteria are most restrictive with regard to the studies of social characteristics associated with schizophrenia. A major aim has been to determine the level of confidence that may be placed in a statement that a particular variable is associated with schizophrenia. Thus we shall be concerned with traditional and frequently asserted propositions linking schizophrenia with social class, social mobility, or migration.

With respect to the distinction between incidence and prevalence as morbidity indexes, we have adopted the position that incidence (the rate at which new cases appear during a given time period) is preferred to prevalence (the number of cases ill during a given time period) for studying the etiological role of sociocultural variables. Kramer's (1957) well-known discussion and his definition of incidence as "the fundamental epidemiologic ratio" is pointed toward clarifying the difference between the two indexes when the duration of illness is neither brief nor constant through different social groupings. As MacMahon (1960) and others have noted, prevalence may be utilized fruitfully to explore etiology only when it is considered as equivalent to incidence. Inasmuch as we believe that one problem in earlier reviews and in the proper evaluation of existing findings has been the lumping together of prevalence and incidence materials, we shall in the section reviewing epidemiological studies restrict systematic examination to those that utilize incidence. However, since there are no cross-cultural or community studies that utilize the incidence of schizophrenia as an index of morbidity, that section of the review will use prevalence data.

It is worth noting that the distinction between incidence and prevalence has received considerably more attention in studies of mental illness than in studies of physical illness, where prevalence measures tend to be the rule and have provided much of the basic data in the field. The main reason for this is that the duration of physical illnesses do not seem to be associated differentially with the basic sociodemographic variables. In the mental illnesses, while definitive data are lacking, there is enough evidence to suggest that duration is associated with such variables as social class (Hollingshead & Redlich, 1958) and marital status (Phillips, 1953) to argue against a casual use of prevalence as if it were equivalent to incidence.

While we have restricted our systematic review to incidence studies, we shall return to the question of other components of prevalence in the final section.

Some confusion exists regarding traditional ecological studies, such as the classic report of Faris and Dunham (1939) for understanding the etiology of schizophrenia. The criticisms of Thorndike (1939) and Robinson (1950) of the use of correlations between group indexes as if they validly represented correlations between characteristics in individuals has led to some misunderstanding of the meaning of the ecological findings. These critics have pointed out that high correlations between total community rates for schizophrenia and other community characteristics, such as median income of the population or median rental value of its homes, do not mean that individuals from these areas who develop schizophrenia actually have the characteristic in question. For example, Faris and Dunham showed that it was the white rather than the Negro residents of predominantly Negro areas who showed particularly high rates for schizophrenia. It is possible to show statistically that ecological and individual correlations are equivalent to each other only under very special conditions and that, on the whole, ecological correlations are likely to be higher than the corresponding individual correlations.

However, the criticism of the ecological studies on statistical grounds does not in itself suffice to dismiss these studies as spurious at the level of individual interpretation. Ecological variables have conceptual as well as operational meaning, and the problem is no different in principle from the problem of correlating occupation with schizophrenia and interpreting occupation as an index of a social-class life style. If, for example, the variable "living in a high-rent census tract" is defined conceptually as an index of social aspirations, then a study of differential rates by rental value of census tracts may be interpreted in terms of psychological as well as ecological theory, and no change in statistical procedures is required to interpret it in one way rather than the other. While available ecological studies are not directly comparable for our purposes to studies using individual analyses and will therefore be used only as background in this review, nevertheless the ecological approach has a valuable role to play in epidemiological research. Some combination of ecological and individual designs would seem to be particularly powerful, a point to which we will return in the final section.

Finally, there is a great deal of controversy in the critical literature as to whether hospital admissions are valid indicators of the "true" incidence of illness. For example, Pugh and MacMahon (1962), in their recent monograph, adopt a cautious position but devote their energies to indicating the usefulness and relevance of hospital admission data. Kramer (1961) and his co-workers, on the other hand, in a detailed analysis conclude that differentials in hospital admission rates are "more a function of differences in a number of external, biological, social, cultural, and environmental factors than of differences in the true incidence and prevalence of mental disorders." Our position in this matter has been to use data reflecting incidence whether it be a hospital admission or other treatment entry rate, but to recognize explicitly the differences among these rates in comparisons of studies and interpretations of findings.

The Incidence of Schizophrenia: Social Characteristics

Social class. Two recent reviews of social-class differentials in rates of schizophrenia, although superficially agreeing in some findings, suggest to us the nature and lack of clarity of accumulated findings and the difficulties associated with comparing different studies. Lemkau and Crocetti (1958, p. 81), basing their remarks on explicit reference only to the early ecological study of Faris and Dunham and on the prevalence rates found in the Eastern Health District Survey of 1936, state: "There is also some evidence that socioeconomic status is a differentiating factor with a disproportionate number of cases being found in the lower socio-economic status."

After reviewing many different types of English and American studies, where the sources of data vary from hospital admission records and army rejection studies to community prevalence surveys, Leacock (1957, p. 337) concludes:

Although the studies of socio-economic status and mental illness are not strictly comparable . . . the general trend is clear and consistent enough to be meaningful. . . . Rates for schizophrenia, like rates for all mental illness, go up in situations associated with situational stress—lower socio-economic status, living in disorganized urban areas, immigration or migration. . . .

Despite the similarity of findings, it is our contention that reports such as these do not advance the understanding of relationships between sociocultural factors and schizophrenia because they do not sufficiently differentiate among the methods and concepts used in different studies. To lump together studies of incidence and prevalence differentials, rates based on hospital admissions and surveys of untreated persons in the community, and studies using markedly different measures and conceptions of social class, is to obscure rather than clarify these relationships.

In the course of preparing this review, many studies were examined that were considered by their authors and by other reviewers to bear on the problem of social-class differences in schizophrenia. We do not wish to dispute their general relevance. However, only nine studies met what we believe are minimal criteria for examining the basic hypothesis that differences in social class are associated with the development of schizophrenia. The analyses of these nine involve comparisons of the social attributes of individuals when they become ill—that is, they are studies of the incidence of schizophrenia in which the individual's own social-class position rather than an ecological characteristic of his community is used as the independent variable.

Of the nine studies, eight use occupation as the measure of social class. Three of the studies include admissions to private as well as state mental hospitals. Typically, although not uniformly, the rates are age-specific or age-standardized, usually controlled for sex, and sometimes controlled for nativity or race. These specific studies are those of Nolan (1917), Odegaard (1932), Clark (1948), Frunkin (two studies) (1952, 1955), Hollingshead and Redlich (1958), Locke and others (1958), Clausen and Kohn (1959), and Jaco[1] (1960).

In view of the importance of the problem and the abundance of review articles and theoretical analyses, the relative scarcity of basic empirical studies is surprising. These nine studies cover a 35-year period. The reference populations are four states, and one large, one medium-sized, and one small city. While the census classification of occupation usually provides the basic coding categories and rank ordering, only two of the nine studies use the same number of categories in their rate comparisons. The number of categories in the different studies—2, 4, 5, 7, 8, 10, 12, and 19—

---

[1] When this article by Mishler and Scotch was originally published, it contained an appendix in which the preceeding articles were abstracted. The appendix can be found in *Psychiatry*, 1963, 26, 344-351.

provides a good index of the low level of basic agreement on methods and procedures.

The most consistent finding, which emerges in eight of the nine studies, is that the highest incidence is associated with the lowest social-class groupings used in each study. In six studies it is the unskilled or laborers category, in a seventh it is the unemployed, and in the eighth it is the lowest of four social classes—defined by an index of occupation, education, and residence—that produces the highest rate.

There are two important specifications to this general finding. First, when male and female rates are computed separately, the female rates are considerably higher within this lowest occupational category. For example, in one study where the highest rates of hospital admissions for schizophrenia are found for metropolitan counties with high over-all hospital usage, the rate for male laborers is 106.5 and for female laborers 479.9 per 100,000 (Locke, 1958). Second, the rates for this category tend to be sharply higher than the rates for the adjacent occupation. The New Haven study (Hollingshead & Redlich, 1958), for example, shows rates for Class V that are twice as high as for Class IV—20 as compared with 10 on the morbidity index used.

A second, almost equally consistent finding (present in six of the studies, one of which includes admissions to private hospitals) is that the lowest rate is associated with the managerial group. This occupational group varies somewhat in definition in the different studies but usually includes proprietors of small businesses and executives of large ones. This finding is stronger among males than females, and seems to be meaningful only for metropolitan areas since too few cases exist in nonmetropolitan areas to compute rates. The differences between rates for this group and adjacent categories are not consistently large, and sometimes another group has an equally low rate.

Only the Hagerstown study (Clausen & Kohn, 1954) reports no differences among occupations. The report focuses more on ecological distributions and social mobility and gives the occupation of patients at admission a minor and secondary role. Two aspects of this study restrict its value for comparison purposes. First, the small number of cases required that occupations be grouped into two broad classes—one including professional, technical, and managerial workers; the other including operatives, service workers, and laborers. Second, rates are not computed separately for males and females. As a result of these procedures, whether or not the differences found in other studies might also be present here cannot be ascertained.

Although all of these investigators use a similar classification of occupations as a set of empirical categories, they do not all share the same conceptual definition of this variable. Earlier writers, where they are explicit, sometimes refer to specific qualities of particular occupations as playing an etiological role in the development of mental disorders. Thus, Nolan (1917) refers to eyestrain and long hours of required concentration as occupationally linked stresses that might induce mental illness; Clark (1948, p. 329) suggests among his hypotheses that "the low prestige aspect of an occupation increases the pre-schizophrenic's negative attitudes toward himself."

In more recent investigations, the specific and differentiating qualities of occupations are not mentioned. Instead, a person's occupation is used as an operational definition of his position in the general system of social stratification. Occupation is seen only as a useful index of social class, which in turn is viewed as a general style of life with clusters of values and behaviors that distinguish the members of one class from the members of other social classes.

As we have already indicated, the ecological studies do not permit direct comparison with the group of studies summarized here. It is worth noting, however, that with the rare exception of the Clausen and Kohn (1954) Hagerstown investigation, the ecological findings show the highest incidence in the poorest or most disorganized areas of the cities (Faris & Dunham, 1939; Lapouse, Monk, & Terris, 1956). There is no evidence in these studies that would contradict the relationships between social class and schizophrenia summarized here.

As indicated earlier, there are several types of alternative explanations of empirical relationships between social variables and the incidence of schizophrenia. Thus, the relationship may be viewed as an error or an artifact arising from the procedures used; both schizophrenia and class position may be thought to reflect or result from the operation of some third variable or process; different rates of remission rather than of onset may produce the associations with social variables; or, finally, social class may be interpreted as a valid etiological variable having a causative role in the development of schizophrenia. Each of these possibilities will be discussed briefly.

Among the many sources of potential error, three in particular deserve attention: The case-finding procedures are not independent of social class, the diagnostic procedures are not independent of social class, and the measurement of social class is unreliable.

It has long been recognized that the use of state hospital admissions as the sole source of data for computing morbidity rates for schizophrenia in different social groups might bias findings. This is because other psychiatric treatment resources such as private mental hospitals, psychiatric units in general hospitals, and outpatient facilities would be used disproportionately by different social groups, and these different usage patterns would be reflected in state hospital admission rates. For this reason, several of the studies have included admissions to private hospitals. This inclusion has not altered the pattern of findings. However, before this source of bias is discounted entirely, two characteristic differences between state hospital and private hospital admissions require further examination.

First, private hospitals may be less likely to diagnose their patients as schizophrenic because of a greater concern with the social stigma carried by such a diagnosis and a greater sensitivity to the family's resistance to this diagnosis. This would depress the schizophrenia rates for groups using these facilities—that is, the higher social-class groups. Second, individuals in the higher class groups are relatively more likely to have had their illness detected early, and if hospitalized to have been released after a short period of treatment. In successive age categories, a higher proportion of their admissions would then be readmissions. This factor would also tend to reduce the apparent incidence in higher class groups since incidence rates in the studies reported are based on first admissions.

Another important possibility is related to this last point— namely, that admissions to hospitals do not constitute a representative sample of persons becoming schizophrenic, but are a sample of those who did not recover quickly. We know that admission to a hospital comes at the end of a series of other attempts to deal with the illness. Studies of the preadmission histories of hospitalized patients indicate that a delay of several months between the onset of symptoms and hospital admission is the typical rather than unusual pattern. During this time family members may either try to deny the illness by "normalizing" the behavior (Clausen & Yarrow, 1955), or may try to adapt to the situation by developing new patterns of relationship (Sampson, Messinger, & Towne, 1962), or may try to cope actively with the illness through various types of professional and nonprofessional help (Cumming, 1962). While the distribution of these patterns by social class is unknown, the relatively greater availability of outpatient treatment facilities for persons in higher social classes may increase the probability of recovery or of maintenance in the community for some proportion of the schizophrenic population, and thus reduce the hospital admission rate for these groups.

There is also the possibility of bias in the diagnostic process. There is some experimental evidence that more severe diagnoses may be attached to working-class patients as compared to middle-class patients where the diagnostic information is the same for both (Hasse, 1955). This is not the same, of course, as demonstrating that the lowest occupational groups are more likely to receive diagnoses of schizophrenia, but the demonstrated low reliability of diagnoses and the complex ways in which social characteristics may be used as cues to diagnosis suggest the need for further attention to this problem.

A third source of potential error lies in the measurement of the social-class variable. Social researchers are aware that the reliable coding of an individual's occupation is an extremely difficult procedure requiring a number of items of information and detailed coding instructions. It is highly unlikely that adequate procedures are followed in hospital admitting offices, and the basic record information undoubtedly contains a large amount of error. This is particularly important for persons in lower-status occupations and for patients whose employment histories may show marked instability. Does one code his most recent occupation? His usual occupation? How long must he have been out of work to be listed as unemployed? These difficulties are further compounded in the occupational classification of women, and it is often unclear in reports of investigations whether their own or their husbands' occupation has been used.

Besides reflecting errors of measurement and procedure, an association between schizophrenia and social class may result from the action of some third variable—that is, the association is not evidence for a direct connection between class and illness but may be an artifact arising from their joint attachment to another variable. Genetic and social drift are the most frequently mentioned hypotheses and suggest processes through which schizophrenics tend to accumulate in certain social groups either through breeding or geographic mobility. These interpretations have been examined in detail by Clausen and Kohn (1954). A related possibility is that the direction of the relationship is from the illness to the social-class position—that is, schizophrenics have difficulty holding good jobs and tend to be downwardly mobile, so that the lower occupational groups have a disproportionately larger number of cases. Investigators have generally been aware of this problem, as indicated in the comment by Locke (1958, p. 187):

Undoubtedly additional studies are needed on the relationship of occupation to mental illness, and of mental illness as a determinant of occupation. . . . The census data and the hospital admission data employed in this study were based on the individual's latest occupational employment. Undoubtedly, studies incorporating occupational histories are needed to clarify the roles that occupation and occupational mobility play in relation to schizophrenia and other mental diseases.

Studies of social mobility will be examined in the next section of this paper.

If the effects of artifacts and errors are removed, one may turn finally to the possibility that the variable of social class is related etiologically to schizophrenia. Earlier, we noted both indirect and direct processes: A differential vulnerability to schizophrenia produced in the early life experiences within the family in different class cultures; or differentials in levels of social and personal stress among various class groups leading to differential rates of schizophrenia. Dunham (1959, p. 258) has recently evaluated the latter hypothesis:

In this review of social structures and mental disorders, I have attempted to concentrate on the various hypotheses that purport to explain significant rate differentials in selected social structures . . . from an environmental perspective, interest is greater for the socalled functional disorders but even here the evidence is highly inconclusive for asserting with any confidence that a high rate in a given position of a social structure is a product of certain stresses, strains, and conflicts in that position.

The role of the parental family in the etiology of schizophrenia has received considerable attention in the clinical literature. Recent reviews of research in this area indicate that interesting speculation still far outruns reliable data (Spiegel & Bell, 1957). Studies have suffered from small and unrepresentative samples, a lack of research controls, and unreliable instruments. Despite the present limitations of family studies, it would seem that a comprehensive theory of social factors in the etiology of schizophrenia would have to include the family's influence on the patient both in his formative and later years, and the family's function as a transmitter of forces in the larger social environment. Studies which attempt to relate patients' living arrangements to their position in the social-class structure are an obvious need (Gerard & Houston, 1953).

We believe that at this time no reasonable decision can be made as to the merits of the alternative explanations of the relationships found between social class and the incidence of schizophrenia. Neither can proper weights be assigned to any set of them taken collectively. The higher rates for schizophrenia found among the lowest social-class groups in the studies reviewed here may be a function of errors of measurement or may be an artifact. Before attributing an etiological role to social class, these more parsimonious though less elegant interpretations should be ruled out through systematic investigation. We shall return to some of the problems of theory and further research in the final section of this review.

Social Mobility. Almost as much attention has been given in theoretical discussions to the question of whether the incidence of schizophrenia is associated with downward social mobility as to the relationship with social class. It is, of course, an important variable in its own right, but it takes on increased importance in view of the finding that the lowest socioeconomic class shows the highest incidence of schizophrenia.

The usual statement of this hypothesis is that schizophrenia-prone persons tend to move down the social-class structure from their point of origin. Therefore, any differentials found among social positions can more reasonably be accounted for by this process than by aspects of the social environment in which schizophrenics are located at the time of hospitalization. While it may seem equally reasonable, and more consistent with the interpretations offered of social-class differentials, to invert this argument and hypothesize that one effect of downward social mobility with its attendant stress might be the development of schizophrenia, this alternative direction of the relationship is found only in the layman's theory of mental illness.

The great difficulty in a study of social mobility is to determine a meaningful base population or standard of comparison in terms of which to evaluate the social histories of schizophrenic patients. In other words, high rates of downward social mobility found among any group of schizophrenics do not permit an interpretation of the relationship until we know the mobility histories of a comparable group of nonschizophrenics.

In their original discussion of the social-drift hypothesis, Faris and Dunham (1939) try to approximate such an analysis by comparing the relative degree of concentration of older and younger patients in the areas of the city with high admission rates. They argue that older people would have had more of an opportunity to drift; not finding any age differences in concentration, they reject the drift hypothesis as being inadequate to account for their findings.

While studies meeting our criteria are rare, we are fortunate in having two recent and well-controlled investigations that are similar in design. Unfortunately, their findings do not agree.

Lystad (1957, p. 291) concludes from her study in New Orleans that schizophrenic patients "show less upward status mobility than matched, non-mentally ill persons." From more intensive control analyses she suggests that this difference is present for whites, females, members of the middle class, and those with more than grammar-school education; the differences disappear among Negroes, males, lower-class members, and those with less than grammar-school education. On the basis of her findings, she stresses ". . . the importance of longitudinal studies of schizophrenic patients and controls in various subcultures of our society" (Lystad, 1957, p. 292).

On the other hand, in a control-group study using both male and female patients matched individually for age, sex, and occupation at a point averaging 16 years before hospitalization, Clausen and Kohn (1959) report that the record of social mobility for this group of first-admission schizophrenics was "approximately equal to that of the normal controls." Fifty-nine percent of the paired controls and 64 percent of the schizophrenics remained in the same occupational class; 16 percent of the controls and 8 percent of the patients moved upward; 2 percent of the controls and 8 percent of the schizophrenics showed marked fluctuations over time in occupational level.

While these two studies are similar in design, comparison remains difficult. The samples, relatively small in both studies, are drawn from different cities and from different types of treatment facilities. Further, Lystad's control analyses suggest that within certain subcultural groups one might not expect differences. Finally, one study uses three and the other uses two occupational classes, and mobility manifested in the former could easily be hidden in the latter.

Two other studies, although ecological in design, deserve mention since they focus on the relationship between social mobility and the incidence of schizophrenia. Both use residential mobility as an index of social mobility. In one study, a group a first-admission white male schizophrenic patients was matched with a control group for age and residential location 25 years prior to their hospitalization; comparisons were then made between the median monthly rentals of the census tract of residence at the two points in time. No significant differences were found in social mobility between the control and patient groups. Thus, this study shows no evidence of downward social drift for schizophrenics as compared to a nonpatient population (Faris, Dunham, 1939; Lapouse, Monk, & Terris, 1956). In another study (Gerard & Houston, 1953), less well-designed than those already noted, there is a suggestion on downward social drift within that subgroup of male schizophrenic patients who live in socially isolated situations. Using the average housing quality of a political ward or housing zone as a socioeconomic index, it was found that for patients living in conjugal or parental family settings at the time of admission there was little evidence of the downward mobility that might be inferred from residential instability and movement into lower economic areas. For example, one year prior to admission 95 percent were living in an area at the same economic level, and five years prior to admission 81 percent were living at the same level. For patients from nonfamily settings (mostly single men), the corresponding figures were 50 percent and 29 percent, and there was a marked concentration of these patients in the poorer areas of the city.

A study of social mobility requires measures of the individual's social class at two different points in time. Interpretations must take into account the previously noted sources of error and artifacts in social-class studies, and must also consider problems specific to the study of social mobility. For example, the investigator's concepts and methods must be adequate for and sensitive to changes that may have taken place over time in the system of social stratification. Thus, being a school teacher today may have a different meaning for women than it did 30 years ago; many occupations did not exist less than a generation ago for which occupations at an equivalent rank must be defined in order to measure social mobility. This point underscores the importance of control-group designs in these investigations.

Studies of social mobility must also define the point of origin to which the individual's later position is to be compared. There are several alternative points that may be used—for example, the social class of the parents, the individual's first occupation on entering the labor market, the social position of his siblings, or the occupational rank of others with comparable education. Which of these is used depends upon the investigator's theory of social class and social mobility. These theories are rarely made explicit, and there appears to be an implicit assumption that all of the possible measures are equivalent in meaning and will produce the same results. This assumption is clearly not tenable.

The success of both the Lystad and Clausen and Kohn studies in using control-group designs and in tracing occupational shifts in both their control and patient samples over a long period of time is encouraging. Further studies of this type would be extremely useful. In order to make firmer statements about the relationship of social mobility to the incidence of schizophrenia, it will be necessary to obtain data on populations larger than those studied thus far. The usefulness of such studies would be markedly increased if they reflected more complex ideas about occupational shifts and mobility than are represented by measuring the amount of change up or down on a single dimension.

Migration. Differentials in rates of mental disorders between migrant and nonmigrant populations have also received considerable attention. In her interpretative review of studies that forms the introduction of Malzberg and Lee's report, Dorothy Thomas concludes:

A variety of approaches suggest that migrants, variously defined, do indeed differ from non-migrants, also variously defined, in respect to the incidence of mental disease; and the weight of evidence favors an interpretation that migrants represent greater "risks" than non-migrants. But many exceptions have been noted and many ingenious attempts have been made to explain them away. Closer examination of both generalizations and exceptions shows so many inconsistencies in definitions, so few adequate bases of controls, so many intervening variables, so little comparability as to time and place, that the fundamental "cause" of the discrepancies may merely be the nonadditive nature of the findings of the different studies (Malzberg & Lee, 1956, p. 41).

The problems noted by Thomas are serious, even though these studies display, on the whole, a high level of rigor and precision in procedures and analyses.

A good example of systematic and careful work is Odegaard's (1932) early study. Striking differences were found between Norwegian-born and native-born residents of Minnesota in over-all rates of mental disorder, with the migrants having higher rates. Unfortunately for our present purposes, his analysis of schizophrenia differentials and migration is limited to a comparison of Norwegian-born persons in Minnesota with Norwegians in Norway—that is, a comparison of emigrants with nonemigrants. The emigrants show higher rates of schizophrenia, with the females showing the more striking difference.

Malzberg and Lee's (1956) investigation of admissions to all psychiatric hospitals in New York State in 1940-41 involves specific controls and uses three different classifications of migration status in order to make a more precise determination of the factors at work. They find that for both sexes in white and nonwhite groups, the hospital admission rates for dementia praecox are higher for both native-born and foreign-born migrants than they are for New York-born residents. Among whites, rates for native-born migrants are equal to or greater than foreign-born rates; among nonwhites, the foreign-born rates are higher. They also find that rates for all psychoses are particularly high for recent migrants (within 5 years prior to the census date), and especially so for nonwhites.

On the other hand, Jaco's (1960) recent study, which compares native-born and non-native-born Texans, reports no systematic differences in rates of schizophrenia between these two groups. In only one subgroup, Spanish-American females, is there any evidence that migrant rates are higher than nonmigrants as defined in this one study. Jaco notes several differences between his and the Malzberg-Lee study that might account for the differences in findings: Different socioeconomic conditions between the two states and at the different periods studied, differentials in over-all rates of migration into Texas and New York, and different case-finding procedures.

Despite the inconsistency among the findings from different studies, there is a general tendency in the literature to assume higher rates for migrants. Thus Lemkau and Crocetti (1958, p. 81) state: "The most striking differentials in the rates of schizophrenia are those between age groups and between mobile and non-mobile populations . . . the more mobile populations frequently have higher rates of the disease than the non-mobile." They go on to note briefly several different interpretations of this differential: "Whether this is because of a tendency for individuals in a pre-schizoid stage to be migratory generally or to migrate to different cultural settings, or whether this is due to the greater stress involved in a person's living in a somewhat mobile sub-culture or a new and alien cultural milieu is not clear" (p. 81).

Malzberg and Lee (1956) in a qualifying note on their findings, point to a possibly important statistical artifact in migrant studies: The population turnover among migrants is relatively high and the population at risk used as the denominator in computing rates may be too low, thus artificially increasing the migrant rates.

The demographic variable of migration is closer in many ways to clinical considerations about the onset of schizophrenia than either social class or social mobility. In clinical theory, ideas of loss, of identity problems, and of lack of involvement with other people enter into discussions of the etiology of schizophrenia. The possible connection between these concepts and the social-psychological position of the migrant is an obvious one; it suggests that future studies must be as concerned with the specific environments from which the migrants come as with their place of destination. Their past and present living arrangements, whether isolated or within a family (as, for example, in the study by Gerard and Houston, 1953), and the social environments of their points of origin and destination must be examined. The evidence on social mobility would also suggest the importance of bringing together ideas and measures of both social and geographic mobility in further work.

Culture and Schizophrenia

There is a sense in which the variables already discussed, such as social class, are "cultural" as well as social. In our organization of this review we are distinguishing more between the units of study and between the directions of theorizing than between variables as either social or cultural. Whereas in the previous sections we investigated whether rates of schizophrenia varied with social class, social mobility rates, or geographic mobility rates, in this portion we begin with the characteristics of cultures and ask whether different characteristics are more or less likely to predispose persons to schizophrenia. An adequate understanding of etiological processes requires a combination of these two broad directions of work and theory; we shall return to this in the closing section of the paper.

In the following sections, we will review materials that treat the relation of "culture as a whole" to the etiology of schizophrenia. As will be seen, although several conceptual models exist as potential starting points for research and there are numerous reports of mental disorders in a great variety of societies, remarkably little systematic data have been collected that bear on the significance of cultural differences for the etiology of schizophrenia.

Several papers (Leighton & Hughes, 1956; Jackson, 1960; Clausen & Kohn, 1954) hypothesize ways in which culture might influence or cause mental illness, but apparently there is very little empirical support for the hypothesized causal relationships. Such evidence as does relate culture to schizophrenia bears more on the question of content, or symptomatology, than on etiology, development, or cause of the illness. Beyond the possibility suggested in the literature that rates vary from society to society, and the implication that this *may* be a function of culture, there is no evidence relating culture in a causal manner to schizophrenia.

There are at least three broad approaches to the problem of studying and demonstrating any relationships that might exist between culture and schizophrenia: The cross-cultural or comparative approach, the study of total communities, and the study of culture change.

The Cross-Cultural Approach. The comparative method, while not uniquely anthropological, has been used to good advantage by anthropologists to examine the universality of various propositions concerning human behavior. It allows a certain degree of scientific control and is therefore particularly useful in the study of phenomena for which alternative methods are not feasible. Clausen (1959, p. 496), in discussing such an approach to the investigation of mental disorders, has stated:

> . . . in attempting to interpret in an etiological framework any observed difference in the incidences of treated or psychiatrically observed mental illness between two population segments (whether these be social classes, ethnic groups, or subcultures), the crucial question is: do some discernible aspects of life processes in one of these segments give rise to more cases of mental illness than are produced in the other? Or, restated, if the two subcultures do differ in the amounts of mental illness produced, what are the specific social and cultural variables or constellations of variables involved, and how do they exercise their effect?

While it is probably true that the comparative cross-cultural approach alone can never lead to definitive answers regarding disease etiology, it appears to be as good a starting point as any other in epidemiological studies of certain diseases. Thus the primary function of such an approach is to provide working hypotheses for further research, and possibly to better delineate the nature of the dependent variable.

A variant of the comparative approach limits the scope of inquiry by focusing on the effect of a particular variable, or set of variables, in diverse cultures. For example, one might look at the relation of social class to the prevalence of schizophrenia in a number of different settings. In this way hypotheses relating such a variable to schizophrenia may be tested and refined.

In such comparative approaches it is of course of paramount importance that the rates be accurate. The problems involved in accurate determination of rates are severe in the United States and Western Europe, but doubly so in those non-Western societies where many of these studies have been carried out. Often these comparative studies are not performed by a single investigator working in two or more different cultures; rather, they involve a comparison of a number of individual studies carried out by as many investigators. More important is the fact that diagnostic comparability is absent when findings from many different societies are assembled. This is true not only for the reasons mentioned earlier (different types of rates, different case-finding procedures, and so forth) but also because of additional questions concerning the cross-cultural applicability of designations of normal and abnormal behavior patterns.

In part for these reasons, a review of the cross-cultural literature, particularly that concerning non-Western societies, is disheartening. For example, Wittkower and his associates (Wittkower, Murphy, Fried, & Ellenburger, 1960, p. 855), in a praiseworthy attempt to build a body of data, organized a "Transcultural Psychiatric Review and Newsletter" and sent questionnaires to psychiatrists and others throughout the world. They received reports from 37 respondents in 25 countries. The questionnaires cover "observed schizophrenic symptomatology, clinical subtypes, cultures and peoples to whom the observations referred, and locale of observation and psychiatric orientation of observer." There are no valid data on rates, either prevalence or incidence, or even on ratios of one type of illness to another, since the returns are based on estimates by the respondents derived from a variety of sources. There is thus no comparability. In the end this survey comprises what the authors call "preliminary observations" or impressions of the ratio of schizophrenia to other mental disorders, and of ratios of schizophrenic subtypes, plus impressions of the cultural effects on symptomatology and delusional content (Wittkower & Fried, 1959).

Recent reviews by Benedict and Jacks (1954), Benedict (1958), and Lemkau and Crocetti (1958) of existing studies on non-Western groups highlight both the lack of substantive findings and many of the methodological problems involved.

Benedict's exhaustive review included studies of Africans, Negroes in Latin and South America, American Indians, Micronesians, Australians, Formosans, Japanese, Fijians, East Indians, and assorted immigrant groups to the United States and Canada. These studies document the noncomparability of incidence and prevalence since, with but few exceptions—such as Lin's (1953) study of Formosa—they use hospital admissions as a reflection of incidence of schizophrenia within the several populations. In fact, most of the writers devote little attention to rates but tend to be concerned with symptoms, ratios of schizophrenia subtypes, and delusional content. Thus one writer points out that his group is high in paranoids but low in catatonics, and other writers point out the reverse.

In passing, Benedict takes up the issue of the possible relativity of symptomatology, and tends to be critical of the "anthropological position" which, as he sees it, almost denies the possibility of abnormality within primitive societies (although he notes that the strength of this position within anthropology seems to wax and wane with time). He points out that the belief, no longer as popular as it once was, that schizophrenia is a disease of civilization is sheer folklore, and that while the rates reported in these studies are questionable, the fact of the existence of the disease in each of these societies is not. Additionally, Benedict, as well as the authors he reviews, asserts that not only are the forms and symptoms of the disease derived from the culture, but also there are obvious "cultural" differences in diagnosis, treatment, hospitalization, admission rates, and tolerance of behavior in the community.

Benedict points out that the majority of studies do not even attempt to deal with the question of etiology. Those that do almost uniformly offer the hypothesis of rapid culture change as the major etiologic influence. The implicit assumption is of course that in the "primitive" state there is no schizophrenia. Benedict is highly skeptical of the evidence offered in support of this position. In a few of these studies low socioeconomic status is cited as being possibly etiologically relevant.

To illustrate the difficulties in utilizing published studies for cross-cultural comparisons it is instructive to focus in some detail on what is frequently cited as one of the better studies of this type. In his review Benedict (1958, p. 698) states:

For schizophrenia among natives of West Africa we can turn to the recent study by Tooth, which is superior in most respects to any of the foregoing. Tooth, working on the Gold Coast, conducted a kind of census survey, collecting data on nonhospitalized cases through surveys by resident officers and examining as many of these cases as he could gain access to. Although he admits that his material is inadequate in many respects and describes the difficulties produced by native resistance, language handicaps, and the like, *this study must be considered the most nearly complete of any for Africa* [italics added].

Both Benedict's and Tooth's caveats notwithstanding, this study is worthless for epidemiological purposes. In the first place the paper is replete with judgmental and unsubstantiated observations on African character and personality. More important for our purposes, however, are methodological shortcomings. This is a general population survey, but the findings come only from *nonhospitalized* cases in the population at large. If conclusions are to be drawn concerning, say, the distribution of schizophrenia or mental illness in general in the different areas of the Gold Coast, and if hospital populations are not included in the obtained rates, then the interpretations are subject to the artifact of possible differences in each area in the willingness to hospitalize, or keep at home, those suffering from disease. Although Tooth does warn against taking these data too seriously, he himself does nonetheless draw conclusions.

How did Tooth find his cases? He asked census enumerators and local chiefs to supply lists of names of "mad" persons. He writes: "But the reactions of Chiefs to this request were erratic and unpredictable and this part of the work furnished an interesting example of the difficulties of organizing even a comparatively *simple* [sic!] project through the native authority." Using such questionable methods, after two years Tooth (1950) assembled 400 cases of mental illness. He writes:

During the period of two years covered by this report approximately 400 examples of mental illness were seen but in less than half this number was it possible to obtain anything approaching a satisfactory record of the illness. Accounts from relatives or persons who had known the subject before the onset of the illness were obtained in 173 instances and although, in many of these, the information available fell short of what is normally desirable, it was sufficient for the purpose of classification. It is with the analysis of these 173 cases that the following section is concerned.

No mention is ever again made of the 227 discarded cases, thus introducing possible biases—sex, age, tribe, and so forth—regarding which cases it is likely to get information on, and which not.

In addition, there are numerous other very considerable shortcomings as regards standards and criteria, methods of observation, and so on. What are left, then, are some characteristics of types of mentally ill Africans, with no reliable way to estimate either rates or differences in rates from tribe to tribe, area to area, sex to sex. We cite this study in some detail not as an example of a poor study, but because, according to the consensus of most reviewers, it is one of the best studies available. Since its publication, Tooth's warnings have rarely been heeded and his conclusions have tended to be accepted at face value.

Lemkau and Crocetti (1958, p. 65), while reviewing much of the literature covered by Benedict, have focused almost completely on schizophrenia; they are more concerned with rates than with symptoms. They summarize their findings as follows:

> There are many descriptions in the literature of psychopathological pictures in other than Western European cultures, but most of these are anecdotal descriptions of a single case or of a group of cases with no relation to a standard population. Many are reports of cases which are clearly comparable to schizophrenia as it is known to Western psychiatrists, and, as a generalization, it may be said that psychiatrists trained in Europe and the United States seem to find cases which fit these diagnostic categories in whatever cultures they work in. As a symptom picture the disease appears to occur in every population that has been thoroughly studied, whatever its cultural background. The rate of occurrence is quite another matter. It is fair to say at the outset that there is no culture outside of the Western European group which has been studied as intensively. There are a great many unsupported statements in the literature that this or that culture has more or less of schizophrenia than others. Most of these data are purely impressionistic and are frequently based on one of two equally undependable indicators: the investigator's prejudices regarding the etiology of schizophrenia or the use of inadequately gathered statistics.

They conclude:

> In summary, there is evidence that schizophrenia, or schizophrenia-like reactions, occur in all known cultures. There is extremely little valid data on the incidence or prevalence of the disease in other than Western European-type cultures; within rough limits, rates are similar in all those which have been carefully studied (p. 66).

From the foregoing it is evident that the literature dealing with schizophrenia among primitive groups is not likely to be a particularly valuable source for rates. On the whole, the comparative cross-cultural approach has until now been of limited value with regard to an understanding of the etiology of schizophrenia.

The study of total communities. The rationale for studying mental illness within "total communities" is both plausible and reasonable. Social variables can best be studied in the context of the larger cultural system in which they are found. Any given variable could have considerably different significance in different societies. Lower socioeconomic status, for example, may be critically important where the range is wide; where the range is narrow, it may be of minor importance. Thus, to study such a variable cross-culturally with the assumption that its cultural meaning and significance is *constant* may very well be unwarranted. The study of total communities would not only measure the relationship of the rate of mental illness to social-class position, but also—by examining the variable in its total cultural context—would attempt to assess the meaning and importance of class membership within this community.

Additionally, a much wider range of social and cultural phenomena are surveyed in community studies than is the case when particular variables or groups of variables are selected in advance for primary or sole attention. Under the former conditions, previously unsuspected variables bearing powerfully on mental disease are more likely to impress themselves upon those conducting the study than if the focus is a priori on particular sets of variables. And while it is less likely that not-so-powerful variables will make themselves known to investigators, there is still a better chance that they will receive attention when the investigator goes into the community than if he relies simply on hospital admission data and the usual demographic indexes.

Finally, among the important advantages of community studies is the increased opportunity to study the healthy as well as the sick. Hospital studies often use control populations, but in community studies one can examine more directly how the ill and the well in the same social environment differ from each other in terms of a range of social and cultural characteristics. The answers should be productive of working hypotheses on a number of levels.

From reviewing the literature it appears that disadvantages must outweigh the advantages, since exceedingly few studies of total communities are reported. What is more discouraging is the lack of comparability of available studies, not only in terms of rates, but also in terms of the social data collected. The existing handful of community studies all rely on prevalence measures, rather than incidence. Most studies group together several different categories of mental illness and do not focus on particular disorders, since the rates for individual diseases tend to be so low that adequate numbers are not obtained unless huge populations are sampled. In some cases, traditional diagnostic categories are not used in major analyses, which means, of course, that the results are of limited value in the study of specific diseases, such as schizophrenia. Even where the diagnoses are kept separate, and the statistical procedures are rigorous, attention to social variables is superficial. In other cases, the social and cultural variables are relatively well handled, but the statistical procedures may be questioned.

It is unfortunate that in neither of the two recent elaborate community studies of mental disorder does schizophrenia receive separate attention. In the Midtown study (Srole, Langner, Michael, Opler, & Rennie, 1962), the primary dependent variable in the analysis of social and cultural variables is a general rating of "impairment," without reference to diagnosis. The Stirling County study will also emphasize general ratings of impairment and psychiatric disorder in the still-unpublished third volume, which will contain data on the distribution of levels of impairment in the several communities studied. These communities have been classified in terms of their level of social disorganization, with the prediction that the more "disorganized" communities will have higher rates of mental disorder than the "integrated" communities (Leighton et al., 1959; Hughes et al., 1960). Comparative studies such as this hold much promise.

The Formosan study by Lin (1953) is generally regarded as one of the better community surveys of mental disorder. Schizophrenia receives separate treatment and analysis, and Lin's methodology, especially his case-finding techniques, is impressive. Using what he calls the "census examination method" Lin carefully studied random samples from three communities in Formosa: a rural village, a small town, and an urban community. The total sample of almost 20,000 was interviewed by psychiatric teams. All cases of suspected mental abnormalities were reviewed by Lin, who was responsible for final diagnosis. Forty-three cases of schizophrenia were uncovered, yielding the following prevalence rates per 1,000: 1.8 in the rural village, 2.5 in the town, and 2.1 in the city. The differences in rates between the three communities appear negligible. However, these cases of schizophrenia tended to concentrate in the center (and most densely populated area) of *each* community (a finding in keeping with earlier ecological studies in the United States). In comparing densely populated areas with sparsely populated areas Lin found a ratio of 29:14. Lin further found that the rates were higher for females, and that they varied by social class (upper 3.5, middle 1.2, lower 4.5), though no interpretation was offered for these variations in rates. Lin did not make it clear exactly how these class categories were established, mentioning only that a number of factors—such as wealth, education, occupation, and appearance of house and furniture—were taken into consideration. Even in this careful study, the independent variables used to study the relation of schizophrenia prevalence to social factors reflect the general poverty of the field, consisting only of sex, ecological distribution, and social class.

In contrast to Lin's study, the investigation by Eaton and Weil (1955) of the mental health of the Hutterites uses somewhat questionable rates and case-finding techniques, but is quite sophisticated with regard to social and cultural factors. Essentially Eaton and Weil were interested in examining the hypothesis held by some observers that mental illness is absent in the Hutterite society, as a result of a culture and system of values that stress conformism, cooperation, and religion and devalues such "American characteristics" as aggression and competition, thought by laymen, at least, to be productive of higher rates of mental illness. Using anthropological techniques (key informants, participant observation, and so forth), the authors constructed an ethnographic description of this group, with the focus on areas of potential interpersonal difficulties. While these investigators found, in contrast to some expectation, that mental disorder was far from absent in this group, they did find a relatively low prevalence of schizophrenia, 1.1 per 1,000.

However, objections to the conclusions may be raised on at least two counts. First, the case-finding techniques represent a mixed bag. Some communities were intensively investigated, with Weil, the psychiatrist, personally examining suspected mentally ill persons; other communities were not even visited and cases were collected from hospital records, correspondence and interviews with physicians, and hearsay from Hutterite community leaders. It is difficult to diagnose an illness like schizophrenia under the best conditions, but to do it on the basis of descriptions by community leaders of the behavior of suspected individuals is highly questionable. Second, the rate used, the "lifetime morbidity rate" (all individuals alive on a given date with any history of schizophrenia), is of limited value regarding the crucial question of etiology. Kramer's (1958, p. 838) comments on this problem also point to a number of important general issues that community researchers must deal with:

In effect, this index is a determination of the proportion of a population alive on a given date who have a history of an attack of mental disorder. It should be apparent that this index is an inappropriate one to use if the focus of the research is to determine the influence of culture on the rate at which mental disorder occurs. The proportion of a population surviving to a given date with a history of a disease is a function of the incidence rate, the mortality of persons who have ever had the disease and the mortality of the non-affected population. The fact that lifetime prevalence would differ between two or more cultural groups does not mean that incidence differs. Indeed, incidence may be equal while the duration of life following attack by the illness differs. For example, there may be two primitive cultures A and B with an equal rate of incidence of mental disorders. Culture A's attitude toward the mentally ill is a protective one and everything possible is done to prolong their lives, whereas culture B's attitude is just the opposite. Thus, in A the interval between onset of illness and death would be considerably longer than in B and as a result, lifetime prevalence in A would be higher than in B.

Culture change. In the study of the relationship of culture to schizophrenia, the study of culture changes differs from the comparative and total community approaches in that it does not constitute a distinct methodological approach. It nevertheless deserves separate attention because of the fascination it seems to hold for a number of writers as a possible key to understanding the pathogenesis of this disease and many others. For example, Leighton and Hughes (1956, p. 363) have written:

In concluding our paper, we should like to return again to a point mentioned earlier. This is our impression that comparative study of change is one of the most fruitful opportunities for uncovering the nature of socio-cultural factors in relation to psychiatric disorder.

There are a number of different processes that may be used to define some aspect of culture change—industrialization, business cycles, acculturation, migration, and so on. Murphy (1959), in reviewing the literature relating social change to mental health, holds that there are two types of hypotheses in this area, one which lays the cause of disorders to the factor of change itself, the other which suggests that social change in certain circumstances combines with other elements in the situation to produce disorder. While Murphy's review deals with mental illness in general and includes only a few studies which focus on schizophrenia, his general statement is nevertheless worth noting: "There are almost as many studies which suggest that social change leads to no increase in mental disorder, or even to a decrease, as there are studies suggesting that an increase is directly traceable to such a cause" (Murphy, 1959, p. 306).

With the exception of the migration studies reviewed earlier, there are exceedingly few studies dealing with the relation of culture change to schizophrenia separately from other mental disorders. For example, probably the most careful and rigorous of these studies, that by Goldhamer and Marshall (1953) deals with psychoses in general and does not treat schizophrenia separately. Nonetheless, Goldhamer and Marshall's findings deserve attention because they run so counter to what had been thought concerning the supposed influence of culture change in Western society on allegedly rising rates of psychosis. Using first admission to a variety of mental institutions in Massachusetts from the years 1840 to 1940, the authors were able ingeniously to calculate age- and sex-specific psychosis rates and found that there had been no long-term increase during the last century in the incidence of the psychoses of early and middle life.

For an example of a recent study purporting to relate culture change to changes in the rates of mental illness in the United States, with schizophrenia rates treated separately, we may turn to the paper by Wilson and Lantz (1957). Using hospital admissions (it is not clear whether they include readmissions), the writers compute rates for whites and Negroes in Virginia for the years 1920 to 1955. On the basis of these rates, they conclude: "It is felt that the fact that there is more mental illness among the Negroes of Virginia than among the whites and more mental illness among the Negroes in 1954 than in 1914 is due to segregation and to the uncertainties of the Negro race as they cross from one culture to another" (Wilson & Lantz, 1957, p. 31). Such a conclusion is unwarranted on at least two counts: The cases are hospital cases only, so that rates are questionable; even more important, there are no systematic measures of the independent cultural variables—these are simply crude impressions.

As expected, the situation is no better in acculturation studies of nonliterate groups. The previously criticized study by Tooth (1950) takes up the question of culture change, and is often cited in this connection as yielding negative evidence for the role of culture change in supposedly increasing rates of mental disorder. Of course, the methodological inadequacies of this study make it clear that any generalizations derived from it are, at best, highly questionable. Nonetheless, Tooth's interpretation is really most curious, for he finds data that would normally lead one to conclude that change does, in fact, lead to higher rates of mental disease, and interprets this data as supporting the opposite conclusion. This has not escaped Benedict's (1958, p. 698) notice:

> . . . he [Tooth] handles this point in a peculiarly inconsistent manner, however, and in fact suggests that the literacy rate is higher than might be anticipated among psychotics. Moreover, the incidence figures cited by him show a considerably higher value for the one relatively urbanized district.

Finally, a study from East Africa by Carothers (1948), which attempts to demonstrate that culture change does lead to higher rates of mental illness, is also highly questionable on a number of counts, not the least of these being that the data consist of hospital admissions in a country where such admissions cannot seriously be taken to be representative, subject as they are to any number of biases.

In short, the study of culture change has not yet been productive of careful studies of substantive data. Very little has been done. But on the basis of studies of change and other diseases (for example, hypertension), and on the basis of studies of acculturation and its known psychological impact, culture change undoubtedly deserves attention.

In summarizing this section, we agree with the consensus that a relationship has not yet been demonstrated between the culture and schizophrenia. There are various possible explanations for this. Most logical, but most difficult to accept, is the possibility that no such relationship exists. More acceptable to social scientists is the likelihood that the relationship is too complex, or too distant, or both, making it extremely difficult to study. Or it may be that the methods of study have so far been inadequate. Or it may simply be that the status of the dependent variable, schizophrenia—and the numerous problems associated with it—has hindered the accumulation of such evidence.

Any or all of the above may explain the dearth of substantive evidence. There is, in addition, the important fact that few systematic studies of culture and schizophrenia have so far been reported in the literature. A number of factors inhibit such research—time, expense, the need for an interdisciplinary team, the lack of psychiatric researchers able to spend large blocks of time in the field, and so on. Further, there seems to be a widespread but insufficiently supported belief that the incidence of schizophrenia is relatively constant from one culture to another. This current belief may be a reaction to the previous belief in the rarity of the illness among primitive groups. Whatever its source, such a belief tends to dampen the enthusiasm of investigators. In sum, the number of acceptable studies that have been conducted on this question are far too few to offer even the most tentative test of the postulated relationships.

Discussion

Writing a concluding section for a review of studies of the social etiology of schizophrenia is like talking with the relatives of the deceased after returning from a funeral. Other than some platitudes, there is little that can be suggested that would remedy, alleviate, or eliminate the trouble.

It is not difficult to criticize the state of the field—few studies are available, concepts and methods are unclear and unstandardized, findings are inconsistent, and speculation abounds in the absence of reliable empirical knowledge. However, it is difficult to make useful recommendations in a field where so little is tied down. How does one decide which end to secure of a billowing canvas? Or in which direction to head if there are no road markers and perhaps no roads?

Faced with this problem, critics and reviewers tend either to examine for the nth time some of the basic methodological issues or to design "ideal" studies for someone else to carry out. The interesting characteristic of the considerable existing commentary and analysis is its generally high level of quality. It is an instructive and serious literature.

One of the striking characteristics of the field is the fact of a small amount of inadequate research combined with a large amount of adequate criticism. The question arises: If we know so much why aren't we doing it? Or, if we're all so smart why aren't we rich? We believe that part of the answer lies in the narrow and restrictive definitions of epidemiologic inquiry that are implied in both the studies and the analyses. With a few noteworthy exceptions, studies in this area are simple in design and fall into the category of descriptive epidemiology. More complex designs that are closer to analytic epidemiology have not been used systematically; the separate components of the prevalence picture, particularly duration of illness, have not been explored; simple summary statistics are used with no attempt made to analyze data with more analytic multivariate techniques; finally, the hypotheses developed in the descriptive studies are not followed up through analytic and experimental studies.

We believe that the "bench-mark" data about the distribution of illness that may be accumulated through descriptive epidemiology are most meaningful when there is a body of basic knowledge about the illness itself; where such knowledge is lacking, as is the case in schizophrenia, the findings of descriptive epidemiology provide little in the way of an understanding of the illness. This does not mean that epidemiologic investigation must await the solution of the clinical questions about onset, natural history, subtypes, and remission patterns. However, in order both to accumulate information that will not be rendered obsolete or worthless by some change in psychiatric practice (such as, for example, the introduction of tranquilizers) and to contribute to the over-all understanding of the illness, epidemiologic investigations should be more analytic in design and more complex in the methods and concepts used than has been true in the past.

Essentially, we believe that epidemiological investigation will come to contribute more to an understanding of schizophrenia if studies are as much concerned with limiting the range of possible interpretation of the findings as with generating the findings themselves. We do not mean that empirically minded epidemiologists should become theory-builders; however, they must build into their designs the types of controls and measuring instruments that will permit alternative and competing interpretations to be evaluated. Thus, studies of social class and schizophrenia that do not permit some comparison of social mobility and social stress hypotheses with each other will have little to contribute to an understanding of the relations between social factors and illness. Arguments between adherents of various theories tend to become sterile without the accumulation of empirical data by means of which the theories can be checked directly; on the other hand, the accumulation of descriptive statistics leads to little progress, since the different studies do not allow for meaningful comparisons if similar control variables have not been included.

Some concrete implications of these general considerations will be noted in this closing section. We will give brief attention to problems that emerge with regard to the diagnostic classification, control variables, morbidity indexes, and sociologic variables used.

As has been pointed out, the nosological and diagnostic problems hampering the study of schizophrenia are still far from solution.

At this point in time, investigators must be concerned with the reliability of the diagnostic procedures used in the series of cases in their study. The use of diagnoses that appear on hospital case records without further examination of the underlying diagnostic procedures is completely inadequate. Studies that include standardized and evaluated diagnosis of cases as part of the investigation are ideal but this is not always feasible or economical. Faced with someone else's diagnosis, investigators should at least try to find out "who" this someone else is—a first-year psychiatric resident, a senior psychiatrist, a staff conference; and the basis on which the diagnosis was assigned—a half-hour admission interview, psychological tests, a month's observation on the psychiatric ward. Where both an admission and a discharge diagnosis are available, cases might be classified usefully as: Schizophrenic at admission only, schizophrenic at discharge only, schizophrenic at both admission and discharge. Obviously, none of these procedures increase the reliability of diagnosis, but they would help investigators to understand more precisely the meanings of both consistent and inconsistent findings from various studies. Further, attention to the problem in this explicit way would be another pressure operating on clinical psychiatry to sharpen its diagnostic processes.

With regard to the problem of the subtypes of schizophrenia, each investigator will presumably have his own preference depending in part on the norms of the clinical subculture in which he carries out his work. We would urge that all investigators use some scheme of classification, whatever its conceptual and clinical basis, so that social variables may be related to one or two or even three types of schizophrenia rather than simply to some general category. This procedure would have several useful effects. First, it would permit an assessment of the limits or generality of influence of a particular social variable. For example: Are there social-class differentials in simple as well as paranoid schizophrenia? Is there a disproportionate incidence among migrants of schizophrenics with good premorbid social adjustment as compared with those of poor premorbid social adjustment? Second, the utility of the subclassification may be determined. If all the subtypes, for example, show the same direction and degree of relationship to a range of social variables, then this would argue against the meaningfulness of the distinction used; however, if the incidence of one subtype is higher among women, but of another subtype is higher among men, then the way is open to a fuller understanding of the illness.

Our own preference is for a distinction on the order of that between good and poor premorbid patients since there is now considerable evidence that these two groups differ in terms of genetic background, social relationships, symptoms, and prognosis (Rodnick & Garmezy, 1957; Rosenthal, 1959; Phillips, 1953; Vaillant, 1962). Indicators of this distinction in hospital case records would include age of onset, premorbid social and sexual adjustment, and improvement or discharge from the hospital.

On the whole, investigators have been aware of the problems of research controls and in most studies analyses are conducted with the control of age and sex; sometimes socioeconomic and marital status are used. However, in order to test the independent effect of the variable under study, these controls are often applied in a mechanical and indiscriminate way that erases the effect of the control variable. For example, two populations will be standardized for age so as to give us rates that are comparable despite the real age composition differences between the two. Knowing that schizophrenia peaks in the under-35 age group and that the mode appears later and drops less sharply for women than for men, we think it would be more interesting and more instructive to look for relations between social variables and schizophrenia separately within under- and over-35 age groups than to obscure such possible differences by a mechanical standardization for age.

We have already discussed a number of issues concerning the index of morbidity used, the different meaning of ecological and individual correlations, and the differing interpretations dependent on whether social variables have been associated with prevalence or incidence measures. Two points merit explicit emphasis. First, attention has been almost exclusively directed toward incidence as measured by first admission to hospitals. Where chronicity is a variable and important component of the disease process—for example, there seem to be at least two types of schizophrenia that vary in terms of chronicity (Vaillant, 1962)—it is equally important to give additional emphasis to this aspect of the over-all prevalence picture. Second, the relative rate for schizophrenia as compared to other major mental illnesses is a matter of great importance for an understanding of the significance of social differentials in schizophrenia itself. For example, is the over-all rate for all mental illnesses relatively the same from one social group to another, with rare differentials for specific illnesses primarily a function of different diagnostic "styles"? Or are schizophrenia and the other mental illnesses related in different ways to different social variables, with the latter having specific rather than general influence? There was some early interest in these comparisons [for example, in the different ratios of schizophrenia to manic-depressive psychosis in different social classes (Lemkau & Crocetti, 1958)], and some reports contain detailed tables that permit such comparisons across a number of social variables (Jaco, 1960).

It has been particularly discouraging to the authors as social scientists to have to recognize the simplistic quality both of the social variables used in epidemiological studies and the forms of analyses into which they have been incorporated. Whereas in the investigation of almost every other problem, a relationship with social class would be the beginning of intensive analysis through a series control and test variables, in the investigation of the epidemiology of schizophrenia it often stands for the complete analysis. In examining the social correlates of any other piece of complex behavior, the ecological and cultural characteristics of the groups in which the individuals are members would become an explicit part of the analysis through designs permitting such cross-comparisons, but in the study of schizophrenia it takes contradictions in findings to force such factors into researchers' awareness.[2]

These last problems are related to the tendency to use only macrosociological variables in these investigations, such as social class or migration, and to pay little or no attention to such microsociological variables as family processes, living arrangements, or peer-group patterns. Few studies have tried to bring together micro- and macro-levels of variables; Gerard and Houston's (1953) work is a notable exception. Recent emphasis on the importance of certain family process variables (Spiegel & Bell, 1957; Jackson, 1960) suggests that it would be particularly useful if measures of these types of variables could be incorporated into more traditional epidemiological work.

Epidemiologists and statisticians have a tendency to think of theory as that vague and uncharted area of the cognitive map which will disappear as one accumulates more hard information; theorists find that the accumulated hard facts are not as relevant to the theoretical issues as might be desired; and the clinicians may be heard to complain that both the ideas and the statistics generated respectively by theorists and researchers are too abstract to be of use in understanding and dealing with the concrete phe-

[2] See, for example, Clausen and Kohn's (1954) comments on size of city, and Locke's (1958) remarks on the disparity between the ecological findings and usual expectations.

nomena of schizophrenia. We do not believe that the basic aim of understanding the etiology of schizophrenia and its ultimate prevention, control, and treatment are served well by the type of insulation that has prevailed among researcher, theorist, and clinician. Neither does it seem to us to be a plea for eclecticism to urge that theory and research findings should be relevant both to each other and to the phenomena of basic interest.

Most of the studies reviewed in this paper were carried out during the last 25 years, many of them during the past decade. The amount of useful and systematic knowledge about social factors in the epidemiology of schizophrenia is disappointingly small. However, it should be clear from the previous pages that it is within investigators' capacity to know much more. Instruments, procedures, and concepts are available that will permit organized and significant research. Whether or not much more will be known at the end of the next decade or 25 years will depend primarily on researchers' willingness to invest in these difficult undertakings.

REFERENCES

American Psychiatric Association. *Diagnostic and statistical manual: mental disorders.* Washington, D.C.: Author, 1952.

Bellak, L. (Ed.). *Schizophrenia: a review of the syndrome.* New York: Logos Press, 1958.

Benedict, P. K. Sociocultural factors in schizophrenia. In L. Bellak (Ed.), *Schizophrenia: a review of the syndrome.* New York: Logos Press, 1958. Pp. 694-729.

Benedict, P. K., & Jacks, I. Mental illness in primitive societies. *Psychiatry*, 1954, 17, 377-389.

Bleuler, Eugen. Dementia praecox or the group of schizophrenias. *Monograph series on schizophrenia.* (Translated from the German Edition, 1911). New York: International University Press, 1950.

Cameron, N. The functional psychoses. In J. M. Hunt (Ed.), *Personality and the behavior disorders.* Vol. 1. New York: Ronald Press, 1944. Pp. 861-921.

Cameron, N. *The psychology of behavior disorders.* Boston: Houghton Mifflin, 1947.

Carothers, J. C. A study of mental derangement in Africans, and an attempt to explain its peculiarities, more especially in relation to the African attitude to life. *Psychiatry*, 1948, 11, 47-85.

Clark, R. E. The relationship of schizophrenia to occupational income and occupational prestige. *American Sociological Review*, 1948, 13, 325-330.

Clausen, J. A.   The sociology of mental illness. In R. K. Merton, L. Broom, and L. S. Cottrell (Eds.), *Sociology today*. New York: Basic Books, 1959. Pp. 485-508.

Clausen, J. A., & Kohn, M. L.   The ecological approach in social psychiatry. *American Journal of Sociology*, 1954, **60**, 140-149.

Clausen, J. A., & Kohn, M. L.   Relation of schizophrenia to the social structure of a small city. In B. Pasamanick (Ed.), *Epidemiology of mental disorder*. Washington, D.C.: American Association for the Advancement of Science, 1959. Pp. 69-86.

Clausen, J. A., & Yarrow, Marian R.   The impact of mental illness on the family. *Journal of Social Issues*, 1955, **11** (No. 4).

Cumming, Elaine.   Phase movement in the support and control of the psychiatric patient. *Journal of Health and Human Behavior*, 1962, **3**, 235-241.

Dunham, H. W.   Social structures and mental disorders: competing hypotheses of explanation. In *Causes of mental disorders: a review of epidemiological knowledge, 1959*. New York: Milbank Memorial Fund, 1961. Pp. 227-265.

Eaton, J. W., & Weil, R. J.   *Culture and mental disorders*. Glencoe, Ill.: Free Press, 1955.

Faris, R. E. L., & Dunham, H. W.   *Mental disorders in urban areas*. Chicago: University of Chicago Press, 1939.

Frumkin, R. M.   Occupation and mental illness. *Ohio Public Welfare Statistics*, September 1952, 4-13.

Frumkin, R. M.   Occupation and major mental disorders. In A. M. Rose (Ed.), *Mental health and mental disorder*. New York: Norton, 1955. Pp. 136-160.

Geiger, H. J., & Scotch, N. A.   The epidemiology of essential hypertension: a review with special attention to psychological and sociocultural factors. I: Biologic mechanisms and descriptive epidemiology. *Journal of Chronic Disease*, 1963, **16**, 1151-1182.

Gerard, D. L., & Houston, L. G.   Family setting and the social ecology of schizophrenia. *Psychiatric Quarterly*, 1953, **27**, 90-101.

Goldhamer, H., & Marshall, A. W.   *Psychosis in civilization*. Glencoe, Ill.: Free Press, 1953.

Haase, W.   Rorschach diagnosis, socio-economic class and examiner bias. Unpublished doctoral dissertation, New York University, 1955.

Hoch, R. H., & Zubin, J. (Eds.).   *Comparative epidemiology of the mental disorders*. New York: Grune & Stratton, 1961.

Hollingshead, A. B., & Redlich, F. C.   *Social class and mental illness*. New York: Wiley, 1958.

Hughes, C. C.   *People of Cove and Woodlot*. New York: Basic Books, 1960.

Jackson, D. D. (Ed.).   *The etiology of schizophrenia*. New York: Basic Books, 1960.

Jackson, D. D.   Introduction. In D. D. Jackson (Ed.), *The etiology of schizophrenia*. New York: Basic Books, 1960. Pp. 3-20.

Jaco, E. G. *The social epidemiology of mental disorders.* New York: Russell Sage, 1960.

Kramer, M. A discussion of the concepts of incidence and prevalence as related to epidemiologic studies of mental disorder. *American Journal of Public Health,* 1957, 47, 826-840.

Kramer, M., Pollack, E. S., & Redick, R. W. Studies of the incidence and prevalence of hospitalized mental disorders in the United States: current status and future goals. In P. H. Hoch & J. Zubin (Eds.), *Comparative epidemiology of the mental disorders.* New York: Grune & Stratton, 1961. Pp. 56-100.

Lapouse, R., Monk, M. A., & Terris, M. The drift hypothesis and socioeconomic differentials in schizophrenia. *American Journal of Public Health,* 1956, 46, 978-986.

Leacock, Eleanor. Three social variables and the occurrence of mental disorder. In A. H. Leighton, J. A. Clausen, & R. N. Wilson (Eds.), *Explorations in social psychiatry.* New York: Basic Books, 1957. Pp. 308-337.

Leighton, A. *My name is legion.* New York: Basic Books, 1959.

Leighton, A. H., & Hughes, Jane H. Cultures as causative of mental disorder. In Milbank Memorial Fund, *Causes of mental disorders: a review of epidemiological knowledge, 1959.* New York: Author, 1961. Pp. 341-365.

Lemkau, P. Y., & Crocetti, G. M. Vital statistics of schizophrenia. In L. Bellak (Ed.), *Schizophrenia: a review of the syndrome.* New York: Logos Press, 1958. Pp. 64-81.

Lin, T. A study of the incidence of mental disorder in Chinese and other cultures. *Psychiatry,* 1953, 16, 313-336.

Locke, B. Z., et al. Problems in interpretation of patterns of first admissions to Ohio state public mental hospitals for patients with schizophrenic reactions. In B. Pasamanick & P. H. Knapp (Eds.), *Psychiatric research reports No. 10: social aspects of psychiatry.* Washington, D.C.: American Psychiatric Association, 1958. Pp. 172-196.

Lystad, Mary H. Social mobility among selected groups of schizophrenic patients. *American Sociological Review,* 1957, 22, 288-292.

MacMahon, B., Pugh, T. F., & Ipsen, J. *Epidemiologic methods.* Boston: Little, Brown, 1960.

Malzberg, B., & Lee, E. S. *Migration and mental disease.* New York: Social Science Research Council, 1956.

Milbank Memorial Fund. *Causes of mental disorders: a review of epidemiological knowledge, 1959.* New York: Author, 1961.

Murphy, H. B. M. Social change and mental health. In Milbank Memorial Fund, *Causes of mental disorders: a review of epidemiological knowledge, 1959.* New York: Author, 1961. Pp. 280-329.

Nolan, W. J. Occupation and dementia praecox. *New York State Hospital Quarterly,* 1917, 3, 127-154.

Nolan, W. J.   Occupation and manic-depressive psychosis. *New York State Hospital Quarterly*, 1918, 4, 75-102.

Norris, Vera.   Mental illness in London. *Maudsley Monograph*. London: Chapman and Hall, 1959, No. 6.

Odegaard, O.   Emigration and insanity: a study of mental disease among the Norwegian-born population of Minnesota. *Acta Psychiatrica et Neurologica*, Supplement IV. Copenhagen, 1932.

Pasamanick, B. (Ed.).   *Epidemiology of mental disorder*. Washington, D.C.: American Association for the Advancement of Science, 1959.

Phillips, L.   Case history data and prognosis in schizophrenia. *Journal of Nervous and Mental Disease*, 1953, 117, 515-525.

Plunkett, R. J., & Gordon, J. E.   Epidemiology and mental illness. *Monograph, Joint Commission on mental illness and health*. New York: Basic Books, 1960, No. 6.

Pugh, T. F., & MacMahon, B.   *Epidemiologic findings in United States hospital data*. Boston: Little, Brown, 1962.

Robinson, W. S.   Ecological correlations and the behavior of individuals. *American Sociological Review*, 1950, 15, 351-357.

Rodnick, E. H., & Garmezy, N.   An experimental approach to the study of motivation in schizophrenia. In M. R. Jones (Ed.), *Nebraska symposium on motivation: 1957*. Lincoln, Nebr.: University of Nebraska Press, 1957. Pp. 104-184.

Rosenthal, D.   Some factors associated with concordance and discordance with respect to schizophrenia in monozygotic twins. *Journal of Nervous and Mental Disease*, 1959, **129**, 1-10.

Sampson, H., Messinger, S. L., & Towne, R. D.   Family processes and becoming a mental patient. *American Journal of Sociology*, 1962, **68**, 88-96.

Sanua, V. D.   Sociocultural factors in families of schizophrenics. *Psychiatry*, 1961, **24**, 246-265.

Scotch, N., & Geiger, H. J.   The epidemiology of rheumatoid arthritis: a review with special attention to social factors. *Journal of Chronic Diseases*, 1962, 15, 1037-1067.

Scotch, N. A., & Geiger, H. J.   The epidemiology of essential hypertension: a review with special attention to psychological and sociocultural factors. II: Psychologic and sociocultural factors in etiology. *Journal of Chronic Diseases*, 1963, 16, 1183-1213.

Spiegel, J. P., & Bell, N. W.   The family of the psychiatric patient. In S. Arieti (Ed.), *American handbook of psychiatry*. Vol. 1. New York: Basic Books, 1957. Pp. 114-149.

Srole, L., Langner, T., Michael, S., Opler, M., & Rennie, T.   *Mental health in the metropolis: the midtown Manhattan study*. Vol. 1. New York: McGraw-Hill, 1962.

Stromgren, E.   Defining the unit of study in field investigations in the mental disorders. In J. Zubin (Ed.), *Field studies in the mental disorders*. New York: Grune & Stratton, 1961. Pp. 173-182.

Thorndike, E. L.   On the fallacy of imputing the correlations found for groups to the individuals or smaller groups composing them. *American Journal of Psychology*, 1939, 52, 122-124.

Tooth, G.   *Studies in mental illness in the Gold Coast.* London: His Majesty's Stationery Office, 1950.

Vaillant, G. E.   The prediction of recovery in schizophrenia. *Journal of Nervous and Mental Disease*, 1962, 135, 534-543.

Wilson, D. C., & Lantz, Edna M.   The effect of culture change on the Negro race in Virginia, as indicated by a study of state hospital admissions. *American Journal of Psychiatry*, 1957, 114, 25-32.

Wittkower, E. D., & Fried, J.   Some problems of transcultural psychiatry. In M. K. Opler (Ed.), *Culture and mental health.* New York: Macmillan, 1959. Pp. 489-500.

Wittkower, E. D., Murphy, H. B., Fried, J., & Ellenberger, H.   Cross-cultural inquiry into the symptomatology of schizophrenia. *Annals of the New York Academy of Sciences*, 1960, 84, 854-863.

Zubin, J. (Ed.).   *Field studies in the mental disorders.* New York: Grune & Stratton, 1961.

10

The Role of the Family in the Development of Psychopathology

INTRODUCTION

Many workers in the field of mental health consider it almost axiomatic to say that psychopathological problems have their genesis in the individual's early family experiences. It has often been suggested that even if the problems do not stem directly from the familial experiences, these experiences predispose the individual to pathological responses when he encounters stresses in later life. Perhaps because of the high level of agreement about the crucial role played by the family, there has been a tendency to accept conclusions based on inadequate or uncontrolled research. In the following article George Frank reviews critically the research efforts of the past forty years which have attempted to relate the family and the development of pathology.

At first glance the idea of researching the relationship between the family and the development of behavior pathology is deceptively simple. It is complicated, however, by a number of factors, one of which is the identification of the relevant family variables to be studied. When studying anything more than the effect of the *presence or absence of family life experiences* on the child's development, one must decide which aspects of the family should be studied. For example, should one look into the *characteristics and adjustment of the parents* or investigate the *child's perception of the parents?* Or the *parents' perception of the child* might be investigated. On another level, one might investigate the effect of *sibling position* within the family, types of *communication* in the family, types of *interactions* between family members, or the overall *emotional climate* of the home. Furthermore, since pathology may not be caused by a single factor, it might be profitable to in-

297

vestigate the interaction of some of the different individual variables.

Once the decision of what to study has been made, an even more difficult problem arises—that of collecting valid observations on the variable in question. A variety of techniques have been used in the past including *direct observation, case studies, psychiatric interviews, questionnaires,* and *projective testing.* When observations, interviews, or questionnaires are used, it is very difficult to conceal that the person is being studied and that he is being studied in relation to his potential knowledge of or involvement in the factors revolving around the development of pathology. Therefore, the measurements taken by observations, interviews, and questionnaires are highly "reactive" in nature. (1966) That is, the data a subject gives through these techniques may be greatly affected by the mere fact that the subject knows he is being studied and why. For example, if the person under study is emotionally involved in the situation (as family members are), distortions may result from the individual's need to defend himself against what he sees as impending criticism or guilt feelings. Alternatively, a subject's report may be subtly distorted as a function of his own theory or by what he has heard from others about the development of abnormal behavior. Reactivity is, of course, not limited to the individual being studied, for the material reported in a case study or noted by an observer may also be selectively screened as a function of the biases and expentancies of the observer. Projective techniques probably suffer least from reactivity because, in theory, the respondent is unaware of the meaning of his responses and thus cannot defend or recall selectively, and, in addition, the test responses can be scored blind by the researcher. The problem with these techniques, however, lies in the question of the validity of the interpretations drawn from the subject's responses.

It would seem, then, that all of the measurement techniques have some problems that result in data distortion. However, data collected through *different techniques* may not be subject to *identical distortions.* That is, different types of measures may be subject to different types of distortions. Firm conclusions may be drawn only when the results of two or more studies are in agreement and when the methodologies used in the studies are different and do not share the same type of possible error. Therefore, to reduce the uncertainty of conclusions concerning the families of disturbed individuals we should look not only at the level of agreement between studies using the same measurement technique but, more importantly, at the level of agreement between studies employing different techniques. In the following paper the research is grouped by the technique employed for the data collection. In reviewing the research results the reader should make his own validity check by comparing the results obtained by different approaches.

In addition to the validity problems raised by the reactivity of the measures and the interpretation of the responses, an investigator is faced with the almost unsolvable *temporal* problem presented by trying to study the development of pathology after that development has taken place. Although we are interested in observing the characteristics and interactions of individuals and families which lead to the development of a disorder, we are in a position to observe only the characteristics and reactions of families who have a disturbed member in their midst at the time they are being studied. There is no guarantee that the way the family responds to a child who has been identified as "sick" is the way they responded to the child during the pathological development. In fact, one would expect a change in orientation or responding as a function of the identification of one member of the family as "sick." For example, the finding that the parents of a disturbed child tend to be more strict or lenient may not be the cause of the child's disturbance but rather a function of the parents' attempt to cope with the disturbance. Because of the temporal problem in measurement, it is difficult to separate cause from effect. One attempt to circumvent this problem has been initiated by Mednick and Schulsinger (1965) who are studying longitudinally a group of children for whom the probability of becoming schizophrenic is high. Because of the generally low incidence of schizophrenia, such a study becomes practical only when a "high-risk" population is examined on the pretest.

Lastly, there is the group of problems posed by the selection of individuals (patients and controls) whose families are to be studied. Since it has usually been assumed that the same cause lies behind the symptoms of all patients with the same diagnoses, most researchers have compared the family characteristics of patients of one diagnostic group to the family characteristics of another diagnostic group or to control families. But because of the low reliability of diagnoses and thus the difficulty of identifying the members of a diagnostic group, patients who belong to other groups may be included in the experimental group. Moreover, as Zigler and Phillips stated in an earlier paper, there are often important individual differences within any one diagnostic group. For example, as is pointed out later in an article by William Heron, "reactive schizophrenics" are characterized by, among other things, a *good* early family history, whereas "process schizophrenics" are characterized by a *poor* family history. The inclusion of both types into the class of "schizophrenic" may well obscure or distort the possible differences between families of patients and controls. At the same time, disregarding these subject differences can lead to what would appear to be contradictory results coming from different studies. If differences in the subjects used in two different studies are not taken into consideration, the conflicting results of the second study may unfortunately be seen as a refutation rather than a refinement of the earlier findings.

After the sick and healthy individuals whose families will be studied are identified, the researcher is faced with the problem of identifying the families. That is, should only the primary family be studied or, as some theorists have suggested, should attention be given to the entire extended family? There is, of course, considerable evidence that in certain classes and cultures individuals outside the primary family often play crucial roles in the child's development.

The problems of what, how, and who should be studied are not necessarily unique to research on the family characteristics of disturbed individuals. They do, however, serve to make research in this area complicated for the researcher to carry out and difficult for the reader to interpret and evaluate. Only some of these problems have been accounted for in the conclusions drawn by the author of the following article. When reviewing this research the reader should keep all of these problems in mind so that he will appreciate the difficulties faced by the researchers and so that he will be aware of possible confounding factors and sources of confusion in this body of literature.

Before turning to the review of the data, the concept of the *schizophrenogenic mother* should be introduced, since this concept has played a central role in much of the research. As a rule, the term *schizophrenogenic* is used to refer to a mother who is *overtly* extremely dominating and oversolicitious of her child's welfare (behavior that has been referred to as "smother love") while at the same time she is *covertly* hostile and rejecting of the child. It has been suggested that this inconsistency disrupts the child's personal development, since it is impossible for him to maintain a relationship with his mother that would be consistent with the way she responds to him. The second type of schizophrenogenic mother is much less subtle in her malignant influence, for she is highly rejecting and sadistically critical of the child, both overtly and covertly. This type of mother demands a very high level of performance on the part of the child in almost all areas. In theory, these excessive demands in combination with her constant disapproval and complete nonacceptance of the child undermine the child's self-confidence and healthy ego development.

Mednick, S., & Schulsinger, F. A longitudinal study of children with a high risk for schizophrenia, a preliminary report. In S. Vandenberg (Ed.), *Methods and goals in human behavior genetics*. New York: Academic Press, 1965.

Webb, E., Campbell, D., Schwartz, R., & Sechrest, L. *Unobtrusive measures: Nonreactive research in the social sciences*. Chicago: Rand McNally, 1966.

10

THE ROLE OF THE FAMILY IN
THE DEVELOPMENT OF PSYCHOPATHOLOGY

GEORGE H. FRANK

As psychopathology came to be viewed as the consequence of the emotional experiences to which the individual was exposed, interest was focused on the earliest of such experiences, those that occur in the family. The human infant is born incapable of sustaining its own life for a considerable length of time following birth, and is, in consequence, dependent upon the mother or a mother substitute for its very existence. There is no wonder, therefore, that the mother-child relationship is a close one and is expected to be influential with regard to the psychological development of the child. Some explanations for the development of psychopathology have therefore focused on this particular relationship as the major etiological factor. Levy (1931, 1932, 1937, 1943) has described a pattern centering around "maternal overprotection," involving a constellation of attitudes which he felt contributed to the development of neurotic disorders, and Despert (1938) focused on a kind of mother-child relationship which seemed to her to be closely associated with the development of schizophrenia, a pattern which has come to be termed the "schizophrenogenic mother."

The hypothesis that the emotional climate of the interpersonal relationships within the family—and between the child and its mother in particular—has a decisive part in the development of the personality of the child would seem to have face validity. In part, support for this hypothesis may be gleaned from the data demonstrating the devastating effects of being brought up in the extreme interpersonal isolation that comes from *not* having a family (Beres & Obers, 1950; Brodbeck & Irwin, 1946; Goldfarb, 1943a, 1943b, 1943c, 1945a, 1945b; Lowrey, 1940; Spitz, 1945) or extreme social isolation within a family (Bartmeier, 1952; Davis, 1940). Moreover, it has been demonstrated that various specific emotional behaviors of the child seem to be correlated causally with factors in

SOURCE. Reprinted with permission of the American Psychological Association and the author from the *Psychological Bulletin*, 1965, **64**, 191-205.

the home. For example, children who could be described as emotionally immature, who are dependent, fearful, negativistic, emotionally labile, etc., have had mothers described as worriers (Pearson, 1931), overattentive (Hattwick, 1936; Hattwick & Stowell, 1936), or punitive (McCord, McCord, & Howard, 1961; Sears, Whiting, Nowlis, & Sears, 1953; Watson, 1934). Children who were described as being overly aggressive were described as having come from homes where mothers were seen as overcontrolling (Bishop, 1951) or punitive (McCord et al., 1961; Sears, 1961).

The evidence thus far suggests that there is, in fact, a correlation between events in the parent-child relationship and resultant personality *traits*. The question arises as to whether there is evidence which supports the hypothesis that there is a correlation between events in the parent-child relationship and the resultant complex patterns of behavior which have been termed personality. More specifically, in light of the theories which relate personality development to social, (i.e., interpersonal) learning, the question is raised as to whether there is any consistent relationship between the emotional experience the child may have in the home and the development of personality pathology, that is, schizophrenia, neurosis, and behavior disorders. Towards this end, the findings of the research that has explored the psychological characteristics of the parents of these people will be analyzed in order to isolate those consistent characteristics of the parents that may emerge from study to study. The analysis will be done with regard to each major type of psychopathology as a group. Moreover, because psychological test data might yield different information than case history analysis, or direct observation of familial interaction as compared to attitudes as elicited by questionnaire, an attempt will be made to analyze the information gleaned from the studies in terms of the method of data collection within the specific psychopathological groupings.

Schizophrenia

Case History

One of the classical methods of data collection in the study of psychiatric illness is the case history, the information for which has generally been gathered by other professionals. The individual conducting a piece of research notes the material in the folders and draws conclusions from the collation of these observations.

In so doing, Despert (1938) observed that approximately 50%

of the mothers of a sample of schizophrenic children, generally between the ages of 7 and 13, had been described as aggressive, overanxious, and oversolicitous and were considered to be the dominant parent. Clardy (1951) noted that 50% of the 30 cases of children between the ages of 3 and 12 diagnosed as schizophrenic had families characterized as overprotective and yet basically rejecting. Frazee (1953) noted the presence of this constellation particularly when the families of schizophrenics were compared with the families of children diagnosed as behavior disorders. Canavan and Clark (1923) and Lampron (1933) noted that 30% of the children of psychotics were themselves emotionally disturbed. Huschka (1941) and Lidz and Lidz (1949) noted that over 40% of their sample of schizophrenics had parents who were psychotic or neurotic. Bender (1936, 1937) and Frazee (1953) noted the high incidence of psychopathology in the children of psychotic parents. Preston and Antin (1932), on the other hand, found no significant differences in the incidence of psychosis and neurosis as a function of parents who were psychotic as compared to parents who were "normal," and Fanning, Lehr, Sherwin, and Wilson, (1938) found that 43% of the children of mothers who were psychotic were observed to be making an adequate social and personal adjustment, with only 11% of that sample classified as maladjusted.

Lidz and Lidz (1949) found that 40% of their sample of schizophrenic patients were deprived of one parent by divorce or separation before they were 19. Plank (1953) found that 63% of his sample of schizophrenics had families where one parent was absent either due to death or marital separation. Wahl (1954, 1956) found that there was a greater incidence of parental loss and rejection early in life for schizophrenics as compared to normals, and Barry (1936) found that from the case histories of 30 rulers adjudged, post facto, insane, 80% of them had lost one of their parents by the time they were 18. However, Barry and Bousfield (1937) found that the incidence of orphanhood in a psychiatric population (19 out of 26) was not much different from the incidence of orphanhood in a normal population (19 out of 24). Moreover, Oltman, McGarry, and Friedman (1952) found that the incidence of broken homes and parental deprivation in the families of schizophrenics (34%) was not very different from that found in the families of hospital employees (32%), alcoholics (31%), and manic-depressives (34%); indeed, in their sampling, neurotics (49%) and psychopaths (48%) showed a greater incidence. Other studies have found that the incidence of broken homes in the history of neurotics is between 20% (Brown & Moore, 1944) and 30% (Madow & Hardy, 1947; Wallace, 1935), and Gerard and Siegel (1950) found no particular incidence of broken homes in the family history of their sample of schizophrenics.

Psychiatric Interview

Another classical method of obtaining information regarding the individual with whom patients have been living is by having interviews with them directly. The quality of the mother-child relationship is then inferred from what the interviewee says. From this research, an overwhelming number of studies (Despert, 1951; Gerard & Siegel, 1950; Guertin, 1961; Hajdu-Gimes, 1940; Kasanin, Knight, & Sage, 1934; Lidz, Cornelison, Fleck, & Terry, 1957a, 1957b, 1957c; Lidz, Cornelison, Terry, & Fleck, 1958; Lidz & Lidz, 1949; Lidz, Parker, & Cornelison, 1956; Tietze, 1949; Walters, 1938) describe a familial pattern characterized by a dominant, overprotective, but basically rejecting mother and a passive, ineffectual father. Yet the data in the study by Schofield and Balian (1959) reflected similarity rather than differences in the families of schizophrenic and nonpsychiatric (general medical) patients, and the data of Gerard and Siegel (1950) indicated that the schizophrenics in their study, according to interpretation of the data gleaned from the interviews, received adequate breast feeding, had no history of particularly difficult toilet training or of obvious feeding problems, did not come from broken homes, and apparently were not unduly rejected or punished. Another factor which seems to emerge from the studies is that a dominant characteristic of the family life of schizophrenics is a quality of inappropriateness of thinking and behaving which seems to infiltrate the entire atmosphere (Fleck, Lidz, & Cornelison, 1963; Lidz et al., 1957b, 1957c; Stringer, 1962). Meyers and Goldfarb (1962), however, found that only 28% of the mothers of 45 children diagnosed as schizophrenic and only 12% of the fathers were themselves manifestly schizophrenic.

Psychological Evaluation

Attitude questionnaires. One of the most widely used questionnaires in this area of research has been the Shoben (1949) Parent-Child Attitude Survey. The Shoben scale consists of 148 items which measure the dimensions of parental rejection, possessiveness, and domination. From the administration of this attitude survey, Mark (1953) and Freeman and Grayson (1955) reported significant differences in attitudes toward child rearing between mothers of schizophrenics and mothers of normal children. In comparison with the mothers of the control subjects, the mothers of schizophrenic patients (Mark, 1953) were revealed as inconsistent in their methods of control. They described themselves as being, at times, overrestrictive and controlling of behavior, but in some instances lax. They frowned on sex play and tended to keep information regarding sex from their children; they also seemed to frown on friends for their children. Their relationship to their children appeared inconsistent; they described what could be interpreted as excessive devotion and interest in the child's activities while at the same time revealing a notable degree of "cool detachment." Freeman and Grayson (1955) found that in comparison to mothers of students in an undergraduate course, mothers of 50 hospitalized schizophrenics (ages 20 to 35) tended to reveal themselves to be somewhat more possessive, but inherently rejecting of their children, and particularly disturbed about sexual behavior in their children. However, according to these same data, the mothers of schizophrenic patients did not reveal themselves to be more dominant, dogmatic, or inconsistent in their attitude than the controls. But most important was the fact that item analysis of these data revealed that the attitudes of the mothers of the schizophrenics and of the controls were distinguished on only 14 of the items, and then, in general, there was so much overlap that even on these items the statistical significance was contributed by a small percentage of each group. Freeman, Simmons, and Bergen (1959) included four items from the Shoben scale among a larger sample of questions posed to parents. These items had been derived from a previous study (Freeman & Simmons, 1958) and were included in the second study because they were the only ones in the first study which were found to discriminate between the attitudes of mothers of schizophrenic patients and those of mothers of normals. The items are:

1. Parents should sacrifice everything for their children.
2. A child should feel a deep sense of obligation always to act in accord with the wishes of his parents.
3. Children who are gentlemanly or ladylike are preferable to those who are tomboys or "regular guys."
4. It is better for children to play at home than to visit other children.

Freeman et al. (1959) found no capacity for these items to differentiate the attitudes of the mothers of schizophrenics from those of other individuals with severe functional disorders.

Zuckerman, Oltean, and Monashkin (1958) utilized another attitude scale, the Parental Attitude Research Inventory (PARI, developed by Schaefer and Bell in their work at the Psychology Laboratory at NIMH). The PARI was administered to mothers of normals and mothers of schizophrenics and it was found that only one of the 20 five-item scales distinguished between the two groups. The mothers of schizophrenics scored significantly lower on the Strictness scale, indicating that these mothers, as opposed to mothers of nonschizophrenics, felt that the ideal child rearing behavior for mothers in general was less strict. While the one difference out of 20 could be interpreted as being due to chance, it should be noted that Tolor and Rafferty (1963) replicated the finding on the Strictness scale. Unlike Zuckerman, et al., however, Tolor and Rafferty (1963) also found that the mothers of schizophrenics had significantly higher scores on the Fostering Dependency, Seclusion, and Intrusiveness scales.

The minimal discrimination value of the several attitude scales should be noted. This would seem to reflect either minimal capacity of the scales to make such distinctions or little in the way of measurable differences between the groups. In either case, it is very difficult to evaluate the meaning of these data since the attitudes of the mothers of schizophrenics seemed to be distinguished from the attitudes of the mothers of nonschizophrenics on only a few scales.[1]

Projective tests. Several studies presented Rorschach data on the mothers of schizophrenic patients (Baxter, Becker, & Hooks, 1963; Prout & White, 1950; Winder & Kantor, 1958). In comparison to those of the mothers of normals, the Rorschach protocols of the mothers of the schizophrenic patients were undistinguished as regards the general degree of immaturity (Winder & Kantor, 1958) and the use of defences which are essentially reality distorting, namely, denial and projection (Baxter et al., 1963).[2] How-

---

[1] In Frank's paper in its original form the study by Zuckerman, Oltean, and Monashkin (1958) was misrepresented and the study by Tolor and Rafferty (1963) was not referenced. These errors were pointed out in a subsequent article by Zuckerman (1966). With the permission of the author the preceding two paragraphs were rewritten to correct these errors.

[2] The conclusion that the Rorschach protocols of the mothers of schizophrenics were undistinguished from the Rorschach protocols of the mothers of normals (as in the research by Winder & Kantor, 1958, Baxter et al., 1963) is an interpretation of the results made by the present author. In fact, in both of these

ever, Prout and White did find more pure color without form and less human and animal movement and shading responses in the Rorschach protocols of mothers of schizophrenic boys as compared to the mothers of a comparable group of boys randomly selected from the community. Perr (1958) found that the parents of schizophrenic children gave responses to the Thematic Apperception Test (TAT) little distinguished from those of parents of normal children, and Fisher, Boyd, Walker, and Sheer (1959) found that the TAT and Rorschach protocols of the parents of schizophrenic patients were measurably different from those of the parents of nonpsychiatric (general medical) patients, but they were not distinguishable from the protocols of the parents of neurotic patients. The mothers of the schizophrenics revealed a higher degree of perceptual rigidity, greater incidence of indicators of maladjustment on the Rorschach, and less definitely conceived parental images on the TAT than the mothers of the normals.

Direct observation of interpersonal behavior. Attempts have been made to study the interpersonal behavior of families of schizophrenics *in vivo;* some investigators have gone into the home, others have brought the family into a hospital setting and observed the interaction between family members for an hour or so at a time, others have brought the family into a laboratory setting (National Institute of Mental Health) where the family lives under actual but known conditions for months at a time.

In the study of the interpersonal relationships in the actual home setting, Behrens and Goldfarb (1958) observed that the personality of the mother seemed to set the tone of the family milieu and that there seemed to be a direct relationship between the degree of pathology that could be seen in the family setting and the degree of psychopathology demonstrated by the child. The homes they observed appeared physically deteriorated and crowded. There was a

---

articles, the authors conclude that there *are* significant differences. However, in the article by Winder and Kantor, the mean rating of the degree of maturity of personality development for the mothers of the schizophrenics was 2.89, for the mothers of the normals, 2.43. In the article by Baxter et al., the means of the ratings of the degree of utilization of psychologically immature defenses on the Rorschach by the parents of poor premorbid schizophrenics, good premorbid schizophrenics, and neurotics are, respectively, 19.43, 19.62, and 19.49. Though in both of these investigations valid statistical significance was demonstrated between the obtained means, the actual means, in both researches, are so similar to each other that the interpretation of *psychologically* significant differences between groups on the basis of the obtained *statistically* significant differences seemed a highly doubtful conclusion.

basic isolation between the mother and father, and the fathers were basically passive. Confusion and disorganization characterized the family atmosphere, with the family demonstrating inadequate mechanisms to handle emotional flareups. The intensive observation of one mother-child interaction (Karon & Rosberg, 1958) yielded the observation that the mother was unempathic. She blocked verbalizations of emotions and tended to live vicariously through the child, but her relationship to the child appeared to involve a basic, though unconscious, hostility and rejection. The mother was an obsessive-compulsive personality, dominated the home, and was unable to accept herself as a woman. The intensive observation of 51 families (Donnelly, 1960) tends to confirm this finding. Observing the mother-child interaction in the home, utilizing the Fels Parent Behavior Scales, Donnelly found that mothers treated a psychotic child differently than their other nonpsychotic children. To the psychotic child, the mother was generally less warm, less accepting, less empathic, more punitive, more controlling, and more overprotective. The father was passive, but more rational than the mother in relation to the child. Psychotic children tended to come from homes characterized as less well adjusted, full of discord, and low in sociability. However, in comparing the family interaction of schizophrenic patients with those of normal controls, both Perr (1958) and Meyers and Goldfarb (1961) found little that could stand as a valid measure of distinction between the two groups of families. Perr found that the parents of schizophrenics tend to show more self-deception and to describe themselves as being more hostile. Meyers and Goldfarb found that the mothers of schizophrenic children appeared less capable of formulating a consistent definition of the world for the child.

A method of directly assessing the interpersonal behavior of husband and wife was introduced by Strodtbeck (1951). He posed questions to each parent individually, then he brought them together and had them discuss those points where their attitudes differed. Farina and his associates (Bell, Garmezy, Farina, & Rodnick, 1960; Farina, 1960; Farina & Dunham, 1963) utilized this method to study the families of schizophrenic patients. The questionnaire they used was the PARI. They found that they could distinguish the interpersonal behavior of schizophrenics otherwise described as having good or poor premorbid adjustment. In these studies, mother dominance was discerned in the families of the poor premorbid group only, with interpersonal conflict greatest in that group. In comparing the family interaction of the schizophrenic patient with those of normal controls, Bell et al. (1960) found that in the family constellation of normals, authority tended to be shared by both parents, and parental conflict was at a minimum, although even here there was a trend towards maternal dominance.

Bishop (1951) reported a method of studying the mother-child interaction under live, yet controlled, conditions. The mother and child were brought into a play room where the interpersonal behavior was observed directly. In 1954, Bowen introduced the principle of this technique to the study of families of schizophrenics. Families were brought into what came to be known as the Family Study Section of NIMH (National Institute of Mental Health), and there they were observed living under actual but known conditions for long periods of time (6 months–2 years). Observations based on families living under these conditions revealed that the mothers of schizophrenics showed extremely domineering, smothering, close relationships with the child (Dworin & Wyant, 1957), with the mothers utilizing threat of deprivation to control the child. Bowen, Dysinger, and Basamanie (1959) observed the presence of marked emotional distance and intense conflict between the parents. The fathers were emotionally immature and unable to define their role in the family and unable to make decisions; the mothers were usually the dominant ones, affecting a close relationship with the child to the exclusion of the father. Brodey (1959) found that the behavior of the families of schizophrenics was characterized by a selective utilization of reality, particularly the use of externalization, and that the interpersonal relationships were highly narcissistic.

Perception of parental behavior by patients. Several studies have indicated that schizophrenics tend to have experienced their mother as having been rejecting (Bolles, Metzger, & Pitts, 1941; Lane & Singer, 1959; Singer, 1954), and dominant, demanding, and overprotective (Garmezy, Clarke, & Stockner, 1961; Heilbrun, 1960; Kohn & Clausen, 1956; McKeown, 1950; Reichard & Tillman, 1950; Schofield & Balian, 1959). However, when one compares the perception of their mothers by normals (Garmezy et al., 1961; Heilbrun, 1960; Lane & Singer, 1959; Singer, 1954) the uniqueness of these attitudes toward the mothers of schizophrenics disappears. Recollections of dominance and overprotectiveness are common for both schizophrenics and normals. Although Heilbrun, Garmezy et al., and Bolles et al. report data which have shown that there is a greater incidence of a feeling of having been rejected on the part of a group of psychiatric patients when compared to medical-surgical controls, the actual incidence of this even in the psychiatric group was only 15% as compared to 1% in the controls. Moreover, Singer and Lane and Singer found that perception of parental relationships during childhood was more a function of the subjects' socioeconomic level than was psychopathology, paralleling a finding by Opler (1957) that familial patterns (parental dominance and attitudes) are a function of cultural factors (Italian versus Irish origin) rather than of psychopathology.

Neurosis

As compared to the research in the area of schizophrenia, investigations of the dynamics of the family life of neurotics are few and generally restricted to data gleaned from case histories. From these studies it appears that the neurotic behavior of the child is a direct function of the neurotic behavior of the mother (e.g., Fisher & Mendell, 1956; Ingham, 1949; Sperling, 1949, 1951; Zimmerman, 1930). Neurotic behavior in children has been seen to have been related to maternal overprotection (Holloway, 1931; Jacobsen, 1947; Zimmerman, 1930), maternal domination (Mueller, 1945), maternal rejection (Ingham, 1949; Newell, 1934, 1936; Silberpfennig, 1941), separation from the mother during the first 3 years of life (Bowlby, 1940; Ribble, 1941), and oral deprivation (Childers & Hamil, 1932). Neurotic involvement with the mother, where the mother needs the child for the satisfaction of her own needs and discourages the development of emotional separation between the child and herself, has been associated with the development in the child of psychosomatic disorders (Miller & Baruch, 1950; Sperling, 1949) and school phobia (e.g., Davidson, 1961; Eisenberg, 1958; Estes, Haylett, & Johnson, 1956; Goldberg, 1953; Johnson, Falstein, & Suzurek, 1941; Suttenfield, 1954; Talbot, 1957; van Houten, 1948; Waldfogel, Hahn, & Gardner, 1954; Wilson, 1955).

Neurosis in children has also been associated with such factors in the home as poverty (Brown & Moore, 1944; Holloway, 1931) and broken homes (Ingham, 1949; Madow & Hardy, 1947; Wallace, 1935). Silverman (1935), however, found that 75% of the children from broken homes were essentially "normal"; 16% were described as conduct disorders, and only 9% were classifiable as personality problems.

Of the studies that did not use the case history method of data collection, McKeown (1950) found that neurotic children perceive their mothers as demanding, antagonistic, and setting inordinately high standards for them to meet. Stein (1944) found that neurotics tended to perceive themselves as having been rejected, particularly as compared to the perception of their family life held by normals (Bolles et al., 1941). Although Kundert (1947) found that whether justified by experience or not (e.g., separation due to hospitalization of mother or child), emotionally disturbed children, in general, fear being deserted by their mothers and cling to them compulsively. The Rorschach protocols of mothers of neurotics reveal that they tend to utilize psychological mechanisms which abrogate reality, for example, denial and projection (Baxter et al., 1963).

Behavior Disorder

The research on the family background of individuals whose personality problems take the form of antisocial behavior is scanty. Shaw and McKay (1932) found no differences in the incidence of broken homes from cases referred to Cook County Juvenile Court (36%) as compared to a random sample of children in the Chicago public school system (42%). Behavior disorders in children have been seen to have been related to neurotic behavior in their parents (Field, 1940; Huschka, 1941), primarily involving maternal rejection, overt and covert. In line with a social learning hypothesis, another interesting finding is that a correlation has been found between antisocial behavior in children and the children's perception of parents' antisocial behavior (Bender, 1937; K. Friedlander, 1945; Williams, 1932).

Discussion

Let us now summarize what conclusions can be drawn from these data which illuminate the role of the family in the development of psychopathology. As regards the families of schizophrenics, from an overview of the research which has investigated the pattern of parent-child interaction of this pathological group considered without reference to any other pathological or control group, several factors emerge which seem to characterize this group, regardless of the method of data collection, that is, whether by case history, interview, psychological test, or direct observation. Families of schizophrenics seem to be characterized by mothers who are dominant, fathers who are passive, and considerable family disharmony. The mother is overprotective, overpossessive, and overcontrolling, yet basically, albeit unconsciously, rejecting. These mothers frown on sex, are inconsistent in their methods of discipline, and introduce modes of thinking, feeling, and behaving which are not reality oriented. In light of the fact that these patterns emerge as a function of almost all methods of data collection, these results seem very impressive. Had our review of these data stopped here, we would have had apparent verification of the thesis that certain kinds of mother-child relationships and family atmospheres indeed account for the development of schizophrenia in the offspring. However, when each of these parental characteristics is compared with those which emerge from the analysis of the family situation of the normal (apparently nonpsychiatrically-involved) individual, each characteristic that is found to be typical of the families of schizophrenics is found to exist in the families of the controls as well. Furthermore, research which has attempted to make direct comparisons between the families of children in different categories of psychopathology (e.g., Baxter et al., 1963; Fisher et al., 1959; Frazee, 1953; Freeman et al., 1959; D. Friedlander, 1945; Inlow, 1933; McKeown, 1950; Oltman et al., 1952; Pollack & Malzberg, 1940; Pollack, Malzberg, & Fuller, 1936) reveals no significant or inconsistent differences in the psychological structure of the families.

The results are the same with regard to the families of the neurotics as well. At first glance, it appears that the mother's neurotic involvement with the child is causally associated with the neurotic behavior of the child. However, the essential characteristics of this involvement—maternal overprotectiveness, maternal domination, maternal rejection, deprivation and frustration, and the mothers fostering an almost symbiotic relationship between themselves and their children—are basically the same as those found in the families of schizophrenics and of children with behavior disorders. Moreover, in many respects, it would be hard, on blind analysis, to distinguish the family which produced an emotionally disturbed child from that which produced the so-called normal or well-adjusted child.

It seems apparent that the major conclusion that can be drawn from these data is that there is no such thing as a schizophrenogenic or a neurotogenic mother or family. At least these data do not permit of the description of a particular constellation of psychological events within the home and, in particular, between mother and child that can be isolated as a unique factor in the development of one or the other kind of personality disorder. If one is looking for *the* factor to account for the development of neurosis or schizophrenia, that one factor does not appear to exist as a clear cut finding in the research.

It is incumbent upon us to wonder why the research literature does not permit support of a hypothesis regarding parental influence on the psychological development of children in the manner we hypothesized. One of the major problems with which we must contend is that human behavior is a very complicated event, determined by many factors, and not clearly understood out of the context in which it occurs, and, in this regard, not everyone reacts in a like manner to similar life experiences. For example, strict discipline is reacted to differently when this occurs in a "warm" or "cold" home atmosphere (Sears, 1961); maternal rejection is reacted to differently where the father is accepting and warm (McCord et al., 1961) as well as where the father can be a buffer between the child and the overprotective mother (Witmer, 1933). Emphasizing the multivariate aspect of the determinants of behavior, one notes that Madow and Hardy (1947) reported that of the soldiers who broke down with neurotic reactions there was a high incidence of those coming from broken homes. Amongst those soldiers who did not break down, the incidence of coming from a broken home was 11-15%; the incidence of broken homes in the history of soldiers who did break down was 36%. Statistically, there is a significant difference between these percentages; however, even the 36% datum leaves 64% of the soldiers who broke down *not* coming from a broken home. Huschka (1941) reported that the incidence of neurotic mothers of problem children is high (42%); however, this leaves 58% of the group *not* accounted for by this factor. Brown and Moore (1944) commented that the incidence of excessive poverty, drunkenness, and family conflict in soldiers who broke down was significant, but this accounted for only 20% of the cases. Although between 30% (Canavan & Clark, 1923; Lampron, 1933) and 40% (Huschka, 1941; Lidz & Lidz, 1949) of the children born to mothers who are psychotic become psychotic themselves, these percentages do not account for the majority of children born to these mothers. Indeed, Fanning et al. (1938) found that 43% of the children born to mothers who were psychotic were observed to be making an adequate social and personal adjustment; only 11% of that sample of children was not. It should be noted that only half of the samples of mothers studied by Despert (1938) and Clardy (1951) resembled the traditional pattern of what has come to be known as the "schizophrenogenic mother." Finally, Beres and Obers (1950) observed that there is a wide reaction to an experience of emotional deprivation (in this instance, institutionalization) ranging from the development of a schizoid personality to schizophrenia itself, and including neurotic reactions and character disorders. Indeed, 25% of their sample of children who were brought up in institutions appeared to be making a satisfactory adjustment in spite of this ostensibly devastating experience.

Over and above the complexity of human behavior contributing to the inconclusiveness of the results, one must look at the way in which these data have been collected. It might be that the criterion measure, that is, the diagnosis, did not provide the investigator with meaningful groupings of subjects so that consistent findings *could* be obtained. As regards the method of data collection: Case histories may be inadequate in providing basic data; Information can be gross and/or inaccurate; The informant has to rely on memory, and this memory might be consciously or unconsciously selective, or the informant might not be aware of the import of or feel shame in giving certain data. Yet, despite the many limitations of this mode of data collection, some of the primary research in schizophrenia has utilized this method, and almost all of the data with respect to the family life of neurotics and behavior disorders were gathered in this way. These same limitations apply to data that are gathered when the informant is asked to fill out an attitude questionnaire. Surely the data on parents elicited from the children are susceptible to distortion even when given by normal children, no less those who already tend to consciously or unconsciously confound their perception of reality with fantasy. The psychiatric interview is a much more sensitive procedure than the case history or attitude questionnaire. Either structured or open-ended interviews enable the interviewer to follow up leads and possibly detect where information is being omitted for one reason or another. The problem here, however, is that there is always the possibility that distorted or inaccurate data are gathered by the interviewer, either through the kinds of questions asked, or the perception of the answer or of the individual being interviewed. For example, it is interesting to note that although the majority of psychiatric interviewers experienced the mothers of schizophrenics as matching the model of the schizophrenogenic mother— the dominant, overprotective, but basically rejecting mother who induces inappropriateness of thinking in her children—the psychological test evaluation of mothers of schizophrenics failed to confirm these findings. One explanation for this is that the interviewer, already acquainted with the literature regarding the mother of schizophrenics, anticipating to experience the mothers in terms of the ideas about schizophrenogenic mothers, did, indeed, experience them in that way, whereas a more objective evaluation of the patterns of thinking and feeling of these mothers did not confirm the more subjective impression.

In order to try and avoid the pitfalls inherent in data gleaned through case history or interview, investigators hypothesized that direct observation of the mother-child interaction might yield more valid information. Unfortunately, here, too, limitations inherent in the mode of data collection become apparent. Observations of the mother-child interaction in the home or in an observation room in a hospital or clinic are generally restricted to a limited time segment, for example, 1 hour once a week. This factor, in and of itself, limits the observations to a fairly restricted aspect of the spectrum of the interaction between mother and child. Here, too, the behavior to which the observer is exposed may be influenced by the conscious or unconscious attitudes and motives of the parent being observed. It is not too difficult for the parent to present only that behavior which, for one reason or another, she feels it safe to display and to control the presence of other behaviors. Direct observation of the family for extensive periods of time, that is, months, and under controlled but as natural as possible living conditions (as in the Family Study Section of NIMH) avoids the restrictiveness and overcomes, to one degree or another, the artificiality of the relatively brief observation. However, the family is still aware that they are being observed and may, to one degree or another, be unable to act "natural." Moreover, unless the observations are independently made by several people whose reliability of observation has already been established, they may also be influenced by the *Zeitgeist* and perceive the family as being "schizophrenogenic" whether it is or not, mutually reinforcing each other's expectations. A more pressing consideration in evaluating the validity of these kinds of observations is the fact that the interaction, no matter how natural, takes place after the development of the psychopathology. It is quite possible that the aspects of the interpersonal relationship within the family, or between the mother and child in particular, that eventuated in the development of the patterns of thinking, feeling, and behaving characteristic of the schizophrenic or the neurotic, are no longer present; they may have occurred at a time of the child's life long since past and/or under conditions of intimacy not even accessible to the observer. There is no reason to assume that the etiological factors are still functioning or that they will be available to the trained observer even over the course of 6 months. Of course, it might be that whatever differentiates the psychological existence of the schizophrenic from that of the neurotic or of the normal might be so subtle that it is imperceptible to the participants themselves or even the trained observer and, hence, escape notice. Here, one is reminded of Freud's comment that "the years of childhood of those who are later neurotic need not necessarily differ from those who are later normal except in intensity and distinctness [Freud, 1938 (orig. publ. 1910), p. 583]."

Theorizing about the etiology of psychopathology has characteristically been of the either/or variety. Nineteenth century scientists sought explanations for neurotic and psychotic disorders in the hereditary background of their patients, working from the assumption that many directly inherited the neurotic or psychotic "illness." On the other hand, the scientist of the twentieth century has sought explanations for psychopathology in the experiential aspect of man's life, in his emotional and interpersonal learning. As with most events in our life, the truth is probably somewhere in between these two positions. Indeed, in spite of the emphasis that is placed on the role of experience in the development of personality in psychoanalysis, Freud did not think, at least as regards the etiology of psychopathology, in such categorically black and white terms. He was able to bridge the gap between the nature-nurture extremes:

We divide the causes of neurotic disease into those which the individual himself brings with him into life, and those which life bring to him—that is to say, into constitutional and accidental. It is the interaction of these as a rule first gives rise to illness [Freud, 1950b (orig. pub. 1913), p. 122].

Let us bear clearly in mind that every human being has acquired, by the combined operation of inherent disposition and of external influences of childhood, a special individuality in the exercise of his capacity to love—that is, in the conditions which he sets up for loving, in the impulses he gratifies by it, and in the aims he sets out to achieve in it. . . . We will here provide against misconceptions and reproaches to the effect that we have denied the importance of the inborn (constitutional) factor because we have emphasized the importance of infantile impressions. Such an accusation arises out of the narrowness with which mankind looks for causes, inasmuch as one single causal factor satisfies him, in spite of the many commonly underlying the face of reality. Psycho-Analysis has said much about the "accidental" component in aetiology and little about the constitutional, but only because it could throw new light upon the former, whereas of the latter it knows no more so far than is already known. We deprecate the assumption of an essential opposition between the two series of aetiological factors; we presume rather a perpetual interchange of both in producing the results observed [Freud, 1950a (orig publ. 1912), p. 312].

Other psychoanalysts have followed Freud in the presumption of an inherent, predetermined characteristic functioning of the nervous system of the human organism which determines reactions to stimuli pre- and post-natally (e.g., Greenacre, 1941).

Augmenting the clinical observations of psychoanalysis, one must juxtapose the experimental evidence in psychology which indicates that (a) individuals reflect characteristic patterns of autonomic activity which are stable and which are typical of them as individuals (Grossman & Greenberg, 1957; Lacey, 1950; Richmond & Lustman, 1955; Wenger, 1941), (b) the characteristic patterns of neural activity are identifiable prenatally and are consistent with the patterns of activity observable postnatally (Richards & Newbery, 1938) (c) these characteristic patterns of autonomic activity consistently emerge in a factor of liability and balance in which specific personality factors are consistently highly loaded (Darling, 1940; Eysenck, 1956; Eysenck & Prell, 1951; Theron, 1948; van der Merwe, 1948; van der Merwe & Theron, 1947), (d) there is greater similarity of autonomic reactivity between identical twins than fraternal twins or ordinary siblings (Eysenck, 1956; Eysenck & Prell, 1951; Jost & Sontag, 1944), and (e) there is a selective influence on personality functioning due to the sex of the individual per se. For example, generally boys outnumber girls 2-1 in being referred for psychological help (Bender, 1937; Wile & Jones, 1937). Sears (1961) found a significant difference in the basic mode of self-reported expression of aggression between boys and girls: Girls appeared higher in socially acceptable forms of aggression and high in anxiety regarding hostility, while boys were significantly higher in aggression that was directed against social control. Sears also found that the more punitive the mother is, the more dependent the son becomes but the less dependent the daughter becomes. Newell (1936) found that maternal rejection affected males more than females: Marked increase in aggressive behavior was noted in the boys who experienced rejection, not so with the females. Baruch & Wilcox (1944) noted that interparental tensions lead to different reactions in boys as compared to girls; in boys, it led to ascendance-submission problems, in girls, to an experience of lack of affection.

We end this survey by concluding that we have not been able to find any unique factors in the family of the schizophrenic which distinguishes it from the family of the neurotic or from the family of controls, who are ostensibly free from evidence of patterns of gross psychopathology. In short, we end by stating that the assumption that the family is *the* factor in the development of personality has not been validated. It is interesting to note that Orlansky (1949), in his review of the literature exploring the relationship between certain childhood experiences, for example, feeding, toilet training, thumbsucking, the degree of tactile stimulation by the mother, etc., upon the development of personality characteristics, was also forced to conclude that the data failed to confirm an invariant relationship between the experience in infancy and the resultant personality. Of course, it might well be that the reality of the family is not the important dimension in determining the child's reactions; rather, it might be the perception of the family members, and this might often have little or no relation to the people as they really are. This would mean, then, that in many instances the important variables in the development of psychopathology might be factors which the child brings to the family, the functioning of the nervous and metabolic systems and the cognitive capacity to integrate stimuli into meaningful perceptual and conceptual schema. Indeed, we are left to wonder, as do the psychoanalysts, whether the proclivity towards fantasy distortion of reality might not be *the* factor in the development of psychopathology, and this proclivity might not be always determined by the child's experiences per se.

Obviously, questions regarding the etiology of patterns of personality behavior which are regarded as pathological, unadaptive, or unadjusted cannot be met with simple answers. Apparently, the factors which play a part in the development of behavior in humans are so complex that it would appear that they almost defy being investigated scientifically and defy one's attempts to draw meaningful generalizations from the exploration which has already been done. It is, of course, conceivable that human behavior is so complex that it cannot be reduced to simple terms or be expected to yield unalterable patterns of occurrences. It might also be that what produces psychopathological reactions in one individual does not in another. All this would be understandable in light of the complexity that is the human being, neurologically as well as socially, but it is unfortunate as regards research endeavors. In 1926, Freud wrote:

Anxiety is the reaction to danger. One cannot, after all, help suspecting that the reason why the affect of anxiety occupies a unique position in the economy of the mind has something to do with the essential nature of danger. Yet dangers are the common lot of humanity; they are the same for everyone. What we need and cannot lay our fingers on is some factor which will explain why some people are able to subject the affect of anxiety, in spite of its peculiar quality, to the normal workings of the mind, or which decides who is doomed to come to grief over the task [Freud, 1936, p. 64].

We end this review of forty years of research without being able to feel that we are any closer to an answer than was Freud.

REFERENCES

Ayer, Mary E., & Bernreuter, R. G. A study of the relationship between discipline and personality traits in little children. *Journal of Genetic Psychology*, 1937, 50, 165-170.

Barry, H. Orphanhood as a factor in psychoses. *Journal of Abnormal and Social Psychology*, 1936, 30, 431-438.

Barry, H., & Bousfield, W. A. Incidence of orphanhood among fifteen hundred psychotic patients. *Journal of Genetic Psychology*, 1937, 50, 198-202.

Bartmeier, L. H. Deprivations during infancy and their effects upon personality development. *American Journal of Mental Deficiency*, 1952, 56, 708-711.

Baruch, Dorothy W., & Wilcox, J. Annie. A study of sex differences in pre-school children's adjustment coexistent with inter-parental tensions. *Journal of Genetic Psychology*, 1944, 64, 281-303.

Baxter, J. C., Becker, J., & Hooks, W. Defensive style in the families of schizophrenics and controls. *Journal of Abnormal and Social Psychology*, 1963, 66, 512-518.

Behrens, Marjorie L., & Goldfarb, W. A study of patterns of interaction of families of schizophrenic children in residential treatment. *American Journal of Orthopsychiatry*, 1958, 28, 300-312.

Bell, R. Q., Garmezy, N., Farina, A., & Rodnick, E. H. Direct study of parent-child interaction. *American Journal of Orthopsychiatry*, 1960, 30, 445-452.

Bender, Lauretta. Reactive psychosis in response to mental disease in the family. *Journal of Nervous and Mental Disease*, 1936, 83, 143-289.

Bender, Lauretta. Behavior problems in the children of psychotic and criminal parents. *Genetic Psychology Monographs*, 1937, 19, 229-339.

Beres, D., & Obers, S. J. The effects of extreme deprivation in infancy on psychic structure in adolescence: A study in ego development. *Psychoanalytic Study of the Child*, 1950, 5, 212-235.

Bishop, Barbara M. Mother-child interaction and the social behavior of children. *Psychological Monographs*, 1951, 65 (11, Whole No. 328).

Bolles, Marjorie M., Metzger, Harriet F., & Pitts, Marjorie W. Early home background and personal adjustment. *American Journal of Orthopsychiatry*, 1941, 11, 530-534.

Bowen, M., Dysinger, R. H., & Basamanie, Betty. The role of the father in families with a schizophrenic patient. *American Journal of Psychiatry*, 1959, 115, 1017-1020.

Bowlby, J. The influence of early environment in the development of neurosis and neurotic character. *International Journal of Psychoanalysis*, 1940, 21, 154-178.

Brodbeck, A. J., & Irwin, O. C. The speech behavior of infants without families. *Child Development*, 1946, 17, 145-156.

Brodey, W. M. Some family operations in schizophrenia. *Archives of General Psychiatry*, 1959, 1, 379-402.

Brown, W. T., & Moore, M. Soldiers who break down—family background and past history. *Military Surgeon*, 1944, 94, 160-163.

Canavan, Myrtelle M., & Clark, Rosamond. The mental health of 463 children from dementia praecox stock. *Mental Hygiene*, 1923, 7, 137-148.

Childers, A. T., & Hamil, B. M. Emotional problems in children as related to the duration of breast feeding in infancy. *American Journal of Orthopsychiatry*, 1932, 2, 134-142.

Clardy, E. R. A study of the development and course of schizophrenic children from dementia praecox stock. *Mental Hygiene*, 1923, 7, 137-148.

Darling, R. P. Autonomic action in relation to personality traits of children. *Journal of Abnormal and Social Psychology*, 1940, 35, 246-260.

Davidson, Susannah. School phobia as a manifestation of family disturbance: Its structure and treatment. *Journal of Child Psychology and Psychiatry*, 1961, 1, 270-287.

Davis, K. Extreme social isolation of a child. *American Journal of Sociology*, 1940, 45, 554-565.

Despert, Louise J. Schizophrenia in children. *Psychiatric Quarterly*, 1938, 12, 366-371.

Despert, Louise J. Some considerations relating to the genesis of autistic behavior in children. *American Journal of Orthopsychiatry*, 1951, 21, 335-350.

Donnelly, Ellen M. The quantitative analysis of parent behavior toward psychotic children and their siblings. *Genetic Psychology Monographs*, 1960, 62, 331-376.

Dworin, J., & Wyant, O. Authoritarian patterns in mothers of schizophrenics. *Journal of Clinical Psychology*, 1957, 13, 332-338.

Eisenberg, L. School phobia: A study in the communication of anxiety. *American Journal of Psychiatry*, 1958, 114, 712-718.

Estes, H. R., Haylett, Clarice H., & Johnson, Adelaide M. Separation anxiety. *American Journal of Psychotherapy*, 1956, 10, 682-695.

Eysenck, H. J. The inheritance of extraversion-introversion. *Acta Psychologica*, 1956, 12, 95-110.

Eysenck, H. J., & Prell, D. B. The inheritance of neuroticism: An experimental study. *Journal of Mental Science*, 1951, 97, 441-465.

Fanning, Aneita, Lehr, Sara, Sherwin, Roberta, & Wilson, Marjorie. The mental health of children of psychotic mothers. *Smith College Studies in Social Work*, 1938, 8, 291-343.

Farina, A. Patterns of role dominance and conflict in parents of schizophrenic patients. *Journal of Abnormal and Social Psychology*, 1960, 61, 31-38.

Farina, A., & Dunham, R. M. Measurement of family relationships and their effects. *Archives of General Psychiatry*, 1963, 9, 64-73.

Field, Minna A. Maternal attitudes found in twenty-five cases of children with primary behavior disorders. *American Journal of Orthopsychiatry*, 1940, 10, 293-311.

Fisher, S., Boyd, Ina, Walker D., & Sheer, Dianne. Parents of schizophrenics, neurotics, and normals. *Archives of General Psychiatry*, 1959, 1, 149-166.

Fisher, S., & Mendell, D. The communication of neurotic patterns over two and three generations. *Psychiatry*, 1956, 19, 41-46.

Fleck, S., Lidz, T., & Cornelison, Alice. Comparison of parent-child relationships of male and female schizophrenic patients. *Archives of General Psychiatry*, 1963, 8, 1-7.

Frazee, Helen E. Children who later became schizophrenic. *Smith College Studies in Social Work*, 1953, 23, 125-149.

Freeman, R. V., & Grayson, H. M. Maternal attitudes in schizophrenia. *Journal of Abnormal and Social Psychology*, 1955, 50, 45-52.

Freeman, H. E., & Simmons, O. G. Mental patients in the community: Family settings and performance levels. *American Sociological Review*, 1958, 23, 147-154.

Freeman, H. E., Simmons, O. G., & Bergen, B. J. Possessiveness as a characteristic of mothers of schizophrenics. *Journal of Abnormal and Social Psychology*, 1959, 58, 271-273.

Freud, S. *Inhibitions, symptoms, and anxiety.* London: Hogarth Press, 1936.

Freud, S. Three contributions to the theory of sex. In A. A. Brill (Ed.), *The basic writings of Sigmund Freud.* (Orig. Publ. 1910) New York: Modern Library, 1938. P. 583.

Freud, S. The dynamics of the transference. (Orig. publ. 1912) In *Collected papers.* Vol. 2. London: Hogarth Press, 1950. Pp. 312-322. (a)

Freud, S. The predisposition to obsessional neurosis. (Orig. publ. 1913) In *Collected papers.* Vol. 2. London: Hogarth Press, 1950. Pp. 122-132. (b)

Friedlander, D. Personality development of twenty-seven children who later became psychotic. *Journal of Abnormal and Social Psychology*, 1945, 40, 330-335.

Friedlander, Kate. Formation of the antisocial character. *Psychoanalytic Study of the Child*, 1945, 1, 189-203.

Garmezy, N., Clarke, A. R., & Stockner, Carol. Child rearing attitudes of mothers and fathers as reported by schizophrenic and normal patients. *Journal of Abnormal and Social Psychology*, 1961, **63**, 176-182.

Gerard, D. L., & Siegal, L. The family background of schizophrenia. *Psychiatric Quarterly*, 1950, **24**, 47-73.

Goldberg, Thelma B. Factors in the development of school phobia. *Smith College Studies in Social Work*, 1953, **23**, 227-248.

Goldfarb, W. The effects of early institutional care on adolescent personality (graphic Rorschach data). *Child Development*, 1943, **14**, 213-223 (a).

Goldfarb, W. Infant rearing and problem behavior. *American Journal of Orthopsychiatry*, 1943, **13**, 249-266. (b)

Goldfarb, W. The effects of early institutional care on adolescent personality. *Journal of Experimental Education*, 1943, **12**, 106-129. (c)

Goldfarb, W. Psychological deprivation in infancy. *American Journal of Psychiatry*, 1945, **102**, 19-33. (a)

Goldfarb, W. Psychological privation in infancy and subsequent adjustment. *American Journal of Orthopsychiatry*, 1945, **15**, 247-255. (b)

Greenacre, Phyllis. The predisposition to anxiety. *Psychoanalytic Quarterly*, 1941, **10**, 66-94.

Grossman, H. J., & Greenberg, N. H. Psychosomatic differentiation in infancy. I. Autonomic activity in the newborn. *Psychosomatic Medicine*, 1957, **19**, 293-306.

Guertin, W. H. Are differences in schizophrenic symptoms related to the mother's avowed attitudes toward child rearing? *Journal of Abnormal and Social Psychology*, 1961, **63**, 440-442.

Hajdu-Grimes, Lilly. Contributions to the etiology of schizophrenia. *Psychoanalytic Review*, 1940, **27**, 421-438.

Hattwick, Berta W. Interrelations between the preschool child's behavior and certain factors in the home. *Child Development*, 1936, **7**, 200-226.

Hattwick, Berta W., & Stowell, Margaret. The relation of parental over-attentiveness to children's work habits and social adjustment in kindergarten and the first six grades of school. *Journal of Educational Research*, 1936, **30**, 169-176.

Heilbrun, A. B. Perception of maternal childbearing attitures in schizophrenics. *Journal of Consulting Psychology*, 1960, **24**, 169-173.

Holloway, Edith. A study of fifty-eight problem children, with emphasis upon the home situation as a causative factor in producing conflict. *Smith College Studies in Social Work*, 1931, **1**, 403.

Huschka, Mabel. Psychopathological disorders in the mother. *Journal of Nervous and Mental Disease*, 1941, **94**, 76-83.

Ingham, H. V. A statistical study of family relationships in psychoneurosis. *American Journal of Psychiatry*, 1949, **106**, 91-98.

Inlow, Ruby S. The home as a factor in the development of the psychosis. *Smith College Studies in Social Work*, 1933, **4**, 153-154.

Jacobsen, Virginia. Influential factors in the outcome of treatment of school phobia. *Smith College Studies in Social Work*, 1947, **19**, 181-202.

Johnson, Adelaide M., Falstein, E. I., Szurek, S. A., & Svendsen, Margaret. School phobia. *American Journal of Orthopsychiatry*, 1941, **11**, 702-711.

Jost, H., & Sontag, L. W. The genetic factor in autonomic nervous system function. *Psychosomatic Medicine*, 1944, **6**, 308-310.

Karon, B. P., & Rosberg, J. Study of the mother-child relationship in a case of paranoid schizophrenia. *American Journal of Psychotherapy*, 1958, **12**, 522-533.

Kasanin, J., Knight, Elizabeth, & Sage, Priscilla. The parent-child relationship in schizophrenia. *Journal of Nervous and Mental Disease*, 1934, **79**, 249-263.

Kohn, M. L., & Clausen, J. A. Parental authority behavior and schizophrenia. *American Journal of Orthopsychiatry*, 1956, **26**, 297-313.

Kundert, Elizabeth. Fear of desertion by mother. *American Journal of Orthopsychiatry*, 1947, **17**, 326-336.

Lacey, J. I. Individual differences in somatic response patterns. *Journal of Comparative and Physiological Psychology*, 1950, **43**, 338-350.

Lampron, Edna M. Children of schizophrenic parents. *Mental Hygiene*, 1933, **17**, 82-91.

Lane, R. C., & Singer, J. L. Familial attitudes in paranoid schizophrenics and normals from two socioeconomic classes. *Journal of Abnormal and Social Psychology*, 1959, **59**, 328-339.

Levy, D. M. Maternal overprotection and rejection. *Archives of Neurology and Psychiatry*, 1931, **25**, 886-889.

Levy, D. M. On the problem of delinquency. *American Journal of Orthopsychiatry*, 1932, **2**, 197-211.

Levy, D. M. Primary affect hunger. *American Journal of Psychiatry*, 1937, **94**, 643-652.

Levy, D. M. *Maternal overprotection.* New York: Columbia Univ. Press, 1943.

Lidz, T., Cornelison, Alice R., Fleck, S., & Terry, Dorothy. The intrafamilial environment of the schizophrenic patient: I. The father. *Psychiatry*, 1957, **20**, 329-342. (a)

Lidz, T., Cornelison, Alice R., Fleck, S., & Terry, Dorothy. The intrafamilial environment of schizophrenic patients: II. Marital schism and marital skew. *American Journal of Psychiatry*, 1957, **114**, 241-248. (b)

Lidz, T., Cornelison, Alice R., Fleck, S., & Terry, Dorothy. The intrafamilial environment of the schizophrenic patient. *Psychiatry*, 1957, **20**, 329-342. (c)

Lidz, T., Cornelison, Alice, Terry, Dorothy, & Fleck, S. Intrafamilial environment of the schizophrenic patient: VI. The transmission of irrationality. *Archives of Neurology and Psychiatry*, 1958, **79**, 305-316.

Lidz, Ruth W., & Lidz, T. The family environment of schizophrenic patients. *American Journal of Psychiatry*, 1949, **106**, 332-345.

Lidz, T., Parker, Neulah, & Cornelison, Alice. The role of the father in the family environment of the schizophrenic patient. *American Journal of Psychiatry*, 1956, **113**, 126-137.

Lowrey, L. G. Personality distortion and early institutional care. *American Journal of Orthopsychiatry*, 1940, **10**, 576-585.

Madow, L., & Hardy, S. E. Incidence and analysis of the broken family in the background of neurosis. *American Journal of Orthopsychiatry*, 1947, **17**, 521-528.

Mark, J. C. The attitudes of the mothers of male schizophrenics toward child behavior. *Journal of Abnormal and Social Psychology*, 1953, **48**, 185-189.

McCord, W., McCord, Joan, & Howard, A. Familial correlates of aggression in nondelinquent male children. *Journal of Abnormal and Social Psychology*, 1961, **62**, 79-93.

McKeown, J. E. The behavior of parents of schizophrenic, neurotic, and normal children. *American Journal of Sociology*, 1950, **56**, 175-179.

Meyers, D. I., & Goldfarb, W. Studies of perplexity in mothers of schizophrenic children. *American Journal of Orthopsychiatry*, 1961, **31**, 551-564.

Meyers, D., & Goldfarb, W. Psychiatric appraisals of parents and siblings of schizophrenic children. *American Journal of Psychiatry*, 1962, **118**, 902-908.

Miller, H., & Baruch, D. A study of hostility in allergic children. *American Journal of Orthopsychiatry*, 1950, **20**, 506-519.

Mueller, Dorothy D. Paternal domination: Its influence on child guidance results. *Smith College Studies in Social Work*, 1945, **15**, 184-215.

Newell, H. W. The psycho-dynamics of maternal rejection. *American Journal of Orthopsychiatry*, 1934, **4**, 387-401.

Newell, H. W. A further study of maternal rejection. *American Journal of Orthopsychiatry*, 1936, **6**, 576-589.

Oltman, Jane E., McGarry, J. J., & Friedman, S. Parental deprivation and the "broken home" in dementia praecox and other mental disorders. *American Journal of Psychiatry*, 1952, **108**, 685-694.

Opler, M. K. Schizophrenia and culture. *Scientific American*, 1957, **197**, 103-110.

Orlansky, H. Infant care and personality. *Psychological Bulletin*, 1949, **46**, 1-48.

Pearson, G. H. Some early factors in the formation of personality. *American Journal of Orthopsychiatry*, 1931, **1**, 284-291.

Perr, H. M. Criteria distinguishing parents of schizophrenic and normal children. *Archives of Neurology and Psychiatry*, 1958, **79**, 217-224.

Plank, R. The family constellation of a group of schizophrenic patients. *American Journal of Orthopsychiatry*, 1953, **23**, 817-825.

Pollock, H. M., & Malzberg, B. Hereditary and environmental factors in the causation of manic-depressive psychoses and dementia praecox. *American Journal of Psychiatry*, 1940, **96**, 1227-1244.

Pollock, H. M., Malzberg, B., & Fuller, R. G. Hereditary and environmental factors in the causation of dementia praecox and manic-depressive psychoses. *Psychiatric Quarterly*, 1936, 10, 495-509.

Preston, G. H., & Antin, Rosemary. A study of children of psychotic parents. *American Journal of Orthopsychiatry*, 1932, 2, 231-241.

Prout, C. T., & White, Mary A. A controlled study of personality relationships in mothers of schizophrenic male patients. *American Journal of Psychiatry*, 1950, 107, 251-256.

Reichard, Suzanne, & Tillman, C. Patterns of parent-child relationships in schizophrenia. *Psychiatry*, 1950, 13, 247-257.

Ribble, Margarethe A. Disorganizing factors of infant personality. *American Journal of Psychiatry*, 1941, 98, 459-463.

Richards, T. W., & Newbery, Helen. Studies in fetal behavior: III. Can performance on test items at six months postnatally be predicted on the basis of fetal activity? *Child Development*, 1938, 9, 79-86.

Richmond, J. B., & Lustman, S. L. Autonomic function in the neonate: I. Implications for psychosomatic theory. *Psychosomatic Medicine*, 1955, 17, 269-275.

Schofield, W., & Ballan, L. A comparative study of the personal histories of schizophrenic and nonpsychiatric patients. *Journal of Abnormal and Social Psychology*, 1959, 59, 216-225.

Sears, R. R. Relation of early socialization experiences to aggression in middle childhood. *Journal of Abnormal and Social Psychology*, 1961, 63, 466-492.

Sears, R. R., Whiting, J. W. M., Nowlis, V., & Sears, Pauline S. Some child-rearing antecedents of aggression and dependency in young children. *Genetic Psychology Monograph*, 1953, 47, 133-234.

Shaw, C. R., & McKay, H. D. Are broken homes a causative factor in juvenile delinquency? *Social Forces*, 1932, 10, 514-524.

Shoben, E. J. The assessment of parental attitudes in relation to child adjustment. *Genetic Psychology Monographs*, 1949, 39, 101-148.

Silberpfennig, Judith. Mother types encountered in child guidance clinics. *American Journal of Orthopsychiatry*, 1941, 11, 475-484.

Silverman, B. The behavior of children from broken homes. *American Journal of Orthopsychiatry*, 1935, 5, 11-18.

Singer, J. L. Projected familial attitudes as a function of socioeconomic status and psychopathology. *Journal of Consulting Psychology*, 1954, 18, 99-104.

Sperling, Melitta. The role of the mother in psychosomatic disorders in children. *Psychosomatic Medicine*, 1949, 11, 377-385.

Sperling, Melitta. The neurotic child and his mother: A psychoanalytic study. *American Journal of Orthopsychiatry*, 1951, 21, 351-362.

Spitz, R. A. Hospitalism: An inquiry into the genesis of psychiatric conditions in early childhood. *Psychoanalytic Study of the Child*, 1945, 1, 53-74.

Stein, Lucille H.   A study of over-inhibited and unsocialized-aggressive children. *Smith College Studies in Social Work*, 1944, 15, 124-125.

Stringer, Joyce R.   Case studies of the families of schizophrenics. *Smith College Studies in Social Work*, 1962, 32, 118-148.

Strodtbeck, F. L.   Husband-wife interaction over revealed differences. *American Sociological Review*, 1951, 16, 468-473.

Suttenfield, Virginia.   School phobia: A study of five cases. *American Journal of Orthopsychiatry*, 1954, 24, 368-380.

Talbot, Mira.   School Phobia: A workshop: I. Panic in school phobia. *American Journal of Orthopsychiatry*, 1957, 27, 286-295.

Theron, P. A.   Peripheral vasomotor reaction as indices of basic emotional tension and lability. *Psychosomatic Medicine*, 1948, 10, 335-346.

Tietze, Trude.   A study of mothers of schizophrenic patients. *Psychiatry*, 1949, 12, 55-65.

van der Merwe, A. B.   The diagnostic value of peripheral vasomotor reactions in the psychoneuroses. *Psychosomatic Medicine*, 1948, 10, 347-354.

van der Merwe, A. B., & Theron, P. A.   A new method of measuring emotional stability. *Journal of General Psychology*, 1947, 37, 109-124.

van Houten, Janny.   Mother-child relationships in twelve cases of school phobia. *Smith College Studies in Social Work*, 1948, 18, 161-180.

Wahl, C. W.   Some antecedent factors in the family histories of 392 schizophrenics. *American Journal of Psychiatry*, 1954, 110, 668-676.

Wahl, C. W.   Some antecedent factors in the family histories of 568 male schizophrenics of the United States Navy. *American Journal of Psychiatry*, 1956, 113, 201-210.

Waldfogel, S., Hahn, Pauline B., & Gardner, G. E.   A study of school phobia in children. *Journal of Nervous and Mental Disease*, 1954, 120, 399.

Wallace, Ramona.   A study of the relationship between emotional tone of the home and adjustment status in cases referred to a travelling child guidance clinic. *Journal of Juvenile Research*, 1935, 19, 205-220.

Walters, Jean H.   A study of the family relationships of schizophrenic patients. *Smith College Studies in Social Work*, 1939, 9, 189-191.

Watson, G. A.   A comparison of the effects of lax versus strict home training. *Journal of Social Psychology*, 1934, 5, 102-105.

Wenger, M. A.   The measurement of individual differences in autonomic balance. *Psychosomatic Medicine*, 1941, 3, 427-434.

Wile, I. S., & Jones, Ann B.   Ordinal position and the behavior disorders of young children. *Journal of Genetic Psychology*, 1937, 51, 61-93.

Williams, H. D.   Causes of social maladjustment in children. *Psychological Monographs*, 1932, 43(1, Whole No. 194).

Wilson, Margaret J.   Grandmother, mother, and daughter in cases of school phobia. *Smith College Studies in Social Work*, 1955, 25, 56-57.

Winder, C. L., & Kantor, R. E.   Rorschach maturity scores of the mothers of schizophrenics. *Journal of Consulting Psychology*, 1958, 22, 438-440.

Witmer, Helen L.   Parental behavior as an index to the probable outcome of treatment in a child guidance clinic. *American Journal of Orthopsychiatry*, 1933, **3**, 431-444.

Zimmerman, Anna C.   Parental adjustments and attitudes in relation to the problems of five- and six-year-old children. *Smith College Studies in Social Work*, 1930, **1**, 406-407.

Zuckerman, M.   Save the pieces! A note on "The role of the family in the development of psychopathology." *Psychological Bulletin*, 1966, **66**, 78-80.

Zuckerman, M., Oltean, Mary, & Monashkin, I.   The parental attitudes of mothers of schizophrenics. *Journal of Consulting Psychology*, 1958, **22**, 307-310.

11

The Process-Reactive
Classification of Schizophrenia

INTRODUCTION

Many of the data obtained from schizophrenics are characterized
by an extreme degree of *variability*. That is, subjects in the schizophrenic group often differ among themselves more than do subjects in nonpsychotic groups. Because the performance of these
patients is so variable and because so many diverse symptoms are
represented within the class of schizophrenia, it is extremely difficult to do research on this class of patients and even more difficult
to draw conclusions or make accurate predictions concerning them.
This is essentially the problem of homogeneity—or lack thereof—
which was discussed in the earlier article by Zigler and Phillips.
They pointed out that "A criticism often leveled against the contemporary diagnostic system is that its categories encompass
heterogeneous groups of individuals, i.e., individuals varying in
respect to symptomology, test scores, prognosis, etc." (p. 31). They
went on to suggest that to increase the homogeneity of the groups
within the larger diagnostic groups. The following article by
with which we deal it might be necessary to develop new subclasses
William Herron is a review of the research on such a subdivision.
This subclassification seems to increase our predictive accuracy with
regard to psychological performance and prognosis.

Herron uses the terms *process* and *reactive* to identify two subclasses of patients within the class of schizophrenia. Another
combination of terms that has been used to describe these types of
patients is benign-malignant. The terms process and reactive probably fit the types of patients in question best because these terms
reflect the difference in the development of the types of schizophrenia, that is, a process or a reaction. As the reader will see, the
dominant factor in determining the degree to which a patient is

process or reactive is the patient's *premorbid personality*, that is, the patient's adjustment *before* he was diagnosed as schizophrenic. It is important to note that this diagnostic approach differs from the usual approach in that for the most part it explicitly uses criteria other than current symptomology. It also differs from the traditional approach in that it does not involve the concept of diagnostic classification per se. That is, rather than being an either-or classification, process and reactive are terms for the two ends of a *continuum*, and rather than merely being called either "process" or "reactive," a patient gets a *score* on the process-reactive continuum. (The fact that they are actually end points on a continuum is often forgotten, because in research extreme groups are usually used, and they tend to be referred to as different "types" of patients.) The assignment of continuous scores to patients, rather than the assignment of patients to discrete classes, leads to greater sensitivity in description, which can in turn lead to increased predictive ability. This is an important step forward.

Judging from the data that are reviewed in the following paper, it is clear that in looking at the results of any research on schizophrenia one should take into consideration what type of schizophrenics is being investigated. It might also be valuable to divide patients other than schizophrenics on the basis of their premorbid adjustment. Such a division of other psychotic and neurotic groups might allow us to account for more of the variance in their performance, symptomology, and etiology. In fact, Zigler and Phillips (1962) have said that "the relationship of achieved level of maturity (defined in terms of premorbid social competence) to certain dimensions of psychopathology is not unique to schizophrenia, but instead cut across all forms of functional mental disorder" (p. 216).

Zigler, E., & Phillips, L. Social competence and the process-reactive distinction in psychopathology. *Journal of Abnormal and Social Psychology*, 1962, 65, 215-222.

11

THE PROCESS-REACTIVE CLASSIFICATION OF SCHIZOPHRENIA

WILLIAM G. HERRON

The heterogeneity of schizophrenic patients and the lack of success in relating variable schizophrenic functioning to diagnostic subtypes (King, 1954) have indicated the serious limitations of the current neuropsychiatric classification of schizophrenia. In response to these limitations interest has arisen in a two-dimensional frame of reference for schizophrenia. Such a conception is based on the patient's life history and/or prognosis. A number of terms—malignant-benign, dementia praecox-schizophrenia, chronic-episodic, chronic-acute, typical-atypical, evolutionary-reactive, true-schizophreniform, process-reactive—have appeared in the literature describing these two syndromes. Process schizophrenia involves a long-term progressive deterioration of the adjustment pattern with little chance of recovery, while reactive schizophrenia indicates a good prognosis based on a history of generally adequate social development with notable stress precipitating the psychosis.

In view of the current favorable interest in this approach to the understanding of schizophrenia (Rabin & King, 1958) the present investigation is designed as an evaluative review of the literature on the process-reactive classification.

Early Prognostic Studies

The process-reactive distinction had its implicit origin in the work of Bleuler (1911). Prior to this the Kraepelinian influence had prevailed, with dementia praecox considered an incurable deteriorative disorder. Bleuler, while adhering to an organic etiology for schizophrenia, nonetheless observed that some cases recovered. This conclusion opened the field to a series of subsequent prognostic studies (Benjamin, 1946; Chase & Silverman, 1943; Hunt & Appel, 1936; Kant, 1940, 1941, 1944; Kretschmer, 1925;

SOURCE. Reprinted with permission of the American Psychological Association and the author from the *Psychological Bulletin*, 1962, 59, 329-343.

Langfeldt, 1951; Lewis, 1936, 1944; Malamud & Render, 1939; Mauz, 1930; Milici, 1939; Paskind & Brown, 1940; Wittman, 1941, 1944; Wittman & Steinberg, 1944a, 1944b) eventuating in formalized descriptions of the process and reactive syndromes in terms of specific criteria.

These early studies can be classified in three general catagories: studies correlating the outcome of a specific type of therapy with certain prognostic variables, studies descriptively evaluating prognostic criteria, and studies validating a prognostic scale.

The first category is illustrated by the attempt of Chase and Silverman (1943) to correlate the results of Metrazol and insulin shock therapy with prognosis, using 100 schizophrenic patients treated with Metrazol and 40 schizophrenic patients treated with insulin shock.

In the first part of this study the probable outcome of each of the 150 patients was estimated on the basis of prognostic criteria. The criteria considered of primary importance for a favorable prognosis were: short duration of illness, acute onset, obvious exogenic precipitating factors, early prominence of confusion, and atypical symptoms (marked by strong mixtures of manic-depressive, psychogenic, and symptomatic trends), and minimal process symptoms (absence of depersonalization, derealization, massive primary persecutory ideas, and sensations of influence, conscious realization of personality disintegration, bizarre delusions and hallucinations, marked apathy, and dissociation of affect). When these conditions were reversed the prognosis was least favorable. The following factors were considered less important for a favorable prognosis: history of previous illness, pyknic body type, extrovert temperament and adequate prepsychotic life adjustment, catatonic and atypical subtypes. Asthenic body type, introversion, inadequacy of prepsychotic reactions to life situations, onset of illness after the age of 40, and hebephrenic and paranoid subtypes were considered indicative of unfavorable prognosis. Age of onset under 40, sex, education, and abilities, and hereditary background were not considered of prognostic importance. An analysis of the prognostically significant factors resulted in the evaluation of the prognosis for each case as good, fair, or poor.

Following termination of shock treatment all patients were followed-up for an average of 10 months and divided into three groups; much improved, improved, and unimproved. A comparison of the prognostic assessments with the results of shock indicated that of 43 cases in which the prognosis was considered good, 33 showed remissions, while of 74 cases with a poor prognosis, 63 did not improve. It was concluded that shock therapies were effective in cases of schizophrenia in which the prognosis was favorable, but were of little value when the prognosis was poor.

The second part of the research involved a reanalysis of the prognostic criteria in the light of the results of shock treatment. Short duration of illness and the absence of process symptoms were the most significant factors for favorable outcome, while long duration of illness (more than 2 years) and the presence of process symptoms were primary in determining poor prognosis.

A descriptive review of prognostic factors is seen in Kant's (1944) description of the benign (reactive) syndrome as cases in which clouding and confusion prevail, or in which the schizophrenic symptoms centered around manic-depressive features or cases with alternating states of excitement and stupor with fragmentation of mental activity. Malignant (process) cases are characterized by direct process symptoms. These include changes in the behavior leading to disorganization, dulling and autism, preceding the outbreak of overt psychosis. The most subtle manifestation of this is the typical schizophrenic thought disturbance. The patient experiences the process as a loss of normal feeling of personality activity and the start of experiencing a foreign influence applied to mind or body.

The third category includes the Elgin Prognostic Scale, constructed by Wittman (1941) to predict recovery in schizophrenia. It is comprised of 20 rating scales weighted according to prognostic importance: favorable factors are weighted negatively, and unfavorable factors are assigned positive weights. Initial validation involved 343 schizophrenic cases placed on shock treatment. Wittman and Steinberg (1944a) performed a follow-up study on 804 schizophrenics and 156 manic-depressive patients. The Elgin scale proved effective in predicting the outcome of therapy in 80–85% of the cases in both studies, and has been utilized in the work of Becker (1956, 1959), King (1958), and McDonough (1960) to distinguish the process-reactive syndrome. Included in the subscales of the Elgin scale are evaluations of prepsychotic personality, nature of onset, and typicality of the psychosis relative to Kraepelin's definition.

Studies with Detailed Process-Reactive Criteria

The synthesis of early studies is found in the research of Kantor, Wallner, and Winder (1953) establishing detailed criteria for distinguishing the two syndromes on the basis of case history material. A process patient would exhibit the following characteristics: early psychological trauma, severe or long physical illness, odd member of the family, school difficulties, family troubles paralleled by sudden changes in the patient's behavior, introverted behavior trends and interests, history of a breakdown of social, physical, and/or mental functioning, pathological siblings, overprotective or rejecting mother, rejecting father, lack of heterosexuality, insidious gradual onset of psychosis without pertinent stress, physical aggression, poor response to treatment, lengthy stay in the hospital, massive paranoia, little capacity for alcohol, no manic-depressive component, failure under adversity, discrepancy between ability and achievement, awareness of a change in the self, somatic delusions, a clash between the culture and the environment, and a loss of decency. In contrast, the reactive patient has these characteristics: good psychological history, good physical health, normal family member, well adjusted at school, domestic troubles unaccompanied by behavioral disruptions in the patient, extroverted behavior trends and interests, history of adequate social, physical, and/or mental functioning, normal siblings, normally protective accepting mother, accepting father, heterosexual behavior, sudden onset of psychosis with pertinent stress present, verbal aggression, good response to treatment, short stay in the hospital, minor paranoid trends, good capacity for alcohol, manic-depressive component present, success despite adversity, harmony between ability and achievement, no sensation of self-change, absence of somatic delusions, harmony between the culture and the environment, and retention of decency.

The first three criteria apply to the patient's behavior between birth and the fifth year; the next seven, between the fifth year and adolescence; the next five, from adolescence to adulthood; the last nine, during adulthood. Using these 24 points to distinguish the two syndromes they tried to answer three questions:

1. Do diagnoses based upon the Rorschach alone label as nonpsychotic a portion of the population of mental patients who are clinically diagnosed as schizophrenic?

2. Can case histories of clinically diagnosed schizophrenics be differentiated into two categories: process and reactive?

3. Are those cases rated psychotic from the Rorschach classed as process on the basis of case histories, and are those cases judged nonpsychotic from the Rorschach classified as reactive from the case histories?

Two samples of 108 and 95 patients clinically diagnosed as schizophrenic were given the Rorschach and rated according to the process-reactive criteria. In the first sample of 108 patients, 57 were classified as psychoic and 51 nonpsychotic on the basis of the Rorschach alone, while in the second sample, of 74 patients who could be rated as process or reactive, 36 were classified as psychotic, and 38 as nonpsychotic from their Rorschach protocols. Those patients who were rated as reactive from their history were most often judged nonpsychotic from the Rorschach, and those rated process from the case histories were most often judged as psychotic from the Rorschach.

Only one judge was used in the second sample to rate the patients as process or reactive, but two judges were used in the first sample. Of the 108 patients in this sample, both judges rated 86 cases, and were in agreement on 64 of these, which is greater than would be expected by chance.

However, the accuracy of the schizophrenic diagnosis is questionable in this study. If the Rorschach diagnosis is followed, then it appears that reactive schizophrenics are not psychotic. Furthermore, the psychiatric diagnosis appears to be somewhat contaminated because it was established on the basis of data collected by all appropriate services of the hospital, including psychological examinations. A similar type of contamination may have been present in classifying patients as process or reactive because one judge had reviewed each case previously and had seen psychological examination and history materials together prior to making his ratings. Three difficulties can be found with the criteria for process-reactive ratings. First, case histories are often incomplete and the patient is unable or unwilling to supply the necessary information. Second, it is difficult to precisely apply some of the criteria. For example, what is the precise dividing line between oddity and normality within the family? Third, in order to classify a patient it is necessary to set an arbitrary cut off point based on the number of process or reactive characteristics a patient has. Such a procedure needs validation.

Nonetheless, the results of this study support the view that schizophrenics can be classified as process or reactive, and that these syndromes differ in psychological functioning.

Another rating scale which has been used extensively to distinguish prognostically favorable and prognostically unfavorable schizophrenics was developed by Phillips (1953). The scale was developed from the case histories of schizophrenic patients who were eventually given shock treatment. The scale evaluates each patient in three areas: premorbid history, possible precipitating factors, and signs of the disorder. Premorbid history includes seven items on the social aspects of sexual life during adolescence and immediately beyond, seven items on the social aspects of recent sexual life, six items on personal relations, and six items on recent premorbid adjustment in personal relations. The sections of the scale which reflect the recent sexual life and its social history are the most successful in predicting the outcome of treatment. The items in the scales are arranged in order of increasing significance for improvement and nonimprovement away from the score of three, which is the dividing point between improved and unimproved groups. The premorbid history subscale has been utilized as the ranking instrument in the studies described by Rodnick and Garmezy (1957; Garmezy & Rodnick, 1959).

Another approach to the separation of schizophrenics into prognostic groups uses the activity of the autonomic nervous system as the basis for division (Meadow & Funkenstein, 1952; Meadow, Greenblatt, Funkenstein, & Solomon, 1953; Meadow, Greenblatt, & Solomon, 1953). Meadow and Funkenstein (1952) worked with 58 schizophrenic patients tested for autonomic reactivity and for abstract thinking. Following therapy the patients were divided into two groups, good or poor, depending on the outcome of the treatment. The battery of psychological tests included the similarities and block design subtests of the Wechsler-Bellevue scale, the Benjamin Proverbs test, and the object sorting tests. The physiological test involved the systolic blood pressure reaction to adrenergic stimulation (intravenous Epinephrine) and cholinergic stimulation (intramuscular Mecholyl). On the basis of the physiological and psychological testing, schizophrenic cases were divided into three types: Type I, characterized by marked response to Epinephrine, low blood pressure, and failure of the blood pressure to rise under most stresses, loss of ability for abstract thinking, inappropriate affect, and a poor prognosis; Type II, characterized by an entirely different autonomic pattern, relatively intact abstract ability, anxiety or depression, and a good prognosis; Type III, showing no autonomic disturbance, relatively little loss of abstract ability, little anxiety, well organized paranoid delusions, and a fair prognosis.

However, as Meadow and Funkenstein (1952) point out, there is considerable overlap of the measures defining these types so that the classification must be tentative. Also, of the psychological tests used, only Proverbs distinguished significantly between the patients when they were classified according to autonomic reactivity, while Block Design failed to distinguish significantly among any of the types. Further research using this method of division (Meadow, Greenblatt, Funkenstein, & Solomon, 1953; Meadow, Greenblatt, & Solomon, 1953) served as a basis for investigations of the process-reactive syndromes by King (1958) and Zuckerman and Grosz (1959).

King (1958) hypothesized that predominantly reactive schizophrenics would exhibit a higher level of autonomic responsiveness after the injection of Mecholyl than predominantly process schizophrenics. The subjects were 60 schizophrenics who were classified as either process or reactive by the present investigator and an independent judge using the criteria of Kantor et al. (1953). Only those subjects were used on which there was classificatory agreement. This resulted in 22 process and 24 reactive patients. In order to consider the process-reactive syndrome as a continuum, 16 subjects were randomly selected from these two groups and were ranked by two independent raters.

While the patient was lying in bed shortly after awaking in the morning the resting systolic blood pressure was determined. The patient then received 10 milligrams of Mecholyl intramuscularly, and the systolic blood pressure was recorded at intervals up to 20 minutes. Then the maximum fall in systolic blood pressure (MFBP) below the resting blood pressure following the injection of Mecholyl was computed for the different time intervals. There was a significant difference in the MFBP score for the reactives as compared with the normals. For the 16 subjects, the correlation between the sets of ranks on the process-reactive dimension and MFBP was —.58.

In a second part of the study 90 schizophrenics, none of whom had participated in the first part, were classified as either process, process-reactive, or reactive, using the criteria of Kantor et al. (1953). On this basis the subjects were divided into three groups of 24. Also, scores for 22 subjects were obtained on the Elgin Prognostic Scale, and 12 of these were rated independently by two raters. The MFBP scores were 17.04 for the process group, 22.79 for the process-reactive group, and 26.62 for the reactive. Using an analysis of variance a significant F score occurs at the .01 level. The correlation between the Elgin Prognostic Scale and the MFBP scores for 22 patients was —.49.

Results of both parts of the study revealed that the patients classified as reactive exhibited a significantly greater fall in blood pressure after the administration of Mecholyl than the process patients. This evidence points to diminished physiological responsiveness in process, but not in reactive schizophrenia. However, Zuckerman and Grosz (1959) found that process schizophrenics showed a significantly greater fall in blood pressure following the administration of Mecholyl than reactives. Since these results contradict King's findings the question of the direction of responsiveness to Mecholyl in these two groups requires further investigation before a conclusion can be reached.

Process-Organic versus Reactive-Psychogenic

Brackbill and Fine (1956) suggested that process schizophrenics suffer from an organic impairment not present in the reactive case. They hypothesized that there would be no significant differences in the incidence of "organic signs" on the Rorschach between a group of process schizophrenics and a group of known cases of central nervous system pathology, and that both organic and process groups would show significantly more signs of organic involvement than the reactive group.

The subjects consisted of 36 patients diagnosed as process schizophrenics and 24 reactive schizophrenics. The criteria of Kantor et al. (1953) were used to describe the patients as process or reactive. Patients were included only when there was complete agreement between judges as to the category of schizophrenia. Also included in the sample were 28 cases of known organic involvement. All patients were given the Rorschach, and the protocols were scored using Piotrowski's (1940) 10 signs of organicity.

Using the criterion of five or more signs as a definite indication of organic involvement there was no significant difference between the organic and process groups, but both groups were significantly different from the reactives. Considering individual signs, four distinguished between the reactive and organic group, while two distinguished between process and reactive groups. The authors concluded that the results supported the hypothesis that process schizophrenics react to a perceptual task in a similar manner to that of patients with central nervous system pathology. No specific hypothesis was made about individual Rorschach signs, but color naming, completely absent in the reactives, was indicated as an example of concrete thinking and inability to abstract, suggesting that one of the critical differences between process and reactive groups is in terms of a type of thought disturbance.

This study does not provide detailed information about the manner of establishing the diagnosis of schizophrenia or about the judges deciding the process and reactive syndromes. Also, a further difficulty is the admitted inadequacy of the organic signs, since 66% of cases with organic pathology in this study were false negatives according to the Rorschach criteria. Thus while the existence of the process and reactive syndromes is supported by the results of this investigation, there is less evidence of an organic deficit in process schizophrenics.

Becker (1956) pointed out that the consistency of the prognostic findings in schizophrenia has led to postulating two kinds of schizophrenia: process, with an organic basis, and reactive, with a psychological basis. He rejects this conclusion because research data in this area shows considerable group overlap, making it clinically difficult and arbitrary to force all schizophrenics into one group or the other. Also, if schizophrenia is a deficit reaction which may be brought about by any combination of 40 or more etiological factors, then the conception of two dichotomous types of schizophrenia is not useful. Finally, he maintains that 20 years of research have failed to find clear etiological differences between any subgroupings.

Instead, Becker stated that process and reactive syndromes should be conceived as end points on a continuum of levels of personality organization. Process reflects a very primitive undifferentiated personality structure, while reactive indicates a more highly organized one. He hypothesized that schizophrenics more nearly approximating the process syndrome would show more regressive and immature thinking processes than schizophrenics who more nearly approximate the reactive syndromes. His sample consisted of 51 schizophrenics, 24 males and 27 females, all under 41 years of age. Their thinking processes were evaluated by the Rorschach and the Benjamin Proverbs test. The 1937 Stanford-Binet vocabulary test was used to estimate verbal intelligence. A Rorschach scoring system was used which presumably reflected the subjects' level of perceptual development, while a scoring system was devised for the Proverbs which reflected levels of abstraction. Since there is a high relationship between intelligence and ability to interpret proverbs, a more sensitive index of a thinking disturbance was considered to be a discrepancy score based on the standard score difference between a vocabulary estimate of verbal intelligence and the proverbs score. Process and reactive ratings were made on the Elgin Prognostic Scale.

The Rorschach mean perceptual level score and the Elgin Prognostic Scale correlated —.599 for men and —.679 for women, indicating a significant relationship between the process-reactive dimension as evaluated from case history data and disturbances of thought processes as measured by the Rorschach scoring system. The proverbs-vocabulary discrepancy score was significantly related to the process-reactive dimension for men, but not for women. No adequate explanation was found for this sex difference, which mitigates the results. A further difficulty occurs because the case history and test evaluations were made by the same person. However, the results in part support the hypothesis, indicating evidence for a measurable dimension of regressive and immature thinking related to the process-reactive dimension.

McDonough (1960), acting on the assumption that process schizophrenia involves central nervous system pathology specifically cortical in nature, hypothesized that brain damaged patients and process schizophrenics would have significantly lower critical flicker frequency (CFF) thresholds and would be unable to perceive the spiral aftereffect significantly more often than reactive schizophrenics and normals. Four groups of 20 subjects each were tested. The organic group consisted of individuals with known brain damage. One hundred and sixty-one schizophrenic case histories were examined, and 76 were chosen from this group to be rated on the Elgin Prognostic Scale. The 20 patients receiving the lowest point totals were selected as being most reactive, while those with the 20 highest scores were considered most process.

Results of the experiment revealed that organic patients were significantly different from all other groups in CFF threshold and ability to perceive the spiral aftereffect. Process and reactive schizophrenics did not differ from each other on either task, but reactive schizophrenics had higher CFF thresholds than normals. These results do not indicate demonstrable cortical defect in either process or reactive schizophrenia.

Process-Poor Premorbid History versus Reactive-Good Premorbid History

Rodnick and Garmezy (1957), discussing the problem of motivation in schizophrenia, reviewed a number of studies in which the Phillips prognostic scale was used to classify schizophrenic patients into two groups, good and poor. For example, Bleke (1955) hypothesized that patients whose prepsychotic life adjustment was markedly inadequate would have greater interferences and so show more reminiscence following censure than patients whose premorbid histories were more adequate.

The subjects were presented with a list of 14 neutrally toned nouns projected successively on a screen. Each subject was required to learn to these words a pattern of pull-push movements of a switch lever. For half the subjects in each group learning took place under a punishment condition, while the remaining subjects were tested under a reward condition. The subjects consisted of 40 normals, 20 poor premorbid schizophrenics, and 20 good premorbid schizophrenics. The results confirmed the hypothesis.

A reanalysis of Dunn's (1954) data indicated that a poor premorbid group showed discrimination deficits when confronted with a scene depicting a mother and a young boy being scolded, but good premorbid and normal subjects did not show this deficit.

Mallet (1956) found that poor premorbid subjects in a memory task for verbal materials showed significantly poorer retention of hostile and nonhostile thematic contents than did good premorbid and normal subjects. Harris (1955) has found that in contrast to goods and normals poor premorbids have more highly deviant maternal attitudes. They attribute more rejective attitudes to their mothers, and are less able to critically evaluate their mothers. Harris (1957) also found differences among the groups in the size estimation of mother-child pictures. The poors significantly overestimated, while the goods underestimated, and the normals made no size error.

Rodnick and Garmezy (1957) reported a study using Osgood's (1952) semantic differential techniques in which six goods and six poors rated 20 concepts on each of nine scales selected on the basis of high loadings on the evaluative, potency, and activity factors. Good and poor groups differed primarily on potency and activity factors. The poors described words with negative value, as more powerful and active. The goods could discriminate among concepts, but the poors tended to see most concepts as powerful and active.

Rodnick and Garmezy (1957) also investigated differences in authority roles in the family during adolescence in good and poor premorbid patients. While results were tentative at that time, they suggested that the mothers of poor premorbid patients were perceived as having been more dominating, restrictive, and powerful, while the fathers appeared ineffectual. The pattern was reversed in the good premorbid patients.

Alvarez (1957) found significantly greater preference decrements to censured stimuli by poor premorbid patients. This result was consistent with the results of Bleke's (1955) and Zahn's (1959) observations of reversal patterns of movement of a switch lever following censure. These experiments suggested an increased sensitivity of the poor premorbid schizophrenic patient to a threatening environment.

These studies reported by Rodnick and Garmezy (1957) indicated that it was possible, using the Phillips scale, to effectively dichotomize schizophrenic patients. However, the Phillips scale had predictive validity only when applied to male patients. Within this form of reference it was also possible to demonstrate differences between goods and poors in response to censure, and in perception of familial figures. Variability in the results of schizophrenic performance was considerably reduced by dichotomizing the patients, but it was often impossible to detect significant differences between the performance of good premorbid schizophrenics and normals. Rodnick and Garmezy (1957) suggest that the results be considered as preliminary findings pending further corroboration, though providing support for the concept of premorbid groups of schizophrenics differing in certain psychological dimensions.

Process-Reactive Empirical-Theoretical Formulations

Fine and Zimet (1959; Zimet & Fine, 1959) used the same population employed by Kantor et al. (1953) and the same criteria for distinguishing the process and reactive patients. For this study only those cases were included where there was complete agreement among the judges as to the category of schizophrenia. They studied the level of perceptual organization of the patients as shown on their Rorschach records. The process group was found to have significantly more immature, regressive perceptions, while the reactive group gave more mature and more highly organized responses. The findings indicated that archaic and impulse-ridden materials break through more freely in process schizophrenia, and that there is less ego control over the production of more regressive fantasies. Zimet and Fine (1959) speculated that process schizophrenia mirrors oral deprivation of early ego impoverishment, so that either regression or fixation to an earlier developmental stage is reflected in his perceptual organization. In contrast, it is possible that the reactive schizophrenic's ego weakness occurs at a later stage in psychosexual development, and any one event may reactivate the early conflict.

An amplification of the process-reactive formation has been suggested by Kantor and Winder (1959). They hypothesized that schizophrenia can be understood as a series of responses reflecting the stage of development in the patient's life at which emotional support was severely deficient. Schizophrenia can be quantitatively depicted in terms of the level in life to which the schizophrenic has regressed, and beyond which development was severely distorted because of disturbing life circumstances. The earlier in developmental history that severe stress occurs, the more damaging the effect on subsequent interpersonal relationships. Sullivan (1947) suggested five stages in the development of social maturity: empathic, prototaxic, parataxic, autistic, and syntaxic. The most malignant schizophrenics are those who were severely traumatized in the empathic stage of development when all experience is unconnected, there is no symbolism, and functioning is at an elementary biological level. The schizophrenic personality originating at this stage may show many signs of organic dysfunction. Prognosis will be most unfavorable, and delusional formation will tend to be profound.

In view of the primitive symbolic conduct and the lack of a self-concept in the prototaxic stage, the schizophrenic personality referable to this stage will be characterized by magical thinking and disturbed communication. The delusion of adoption often occurs. However, these patients are more coherent than those of the previous level.

The parataxic schizophrenic state involves the inability of the self-system to prevent dissociation. The autonomy of the dissociations result in the patient's fear of uncontrollable inward processes. Schizophrenic symptoms appear as regressive behavior attempting to protect the self and regain security in a threatening world. Delusional content usually involves world disaster coupled with bowel changes. Nihilistic delusions are common. While there is evidence of a self-system in these patients, prognosis remains unfavorable.

The patient who has regressed to the autistic stage, although more reality oriented than in the previous stages, is characterized by paranoid suspiciousness, hostility, and pathological defensiveness against inadequacy feelings. A consistent system of delusions will be articulated and may bring the patient into conflict with society. However, prognosis is more favorable at this stage than previously.

An individual at the syntaxic level has reached concensus with society, so that if schizophrenia occurs it will be a relatively circumscribed reaction. Onset will be sudden with plausible environmental stresses, and prognosis is relatively good.

Becker (1959) also elaborated on the lack of a dichotomy in schizophrenia. Individual cases spread out in such a way that the process syndrome moves into the reactive syndrome, so that the syndromes probably identify the end points of a dimension of severity. At the process end of the continuum the development of personality organization is very primitive, or involves severe regression. There is a narrowing of interests, rigidity of structure, and inability to establish normal heterosexual relationships and independence. In contrast, the reactive end of the continuum represents a higher level of personality differentiation. The prepsychotic personality is more normal, heterosexual relations are better established, and there is greater tolerance of environmental stresses. The remains of a higher developmental level are present in regression and provide strength for recovery.

Becker (1959) factor analyzed some of the data from his previous study (Becker, 1956). The factored matrix included a number of background variables, the 20 Elgin Prognostic Scale subscores, and a Rorschach genetic level score (*GL*) based on the first response to each card. Seven centroid factors were extracted from the correlation matrix. Factors 4, 6, and 7 represented intelligence, cooperativeness, and marital status of parents, respectively. The highest loadings on Factor 5 were history of mental illness in the family, excellent health history, lack of precipitating factors, and clouded sensorium. The Rorschach *GL* score and the Elgin scales did not load significantly on Factors 4 through 7.

The remaining three factors parallel the factors Lorr, Wittman, and Schanberger (1951) found with 17 of the 20 Elgin scales using an oblique solution instead of the orthogonal solution used in this study. Factor 1 is called schizophrenic withdrawal, loading on defect of interest, insidious onset, shut-in personality, long duration of psychosis, and lack of precipitating factors. At one end this factor defines the typical process syndrome, while the other end describes the typical reactive syndrome. The Rorschach *GL* score loaded —.46 on Factor 1.

Factor 2, reality distortion, loads on hebephrenic symptoms, bizarre delusions, and inadequate affect. Rorschach *GL* score loaded —.64 on this factor. Factor 3 loaded on indifference and exclusiveness-stubbornness. The opposite pole of this factor involves insecurity, inferiority, selfconsciousness, and anxiety. Rorschach *GL* score loaded .25 on this factor.

Further analysis indicated that when Factors 1 and 2 were plotted against each other an oblique rotation was required, introducing a correlation of from .60 to .70 between schizophrenic withdrawal and reality distortion factors. Similar obliqueness was found between Factors 2 and 3, suggesting the presence of a second-order factor.

However, the sampling of behavior manifestations in the Elgin scale overweights the withdrawal factor, which gives Factor 1 undue weight and biases the direction of a second-order factor toward the withdrawal factor. Also, it is not possible to accurately locate second-order factors with only seven first-order factors as reference points. In addition, sample size and related sampling errors limited inferences about a second-order factor. There is the suggestion, however, of the existence of a general severity factor, loading primarily schizophrenic withdrawal and reality distortion.

The author suggests utilizing the evidence from this study to form an index of severity of psychosis which could be used to make diagnoses with prognostic significance. This diagnostic procedure would include factor estimates of schizophrenic withdrawal and emotional rigidity, based on Elgin scale ratings, and reality distortion, based on the Rorschach GL score.

Garmezy and Rodnick (1959) pointed out that despite failure to find support for a fundamental biological deviation associated with schizophrenia (Kety, 1959), the view of schizophrenia as a dichotomous typology influenced either by somatic or psychic factors has continuously been advanced. They maintain that on the basis of empirical evidence there is little support for a process-organic versus reactive-psychogenic formulation of schizophrenic etiology.

Reviewing a series of studies using the Phillips scale as a dichotomizing instrument (Alvarez, 1957; Bleke, 1955; Dunham, 1959; Dunn, 1954; Englehart, 1959; Farina, 1960; Garmezy, Stockner, & Clarke, 1959; Harris, 1957; Kreinik, 1959; Rodnick & Garmezy, 1957; Zahn, 1959) Garmezy and Rodnick concluded that the results indicate two groups of schizophrenic patients differing both in prognostic potential and sensitivity to experimental cues. There is an interrelationship among the variables of premorbid adequacy, differential sensitivity to censure, prognosis, and types of familial organization. This suggests a relationship between varying patterns of early experience and schizophrenia, though it does not embody the acceptance of a given position regarding psychological or biological antecedents in schizophrenia.

Reisman (1960), in an attempt to explain the heterogeneous results of psychomotor performance in schizophrenics, suggested that there were two groups of schizophrenics, process and reactive, differing in motivation. The process group was seen as more withdrawn and indifferent to their performance, and consequently reflecting a psychomotor deficit not present in reactives. In order to test this hypothesis 36 reactives, 36 process patients, and 36 normals performed a card-sorting task. The groups were distinguished according to the criteria of Kantor, Wallner, and Winder (1953). On Trial 1 all subjects were requested to sort as rapidly as possible. Then the subjects were assigned to one of four experimental conditions, with an attempt made to equate across the experimental conditions for age, estimated IQ, length of hospitalization, and initial sorting time. Condition 1 (FP) involved sorting the cards seven more times and if the sort was fast the subjects were shown stress-arousing photographs. If they sorted slowly no photographs were shown. Condition 2 (SP) was the reverse of this. Condition 3 (FL) and Condition 4 (SL) were similar to the first two conditions except that a nonreinforcing light was used instead of the pictures. After Trial 8 all subjects were informed that there would be no more pictures or light, but were asked to sort rapidly for three more trials. With four conditions on Trials 2 through 8, 10 subjects from each of the three groups participated in each of the two picture conditions, while eight subjects from each group participated in each of the light conditions.

The results indicated that the normals performed about the same under all conditions. The process group under FP sorted as fast as normals, but performed slowly under the other three conditions, while the reactives were slowest under FP but were as fast as normals under the other three conditions. Within all three groups performance under FL did not differ significantly from performance under SL. Under FL and SL, however, reactives and normals sorted more rapidly than the process group. These results supported the hypothesis of a motivational deficit for process schizophrenics. The results also indicated that the pictures were negatively reinforcing for the reactives, while the process patients were motivated to see them. This suggested a withdrawal differential. The withdrawal of the process patients is of such duration that supposedly threatening photographs cause little anxiety. In contrast, reactive withdrawal is motivated by an environment that recently became unbearable. Confronted with pictures representing this environment the reactive patient experiences anxiety and avoidance. However, the results of this experiment are in contrast to the findings of Rodnick and Garmezy (1957) that prolonged exposure to social censure will result in greater sensitivity to that stimulation.

Summary

This review of all the research on the process-reactive classification of schizophrenia strongly indicates that it is possible to divide schizophrenic patients into two groups differing in prognostic and life-history variables. Using such a division it is also possible to demonstrate differences between the two groups in physiological measures and psychological dimensions.

The result of such an approach has been to clarify many of the heterogenous reactions found in schizophrenia. It also appears that the dichotomy is somewhat artificial and really represents end points on a continuum of personality organization. The most process patient represents the extreme form of personality disintegration, while the most reactive patient represents the extreme form of schizophrenic integration. The reactions of this type of patient are often difficult to distinguish from behavior patterns of normal subjects. There does not appear to be any significant evidence to support the contention of a process-organic versus a reactive-psychogenic formulation of schizophrenic etiology.

It is difficult to decide on the most appropriate criteria for selecting schizophrenic subjects so as to reduce their response variability. Preferences are generally found for one of three sets of criteria: Kantor, Wallner, and Winder's (1953) items, the Elgin Prognostic Scale (1944), or the Phillips scale (1953). The criteria of Kantor et al. (1953) does not provide a quantitative ordering of the variables, and is descriptively vague in several dimensions as well as depending upon life history material which is not always available. While the Elgin scale does provide a quantitative approach, it also has the disadvantages of descriptive vagueness and excessive dependence upon life history material. The Phillips scale eliminates some of these difficulties, but its validity is limited to the adequacy or inadequacy of social-sexual premorbid adjustment. The need for more feasible criteria may be met by the factor analysis of pertinent variables to obtain a meaningful severity index (Becker, 1959), or by using rating scales in which the patient verbally supplies the necessary information. An example of the latter is the Ego Strength scale (Barron, 1953), recently utilized in distinguishing two polar constellations of schizophrenia; a process type with poor prognosis and grossly impaired abstract ability, and a reactive type characterized by good prognosis and slight abstractive impairment (Herron, in press).

This need for more efficient differentiating criteria mitigates some of the significance of present findings using the process-reactive dimension. Nonetheless, the process-reactive research up to this time has succeeded in explaining schizophrenic heterogeneity in a more meaningful manner than previous interpretations adhering to various symptom pictures and diagnostic subtypes. Consequently, there appears to be definite value in utilizing the process-reactive classification of schizophrenia.

REFERENCES

Alvarez, R. R.   A comparison of the preferences of schizophrenic and normal subjects for rewarded and punished stimuli. Unpublished doctoral dissertation, Duke University, 1957.

Barron, F.   An ego-strength scale which predicts response to psychotherapy. *Journal of Consulting Psychology*, 1953, **17**, 327-333.

Becker, W.   A genetic approach to the interpretation and evaluation of the process-reactive distinction in schizophrenia. *Journal of Abnormal and Social Psychology*, 1956, **53**, 229-236.

Becker, W. C.   The process-reactive distinction: A key to the problem of schizophrenia? *Journal of Nervous and Mental Disorders*, 1959, **129**, 442-449.

Benjamin, J. D.   A method for distinguishing and evaluating formal thinking disorders in schizophrenia. In J. S. Kasanin (Ed.), *Language and thought in schizophrenia*. Berkeley: University of California Press, 1946. Pp. 66-71.

Bleke, R. S.   Reward and punishment as determiners of reminiscence effects in schizophrenics and normal subjects. *Journal of Personality*, 1955, **23**, 479-498.

Bleuler, E.   *Dementia praecox*. New York: International University Press, 1911.

Brackbill, G., & Fine, H.   Schizophrenia and central nervous system pathology. *Journal of Abnormal and Social Psychology*, 1956, **52**, 310-313.

Chase, L. S., & Silverman, S.   Prognosis in schizophrenia: An analysis of prognostic criteria in 150 schizophrenics treated with Metrazol or insulin. *Journal of Nervous and Mental Disorders*, 1943, **98**, 464-473.

Dunham, R. M.   Sensitivity of schizophrenics to parental censure. Unpublished doctoral dissertation, Duke University, 1959.

Dunn, W. L.   Visual discrimination of schizophrenic subjects as a function of stimulus meaning. *Journal of Personality*, 1954, **23**, 48-64.

Englehart, R. S.   Semantic correlates of interpersonal concepts and parental attributes in schizophrenia. Unpublished doctoral dissertation, Duke University, 1959.

Farina, A.   Patterns of role dominance and conflict in parents of schizophrenic patients. *Journal of Abnormal and Social Psychology*, 1960, **61**, 31-38.

Fine, H. J., & Zimet, C. N.   Process-reactive schizophrenia and genetic levels of perception. *Journal of Abnormal and Social Psychology*, 1959, **59**, 83-86.

Garmezy, N., & Rodnick, E. H.   Premorbid adjustment and performance in schizophrenia: Implications for interesting heterogeneity in schizophrenia. *Journal of Nervous and Mental Disorders*, 1959, **129**, 450-466.

Garmezy, N., Stockner, C., & Clarke, A. R.   Child-rearing attitudes of mothers and fathers as reported by schizophrenic and normal control patients. *American Psychologist*, 1959, 14, 333. (Abstract)

Harris, J. G., Jr.   A study of the mother-son relationship in schizophrenia. Unpublished doctoral dissertation, Duke University, 1955.

Harris, J. G., Jr.   Size estimation of pictures as a function of thematic content for schizophrenic and normal subjects. *Journal of Personality*, 1957, **25**, 651-672.

Herron, W.   Abstract ability in the process-reactive classification of schizophrenia. *Journal of Genetic Psychology*, 1962, **67**, 147-154.

Hunt, R. C., & Appel, K. E.   Prognosis in psychoses lying midway between schizophrenia and manic-depressive psychoses. *American Journal of Psychiatry*, 1936, **93**, 313-339.

Kant, O.   Differential diagnosis of schizophrenia in light of concepts of personality stratification. *American Journal of Psychiatry*, 1940, **97**, 342-357.

Kant, O.   A comparative study of recovered and deteriorated schizophrenic patients. *Journal of Nervous and Mental Disorders*, 1941, **93**, 616-624.

Kant, O.   The evaluation of prognostic criteria in schizophrenia. *Journal of Nervous and Mental Disorders*, 1944, **100**, 598-605.

Kantor, R., Wallner, J., & Winder, C.   Process and reactive schizophrenia. *Journal of Consulting Psychology*, 1953, **17**, 157-162.

Kantor, R. E., & Winder, C. L.   The process-reactive continuum: A theoretical proposal. *Journal of Nervous and Mental Disorders*, 1959, **129**, 429-434.

Kety, S. S.   Biochemical theories of schizophrenia. *Science*, 1959, **129**, 1528-1532, 1590-1596, 3362-3363.

King, G.   Differential autonomic responsiveness in the process-reactive classification of schizophrenia. *Journal of Abnormal and Social Psychology*, 1958, **56**, 160-164.

King, G. F.   Research with neuropsychiatric samples. *Journal of Psychology*, 1954, **38**, 383-387.

Kreinik, P. S.   Parent-child themes and concept attainment in schizophrenia. Unpublished doctoral dissertation, Duke University, 1959.

Kretschmer, E.   *Physique and character.* New York: Harcourt & Brace, 1925.

Langfeldt, G.   The diagnosis of schizophrenia. *American Journal of Psychiatry*, 1951, **108**, 123-125.

Lewis, N. D. C. *Research in dementia praecox.* New York: National Committee for Mental Hygiene, 1936.

Lewis, N. D. C. The prognostic significance of certain factors in schizophrenia. *Journal of Nervous and Mental Disorders,* 1944, **100**, 414-419.

Lorr, M., Wittman, P., & Schanberger, W. An analysis of the Elgin Prognostic Scale. *Journal of Clinical Psychology,* 1951, **7**, 260-263.

McDonough, J. M. Critical flicker frequency and the spiral aftereffect with process and reactive schizophrenics. *Journal of Consulting Psychology,* 1960, **24**, 150-155.

Malamud, W., & Render, N. Course and prognosis in schizophrenia. *American Journal of Psychiatry,* 1939, **95**, 1039-1057.

Mallet, J. J. Verbal recall of hostile and neutral thematic contents by schizophrenic and normal subjects. Unpublished doctoral dissertation, Duke University, 1956.

Mauz, F. *Die Prognostik der endogen Psychosen.* Leipzig: G. Theime, 1930.

Meadow, A., & Funkenstein, D. H. The relationship of abstract thinking to the automatic nervous system in schizophrenia. In P. H. Hoch and J. Zubin (Eds.), *Relation of psychological tests to psychiatry.* New York: Grune & Stratton, 1952. Pp. 131-144.

Meadow, A., Greenblatt, M., Funkenstein, G. H., & Solomon, H. C. The relationship between the capacity for abstraction in schizophrenia and the physiologic response to autonomic drugs. *Journal of Nervous and Mental Disorders,* 1953, **118**, 332-338.

Meadow, A., Greenblatt, M., & Solomon, H. C. "Looseness of association" and impairment in abstraction in schizophrenia. *Journal of Nervous and Mental Disorders,* 1953, **118**, 27-35.

Milici, P. Postemotive schizophrenia. *Psychiatric Quarterly,* 1939, **13**, 278-293.

Osgood, C. E. The nature and measurement of meaning. *Psychological Bulletin,* 1952, **49**, 197-237.

Paskind, J. A., & Brown, M. Psychosis resembling schizophrenia occurring with emotional stress and ending in recovery. *American Journal of Psychiatry,* 1940, **96**, 1379-1388.

Phillips, L. Case history data and prognosis in schizophrenia. *Journal of Nervous and Mental Disorders,* 1953, **117**, 515-525.

Piotrowski, Z. A. Positive and negative Rorschach organic reactions. *Rorschach Research Exchange,* 1940, **4**, 143-151.

Rabin, A. J., & King, G. F. Psychological studies. In L. Bellak (Ed.), *Schizophrenia: A review of the syndrome.* New York: Logos, 1958. Pp. 216-278.

Reisman, J. M. Motivational differences between process and reactive schizophrenics. *Journal of Personality,* 1960, **28**, 12-25.

Rodnick, E. H., & Garmezy, N. An experimental approach to the study of motivation in schizophrenia. In M. R. Jones (Ed.), *Nebraska symposium on motivation: 1957.* Vol. V. Lincoln: University of Nebraska Press, 1957. Pp. 109-184.

Sullivan, H. S. *Conceptions of modern psychiatry.* Washington: W. A. White Psychiatric Foundation, 1947.

Wittman, P.   A scale for measuring prognosis in schizophrenic patients. *Elgin State Hospital Paper*, 1941, 4, 20-33.

Wittman, P.   Follow-up on Elgin prognosis scale results. *Illinois Psychiatric Journal*, 1944, 4, 56-59.

Wittman, P., & Steinberg, L.   Follow-up of an objective evaluation of prognosis in dementia praecox and manic-depressive psychoses. *Elgin State Hospital Paper*, 1944, 5, 216-227. (a)

Wittman, P., & Steinberg, D. L.   Study of prodromal factors in mental illness with special references in schizophrenia. *American Journal of Psychiatry*, 1944, 100, 811-816. (b)

Zahn, T. P.   Acquired and symbolic affective value as determinant of size estimation in schizophrenic and normal subjects. *Journal of Abnormal and Social Psychology*, 1959, 58, 39-47.

Zimet, C. N., & Fine, H. J.   Perceptual differentiation and two dimensions of schizophrenia. *Journal of Nervous and Mental Disorders*, 1959, 129, 435-441.

Zuckerman, M., & Grosz, H. J.   Contradictory results using the mecholyl test to differentiate process and reactive schizophrenia. *Journal of Abnormal and Social Psychology*, 1959, 59, 145-146.

12

Psychological Deficit in Schizophrenia: I. Affect, Reinforcement, and Concept Attainment

INTRODUCTION

In the following two papers Arnold Buss and Peter Lang review the research on the various factors that may cause the psychological deficit in schizophrenia. Psychological deficit does not refer to the presence of such symptoms as hallucinations and delusions but rather to inadequate functioning in such areas as learning, concept formation, and perception. Abnormalities in these areas constitute a large proportion of the symptomology in schizophrenia. In addition, of course, deficits in these areas can provide a basis for further departures from normal functioning. That is, the psychological deficits are usually considered to be symptoms, but these symptoms can lead to other problems. Since these deficits play such a prominent role in schizophrenia (both as symptoms and as possible secondary causes), an understanding of the factors causing these deficits is crucial to understanding schizophrenia.

In the first paper Buss and Lang begin by reviewing the evidence for the effects of affect and reinforcement on functioning in schizophrenia. They first discuss the social censure hypothesis, which suggests that schizophrenics are upset by criticism and that this leads to poor performance. Since the evidence indicates that the concept of social censure does not seem to be encompassing enough, the explanation is broadened and the evidence related to whether or not affective or emotional stimuli, either negative *or* positive, disrupt the schizophrenic's performance. As the reader will see, this question is complicated by the problem of defining what stimuli are affective or emotional.

Following the consideration of the effects of censure, and emotional stimuli in general, evidence for a motivational deficit is reviewed. This research explores the question of whether insufficient motivation or lack of interest in social contacts may be used to account for the deficits. The motivational deficit hypothesis has been tested by varying motivation to determine whether increasing the schizophrenic's motivational level would result in performance comparable to the normal's. Motivational level was manipulated by the degree to which a subject was rewarded or punished for his responses. Elsewhere Buss (1966) has suggested that the hypotheses that relate the schizophrenic deficit to the presence of affect-laden stimuli in the environment and the hypotheses that relate the deficit to lack of motivation can both be considered to be motivational approaches to understanding the psychological deficit. In the first instance the schizophrenic is overmotivated and therefore overreacts to stimuli connoting affect; in the second, the schizophrenic is undermotivated, and his insusceptibility to the usual rewards leads to his inefficient behavior. After reviewing the data relevant to the affect and reinforcement hypothses, Buss and Lang offer some alternative explanations of the results in terms of the information or attentional focusing value of some of the experimental procedures.

The second half of the article is devoted to reviewing research on the factors that may cause the schizophrenic's impaired ability in concept attainment, that is, loss of abstractness, loss of communication, regression to childish thinking, and interference. Although the data reviewed in this section are quite clear, it might be helpful to identify briefly the terms *public-private* and *open-closed* as they relate to dimensions on which concepts may be classified. A *public* concept is one that is easily communicated to or usable by other persons, whereas a *private* concept is highly idiosyncratic or limited to the individual using it. An *open* concept is one that uses a minimum of defining attributes, so that numerous items can be included within it, whereas a *closed* concept is one in which all of the attributes are defined, so that only identical items can be added to the concept group. For example, a closed-private concept to encompass *green square, matches, and cigarette* might be "have on my desk at home," and an open-public concept for *red circle, red ball, red eraser* might be "They're red" (McGaughram and Moran 1956).

In reading the review of this research, the reader should note the differences that are often reported between different types of patients within the schizophrenic groups. The authors often refer to good premorbid and poor premorbid patients. For the most part, these terms are synonymous with reactive and process, which were discussed earlier. As the reader will see, these two types of patients often perform differently, thus offering more support for the contention that if progress in understanding behavior pathology is to be made, we need finer or different diagnostic classes.

Buss, A. *Psychopathology.* New York: Wiley, 1966.

McGaughram, L. S., & Moran, L. J. "Conceptual levels" versus "conceptual area" analysis of object sorting behavior of schizophrenic and neuropsychiatric groups. *Journal of Abnormal and Social Psychology,* 1956, 52, 43-50.

12

PSYCHOLOGICAL DEFICIT IN SCHIZOPHRENIA: I. AFFECT, REINFORCEMENT, AND CONCEPT ATTAINMENT

ARNOLD H. BUSS AND PETER J. LANG

The term *psychological deficit* was coined by Hunt and Cofer (1944) who wanted a neutral phrase to describe the decrement shown by psychiatric patients in comparison to normals on various laboratory and intellectual tasks. They reviewed the substantial body of research accumulated prior to World War II.

Since that time there has been a prolific output of research on deficit, too much to encompass within a single review. Therefore we shall consider only laboratory studies of psychological deficit in schizophrenia, omitting reports of tests and clinical observations.

Organizing the voluminous literature proved to be a difficult task. One possibility was to group studies on the basis of the major theoretical approaches to deficit, since theories of deficit are essentially theories of schizophrenia; but this would have led to excessive repetition. Therefore the literature has been organized around seven areas defined in part by theory but more broadly in terms of issues and methods of investigation: (*a*) affect and reinforcement, (*b*) concept attainment, (*c*) attention, (*d*) set, (*e*) associative interference, (*f*) drive, and (*g*) somatic arousal.

The dominant orientation in the affect and reinforcement area might be called a social-motivational view, which has two main variants. One suggests that schizophrenics are oversensitive to punishing and/or affective stimuli, which cause them to withdraw and which produce performance deficit. The other assumes that schizophrenics are already so withdrawn from interpersonal situations that the usual incentives, rewards, and punishments employed in experimental situations do not motivate them, and their performance suffers.

In the concept attainment area, research relevant to four ex-

SOURCE. Reprinted with permission of the American Psychological Association and the authors from the *Journal of Abnormal Psychology*, 1965, **70**, 2-24.

planatory concepts is reviewed. The first approach holds that both schizophrenics and brain-damaged patients suffer from a loss of the "abstract attitude." A second view argues that deficit is attributable to a communication disturbance, and a third emphasizes regression: later, more mature modes of functioning are ostensibly given up for earlier, more concrete, and less efficient modes. Finally, more recent research suggests that differences in the concepts of normals and schizophrenics occur because the latter are distractible and respond to irrelevant cues.

Research on attention, set, and association further emphasizes the importance of interference effects in deficit. The schizophrenic is regarded as being excessively distracted by both incidental, external stimuli and intrusive associations, as failing to maintain a proper set or orientation, and as failing to alter the set when such a change is appropriate.

Two drive theories are evaluated. The better known theory assumes that the schizophrenic is extremely anxious, this anxiety being a high drive state that worsens performance, especially on complex tasks. The lesser known theory suggests that in schizophrenia there is a protective (cortical) inhibition that slows down learning and increases reminiscence. Interpretations of deficit in terms of the neurophysiological concept of arousal are also considered, and the relevant research on the somatic responses of schizophrenics is evaluated.

The exposition is divided into two papers. In this first paper we review the affect-reinforcement and concept-regression areas. A subsequent paper considers research on interference effects (attention, set, and associative interference) and activation (drive and arousal) as well as general problems of method in deficit research.

Affect and Reinforcement

Social Censure

Rodnick and Garmezy (1957) have been the most forceful advocates of the censure hypothesis:

We have indicated that clinical psychiatric reports stress the sensitivity of the schizophrenic patient to the threat of criticism or rebuff inherent in almost any social situation. If such criticism does accentuate the patient's difficulty in differentiating cues in his environment, then it would follow that the experimental introduction of censure should produce greater discrimination decrements in schizophrenic patients than in normal individuals [p. 118].

Rodnick and Garmezy have attempted to confirm the censure

hypothesis in a series of experiments conducted by themselves or by their students. Garmezy (1952) showed that after censure (the word WRONG flashed after a response) schizophrenics had flatter generalization gradients and more errors than after praise (the word RIGHT flashed after a response) ; the performance of normals improved with censure. Webb (1955) found that failure led to poorer performance on a conceptual task, whereas a control group *improved* in their performance. All subjects were schizophrenics, and it is not known whether failure would have led to poorer performance in normals.

Bleke (1955) compared normals, good premorbid, and poor premorbid schizophrenics on a memory task. The subjects were either rewarded (RIGHT) or punished (WRONG) during learning. The poor premorbid schizophrenics manifested significantly better reminiscence and relearning than did good premorbids or normals. This was interpreted in terms of the effect of censure: criticism interfered with the learning of the poor premorbids, but on later testing for recall in the absence of censure they improved.

Smock and Vancini (1962) followed up Bleke's study, using a similar task but without differentiating between good and poor premorbid schizophrenics. After a practice session, half the subjects were rewarded (told they had done well), and half were censured (told they had done poorly). The practice was followed by learning without reinforcement, and then recall. There were no differences between normals and schizophrenics or between praised and censured subjects in original learning, but the censured schizophrenics had significantly *less* reminiscence than both the praised schizophrenics and the normal subjects. These findings are opposed to Bleke's, but there are differences between the studies that might be important: the makeup of the schizophrenic sample (good and poor premorbid versus a mixed group), the task, and the way praise and censure were delivered (after each response versus after practice trials). The discrepancy in findings and the possible reasons for it suggest that the effects of praise and censure may be too complex to be handled within the Rodnick-Garmezy framework.

Alvarez (1957) had normals, good premorbids, and poor premorbids make judgments about pictures. The judgments were either censured (WRONG) or praised (RIGHT), and later preference for the pictures was assessed. Poor premorbid schizophrenics were more susceptible to the effects of censure than good premorbids or normals, that is, the poor premorbids showed the greatest decline in preference for the pictures associated with WRONG. Thus the poor premorbids were more sensitive to WRONG, as judged by their preference scores; note that this does not mean that WRONG disrupted their performance, for this was not assessed. Similar results have been reported by Neiditch (1963), who found that functional psychotics lowered their preference for tasks which followed a failure situation significantly more than normals. He interpreted these data in terms of an inappropriate set.

Finally, Zahn (1959) tested the perceived size of pictures denoting scolding and feeding of a child by a mother. The size estimates were rewarded (RIGHT) for some subjects and punished (WRONG) for others. Good premorbid schizophrenics tended to *overestimate* the size of the punished pictures, whereas normals and poor premorbids did not.

The results are interpreted in terms of a high degree of anxiety or affective responsivity in the Goods and the predominance of avoidance and withdrawal mechanisms in the Poors [Zahn, 1959, pp. 46-47].

Most of these experiments were conducted under the aegis of Rodnick and Garmezy (1957). Taken at face value, they offer some support for the social censure hypothesis: failure or being told WRONG seems to produce schizophrenic deficit, an effect more striking in poor premorbid than in good premorbid schizophrenics. However, the evidence is weak, and individual experiments are open to a variety of interpretations. We shall return to these issues in the larger context of reward and punishment.

"Affective Stimuli"

Censure stimuli. The social censure hypothesis has a corollary pertaining to stimuli: schizophrenics are oversensitive to, and therefore disrupted by, stimuli connoting parental punishment or negative parent figures. This corollary has been tested mainly by students of Rodnick and Garmezy.

Dunn (1954) presented pictures of scolding, whipping, feeding, and neutral objects to schizophrenics and normals. For each scene there was a standard picture and five variations; the task was to judge whether the standard and the variations (presented in pairs) were the same or different. The schizophrenics judged more of the scolding variations as being the same as the standard than did the normals, but the other scenes yielded no differences. Dunn also discovered that a history of maternal conflict led to more judgments of "same" on the scolding scene. Two issues make it difficult to interpret these findings. First, the scolding scene is less clearly represented and might depict a number of different interactions, whereas the raised whip and the food in hand leave no doubt about the relationships presented. Thus ambiguity might account for the results, assuming that schizophrenics have more difficulty with complex stimuli which elicit many alternate responses. Second, if it were established that scolding (but not whipping or feeding) is the major trauma in the parent-child interactions of schizophrenics, the social censure hypothesis might be supported by these data. However, there is at present no basis for assuming that scolding is a more prominent problem for schizophrenics than whipping or feeding difficulties.

Dunn's results are only partially corroborated by those of Turbiner (1961), whose procedure was almost identical. In addition to neutral pictures, Turbiner had pictures of scolding and of affection. The schizophrenics' judgments were the same as the normals' for neutral stimuli but poorer than normals' for *both* positive and negative affective pictures.

Garmezy and Rodnick (1959) suggested that good and poor premorbid schizophrenics are not equally sensitive to censure from both parents. Specifically, they proposed that good premorbid schizophrenics are disrupted by paternal censure and poor premorbids by maternal censure. Two of their students, Dunham (1959) and Kreinik (1959), attempted to verify this hypothesis.

Dunham repeated Dunn's experiment, with minor modifications. Compared to normal subjects, good premorbid schizophrenics showed deficit only on slides depicting father censure and poor premorbids showed deficit on both mother censure and neutral slides. These are positive findings, but the poor premorbids' deficit with neutral slides is difficult to reconcile with the hypothesis.

Kreinik's experiment is open to two interpretations. She employed a conceptual task in which all subjects were presented with stimuli connoting positive fathers, negative fathers, positive mothers, negative mothers, and neutrality (nonhuman). There were two sessions, and only two groups failed to show improvement in the second session. These were the good premorbids with positive father stimuli and the poor premorbids with positive mother stimuli. Kreinik attributed these results to sequence effects. The Goods presented with negative father stimuli in the first session failed to improve with positive father stimuli in the second session. The results were the same for Poors with mother stimuli. Kreinik assumed that the deleterious effects of the negative parental stimuli carried over to the session with the positive stimuli. The problem with this interpretation is that the sessions were 1 day apart, and it appears doubtful that any effects would be sustained for 24 hours. The alternate explanation is more parsimonious: Goods and Poors are negatively affected by positive father and mother figures, respectively.

Two other studies are relevant. Baxter and Becker (1962) used TAT cards depicting mother-son and father-son relationships, scoring the stories for anxiety. Poor premorbids scored higher in anxiety than good premorbids on the mother-son picture, and the reverse was true for the father-son picture. However, two issues make it difficult to interpret these results unequivocally. First, the Goods scored approximately the same in anxiety on the mother-son and father-son pictures. Second, there was no control group of normal subjects, which means we do not know how much anxiety ordinarily appears in stories about these pictures.

Lebow and Epstein (1963) used TATlike stimuli depicting mother, father, and peer interactions in nurturant, rejecting, and ambiguous situations. The subjects were good premorbid schizophrenics and medical patients. In the present context the only relevant measure was a rating of the stories, called goodness of response. Concerning this measure,

there was a strong tendency for the schizophrenics to tell their poorest stories to the nurturant cues and their best stories to the ambiguous cues. Thus, if anything, the schizophrenics find nurturant as well as rejecting cues disruptive, and the former more so. Rather than a specific censure-cue deficit, the schizophrenic exhibits a general deficit for cues associated with emotional involvement, whether of a positive or a negative nature [p. 32].

Size estimation has also been used as an index of the distorting effects of affective stimuli. Harris (1957) presented pictures of the mother-son interaction. Normals made few mistakes in size estimation, and good premorbids underestimated the size of the pictures. In a similar study Zahn (1959) tested perceived size of scolding and feeding pictures. In addition the pictures were associated with RIGHT for some subjects and with WRONG for others. Good premorbids, in relation to the rewarded and the feeding pictures, overestimated the size of scolding pictures and pictures associated with WRONG. There were no similar relationships for normals or poor premorbids. In attempting to explain the discrepancy (Harris' good premorbids *under*estimated, Zahn's good premorbids *over*estimated), Zahn pointed out that his schizophrenics had been hospitalized longer than Harris', although it is not clear how this accounts for the discrepancy.

Moriarty and Kates (1962) matched normals, good premorbid, and poor premorbid schizophrenics for concept attainment with neutral stimuli and tested them with stimuli connoting parental approval and disapproval. For *both* approval and disapproval stimuli the normals performed significantly better than the good premorbids, who performed significantly better than the poor premorbids. Evidently, "social" stimuli disrupted the performance of the schizophrenics. Concerning specific effects of parental disapproval,

all groups show deficit behavior on social materials suggesting censure, with the psychiatric and the normal groups showing about the same relative decrements on the disapproval cards [p. 362].

Taken together, these studies do not support the hypothesis that the performance of schizophrenics is disrupted by stimuli connoting censure, especially parental censure. Positive findings have been reported, but they have been open to alternate interpretations because of methodological problems (e.g., Dunn, 1954; Kreinik, 1959) or unclear results (e.g., Dunham, 1959; Baxter & Becker, 1962). Early positive results have been either contradicted by later results (e.g., Harris, 1957; Zahn, 1959) or only weakly corroborated by later results (e.g., Dunn, 1954; Turbiner, 1961). There have also been negative findings: schizophrenics are adversely affected not only by censure stimuli but also by stimuli connoting affection, nurturance, and approval.

Affective stimuli in general. If the social censure hypothesis is correct, deficit should be produced *only* by stimuli associated with censure or parental punishment. An alternate hypothesis is that schizophrenics are oversensitive to *all* affective stimuli, not merely those connoting censure. A number of studies have attempted to test this hypothesis.

Culver (1961) had subjects estimate the size of pictures of a mother and a neutral object. *Both* good and poor premorbids underestimated the size of the mother, whereas normals did not. All three groups were similar in size estimation of the square. Raush (1956) tested for perceived size of a neutral object (overcoat button) and symbolic objects (ice cream cone and cigar). Using the estimated size of the neutral object as a base, he found that schizophrenics overestimated the size of the symbolic objects in comparison to the normals. Ehrenworth (1960) had subjects estimate the relative size of drawings of geometric figures and themes of heterosexuality, autonomy, competition, affiliation, and authority (all affective themes). Schizophrenics' size estimates of the affective stimuli were significantly poorer than both their estimates of the neutral stimuli and normals' estimates of the affective stimuli.

Pishkin, Smith, and Leibowitz (1962) used figures dressed as psychiatric aides or patients, and the subjects judged the relative size of the figures versus a silhouette. For the aide figure the errors of schizophrenics and normals were similar; for the patient figure the schizophrenics made significantly more errors. Assuming the patient figure was more symbolic, Pishkin et al. concluded that

it is the symbolic or emotional value of the stimulus which accounts for schizophrenic deficit on perceptual tasks [p. 329].

De Wolfe (1962) showed that good premorbids are more emotionally responsive to affective words than both poor premorbids and normals in a verbal conditioning task. Feldstein (1962) tested speech disturbance to affective and neutral materials and found no differences between schizophrenics and normals.

Four studies reported significant results using the human-nonhuman dichotomy. Davis and Harrington (1957) matched subjects on the basis of their ability to utilize information about nonhuman stimuli in a conceptual-discrimination problem. Schizophrenics were severely disrupted by human stimuli in a comparable problem, whereas normals were not. Marx (1962) divided his schizophrenic subjects into "early" and "late" patients (similar to acute versus chronic). In a conceptual task, human stimuli disrupted the early schizophrenics more than the late schizophrenics. Whiteman (1954) had subjects learn formal concepts (based on physical properties or size relationships) and social concepts (based on interactions among people, such as cooperation or encouragement). Although the schizophrenics were poorer than normals on the formal, nonhuman concepts, their performance significantly worsened on the social, human concepts. Brodsky (1961) compared schizophrenics and nonpsychotic hospital patients on a conceptual task involving people and nonhuman stimuli. The schizophrenics' conceptual performance was less adequate than normals' only with human stimuli.

Feffer (1961) tested the perception of affective and neutral words. He divided his schizophrenic subjects into "pathologically-concrete" and "adequately-conceptualizing" groups on the basis of tests of conceptual thinking. On the perceptual task the adequately-conceptualizing schizophrenics were especially vigilant in the presence of affective stimuli; the pathologically-concrete schizophrenics tended to avoid affective stimuli; and the normals showed no particular reaction to affective stimuli.

Silverman (1963) reported similar findings when words were presented tachistoscopically. Schizophrenics were especially sensitive to unpleasant words, identifying them more correctly than did normals. There were two kinds of schizophrenics, paranoid and nonparanoid. The paranoids placed between nonparanoids and normals in their differential sensitivity to unpleasant words. These results raise the possibility that Feffer's pathologically-concrete and adequately-conceptualizing schizophrenics may have been nonparanoid and paranoid, respectively.

One study failed to find a difference in perception between schizophrenics and normals. Nelson and Caldwell (1962) measured depth perception, using as stimuli drawings of a man, a woman, a dog, and a circle. There were no significant differences in perception for different stimuli or between normals and schizophrenics.

Arey (1960) tested subjects for recognition of sexual and neutral pictures. He found that schizophrenics were more affected by the sexual pictures, i.e., their recognition performance on sexual pictures compared to nonsexual pictures was significantly poorer than normals.

These various studies indicate that schizophrenic deficit occurs in response to many different kinds of stimuli, not merely those connoting censure. Thus the censure hypothesis is not sufficiently encompassing to account for the data. The results can be better explained by the alternate hypothesis that schizophrenics are oversensitive to all affective stimuli.

This latter hypothesis suggests that schizophrenics are disturbed by certain kinds of stimuli and that such disturbance leads to a deterioration in performance. The central problem is to define the term *affective,* whose meaning appears to change from one experiment to the next. It can have taboo aspects, as in the sexual stimuli used by Arey (1960); it may refer to human, as opposed to non-human stimuli; it may be symbolic, as opposed to nonsymbolic stimuli (Raush, 1956); or it may be defined empirically, by means of Luria free association indices (Feffer, 1961). In the face of such diverse operational definitions, it is difficult to maintain a clear referent for "affective stimuli."

Another way of approaching this issue is to regard affective stimuli as being better able to elicit associations from subjects. It is reasonable to assume that human, symbolic, sexual, and aggressive stimuli are more capable of setting off a train of personal and idiosyncratic associations than are more neutral and impersonal stimuli. One way of accounting for the deleterious effect of affective stimuli is to assume that they trigger more associations than do neutral stimuli. This assumption has been verified by Deering (1963), who had subjects associate to affective (pleasant and unpleasant) and neutral words matched for familiarity. Schizophrenics gave significantly more associations to affective words than did normals, but the groups did not differ in the number of associations to neutral words. Presumably, the greater the number of associations to any stimuli, the more the responder will be distracted and the more his performance will suffer.

Insufficient Motivation

Clinical descriptions of schizophrenics usually include apathy and isolation, or at least a tendency to withdraw from interpersonal contacts. The social censure hypothesis attempts to explain the withdrawal (as well as psychological deficit) in terms of the schizophrenic's inordinate sensitivity to rejection. The insufficient motivation hypothesis accepts the disinterest in social contacts as a given and uses it to account for deficit. The schizophrenic is ostensibly unmotivated to perform well on experimental tasks, whereas the normal subject tries to please the experimenter and perseveres at meaningless tasks in the face of boredom and fatigue (Orne, 1962). The schizophrenic, it is suggested, tends to be uncooperative, disinterested, and relatively unmotivated by laboratory criteria of success or by pleasing the experimenter. Supporting this view, Slechta, Gwynn, and Peoples (1963) showed that when such casual social reinforcers as nods of the interviewer's head or "mmm-hm" follow particular verbal behaviors, normal subjects yield a significantly greater percentage of criterion responses than do schizophrenics.

The deficit, then, is not in the schizophrenic's ability but in his motivation. It follows that if the schizophrenic could be urged to cooperate or if he were given appropriate incentives, rewards, or punishments, his performance would equal that of normals.

Cooperation and urging. Wittman (1937) estimated the cooperativeness of schizophrenics, paretics, and nonpsychiatric patients from the response of attendants and physicians to rating scales and checklists. The schizophrenics' cooperativeness scores were generally lower than those of the other two groups, and the schizophrenics were the only group to have high negative correlations between cooperativeness ratings and a memory-reasoning test. Similar findings have been reported by Shakow (1962) for a variety of tasks, and Spohn and Wolk (1963) and Wing and Freudenberg (1961) showed that sustained social stimulation can lead to improved performance and improved ward behavior.

Several experiments were based on the following line of reasoning: (a) schizophrenics perform worse than normals, (b) schizophrenics are less cooperative or less motivated than normals, (c) therefore schizophrenics should improve more than normals when both are urged.

Stotsky (1957) studied the effect of a "motivational incentive" on the psychomotor performance of remitted, regressed schizophrenics and normal subjects. The incentive took the form of encouragement, from their psychotherapist for the patients and from the experimenter for the normal subjects, during an interim between tasks. Both patients and normals were responsive to the motivational condition: the regressed schizophrenics showed significantly greater improvement than normals in simple reaction time (RT), but the normals showed significantly greater improvement than the patients on the disjunctive RT task. D'Alessio and Spence (1963) reported no difference in degree of improvement on a simple motor task between normal and chronic schizophrenic patients. Benton, Jentsch, and Wahler (1960) found that both normal and schizophrenic subjects improved RT performance equally when administered positive "motivating" instructions, and the improvement of the schizophrenic subjects was not significantly different from that of a group of similarly-treated brain-damaged patients (whose date were available from Blackburn, 1958). Olson (1958) reported that schizophrenics improved their performance on a digit-symbol task following either depreciation or praise of a previous performance, whereas normals improved only after praise. However, Goodstein, Guertin, and Blackburn (1961) found no difference in the RT improvement of schizophrenics and normals, both groups improving most following failure instructions. Shankweiler (1959) reported that like schizophrenics, brain-damaged subjects also improve on a psychomotor task subsequent to failure instructions.

Johannsen (1962) had nonparanoid and paranoid schizophrenics and normals cancel the letter f in prose material. At the end of each 2-minute trial subjects were told their performance was good or poor, or they were told nothing. The criticized subjects showed the greatest improvement, the praised subjects were next, and the control subjects were last; these results held for both schizophrenic and normal subjects. The order of improvement for diagnostic groups was: normals, paranoids, and nonparanoids.

Schooler and Spohn (1960) studied schizophrenics and normals in an Asch situation and found both groups equally responsive to social pressure. Felice (1961) examined the effects of interpersonal (experimenter present) and impersonal (experimenter absent) administration on the performance of normals and schizophrenics on a variety of laboratory tasks. Task, diagnosis, and method of administration interacted to produce highly variable results. On some tests schizophrenic performance was depressed by the presence of the experimenter, on other tasks it made no difference, and on some the normals did poorest during the interpersonal administration. However, in these experiments the experimenter's status as a social or affective stimulus may not be the relevant variable. He may simply be an additional distracting element or a source of reduced cues which aid the subject in his task.

In summary, the data on both positively and negatively oriented urging do not support a motivational interpretation of deficit. Normals, schizophrenics, and brain-damaged patients all tend to respond with equal improvement on these conditions. At least one researcher has reported urging instructions to be completely ineffective in modifying schizophrenic psychomotor behavior (Ladd, 1960). In any event, the schizophrenic's deficit has never been completely overcome by these methods. Only Stotsky's (1957) "remitted" group could not be differentiated from normals, and this occurred on some tasks before additional motivations were introduced.

Nonverbal reward and punishment. While the schizophrenic may be insensitive to the rewards of social interaction (pleasing the experimenter, etc.), he might still be affected by more tangible or biologically pertinent reinforcers. Thus an attempt may be made to eliminate his performance deficit by using such nonverbal rewards (cigarettes, money, pleasant stimuli) or punishments (electric shock and "white noise").

Peters (1953) and Peters and Jenkins (1954) studied the motor learning and problem-solving behavior of schizophrenics receiving subshock insulin, providing a "sweet nutrient" as a reward for correct responses. On the basis of his first study, Peters concluded that although the reward did increase operant rate, it did little to eliminate errors. In the second study, using the same incentive condition, an attempt was made to use rewarded problem-solving as an adjunct to therapy. It was anticipated that rewarded achievement on simple motor tasks would provide a base for success in more complex social tasks, and hence would transfer to routine, day to day behavior. It was found that the experimental group had significantly fewer "negative ward incidents" than the control group, but the ratings of ward personnel did not distinguish between the groups. The weak effect found in these studies is consistent with Michaux's (1955) study of apperception as a function of hunger. He reported that unlike normals, schizophrenics show no increase in food completions on a verbal task under hunger conditions.

Schizophrenics, brain-damaged patients, and medical controls were promised money for better performance in a study by Burday (1962). The task involved conceptual sorting, and the money incentive yielded no significant differences among the three groups. However, Rodnick and Garmezy (1957) reported informally that candy, cigarettes, and an attractive scoreboard raise the performance level of schizophrenic subjects. At the beginning of their experiments the performance of good premorbid patients has frequently been no different from that of normal subjects.

Lindsley and Skinner (1954) found results similar to those for dogs, rats, and pigeons, in schizophrenic patients conditioned to pull levers for candy, cigarettes, or projected colored slides. They concluded that psychotic behavior is controlled "to some extent" by the reinforcing properties of the immediate physical environment. Isaacs, Thomas, and Goldiamond (1960) reinstated verbal behavior in two catatonic patients, using operant conditioning methods, and Tilton (1956) reported an improved "general level of functioning" in schizophrenics treated by instrumental learning. However, in Lindsley's study (1960) schizophrenics sometimes abruptly ceased their operant responding without the introduction of any extinction procedure. Furthermore, King, David, and Lovinger (1957) failed to confirm the hypotheses that severity of neuropsychiatric illness is inversely related to rewarded operant rate and that clinical improvement is positively related to this variable. Contrary to Lindsley and Skinner, they concluded that "operant motor behavior seems best classified as a peripheral variable in terms of psychopathology [1957, p. 325]."

As with urging instructions, tangible positive rewards appear somewhat to ameliorate the poor performance of schizophrenics, and less severely disturbed patients may approach the performance of normals on some tasks. However, there is no clear evidence that for schizophrenics, positive tangible rewards are superior to verbal encouragement. Killberg (1962) found that improvement in a verbal learning task was greater for verbally reinforced normal subjects than for similarly treated schizophrenics and that schizophrenics and normals did not differ in improvement when cigarettes were used as a reinforcer. However, the difference between the schizophrenic subjects under the two conditions of reinforcement was not significant.

Whereas monetary reward improved the performance of normals on a serial anticipation task, Topping and O'Connor (1960) found that nonparanoids did not improve and paranoid schizophrenics worsened under the same conditions. Clearly, positive rewards do not exert any consistent control over schizophrenic behavior and probably vary considerably in their consequences with changes in population and experimental setting.

Physical punishment has proved to be the most consistent and effective reinforcer of behavior in schizophrenic subjects. Pascal and Swenson (1952) found no difference between a group of schizophrenic and normal subjects on initial trials of a complex, discrimination RT task, but on subsequent trials the normals improved and the schizophrenics did not. At this point a strong, aversive stimulus was introduced in the form of high intensity noise delivered through earphones, and subjects were told that the noise would be turned off only after a correct response. Under these conditions both groups improved, the schizophrenics showing a greater reduction in latency scores than the normal subjects. Analysis of the final trials revealed no significant difference between the schizophrenic and normal groups.

Cohen (1956) evaluated the performance of chronic schizophrenic and normal subjects on an apparatus which presented patterned visual stimuli. Subjects responded by moving a handle either left or right, depending on the pattern. After a number of trials under the usual conditions of administration, half of the normal group and half of the schizophrenics received a shock at stimulus onset, which was terminated by a correct response. The schizophrenics consistently required more trials to learn and made more errors than did the normals. However, although the unshocked schizophrenics showed a decrement in performance on later trials, the shocked schizophrenics maintained their previous level of performance. This difference between control and experimental groups was not present in the results of the normals.

A study of RT in schizophrenia by Rosenbaum, Mackavey, and

Grisell (1957a) suggests that schizophrenics are able to improve their performance under shock conditions. Male and female schizophrenics and hospital employees were first tested in a simple RT situation under standard conditions. Half of each group was then tested under shock conditions, while the remainder continued responding in the previous manner. The task was a simple finger lift from a key in response to an auditory stimulus. In the shock condition subjects were stimulated electrically in the finger to be withdrawn, simultaneously with the sounding of the buzzer. The hospital employees were significantly faster than the psychotics under all conditions of the experiment, but the schizophrenics showed significantly greater improvement than the normals from nonshock to shock conditions. In fact, the electric shock raised the scores of the schizophrenic men to the level of the normals. These results cannot be attributed to an increased "need" to respond quickly because the shock, which was administered to the responding finger, actually replaced sound as the discriminative stimulus. The improvement can as easily be assigned to an increased stimulus dynamism.

In a subsequent study Rosenbaum, Grisell, and Mackavey (1957b) tested the RTs of female schizophrenics and college students. There were several conditions, involving particular combinations of "ready" interval (regular or irregular) and shock. The conditions were called "social motivation," "anxiety motivation," and "biological motivation," respectively. The authors report that:

> The normals were superior to the schizophrenics on all measures, but could be significantly differentiated from the younger, privileged group only on anxiety reaction time [during the anxiety reaction time trials, the shock was presented in an unpredictable manner] [p. 206].

Two other studies are particularly worthy of mention in that a concept formation rather than a psychomotor test provided the experimental task. Cavanaugh (1958) compared the performance of chronic schizophrenics and nonpsychiatric patients and found that under the usual conditions of administration, schizophrenics were inferior. However, when an aversive stimulus was introduced (high intensity noise presented with the concept materials and terminated by a correct response), schizophrenic experimental subjects performed significantly better (in terms of the number of correct concepts and latency scores) than a control (no noise) group. Furthermore, there was no difference in performance between this schizophrenic noise group and a group of similarly treated nonpsychiatric patients. Brown (1961) substantially confirmed Cavanaugh's findings in a study in which incorrect responses were followed by aversive noise.

In brief, in all studies employing physical punishment as an incentive there has been a definite reduction, and in a few instances the temporary elimination, of psychological deficit. These results are consistent with this variant of motivation theory: deficit is a consequence of lowered social motivation, and thus may be reduced when biologically intense reinforcers are used. However, they can also be explained by interference theory: the important fact in the introduction of intense stimuli may be the change in attention and set, with a sharper differentiation between relevant and irrelevant inputs being created.

Verbal reward and punishment. Many studies of schizophrenia have been designed to evaluate the effects of specific verbal cues or reinforcers on the course of psychological tasks. This research has been less concerned with overcoming deficit than with the differential effects of verbal reward and punishment. It will be recalled that Rodnick and Garmezy (1957) hold that social censure or disapproval disrupts the performance of schizophrenics. However, studies of physical punishment and studies which found improvement after negatively oriented urging suggest that the schizophrenic's performance is specifically facilitated by censure.

In a series of experiments Buss and colleagues (Buss & Buss, 1956; Buss, Braden, Orgel, & Buss, 1956; Buss, Wiener, & Buss, 1954) found that the word WRONG, following an incorrect response, yields more effective learning than RIGHT for correct answers. The subjects were mixed groups of psychiatric patients, the majority being schizophrenic. Leventhal (1959) confirmed these findings in a study of diagnosed schizophrenics; "Not so good" was more effective in facilitating verbal conditioning than "Good." Atkinson and Robinson (1961) and Koppenhaver (1961) compared verbal reward and punishment in a paired-associates learning task and found that punishment improved schizophrenic learning, relative to that obtained with reward.

Losen (1961) matched good premorbid schizophrenics with normals on the basis of arithmetic ability and tested them on arithmetic and short-term memory tasks. There were four experimental groups. One group was shown their scores without comment following each response; the other three groups were administered 100%, 50%, and 0% censure schedules. The censure was verbal: "No that was wrong." None of the experimental conditions significantly altered the performance of normal subjects. For schizophrenics, the 0% censure group and the group that was simply shown their scores did not change, but both the 100% and 50% censure groups showed significant improvement. In all of the above studies mild verbal censure of the type used by Garmezy and Rodnick and their students *facilitated* the performance of schizophrenics.

A number of experiments suggest that the ameliorative effects of censure cannot be attributed to the personal or social character of these reinforcers. Lang (1959) found that chronic schizophrenics significantly improved RT scores when a neutral tone followed responses slower than a previously established standard. A subsequent study (Cavanaugh, Cohen, & Lang, 1960) showed that verbal reward was ineffective in improving RT but that verbal censure and the same information about errors used in the previous experiment led to nearly equal improvement. Atkinson and Robinson (1961) found no difference between the facilitating effect of verbal censure and the results obtained when incorrect responses were followed by the sound of an adding machine in operation. On the other hand, Maginley (1956) employed a visual rather than an auditory cue as a nonsocial reinforcer and found that schizophrenics performed less well than normals on the later trials of a concept formation task. However, he attributed this effect to the "diminished interest and attention" occasioned by the light. Johannsen (1961) studied the performance of normals and two schizophrenic groups on a double alternation task. The reinforcers were either verbal right and wrong or differentially colored light. Paranoid schizophrenics were no different under conditions of social and nonsocial reinforcement but the performance of nonparanoid schizophrenics was significantly poorer when social reinforcers were employed.

The thesis that punishment invariably disrupts performance is clearly not tenable. Both a negative evaluation and specific verbal or physical punishment for errors can lead to significant improvement in performance rather than further deficit. The fact that this improvement occurs in both the presence and absence of socially or personally punitive conditions suggests that the significant factor is information about inadequate responses rather than the interpersonal context.

Knowledge of results is important to any task in which improvement is expected with practice, and in general the normal subject recognizes the correctness or wrongness of a response as soon as it occurs, and no assistance is required. However, schizophrenics seem to be less able to instruct themselves and less able to maintain or usefully alter a response set (Shakow, 1962). Furthermore, studies of incidental learning (Greenberg, 1954; Winer, 1954) reveal that relative to normals, schizophrenics fail to observe objects or relationships towards which their attention has not been specifically directed. Thus, informational cues introduced by the experimenter have greater importance for the psychotic subject in certain tasks.

In the experiments of Lang (1959), Cavanaugh et al. (1960), and Losen (1961) normal subjects performed asymptote under the usual conditions of administration; additional cues did not lead to improvement. Starting at a lower performance level, schizophrenics were able to profit from information about errors and thereby improve their performance. On a task with more ceiling, however, normal subjects can accomplish the same result, Buss and Buss (1956) demonstrated that in concept formation, normals yield a reward-punishment hierarchy no different from that originally found with patients, i.e., punishing errors is more effective in improving performance than rewarding correct responses.

Studies of normal subjects indicate there is considerable difference in the effectiveness of reward and punishment, depending on the experimental task (Meyer & Offenbach, 1962). If the task is a simple one (few alternate responses) and the correct response is already in the respondent's behavioral repertoire, reward is likely to be effective in maintaining the wanted behavior. However, if the task is complex (many alternate responses) and if the correct response is not currently in the subject's repertoire or readily elicited, punishment will provide the better guide. In essence, verbal approval confirms the aptness of a response already made; punishment signals a need for change. In nearly all the experiments under consideration the question raised was to what extent could subjects improve or change, and information about errors generally proved to be the most valuable experimental manipulandum for *both* normal and schizophrenic subjects.

Nevertheless, diagnosis and the specific experimental task interact, and results at variance with this trend are not surprising. Both Atkinson and Robinson (1961) and Leventhal (1959) report that schizophrenics learn fastest when punished for errors, while nonpsychotics show most rapid learning with reward. The former authors attribute these findings to the fact that punishment tends to break up the perseverative behavior unique to schizophrenic subjects, an interpretation consistent with the set hypothesis proposed earlier.

Garmezy's study of generalization (1952) can also be interpreted as suggesting that punishing errors is a more effective method for schizophrenic than normal subjects. The subjects were instructed either to pull a lever if a tone was the same as a training stimulus or to push the lever if it was different. Extreme incorrect pull responses were punished, and correct pull responses were rewarded: in effect, the subject was both rewarded and punished for the same behavior. Under these circumstances the incidence of pull responses among schizophrenic subjects dropped to all tones. They simply learned to avoid the word WRONG, rather than to make the discrimination accomplished by the normal subjects. Maginley (1956) reported similar data in a concept formation task. Reward was superior to a combination of punishment for errors and reward for correct responses, and this held for *both* normal and schizophrenic subjects. It is not clear whether the performance difference may be attributed to censure or the different information provided by the two kinds of cues.

Waters (1962) attempted to separate the effects of censure and information about errors in a two-choice learning task. As might be expected, chronic schizophrenics performed best when provided with maximal cues. Paradoxically, the acute patients had fewer errors under the minimal cue condition. Both groups showed poorer performance when social censure was introduced.

Fischer (1963) used both specific criticism for responses and general criticism for performance, as well as specific praise, general praise, and a control. The task was to repeat a series of lights, and the performance measure was response speed. All subjects improved from the first series to the second, and in order of improvement the conditions were criticism (general and specific), praise (general and specific), and the control. An additional finding was that the subjects performed better in the experimenter's absence (comments delivered via earphones) than in his presence.

In neither Waters' nor Fischer's experiment were there normal subjects, but there were normals in a related study by Brooker (1962), who compared task-relevant criticism (WRONG) and praise (RIGHT) with task-irrelevant criticism and praise. The relevant task was the Wisconsin Card Sorting Test, and the irrelevant task was judging a weight every five trials of the card sorting. Normals and schizophrenics both learned better with task-relevant criticism than with task-relevant praise. In the task-irrelevant condition, criticism led to poorer learning than reward for schizophrenics, but there were no differences for normals. These results can be interpreted as supporting both the social censure and interference theories. In light of the complexities that have cropped up in previous research, the separation of censure from information about errors should be part of any experiment on verbal punishment and deficit.

Summary

The research on affect and reinforcement will be summarized under four headings: affective stimuli, information, punishment, and diagnosis.

Affective stimuli. Certain "affective" stimuli disturb schizophrenics enough to produce psychological deficit, but the stimuli are so varied that this term has no precise referent. Concerning affective stimuli, the social censure hypothesis appears to be incorrect. Schizophrenic deficit occurs not only with stimuli connoting censure but also with human, symbolic, and taboo stimuli. A promising hypothesis is that affective stimuli elicit more associations from schizophrenics and that these associations interfere with performance.

Information. It is clear that schizophrenic subjects improve when they are given information about their responses, and they can profit from cues that may be superfluous to normals. Lang (1959) and Losen (1961) have pointed out that schizophrenics, unlike normals, fail to make statements during tasks which suggest self-guidance (e.g., "I got that one wrong"; "I'll have to watch it next time."). It seems likely that external reinforcing cues serve a directive purpose in schizophrenics that normal subjects accomplish for themselves.

The task usually determines whether positive or negative information is more valuable in improving performance. Most tasks have been complex (initiate many alternate responses), and change (improvement), rather than the maintenance of an initially offered response, has been the desired result. If the task also has sufficient ceiling, both normals and schizophrenics profit more from information about errors than they do from knowledge of successes.

Punishment. In some tasks psychotics make more use of punishment than reward, relative to normal subjects, but there is little evidence to suggest this is due to schizophrenics' personal reaction to social censure. Punishment seems to assist the schizophrenic by breaking up perseverative tendencies, whereas reward maintains a previously correct response that is wrong on subsequent trials. This could happen in paired-associate learning, in which a correct response to one stimulus word is wrong for every other stimulus. The process is probably dependent on instructions the subject gives to himself, and it is here that schizophrenics appear to be deficient.

Physical punishment facilitates the performance of schizophrenics, and in fact it is the only contingency that has led to a complete elimination of deficit on some tasks (concept formation). However, it is conceivable that "noise" and shock serve a focusing or arousal function, rather than the traditional role of incentive or reinforcer.

Diagnosis. Response to motivating instructions, social stimuli, and information about performance all seem to vary with diagnosis. These variables are sensitive to personality differences in normal subjects, and perhaps at least an equal effect should be anticipated in schizophrenics. Because of the variety of populations and experimental situations employed, generalizations about the consequences of motivational factors are difficult. However, paranoid-nonparanoid, good premorbid versus poor premorbid, and the acute-chronic typologies have all proved to be experimentally distinct and cannot be ignored in research with schizophrenics.

Concept Attainment

Schizophrenics show deficit in conceptual tasks, just as they do in tasks involving simple learning, perception, and psychomotor behavior. In fact, studies on concept learning predominate in the older literature on deficit. There are four main hypotheses in this area: loss of abstractness, loss of communication, regression, and interference.

Loss of Abstractness

Goldstein (1946), analogizing from his research with brain-damaged patients, suggested that the fundamental thinking disorder in schizophrenia is the inability to form abstract concepts. He postulates a disturbance of the "abstract attitude," which has the following characteristics:

1. To assume a mental set voluntarily.
2. To shift voluntarily from one aspect of the situation to another.
3. To keep in mind simultaneously various aspects.
4. To grasp the essentials of a given whole; to break up a given whole into parts and to isolate them voluntarily.

5. To generalize; to abstract common properties; to plan ahead ideationally; to assume an attitude toward the "mere possible," and to think or perform symbolically.

6. To detach our ego from the outer world [p. 19].

The ability to assume the abstract attitude develops gradually being preceded by the "concrete attitude," which is merely a response to immediate sense impression. Goldstein's (1959) major hypothesis is that both organic brain-damaged patients and schizophrenics have lost the abstract attitude and can function in thought and language only at the concrete level. He was careful not to conclude that schizophrenia is the same as organic brain damage, but it is clear from his writings that he attributed schizophrenic deficit in conceptual tasks to a loss of function similar to that seen in neurological conditions.

Goldstein cited as evidence for this theory the relatively poor performance of schizophrenics on the Goldstein-Scheerer test (Bolles & Goldstein, 1938; Goldstein & Scheerer, 1941). Similar results were obtained with the Vigotsky blocks, a test of concept formation (Hanfmann & Kasanin, 1937, 1942; Kasanin, 1946). However, Fisher (1950) found that schizophrenics and hysterics were not significantly different in their performance with the Vigotsky blocks. It is difficult to interpret this body of data. The Goldstein-Scheerer test is nonquantitative and requires a rating of concreteness by the experimenter. The Vigotsky test uses a combination time-help score that confounds slowness with poor performance. Furthermore, in many of the studies adequate control groups were absent. Thus these early studies are inconclusive.

Later investigators, using quantitative techniques and adequate control groups, have demonstrated that schizophrenics are *not* abnormally concrete (Chapman & Taylor, 1957; Fey, 1951; Lothrop, 1960; McGaughran, 1954; McGaughran & Moran, 1956, 1957; Rashkis, 1947; White, 1949; Williams, 1962). They showed that schizophrenics are capable of responding with abstract concepts, but the concepts are often unusual and idiosyncratic. The problem with schizophrenics is therefore not a loss of the abstract attitude but a tendency to verbalize concepts that are deviant and difficult for normals to understand. One way of interpreting these results is to assume an inability to communicate with others.

Loss of Communication

This theory holds that the problem in schizophrenia is not a loss but a basic lack of communication. The schizophrenic's concepts are bizarre and unacceptable to others because he is withdrawn and asocial. The first one to advance this view was Sullivan (1946), who emphasized language problems. Cameron (1946) elaborated it in terms of fantasy:

> Social communication is gradually crowded out by fantasy; and fantasy itself, because of its nonparticipation in and relation to action, becomes in turn less and less influenced by social patterns. The result is a progressive loss of organized thinking . . . [pp. 51-52].

As McGaughran (1954; McGaughran & Moran, 1956) has indicated loss of communication and loss of abstractness represent two dimensions of concepts: public-private and open-closed. The public-private dimension is the one emphasized by Sullivan and later Cameron (1946). Schizophrenics ostensibly give an idiosyncratic, private basis for the way they sort objects, whereas normals give a common, public basis. The open-closed dimension is the one emphasized by Goldstein and Kasanin. Schizophrenics give a more closed, narrow, stimulus-bound basis for sorting objects, whereas normals give an open, more inclusive, stimulus-free basis for sorting.

McGaughran and Moran (1956) used a quantified object-sorting task to test these two theories. Sorting performance was scored for both the open-closed and public-private dimensions. Schizophrenics gave slightly fewer public bases for sorting and slightly more open bases than matched normals, but neither difference met the usual level of statistical significance. Furthermore, intelligence was found to be related to the public-private dimension: the more intelligent schizophrenics gave more public bases for sorting than did the less intelligent schizophrenics.

Some of these results were corroborated by Payne and Hewlitt (1960), who included in their battery tests of concreteness. While schizophrenics did perform relatively poorly on three measures of concreteness, performance on these measures was determined mainly by intelligence. These authors also noted that many of the unusual responses of schizophrenics tend to be scored as concrete.

Not all investigators have demonstrated conceptual deficit in schizophrenics. Nathan (1962) compared acute and chronic schizophrenics and normals on eight conceptual tasks, which varied on three dichotomous dimensions: formal versus social, verbal versus nonverbal, and abstract versus subsuming. There were no significant differences between schizophrenics in these tasks.

Evidence that schizophrenics are abnormally concrete is again weak. Their concepts do tend to be eccentric and thus difficult for normals to understand. However, this is a property of the concepts, not a defect in the manner in which they are communicated. Furthermore, both dimensions appear to be related to general intelligence, suggesting that evidence for the concreteness or privacy of concepts is confounded with a more general intellectual disability.

Regression to Childish Thinking

Goldman (1962) elaborated Werner's (1948) developmental approach, combining the loss of abstractness and the loss of communication views into a single theory. He distinguished three dimensions believed to be important in the development of thinking in children. First, the child's concepts and ideas are initially personal and idiosyncratic, but they gradually become more public and common. Second, early concepts are labile and shifting, whereas later ones are more stable. Third, early concepts are more concrete and tied to the stimulus context, but later concepts are more abstract and free of the stimuli or events with which they were originally associated.

In support of his position Goldman cited qualitative findings with children and clinical reports on schizophrenics' concreteness (Arieti, 1955; Cameron, 1938; and Kasanin, 1946). Unfortunately these findings lack quantification or adequate controls. As additional evidence Goldman noted that schizophrenics tend to define words more concretely than normals (Choderkoff & Mussen, 1952; Feifel, 1949; Flavell, 1956; Harrington & Ehrmann, 1954). However, as we noted above, bizarre and eccentric responses tend to be scored as concrete, which renders such evidence inconclusive. Furthermore, a number of experiments have demonstrated that schizophrenics give abstract concepts.

Going beyond these considerations, there is the more general issue of the regression hypothesis: does the thinking of schizophrenics resemble that of children? Feifel (1949) showed that children and schizophrenics defined words in a similar pattern that deviated from normal adult definitions. Ellsworth (1951) found that children and schizophrenics were similar in the way they used different parts of speech. Burstein (1959, 1961) demonstrated that children and schizophrenics both tended to equate antonyms with synonyms to a greater extent than normals. On the other hand, Cameron (1938) found that children were very different from schizophrenics in the way they completed incomplete sentences involving causality.

Chapman, Burstein, Day, and Verdone (1961) pointed out a possible artifact in these studies:

> the tasks were such that both children and schizophrenics were characterized by deviant performance relative to normal adults. However, as a result of restrictions either on the response alternatives available or on the investigator's categorization of the responses, each task provided relatively few avenues along which deviations could occur. The tasks tended to measure undifferentiated deviation rather than different kinds of specific deviation. Therefore the likelihood that schizophrenics and children would appear similar was very great [p. 541].

Chapman et al. administered two different thinking tasks to children, schizophrenics, and brain-damaged patients. On one task the younger children resembled schizophrenics but not brain-damaged patients. On the other task the younger children resembled brain-damaged patients but not schizophrenics. They concluded:

> There is no blanket similarity between the error patterns of children and of either schizophrenics or brain-damaged patients, and the use of the term "regression" to imply such a blanket similarity is not justified [p. 545].

To the extent that these comments are true, we may question the conclusion that the thinking of schizophrenics and children is similar. In brief, the evidence for regression of thought processes is equivocal, and there are opposing findings; we regard the regression hypothesis as not proved.

Interference Theory

In searching for an approach to conceptual deficit, one possibility is interference theory. There are two variants, one emphasizing overinclusion or excessive generalization and the other a deficit in attention.

Overinclusion. Overinclusion is the tendency to include irrelevant and extraneous aspects in responding to stimuli. In Cameron's (1938) early work he demonstrated that schizophrenics have difficulty in maintaining boundaries, their concepts spilling over into nontask stimuli such as objects in the room and even the experimenter. Cameron labeled this *interpenetration:* the intrusion of personal and idiosyncratic themes into the schizophrenic's speech and concepts.

Cameron and Magaret (1951) have pointed out that *exclusion* is necessary for success on a given task. At first the subject attends to too many aspects of the stimulus situation, and much of his response is superfluous. Gradually he focuses on the crucial aspects of the stimulus situation, ignoring irrelevant aspects; similarly, he drops out motor responses he does not need. Presumably the schizophrenic cannot exclude nonessential stimulus elements, and his overinclusiveness impairs performance on conceptual tasks.

That schizophrenics are overinclusive has been established by a number of experiments since Cameron's original observations. Zaslow (1950) showed that schizophrenics included more stimuli in the concepts of circularity and triangularity than did normals, although Kugelmass and Fondeur (1955) did not replicate these results with early schizophrenics.

Epstein (1953) and Moran (1953) presented subjects with a stimulus word and a number of response words. The task was to underline response words that were an essential part of the concept denoted by the stimulus. In both studies schizophrenics underlined significantly more response words, especially more distantly related words, than did normals. In addition Moran found that the schizophrenics' associations to the stimulus words were more distant and their synonyms were less precise than those of normals.

Lovibond (1954) quantified object-sorting performance and found that schizophrenics were more overinclusive than normals. Chapman (1956) and Chapman and Taylor (1957) presented pictures of different objects and had subjects sort them under specific headings or concepts such as clothing, furniture, and fruit. In comparison to normals, schizophrenics were more influenced by irrelevant and distracting elements, their conceptual performance being severely impaired by extraneous stimuli.

Payne and his collaborators (Payne & Hewlitt, 1960; Payne, Matussek & George, 1959) used as conceptual tasks a set of proverbs, two sorting tests, and Epstein's word-grouping test. The results were in the expected direction and for the most part significant: schizophrenics were overinclusive in comparison to normals. A number of the schizophrenics were no more overinclusive than the normals, but they were somewhat slow in their motor responses. Payne and Hewlitt speculated that paranoid and catatonic schizophrenics behave differently in these tasks. Paranoids, they suggested, tend to overgeneralize, their overinclusiveness showing up both in ideas of reference and in laboratory conceptual tasks; but they are neither slower nor less abstract than normals. Catatonics do not overgeneralize and are not overinclusive, but they tend to be slower and less abstract than normals.

Attention. Chapman (1961), who reported strong evidence for the overinclusion hypothesis, was not completely satisfied with it. He argued that schizophrenic concreteness is really *underinclusion* (overexclusion), which means that schizophrenics are both overinclusive and underinclusive:

what may in part underlie the frequently observed inappropriate enlarging or restricting of the application of common concepts is in fact a preference for concepts of a particular breadth [p. 514].

He used two kinds of tasks, one tending to elicit errors of overinclusion and one tending to elicit errors of overexclusion. Schizophrenics were found to make both kinds of errors, although there was a predominance of overinclusion errors. When the task called for broad concepts, there were more overexclusion errors and fewer overinclusion errors. The same tendency was observed in normals, although greatly diminished. Thus the schizophrenics' predilection for concepts of a particular breadth may be merely an exaggeration of a similar finding in normals.

This suggestion is supported by a study by Seth and Beloff (1959) on schizophrenics and tubercular controls. The schizophrenics, who were inferior on verbal tasks, manifested a language decrement and a tendency not to use abstract concepts spontaneously. The errors made by the schizophrenics were exaggerations of the error tendencies of the controls, and the authors suggested that the underlying reason for this was a lowering or alternation of the attention process.

These results lead to the second variant of the interference hypothesis:

Both disorders of perception and thinking in schizophrenic patients are secondary to a disorder of the span of attention, which can be too broad or too narrow, or may alternate between the two. Constancy of perception . . . depends on the ability to perceive a thing in its context, or to take into account all the "cues" existing in the whole perceptual field. Thus it is related to "broadness of attention." "Overinclusiveness" or wide span of schizophrenic concepts is related also to "overbroadness" of their attention, which makes them incapable of excluding irrelevant stimuli. On the other hand, the ability to perceive embedded figures is related to "narrowness" of attention which causes the distracting, embedded figure to be excluded [Weckowicz & Blewitt, 1959, p. 914].

Note that this hypothesis, introduced before Chapman's results appeared, explains his results. Excessively broad attention should lead to overinclusive concepts; excessively narrow attention should lead to overexclusive concepts; alternating between too-broad and too-short attention should lead to both overinclusive errors and overexclusive errors, such as were found in schizophrenics by Chapman (1961).

Weckowicz and Blewitt were able to test one implication of their hypothesis. In maintaining constancy of perception it is necessary to accept certain cues and reject others. There must be some kind of "filter" mechanism that avoids the errors of both overinclusiveness and overexclusiveness in conceptual performance as well as in size perception. They obtained high correlations (in the fifties) between abstraction scores on a sorting test and size constancy, thus substantiating the hypothesis. More evidence of this kind is needed, but at present this second variant of the interference hypothesis appears to be a promising explanation of schizophrenic deficit in the conceptual area.

Summary

This section has considered four interpretations of schizophrenic deficit in concept attainment. The loss of abstractness theory appears to be incorrect: schizophrenics' concepts are not especially concrete although they tend to be eccentric and deviant. Schizophrenics' concepts are not necessarily childlike, and the evidence for such regression may be attributed to both the limited responses available on the tasks used and to the scoring of idiosyncratic responses as concrete.

Concerning lack of communication, there is no doubt that schizophrenics have difficulty in making their concepts comprehensible to others. However, this appears to be due to the bizarre nature of the concepts rather than an inability to communicate them. Thus the disorder appears to involve thought processes rather than communication skills.

Interference theory appears to be the most promising approach. The overinclusion hypothesis has been sustained by a number of studies: schizophrenics' concepts are excessively broad, and they suffer from the intrusion of extraneous and irrelevant elements. Whether this is true of all schizophrenics or mainly of paranoids is an interesting question. One possibility is that paranoids are more inclusive and less deteriorated than nonparanoids (catatonics and hebephrenics).

Discussion

This section will focus on five theories that attempt to explain schizophrenic deficit in the two research areas covered in this paper. Three theories emphasize interpersonal and social aspects: social censure, sensitivity to affective stimuli, and insufficient motivation. The other two, while not ignoring interpersonal aspects completely, emphasize more impersonal aspects of psychological functioning: regression and interference.

Social Censure

This theory exists in two basic forms, one general and the other a specific corollary. The general theory holds that schizophrenics are abnormally sensitive to, and disrupted by, social censure and stimuli connoting censure. In its support is the fact that in some experiments deficit has been found to increase when censure stimuli are introduced. However, other research has found no difference in the censure response of schizophrenics and normals, or effects for one type of schizophrenic and not for another. Furthermore, data interpreted in support of censure theory are often more parsimoniously explained in other terms (differential information or the saliency of cues). The strongest negative evidence is that on a great variety of tasks social censure *reduces* deficit in schizophrenia rather than increases it, i.e., facilitates performance relative to praise or no reinforcement.

The specific censure theory argues that schizophrenics with good and poor premorbid histories are differentially responsive to parental chastisement: the former are disturbed by paternal and the latter by maternal censure. While there are data consistent with this view, replication has infrequently supported original studies, and methodological problems abound. Both schizophrenic groups have shown disturbance with parental stimuli, regardless of whether the stimuli were positive or negative; both types of schizophrenics have, in specific experiments, been similar to normals in their response to censure.

Furthermore, while distinctions are made within the schizophrenic group, control subjects are treated as a homogeneous population. We cannot help but speculate that the subdivision of a hospital attendant or neurotic group—following similar criteria of general social or sexual adequacy—might yield similar differences in response to parental stimuli. In other words, we do not know that the findings are in any way unique to schizophrenia. In fact, while good and poor premorbid patients are treated as subtypes of schizophrenia, group assignment is actually determined by a scale defining a continuous dimension of social maturity (Phillips, 1953). The scales' author has already provided strong evidence:

that the relationship of achieved level of maturity (defined in terms of premorbid social competence) to certain dimensions of psychopathology is not unique to schizophrenia, but instead cuts across all forms of functional mental disorder [Zigler & Phillips, 1962, p. 216].

As a general theory of deficit the social censure approach is not sufficiently comprehensive and involves a major inconsistency: stimulus conditions other than censure have been found to yield deficit in schizophrenia, and censure may reduce rather than increase deficit. The specific theory involves a questionable typology. It also needs the support of less equivocal experiments. Dividing schizophrenics into good and poor premorbid groups does not account for the variable effects of censure, a full explanation of which must include *task variables.*

This evaluation does not necessarily negate the clinical theory from which the social censure hypothesis originated. Parental censure may still be an important variable in the histories of schizophrenics and may shape some symptoms. However, social censure does not provide a general explanation for schizophrenic deficit in the laboratory.

Sensitivity to Affective Stimuli

This theory resembles social censure theory, but it is broader in that it assumes that schizophrenics are especially sensitive to, and disrupted by, *all* affective stimuli. This assumption has been verified in many experiments which have demonstrated poorer performance by schizophrenics with affective stimuli than with neutral stimuli. The difficulty with this evidence is that so many stimuli have been labeled *affective* that the term no longer has precise referents. The underlying assumption in this theory is that past events in schizophrenics' lives have rendered them abnormally sensitive to stimuli that connote traumatic situations or anxiety-laden interpersonal relationships. While some of the affective stimuli that lead to deficit pertain to special areas of maladjustment such as sexuality, censure, or competition, others have only a vague connection with personal adjustment or emotion, e.g., human-nonhuman, symbolic-nonsymbolic, and patient-attendant stimulus dimensions have all been shown to influence the performance of schizophrenics. Furthermore, as we have seen with censure stimuli, the effect of specific affective contents varies considerably from experiment to experiment, and perhaps from subject to subject.

The dilemma is as follows. If the term affective is loosely defined, the theory can account for all the data, but it lacks precision. If the term affective is restricted to a narrow, precise meaning, then the reliability of the phenomenon must be questioned; furthermore, nonaffective stimuli have been found to produce deficit. Shakow (1962) has suggested that the associations of schizophrenics constitute a kind of apperceptive mass,

full of elements—both affective and nonaffective—of past experience. For the schizophrenic, many of these elements are floating around on top of the barrel, ready to be attached to almost any new situation [p. 9].

This conception accommodates the data and provides the basis for an interference explanation. Evidence for this view will be assessed in the next paper. However, the psychodynamic concept of affective stimuli is clearly not a sufficient theory of schizophrenic deficit.

Insufficient Motivation

Another group of theorists argue that schizophrenic deficit is attributable not to an oversensitivity to social stimuli but to a reduced sensitivity to such inputs. Schizophrenics are held to be unmotivated, uninterested in pleasing the experimenter, or uninterested in meeting task requirements; Hunt and Cofer (1944) suggested that responses to social stimuli have been extinguished in schizophrenic patients. In general, the evidence is against this formulation. Testable schizophrenics are as responsive to persuasion as normals or brain-damaged patients whether the social pressure is based on encouragement or on critical admonishment. Many studies stimulated by this theory have confounded the effects of praise and criticism or reward and punishment with the effects of giving subjects different information about their task performance. Evaluating their separate effects is difficult. Nevertheless, schizophrenics and normals generally show a similar pattern of responding: on most tasks information about errors leads to better performance than the signaling of correct responses. However, the importance of this additional information seems to be greater for schizophrenics than for normal subjects. Schizophrenics show relatively greater improvement with clear supplementary cues than do normals, and there is some evidence that information about errors is particularly useful to schizophrenics. The effect of these cues does not appear to be social motivational but rather to help maintain attention and guide responding. It has been suggested that the schizophrenic fails to instruct himself as normals do, and the additional information provided after each response fulfills this guidance function.

Physical punishment tends to facilitate the performance of schizophrenics, and it has occasionally eliminated schizophrenic deficit. This fact has been used to support the lowered motivation hypothesis: if schizophrenics are able to approach normal functioning when reinforced with pain termination but not when social reinforcers are administered, a deficit in social motivation is implied. An alternate view is that physical punishment may be a better source of information about errors, breaking up incorrect sets, and guiding responding. The importance of cue emphasis as opposed to motivational instigation has been demonstrated in studies of normal subjects, in which improvement was occasioned by delivering electric shock for correct responses. Furthermore, when intense stimuli are coincident with important discriminative stimuli, the latter are lent emphasis and more clearly separated from the irrelevant cues in the situation. Evidence for these alternate motivation and interference interpretations of studies employing aversive stimuli will be evaluated in the subsequent paper.

Regression

The loss of abstractness theory received support mainly from early studies, but later work revealed that the excessive concreteness of schizophrenics may be attributed to methods of scoring responses rather than to a loss of the abstract attitude. Schizophrenics are capable of attaining abstract concepts, although their concepts may be bizarre, eccentric, and deviant from those given by normals.

The loss of abstractness theory is but one variant of regression theory, which includes not only Goldstein's formulation but those of Freud, Arieti (1955), and Werner (1948). Regression theory makes two fundamental assumptions: (a) there is a fixed sequence of developmental stages that ends in maturity or adult normality, and (b) psychopathology represents a retracing of these developmental steps. Concerning deficit, the theory should demonstrate: (a) a fixed sequence or hierarchy of psychomotor learning and thinking behavior in childhood, and (b) a retracing of the sequence in psychopathology. The only one to attempt such a specific formulation with respect to schizophrenic deficit has been Goldman (1962), using Werner's developmental approach. Whether or not one accepts Goldman's developmental sequence of learning and thinking, there is considerable doubt that the learning and thinking of schizophrenics resembles those of children of any given age. There are occasional similarities between schizophrenics' concepts and those of children: tendencies toward more primitive concepts and deviance from adult concepts. However, there are also marked differences between children's and schizophrenics' concepts: those of schizophrenics are usually more abstract, bizarre, and eccentric than those of children.

Furthermore, it is not sufficient to demonstrate vague similarities between schizophrenics and children. It must be shown that as an individual becomes schizophrenic, he retraces the developmental sequence (if there is one) of learning and thinking; as he recovers, he again moves forward toward demonstrably more mature modes of learning and thinking. These corollaries of regression theory have yet to be established empirically, and therefore we conclude that the regression theory of schizophrenic deficit is unproved.

Interference

This theory assumes that when a schizophrenic is faced with a task, he cannot attend properly or in a sustained fashion, maintain a set, or change the set quickly when necessary. His ongoing response tendencies suffer interference from irrelevant, external cues and from "internal" stimuli which consist of deviant thoughts and associations. These irrelevant, distracting, mediated stimuli prevent him from maintaining a clear focus on the task at hand, and the result is psychological deficit.

If the schizophrenic has difficulty in shifting to a new set, he should benefit from stimuli that break the old set. This is precisely what has been established. Schizophrenics benefit from punishment, which eliminates previously correct response tendencies that are no longer appropriate. Physical punishment, in some instances, has been found to eliminate schizophrenic deficit entirely.

If the presence of distracting, internal stimuli prevents the schizophrenic from giving self-instructions (as normals do), he should benefit from external cues. It has been established that schizophrenics are helped more than normals by external reinforcing cues which help direct responses, although normals are also helped. Thus interference theory has an explanation for the effects of punishment and of the rewarding and punishing stimuli that follow responses.

Interference theory can account for schizophrenic deficit with affective stimuli. The theory assumes that the schizophrenics' associations distract him, thereby producing disturbance of performance. The more associations, the greater the deficit. Since affective stimuli elicit more associations than neutral stimuli (Deering, 1963), it follows that they should produce more schizophrenic deficit.

Conceptual deficit is explained by assuming excessive variability in attention. The schizophrenic is either overinclusive because he allows irrelevant stimuli to intrude or overexclusive because he attempts to defend against the distracting, internal stimuli. It follows that some schizophrenics should be overinclusive, some overexclusive, and some alternating between the two; all three possibilities have been found to exist in schizophrenics when they are confronted with conceptual tasks.

Interference theory may be viewed as a devil's advocate in that in each research area it offers an alternative to the theories of social censure, sensitivity to affective stimuli, insufficient motivation, and regression. Obviously, the theory is sufficiently comprehensive, but a theory must do more than merely offer alternatives. Also needed is evidence that tests specific hypotheses, in this instance about the particular interfering effects of environmental, associational, and also somatic stimuli. Such evidence is reviewed in the subsequent paper.

REFERENCES

Alvarez, R. R. A comparison of the preferences of schizophrenic and normal subjects for rewarded and punished stimuli. Unpublished doctoral dissertation, Duke University, 1957.

Arey, L. B. The indirect representation of sexual stimuli by schizophrenic and normal subjects. *Journal of Abnormal and Social Psychology*, 1960, **61**, 424-431.

Arieti, S. *Interpretation of schizophrenia*. New York: Bruner, 1955.

Atkinson, Rita L., & Robinson, Nancy M. Paired-associate learning by schizophrenic and normal subjects under conditions of personal and impersonal reward and punishment. *Journal of Abnormal and Social Psychology*, 1961, **62**, 322-326.

Baxter, J. C., & Becker, J. Anxiety and avoidance behavior in schizophrenics in response to parental figures. *Journal of Abnormal and Social Psychology*, 1962, **64**, 432-437.

Benton, A. L., Jentsch, R. C., & Wahler, H. J. Effects of motivating instructions on reaction time in schizophrenia. *Journal of Nervous and Mental Disease*, 1960, **130**, 26-29.

Blackburn, H. L. Effects of motivating instructions on reaction time in cerebral disease. *Journal of Abnormal and Social Psychology*, 1958, **56**, 359-366.

Bleke, R. C.   Reward and punishment as determiners of reminiscence effects in schizophrenic and normal subjects. *Journal of Personality*, 1955, **23**, 479-498.

Bolles, Marjorie, & Goldstein, K.   A study of schizophrenic patients. *Psychiatric Quarterly*, 1938, **12**, 42-65.

Brodsky, M. J.   Interpersonal stimuli as interference in a sorting task. *Dissertation Abstracts*, 1961, **22**, 2068.

Brooker, H.   The effects of differential verbal reinforcement on schizophrenic and non-schizophrenic hospital patients. Unpublished doctoral dissertation, Indiana University, 1962.

Brown, R. L.   The effects of aversive stimulation on certain conceptual error responses of schizophrenics. *Dissertation Abstracts*, 1961, **22**, 629.

Burday, G.   The performance of schizophrenic, brain-damaged and nonpsychiatric patients on a modified matching concept formation test and the effects of positive motivation on concept formation performance. Unpublished doctoral dissertation, Temple University, 1962.

Burstein, A. G.   Primary process in children as a function of age. *Journal of Abnormal and Social Psychology*, 1959, **59**, 284-286.

Burstein, A. G.   Some verbal aspects of primary process thought in schizophrenia. *Journal of Abnormal and Social Psychology*, 1961, **62**, 155-157.

Buss, A. H., Braden, W., Orgel, A., & Buss, Edith H.   Acquisition and extinction with different verbal reinforcement combinations. *Journal of Experimental Psychology*, 1956, **52**, 288-295.

Buss, A. H., & Buss, Edith H.   The effect of verbal reinforcement combinations on conceptual learning. *Journal of Experimental Psychology*, 1956, **52**, 283-287.

Buss, A. H., Wiener, M., & Buss, Edith H.   Stimulus generalization as a function of verbal reinforcement combinations. *Journal of Experimental Psychology*, 1954, **48**, 433-436.

Cameron, N. S.   Reasoning, regression and communication in schizophrenics. *Psychological Monographs*, 1938, **50**(1, Whole No. 221).

Cameron, N. S.   Experimental analysis of schizophrenic thinking. In J. S. Kasanin (Ed.), *Language and thought in schizophrenia*. Berkeley: Univer. California Press, 1946. Pp. 50-64.

Cameron, N., & Magaret, Ann.   *Behavior pathology*. Boston: Houghton Mifflin, 1951.

Cavanaugh, D.   Improvement in the performance of schizophrenics on concept formation tasks as a function of motivational change. *Journal of Abnormal and Social Psychology*, 1958, **57**, 8-12.

Cavanaugh, D., Cohen, W., & Lang, P. J.   The effect of "social censure" and "social approval" on the psychomotor performance of schizophrenics. *Journal of Abnormal and Social Psychology*, 1960, **60**, 213-218.

Chapman, L. J.   The role of type of distracter in the "concrete" performance of schizophrenics. *Journal of Personality*, 1956, **25**, 130-141.

Chapman, L. J. A reinterpretation of some pathological disturbances in conceptual breadth. *Journal of Abnormal and Social Psychology*, 1961, **62**, 514-519.

Chapman, L. J., Burstein, A. G., Day, Dorothy, & Verdone, P. Regression and disorders of thought. *Journal of Abnormal and Social Psychology*, 1961, **63**, 540-545.

Chapman, L. J., & Taylor, Janet A. The breadth of deviate concepts used by schizophrenics. *Journal of Abnormal and Social Psychology*, 1957, **54**, 118-123.

Choderkoff, B., & Mussen, P. Qualitative aspects of the vocabulary responses of normals and schizophrenics. *Journal of Consulting Psychology*, 1952, **16**, 43-48.

Cohen, B. D. Motivation and performance in schizophrenia. *Journal of Abnormal and Social Psychology*, 1956, **52**, 186-190.

Culver, C. M. The effect of cue value on size estimation in schizophrenic subjects. Unpublished doctoral dissertation, Duke University, 1961.

D'Alessio, G. R., & Spence, Janet T. Schizophrenic deficit and its relation to social motivation. *Journal of Abnormal and Social Psychology*, 1963, **66**, 390-393.

Davis, R. H., & Harrington, R. W. The effect of stimulus class on the problem-solving behavior of schizophrenics and normals. *Journal of Abnormal and Social Psychology*, 1957, **54**, 126-128.

Deering, Gayle. Affective stimuli and disturbance of thought processes. *Journal of Consulting Psychology*, 1963, **27**, 338-343.

DeWolfe, A. S. The effect of affective tone on the verbal behavior of process and reactive schizophrenics. *Journal of Abnormal and Social Psychology*, 1962, **64**, 450-455.

Dunham, R. M. Sensitivity of schizophrenics to parental censure. Unpublished doctoral dissertation, Duke University, 1959.

Dunn, W. L. Visual discrimination of schizophrenic subjects as a function of stimulus meaning. *Journal of Personality*, 1954, **23**, 48-64.

Ehrenworth, J. The differential responses to affective and neutral stimuli in the visual-motor performance of schizophrenics and normals. Unpublished doctoral dissertation, Boston University, 1960.

Ellsworth, R. B. The regression of schizophrenic language. *Journal of Consulting Psychology*, 1951, **15**, 378-391.

Epstein, S. Overinclusive thinking in a schizophrenic and a control group. *Journal of Consulting Psychology*, 1953, **17**, 384-388.

Feffer, M. H. The influence of affective factors on conceptualization in schizophrenia. *Journal of Abnormal and Social Psychology*, 1961, **63**, 588-596.

Feifel, H. Qualitative differences in the vocabulary response of normals and abnormals. *Genetic Psychology Monographs*, 1949, **39**, 151-204.

Feldstein, S. The relationship of interpersonal involvement and affectiveness of content to the verbal communication of schizophrenic patients. *Journal of Abnormal and Social Psychology*, 1962, **64**, 39-45.

Felice, A.   Some effects of subject-examiner interaction on the task performance of schizophrenics. Unpublished doctoral dissertation, Temple University, 1961.

Fey, Elizabeth T.   The performance of young schizophrenics on the Wisconsin Card Sorting Test. *Journal of Consulting Psychology*, 1951, 15, 311-319.

Fischer, E. H.   Task performance of chronic schizophrenics as a function of verbal evaluation and social proximity. *Journal of Clinical Psychology*, 1963, 19, 176-178.

Fisher, S.   Patterns of personality rigidity and some of their determinants. *Psychological Monographs*, 1950, 64(1, Whole No. 307).

Flavell, J. H.   Abstract thinking and social behavior in schizophrenia. *Journal of Abnormal and Social Psychology*, 1956, 52, 208-211.

Garmezy, N.   Stimulus differentiation by schizophrenic and normal subjects under conditions of reward and punishment. *Journal of Personality*, 1952, 21, 253-276.

Garmezy, N., & Rodnick, E. H.   Premorbid adjustment and performance in schizophrenia: Implications for interpreting heterogeneity in schizophrenia. *Journal of Nervous and Mental Disease*, 1959, 129, 450-466.

Goldman, A. E.   A comparative-developmental approach to schizophrenia. *Psychological Bulletin*, 1962, 59, 57-69.

Goldstein, K.   Methodological approach to the study of schizophrenic thought disorder. In J. S. Kasanin (Ed.), *Language and thought in schizophrenia*. Berkeley: Univer. California Press, 1946. Pp. 17-40.

Goldstein, K.   Concerning the concreteness in schizophrenia. *Journal of Abnormal and Social Psychology*, 1959, 59, 146-148.

Goldstein, K., & Scheerer, M.   Abstract and concrete behavior: An experimental study with special tests. *Psychological Monographs*, 1941, 53(2, Whole No. 239).

Goodstein, L. D., Guertin, W. H., & Blackburn, H. L.   Effects of social motivational variables on choice reaction time in schizophrenics. *Journal of Abnormal and Social Psychology*, 1961, 62, 24-27.

Greenberg, A.   Directed and undirected learning in chronic schizophrenia. *Dissertation Abstracts*, 1954, 14, 1457-1458.

Hanfmann, Eugenia, & Kasanin, J.   A method for the study of concept formation. *Journal of Psychology*, 1937, 3, 521-540.

Hanfmann, Eugenia, & Kasanin, J. S.   Conceptual thinking in schizophrenia. *Nervous and Mental Disease Monographs*, 1942, No. 67.

Harrington, R., & Ehrmann, J. C.   Complexity of response as a factor in the vocabulary performance of schizophrenics. *Journal of Abnormal and Social Psychology*, 1954, 49, 362-364.

Harris, J. G., Jr.   Size estimation of pictures as a function of thematic content for schizophrenic and normal subjects. *Journal of Personality*, 1957, 25, 651-671.

Hunt, J. McV., & Cofer, C.   Psychological deficit in schizophrenia. In J. McV. Hunt (Ed.), *Personality and the behavior disorders*. Vol. 2. New York: Ronald Press, 1944. Pp. 971-1032.

Isaacs, W., Thomas, J., & Goldiamond, I.   Application of operant conditioning to reinstate verbal behavior in psychotics. *Journal of Speech and Hearing Disorders*, 1960, **25**, 8-12.

Johannsen, W. J.   Responsiveness of chronic schizophrenics and normals to social and nonsocial feedback. *Journal of Abnormal and Social Psychology*, 1961, **62**, 106-113.

Johannsen, W. J.   Effect of reward and punishment on motor learning by chronic schizophrenics and normals. *Journal of Clinical Psychology*, 1962, **18**, 204-207.

Kasanin, J. S.   The disturbance of conceptual thinking in schizophrenia. In J. S. Kasanin (Ed.), *Language and thought in schizophrenia*. Berkeley: Univer. California Press, 1946. Pp. 41-49.

Killberg, J.   The differentiating effects of nonverbal and verbal rewards in the modification of verbal behavior of schizophrenic and normal subjects. Unpublished doctoral dissertation, Columbia University, 1962.

King, G., David, M., & Lovinger, E.   Operant motor behavior in acute schizophrenics. *Journal of Personality*, 1957, **25**, 317-326.

Koppenhaver, N. D.   The effects of verbal and nonverbal reinforcement on the performance of schizophrenic subjects. Unpublished doctoral dissertation, Purdue University, 1961.

Kreinik, Phyllis S.   Parent-child themas and concept attainment in schizophrenia. Unpublished doctoral dissertation, Duke University, 1959.

Kugelmass, S., & Foundeur, M. P.   Zaslow's test of concept formation: Reliability and validity. *Journal of Consulting Psychology*, 1955, **19**, 227-229.

Ladd, C. E.   The digit symbol performance of schizophrenic and nonpsychiatric patients as a function of motivational instructions and task difficulty. Unpublished doctoral dissertation, University of Iowa, 1960.

Lang, P. J.   The effect of aversive stimuli on reaction time in schizophrenia. *Journal of Abnormal and Social Psychology*, 1959, **59**, 263-268.

Lebow, K. E., & Epstein, S.   Thematic and cognitive responses of good premorbid schizophrenics to cues of nurturance and rejection. *Journal of Consulting Psychology*, 1963, **27**, 24-33.

Leventhal, A. M.   The effects of diagnostic category and reinforcer on learning without awareness. *Journal of Abnormal and Social Psychology*, 1959, **59**, 162-166.

Lindsley, O.   Characteristics of the behavior of chronic psychotics as revealed by free-operant conditioning methods. *Diseases of the Nervous System Monograph Supplement*, 1960, **21**.

Lindsley, O., & Skinner, B. F.   A method for the experimental analysis of the behavior of psychotic patients. *American Psychologist*, 1954, **9**, 419-420.

Losen, S. M.   The differential effect of censure on the problem solving behavior of schizophrenics and normal subjects. *Journal of Personality*, 1961, **29**, 258-272.

Lothrop, W. W.   Psychological test covariates of conceptual deficit in schizophrenia. *Journal of Consulting Psychology*, 1960, **24**, 496-499.

Lovibond, S. H.   The Object Sorting Test and conceptual deficit in schizophrenia. *Australian Journal of Psychology*, 1954, **6**, 52-70.

McGaughran, L. S.   Predicting language behavior from object sorting. *Journal of Abnormal and Social Psychology*, 1954, **49**, 183-195.

McGaughran, L. S., & Moran, L. J.   "Conceptual level" vs. "conceptual area" analysis of object sorting behavior of schizophrenic and nonpsychiatric groups. *Journal of Abnormal and Social Psychology*, 1956, **52**, 43-50.

McGaughran, L. S., & Moran, L. J.   Differences between schizophrenic and brain-damaged groups in conceptual aspects of object sorting. *Journal of Abnormal and Social Psychology*, 1957, **54**, 44-49.

Maginley, H. J.   The effect of "threats" of failure upon the conceptual learning performance of hospitalized mental patients. Unpublished doctoral dissertation, University of Pittsburgh, 1956.

Marx, A.   The effect of interpersonal content on conceptual task performance of schizophrenics. Unpublished doctoral dissertation, University of Oklahoma, 1962.

Meyer, W. J., & Offenbach, S. I.   Effectiveness of reward and punishment as a function of task complexity. *Journal of Comparative and Physiological Psychology*, 1962, **55**, 532-534.

Michaux, W.   Schizophrenic apperception as a function of hunger. *Journal of Abnormal and Social Psychology*, 1955, **50**, 53-58.

Moran, L. J.   Vocabulary knowledge and usage among normal and schizophrenic subjects. *Psychological Monographs*, 1953, **67**(20, Whole No. 370).

Moriarty, D., & Kates, S. L.   Concept attainment on materials involving social approval and disapproval. *Journal of Abnormal and Social Psychology*, 1962, **65**, 355-364.

Nathan, P.   A comparative investigation of conceptual ability in relation to frustration tolerance. Unpublished doctoral dissertation, Washington University, 1962.

Neiditch, S. J.   Differential response to failure in hospital and nonhospital groups. *Journal of Abnormal and Social Psychology*, 1963, **66**, 449-453.

Nelson, Sandra, & Caldwell, W. E.   Perception of affective stimuli by normal and schizophrenic subjects in a depth perception task. *Journal of General Psychology*, 1962, **67**, 323-335.

Olson, G. W.   Failure and subsequent performance of schizophrenics. *Journal of Abnormal and Social Psychology*, 1958, **57**, 310-314.

Orne, M.   On the social psychology of the psychological experiment: With particular reference to demand characteristics and their implications. *American Psychologist*, 1962, **17**, 776-783.

Pascal, C., & Swensen, G.   Learning in mentally ill patients under unusual motivation. *Journal of Personality*, 1952, **21**, 240-249.

Payne, R. W., & Hewlitt, J. H. G.   Thought disorder in psychotic patients. In H. J. Eysenck (Ed.), *Experiments in personality*. Vol. II. London: Routledge & Kegan Paul, 1960. Pp. 3-104.

Payne, R. W., Mattussek, P., & George, E. I.   An experimental study of schizophrenic thought disorder. *Journal of Mental Science,* 1959, **105,** 627-652.

Peters, H. N. Multiple choice learning in the chronic schizophrenic. *Journal of Clinical Psychology,* 1953, **9,** 328-333.

Peters, H. N., & Jenkins, R. L. Improvement of chronic schizophrenic patients with guided problem-solving motivated by hunger. *Psychiatric Quarterly,* 1954, **28,** 84-101.

Phillips, L. Case history data and prognosis in schizophrenia. *Journal of Nervous and Mental Disease,* 1953, **117,** 515-525.

Pishkin, V., Smith, T. E., & Leibowitz, H. W. The influence of symbolic stimulus value on perceived size in chronic schizophrenia. *Journal of Consulting Psychology,* 1962, **26,** 323-330.

Rashkis, H. A. Three types of thinking disorder. *Journal of Nervous and Mental Disease,* 1947, **106,** 650-670.

Raush, H. L. Object constancy in schizophrenia: The enhancement of symbolic objects and conceptual stability. *Journal of Abnormal and Social Psychology,* 1956, **52,** 231-234.

Rodnick, E. H., & Garmezy, N. An experimental approach to the study of motivation in schizophrenia. In M. R. Jones (Ed.), *Nebraska symposium on motivation: 1957.* Lincoln: Univer. Nebraska Press, 1957. Pp. 109-184.

Rosenbaum, G., Mackavey, W. R., & Grisell, J. L. Effects of biological and social motivation on schizophrenic reaction time. *Journal of Abnormal and Social Psychology,* 1957, 54, 364-368. (a)

Rosenbaum, G., Grisell, J. L., & Mackavey, W. R. The relationship of age and privilege status to reaction time indices of schizophrenic motivation. *Journal of Abnormal and Social Psychology,* 1957, **55,** 202-207. (b)

Schooler, C., & Spohn, H. E. The susceptibility of chronic schizophrenics to social influence in the formation of perceptual judgments. *Journal of Abnormal and Social Psychology,* 1960, **61,** 348-354.

Seth, G., & Beloff, Halla. Language impairment in a group of schizophrenics. *British Journal of Medical Psychology,* 1959, **32,** 288-293.

Shakow, D. Segmental set: A theory of the formal psychological deficit in schizophrenia. *Archives of General Psychiatry,* 1962, **6,** 17-33.

Shankweiler, D. P. Effects of success and failure instructions on reaction time in brain-injured patients. *Journal of Comparative and Physiological Psychology,* 1959, **52,** 546-549.

Silverman, J. Noxious cue sensitivity in schizophrenia. Paper read at American Psychological Association, Philadelphia, August 1963.

Slechta, Joan, Gwynn, W., & Peoples, C. Verbal conditioning of schizophrenics and normals in a situation resembling psychotherapy. *Journal of Consulting Psychology,* 1963, **27,** 223-227.

Smock, C. D., & Vancini, J. Dissipation rate of the effects of social censure in schizophrenics. *Psychological Reports,* 1962, **10,** 531-536.

Spohn, H. E., & Wolk, W. Effect of group problem solving experience upon social withdrawal in chronic schizophrenics. *Journal of Abnormal and Social Psychology,* 1963, **66,** 187-190.

Stotsky, B.   Motivation and task complexity as factors in the psychomotor responses of schizophrenics. *Journal of Personality*, 1957, **25**, 327-343.

Sullivan, H. S.   The language of schizophrenia. In J. S. Kasanin (Ed.), *Language and thought in schizophrenia.* Berkeley: Univer. California Press, 1946. Pp. 4-16.

Tilton, J. R.   The use of instrumental motor and verbal learning techniques in the treatment of chronic schizophrenics. *Dissertation Abstracts*, 1956, **16**, 1180-1181.

Topping, Gillian, & O'Connor, N.   The response of chronic schizophrenics to incentives. *British Journal of Medical Psychology*, 1960, **33**, 211-214.

Turbiner, M.   Choice discrimination in schizophrenic and normal subjects for positive, negative, and neutral affective stimuli. *Journal of Consulting Psychology*, 1961, **25**, 92.

Waters, T. J.   Censure reinforcement, cue conditions and the acute-chronic schizophrenia distinction. Unpublished doctoral dissertation, University of Missouri, 1962.

Webb, W. W.   Conceptual ability of schizophrenics as a function of threat of failure. *Journal of Abnormal and Social Psychology*, 1955, **50**, 221-224.

Weckowicz, T. E., & Blewitt, D. B.   Size constancy and abstract thinking in schizophrenic patients. *Journal of Mental Science*, 1959, **105**, 909-934.

Werner, H.   *Comparative psychology of mental development.* Chicago: Follett, 1948.

White, Mary A.   A study of schizophrenic language. *Journal of Abnormal and Social Psychology*, 1949, **44**, 61-74.

Whiteman, M.   The performance of schizophrenics on social concepts. *Journal of Abnormal and Social Psychology*, 1954, **49**, 266-271.

Williams, E. B.   Deductive reasoning in schizophrenia. Unpublished doctoral dissertation, Columbia University, 1962.

Winer, H. R.   Incidental learning in schizophrenics. *Dissertation Abstracts*, 1954, **14**, 1002-1003.

Wing, J. K., & Freudenberg, R. K.   The responses of severely ill chronic schizophrenics to social stimulation. *American Journal of Psychiatry*, 1961, **118**, 311-322.

Wittman, Phyllis.   An evaluation of opposed theories concerning the etiology of so-called "dementia" in dementia praecox. *American Journal of Psychiatry*, 1937, **93**, 1363-1372.

Zahn, T. P.   Acquired and symbolic affective value as determinants of size estimation in schizophrenic and normal subjects. *Journal of Abnormal and Social Psychology*, 1959, **58**, 39-47.

Zaslow, R. W.   A new approach to the problem of conceptual thinking in schizophrenia. *Journal of Consulting Psychology*, 1950, **14**, 335-339.

Zigler, E., & Phillips, L.   Social competence and the process-reactive distinction in psychopathology. *Journal of Abnormal and Social Psychology*, 1962, **65**, 215-222.

13

Psychological Deficit in Schizophrenia: II. Interference and Activation

INTRODUCTION

In the following paper Lang and Buss review the research evidence for two other possible explanations of psychological deficit in schizophrenia—interference and activation. Both of these general explanations can be broken down into more specific hypotheses. With regard to interference, some researchers have speculated that the schizophrenic's deficit stems from the fact that he does not carefully attend to the important stimuli in the task that he is to perform. That is, his *attention* to the relevant stimuli is interfered with by other stimuli which, if he is to perform well, he should ignore. This hypothesis has been investigated in the laboratory by directing the subject's attention or by limiting the number of irrelevant stimuli that are available to distract the subject. A similar explanation is based on the hypothesis that the cause of the deficit is not distraction by other stimuli in the situation, but the deficit is the result of the schizophrenic's beginning to respond in a particular way and then not changing his approach or set despite a change in the demands of the situation. In this way the previous *set* would interfere with successful performance. The last hypothesis relevant to interference suggests that the idiosyncratic meanings and associations that the schizophrenic has for various stimuli will handicap him in making appropriate responses to the stimuli. That is, *associative interference* will be caused by the abnormal meanings that the schizophrenic has for stimuli, and because of these unusual meanings the schizophrenic cannot perform as he is expected to perform.

Lang and Buss also review the large and complex body of data relating drive level and somatic arousal (i.e., activation) to psychological deficit in schizophrenia. The *positive drive* hypothesis suggests that the schizophrenic's poor performance results from an excessively *high anxiety* (drive) *level,* which disrupts his performance in complex situations. The positive drive theory approach also suggests that the schizophrenic's associative disturbance (discussed earlier as an interference hypothesis) stems from the patient's attempt to reduce his anxiety level. That is, the remote and tangential associations of schizophrenics have been interpreted as attempts to avoid associations that are related to high anxiety or drive. The use of irrelevant associations that are not associated with anxiety or drive would be drive-reducing, hence the use of these remote associates would be reinforcing.

The *negative drive* hypothesis suggests that the schizophrenic develops *inhibition* more rapidly than normals and dissipates it more slowly than normals. This inhibition has been conceptualized in various ways, but on the simplest level it might be thought of as a *negative drive* or *neurological fatigue.* The hypothesized rapid buildup of inhibition in schizophrenics can then be used to explain slower learning in schizophrenics.

Because of the large variety of physiological measures that have been employed, the data on *somatic arousal* as it relates to schizophrenia, and specifically to the performance deficit, is very complex. Many of the measures tap different aspects of arousal and therefore are not directly related to one another. Research has dealt with either the *habitual level of somatic activity* (i.e., comparisons of the base rate of arousal of schizophrenics and normals) or with *somatic reactivity* (i.e., comparisons of the way schizophrenics and normals react to stimuli). At first these two approaches seem to offer contradictory evidence when chronic patients are used as subjects, because these subjects seem to have a *higher basal level of arousal* than normals, but at the same time they seem to be *hyporeactive to stimuli.* The reader should be careful to note, however the discussion of the *law of initial values,* which suggests that if a subject has a high base rate of arousal he will necessarily be more limited by the ceiling of arousal than a subject who has a lower base level of arousal and who therefore has more room to react before reaching the ceiling. When this is taken into consideration, the data become more consistent.

At the end of the paper the authors briefly summarize the various hypotheses and the evidence for them. In reading this article, the reader should pay special attention to the differences in results that are obtained when different types of patients are used, that is, acute versus chronic, paranoid versus nonparanoid, process versus reactive, and so on. These differences seem to indicate that a number of rather different types of problems may result from various causes. Thus if we are to make progress in our research on and treatment of patients, we must increase our specificity in classifying patients. This problem, and other methodological issues, is discussed by the authors at the conclusion of the paper.

13

PSYCHOLOGICAL DEFICIT IN SCHIZOPHRENIA: II. INTERFERENCE AND ACTIVATION[1]

PETER J. LANG AND ARNOLD H. BUSS

During the last 20 years a voluminous research literature has appeared on the subject of psychological deficit in schizophrenia, and the relative incapacity of this patient group has been demonstrated with a host of different laboratory tasks. In a previous paper (Buss & Lang, 1965), the authors reviewed deficit experiments concerned with concept formation, the possible disrupting character of social censure and affective stimuli, and the enhancing effect on performance of various reinforcers and motivational devices.

These findings revealed that testable schizophrenics are about as responsive to social pressure (reward or punishment) as other patients and normal controls. The hypothesis that in schizophrenia social censure invariably leads to deficit is not tenable. Regression theory interpretations of psychotic behavior receive little specific empirical corroboration.

A large body of literature indicates that affective stimuli in general disrupt the functioning of schizophrenics, but this may be due to a broader inability to inhibit any interfering stimulus. Similarly, while schizophrenics do not appear to have lost the capacity to form concepts, the concepts achieved are deviant—overinclusive or overexclusive—a flaw often traceable to the intrusion of task-irrelevant events. On the positive side, deficit can be significantly reduced by extra instructions, feedback about responses, and intense, physical reinforcers.

Guided by these considerations, the present paper is oriented around two broad conceptions: interference and activation. The first of these directly concerns schizophrenics' ability to attend to

SOURCE. Reprinted with permission of the American Psychological Association and the authors from the *Journal of Abnormal Psychology*, 1965, 70, 77-106.
[1] The following abbreviations will be used: reaction time (RT), preparatory interval (PI), critical flicker frequency (CFF), galvanic skin response (GSR), electroencephalograph (EEG), electromyograph (EMG), autonomic nervous system (ANS), and stimulus generalization (SG).

specific stimuli and to inhibit inappropriate responses. The relevant literature on attention, set, and association is explored. In general, schizophrenics show interference effects in all three of these areas. They are distracted by external stimuli. Responses are more likely to be determined by incidental physical properties of the perceptual field than by meaningful relationships. There is difficulty in initiating and maintaining a set over time and in changing a set that is no longer suitable to the experimental task. Finally, schizophrenics' associations are uncommon, intrusive, and interfere with performance.

While the first paper suggested that social motivational constructs have limited value, the fact of greatly reduced responsivity in schizophrenia argues for a thorough exploration of formal theories of motivation or activation. Experimental studies relevant to two classical drive theories are reviewed. One holds that the associational disturbance of schizophrenics is a consequence of high-anxiety drive; the other stresses reactive inhibition, which slows down learning and increases reminiscence. The drive approach is complemented by the neurophysiological concept of arousal. From this perspective, schizophrenics have been viewed both as under-aroused and as so hyperactivated that effective responding is impossible. Evidence for these conceptions is evaluated in a review of research on the somatic response system in schizophrenia.

Thus, the present paper considers five specific topics: attention, set, associative interference, drive, and somatic arousal. A final discussion of deficit theory and a consideration of methodological problems follows the research review.

Attention

The improvement of schizophrenics under aversive stimulus conditions has generally been explained in terms of an increase in motivation or "need" to respond. However, Lang (1959) suggested that the improvement is attributable to a stimulus-intensity dynamism and undertook a test of this hypothesis. Schizophrenics and normals performed a visual disjunctive reaction-time (RT) task under five conditions: escape, excitation, avoidance, information, and control. Following a pretest series the escape subjects were administered an aversive white noise stimulus, simultaneous with the onset of the visual cue and terminated by a correct response. Excitation subjects received the same ancillary stimulus, but the noise was terminated at random intervals unrelated to the subject's response. Escape and excitation both yielded significantly greater improvement in RT than did the control condition. Avoidance training subjects were administered aversive noise following responses slower than their pretest median. Information subjects received a nonaversive signal under the same conditions. The information group significantly lowered their RT; the avoidance procedure did not lead to significantly greater improvement than that obtained for control subjects. While the positive effects of the escape and excitation conditions did not persist into a posttest series, the positive effects of information did. These data strongly suggest that aversive stimuli improve the performance of schizophrenics via a stimulus-intensity dynamism or better definition of the task-relevant stimuli rather than via an alteration of the subject's need to respond.

Tizard and Venables (1957) found that schizophrenics improved visual RT on trials accompanied by white noise. They also found regular decreases in auditory RTs to pure tones or white noise with increases in the physical intensity of the stimulus (Venables & Tizard, 1958). King (1962b) and Grisell and Rosenbaum (1963) confirmed this result and showed that the intensity-latency gradient is steeper for chronic schizophrenics than for normal subjects. However, King reported that in both chronic schizophrenics and normals the degree of RT reduction attendant on intensity increase covaried with the subject's base latency at more moderate stimulus intensities. Furthermore, both populations showed a similar reduction in intraindividual variability with stimulus-intensity increase. King (1962b) concluded that schizophrenics and normals

are equally sensitive to change in the variable, in a relative sense, although patient response is initially slower and thereby subject to greater reduction in absolute value [p. 304].

The effects of intensity on visual RT are not clear.[2] An initial experiment yielded variable results for different light intensities but no regular order (Venables & Tizard, 1956a). A second investigation (Venables & Tizard, 1956b) reported paradoxical effects, but these did not hold up on retest. The variable results may be due to the short intertrial period (8 seconds) used in these

---

[2] Venables and O'Connor (1959) reported that unlike normal subjects, schizophrenics yield relatively faster RTs to light than to an auditory stimulus. Analysis of the data revealed this to be an artifact of relative speed. Slow normals also showed the light stimulus superiority, whereas fast schizophrenics had relatively better auditory RTs. However, cross modality investigations involve many procedural problems, and further study is needed before the importance of these results can be assessed.

experiments, and possible differences between normal and schizophrenic subjects in recovery time to visual stimuli should be explored. Cohen (1949a, 1949b) reported anomalies in the eye grounds of schizophrenic patients and suggested that their visual pathways may be affected by some pathological process. In any event, withdrawn schizophrenics did yield significantly faster auditory RTs in a bright room than under conditions of dim illumination (Tizard & Venables, 1957). These authors proposed that schizophrenics suffer from a deficit in the arousal system, and that

an increase in sensory input might be expected to have nonspecific facilitatory effects on cortical and sub-cortical activities [p. 303].

Karras (1962) attempted to test the alternate reinforcement and arousal interpretations of the deficit reduction attendant on aversive stimulation. Chronic male schizophrenics responded in a visual RT task under one of five experimental conditions. The first two groups escaped from either a low- or an intense-noise stimulus; two other groups performed while either a low- or an intense-noise was continuously administered. All four groups were compared with a no-noise control. Both escape groups had faster RTs than the two stimulation conditions, and Karras held that these findings favored a reinforcement interpretation. However, another conclusion is suggested by comparison with other data. In the previously considered experiments (Lang, 1959; Tizard & Venables, 1957) the sound was not on continuously. Tizard and Venables administered the sound only during a few trials in a long series. In the Lang experiment it was initiated at the same time as the visual stimulus and thus may have functioned both as a stimulus dynamism (arousal) and as a signal to emphasize the appropriate instant for a response (a focusing function). In the Karras (1962) experiment the continuous white noise might have aroused the subject, but it was also an irrelevant stimulus, unrelated to the task at hand. As such, it would be expected to initiate competing responses. Consistent with this interpretation is the fact that Karras's low-stimulation group yielded slower RTs than the high-stimulation group. Both the high and low stimuli were distracting, but it appears that the high-intensity sound also served a positive arousal function. Furthermore, the low-intensity stimulus was not reported as unpleasant when presented suddenly. Nevertheless, when presented coincident with the discriminative stimulus (escape), the low-intensity stimulus yielded faster RTs than the two general stimulation conditions and consistently faster RTs than the control group, although this latter difference was not significant. These effects cannot be attributed to escape from an aversive stimulus and must therefore be attributed to the increased focusing of a more marked onset change.[3]

Wienckowski (1959) also re-examined the effects of collateral stimuli on the RT task, using a modification of Lang's apparatus (1959). In addition to a control situation, the performances of acute and chronic schizophrenics and normals were evaluated under three experimental conditions: (a) a light and a brief buzzer initiated the preparatory interval (PI); the light alone was maintained throughout the PI and terminated with the onset of the discriminative stimulus; (b) both buzzer and center light continued throughout the foreperiod and were terminated with discriminative stimulus onset; (c) the buzzer and center light were not terminated until the subject completed his response. Under Condition b, both the chronic and acute schizophrenics showed a greater reduction in RT than either schizophrenic controls or normals performing under the same experimental condition. Neither Condition a nor c resulted in improved scores for any group, although the latter condition resulted in a nonsignificant lengthening of the mean RT of the chronic patients. Thus schizophrenics showed positive effects from collateral stimuli only when there was a significant net change in total stimulation at the onset of the discriminative stimulus (Condition b). Stimuli introduced at other times were ineffective or, in the case of the chronic group, showed a tendency to disrupt performance when they continued throughout the trial period (Condition c).

On the basis of their clinical observations, McGhie and Chapman (1961) attributed schizophrenic deficit to a disturbance of "selective attention," the disturbance being greatest when the patient must inhibit information in one sensory channel and attend to another. They noted that schizophrenics are particularly distracted by irrelevant auditory stimuli but that any unrelated sensory input disturbs a smooth sequence of motor responses. Substantial support for this view was obtained in an experimental study (Chapman & McGhie, 1962). When a sporadic, high-pitched noise was introduced, schizophrenics displayed a greater increase in errors on a visual tracking task than either normals or nonschizophrenic psychiatric patients. Similar differences were found when subjects were instructed to spin a wheel at a constant rate while listening

[3] An alternate interpretation of the Lang and Karras studies is offered by Silverman (1963).

to varying rates from a taped metronome. Shakow (1950) also reported interfering effects of distracting stimuli. Chapman and McGhie (1962) found the same effects for visual distractors: when subjects were instructed to attend only to auditory information while being simultaneously presented with competing visual cues, schizophrenics showed great disturbance of performance relative to normals or other psychiatric patients. Sutton, Hakerem, Zubin, and Portnoy (1961) studied a serial RT task and found that schizophrenics showed greater lengthening of RT to a second stimulus in a different modality than did normal subjects.

The inability of schizophrenics to exclude distracting stimuli has also been observed in cognitive tasks. Chapman (1956) had schizophrenic and normal subjects sort cards according to concepts. In addition to a "correct" figure the cards shared communalities that were not appropriate to the correct response. The schizophrenics used the incorrect distractor communalities as a basis for the sorting more than did normals. Weckowicz (1960) found that schizophrenics and brain-damaged patients performed worse than other nonschizophrenic psychiatric patients on a Hidden Figure Test, which required subjects to select relevant and disregard irrelevant information. Recently, Draguns (1963) studied a task in which subjects interpreted pictures that became progressively clearer with successive presentations. In addition to making more recognition errors, chronic schizophrenics were less able than normals to inhibit responses to the earlier, ambiguous pictures.

In addition to their inability to exclude or inhibit unwanted sensory inputs, schizophrenics have difficulty in integrating related stimuli. When this is done by the experimenter's presenting stimuli simultaneously as in the Lang and Wienckowski studies, a marked facilatory effect is observed. However, when stimuli are only slightly out of phase, the schizophrenic is unable to compensate and relative deterioration results. Chapman and McGhie (1962) found schizophrenics' performance to be markedly disturbed when they were required to repeat information presented on alternate visual and auditory channels. Schizophrenics also had greater discrepancies than other psychiatric patients between their scores on a dual task (they were instructed to indicate which figures appeared in a series twice *and* locate their position) and performance when instructed to do only one of these tasks.

Distractibility and disrupted information processing may underly schizophrenic deficit in a variety of perceptual tasks. Cohen, Senf, and Huston (1956) and Johannsen, Friedman, and Liccione

(1963b) studied pattern recognition in schizophrenics, using the Street Visual Gestalt Test. They found inferior closure in chronic patients relative to both acute schizophrenics and normal controls. Eysenck, Granger, and Brengelmann (1957) reported a lower than normal (although not significant) mean Street Test score for a small group of psychotics; a significant closure deficit was found on a Kohs blocks task when these patients were compared to either normals or neurotics. Snyder, Rosenthal, and Taylor (1961) reported a closure deficit in schizophrenics, based on drawings of incomplete figures. However, Snyder (1961) found a greater than normal tendency to closure in a group of acute, paranoid patients, which he attributed to emotionality associated with disease onset. Johannsen et al. (1963b) reported a significant interaction between the paranoid-nonparanoid dimension and chronicity. Their paranoid subjects maintained normal closure test scores except for the most extreme chronic group, but nonparanoid schizophrenics showed progressive deterioration with chronicity.

Although evidence is limited, a few studies suggest differences between schizophrenics and normal controls in critical flicker frequency (CFF). Dillon (1959) reported higher CFF thresholds in functional psychotics than in a control group, but the patients were a specially selected treatment sample. McDonough (1960) also found higher than normal mean CFFs in reactive schizophrenics but no differences between process schizophrenics and normals. Recently, Johannsen et al. (1963b) reported that acutes showed a high CFF, but with increasing chronicity there was a progressive reduction in thresholds to a point well below that of normal subjects. The conflicting findings may be due to the competing effects of high distractibility and high activation level in schizophrenia. These two factors tend to influence CFF thresholds in opposite ways. The most extensive study (Johannsen et al., 1963b) is consistent with the hypothesis of decreased vigilance in chronic patients.

A number of researchers report deficit in size or distance constancy in chronic schizophrenics (Cooper, 1960; Crooks, 1957; Lovinger, 1956; Reynolds, 1954; Weckowicz, 1957, 1958, 1960; Weckowicz & Blewitt, 1959; Weckowicz & Hall, 1960; Weckowicz, Sommer, & Hall, 1958). Nevertheless, Reisman (1961) failed to find differences in size constancy between normals and two schizophrenic groups. Raush (1952, 1956) found that "fairly young, fairly well oriented" paranoid schizophrenics showed higher constancy scores than normal subjects. Sanders and Pacht (1952) also reported what amounts to "overconstancy" (distant objects seen as larger than they actually were) in a group of psychotic outpatients. However, Kidd (1964) found subnormal monocular depth perception in schizophrenics within 48 hours after they were admitted to a state hospital. Unfortunately, it is not clear whether these were first admissions, nor is there information on the subtype or chronicity of these patients. Perhaps the most comprehensive data on these variables is provided by Johannsen et al. (1963b) who studied depth perception in a large group of schizophrenics classified according to duration of illness. They found a low mean error score for acute patients; chronic patients generally made significantly more errors than either acute psychotics or normal controls, although the most extreme chronic group evidenced some restitution of ability.

Thus, the closure, size constancy, and distance constancy studies reviewed here found deficit in schizophrenics more often than not. However, experiments with acute schizophrenics, and particularly with early paranoid patients, suggest the presence of compensatory efforts in these subjects, which result in normal or occasionally above-average functioning. Chronic patients show the greatest deterioration, but even this result is not wholly reliable.

Perhaps much of this variability between experiments reflects the schizophrenic's response to characteristics of the specific task or task setting that do not affect normal subjects. The perceptual judgments of schizophrenics appear to be readily manipulated by minor alterations of experimental stimuli. Weckowicz (1964) found inferior shape constancy in schizophrenics when the stimulus objects were inclined at 60 degrees, but not when the angle of inclination was only 30 degrees. The findings of Raush (1956) and Pishkin, Smith, and Leibowitz (1962) among others, show significant constancy differences attributable to the symbolic value of stimulus objects. It has already been suggested (Buss & Lang, 1965) that these results are due to the greater number of associations occasioned in schizophrenics by these stimuli and their intrusion into the task at hand. Salzinger (1957) reported no initial differences between schizophrenics and normals in ability to discriminate weights. However, when required to make estimates following the lifting of a heavy anchor stimulus, the patient group showed a significantly greater shift in judgment than controls. Lovinger (1956) found deterioration in the size constancy of schizophrenics only under minimal cue conditions. Leibowitz and Pishkin (1961) reported no size constancy deficit in schizophrenics under maximum cue conditions, but a follow-up investigation (Pishkin et al., 1962) revealed a significant difference in size estimation errors between normals and chronic schizophrenics. In this latter experiment the subjects had to illuminate the stimulus objects themselves by closing a switch; in addition to making more errors, schizophrenics tended to illuminate the field significantly more often than controls. Pishkin and his associates attributed these differences to the schizophrenics' greater difficulty in selecting and attending to relevant cues. Further evidence for an attention deficit is provided by tachistoscopic studies, e.g., McGinnies and Adornetto (1952) found that schizophrenics have higher recognition thresholds than normal for *both* emotionally toned and neutral verbal material.

Schizophrenics appear to live in a subjective world determined by the physical size and intensity of stimuli, poorly integrated with the information about relationships between objects, which modulates the perception of normal subjects. Perhaps because attention is so wavering, the static, formal characteristics of the physical field determine behavior, and schizophrenics fail to show normals' flexible, meaningful perceptual experience. Thus, deficit is greatest when the schizophrenic must pay attention to more than one stimulus input, switch his attention from one stimulus to another, or ignore irrelevant stimuli in favor of physically weak, task-relevant inputs. Deficit is least when the irrelevant stimuli are few, the task stimulus is intense and unequivocal, or any collateral inputs are temporally in phase. Under these latter conditions chronic schizophrenics may approach the functioning level of normal subjects.

Set

Analogous to the difficulty with concurrent stimuli described above is the schizophrenic's frequent failure to inhibit inappropriate responses initiated by sequences in time. This was already suggested by the Chapman and McGhie (1962) experiment in which patients failed to spin a wheel at a constant speed while listening to varied tempi from a metronome. A number of studies indicate a time estimation deficit in schizophrenia. Rabin (1957) found schizophrenics to be significantly poorer than nonpsychotics in estimating the length of a psychological interview. Lhamon and Goldstone (1956), H. E. King (1962a), and Pearl and Berg (1963) all reported that schizophrenics systematically overestimate short time intervals (.5 to 30 seconds). King's interval-matching study indicated that normal subjects consistently underestimate the same intervals, and he suggested that the deficit of schizophrenics may be attributed to their characteristic psychomotor retardation. Pearl and Berg (1963) had schizophrenics and normals estimate the presentation time of neutral and affect arousing pictures and found that psychotics displayed greater overestimation to the affective materials.

The schizophrenic's performance is markedly disturbed whenever he must initiate a response at a fixed point in time. Shakow (1962) has noted that schizophrenics show less deficit on tasks such as tapping, in which time of onset and termination is not important to adequate performance, than on tasks like RT, which require preparation for a response at the discretion of the experimenter. Furthermore Rosenthal, Lawlor, Zahn, and Shakow (1960), and H. E. King (1954, 1961) have demonstrated a high positive relationship between RT and mental health ratings.

The latencies of schizophrenics are readily manipulated by slight variations in the foreperiod or preparatory interval (PI). The RT of chronic patients increases disproportionately with the lengthening of a regular PI (Huston, Shakow, & Riggs, 1937; Rodnick & Shakow, 1940). Zahn, Shakow, and Rosenthal (1961) demonstrated that this effect is attributable not to the slower pace of the task but to foreperiod length; it is also partially a function of the preceding sequence of foreperiods. When a single long PI occurs in a series of shorter ones, the RT latency is relatively shorter than if the preceding foreperiods were of equal length (Rodnick & Shakow, 1940; Tizard & Venables, 1956). Similarly,

when a single long PI trial was followed by a single short PI trial, RT on the latter trial was disproportionately lengthened in schizophrenic as compared with normal subjects [Zahn, Rosenthal, & Shakow, 1961, p. 167].

Zahn et al. (1961, 1963) demonstrated that if the length of the PI is systematically varied during the task, the RT of schizophrenics changes in characteristic ways. When successive PIs were administered in order of increasing length, RT was an increasing function of foreperiod length for both schizophrenics and normals, but the slope of the curve was significantly greater for the former population. The RTs of the schizophrenics tended to be the same for all PIs and relatively slow when a descending order of administration was employed, whereas the curve for normal subjects was virtually identical to that when length was increased.

In summary, the RT of schizophrenics is controlled to a great extent by the context of PIs and more particularly by the immediately preceding foreperiod. As with concurrent stimuli, temporal sequence may be manipulated to produce increases or decreases in deficit.

Blaufarb (1962) demonstrated a facilatory effect of context on a verbal task. Schizophrenics and normals were administered proverb tasks in two sessions. In one session they were asked to give the meaning of a single proverb, and in the other session they were asked to give the meaning of a set of proverbs, all of which had the same meaning. The chronic schizophrenics were significantly poorer than normals under the single proverb condition. Schizophrenics showed significantly greater improvement with proverb sets and under this condition could not be distinguished from the normal group.

However, tasks may be selected so as to produce inappropriate sets, thereby increasing deficit. Mandl (1954) found that paranoid schizophrenics showed greater rigidity than normals on a perceptual task. Shakow (1950) noted that distractors disrupted the performance of both normals and schizophrenics, but the deleterious effects carried over to subsequent nonstress trials only for the psychotic patients. In W. O. Smith's (1959) study of the pursuit rotor task, process schizophrenics showed less improvement with modification of the experimental conditions than did reactive patients. Similarly, Crumpton (1963) showed that schizophrenics persisted in a previously rewarded but now incorrect response for significantly more trials than a normal control sample. Furthermore, this tendency to persist with a maladaptive response appeared to be related to the severity of the schizophrenic process.

Associative Interference

It was Bleuler (1950) who first pointed to association as the crucial issue in schizophrenia. He believed that many schizophrenic symptoms (hallucinations, delusions, etc.) were only elaborations of, and secondary to, the primary disturbance in association. This disturbance in association may be seen in bizarre ideas, loose associations, fragmented thinking, and the blocking of the usual and common chains of associations and ideas.

What is the role of associative disturbance in schizophrenic deficit? Specifically, how would difficulty in association disturb attention or set and therefore worsen performance on psychomotor, perceptual, and learning tasks? The answer may be framed in the context of the psychological demands of such tasks. The subject is required to maintain a state of vigilance, a readiness to respond to oncoming stimuli. He must also react to stimuli and instructions in a normative manner, that is, on the basis of the common meanings of stimuli and instructions. To the extent, that stimuli have individual, idiosyncratic meanings (associations) for the subject, he will be handicapped in responding to them. For example, stimuli seen as relatively neutral by normals, may be provocative for schizophrenics, who perceive simple stimuli in idiosyncratic ways (Feldman & Drasgow, 1951).

In maintaining a state of vigilance as preparation for oncoming stimuli, the subject needs to be free from distractions. He must inhibit responses not only to inappropriate external stimuli but also to extraneous thoughts and associations that may divert his attention. The research on psychomotor performance discussed earlier shows that the schizophrenic is unable to accomplish the first of these tasks. Clinical reports suggest that he also cannot prevent the intrusion of bizarre ideas and associations that pull his attention from the task at hand. The idiosyncratic associations of schizophrenics distract them, thus degrading their performance. This formulation leads to two testable hypotheses.

The Associations of Schizophrenics Are Uncommon

Several studies have sustained this assertion. Moran (1953) tried a word association task with schizophrenics and normals, the stimulus words having previously been defined by the subjects. The schizophrenics' associations were significantly less related to the stimulus words than the associations of the normals. These findings were corroborated by Johnson, Weiss, and Zelhart (1964) who found that schizophrenics produced more idiosyncratic word associations than normals.

Sommer, Dewar, and Osmond (1960) compared the associations of schizophrenics and normals to the words on the Kent-Rosanoff list. Schizophrenics gave significantly more uncommon associations, and they were extremely variable in terms of both stability of responses over time and comparisons between subjects. Sommer, Witney, and Osmond (1962) followed up this experiment by trying to condition common associations. While alcoholics conditioned rapidly, schizophrenics showed very little conditioning.

Wynne (1963) found that the free associations of acute schizophrenics differed little from those of normals. However, when instructed to give the associations "most people do," normals gave more common associations but schizophrenics did not. Maltzman,

Seymore, and Licht (1962) attempted to condition normal subjects to give common or uncommon associations. They learned to give more common associations but did not learn to give more uncommon associations. Maltzman, Cohen, and Belloni (1963) found that schizophrenic children give more uncommon associations than normal children.

On the basis of these various studies, we may conclude that schizophrenics tend to give uncommon associations but cannot learn common associations, whereas normals tend to give common associations but cannot learn uncommon associations.

Intrusive Associations Worsen the Performance of Schizophrenics More Than of Normals

Chapman (1958) used a verbal concept formation task, with a stimulus word and three response words. One response was the correct concept, one an (irrelevant-to-the-task) association, and one neither. The associations were of high and low strength. Schizophrenics showed significantly more associative intrusions than normals.

Donahoe, Curtin, and Lipton (1961) questioned whether associative intrusions in schizophrenics occurred only with meaningful stimuli (words) or with all stimuli (words and nonsense syllables). They tested the effect of experimentally built-in intrusive associations on the learning of nonsense syllables and found an equal decrement in normals and schizophrenics. Downing, Ebert, and Shubrooks (1963) studied the number of errors schizophrenics produced on a concept test by different types of distractor words. Associatively linked words produced more errors than either contiguity or rhyme-clang distractors. Thus it is the restrictive hypothesis that appears to be correct: schizophrenics suffer especially from the intrusion of meaningful irrelevant associations and not all types of irrelevant associations.

A number of studies have produced more direct evidence on the intrusion of associations in schizophrenia. Lang and Luoto (1962) had subjects learn two lists of paired associates (words). On the second list, half the response terms were associates of the response terms used in the first list. The response terms of the other half were also associates, but they were not assigned to the correct stimulus term, thereby creating an interference list. The results showed that the schizophrenics' mediational processes were not significantly different from the normals. However, schizophrenics showed significantly poorer performance than normals on the early trials of the interference list. Furthermore, while normals seldom again offered the response terms of pairs already learned, these words tended to persist as responses for schizophrenics, interfering with subsequent learning.

Spence and Lair (1964) failed to find differences between the paired-associate learning of normals and schizophrenics, consistent with Mednick's theory (1958). However, an analysis of errors did differentiate the two groups. Acute schizophrenics tended to give more overt, inappropriate responses, stemming from both intralist and extralist sources. Normals produced more errors of omission. Thus, schizophrenics seem unable to inhibit the overt expression of intruding associations.

Further evidence of intrusiveness comes from an experiment by Lauro (1962), who used words that varied in clustering tendency. There were no differences in recall between normals and schizophrenics in the easy clustering list, but in the difficult clustering list the schizophrenics "imported" more irrelevant words than did normals.

There should be more associative interference when words have several meanings than when they have only one meaning. Faibish (1961) had normals and schizophrenics define and free associate to words with either one meaning or multiple meanings. Both normals and schizophrenics showed poorer word association and vocabulary performance with the multiple-meaning words, but the schizophrenics' decrement was greater than the normals. The schizophrenics were disrupted by the multiple meanings, and Faibish concluded that "the majority of the results can be understood in terms of interference effects [p. 423]."

Finally, Lester (1960) studied restricted association in normals, hebephrenic and paranoid schizophrenics, and epileptics. The patient groups showed more interference than the normals in the selection of associates, the interference occurring because of the intrusion of extraneous associations. The interference was greatest for epileptics, followed by hebephrenics, paranoids, and normals, in decreasing order.

In brief, the hypothesis of associative interference has been verified. Schizophrenics have more unique, nonshared associations, and these associations, like external distractors, serve to deteriorate performance because of their intrusive nature. Shakow's (1962) summation of his RT studies aptly describes both inner (associational) and outer distractors:

Here we see particularly the various difficulties created by *context*, the degree to which the schizophrenic is affected by irrelevant aspects of the stimulus surroundings—inner and outer—which prevent his focusing on the "to-be-responded-to" stimulus. It is as if, in the scanning process which takes place before the response to a stimulus is made, the schizophrenic is unable to select out the material relevant for optimal response. He apparently cannot free himself from the irrelevant among the numerous possibilities available for choice. In other words, that function which is of equal importance as the response *to* stimuli, namely, the protection *against* the response to stimuli, is abeyant [p. 25].

Drive

Two drive theories of schizophrenic deficit have been proposed, each associated with different behaviors. Positive drive theory, which identifies anxiety as the crucial variable, is intended to explain aspects of the schizophrenic's associational disturbance. Negative drive theory focuses on inhibition during conditioning and the phenomenon of reminiscence.

Anxiety and Associational Deficit

The hypothesis of continuity between neurosis and psychosis has long been popular with theorists and practicing clinicians. From this perspective, the symptoms of schizophrenia result from a failure of neurotic defenses. The individual is finally overwhelmed by social or personal anxiety, and he retreats to the pseudoworld of psychosis. Fenichel (1945) and Arieti (1955) provide classical examples of this approach to clinical phenomena.

Mednick (1958) has recently attempted an analogous, though more rigorous, explanation of the schizophrenic's associational disturbance. Anxiety is again taken to be the central construct, but it is equated with the Hull-Spence concept of drive.

The term *drive* is frequently used to denote physiological activation; it is not considered here in that context (see the following section on arousal). In the Hull-Spence framework, drive is generally defined by deprivation time or stimulus intensity and measured by performance. As an intervening variable it bears a mathematical relationship to response strength, learning, and generalization; Mednick's hypotheses are deduced within this theoretical system. Experimental evidence is sought at a number of crucial points, and the following review is concerned mainly with this empirical support.

Mednick (1958) assumes anxiety to be intense in the schizophrenic. High drive (intense anxiety) leads to excessive stimulus generalization and associative generalization. A phobic defense may be successful in maintaining a precarious balance, as seen in schizoid, withdrawing personalities, but the balance may be upset by a precipitating event, which elevates the anxiety level. This increase in drive leads to still more generalization, and now many more stimuli are fear-invoking. Furthermore, the higher drive level increases the intensity of previously present fear responses.

As the spiral of anxiety and generalization mounts, his drive level may increase to an almost insupportable degree. As this is taking place, his ability to discriminate is almost totally eclipsed by his generalization tendencies. Any unit of a thought sequence might call up [still another] remote associate. . . . Clang associates based on stimulus-response generalization may be frequent. . . . His speech may resemble a "word salad." He will be an acute schizophrenic with a full-blown thinking disorder [p. 322].

Mednick recognized that, in contrast to acute schizophrenics, chronic schizophrenics tend not to give overt evidence of intense anxiety. Therefore he proposed the following transition from acute to chronic schizophrenia. The excessive generalization of the high drive (anxiety) state may lead to a "highly generalized, remote, irrelevant, tangential associate." A remote association diverts the individual's attention from anxiety-provoking stimuli, and the resulting drive (anxiety) reduction is reinforcing. Continued repetition of the strongly reinforced tendency to escape anxiety via remote associations leads to deviant, disorganized thinking. Thinking irrelevant thoughts proves to be so effective in reducing anxiety that the schizophrenic may appear emotionally phlegmatic. Now the well-learned tendency toward remote and tangential associations is maintained even in the absence of a high anxiety level. In deriving his theory Mednick made four assumptions.

Schizophrenics acquire classically conditioned responses faster than normals. Two studies support this assumption. Pfaffman and Schlosberg (1936) demonstrated more frequent conditioned patellar tendon reflexes in schizophrenics than in normals. Spence and Taylor (1953) reported similar results for eyelid conditioning.

On the other hand, six studies have shown that normals condition at least as well as, or better than, schizophrenics. Shipley (1934) and Pishkin and Hershiser (1963) found better conditioning for normals with the GSR, and Howe (1958), also using GSR conditioning, failed to obtain significant differences between normals and schizophrenics. Franks (1954), Peters and Murphree (1954), and O'Connor and Rawnsley (1959) also found that schizophrenics fail to learn faster or better than normals on a variety of conditioning tasks. Thus the weight of evidence is against the hypothesis, which receives little support from the studies just cited.

In more complex situations schizophrenics learn slower. This assumption is linked to the first one in an attempt to apply drive theory to two types of learning situations. In simple situations (e.g., classical conditioning) high drive leads to faster learning; in complex situations high drive enhances irrelevant and incorrect responses, causing a decrement in learning. Schizophrenics, having greater anxiety and therefore higher drive, should learn faster in simple situations and slower in complex situations. The second part of this statement is true: schizophrenics do learn slower in complex situations. However, the first part is probably untrue. Except for classical conditioning, where the evidence is admittedly equivocal, schizophrenics learn *slower* than normals in simple situations. (See the sections on Insufficient Motivation, Attention, Set, and Associative Interference.)

Actually the facts already reviewed are a good deal more complex than the hypothesis allows. While chronic schizophrenics rarely show superior learning to normals, they may approach normal functioning when the response alternatives are reduced and distractions are few. If such conditions define task simplicity, these facts may bring the drive theorist some solace. Furthermore, in a few experiments acute paranoid patients have actually emerged superior to their normal controls. Unfortunately, one must pick and choose among the data to find support for what pretends to be a comprehensive theory. Since schizophrenics in general learn both simple and complex tasks more slowly than normals, the evidence is not consistent with drive theory.

Schizophrenics overgeneralize in comparison to normals. Mednick cited four experiments that ostensibly found elevated generalization gradients in schizophrenics. The first is a study by Bender and Schilder (1930), who present data that are difficult to interpret in terms of generalization gradients and who did not employ normal controls. The second is Garmezy's study (1952), which is open to several interpretations, as we showed in the previous paper (Buss & Lang, 1965). The third is Mednick's (1955) doctoral dissertation, in which he wrote:

> With respect to the hypothesis that schizophrenics would display a more elevated GSR (gradient of stimulus generalization) than normals, the results are not conclusive. While the C (normal) and S (schizophrenic) groups differ, the differences occur both in the predicted direction and counter to it [p. 540].

The fourth study is that of Dunn (1954) who found an elevated generalization gradient in schizophrenics in one experimental condition and no differences between the gradients of schizophrenics and normals in three other conditions. The most neutral comment to be made about these four studies is that they do not offer support for this third hypothesis.

There is considerable evidence that schizophrenics tend to be overinclusive, including in their vocabulary definitions and conceptual sortings more stimuli than do normals (Buss & Lang, 1965).

Phenomena of this sort tempt one to describe schizophrenics as showing a heightened and broadened gradient of secondary stimulus generalization. However, the experimental evidence seems to contradict this interpretation. At least three different investigators have compared schizophrenics and normals on tasks which are usually thought of as measuring propensities toward heightened semantic generalization. All of these studies have uniformly obtained negative results, that is, they find no difference between schizophrenics and normals on semantic generalization [Chapman, 1962].

Chapman went on to report an experiment demonstrating that schizophrenics were *less* inclusive than normals. Thus the assumption that schizophrenics overgeneralize is not supported by the evidence.

High anxiety leads to overgeneralization and to faster conditioning. This assumption receives some support from the literature, which is too remote from schizophrenic deficit to review here. It should be noted that research with the Taylor Manifest Anxiety scale (the major instrument in these studies) has tended to produce controversial and, at times, unreliable results. Mednick himself (1957) found that middle-anxious subjects had flatter stimulus generalization (SG) gradients than did high- and low-anxious psychiatric patients. Thus there has been both positive and negative evidence on the relationship between anxiety and overgeneralization.

The results concerning anxiety and classical conditioning have been more clearly positive: high-anxious subjects do condition faster than low-anxious subjects. However, the potency of anxiety as a determiner of conditioning is slight, a fact that is admitted by drive theorists:

While previous studies have demonstrated a relationship between conditioning and manifest anxiety, variously defined, correlation coefficients that have been reported between those two variables indicate that a relatively small amount of the variability among Ss can be accounted for in terms of anxiety [Taylor & Spence, 1954, p. 502].

Thus the evidence of this fourth assumption tends to be equivocal.

Examination of Mednick's four assumptions indicates that supporting evidence is either equivocal or lacking. Since these assumptions are the base of his drive theory, the theory itself it weakened to the extent that the assumptions lack verification.

The theory places all its eggs in one basket in that it accounts for schizophrenia solely in terms of anxiety. The difficulty is that, with anxiety so prevalent, it is necessary to explain why schizophrenia is still relatively rare in the population. Mednick (1958) was aware of this issue of "over-explanation":

Why doesn't everybody proceed to schizophrenia after an extremely anxiety provoking event? The answer lies in three factors: the individual's original drive level, his rate of recovery from anxiety states, and the number of stimuli that elicit anxiety responses from the individual . . . high drive, slow recovery rate, and the number of fear arousing stimuli are highly correlated factors [p. 323].

Only those with all three factors tend to become schizophrenic, but Mednick himself admitted that the three factors are all highly correlated. Thus an extremely anxious individual, being high on all three factors, should become schizophrenic. Clearly, Mednick has not answered his own question. We may guess that he cannot answer it because he identifies anxiety as the sole cause of the thinking disorder in schizophrenia. This explanation will not be acceptable to the majority of psychologists. It is evident that many individuals with extremely high levels of anxiety never become schizophrenic, whereas Mednick's drive theory clearly implies that they should.

Reactive Inhibition and Reminiscence

Pavlov (1941) suggested that in schizophrenia inhibition predominates over excitation, the theory being labeled "protective inhibition." Several English investigators have developed this idea in terms of a negative drive, reactive inhibition (Claridge, 1960; Eysenck, 1961; Rachman, 1963; Venables & Tizard, 1956c). Thus schizophrenics are believed to develop reactive inhibition faster than normals and to dissipate it slower. If this is true, schizophrenics should learn more slowly than normals, and, more important, show greater reminiscence. The prediction is straightforward: after a rest period schizophrenics should have a greater increment in performance (reminiscence) than do normals.

This prediction has been unequivocally confirmed in only one study. Huston and Shakow (1948, 1949) tested schizophrenics and normals on a pursuit rotor task at 3-month intervals. Normals performed significantly better than schizophrenics, but whereas normals showed no reminiscence after a 3-month interval, schizophrenics manifested a clear improvement in performance.

Venables and Tizard (1956c) used a repetitive choice task and a 1-minute rest period. Schizophrenics showed slightly more reminiscence than psychotic depressives; there were no normal subjects. Bleke (1955) used a memory task under conditions of reward or punishment. With verbal punishment, poor premorbid schizophrenics showed more reminiscence than either good premorbid schizophrenics or normals. With verbal reward, there were only chance differences in reminiscence. Smock and Vancini (1962) obtained *less* reminiscence in schizophrenics after censure; after reward there were no differences in reminiscence between schizophrenics and normals. Higgins and Mednick (1963) had early and advanced schizophrenics copy the alphabet upside down and backward. They found more reminiscence in early than in advanced schizophrenics. The discrepancies among these last three studies may be due to the way punishment was administered, the difference in tasks, or sampling differences in the subjects.

Taken as a whole, these studies offer little support for the hypothesis that schizophrenics build up reactive inhibition faster than normals and therefore show greater reminiscence. Six experiments have yielded clearly negative results. Campbell (1957) used paper-and-pencil mazes, Rosenbaum, Cohen, Luby, Gottlieb, and Yelen (1959) employed the pursuit rotor, and Venables (1959) used a repetitive choice task; none of these workers found any difference in reminiscence between normals and schizophrenics. O'Connor (1957), Claridge (1960), and Rachman (1963), with varying tasks and rest periods, all found greater reminiscence in normals than in schizophrenics.[4]

[4] Rachman studied length of the intervening time period and amount of reminiscence. He found that schizophrenics show greater reminiscence after 24 hours than they do after 10 minutes. Furthermore, a comparison with data published elsewhere (Rachman, 1962) suggests that the degree of reminiscence, when measured at the first trial following a 10 minute rest period, is less for schizophrenics than for normal subjects. The relationship between time interval and reminiscence is complex and in general outside the scope of the present review. The reader is referred to the Rachman papers for a discussion of these issues and the related topic of disinhibition.

In summary, there appear to be no consistent reminiscence differences between schizophrenics and normals. Some of the discrepancies among results are undoubtedly due to variations in task, in rest period, and in composition of the subject samples. Regardless of methodological considerations, it seems safe to conclude that the negative drive hypothesis has not been corroborated.

Somatic Arousal

Autonomic, cortical, and neuromuscular response systems are of considerable relevance to both activation and interference interpretations of schizophrenic deficit. The basic concept of an arousal system in the lower brain was initially dependent on electroencephalogram (EEG) findings rather than on overt behavioral data. Malmo (1958) has stressed the importance of peripheral physiological responses (GSR, EMG, cardiac rate, and blood pressure) as concomitant estimates of drive or the aroused state. Furthermore, the work of Lacey and Lacey (1958a), Gellhorn (1957), and Barratt (1962) indicates that feedback from autonomic nervous system (ANS) activity and muscle tension may have important effects on cortical functioning and thus determine temperament, alertness, and adequacy of psychomotor control. It has been suggested that schizophrenic deficit is attributable to *diminished* feedback from peripheral sensors or effector systems, with a resultant disturbance of control and orientation. Others propose that *excessive* feedback of ANS activity interferes with organized behavior in a manner analogous to that of irrelevant associations or intrusive external stimuli.

Research on these covert responses in schizophrenics may be divided into two broad areas: *habitual levels of activity* and *reactivity*. The first term refers to the base amount of ANS or neuromuscular responding characteristic of an individual at rest, when external stimuli are abeyant. The second term refers to the form or amplitude of responses to specific stimuli introduced by the experimenter.

Habitual Level of Activity

At the time Hunt and Cofer (1944) reviewed literature on psychological deficit, no consistent differences between normal and schizophrenic subjects in resting ANS response level had been found (Freeman & Pathman, 1943). A later review (Hoskins, 1946) noted that schizophrenics were less variable than normals in blood pressure and the oral-rectal temperature differential.

Early investigators sought unsuccessfully for evidence of ANS hypoactivity to parallel the clinically observed withdrawal and flattened affect. In addition to this theoretical bias they were hampered by a tendency to consider single measures of specific physiological functions—heart rate of skin resistance—both as adequate estimates of overall ANS functioning and as indicants of general emotionality or arousal. However, the experimental literature (Lacey & Lacey, 1958b) suggests that the relationships between somatic responses are complex and that more than one system must be considered in such evaluations. In the subsequent few paragraphs studies of basal skin resistance, cardiovascular and respiration responses, and muscle activity in schizophrenia are reviewed.

Basal skin resistance. Hock, Kubis, and Rouke (1944) note that withdrawn psychotics show increasing skin resistance over time periods in which normals are relatively stable. Experiments by Jurko, Jost, and Hill (1952) and Howe (1958) found higher resting resistance levels for schizophrenic patients than for normal controls. Malmo and Shagass (1949), DeVault (1957), Ray (1963) in a study of female patients, and Pishkin and Hershiser (1963) reported no difference in resistance between normals and schizophrenics. Only two studies found low basal skin resistance in schizophrenics. Zahn, Rosenthal, and Lawlor (1963) report both lower than normal skin resistance and greater spontaneous activity in schizophrenics. Williams (1953) also found lower than normal resting levels for what he described as an "early chronic schizophrenic" group. However, this difference barely reached significance and was not maintained during the experimental conditions. Previous studies by Syz (1926) and Syz and Kinder (1928) attempted to distinguish between patient subtypes. They found high basal resistance for catatonics, the paranoids' mean fell between those obtained from two normal control samples, and there was more spontaneous activity in paranoids than catatonic patients.

Cardiovascular system and respiration. Gunderson (1953), Williams (1953), and Jurko et al. (1952) reported faster resting heart rates for schizophrenics than normal controls. DeVault (1957) obtained similar results for chronic, reactive patients but not for process schizophrenics. However, Reynolds (1962) found process schizophrenics had a significantly higher basal pulse than reactive patients, and normal controls yielded the lowest rates.

Altschule and Sulzbach (1949) reported vasoconstriction, particularly of the hand, to be a habitual condition in many schizophrenics. Data collected by Henschel, Brozek, and Keys (1951) also suggested that the skin vessels of schizophrenics have a high resting tonus level. Consistent with these views, Malmo and Shagass (1952) found habitual high diastolic pressure in chronic schizophrenics, combined with lowered pulse pressure. Both diastolic and systolic pressures tended to be higher in process schizophrenics than normal subjects in the Reynolds (1962) experiment, but a significant difference was obtained for only one of four resting samples.

Gunderson (1953), Jurko et al. (1952), and Williams (1953) reported that schizophrenics had faster respiration rates than normals. Reynolds' data show a nonsignificant tendency for process schizophrenics to have faster rates.

Muscle activity. Malmo and his associates (Malmo & Shagass, 1949; Malmo, 1950; Malmo, Shagass, & Smith, 1951) reported a high resting electromyograph (EMG) in schizophrenics, with the highest levels among chronic patients. Martin (1956), Whatmore and Ellis (1958), and Petursson (1962) also found evidence of higher than normal muscle tension in schizophrenics. Reynolds (1962) reported a significantly higher resting EMG response in process schizophrenics than normal subjects; reactive patients fell between these two groups. Jurko et al. (1952) found considerable adventitious muscle activity in schizophrenics relative to normals. Malmo and Shagass (1949), Edwards and Harris (1953) and later Gindis (1960) reported disturbance of finger movement in a variety of schizophrenics.

EMG investigations parallel psychomotor studies (King, 1962b) in that schizophrenics show high intraindividual variability. Malmo et al. (1951) found that increases in painful stimuli yielded increased action potentials in the neck muscles of schizophrenic patients, but unlike normals, these subjects failed to show such changes in potentials taken from arm electrodes. Reynolds (1962) also reported high variability in response to stressors and within and between subjects during rest.

The psychophysiological studies described above generally included only one testing session, and little information is available on trends in variability. Recently Carrigan (1963) reported that daily polygraph tests yielded few differences in intraindividual variability between a group of nonparanoid schizophrenics and normal controls. Acker (1963) compared a small group of schizophrenics on tranquilizers and normal subjects. The two groups yielded different trends for different physiological systems. Schizophrenics showed heart rate adaptation over sessions, but unlike the normal controls, blood pressure measures did not show this effect. Both psychophysiological variability and adaptation effects in schizophrenia deserve further study.

In summary, the habitual level of somatic activity in schizophrenics appears to have the following characteristics. Skin resistance levels are generally similar to those of normals, although two samples were clearly higher and at least one was lower than those of control subjects. During experiments the cardiovascular systems of schizophrenics tend to be at a higher activation level than those of normal controls. However, the relationship between cardiac functioning and such dimensions as process-reactive or chronic-acute is not yet clear. All reports indicate higher than normal muscle tension in schizophrenics, the highest levels being associated with chronicity and the process label.

The conclusion that schizophrenics are underaroused or at a normal level of arousal during experiments (i.e., Ray, 1963) is not consistent with a major part of the data. Only the skin resistance findings lend support to this position, while the cardiovascular and neuromuscular systems point to a heightened level of activation. The reason for this division has been variously interpreted. Jurko et al. (1952) point out the close relationship between sweat gland activity, attention, and ideation—functions particularly disturbed in schizophrenics. They suggest that energy discharge via muscular tension represents a phylogenetically more primitive way of maintaining energy balance than through the electrodermal response.

The skin resistance findings seem inconsistent with Wenger's (Wenger, 1956; Wenger, Jones, & Jones, 1959) conclusion that the autonomic activity of schizophrenics is dominated by the sympathetic system. However, Solomon, Darrow, and Blaurock (1939) remind us that sweat gland activity, though sympathetically activated, is a cholinergic mechanism. They suggest that the neurohormonal inhibition of cholinergic response systems may be related to psychotic withdrawal. More recently, Rubin (1962) has suggested that an adrenergic-cholinergic unbalance is an important aspect of functional psychosis. Perhaps sweat gland activity is a sensitive measure of small increases in arousal level, but the action of adrenin inhibits this system under high levels of sympathetic activation.

The cardiovascular results and particularly the muscle tension findings suggest that the level of "biological noise" is quite high in schizophrenics. A number of authors have proposed that this directly accounts for schizophrenic symptoms. Angyal (1935, 1936) suggested that disturbance of muscle tension may be the perceptual basis of somatic delusions in schizophrenia, and Gould (1950) proposed that auditory hallucinations could be traced to a motor disturbance of the speech mechanism. Furthermore, diffuse neuromuscular activity may contribute to deficit in psychomotor or perceptual tasks by interfering directly with coordinated behavior (Freeman, 1948; Luria, 1932). Wishner (1955, 1962) has maintained that an increase in degree of psychopathology is signaled by a decrease in efficiency, with efficiency defined as the ratio of focused to diffuse activity. Normals orient their activity to the task requirements, and there is a minimum of diffuse random activity in either the musculature or the ANS. In psychopathology less of the total activity is directed to the task at hand, and more of the total behavior output is diffuse and random. Schizophrenia represents the extreme of inefficiency.

Reynolds (1962) found that in process schizophrenics stress sometimes produces a decrease rather than the normal's increase in muscle tension level. He interpreted studies which show chronic schizophrenics improve under conditions of aversive stimulation (Cohen et al., 1956; Lang, 1959) in a manner that parallels Wishner's theory. Reynolds suggested that aversive stimuli reduce the general tension level in chronic schizophrenics, producing a temporarily favorable ratio of directed to diffuse muscular activity and an associated amelioration of psychomotor performance.

Reactivity and pathology. Many studies of reactivity of stimulation reveal a diminished ANS response in chronic schizophrenia. Stressors that have yielded hyporeactivity include the inhalation of heated air (Freeman & Rodnick, 1940) and cold baths (Buck, Carscallen, & Hobbs, 1950). Schizophrenics show reduced rotational and caloric nystagmus (Angyal & Blackman, 1940, 1941; Angyal & Sherman, 1942; Colbert, Koegler, & Markham, 1959; Freeman & Rodnick, 1942; Leach, 1960) and pupillary hypofunction in response to pain, light, or exercise (May, 1948). Astrup (1962) found inadequate vascular responses to cold in all types of schizophrenia, and Hall and Stride (1954) reported higher thresholds to thermal pain. Reduced GSR responses have been noted to Hock, Kubis, and Ronke (1944), Jurko et al. (1952) and Solomon et al. (1939).

Execpt for the GSR, hyporeactivity in chronic patients may be partly a function of their higher basal levels. The "law of initial values" (Lacey, 1956; Wilder, 1950) predicts reduced responses when psychological systems approach homeostatic limits. Williams' (1953) and Reynolds' (1962) data are consistent with this hypothesis. The latter author found that normals had the lowest basal levels and showed a typical increase in functioning under stress. Reactive schizophrenics displayed a reduced response but a higher base level; process patients yielded the highest initial values and showed the least change. Separating reactivity from base level will prove to be even more difficult if, as Shakow (1963) suggests, the rate of adaptation to stimuli is significantly slower in schizophrenics than normals.

Reactivity is often less in chronic than acute schizophrenics, and lower in process than reactive patients. Malmo and Shagass (1949) reported that early schizophrenics are hyperreactive and resemble anxiety neurotics in the EMG response to pain. Chronic patients showed a reduced muscular response to the same stimulus, although this was not true for heart rate (Malmo et al., 1951). King (1958) found reactive schizophrenics hospitalized less than 8 weeks to be hyperreactive to mecholyl. Process schizophrenics proved to be hyporeactive. DeVault (1957) reported negative heart rate changes to his experimental stimuli in process patients, while reactive schizophrenics tended to show the same positive increases as normal controls.

Venables and Wing (1962) studied the relationship between arousal and ratings on a withdrawal scale (Venables & O'Connor, 1959) by schizophrenic patients' charge nurse. Arousal was measured by the two-flash threshold and the skin potential response. With the exception of those deluded patients who showed no incoherence of speech (essentially intact paranoid schizophrenics), increased physiological arousal was associated with increased ratings of social withdrawal.

The above findings are provocative but difficult to relate to other research. Most workers have measured resistance to an exosomatic current, a procedure not directly comparable with the recording of endosomatic potentials. Furthermore, the visual threshold measure has been infrequently used with psychiatric patients. In one study King (1962c) found no difference between schizophrenics and normals on the two-flash threshold, but his sample was small and distinctions within schizophrenics were not made. More recently Venables (1963b) repeated his results for withdrawal and found the two-flash threshold to be significantly related to the extent irrelevant information disturbed the card sorting behavior of nonparanoid schizophrenics. He also reported

(Venables, 1963a) that, while normals are unaffected, the thresholds of schizophrenic patients are significantly altered by coincident noise. Further study of these phenomena is needed.

Funkenstein (1951) reported that amelioration of schizophrenic pathology is associated with a reduction in basal systolic blood pressure. Gellhorn (1953) and Gunderson (1953) also found that improvement in schizophrenia is correlated with a reduction in the ANS basal level of functioning. Weckowicz (1958) reported that reduced blood pressure response to the mecholyl test is associated with deteriorated size constancy. He suggested that the hyporeactivity in these patients is attributable to higher basal levels of sympathetic activity. An increase in GSR with clinical improvement has been noted by Solomon et al. (1939) and Hock et al. (1944). Finally, Reynolds (1962) found that polygraph profiles of schizophrenics receiving tranquilizing medication were more like those of normals than those of patients off medication at the time of his experiment.[5]

Reactivity and the properties of the stimulus. Paintal (1951) reported that psychotics gave a reduced GSR response to threat of pain. Ray (1963) failed to confirm this finding in a study of female schizophrenics, but he obtained significant set differences. With instructions simply to listen to a list of "loaded" and "neutral" words, no difference in GSR between schizophrenics and normals was noted; with instructions to respond with an association, however, the normal GSR increased considerably more than that of the schizophrenics. This was true regardless of whether the schizophrenics proved to be "adequate" or "inadequate" verbal responders. Furthermore, while the GSRs of normals were greatest to the loaded words under both conditions, the schizophrenics yielded differential responses only when actually responding.

Venables (1960) found that the GSR of schizophrenic subjects varies with the stimulus context in a manner similar to RT. Schizophrenic and normal subjects were presented discrete visual and auditory stimuli, with or without a continuous, collateral stimulus of the opposite modality. The experimental conditions did

---

[5] Tourney et al. (1962) reported that chronic schizophrenics show a disturbance in the mechanism concerned with the transformation of chemical to kinetic energy which seems to parallel the findings cited in this section. The specific activity of chemicals involved in carbohydrate breakdown is greater under basal conditions in chronic schizophrenic patients than normal subjects. However, the mobilization of these products in response to stimulation was significantly less in those patients than in normal controls.

not significantly affect the GSR of normal subjects. A low illumination and quiet condition was compared with a bright illumination and noisy condition; in "active schizophrenics" the former yielded more GSRs which were of greater intensity and shorter latency. In withdrawn schizophrenics the bright, noisy condition produced the same number of GSRs as the quiet condition, but latency was shorter. Thus, as with RT, additional stimuli appear to modify the speed of response, with the most intense stimuli affecting withdrawn schizophrenics the most.

Venables recalled that any sensory input may serve both a cue and a nonspecific arousal function (Hebb, 1955) and that this latter dimension may describe an inverted ∪ function (Malmo, 1958). He suggested that with moderate stimulation active schizophrenics function at an optimal level. With increased intensity there is a paradoxical depression of response. On the other hand, moderate stimuli are less effective for withdrawn patients, and increases in stimulus intensity improve performance in a linear fashion. Unfortunately, no information was provided about basal potentials under both conditions of stimulation, rendering the results and the interpretation inconclusive.

Leach (1960) studied ocular nystagmus in response to rotation at various acceleration speeds. He reported that

with increasing intensity of the stimulus schizophrenic deficit decreased. This tendency is demonstrated most clearly in latency of nystagmus to onset rotation. Schizophrenic deficit was less than one-fourth for moderate and strong intensities than for a mild intensity [p. 308].

The response of normals remained relatively constant in relation to changes in stimulus intensity. These findings parallel those of Venables and Tizard (1958), Lang (1959), and King (1962b), who reported a decrease in relative psychomotor deficit with increases in the physical intensity of the stimulus. The fact that the semicircular canals regulate muscle tonus in the body lends added meaning to this parallel. Furthermore, Angyal and Blackman (1940) showed an association within schizophrenia between nystagmic deficit and disturbance in muscular tonus.

Reduced caloric and rotational nystagmus has also been reported in childhood schizophrenia. Colbert, Koegler, and Markham (1959) found that all the subjects in the sample for whom nystagmus was absent carried the schizophrenic diagnosis. When nystagmus was present, the shorter its duration, the greater the probability of schizophrenia. It is interesting to note that, as with psychomotor behavior (King, 1954, 1961), intraindividual variability was as pathognomic for schizophrenia as the reduced response. These authors ruled out the possibility that a lesion in the major vestibular pathways could be the causal agent because none of the usual collateral symptoms were observed. They speculated that vestibular activity may be inhibited at the level of the caudal midbrain, in a manner neurologically analogous to the inhibition of auditory attention demonstrated by Hernandez-Péon and Associates (1956).

Another approach suggests that both vestibular and psychomotor deficit are attributable to a disturbance of proprioception. Rosenbaum et al. (1959) using shock and no shock conditions studied simple RT of chronic schizophrenics and normal subjects who were administered either LSD-25, amobarbital sodium, or phencyclidine hydrochloride (sernyl). Under nonshock conditions, the sernyl normals and schizophrenics had significantly slower latencies than the other two drug groups. With shock, both the schizophrenics and the sernyl subjects reduced their scores to the level of the other subjects. Similar parallels between schizophrenic and sernyl normals were noted in rotary pursuit learning and weight discrimination. Unlike LSD-25, sernyl seems to produce primary, rather than secondary, schizophrenic symptoms. Furthermore, when it is administered to schizophrenic patients, pathology is markedly exacerbated, and this condition may last for several weeks (Luby, Gottlieb, Cohen, Rosenbaum, & Domino, 1962).

In normal subjects sernyl depresses "central integrating mechanisms involving various sensory modalities such as touch, pain, and proprioception [Luby et al., 1962, p. 64]"; subjects report alterations of body image and feelings of estrangement and unreality, and they display progressive disorganization of thought, inability to maintain set, and impairment of abstract thinking. The drug effects show a further parallel to schizophrenia in that increased levels of respiratory and cardiovascular activity have been reported (Meyer, Greifenstein, & Devault, 1959). Cohen, Rosenbaum, Luby, & Gottlieb (1962) studied the effects of schizophrenia, sernyl, LSD, and amytal on proverb interpretation and a serial sevens task. Under nondrug conditions, the normal groups were superior to the schizophrenic patients. LSD and amytal produced insignificant decrements in the performance of the normals. However, sernyl subjects approximated the level of the patients. Cohen et al. (1962) proposed that both sernyl normals and schizophrenics suffer from a basic proprioceptive deficit, this failure of feedback accounting for both psychomotor and cognitive disturbance.

The S is impaired in his ability to provide himself with those response-produced cues which normally function to enhance stimulus discrimination and relevant response selection [p. 84].

This formulation meaningfully parallels the hypothesized breakdown in self-instruction previously raised to account for the findings of verbal reinforcement studies (Buss & Lang, 1965).

The fact that schizophrenics display increased deficit when many competing stimuli are present has already been amply documented. Recently a number of researchers have reported a decrease in behavior disturbance under conditions of decreased stimulation. Cohen, Rosenbaum, Dobe, and Gottlieb (1959), Harris (1959), and Smith, Thakurdas, and Lawes (1961) all found that schizophrenics who have experienced sensory deprivation show less discomfort and some improvement under these conditions. Reitman and Cleveland (1964) reported that schizophrenics showed an increase in tactile sensitivity and gave more accurate estimates of body size, following sensory deprivation. These positive effects were not observed in similarly treated normal subjects.

Cohen, Luby, Rosenbaum, and Gottlieb (1960) and Lawes (1963) studied the effects of sensory deprivation on normal subjects who had been administered sernyl. Like schizophrenics, sernyl normals evidenced less disorder of thought, attention, and perception under deprivation conditions than under normal conditions of stimulation. Lawes suggested that the schizophrenic is overwhelmed by normal levels of external stimulation and incapable of managing sensory inputs. Callaway and Dembo (1958) described a narrowing of attention which they related to a kind of crowding out of meaningful stimuli by the high level of central sympathetic activity. These authors also reported disturbance of size constancy, reduced EMG, GSR reactivity, and learning deficit produced by drugs that initiate widespread sympathetic activity (nerve gas, amylnitrite, and amphetamine).

There are few studies of cortical responsivity in schizophrenia that can be meaningfully related to psychological deficit. EEG abnormalities have frequently been reported (Ellingson, 1954), but differences have too often been judged rather than measured. Gromoll (1961) tested the hypothesis that reactive schizophrenics would be more responsive and show higher levels of cortical arousal than process patients or controls. No significant difference between groups were obtained on such measures as alpha blocking. However, the author reported that process subjects, rather than reactive schizophrenics, tended to maintain the highest activation levels.

Shagass and Schwartz (1961) have developed techniques for studying evoked responses in the somatosensory cortex of man. Subjects receive electric shock to the wrist, and potentials are recorded from EEG surface electrodes. By repeating the stimulation and averaging across trials, the form of evoked potentials may be determined. In a number of experiments a trial has consisted of two shocks separated by an interval varying in milliseconds. Normal subjects, neurotic depressives, and anxiety patients showed a response to the second shock at around 20 milliseconds that equalled the initial evoked potential. Psychotic depressives and schizophrenics showed a much reduced response in this early recovery phase (Shagass & Schwartz, 1961, 1962). Data consistent with these findings were reported by Purpura, Pool, Ransohoff, Freeman, and Houspian (1957), who found that the direct stimulation of the exposed human cortex yielded much later recovery in two schizophrenic patients than in the nondiseased cortex of a patient with a tumor.

Shagass and Schwartz (1963) also studied the effects of shock intensity on evoked cortical potentials in different psychiatric patients. They reported that the intensity response gradients of a mixed group of patients (including schizophrenics and psychotic depressives) were steeper than those of normal subjects or dysthymic patients. These data parallel the intensity gradients obtained for RT and suggest that studies relating cortical potentials and psychomotor behavior may be of considerable value in studying schizophrenia.

Summary

The picture of schizophrenic deficit that emerges from these findings is remarkably consistent across a number of very different response systems. Latency and/or amplitude of psychomotor, vestibular, cardiovascular, sweat gland, and cortical EEG responses are reduced, relative to normal subjects. In at least three of the above systems and in verbal association, excessive intraindividual variability of response has also proved to be pathognomic of schizophrenic disorder. In addition, the levels of cardiovascular activity and muscular tension are unusually high among these patients. All these behaviors—reduced responsivity, deterioration of associational or psychomotor control, and high somatic tension—are positively related to increased withdrawal or clinically judged exacerbation of the illness. They are more marked for chronic and process schizophrenics than for acute and reactive patients. These relationships do not appear to hold for relatively intact paranoids, and perhaps not for early schizophrenics (recent, first admissions).

The experimental manipulation of stimulus intensity has yielded consistent data in studies of RT, ocular nystagmus, and cortical potentials. Deficit in chronic schizophrenia is greatest for low-intensity inputs and least when stimulus amplitude is high. Related to these findings are results of distractibility experiments, which reveal both the schizophrenic's susceptibility to irrelevant cues and his improved performance when background noise is reduced.

A host of studies indicate set disturbances in schizophrenia. On the one hand, schizophrenics are unable to maintain response readiness, and response latency increases if stimuli are presented in more than one modality. On the other hand, these patients seem unduly influenced by a previous set, and responses persist long after they are demonstrably ineffective.

In general, the hypothesis that schizophrenic deficit is attributable to the interference of competing stimuli, internal or external, receives considerable support. The theory that schizophrenics are underaroused may be maintained only if studies of activity level are ignored. This latter research argues that even long-term chronic patients may be physiologically hyperaroused relative to normal subjects, although the frequency and amplitude of overt behavior is greatly reduced.

Discussion

Theory

In the previous review (Buss & Lang, 1965) three general theories of schizophrenic deficit were considered. The first of these can be roughly described as social or interpersonal in emphasis: deficit is variously attributed to social censure, oversensitivity to affective stimuli, or lowered social motivation. The second approach holds that schizophrenic deficit is a consequence of regression. A third view argues that associative interference underlies many instances of the schizophrenic's behavior disturbance.

Regression theory received little support from data summarized in the first paper, and the current review adds nothing that alters conclusions drawn there. In this discussion, three motivational constructs (social motivation, drive, and arousal) and a more broadly conceived interference theory will be considered as explanations of schizophrenic deficit.

Social motivation. The hypothesis that schizophrenics suffer from lowered social motivation was examined in the previous review. It was seen that schizophrenics and normals respond similarly to general encouragement or chastisement on laboratory tasks. Furthermore, when specific responses are reinforced, differences between groups may be attributed to the greater value of information about performance for the schizophrenic subject. A guidance function is served for patients, which normals apparently provide for themselves. For example, punishment breaks up the perseverative behavior of psychotics, resulting in a closer approximation of normal performance.

The fact that schizophrenics improve more than normals when aversive, physical reinforcers are used has been interpreted to mean that schizophrenics' response to social reward is reduced. However, the research reviewed in the present paper suggests that the intense stimuli employed in these experiments serve to emphasize relevant cues and focus attention, rather than function as special motivators for an indifferent patient.

Some theorists argue that the schizophrenic's problem is not *undersensitivity* to social motivators; it is held that their *oversensitivity* to the affective meaning of stimuli disrupts performance. While affective stimuli may increase deficit, this property is not restricted to one type, such as social censure. In fact, the considerable variety of stimuli (symbolic, human versus nonhuman, etc.) capable of producing these effects calls into questions the value of a category so loosely defined. In the previous paper, the authors suggested that the deficit produced by so-called affective or emotionally arousing stimuli is due to an inability to inhibit irrelevant associations. Most of these stimuli instigate more associations than do the neutral comparison stimuli. Evidence presented here indicates that the capacity to suppress *any* intruding cognition is greatly reduced in schizophrenia.

In summary, the hypotheses that schizophrenics are indifferent to social stimuli or particularly sensitive to the affective meaning of stimuli, have very limited value. Experiments relevant to both views are more parsimoniously interpreted in the context of interference theory, which will be reconsidered after a discussion of drive and arousal.

Drive. Negative drive theory applies Pavlov's notion of protective inhibition in schizophrenia to the learning process. Specifically, schizophrenics are held to develop reactive inhibition faster than normals and should therefore show greater reminiscence. Concerning reactive inhibition, there is no consistent evidence that schizophrenics classically condition slower than normals. Concerning reminiscence, the results are similar: no established difference between schizophrenics and normals. It seems safe to conclude that negative drive theory is incorrect.

Mednick, labeling the potential schizophrenic as high-anxious, used the Spence-Taylor approach in making predictions: faster conditioning in simple situations, slower conditioning in complex situations, and flattened generalization gradients. As we showed earlier, these predictions have received only weak support, and there is strong opposing evidence. Thus Mednick's theory has, in general, not been sustained by research findings.

What appears to be wrong with the theory is its specification of anxiety as the crucial drive that leads to schizophrenia. While it is true that many schizophrenics appear anxious, this could as readily be a reaction to incapacity as a cause of it. The theory is embarrassed not only because the predictions from anxiety theory are not supported but also because more chronic and severe schizophrenics show less clinical anxiety. The fact that chronic, withdrawn patients frequently have high-somatic activity levels appears partially to save the theory. However, Mednick has already explained that the chronic schizophrenic's associational defense successfully eliminates anxiety!

These weaknesses of Mednick's theory do not necessarily apply to all drive theories. In fact, drive theory can be shown to be consistent with much research evidence if it is assumed that: (a) it is a generalized drive state rather than a specific one such as anxiety, and (b) generalized drive can be measured by, or is the same as, physiological arousal. Two sets of facts seem to fit a generalized drive theory. First, schizophrenics tend to be over-aroused, the physiological hyperactivity varying directly with chronicity and/or severity. Second, schizophrenic deficit also varies directly with chronicity and/or severity. These facts can be combined in a causal sequence: schizophrenic deficit is due to the disruptive effects of an excessively high arousal or generalized drive state. Stated this way drive theory can be seen to be one variant of interference theory.

Arousal. Complementary to drive theory is what may be called arousal theory. This view was originally based on the neurological speculations of Hebb (1955) and Lindsley (1951), the EEG work of the latter, and studies of the ANS and muscle tension system by Freeman (1948), Duffy (1962) and Malmo (1958). This conception orders behavior on a continuum from deep sleep to intense excitement. These behavioral states are held to be a function of the degree of diffuse activity in the lower brain, particularly in the reticular formation. From this site collateral impulses ascend to the cortex and descend to the ANS. Alertness, attention, and reactivity are thus determined by the organism's level of "arousal." As with the social motivational point of view, schizophrenics have been held to be both overaroused and underaroused.

The hypothesis that schizophrenics suffer from an underactive arousal mechanism would seem to receive support from studies demonstrating psychomotor and physiological hyporeactivity in chronic patients. However, Malmo (1958) argues cogently that activation is measured more directly in studies of basal physiological level than in research on responsivity. Thus, studies showing high resting somatic activity in schizophrenia would indicate that schizophrenics are generally hyperaroused rather than the opposite. Furthermore, their reduced responsivity is not inconsistent with this view. Malmo (1958), Lacey (1956), and Wilder (1950) have all presented evidence that responsivity progressively decreases when plotted on an abscissa of increasing activation (defined by base activity level). A similar function is obtained in normal subjects when "adequacy of performance" in a complex psychological task replaces responsivity on the ordinate. These facts not only argue that testable chronic schizophrenics are habitually in a hyperaroused state, but in this context the performance deterioration of schizophrenics appears to be analogous to the psychological stress response of a normal subject. However, the symmetry of this analogy is only apparent. Whereas it is complex functioning of normal subjects that mainly suffers under stress (while perhaps more primitive and less adequate but well organized responses emerge), the schizophrenic patient shows deterioration of the simplest and most fundamental behaviors. For example, the schizophrenic performs poorly on a RT task, not because he is anxious, an overready impulsive responder, but because the stimulus seems to arrive unexpectedly. He is not prepared or set, and the response is slow and reduced in amplitude. The psychomotor performance of chronic schizophrenics is more similar to that of aged normals or young adults with general cerebral damage than to that of psychologically stressed normals or anxiety neurotics.

In summary, the underarousal theory of schizophrenia, in terms of the nonspecific projection system, is directly contradicted by most of the psychophysiological research reviewed here, and it may be considered incorrect. The hypothesis that schizophrenics are overaroused receives some support. However, the exact mechanism by which overarousal can produce hyporesponsivity, high-response variability, inattention, disturbances of set and association, and the other symptoms of chronic schizophrenia is yet to be explained.

Interference theory. Interference theory has focused mainly on association and attention-set. The associations of schizophrenics are idiosyncratic and deviant, and they deteriorate performance because they serve as distractors. Schizophrenics have difficulty in focusing on relevant stimuli and excluding irrelevant stimuli, in maintaining a set over time, in shifting a set when it is necessary, in instructing themselves and in pacing themselves, and generally in performing efficiently, in Wishner's sense (1955). These difficulties are pervasive, occurring over a wide range of perceptual, motor, and cognitive tasks. In brief, interference theory, as a broad explanation of schizophrenic deficit, has clearly been supported by research findings and appears to be the only theory comprehensive enough to account for what is known.

The generality of interfering effects suggests a fundamental sensori-motor defect. However, the reactions of patients vary somewhat according to subtype. The defect is seen most clearly in the behavior of chronic, withdrawn patients; acute schizophrenics and particularly early paranoids seem to be compensating for their disability. In many tasks they are overprecise or overresponsive. The fact that in some experiments, among paranoid schizophrenics only the most chronic cases show deficit, suggests that their bizarre attempts at organizing the world may have functional value. Support is gained for Bleuler's contention that many of these behaviors are secondary symptoms—responses to the fundamental disturbance, rather than intrinsic expressions of it.

The locus of the sensori-motor defect is a matter for speculation. It seems clear that the defect is not at the level of the peripheral sensors[6] or effectors, although feedback from the musculature and the ANS may contribute to the disturbance. Lacey and Lacey (1958a) suggest that attention, set, and psychomotor control are directly influenced by autonomic feedback. They propose the carotid sinus as one such steering mechanism: blood pressure changes stimulate the carotid, which has "a profound tonic and inhibitory effect" on cortical electrical activity, and thus alters the organism's orientation to the environment. Furthermore, these re-

---

[6] Schizophrenics are no different from normals in pure tone threshold and speech reception but are disrupted more quickly and easily by auditory feedback and noise (Ludwig, Wood, & Downs, 1962).

searchers have demonstrated a relationship between cardiac variability and failure to inhibit psychomotor responses. Recently, they have also shown that heart rate changes correlate with RT fore-period effects. This raises the interesting possibility that the motor and perceptual symptoms of schizophrenia are related to defects in this carotid-cortical mechanism.

The disturbance that appears in all studies of deficit concerns the initiation of responses to selected stimuli and the inhibition of inappropriate responses. All intelligent behavior represents a compromise between the demands of the immediate environment and a previously established set of the organism, but the schizophrenic makes a uniquely poor bargain. External stimuli, associational and biological "noise," routinely suppressed by normal subjects, intrude, and responses to the appropriate stimuli are not made.

These facts suggest that researchers in schizophrenia should concentrate on the processes by which stimuli adapt out or habituate and response competition is resolved. The ascending reticular activating system is the neurological site of greatest relevance. In addition to general arousal, this system appears to have a specific alerting or focusing function. Hernandes-Péon and his associates (1956) demonstrated that cortical potentials in the cochlear nucleus of the cat, normally elicited by a tone, were suppressed when a competing odor of fish or a jar of mice was simultaneously presented. These authors write:

> Attention involves the selective awareness of certain sensory messages with the simultaneous suppression of others. . . . During the attentive state, it seems as though the brain integrates for consciousness only a limited amount of sensory information, specifically, those impulses concerned with the object of attention [p. 332].

The data on schizophrenic deficit are consistent with the hypothesis that such sensory inhibition centers are defective. These centers and the related behavior should be given extensive study in schizophrenic patients.

Methodological Considerations

It is appropriate that a research review should conclude on a methodological note. The issues raised are many, and their listing amounts to a set of guidelines and admonishments to future investigators.

1. A number of studies have shown that schizophrenics as a group are more variable than normals, and no one regards the

nonpsychiatric population as being especially homogeneous. Furthermore, schizophrenics are known to vary in the extent of deficit in relation to several variables which are usually dichotomized: mild-severe, acute-chronic, reactive-process, good premorbid-poor premorbid, and paranoid-nonparanoid. It seems likely that these variables overlap, but empirical data are limited. We need studies relating these dimensions of schizophrenia to each other, as well as more precise data on their relation to deficit.

The paranoid-nonparanoid dichotomy is of special interest. For over a century there has been doubt about including paranoids under the heading of schizophrenia or keeping them separate as "paranoid conditions." Paranoids have been found to show less deficit (e.g., Payne & Hewlitt, 1960), and clinically they have been observed to show less thought disorder and less deterioration over time than have schizophrenics of other subgroups. However, these statements are not true of all paranoids; some patients with delusions do manifest considerable deficit and deterioration of thought processes. Perhaps the presence of delusions is less important than the relative absence of deficit. Stated another way, perhaps the important dimension is intactness of sensori-motor and intellectual processes, and the paranoid-nonparanoid distinction partially reflects or is partially correlated with this dimension.

Recently Johannsen and his associates (1963) examined correlations between different measures used to describe schizophrenics. High correlations were found between placement on process-reactive, acute-chronic, and good-poor premorbid scales. Only the paranoid-nonparanoid dimension appeared to be an independent dimension. Furthermore, this latter dichotomy was the only one that yielded a significant difference on a double alternation learning task. Whether delusional behavior is an epiphenomenon in low-deficit schizophrenics or a positive effort to reduce deficit as was suggested earlier, future investigators must consider paranoid symptoms in selecting experimental samples.

A less known source of variability among schizophrenics may be found in sex differences. The subjects in most research have been men, with a minority of experiments including both sexes or using women only. It is possible that results found with men cannot be generalized to women, and sex differences might account for some of the discrepancies in results that occur among studies otherwise comparable.

The importance of this issue is pointed up by Schooler's (1963) study of affiliation. He found that the relationships that held for men did not hold for women, and vice versa, which led him to conclude:

A major implication of the study is that theories based on experimental findings with one sex cannot be generalized to explain the behavior of chronic schizophrenics of the other sex [p. 445].

2. In many instances the range of tasks used to study deficit is not sufficient to sustain the broad conclusions of the investigators. For example, on the basis of demonstrated deficiency on conceptual tasks, some researchers have concluded that the basic problem of schizophrenic deficit is an inability to handle concepts. Taken at face value, this conclusion is an overgeneralization because of the absence of evidence that schizophrenics show no deficit on non-conceptual tasks. In the light of the evidence with nonconceptual tasks, the conclusion is patently false. Generalizations about schizophrenic deficit require a sampling of tasks that tap a variety of psychological functions.

It would be of considerable help if we knew more about what various tasks are measuring and their relations to each other. The appropriate tool is factor analysis, which has been employed mainly by English researchers such as Payne and his collaborators (Payne, Mattussek, & George, 1959; Payne & Hewlitt, 1960).

3. When the investigator is interested in particular characteristics of his stimuli, a special problem may arise. He may assume, for example, that some of his stimuli are "affect-laden" without having any evidence for this assertion. A priori statements that stimuli differ along a dimension such as "emotionally arousing" cannot be accepted. It behooves the investigator to present evidence on this point, and the evidence must be independent of the effects obtained with his dependent variable. A similar problem appeared in studies of positive and negative incentives. These experiments were generally interpreted in a social-motivational context, while the more important differences in the degree of information conveyed by these stimuli were largely ignored.

4. General methodological problems in psychophysiological research have been adequately described elsewhere (Lacey, 1956; Lacey & Lacey, 1958b). However, these difficulties are accentuated when schizophrenics are the experimental subjects. For example, the low-positive correlations between physiological measures noted in studies of normal subjects may be lower or even negative in schizophrenics. Single measures of arousal or drive are necessarily

misleading. Thus, hypoactivity in schizophrenia is frequently found for skin resistance, while muscle tension is generally reported to be high. Such results are provocative, and further study of relationships between sweat gland, cardiovascular, and muscle tension systems may prove valuable.

The pervasive use of drugs in the treatment of psychosis creates problems for both the behavioral and psychophysiological investigator. For example, Reynolds (1962) found a significant interaction between diagnostic subtype (process-reactive) and tranquilizer-nontranquilizer conditions in a study of somatic responses in schizophrenia. No research should be undertaken unless the drug variable is properly controlled.

Researchers have begun to emphasize individual variability in behavioral studies of schizophrenia. Investigations of somatic inter- and intrasession variability are also needed. Furthermore, there may be profit in studying somatic responses recorded concurrently with tasks that elicit deficit. Lacey and Lacey (1958a) have reported important relationships between autonomic activity and psychomotor functioning in normals, and studies cited here encourage this experimental strategy.

Better estimates are needed of resting somatic activity levels. Despite the elaborate care of some investigators, what purport to be differences in basal levels between psychotics and normals may actually be differences in reaction to the laboratory situation. Long-term studies are needed in which information is telemetered from patients while they proceed with the usual hospital routine.

5. While only psychological deficit in schizophrenia has been considered in this review, it is important to reaffirm that these patients share many of the characteristics of deficit with other psychiatric disorders and cases of cerebral damage. The psychomotor retardation, inattention, increased response variability, muscle tension and ANS hyperactivity, and even to some extent the associative disturbance, may be found in many aged, paretic, severe epileptic, or arterial sclerotic patients. Deficit behavior can be produced in normal subjects through the administration of drugs or surgical intervention, and there is some evidence that it may be manipulated by brain stimulation (Heath, 1954).

There is ample evidence that severity of psychopathology and psychological deficit are positively related. Some theorists hold that this is the only meaningful relationship between deficit and diagnosis, and they argue that specific consideration of schizophrenia is superfluous. They emphasize the unity of deficit in psychiatric illness and suggest a common neurological defect underlies all its manifestations.

Certainly, further demonstrations that schizophrenics differ from normals are not needed. If the schizophrenic label has experimental validity, the deficit specific to this diagnosis must be more clearly defined. Are variables such as maternal censure or pictures of hospital aids uniquely important to the behavior of schizophrenics, or might they similarly influence the responses of other patient groups? An answer to this question can only come from studies employing control subjects other than normals, i.e., anxiety neurotics, aged, epileptic, brain-damaged or other chronically ill patients. While some experiments have compared schizophrenics to these groups, the evidence is fragmentary and the interpretations usually emphasize the safer, more reliable distinction between normality and psychosis.

The theoretical point of studies in this area often needs sharpening. Deficit is simply performance decrement. In trying to explain it we must distinguish between what is basic to the disorder and what is epiphenomenal. For example: Is the schizophrenic's anxiety the instigator of deficit, or is it an individual reaction to an insidious and pervasive sensori-motor defect? Issues of this type will tax the ingenuity of the behavioral researcher.

In summary, the problem of psychological deficit remains as broad and as challenging now as in 1944. However, the last 20 years have done much to clarify fundamental symptoms and define conditions which increase or decrease deficit. Many theories have failed to receive empirical support and may now be discarded. Fruitful lines of investigation have also been revealed, and the researcher today, guided by this work, is better equipped to discover the basic nature of schizophrenia.

REFERENCES

Acker, C. W. An investigation of the variability in repeated psychophysiological measurements in tranquilized mental patients. *American Psychologist*, 1963, **18**, 454. (Abstract)

Altschule, M. D., & Sulzbach, W. M. Effect of carbon dioxide on acrocyanosis in schizophrenia. *Archives of Neurology and Psychiatry*, 1949, **61**, 44-55.

Angyal, A. The perceptual basis of somatic delusions in a case of schizophrenia. *Archives of Neurology and Psychiatry*, 1935, **34**, 270-279.

Angyal, A. The experience of the body-self in schizophrenia. *Archives of Neurology and Psychiatry*, 1936, **35**, 1029-1053.

Angyal, A., & Blackman, N. Vestibular reactivity in schizophrenia. *Archives of Neurology and Psychiatry*, 1940, **44**, 611-620.

Angyal, A., & Blackman, N. Paradoxical vestibular reactivity in schizophrenia under influence of alcohol, of hyperpnea and CO_2 inhalation. *American Journal of Psychiatry*, 1941, **97**, 894-903.

Angyal, A., & Sherman, N. A. Postural reactions to vestibular stimulation in schizophrenics and normal subjects. *American Journal of Psychiatry*, 1942, **98**, 857-862.

Arieti, S. *Interpretation of schizophrenia.* New York: Bruner, 1955.

Astrup, C. *Schizophrenia: Conditional reflex studies.* Springfield, Ill.: Thomas, 1962.

Barratt, E. S. CNS correlates of intra-individual variability of ANS activity. Paper read at American Psychological Association, St. Louis, September 1962.

Bender, Lauretta, & Schilder, P. Unconditioned and conditioned reactions to pain in schizophrenia. *American Journal of Psychiatry*, 1930, **87**, 365-384.

Blaufarb, H. A demonstration of verbal abstracting ability in chronic schizophrenics under enriched stimulus and instructional conditions. *Journal of Consulting Psychology*, 1962, **26**, 471-475.

Bleke, R. C. Reward and punishment as determiners of reminiscence effects in schizophrenic and normal subjects. *Journal of Personality*, 1955, **23**, 479-488.

Bleuler, E. *Dementia praecox or the group of schizophrenias.* New York: International University Press, 1950.

Buck, C. W., Carscallen, H. B., & Hobbs, G. E. Temperature regulation in schizophrenia: I. Comparison of schizophrenic and normal subjects. II. Analysis by duration of psychosis. *Archives of Neurology and Psychiatry*, 1950, **64**, 828-842.

Buss, A. H., & Lang, P. J. Psychological deficit in schizophrenia: I. Affect, reinforcement, and concept attainment. *Journal of Abnormal Psychology*, 1965, **70**, 2-24.

Calloway, E., III, & Dembo, D. Narrowed attention. *Archives of Neurology and Psychiatry*, 1958, **79**, 74-90.

Campbell, D. A study of some sensorimotor functions in psychiatric patients. Unpublished doctoral dissertation, University of London, 1957.

Carrigan, P. M. Selective variability in schizophrenia. *American Psychologist*, 1963, **18**, 427. (Abstract)

Chapman, L. J. Distractibility in the conceptual performance of schizophrenics. *Journal of Abnormal and Social Psychology*, 1956, **53**, 286-291.

Chapman, L. J. Intrusion of associative responses into schizophrenic conceptual performance. *Journal of Abnormal and Social Psychology*, 1958, **56**, 374-379.

Chapman, L. J.   Stimulus generalization and verbal behavior in schizophrenia. Paper read at Midwestern Psychological Association, Detroit, May 1962.

Chapman, J., & McGhie, A.   A comparative study of disordered attention in schizophrenia. *Journal of Mental Science*, 1962, **108**, 487-500.

Claridge, G.   The excitation-inhibition balance in neurotics. In H. J. Eysenck (Ed.), *Experiments in Personality*. Vol. 2. London: Routledge & Kegan Paul, 1960. Pp. 107-154.

Cohen, B. D., Ludy, E. E., Rosenbaum, G., & Gottlieb, J. S.   Combined sernyl and sensory deprivation. *Comprehensive Psychiatry*, 1960, **1**, 345-348.

Cohen, B. D., Rosenbaum, G., Dobe, Shirley I., & Gottlieb, J. S.   Sensory isolation: Hallucinogenic effects of a brief procedure. *Journal of Nervous and Mental Diseases*, 1959, **129**, 486-491.

Cohen, B. D., Rosenbaum, G., Luby, E. D., & Gottlieb, J. S.   Comparison of phencyclidine hydrochloride (sernyl) with other drugs. *Archives of General Psychiatry*, 1962, **6**, 395-401.

Cohen, B. D., Senf, Rita, & Huston, P. E.   Perceptual accuracy in schizophrenia, depression, and neurosis, and effects of amytal. *Journal of Abnormal and Social Psychology*, 1956, **52**, 363-367.

Cohen, M.   Ocular findings in 323 patients with schizophrenia: Preliminary report. *Archives of Opthalmology*, 1949, **41**, 697-700. (a)

Cohen, M.   Preliminary report on ocular findings in 323 schizophrenic patients. *Psychiatric Quarterly*, 1949, **23**, 667-671. (b)

Colbert, E. G., Koegler, R. R., & Markham, C. H.   Vestibular dysfunction in childhood schizophrenia. *Archives of General Psychiatry*, 1959, **1**, 600-617.

Cooper, R.   Objective measures of perception in schizophrenics and normals. *Journal of Consulting Psychology*, 1960, **24**, 209-214.

Crookes, T. G.   Size constancy and literalness in the Rorschach test. *British Journal of Medical Psychology*, 1957, **30**, 99-106.

Crumpton, Evelyn.   Persistence of maladaptive responses in schizophrenia. *Journal of Abnormal and Social Psychology*, 1963, **66**, 615-618.

DeVault, S.   Physiological responsiveness in reactive and process schizophrenia. *Dissertation Abstracts*, 1957, **17**, 1387.

Dillon, D.   Differences between ascending and descending flicker-fusion thresholds among groups of hospitalized psychiatric patients and a group of normal control persons. *Journal of Psychology*, 1959, **48**, 255-262.

Donahoe, J. W., Curtin, Mary E., & Lipton, L.   Interference effects with schizophrenic subjects in the acquisition and retention of verbal material. *Journal of Abnormal and Social Psychology*, 1961, **62**, 553-558.

Downing, R. W., Ebert, J. N., & Shubrooks, S. J.   Effects of three types of verbal distractors on thinking in acute schizophrenia. *Perceptual and Motor Skills*, 1963, **17**, 881-882.

Draguns, J. G.   Responses to cognitive and perceptual ambiguity in chronic and acute schizophrenics. *Journal of Abnormal and Social Psychology*, 1963, **66**, 24-30.

Duffy, Elizabeth. *Activation and behavior.* New York: Wiley, 1962.

Dunn, W. L.   Visual discrimination of schizophrenic subjects as a function of stimulus meaning. *Journal of Personality,* 1954, **23,** 48-64.

Edwards, A. S., & Harris, A. C.   Laboratory measurements of deterioration and improvement among schizophrenics. *Journal of General Psychology,* 1953, **49,** 153-156.

Ellingson, R. J.   Incidence of EEG abnormality among patients with mental disorders of apparently nonorganic origin: Critical review. *American Journal of Psychiatry,* 1954, **111,** 263-275.

Eysenck, H. J.   Psychosis, drive, and inhibition: A theoretical and experimental account. *American Journal of Psychiatry,* 1961, **118,** 198-204.

Eysenck, H. J., Granger, G. W., & Brengelmann, J. C.   *Perceptual processes and mental illness.* New York: Basic Books, 1957.

Faibish, G. M.   Schizophrenic response to words of multiple meaning. *Journal of Personality,* 1961, **29,** 414-427.

Feldman, M. J., & Drasgow, J.   A visual-verbal test for schizophrenia. *Psychiatric Quarterly Supplement,* 1951, Part I, 1-10.

Fenichel, O.   *The psychoanalytic theory of neurosis.* New York: Norton, 1945.

Franks, C. M.   An experimental study of conditioning as related to mental abnormality. Unpublished doctoral dissertation, University of London, 1954.

Freeman, G. L.   *The energetics of human behavior.* Ithaca: Cornell Univer. Press, 1948.

Freeman, G. L., & Pathman, J. H.   Physiological reactions of psychotics to experimentally induced displacement. *American Journal of Psychiatry,* 1943, **100,** 406-412.

Freeman, H., & Rodnick, E. H.   Autonomic and respiratory responses of schizophrenics and normal subjects to changes of intrapulmonary atmosphere. *Psychosomatic Medicine,* 1940, **2,** 101-109.

Freeman, H., & Rodnick, E. H.   Effect of rotation on postural steadiness in normal and schizophrenic subjects. *Archives of Neurology and Psychiatry,* 1942, **48,** 47-53.

Funkenstein, D. H., Greenblatt, M., & Solomon, H. C.   Autonomic changes paralleling psychological changes in mentally ill patients. *Journal of Nervous and Mental Diseases,* 1951, **114,** 1-18.

Garmezy, N.   Stimulus differentiation by schizophrenic and normal subjects under conditions of reward and punishment. *Journal of Personality,* 1952, **21,** 253-276.

Gellhorn, E.   *Physiological foundations of neurology and psychiatry.* Minneapolis: Univer. Minnesota Press, 1953.

Gellhorn, E.   *Autonomic imbalance and the hypothalamus.* Minneapolis: Univer. Minnesota Press, 1957.

Gindis, I. Z.   The pathological changes in higher nervous activity in the various forms of schizophrenia. *Pavlov Journal of Higher Nervous Activity,* 1960, **10,** 434-439.

Gould, L. N. Verbal hallucinations as automatic speech. The reactivation of dormant speech habits. *American Journal of Psychiatry*, 1950, **107**, 110-119.

Grisell, J. L., & Rosenbaum, G. Effects of auditory intensity on schizophrenic reaction time. *American Psychologist*, 1963, **18**, 394. (Abstract)

Gromoll, H. F., Jr. The process-reactive dimension of schizophrenia in relation to cortical activation and arousal. Unpublished doctoral dissertation, University of Illinois, 1961.

Gunderson, E. K. Autonomic balance in schizophrenia. Unpublished doctoral dissertation, University of California, Los Angeles, 1953.

Hall, K., & Stride, E. The varying responses to pain in psychiatric disorders: A study in abnormal psychology. *British Journal of Medical Psychology*, 1954, **27**, 48-60.

Harris, A. Sensory deprivation and schizophrenia. *Journal of Mental Science*, 1959, **105**, 235-237.

Heath, R. (Ed.) *Studies in schizophrenia*. Cambridge: Harvard Univer. Press, 1954.

Hebb, D. O. Drives and the CNS (conceptual nervous system). *Psychological Review*, 1955, **62**, 243-254.

Henschel, A., Brozek, J., & Keys, A. Indirect vasodilation in normal man and in schizophrenic patients. *Journal of Applied Physiology*, 1951, 4, 340-344.

Hernandez-Péon, R., Scherrer, H., & Jouvet, M. Modification of electrical activity in cochlear nucleus during "attention" in unanesthetized cats. *Science*, 1956, **123**, 331-332.

Higgins, J., & Mednick, S. A. Reminiscence and stage of illness in schizophrenia. *Journal of Abnormal and Social Psychology*, 1963, **66**, 314-317.

Hock, P., Kubis, J. F., & Rouke, F. L. Psychogalvanometric investigations in psychoses and other abnormal states. *Psychosomatic Medicine*, 1944, **6**, 237-243.

Hoskins, R. G. *The biology of schizophrenia*. New York: Norton, 1946.

Howe, E. S. GSR conditioning in anxiety states, normals, and chronic functional schizophrenic subjects. *Journal of Abnormal and Social Psychology*, 1958, **56**, 183-189.

Hunt, J. McV., & Cofer, C. Psychological deficit in schizophrenia. In J. McV. Hunt (Ed.), *Personality and the behavior disorders*. New York: Ronald Press, 1944. Pp. 971-1032.

Huston, P. E., & Shakow, D. Learning in schizophrenia: I. Pursuit learning. *Journal of Personality*, 1948, **17**, 52-74.

Huston, P. E., & Shakow, D. Learning capacity in schizophrenia. *American Journal of Psychiatry*, 1949, **105**, 881-888.

Huston, P. E., Shakow, D., & Riggs, L. A. Studies of motor function in schizophrenia: II. Reaction time. *Journal of General Psychology*, 1937, **16**, 39-82.

Johannsen, W. J., Friedman, S. H., Leitschuh, T. H., & Ammons, Helen. A study of certain schizophrenic dimensions and their relationship to double alternation learning. *Journal of Consulting Psychology*, 1963, **27**, 375-382. (a)

Johannsen, W. J., Friedman, S. H., & Liccione, J. V.   Visual perception as a function of chronicity in schizophrenia. *American Psychologist*, 1963, **18**, 364-365. (b) (Abstract)

Johnson, R. C., Weiss, R. L., & Zelhart, P. F.   Similarities and differences between normal and psychotic subjects in response to verbal stimuli. *Journal of Abnormal and Social Psychology*, 1964, **68**, 221-226.

Jurko, M., Jost, H., & Hill, T. S.   Pathology of the energy system: An experimental clinical study of physiological adaptiveness capacities in a non-patient, a psychoneurotic, and an early paranoid schizophrenic group. *Journal of Psychology*, 1952, **33**, 183-189.

Karras, A.   The effects of reinforcement and arousal on the psychomotor performance of chronic schizophrenics. *Journal of Abnormal and Social Psychology*, 1962, **65**, 104-111.

Kidd, Aline H.   Monocular distance perception in schizophrenics. *Journal of Abnormal and Social Psychology*, 1964, **68**, 100-103.

King, G. F.   Differential autonomic responsiveness in the process-reactive classification of schizophrenia. *Journal of Abnormal and Social Psychology*, 1958, **56**, 160-164.

King, H. E.   *Psychomotor aspects of mental disease.* Cambridge: Harvard Univer. Press, 1954.

King, H. E.   Some explorations in psychomotility. *Psychiatric Research Reports*, 1961, **14**, 62-86.

King, H. E.   Anticipatory behavior: Temporal matching by normal and psychotic subjects. *Journal of Psychology*, 1962, **53**, 425-440. (a)

King, H. E.   Reaction-time as a function of stimulus intensity among normal and psychotic subjects. *Journal of Psychology*, 1962, **54**, 299-307. (b)

King, H. E.   Two flash and flicker fusion thresholds for normal and schizophrenic subjects. *Perceptual and Motor Skills*, 1962, **14**, 517-518. (c)

Lacey, J. I.   The evaluation of autonomic responses: Toward a general solution. *Annals of the New York Academy of Sciences*, 1956, **67**, 123-164.

Lacey, J. I., & Lacey, Beatrice C.   The relationship of resting autonomic activity to motor impulsivity. *Research Publications of the Association for the Study of Nervous and Mental Diseases*, 1958, **36**, 144-209. (a)

Lacey, J. I., & Lacey, Beatrice C.   Verification and extension of the principle of autonomic response stereotypy. *American Journal of Psychology*, 1958, **71**, 50-73. (b)

Lang, P. J.   The effect of aversive stimuli on reaction time in schizophrenia. *Journal of Abnormal and Social Psychology*, 1959, **59**, 263-268.

Lang, P. J., & Luoto, K.   Mediation and associative facilitation in neurotic, psychotic, and normal subjects. *Journal of Abnormal and Social Psychology*, 1962, **64**, 113-120.

Lauro, L. P.   Recall of nouns varying in clustering tendency by normals and schizophrenics. Unpublished doctoral dissertation, New York University, 1962.

Lawes, T. C. G.   Schizophrenia, "sernyl" and sensory deprivation. *British Journal of Psychiatry*, 1963, **109**, 243-250.

Leach, W. W.   Nystagmus: An integrative neural deficit in schizophrenia. *Journal of Abnormal and Social Psychology*, 1960, **60**, 305-309.

Leibowitz, H. W., & Pishkin, V.   Perceptual size constancy in chronic schizophrenia. *Journal of Consulting Psychology*, 1961, **25**, 196-199.

Lester, J. R.   Production of associative sequences in schizophrenia and chronic brain syndrome. *Journal of Abnormal and Social Psychology*, 1960, **60**, 225-233.

Lhamon, W. T., & Goldstone, S.   The time sense. *Archives of Neurology and Psychiatry*, 1956, **76**, 625-629.

Lindsley, D. B.   Emotion. In S. S. Stevens (Ed.), *Handbook of experimental psychology*. New York: Wiley, 1951. Pp. 473-516.

Lovinger, E.   Perceptual contact with reality. *Journal of Abnormal and Social Psychology*, 1956, **52**, 87-91.

Luby, E. D., Gottlieb, J. S., Cohen, B. D., Rosenbaum, G., & Domino, E. F.   Model psychoses and schizophrenia. *American Journal of Psychiatry*, 1962, **119**, 61-67.

Ludwig, A. M., Wood, B. S., & Downs, M. P.   Auditory studies in schizophrenia. *American Journal of Psychiatry*, 1962, **119**, 122-127.

Luria, A. R.   *The nature of human conflicts*. New York: Liveright, 1932.

McDonough, J. M.   Critical flicker frequency and the spiral aftereffect with process and reactive schizophrenia. *Journal of Consulting Psychology*, 1960, **24**, 150-155.

McGhie, A., & Chapman, J.   Disorders of attention and perception in early schizophrenia. *British Journal of Medical Psychology*, 1961, **34**, 103-116.

McGinnies, E., & Adornetto, J.   Perceptual defense in normal and schizophrenic observers. *Journal of Abnormal and Social Psychology*, 1952, **47**, 833-837.

Malmo, R. B.   Experimental studies of mental patients under stress. In M. L. Reymert (Ed.), *Feelings and emotions*. New York: McGraw-Hill, 1950. Pp. 229-265.

Malmo, R. B.   Measurement of drive: An unsolved problem in psychology. In M. R. Jones (Ed.), *Nebraska Symposium on motivation*. Lincoln: Univer. Nebraska Press, 1958. Pp. 44-105.

Malmo, R. B., & Shagass, C.   Physiological studies of reaction to stress in anxiety states and early schizophrenia. *Psychosomatic Medicine*, 1949, **11**, 9-24.

Malmo, R. B., & Shagass, C.   Studies of blood pressure in psychiatric patients under stress. *Psychosomatic Medicine*, 1952, **14**, 82-93.

Malmo, R. B., Shagass, C., & Smith, A. A.   Responsiveness in chronic schizophrenia. *Journal of Personality*, 1951, **19**, 359-375.

Maltzman, I., Cohen, S., & Belloni, Marigold.   Associative behavior in normal and schizophrenic children. Technical report No. 11, 1963, University of California, Los Angeles, Contract Nonr 233 (50), Office of Naval Research.

Maltzman, I., Seymore, S., & Licht, L.   Verbal conditioning of common and uncommon word associations. *Psychological Reports*, 1962, **10**, 363-369.

Mandl, Bille Sue T.   An investigation of rigidity in paranoid schizophrenics as manifested in a perceptual task. *Dissertation Abstracts*, 1954, **14**, 2401-2402.

Martin, I.   Levels of muscle activity in psychiatric patients. *Acta Psychologia*, Amsterdam, 1956, **12**, 326-341.

May, P. R.   Pupillary abnormalities in schizophrenia and during muscular effort. *Journal of Mental Science*, 1948, **94**, 89-98.

Mednick, S. A.   Distortions in the gradient of stimulus generalization related to cortical brain damage and schizophrenia. *Journal of Abnormal and Social Psychology*, 1955, **51**, 536-542.

Mednick, S. A.   Generalization as a function of manifest anxiety and adaptation to psychological experiments. *Journal of Consulting Psychology*, 1957, **21**, 491-494.

Mednick, S. A.   A learning theory approach to research in schizophrenia. *Psychological Bulletin*, 1958, **55**, 316-327.

Meyer, J. S., Griefenstein, F., & Devault, M.   A new drug causing symptoms of sensory deprivation. *Journal of Nervous Mental Diseases*, 1959, **129**, 54-61.

Moran, L. J.   Vocabulary knowledge and usage among normal and schizophrenic subjects. *Psychological Monographs*, 1953, **67**(20, Whole No. 370).

O'Conner, N.   Reminiscence and work decrement in catatonic and paranoid schizophrenics. *British Journal of Medical Psychology*, 1957, **30**, 188-193.

O'Connor, N., & Rawnsley, K.   Two types of conditioning in psychotics and normals. *Journal of Abnormal and Social Psychology*, 1959, **58**, 157-161.

Paintal, A. S.   A comparison of the GSR in normals and psychotics. *Journal of Experimental Psychology*, 1951, **41**, 425-428.

Pavlov, I. P.   *Conditioned reflexes and psychiatry*. Oxford: Oxford Univer. Press, 1941.

Payne, R. W., & Hewlitt, J. H. G.   Thought disorder in psychotic patients. In H. J. Eysenck (Ed.), *Experiments in personality*. London: Routledge & Kegan Paul, 1960, Volume II. Pp. 3-104.

Payne, R. W., Mattussek, P., & George, E. I.   An experimental study of schizophrenic thought disorder. *Journal of Mental Science*, 1959, **105**, 627-652.

Pearl, D., & Berg, P. S. D.   Time perception and conflict arousal in schizophrenia. *Journal of Abnormal and Social Psychology*, 1963, **66**, 332-338.

Peters, H. N., & Murphree, O. D.   The conditioned reflex in the chronic schizophrenic. *Journal of Clinical Psychology*, 1954, **10**, 126-130.

Petursson, E.   Electromyographic studies of muscular tension in psychiatric patients. *Comprehensive Psychiatry*, 1962, **3**, 29-36.

Pfaffman, C., & Schlosberg, H.   The conditioned knee jerk in psychotic and normal individuals. *Journal of Psychology*, 1936, **1**, 201-206.

Pishkin, V., & Hershiser, D.   Respiration and GSR as functions of white sound in schizophrenia. *Journal of Consulting Psychology*, 1963, **27**, 330-337.

Pishkin, V., Smith, T. P., & Leibowitz, H. W. The influence of symbolic stimulus value on perceived size in chronic schizophrenia. *Journal of Consulting Psychology*, 1962, **26**, 323-330.

Purpura, D. P., Pool, J. L., Ransohoff, J., Freeman, H. J., & Housepian, E. M. Observations on evoked dendritic potentials of the human cortex. *EEG and Clinical Neurophysiology*, 1957, **9**, 453-459.

Rabin, A. I. Time estimation of schizophrenics and nonpsychotics. *Journal of Clinical Psychology*, 1957, **13**, 88-90.

Rachman, S. Disinhibition and the reminiscence effect in a motor learning task. *British Journal of Psychology*, 1962, **53**, 149-157.

Rachman, S. Inhibition and disinhibition in schizophrenics. *Archives of General Psychiatry*, 1963, **8**, 91-98.

Rausch, H. L. Perceptual constancy in schizophrenia: 1. Size constancy. *Journal of Personality*, 1952, **21**, 176-187.

Raush, H. L. Object constancy in schizophrenia: The enhancement of symbolic objects and conceptual stability. *Journal of Abnormal and Social Psychology*, 1956, **52**, 231-234.

Ray, T. S. Electrodermal indications of levels of psychological disturbance in chronic schizophrenia. *American Psychologist*, 1963, **18**, 393. (Abstract)

Reisman, M. N. Size constancy in schizophrenics and normals. Unpublished doctoral dissertation, University of Buffalo, 1961.

Reitman, E. E., & Cleveland, S. E. Changes in body image following sensory deprivation in schizophrenic and control groups. *Journal of Abnormal and Social Psychology*, 1964, **68**, 168-176.

Reynolds, D. J. An investigation of the somatic response system in chronic schizophrenia. Unpublished doctoral dissertation, University of Pittsburgh, 1962.

Reynolds, G. A. Perceptual constancy in schizophrenics and "normals." *Dissertation Abstracts*, 1954, **14**, 1000-1001.

Rodnick, E. H., & Shakow, D. Set in the schizophrenic as measured by a composite reaction time index. *American Journal of Psychiatry*, 1940, **97**, 214-225.

Rosenbaum, G., Cohen, B. D., Luby, E. D., Gottleib, J. S., & Yelen, D. Comparison of sernyl with other drugs. *Archives of General Psychiatry*, 1959, **1**, 651-656.

Rosenthal, D., Lawlor, W. G., Zahn, T. P., & Shakow, D. The relationship of some aspects of mental set to degree of schizophrenic disorganization. *Journal of Personality*, 1960, **28**, 26-38.

Rubin, L. Patterns of adrenergic-cholinergic imbalance in the functional psychoses. *Psychological Review*, 1962, **69**, 501-519.

Salzinger, K. Shift in judgement of weights as a function of anchoring stimuli and instructions in early schizophrenics and normals. *Journal of Abnormal and Social Psychology*, 1957, **55**, 43-49.

Sanders, R., & Pacht, A. R.   Perceptual size constancy in known clinical groups. *Journal of Consulting Psychology*, 1952, **16**, 440-444.

Schooler, C.   Affiliation among schizophrenics: Preferred characteristics of the other. *Journal of Nervous and Mental Diseases*, 1963, **137**, 438-446.

Shagass, C., & Schwartz, M.   Reactivity cycle of somatosensory cortex in humans with and without psychiatric disorder. *Science*, 1961, **134**, 1757-1759.

Shagass, G., & Schwartz, M.   Some drug effects on evoked cerebral potentials in man. *Journal of Neuropsychiatry*, 1962, **3**, 49-58.

Shagass, C., & Schwartz, M.   Cerebral responsiveness in psychiatric patients. *Archives of General Psychiatry*, 1963, **8**, 177-189.

Shakow, D.   Some psychological features of schizophrenia. In M. L. Reymert (Ed.), *Feelings and emotions*. New York: McGraw-Hill, 1950. Pp. 383-390.

Shakow, D.   Segmental Set: A theory of the formal psychological deficit in schizophrenia. *Archives of General Psychiatry*, 1962, **6**, 17-33.

Shakow, D.   Psychological deficit in schizophrenia. *Behavioral Science*, 1963, **8**, 275-305.

Shipley, W. C.   Studies of catatonia: VI. Further investigation of the perseverative tendency. *Psychiatric Quarterly*, 1934, **8**, 736-744.

Silverman, J.   Psychological deficit reduction in schizophrenia through response contingent noxious reinforcement. *Psychological Reports*, 1963, **13**, 187-210.

Smith, S., Thakurdis, H., & Lawes, T. G. G.   Perceptual isolation and schizophrenia. *Journal of Mental Science*, 1961, **107**, 839-844.

Smith, W. O.   Rotary pursuit performance in reactive and process schizophrenics. Unpublished doctoral dissertation, Michigan State University, 1959.

Smock, C. D., & Vancini, J.   Dissipation rate of the effects of social censure in schizophrenics. *Psychological Reports*, 1962, **10**, 531-536.

Snyder, S.   Perceptual closure in acute paranoid schizophrenics. *Archives of General Psychiatry*, 1961, **5**, 406-410.

Snyder, S., Rosenthal, D., & Taylor, I. A.   Perceptual closure in schizophrenia. *Journal of Abnormal and Social Psychology*, 1961, **63**, 131-136.

Solomon, A. P., Darrow, C. W., & Blaurock, M.   Blood pressure and palmer sweat (galvanic) responses of psychotic patients before and after insulin and metrazol therapy. *Psychosomatic Medicine*, 1939, **1**, 118-137.

Sommer, R., Dewar, R., & Osmond, H.   Is there a schizophrenic language? *Archives of General Psychiatry*, 1960, **3**, 665-673.

Sommer, R., Witney, Gwynneth, & Osmond, H.   Teaching common associations to schizophrenics. *Journal of Abnormal and Social Psychology*, 1962, **65**, 58-61.

Spence, Janet T., & Lair, C. V.   Associative interference in the verbal learning performance of schizophrenics and normals. *Journal of Abnormal and Social Psychology*, 1964, **68**, 204-209.

Spence, K. W., & Taylor, Janet A.   The relation of conditioned response strength to anxiety in normal, neurotic, and psychotic subjects. *Journal of Experimental Psychology*, 1953, 45, 265-277.

Sutton, S., Hakerem, G., Zubin, J., & Portnoy, M.   The effect of shift of sensory modality on serial reaction-time: A comparison of schizophrenics and normals. *American Journal of Psychology*, 1961, 74, 224-232.

Syz, H. C.   Psychogalvanic studies in schizophrenia. *Archives of Neurology and Psychiatry*, 1926, 16, 747-760.

Syz, H. C., & Kinder, E. F.   Electrical skin resistance in normal and in psychotic subjects. *Archives of Neurology and Psychiatry*, 1928, 19, 1026-1035.

Taylor, Janet A., & Spence, K. W.   Conditioning level in the behavior disorders. *Journal of Abnormal and Social Psychology*, 1954, 49, 497-502.

Tizard, J., & Venables, P. H.   Reaction time responses by schizophrenics, mental defectives, and normal adults. *American Journal of Psychiatry*, 1956, 112, 803-807.

Tizard, J., & Venables, P. H.   The influence of extraneous stimulation on the reaction time of schizophrenics. *British Journal of Psychology*, 1957, 48, 299-305.

Tourney, G., Frohman, C. E., Beckett, P. G. S., & Gottlieb, J. S.   Biochemical mechanisms in schizophrenia. In R. Roessler and N. S. Greenfield (Eds.), *Physiological correlates of psychological disorder*. Madison: Univer. Wisconsin Press, 1962.

Venables, P. H.   Factors in the motor behavior of functional psychotics. *Journal of Abnormal and Social Psychology*, 1959, 58, 153-156.

Venables, P. H.   The effect of auditory and visual stimulation on the skin potential response of schizophrenics. *Brain*, 1960, 83, 77-92.

Venables, P. H.   Changes due to noise in the threshold of fusion of paired light flashes in schizophrenics and normals. *British Journal of Social and Clinical Psychology*, 1963, 2, 94-99. (a)

Venables, P. H.   Selectivity of attention, withdrawal, and cortical activation. *Archives of General Psychiatry*, 1963, 9, 74-78. (b)

Venables, P. H., & O'Connor, N.   Reaction times to auditory and visual stimulation in schizophrenic and normal subjects. *Quarterly Journal of Experimental Psychology*, 1959, 11, 175-179.

Venables, P. H., & Tizard, J.   The effects of stimulus light intensity on the reaction time of schizophrenics. *British Journal of Psychology*, 1956, 47, 144-145. (a)

Venables, P. H., & Tizard, J.   Paradoxical effects in the reaction time of schizophrenics. *Journal of Abnormal and Social Psychology*, 1956, 53, 220-224. (b)

Venables, P. H., & Tizard, J.   Performance of functional psychotics on a repetitive task. *Journal of Abnormal and Social Psychology*, 1956, 53, 23-26. (c).

Venables, P. H., & Tizard, J.   The effect of auditory stimulus intensity on the reaction time of schizophrenics. *Journal of Mental Science*, 1958, 104, 1160-1164.

Venables, P. H., & Wing, J. K.   Level of arousal and the subclassification of schizophrenia. *Archives of General Psychiatry*, 1962, **7**, 114-119.

Weckowicz, T. E.   Size constancy in schizophrenic patients. *Journal of Mental Science*, 1957, **103**, 475-486.

Weckowicz, T. E.   Autonomic activity as measured by the Mecholyl test and size constancy in schizophrenic patients. *Psychosomatic Medicine*, 1958, **20**, 66-71.

Weckowicz, T. E.   Perception of hidden pictures by schizophrenic patients. *Archives of General Psychiatry*, 1960, **2**, 521-527.

Weckowicz, T. E.   Shape constancy in schizophrenic patients. *Journal of Abnormal and Social Psychology*, 1964, **68**, 177-183.

Weckowicz, T. E., & Blewitt, D. B.   Size constancy and abstract thinking in schizophrenic patients. *Journal of Mental Science*, 1959, **105**, 909-939.

Weckowicz, T. E., & Hall, R.   Distance constancy in schizophrenics and non-schizophrenic mental patients. *Journal of Clinical Psychology*, 1960, **16**, 272-276.

Weckowicz, T. E., Sommer, R., & Hall, R.   Distance constancy in schizophrenic patients. *Journal of Mental Science*, 1958, **104**, 1174-1182.

Wenger, M. A., Jones, N. F., & Jones, M. H.   *Physiological psychology.* New York: Holt, 1956.

Wenger, M. A.   *Evaluation of project 6, summary of proceedings: second cooperative psychological research conference.* Cincinnati: Veterans Administration Hospital, 1959.

Whatmore, C. B., & Ellis, R. M., Jr.   Some motor aspects of schizophrenia: An EMG study. *American Journal of Psychiatry*, 1958, **114**, 882-889.

Wienckowski, L. A.   Stimulus factors influencing the disjunctive reaction time of schizophrenic and "normal" subjects. Unpublished doctoral dissertation, University of Buffalo, 1959.

Wilder, J.   The law of initial values. *Psychosomatic Medicine*, 1950, **12**, 392-401.

Williams, M.   Psychophysiological responsiveness to psychological stress in early chronic schizophrenic reactions. *Psychosomatic Medicine*, 1953, **15**, 456-462.

Wishner, J.   The concept of efficiency in psychological health and in psychopathology. *Psychological Review*, 1955, **62**, 69-80.

Wishner, J.   Efficiency: Concept and measurement. In, Proceedings of the XIVth International Congress of Applied Psychology, Vol. 2. *Personality research.* Copenhagen: Munksgaard, 1962. Pp. 161-187.

Wynne, R. D.   Can schizophrenics give the associations that "most people" do? Paper read at Eastern Psychological Association, New York, April 1963.

Zahn, T. P., Rosenthal, D., & Lawlor, W. G.   GSR orienting reactions to visual and auditory stimuli in chronic schizophrenic and normal subjects. *Psychophysiological Newsletter*, 1963, **9**, 43-50.

Zahn, T. P., Rosenthal, D., & Shakow, D.   Reaction time in schizophrenic and normal subjects in relation to the sequence of series of regular preparatory intervals. *Journal of Abnormal and Social Psychology*, 1961, **63**, 161-168.

Zahn, T. P., Rosenthal, D., & Shakow, D.   Effects of irregular preparatory intervals on reaction time in schizophrenia. *Journal of Abnormal and Social Psychology*, 1963, **67**, 44-52.

Zahn, T. P., Shakow, D., & Rosenthal, D.   Reaction time in schizophrenics and normal subjects as a function of preparatory and intertrail intervals. *Journal of Nervous and Mental Diseases*, 1961, **133**, 283-287.

14

Russian Theory and Research on Schizophrenia

INTRODUCTION

Russian theory and research concerning schizophrenia revolves primarily around the concept of *protective inhibition*. This concept stems from the Pavlovian hypothesis that when a nerve is subjected to excessive stimulation, it will stop transmitting impulses so as to avoid permanent damage. That is, the nerve is protectively inhibited. Russian researchers have hypothesized that the majority of schizophrenics are characterized by higher levels of protective inhibition than normal individuals. Since high levels of protective inhibition reduce neural transmission, and since all forms of mental activity depend on neural transmission, the schizophrenic's higher level of protective inhibition can be used to explain the fact that they perform differently than normals. For example, persons with higher levels of protective inhibition show a lower level of arousal and evidence slower learning or conditioning.

Protective inhibition can also interact with another type of inhibition, *internal inhibition,* to retard discrimination training or extinction. Pavlov hypothesized that internal inhibition is developed whenever an individual makes a response that is not reinforced. It was further hypothesized that eventually the accumulation of internal inhibition would result in the cessation of the nonreinforced response. Since the development of internal inhibition is thought to be an *active* process, individuals whose neurological functioning is generally inhibited by high protective inhibition cannot develop internal inhibition. Therefore, these individuals cannot learn which responses to inhibit and consequently emit inappropriate responses that should have been inhibited or extinguished.

Excessive protective inhibition has also been used as an explanation of sudden uncontrollable behavioral outbursts or somatic

453

reactions: inhibition in those areas of the cortex that regulate the functions of the subcortical areas may result in a lapse in control of the subcortical areas, which would allow the manifestation of "primitive" behavior or aberrant somatic reactions. That is, inhibition of restraint would result in uncontrollable behaviors. Lastly, it has been suggested that when there is an extreme degree of protective inhibition, the inhibition may invade the subcortical as well as cortical areas and result in a more pervasive retardation of behavior, possibly similar to that seen in catatonia.

Researchers have used a variety of methods to measure inferentially the effects of protective inhibition. These methods include measurement of motor responsivity (subjects turning toward a stimulus), measurement of the arousal of the sympathetic nervous system (reflected in the dilation of pupils of the eyes), and the measurement of the electrical potentials in the brain [indicated by the EEG (electroencephalogram)]. In each instance higher levels of protective inhibition should result in less responsiveness. Although the reader is probably familiar with most of these measures, a comment might be made concerning the EEG. While the normal individual is at rest the EEG indicates between 8 and 13 waves of current per second. This is referred to as the *alpha rhythm*. When the individual responds to a stimulus, the alpha rhythm disappears. This phenomenon, known as *alpha blocking,* is often taken as a measure of the organism's responsivity to stimulation. Since these EEG measures reflect the level or threshold for cortical activity, they have considerable potential value in studying protective inhibition.

In reviewing the results of the research, the reader should note the differences between the findings for schizophrenics and those for paranoiacs. The inconsistencies in the data should not be interpreted as the fault of the theory or as the result of errors in measurement, but rather as evidence that different types of disorders may have different causes or correlates. In fact, it might be suggested that the theory would be weakened by identical findings in groups with highly different types of symptoms. The reader should also note that occasionally it is reported that not all schizophrenics seem to be characterized by high levels of protective inhibition. A small proportion seems to be equally deviant in the opposite direction. These differences may reflect the large and important differences within the class of schizophrenia (process versus reactive, manic versus depressive types, etc.) that have been pointed out in earlier articles.

Lastly, it should be noted that although the data seem relatively clear, a number of investigators have raised questions about the conceptualization of the nervous system upon which the theory is based and have suggested that a good deal of refinement and definition is still needed. In its present stage it does provide an interesting approach to understanding the disorder, especially with regard to the various somatic therapeutic adjuncts that are used with schizophrenics.

14

RUSSIAN THEORY AND RESEARCH
ON SCHIZOPHRENIA

R. LYNN

In the past few years a number of investigators in the West have advanced theories of schizophrenia in terms of disorders of arousal (e.g., Lynn, 1962; Venables, 1960) or some related concept such as anxiety (Mednick, 1958), sympathetic tone and reactivity (Gellhorn, 1958), or some biochemical disturbance affecting these (e.g., Hoffer & Osmond, 1960). Russian investigators have made a considerable number of studies along somewhat similar lines, although presented in Pavlovian terminology, and the object of the present paper is to review the work of the last decade for Western readers.

Pavlov's Theory of Schizophrenia

Russian research on schizophrenia is still almost entirely dominated by Pavlovian theory and a brief account of this is necessary for an understanding of the rationale of the researches to be described. Pavlov (1941) held that intense or prolonged stimulation of the nerve cells induces a state of protective or transmarginal inhibition, the purpose of which is to protect the cells from further stimulation which would be harmful to them. When nerve cells are in a state of protective inhibition, they do not conduct excitation. It is important in following Pavlovian theory to distinguish between protective inhibition and internal (active) inhibition, which is responsible for the extinction of conditioned reactions with absence of reinforcement and for discrimination ("differentiation"). Protective inhibition has the effect of weakening both the excitatory and (internal) inhibitory processes. Hence, there are certain conditions in which internal inhibition cannot be generated readily because the process has been weakened by protective inhibition.

Pavlov put forward the theory that schizophrenia results from

SOURCE. Reprinted with permission of the American Psychological Association and the author from the *Psychological Bulletin*, 1963, **60**, 486-498.

the generation of protective inhibitions in the cerebral cortex. The protective inhibition can be generated as a result of various kinds of shock, drugs, or physical illnesses. There is also an important constitutional factor in liability to schizophrenia, namely, the strength of the nervous system. This is the extent to which the nervous system is sensitive to stimulation, weak nervous systems being those that are most sensitive. A weak nervous system that is sensitive to stimulation is more likely to become overstimulated, generate protective inhibition, and hence, succumb to schizophrenia. The presence of protective inhibition in the cortex accounts for the slowness and poor conditionability of schizophrenics. The other variegated symptoms of schizophrenia are determined by the effect of protective inhibition in the cortex or the other parts of the brain. In cases of catatonic stupor the protective inhibition spreads down to the subcortex and affects also the sympathetic nervous system. But in those schizophrenic states in which violent outbursts occur, Pavlov suggested that the subcortex is overexcited, due to the removal of cortical control and the operation of the law of positive induction, according to which inhibition in one region of the brain induces excitation in other areas. Pavlov compared this process with the excited outbursts of tired children and intoxicated adults, arguing that in both cases the cerebral cortex is weakened, its control on the subcortex diminished, and hence, the subcortex is freed and activates the emotional outbursts.

Orientation Reactions

A considerable volume of work has been done recently in Russia on the so-called orientation reaction. The orientation reaction covers what is sometimes called in the West the arousal reaction; i.e., the reaction by which the organism pays attention to new stimuli and is mobilized to deal with them. It has three chief components. First, there are changes in skeletal muscles, the animal pricks up its ears, turns its body or head toward the new stimulus, muscle tonus rises, and there is an increase in muscular electrical activity. Secondly, the sympathetic division of the autonomic nervous system is activated: there is an increase in palmar skin conductance and pupil dilation, vasoconstriction in the limbs and vasodilation in the head, and variable changes in heart and respiration rates. Thirdly, the electroencephalogram (EEG) shows an increase in frequency and the alpha rhythm is blocked.

The orientation reaction is distinguished from the defensive reaction which occurs if the stimuli are intense, moderately intense and prolonged, or if the subject is in a state of tension. In the defensive reaction the subject shows signs of being frightened by the stimulus rather than interested in it, and there is vasoconstriction in the head as well as in the limbs.

A number of the components of the orientation reaction in schizophrenics were recorded by Traugott, Balonov, Kauffman, and Luchko (1958), namely, movements of eyes and head, galvanic skin response (GSR), respiration rates, heart rates, and vascular reactions from the shoulder. The stimuli used were auditory (a tone, bell, and whistling sound), visual (lights), and tactile. In chronic deteriorated schizophrenics there were often no orientation reactions of any kind; where reactions were present, however, the autonomic reactions were much weaker than the motor components. In hallucinated-paranoid patients the size of the orientation reaction and its extinction with repeated presentation of the stimulus were very variable, sometimes being stronger and sometimes weaker than in normal subjects. Some patients showed a defensive reaction, while others showed a poor orientation reaction. Reactions to stimulations were also observed during the course of insulin treatment. It was found that in the initial stages of treatment the patients became overactive and gave defensive reactions to the stimuli. Later, with recovery, the stimuli elicited normal orientation reactions.

A similar experiment is reported by Gamburg (1958) on 69 schizophrenics, mainly simple and paranoid. Motor and autonomic components of the orientation reaction were recorded to auditory stimuli and electric shock to the fingers. It was found that very few of the schizophrenics gave normal orientation reactions. Patients diagnosed as simple schizophrenics tended to give no reaction at all, while paranoiacs tended to give defensive reactions. In four out of five catatonic patients the initial stimulus elicited a defensive reaction, but subsequent stimuli elicited no reaction at all. It was also found that when the schizophrenics did give an autonomic reaction, the autonomic disturbance continued much longer than is usual in normal subjects. In those patients who had not given any orientation reactions to stimulation, caffeine restored the reactivity, but bromine and luminal had no effect. The author interprets this finding as supporting Pavlov's theory that the lack of reactivity is a result of excess inhibition, since it is assumed that caffeine dissipates the inhibition but bromine and luminal further increase it.

Sympathetic Nervous System

A number of Russian investigations indicate that there is a depression of the sympathetic nervous system in schizophrenia, both in its level and its reactivity to stimulation (Ekolova-Bagalei, 1955; Stanishevskaya, 1955; Streltsova, 1955; Vertogradova, 1955). Ekolova-Bagalei (1955) investigated 85 catatonic patients and reported low sympathetic tone as assessed by pulse rate, respiration rates, blood pressure, pupil diameter, sweating and vasometer tone; there was also little reactivity to stimulation. Similar results using the plethysmograph to measure vascular reflexes to hot and cold stimuli were reported by Vertogradova (1955) on 30 early cases of paranoid and simple schizophrenia.

In an investigation by Streltsova (1955) four studies were made of effects of stimulation on the pupil reaction in schizophrenic patients, the first being concerned with determining how far stimulation produces the normal reaction of pupil dilation in schizophrenics. The patients studied were 136 schizophrenics of different kinds (85 men, 50 women, aged 14-55 years, length of illness 2 months to 25 years). The stimuli used to elicit pupil reactions were hot and cold pricks (at 45° and 15°C.), a bell, and an olfactory stimulus. In normal subjects it was found that these stimuli elicit pupil dilation of the order of an increase of one-eighth over the initial pupil diameter. Of the schizophrenics, 27.4% reacted normally. The majority of the patients, 65%, showed strikingly subnormal reactions to stimulation; 40% showed no reactions at all and in 25% it was greatly reduced. These patients were long standing hebephrenics and hallucinated paranoiacs, and simple schizophrenias independent of the duration of the illness. The remaining 7.6% of patients showed other abnormal pupil reactions. An excessively large pupil dilation was shown by 3.9% to the extent of an increase of 40%-50% over the original pupil diameter. Streltsova states that increases of this size never occur in normal subjects. These patients were tense and anxious and had confused thought processes. The final group of 3.7% of the patients showed pupil constriction. This reaction is said never to occur in normal subjects except when they are in pain or ill. Streltsova argues that the low reactivity of the majority of her schizophrenics is a result of the high level of inhibition (she does not explain the high reactivity of the small minority of schizophrenics).

In a second experiment, Streltsova (1955) goes on to investigate the extinction of the pupil reaction in schizophrenics using as subjects 50 patients in whom it had been possible to elicit a reaction. In this experiment a bell was used as a stimulus and was presented in two conditions: continuously, and a number of times in short bursts. The results showed that the schizophrenics fell into two groups. Thirty-four out of the 50 patients failed to extinguish the pupil reaction. In normal subjects the pupil reaction is extinguished after an average of 15 seconds when the stimulus is presented continuously, and after 4-25 presentations when it is presented successively for short intervals, but in the schizophrenic patients the reaction had not extinguished after 3 minutes in the continuous condition or after 50 presentations in the successive condition. A paradoxical result is now reported. After this failure of extinction the intensity of the stimulus was raised considerably. In normal subjects this procedure increases the size of the orientation reaction, but in the schizophrenics the reaction promptly extinguished and remained extinguished for 40 or more minutes.

The second group of 16 patients extinguished the orientation reaction as quickly or nearly as quickly as normal subjects, but these subjects took much longer than normal to recover from the extinction procedure and it was not possible to restore the reaction through the presentation of an intense (disinhibiting) stimulus, as it is in normals. In considering her results Streltsova favors an explanation in terms of the tendency of schizophrenics to generate "protective inhibition." She argues that this accounts for (a) the sudden appearance of inhibition, previously absent, when an intense stimulus is presented; and (b) the length of time schizophrenics take to recover from the effects of extinction once their orientation reaction has been extinguished.

In a third experiment Streltsova (1955) investigated the effects of caffeine on the orientation reaction in schizophrenics. The rationale of this investigation springs from the hypothesis that the absence of reaction characteristic of most schizophrenics is a result of the strong inhibitory state of the nervous system. It is assumed that caffeine dissipates inhibition and hence, the hypothesis is advanced that if schizophrenics are given caffeine their orientation reactions should be restored. Fifteen patients who had shown the most persistent failure to give pupil reactions were taken as subjects. They were given doses of .1, .3, .8, and 1.3 milliliters of caffeine and were tested before and at intervals of 15, 30, 45, and 60 minutes after injection.

Thirteen of the subjects showed a normal orientation reaction or pupil contraction after .1 and .3 milliliter of caffeine. Streltsova argues that this supports her hypothesis that the schizophrenics were previously in an inhibited state. However, only 3 patients gave orientation reactions after doses of .8 and 1.3 milliliter of caffeine, the other 12 failing to respond. This failure to respond with the higher doses is attributed to protective inhibition.

In her fourth study Streltsova (1955) compared the reactivity of patients early in the morning with that obtained later in the day. She based this investigation on the Pavlovian view that protective inhibition accumulates during the day, as a result of the stimulation received, and is dissipated during sleep. If this is so, an implication of the theory that schizophrenics are characterized by high levels of protective inhibition would seem to be that, if patients were tested immediately on waking in the morning, they would not have time to generate protective inhibition to any appreciable extent and should react more like normals. In this connection Streltsova cites an observation by Naumova to the effect that catatonic symptoms are less marked early in the morning and increase in the course of the day. Streltsova tested this theory using the pupil dilation measure of reactivity. Twenty-two schizophrenics were tested immediately on waking in the morning and again 2-5 hours later. Twenty-one of the patients responded normally immediately on waking, or occasionally with overreactivity, but later in the day they failed to respond.

An investigation of the characteristics of the vascular system in schizophrenics has been reported by Stanishevskaya (1961). Young simple schizophrenics and anxious hallucinated paranoiacs gave an unusually great number of spontaneous reactions, which is interpreted as indicating a high level of excitation. This in turn is due to the weakening of the cortical inhibitory control over the subcortical areas. In catatonic schizophrenics and in hallucinated paranoiacs who were not anxious, there was very little or no spontaneous activity. When the patients were stimulated, catatonics gave no reactions, hallucinated paranoiacs gave normal reactions, and simple schizophrenics gave generalized vascular reactions but not the local vascular pressor reaction which in normal subjects succeeds the generalized reaction when stimuli are presented a number of times.

Several investigators have reported that sympathetic tone and reactivity are improved in schizophrenics by stimulants including caffeine (Gamburg, 1958; Trekina, 1955), cocaine (Ekolova-Bagalei, 1955), and atropin (Taranskaya, 1955).

EEG

The EEG activity characteristic of schizophrenia reported by a number of Russian workers includes low frequency or absent alpha rhythm, a reduction or absence of blocking of the alpha rhythm to light and other stimuli, large latencies in alpha blocking when it can be obtained, and the presence of "constellations" and "overflows" (Belenkaya, 1960, 1961; Frenkel, 1958; Gavrilova, 1960; Segal, 1955; Trekina, 1955). In Gavrilova's experiment 10 normal subjects were compared with 14 schizophrenics (5 cases of simple schizophrenia, 2 catatonic, and 7 paranoids; duration of the schizophrenia was 8-12 years). The EEGs were recorded when the patients were relaxed and after the presentation of visual and auditory stimuli. When the patients were relaxed, a low frequency alpha rhythm was present in the paranoiacs; but in the simple and catatonics the frequency was below that of the alpha rhythm. No reaction to auditory and visual stimuli was obtained in the simple and catatonic patients, but some reaction occurred in the paranoiacs. With auditory stimuli, a low intensity stimulus produced increased EEG frequency; but when the intensity of the stimulus was increased the reaction disappeared. The results are interpreted as indicating the inhibited state of the cortex in schizophrenics, especially in the simple and catatonic forms and to a lesser extent in paranoia. In paranoid patients weak stimuli evoke some EEG reaction, but strong stimuli increase the inhibition and hence no reaction is obtained.

Gavrilova (1960) also notes the presence in her paranoiacs (but not in the simple or catatonic patients) of frequent constellations, i.e., apparently causeless bursts of high amplitude potentials lasting .5-2 seconds from one cortical area accompanied by low amplitude potentials from another.

These constellations have also been reported in acute, tense, and delirious schizophrenics by Belenkaya (1960). The suggested explanation of these constellations is as follows. The development of protective inhibition in schizophrenia attacks both excitatory and inhibiting processes. It first weakens the process of internal inhibition in the cortex, thereby upsetting the balance between excitatory and inhibitory processes and increasing the strength of excitation. Strong excitatory stimuli increase the protective inhibition and prevent any reaction, but weak stimuli can still "get through" in the less advanced (paranoid) forms of schizophrenia. When these weak stimuli do get through they produce a violent effect. The reason for this is that the cortical process of internal inhibition is normally concerned with damping down incoming stimuli, and since this process has been weakened, the incoming stimuli can no longer be contained.

In paranoid forms of schizophrenia the presence of overflows has been reported; i.e., a burst of activity in one cortical area appears to spread and is followed by bursts of activity in other cortical areas. These overflows rarely occur in normal subjects when they are awake; but are present in falling asleep and during sleep, and also occur in epileptic cases and in patients with subcortical tumors. Gavrilova observed that external stimuli can induce overflows in paranoiacs, and argues that overflows are caused by subcortical stimuli acting on the cortex and inducing excitation which spreads to other areas. She argues from the absence of overflows in her groups of schizophrenics that subcortical-cortical relations are impaired. But Belenkaya (1960) reported overflows in all stages of paranoia, from the initial acute delirium to the final "secondary catatonic" stage.

A number of Russian investigators have followed the course of EEG changes during the administration of drugs to schizophrenics. Trekina (1955), working with 35 chronic deteriorated schizophrenics, reports absence of alpha rhythm, lack of any reaction to light stimuli, and unsynchronized random oscillations which are interpreted as indicating excitation in the reticular formation. Moderate doses of caffeine brought general improvement and restored the alpha rhythm and the reaction to light stimuli, and abolished or decreased the pathological activity from the subcortex.

A similar experiment by Ekolova-Bagalei (1955) reports the EEG activity of 85 catatonic patients (aged 17-45, duration of illness from a few days to several years) before treatment and after administration of cocaine. The cocaine improved the patients' behavior, so that in the majority of cases they began to move to instructions, speak, and negativism and waxy flexibility disappeared. (In eight cases of very long standing schizophrenia, no improvement was obtained even with increased and extended dosage.) At the same time the cocaine had the effect of increasing the alpha frequency. In a small number of cases, however, large doses of cocaine made the patients worse than before. The explanation of the findings is that small doses of cocaine reduce the amount of cortical inhibition, but larger doses induce protective inhibition, which further intensifies the inhibited state of the cortex. It was noted that cocaine acted first by increasing alpha frequency, then by increasing sympathetic tone, and finally by bettering the patient's voluntary behavior. It is argued that this indicates that cocaine acts first on the cortex and that an effective attack on schizophrenia can be made by restoring the cortical excitatory processes.

Two papers of Belenkaya (1960, 1961) report the effects of chlorpromazine and the stimulant meratran on the EEG activity of paranoid schizophrenics. It is argued that there are typically four successive stages in the evolution of paranoid schizophrenia: first, paranoid delirium without hallucinations; secondly, with hallucinations; thirdly, paraphrenic delirium; and fourthly, a state of secondary catatonia with hallucinations. Forty patients were divided into the four groups, and without drugs the increasingly advanced stages showed decreasing EEG activity and lesser reactivity to light (in these experimental conditions normal subjects gave a reaction to light on all testings compared with 24% of the first group of patients and only 5% of the last group). All the groups showed overflows. Both meratran and chlorpromazine had a beneficial effect on the first group and to some extent on the second, improving their general condition and making their EEG records more normal. With chlorpromazine, however, there was a delayed effect. For 2 or 3 weeks the pathological features of the EEG increased, especially the number of overflows. After this time the EEG became normal. Belenkaya explains these results in the following way. Chlorpromazine depresses the excitation in the reticular formation, and during the 2- or 3-week period this depression of reticular excitation allows the internal inhibitory processes to be restored. The increased presence of overflows is a sign of the increasing restoration of the inhibitory processes (assuming the equivalence of inhibition, sleep, and the occurrence of overflows). In the next stage, the reticular formation recovers from the effects of chlorpromazine and exerts a normal excitatory effect on the cortex, controlled by the restored inhibitory processes. Patients with the severer forms of paranoia did not benefit from either drug and showed paradoxical reactions to them, viz., after meratran EEG activity decreased and after chlorpromazine it increased.

Fedorovsky (1955) compared the EEG activity of normal subjects and 36 schizophrenics (hallucinated paranoiacs and simple) during sleep therapy. He found that the schizophrenic records tended to show slow alpha rhythms when they were awake, but that during sleep they showed lower amplitude slow waves than normals. It is suggested that this indicates that schizophrenics sleep less deeply than normal people. A similar result is reported with catatonic patients by Popov (1955).

Conditioning

Both autonomic and motor conditioning techniques have been used on schizophrenics by Russian investigators (Dobrzhanskaya, 1955; Kostandov, 1955; Saarma, 1955; Sinkevitch, 1955; Vertogradova, 1955).

All investigators have found that conditioning is poor or cannot be obtained in schizophrenics. An attempt to condition vascular reactions has been reported by Vertogradova (1955), working with 30 schizophrenics (mainly paranoid and simple, duration of illness 1 month to 3 years). Unconditioned vascular reactions to heat and cold were less than normal. A light was used as a conditioned stimulus and conditioned vascular reactions were typically acquired after 2-18 pairings of the light with the unconditioned stimuli. However, the conditioning was not stable; i.e., frequently the presentation of the conditioned stimulus did not elicit a response, and generally the conditioned response had disappeared on subsequent days. Firm conditioned responses could not be acquired with up to 100 pairings. It was also observed that in a number of cases the presentation of the light during the conditioning procedure inhibited the vascular reaction, so that it was either reduced or disappeared entirely. Thirteen patients were retested after a course of insulin, and in the 10 of these who improved, the vascular reactions became stronger and the inhibiting effect of the light during conditioning disappeared. In the other three patients the lack of behavioral improvement was accompanied by a corresponding absence of increase in the vascular reactions.

A somewhat similar experiment has been reported by Trekina (1955) on 35 chronic deteriorated schizophrenics subject to excited outbursts. Plethysmograph recordings were made of the reactions to the unconditioned stimuli of cold, heat, pain, light, and touch. Some vascular reactivity was present, and it is argued that this indicates that excitatory processes are present in the subcortex. It was found that on the second or third day of the investigation the unconditioned vascular reactions extinguished much more quickly than is normal, i.e., after 4-6 presentations. This is taken as evidence for the strong cortical inhibitory processes in schizophrenics. Attempts were then made to condition the vascular reactions to light and to verbal stimuli, but the conditioning was very slow and the conditioned reactions, once established, were very unsteady and kept disappearing and reappearing. This again is taken as evidence for the strong inhibitory processes in the cortex.

A number of experiments use some variety of motor conditioning in which the subject is instructed to give a response to a certain stimulus (e.g., pressing a buzzer to a light) and is given verbal reinforcements when the response is made correctly. This conditioning procedure is then made more elaborate by investigating the discrimination of the stimulus from similar stimuli, extinction of the response through nonreinforcement, effects of extraneous stimulation, and developments of conditioned disinhibition. The findings most commonly reported using these techniques on schizophrenics are as follows:

1. The speed of conditioning is impaired in all schizophrenics, but more in catatonic patients than in paranoiacs. Several investigators have found it impossible to condition catatonics whereas the conditioning of paranoiacs is possible, but slow. Typically 3-5 trials are required to condition normal subjects and 15-20 trials in schizophrenics.

2. The associations are very unstable, but can be stabilized with a very large number of reinforcements (100 or more).

3. The conditioned reaction is very easily inhibited by extraneous stimuli i.e., changes in laboratory conditions, etc., even though these are quite slight.

4. There is a great variability in response latency.

5. Discriminations are very difficult for schizophrenics to make. Many investigators found only a minority of patients would make correct discriminations.

6. Improvements in behavior following treatment are paralleled by improvements in conditionability.

The impairment of schizophrenics in this type of conditioning is generally interpreted as reflecting the inhibited state of the cerebral cortex. The instability of the conditioned reactions, inhibition by extraneous stimuli and variability in response latencies are regarded as due to the strengthening of cortical inhibition through negative induction from the subcortex. Saarma (1955) reports two further findings consistent with this explanation. When discrimination is attempted the schizophrenic frequently ceases to respond at all. It is inferred from this that inhibition has readily become attached to the stimulus to be discriminated and has spread to the original stimulus. Secondly, when reversal shifts (i.e., the positive stimulus is changed to a negative and the negative stimulus to positive) are attempted on schizophrenics, the positive stimulus can easily be changed to negative, but in many cases it was impossible to change the negative stimulus to positive. A similar finding is reported by Sinkevich (1955).

A possibly unexpected finding from this point of view is that two groups of paranoid schizophrenics, while showing the typical features of poor conditioning listed above, take a large number of nonreinforced trials before the conditioned response is extinguished. This finding has been reported by Dobrzhanskaya (1955) and Kostandov (1955). The explanation advanced by both authors is that the slow conditioning of schizophrenics is due to the protective inhibition. Extinction and discrimination are brought about by the accumulation of internal inhibition and the process of generating internal inhibition has itself been weakened by the protective inhibition. Hence, the slow extinction and discrimination characteristic of schizophrenia.

The effect of drugs on motor conditioning has been reported by Taranskaya (1955). Moderate doses of the stimulant atropin improved schizophrenics' performance on a motor conditioning task, increasing speed of conditioning, the stability of the response, and reducing the latency. At the same time hallucinations disappeared. Larger doses produced less beneficial effect on conditioning and increased hallucinations. The inhibitory drug phenamin further impaired conditionability and increased hallucinations.

Word Association Tests

Apart from conditioning, word association tests are sometimes used in Russian research on schizophrenia. A typical experiment is that of Dokuchaeva (1955). The method consists in presenting a stimulus word, to which the patient has to give a response. The response is scored both for the time taken to give it and for its adequacy; e.g., repetitions of the word, etc., are scored as inadequate. The general findings are that schizophrenics are slow and give inadequate responses. In Dokuchaeva's experiment 60 schizophrenics were given the word association test before and after varying doses of caffeine. It was found that moderate doses of caffeine increased the speed of the response and improved the quality of the associations. This improvement appeared to depend on the reactivation of the sympathetic system, since in cases where caffeine had no sympathetic effect the associative reactions remained unchanged. With large doses of caffeine the speed of reaction became slower and the adequacy of the responses deteriorated.

Treatment

As a logical implication of his theory of schizophrenia, Pavlov recommended and experimented with prolonged sleep as a therapeutic measure. The rationale of this procedure was that it strengthened the protective inhibition and allowed the cortical cells to recover from their exhausted state. The most common drugs used to induce prolonged sleep in the '30s were Cloetta's mixture and sodium amytal, and many Russian psychiatrists have been impressed with the success of these treatments. On the other hand, stimulants have also been used for therapeutic purposes, some of the most common being insulin, convulsive therapy, and caffeine. Ivanov-Smolenskii (1954) considers that the best results are given by combined sleep and stimulant treatment and gives the explanation that sleep allows the cortex to recover, while stimulants reactivate the sympathetic system. Combined administration of bromide with caffeine has also been used successfully in the treatment of dogs with experimental neurosis (Ivanov-Smolenskii, 1954).

In the past few years chlorpromazine has been widely used in the treatment of schizophrenia and a large number of experiments have been published on its site and mode of action. It is generally agreed that chlorpromazine has an inhibiting effect on both conditioned and unconditioned reflexes; according to Savchuk (1960) dogs and rabbits given 1 milligram per kilogram chlorpromazine give weaker salivatory reactions, but 4 to 5 days after administration these increase. There is no agreement among Russian investigators about whether chlorpromazine acts first on the cerebral cortex or on the reticular formation, but it is generally held that both are depressed by large doses.

A theory to account for the therapeutic effects of chlorpromazine on catatonic schizophrenia has been put forward by Zurabashvili (1960). He assumes that this variety of schizophrenia is initially induced by some toxic substance in the blood, citing as evidence in favor of this view experiments showing that the injection of catatonics' blood into dogs has an impairing effect. In these experiments, dogs were trained on a discrimination task; after injection with catatonics' blood, the learned discrimination broke down and the dogs reacted to the negative as well as to the positive stimulus (this breakdown was not obtained after injection with the blood of normal adults). However, if before injection with catatonics' blood the dogs were injected with chlorpromazine, the impairing effect of the catatonics' blood was counteracted. Since it is known that chlorpromazine has a depressant effect on the reticular formation, he infers from this that the toxic substance in schizophrenia has an excitatory effect on the reticular formation. During the development of schizophrenia the toxic agent raises the level of reticular excitation, which in turn stimulates the thalamic areas and the cerebral cortex. This stimulation becomes "above strength" and induces protective inhibition in both the cortex and the thalamic areas, and hence, the signs of inhibition in the cortex (low frequency EEG activity and slow conditioning) and the low sympathetic tone and reactivity. The effect of chlorpromazine is to depress the reticular excitation; reticular stimulation of the thalamic region and the cortex is thereby reduced and the protective inhibition dissipates. As a result of this, there is clinical improvement and the sympathetic system becomes more active. In support of the last point, Zurabashvili cites evidence that in catatonics receiving chlorpromazine there is a fall in the number of erythrocytes and increases in hemoglobins, sweating, and pulse rate. This theory is a departure from the commonly held Pavlovian view that protective inhibition in the cortex is the primary cause of breakdown in schizophrenia, and is an indication that Russian workers in this field are not necessarily fettered by strict observance of Pavlov's original theory.

Conclusion

At an empirical level, Russian work on schizophrenia at some points coincides with that in the West; and at others, breaks entirely new ground. From this point of view the principal findings can be summarized as follows:

1. The Russian evidence as a whole indicates that there are two types of schizophrenics: a majority group characterized by low sympathetic tone and reactivity; and a minority group, in whom sympathetic tone and reactivity are unusually high. The majority group would appear to consist mainly of cases of catatonic and simple schizophrenia and the minority group mainly of acute and agitated patients, especially paranoiacs. In this respect, Russian investigators seem to have arrived independently at similar conclusions to those of several workers in the West who have reported

two groups of schizophrenics characterized by high and low sympathetic reactivity (Gellhorn, 1958), high and low arousal (Venables, 1960), and high and low anxiety (Mednick, 1958).

2. The Russian findings on the EEG of schizophrenics indicate patterns characteristic of low arousal and drowsy states. There are a small number of similar Western findings although many investigators have failed to find EEG differences between schizophrenics and normals (Brackbill, 1956). This is possibly because Western investigators have not looked for the overflows and constellations described in the Russian literature.

3. Behaviorally, the Russian work showing slow reactions in conditioning experiments is to some extent paralleled by the findings of Eysenck and his associates (Eysenck, 1952; Payne & Hewlett, 1960) of slowness in schizophrenics over a variety of tasks. In general, however, Russian conditioning techniques have been very little used in Western research on schizophrenia.

4. A large number of Russian experiments show that schizophrenics are unusually sensitive to stimulants, being improved by small quantities but impaired by large. If these results are interpreted as being due to the effects of stimulants on arousal, they accord quite well with the somewhat similar results of Venables and Tizard (1956) and Venables (1960), which showed that schizophrenics are unusually affected by intense stimuli and by the level of background stimulation. In this respect, the Russian findings support the hypothesis advanced by Venables (1960) that schizophrenics can only operate efficiently within a narrower range of arousal than normals.

At a theoretical level, it will be evident that Russian work on schizophrenia is strongly tied to Pavlov's theory and is largely concerned with demonstrating in detail the truth of Pavlov's hypotheses or of making modifications to explain discrepant findings within the Pavlovian framework. It would appear that the recent experimental results can be made to fit reasonably well with Pavlovian theory and the theoretical significance of the Russian work on schizophrenia depends on the acceptability of general Pavlovian theory, especially on the concepts of protective inhibition and induction. A critical appraisal of Pavlovian theory as a whole would demand a long essay and would be out of place in this review. But it is apparent that, at any rate in the eyes of Russian investigators, Pavlovian theory has withstood the attacks of its critics.

REFERENCES

Belenkaya, N. Ya. Elektroentsephaloskopicheskie issledovaniya bolnykh paranoidnoi formoi schizophrenii pri primenenii meratrana. [Electroencephaloscopic investigations of paranoid schizophrenics using meratran.] *Zh. Nevorpat. Psikhiat.*, 1960, **60**, 224-330.

Belenkaya, N. Ya. Resultaty elektroencephaloscopicheskovo issledovaniya bolnykh paranoidnoi formoi schizophrenii vo vremya lecheniya aminazinom. [The result of an electroencephaloscopic investigation of paranoid schizophrenics under aminazin therapy.] *Zh. Nevropat. Psikhiat.*, 1961, **61**, 218-227.

Brackbill, G. A. Studies of brain dysfunction in schizophrenia. *Psychol. Bull.*, 1956, **53**, 210-226.

Dobrzhanskaya, A. K. Issledovanie neirodinamiki pri ostroi schizophrenii. In, *Trudy Vsesoyuznoi Nauchno-Prakticheskoi Konferentsii posviyaschenoi 100 letiyu so dnya rozhdeniya S. S. Korsakova i aktualnym voprosam psikhologii, 20-27 Maya 1954.* [An investigation of the neurodynamics of acute schizophrenia. In Proceedings of the All Union Theoretical-Practical Conference dedicated to the Centenary of S. S. Korsakov and to current psychological problems.] Moscow: Medgiz, 1955.

Dokuchaeva, O. N. Osobennosti associativnykh reaktii i ikhizmeneniya pod vlianem kofeina u bolnykh schizophreniei. In *Trudy Vsesoyuznoi Nauchno-Prakticheskoi Konferentsii posviyaschenoi 100 letiyu so dnya rozhdeniya S. S. Korsakova i aktualnym voprosam psikhologii, 20-27 Maya 1954.* [The special features of the associative reactions of schizophrenics under the influence of caffeine. In, Proceedings of the All Union Theoretical-Practical Conference dedicated to the Centenary of S. S. Korsakov and to current psychological problems.] Moscow: Medgiz, 1955.

Ekolovia-Bagalei, E. M. Deistvie kokaina na katatonikov. In, *Trudy Vsesoyuznoi Nauchno-Prakticheskoi Konferentsii posviyaschenoi 100 letiyu so dnya rozhdeniya S. S. Korsakova i aktualnym voprosam psikhologii, 20-27 Maya 1954.* [The effect of cocaine on catatonics. In, Proceedings of the All Union Theoretical-Practical Conference dedicated to the Centenary of S. S. Korsakov and to current psychological problems.] Moscow: Medgiz, 1955.

Eysenck, H. J. *The scientific study of personality.* London: Routledge & Kegan Paul, 1952.

Fedorovsky, Yu. N. O nekotorykh elektroensephalographicheskikh osobennostyakh u bolnykh shizophreniei pri udlineniem medikamentoznym snom. In, *Trudy Vsesoyuznoi Nauchno-Prakticheskoi Konferentsii posviyaschenoi 100 letiyu so dnya rozhedeniya S. S. Korsakova i aktualnym voprosam psikhologii, 20-27 Maya 1954.* [Some electroencephalographic features of schizophrenics during induced sleep. In, Proceedings of the

All Union Theoretical-Practical Conference dedicated to the Centenary of S. S. Korsakov and to current psychological problems.] Moscow: Medgiz, 1955.

Frenkel, G. M. E. Electroencephalographic investigation of schizophrenics with hypochondriac syndromes. *Pavlov J. higher nerv. Activ.*, 1958, **8**, 515-590.

Gamburg, A. L. Orientivochnaya i oboronitelnaya reaktsia pri prostoi i paranoidnoi formakh schizophrenii. In L. G. Voronin (Ed.), *Orientirovochnyi refleks i orientirovochno-issledovatelskaya deyatelnost.* [The orientating and defensive reaction in simple and paranoid forms of schizophrenia. In, The orientating reflex and orientating investigating activity.] Moscow: Academy of Pedagogical Sciences of R.S.R.S.R., 1958.

Gavrilova, N. A. *Issledovanie korkovoi mosaiki pri razlichnykh formakh schizophrenii.* [Investigations of the cortical mosaic in different forms of schizophrenia.] *Zh. Nevropat. Psikhat.*, 1960, 4, 453-460.

Gellhorn, E. *Autonomic imbalance and the hypothalamus.* Minneapolis: Univer. Minnesota Press, 1958.

Hoffer, A., & Osmond, H. *The chemical basic of clinical psychiatry.* Springfield, Ill.: Charles C Thomas, 1960.

Ivanov-Smolenskii, A. G. *Essays on the patho-physiology of the higher nervous activity.* Moscow: Foreign Languages Publishing House, 1954.

Kostandov, Z. A. Neirodinamiki i osobenno vzaimodeistviya korkovykh signalnykh sistem pri paranoidnoi forme schizophrenii. [The neurodynamics and the special interaction of the cortical signal systems in the paranoid form of schizophrenia.] *Trud. Inst. Vyssh. Nervn. Deyatel.*, 1955, 1, 26-27.

Lynn, R. Aging and expressive movements: An interpretation of aging in terms of Eysenck's construct of psychotism. *J. genet. Psychol.*, 1962, **100**, 77-84.

Mednick, S. A learning theory approach to research in schizophrenia. *Psychol. Bull.*, 1958, 55, 316-327.

Pavlov, I. P. *Lectures on conditioned reflexes.* New York: International Press, 1941.

Payne, R. W., & Hewlett, J. H. G. Thought disorder in psychotic patients. In H. J. Eysenck (Ed.), *Experiments in personality.* London: Routledge & Kegan Paul, 1960.

Popov, E. A. *O nekotorykh patophyziologicheskikh esobennostiyakh schizophrenii.* In, *Trudy Vsesoyuznoi Nauchno-Prakticheskoi Konferentsii Posviyaschenoi 100 letiyu so dnya rozhdeniya S. S. Korsakova i aktualnym voprosam psikhologii, 20–27 Maya 1954.* [On some of the pathophysiological peculiarities of schizophrenia. In, Proceedings of the All Union Theoretical-Practical Conference dedicated to the Centenary of S. S. Korsakov and to current psychological problems.] Moscow: Medgiz, 1955.

Saarma, Yu. M. Ob izieneniyakh neirodinamiki u bolnykh schizophreniei pod vliyaniem lecheniya insulinom. In, *Trudy Vsesoyuznoi Nauchno-Prakti-*

cheskoi Konferentsii posviyaschenoi 100 letiyu so dnya rozhdeniya S. S. Korsakova i aktualnym voprosam psikhologii, 20–27 Maya 1954. [On the changes in the neurodynamics of schizophrenics during insulin therapy. In, Proceedings of the All Union Theoretical-Practical Conference dedicated to the Centenary of S. S. Korsakov and to current psychological problems.] Moscow: Medgiz, 1955.

Savchuk, V. I.   Deistvie aminazin na razlichnye otdely golovnovo mozga no dannym eksperimentalnovo issledovaniya. [The effect of aminazin on different sections of the brain as shown by the data of an experimental investigation.] *Zh. Nevropat. Psikhiat.*, 1960, **2**, 182-190.

Segal, Yu. E.   Kliniko-phiziologicheskie issledovaniya narushenii vnytrennykh analizatorov pri shizophrenii. In, *Trudy Vsesoyuznoi Neuchno-Prakticheskoi Konferentsii posviyaschenoi 100 letiyu so dnya rozhdeniya S. S. Korsakova i aktualnym voprosam psikhologii, 20–27 Maya 1954.* [Clinical-physiological investigations of the destruction of the internal analysors in schizophrenia. In, Proceedings of the All Union Theoretical-Practical Conference dedicated to the Centenary of S. S. Korsakov and to current psychological problems.] Moscow: Medgiz, 1955.

Sinkevich, Z. L.   Opyt issledovaniya uslovnovo rastormazhivaniya pri shizophrenii. [An experiment investigating conditioned disinhibition in schizophrenia.] *Trud. Inst. Vyssh. Nervn. Deyatel.*, 1955, **1**, 11-25.

Stanishevskaya, N. N.   Pletizmographicheskoe issledovanie bolnykh katatonicheskoi formoi shizophrenii. In, *Trudy Vsesoyuznoi Nauchno-Prakicheskoi Konferentsii posviyaschenoi 100 letiyu so dnya rozhdeniya S. S. Korsakova i aktualnym voprosam psikhologii, 20–27 Maya 1954.* [A plethismographic investigation of catatonic schizophrenics. In, Proceedings of the All Union Theoretical-Practical Conference dedicated to the Centenary of S. S. Korsakov and to current psychological problems.] Moscow: Medgiz, 1955.

Streltsova, N. L.   Kharakteristike nekotorykh bezuslovnykh refleksov u bolnykh shizohreniei. In, *Trudy Vsesoyuznoi Nauchno-Prakticheskoi Konferentsii posviyaschenoi 100 letiyu so dnya rozhdeniya S. S. Korsakova i aktualnym voprosam psikhologii, 20–27 Maya 1954.* [The characteristics of some unconditioned reflexes in schizophrenics. In, Proceedings of the All Union Theoretical-Practical Conference dedicated to the Centenary of S. S. Korsakov and to current psychological problems.] Moscow: Medgiz, 1955.

Taranskaya, A. D.   Bliyanie nekotorykh pharmakologicheskikh vecshestv na gallutsinatsii. In, *Trudy Vsesoyuznoi Nauchno-Prakticheskoi Konferentsii posviyaschenoi 100 letiyu so dnya rozhdeniya S. S. Korsakova i aktualnym voprosam psikhologii, 20–27 Maya 1954.* [The effect of certain drugs on hallucinations. In, Proceedings of the All Union Theoretical-Practical Conference dedicated to the Centenary of S. S. Korsakov and to current psychological problems.] Moscow: Medgiz, 1955.

Traugott, N. N., Balonov, L. Ya., Kauffman, D. A., & Luchko, A. E.   O dinamike narushenii orientirovochnykh refleksov pri nekotorykh psikhoticheskikh sindromakh. In L. G. Voronin (Ed.), *Orientirovochnyi refleks i orientirovochno-issledovatelskaya deyatelnost.* [On the dynamics of the destruction of orientating reflexes in certain psychotic syndromes. In, The orientating reflex and orientating investigating activity.] Moscow: Academy of Pedagogical Sciences of R.S.F.S.R., 1958.

Trekina, T. A.   Klinika i techenie shizofrenii s maniakalnym sindromom. In, *Trudy Vsesoyuznoi Nauchno-Prakticheskoi Konferentsii posviyaschenoi 100 letiyu so dyna rozhdeniya S. S. Korsakova i aktualnym voprosam psikhologii, 20–27 Maya 1954.* [The clinical manifestations and course of schizophrenia with the maniacal syndrome. In, Proceedings of the All Union Theoretical-Practical Conference dedicated to the Centenary of S. S. Korsakov and to current psychological problems.] Moscow: Medgiz, 1955.

Venables, P. H.   The effect of auditory and visual stimulation on skin potential response of schizophrenics. *Brain,* 1960, **83,** 77-92.

Venables, P. H., & Tizzard, J.   Paradoxical effects in the reaction time of schizophrenics. *J. abnorm. soc. Psychol.,* 1956, **53,** 220-224.

Vertogradova, O. P.   Sosudistie uslovnie i bezuslovnie refleksi pri shizophrenii. In, *Trudy Vsesoyuznoi Nauchno-Prakticheskoi Konferentsii posviyaschenoi 100 letiyu so dnya rozhdeniya S. S. Korsakova i aktualnym voprosam psikhologii, 20–27 Maya 1954.* [Conditioned and unconditioned vasoreflexes in schizophrenia. In, Proceedings of the All Union Theoretical-Practical Conference dedicated to the Centenary of S. S. Korsakov and to current psychological problems.] Moscow: Medgiz, 1955.

Zurabashvili, A. D.   Nekotorye voprosy ucheniya o retikuliyarnoi formatsii v sviyazi c teorei i praktikoi psikhiatrii. [Some questions arising from the study of the reticular formation and their relation to psychiatric theory and practice.] *Zh. Nevropat. Psikhiat.,* 1960, **5,** 632-636.

15

Biochemical Theories of Schizophrenia

INTRODUCTION

The primary focus of this book has been on the psychological aspects of behavior pathology. This should not suggest that all behavior pathology is psychogenic in nature, which would be as inaccurate as the position that all behavior pathology is solely determined by biochemical factors. It would appear best to view the psychological and physiological aspects of behavior pathology as falling on a continuum. At the extremes of the continuum are the disorders that are the result of *either* psychological *or* physiological causes, while in the center would be the disorders that are the result of both psychological *and* physiological causes. A psychosis stemming from a syphilitic infection is an example of both physiological and psychological determinants of pathology. Neurosyphilitic conditions are known to result from the invasion of the brain by spirochetes, but the form that the symptom pattern takes is a function of the individual's personality structure prior to the infection.

One might expect that research on biochemical factors would be easier, and the results clearer, than research on psychological factors. However, as the reader will see in Part I of the paper by Seymour Kety, a number of the same methodological problems are involved in the investigation of both chemical factors and psychological factors. For example, research on chemical factors, like that on psychological factors, has been complicated by the problems resulting from drawing subjects from heterogeneous populations. Physiological research, like psychological research, is also complicated by the issue of single or multiple causation. Another problem arises because patients used in biochemical research,

475

unlike their normal controls, have been exposed to numerous infections, have been subjected to different diets and living conditions, and have often received a variety of somatic treatments. Any of these factors might affect the patients in such a way that subsequent physiological measures would be confounded. Interestingly enough, the same problem could be raised with regard to research on psychological factors (e.g., hospitalization per se may have important effects on patients), but unfortunately very little attention has been given to this possibility in the research on psychological factors. Since there seems to be a correspondence between the problems in researching the biochemical and psychological variables, the reader might consider which of the other methodological problems that have come to light in researching psychological variables might be relevant when evaluating research on biochemical variables.

The reader should note the relationship between some of the hypotheses discussed here and those discussed in the articles devoted to hypotheses concerning psychological factors. A number of the hypotheses dealing with biochemical factors can be considered to be directly or indirectly related to the concept of arousal that was used in some of the psychological explanations of schizophrenia or schizophrenic deficit. In the present article, however, rather than attempting to demonstrate the effects of differences in arousal as they may be related to schizophrenia, Kety emphasizes the attempts to determine whether or not there are biochemical differences between patients and normals that might lead to arousal differences and/or schizophrenia.

The reader whose primary interest is in understanding the psychological aspects of behavior pathology should not ignore the hypotheses, results, and problems of biochemical research on behavior pathology. An understanding of biochemical research is essential if psychological research is to be put into proper perspective, for there is little doubt that the solution of the problems posed by behavior pathology will only be achieved by interdisciplinary understanding and cooperation.

15

BIOCHEMICAL THEORIES OF SCHIZOPHRENIA

SEYMOUR S. KETY

PART I

The concept of a chemical etiology in schizophrenia is not new. The Hippocratic school attributed certain mental aberrations to changes in the composition of the blood and disturbances in the humors of the brain, but it was Thudichum (1884), the founder of modern neurochemistry, who in 1884 expressed the concept most cogently: "Many forms of insanity are unquestionably the external manifestations of the effects upon the brain substance of poisons fermented within the body, just as mental aberrations accompanying chronic alcoholic intoxication are the accumulated effects of a relatively simple poison fermented out of the body. These poisons we shall, I have no doubt, be able to isolate after we know the normal chemistry to its uttermost detail. And then will come in their turn the crowning discoveries to which our efforts must ultimately be directed, namely, the discoveries of the antidotes to the poisons and to the fermenting causes and processes which produce them." In these few words were anticipated and encompassed most of the current chemical formulations regarding schizophrenia.

It may be of value to pause in the midst of the present era of psychochemical activity to ask how far we have advanced along the course plotted by Thudichum. Have we merely substituted "enzymes" for "ferments" and the names of specific agents for "poisons" without altering the completely theoretical nature of the concept? Or, on the other hand, are there some well-substantiated findings to support the prevalent belief that this old and stubborn disorder which has resisted all previous attempts to expose its etiology is about to yield its secrets to the biochemist?

An examination of the experience of another and older discipline may be of help in the design, interpretations, and evaluation

SOURCE. Reprinted with permission of the American Association for the Advancement of Science and the author from *Science*, 1959, **129**, 1528-1532, 1590-1596.

of biochemical studies. The concepts of the pathology of schizophrenia have been well reviewed recently (Peters, 1956; David,
1957; Dastur, 1959). As a result of findings of definite histological
changes in the cerebral cortex of patients with schizophrenia
which were described by Alzheimer at the beginning of the present
century and confirmed by a number of others, an uncritical enthusiasm for the theory of a pathological lesion in this disease developed, and this enthusiasm penetrated the thinking of Kraepelin
and Bleuler and persisted for 25 years. This was followed by a
period of questioning which lead to the design and execution of
more critically controlled studies, and eventually, to the present
consensus that a pathological lesion characteristic of schizophrenia
or any of its subgroups remains to be demonstrated.

Earlier biochemical theories and findings related to schizophrenia have been reviewed by a number of authors, of who Mc-
Farland and Goldstein (1938), Keup (1954), and Richter (1957)
may be mentioned (Benjamin, 1958). Horwitt and others (Horwitt, 1956; Evarts, 1958; McDonald, 1958) have pointed out some
of the difficulties of crucial research in this area. It is the purpose
of this review to describe the biochemical trends in schizophrenia
research of the past few years, to discuss current theories, and to
examine the evidence which has been used to support them.

Sources of Error

Because of the chronicity of the disease, the prolonged periods
of institutionalization associated with its management, and the
comparatively few objective criteria available for its diagnosis and
the evaluation of its progress, schizophrenia presents to the investigator a large number of variables and sources of error which he
must recognize and attempt to control before he may attribute to
any of his findings a primary or characteristic significance.

Despite the phenomenological similarities which permitted the
concept of schizophrenia as a fairly well defined symptom complex
to emerge, there is little evidence that all of its forms have a common etiology or pathogenesis. The likelihood that one is dealing
with a number of different disorders with a common symptomatology must be recognized and included in one's experimental design
(Evarts, 1958; Perlin & Lee, in press; Freedman, 1958). Errors
involved in sampling from heterogeneous populations may help to
explain the high frequency with which findings of one group fail
to be confirmed by those of another. Recognition that any sample
of schizophrenics is probably a heterogeneous one would seem to

indicate the importance of analyzing data not only for mean values but also for significant deviations of individual values from group values. The biochemical characteristics of phenylketonuria would hardly have been detected in an average value for phenylalanine levels in blood in a large group of mentally retarded patients.

Most biochemical research in schizophrenia has been carried out in patients with a long history of hospitalization in institutions where over-crowding is difficult to avoid and where hygienic standards cannot always be maintained. It is easy to imagine how chronic infections, especially of the digestive tract, might spread among such patients. The presence of amebiasis in a majority of the patients at one large institution has been reported (Vestergaard, Abbott, Kline, & Stanley, 1958), and one wonders how often this condition or a former infectious hepatitis has caused the various disturbances in hepatic function found in schizophrenia. Even in the absence of previous or current infection, the development of a characteristic pattern of intestinal flora in a population of schizophrenic patients living together for long periods and fed from the same kitchen is a possibility which cannot be dismissed in interpreting what appear to be deviant metabolic pathways.

In variety and quality the diet of the institutionalized schizophrenic is rarely comparable to that of the nonhospitalized normal control. Whatever homeostatis function the process of free dietary selection may serve is often lost between the rigors of the kitchen or the budget and the overriding emotional or obsessive features of the disease. In the case of the "acute" schizophrenic, the weeks and months of emotional turmoil which precede recognition and diagnosis of the disease are hardly conducive to a normal dietary intake. Kelsey, Gullock, and Kelsey (1957) confirmed findings of certain abnormalities in thyroid function previously reported in schizophrenia and showed that in their patients these abnormalities resulted from a dietary deficiency of iodine, correctable by the introduction of iodized salt into the hospital diet. It is not surprising that a dietary vitamin deficiency has been found to explain at least two of the biochemical abnormalities recently attributed to schizophrenia (McDonald, 1958; McDonald, 1957; Aprison & Grosz, 1958; Angel, Leach, Martens, Cohen, & Heath, 1957). It is more surprising that the vitamins and other dietary constituents, whose role in metabolism has become so clearly established, should so often be relegated to a position of unimportance in consideration of the intermediary metabolism of schizophrenics. Horwitt (1953) has found signs of liver dysfunction during ingestion of a diet containing borderline levels of protein, while nonspecific vitamin therapy accompanied by a high protein and carbohydrate diet has been reported to reverse the impairment of hepatic function in schizophrenic patients (Fischer, Georgi, Weber, & Piaget, 1950).

Another incidental factor which sets the schizophrenic apart from the normal control is the long list of therapies to which he may have been exposed. Hypnotic and ataractic drugs and their metabolic products or effects produce changes which have sometimes been attributed to the disease. Less obvious is the possibility of residual electrophysiological or biochemical changes resulting from repeated electroshock or insulin coma.

Emotional stress is known to cause profound changes in man—in adrenocortical and thyroid function (Board, Persky, & Hamburg, 1956), in the excretion of epinephrine and norepinephrine (Elmadjian, Hope, & Lamson, 1957), and in the excretion of water, electrolytes, or creatinine (Schottstaedt, Grace, & Wolff, 1956), to mention only a few recently reported findings. Schizophrenic illness is often characterized by marked emotional disturbance even in what is called the basal state and by frequently exaggerated anxiety in response to routine and research procedures. The disturbances in behavior and activity which mark the schizophrenic process would also be expected to cause deviations from the normal in many biochemical and metabolic measures—in volume and concentration of urine, in the size and function of numerous organic systems. The physiological and biochemical changes which are secondary to the psychological and behavioral state of the patient are of interest in themselves, and an understanding of them contributes to total understanding of the schizophrenic process; it is important, however, not to attribute to them a primary or etiological role.

An additional source of error which must be recognized is one which is common to all of science and which it is the very purpose of scientific method, tradition, and training to minimize—the subjective bias. There are reasons why this bias should operate to a greater extent in this field than in many others. Not only is the motivation heightened by the tragedy of this problem and the social implications of findings which may contribute to its solution, but the measurements themselves, especially of the changes in mental state or behavior, are so highly subjective, and the symptoms are so variable and so responsive to nonspecific factors in the milieu, that only the most scrupulous attention to controlled design will permit the conclusion that a drug, or a diet, or a protein fraction of the blood, or an extract of the brain is capable of causing or ameliorating some of the manifestations of the disease. This is not to suggest that the results of purely chemical determinations are immune to subjective bias; the same vigilance is required there to prevent the hypothesis from contaminating the data. In a field with as many variables as this one, it is difficult to avoid the subconscious tendency to reject for good reason data which weaken a hypothesis while uncritically accepting those data which strengthen it. Carefully controlled and "double blind" experimental designs which are becoming more widely utilized in this area can help to minimize the bias.

Obvious as many of these sources of error are, it is expensive and difficult, if not impossible, to prevent some of them from affecting results obtained in this field, especially in the preliminary testing of interesting hypotheses. It is in the interpretation of these results, however, and in the formulating of conclusions, that the investigator has the opportunity, and indeed the responsibility, to recognize and evaluate his uncontrolled variables rather than to ignore them, for no one knows better than the investigator himself the possible sources of error in his particular experiment. There are enough unknowns in our guessing game with nature to make it unnecessary for us to indulge in such a sport with one another.

Schizophrenia Program of the Laboratory of Clinical Science

Since 1956, the Laboratory of Clinical Science of the National Institute of Mental Health has been developing and pursuing a program of biological research in schizophrenia designed to minimize many of the sources of error discussed above while increasing the opportunity to detect, and to correlate with psychiatric and behavioral information, true biological characteristics if they exist. One of the wards houses a group of approximately 14 clearly diagnosed schizophrenic patients, representative of as many clinical subgroups as possible, chosen from a patient population of 14,000. In selecting these patients an attempt was made to minimize the variable of age, sex, race, and physical illness and, on the basis of careful family surveys, to maximize the likelihood of including within the group individuals representative of whatever genetic subgroups of the disease may exist (Perlin & Lee, in press). These patients are maintained for an indefinite period of time on a good diet, receiving excellent hygienic, nursing, medical, and psychiatric care. Each patient receives a careful and sophisticated psychiatric and genealogical characterization, and detailed daily records are kept on his psychiatric and behavioral status; these, it is hoped, will be of value in a more complete interpretation of biological findings. No specific therapy is employed or even found to be necessary, and drugs or dietary changes are introduced only for research purposes and for short periods of time. The other ward houses a comparable number of normal controls, who volunteer to remain for protracted periods of time on the same diet and in a reasonably similar milieu. We recognize, of course, that only a few of the variables are thus controlled and that any positive difference which emerges in this preliminary experiment between some or all of the schizophrenics and the normal population will have to be subjected to much more rigorous examination before its significance can be evaluated. Such reexamination has rarely been necessary, since our schizophrenic patients, individually or as a group, have shown little abnormality in the biological studies which have thus far been completed (McDonald, 1958; McDonald, 1957; Szara, Axelrod, & Perlin, 1958; Kopin, 1959; Kornetsky, personal communication; Mann & Labrosse, in press).

Oxygen, Carbohydrate, and Energetics

A decrease in basal metabolism was found in schizophrenia by earlier workers, although more recent work has not confirmed this (Richter, 1957), and theories attributing the disease to disturbances in the fundamental mechanisms of energy supply or conversion in the brain have enjoyed some popularity, but on the basis of extremely inadequate evidence, such as spectroscopic oximetry of the ear lobe or nail bed (Lovett Doust, 1952). Our finding of a normal rate of cerebral circulation and oxygen consumption in schizophrenic patients (Kety, Woodford, Harmel, Freyhan, Appel, Schmidt, 1948) was confirmed by Wilson, Schieve, and Scheinberg (1952) and, more recently, in our laboratory by Sokoloff and his associates (Sokoloff, Perlin, Kornetsky, Kety, 1957), who also found a normal rate of cerebral glucose consumption in this condition. These studies make it appear unlikely that the moderate decrease in these functions reported by Gordan and his associates (Gordan, Estess, Adams, Bowman, Simon, 1955), but only in patients with long-standing disease, is fundamental to the disease process. These studies do not, of course, rule out a highly localized change in energy metabolism somewhere in the brain, but cogent evidence for such a hypothesis has yet to be presented.

Richter (1957) has pointed out the uncontrolled factors in earlier work which indicated that a defect in carbohydrate metabolism was characteristic of the schizophrenic disease process. The finding in schizophrenia of an abnormal glucose tolerance in conjunction with considerable other evidence of hepatic dysfunction (Longo, Buscaino, D'Andrea, Uras, Ferrari, Rinaldi, & Pasolini, 1953), or evidence of an abnormally slow metabolism of lactate in the schizophrenic (Altschule, Henneman, Holliday, Goncz, 1956), do not completely exclude incidental hepatic disease or nutritional deficiencies as possible sources of error. Horwitt and his associates (Horwitt, Liebert, Kreisler, Wittman, 1948) were able to demonstrate and correct similar abnormalities by altering the dietary intake of the B group of vitamins.

Evidence for greater than normal anti-insulin or hyperglycemic activity in the blood or urine of a significant segment of schizophrenic patients was reported in 1942 by Meduna, Gerty, and Urse and as recently as 1958 by Moya and his associates (Moya, Dewar, MacIntosh, Hirsch, Townsend, 1958). Some progress has been made in concentrating or characterizing such factors in normal urine (Moya, Szerb, MacIntosh, 1956) as well as in urine from schizophrenics (Morgan & Pilgrim, 1952). Harris (1942) has thrown some doubt on the importance of such anti-insulin mechanisms in the pathogenesis of schizophrenia, and it is hoped that further investigation may clarify the nature of the substance or substances involved and their relevance to schizophrenia.

Defects in oxidative phosphorylation have been thought to occur in this disease. Reports of alterations in the phosphorus metabolism of the erythrocyte (Boszormenyi-Nagy, Gerty, Kueber, 1956; Boszormenyi-Nagy & Gerty, 1955) await further definition and independent confirmation.

Two recent reports of a more normal pattern of carbohydrate metabolism and of clinical improvement following the infusion of glutathoine (Altschule, Henneman, Holliday, Goncz, 1957; Surikov, Ushakov, Il'ina, Verbliunskaia, Khokhlov, 1957) in psychotic patients, some of whom were schizophrenic, are perhaps of interest. There is little verifiable evidence for a reduction in the blood glutathione index in schizophrenia (McDonald, 1958); one group which has repeatedly postulated this reduction has done so on the basis of decreasingly convincing data (Angel, Leach, Martens, Cohen, & Heath, 1957; Martens, Leach, Heath, Cohen, (1956), while our laboratory has failed to find it at all (McDonald, 1957), and a very recent report publishes identical figures for the schizophrenic and normal groups (Barak, Humoller, Stevens, 1958). Clinical and biochemical improvement in a variety of psychoses following glutathione infusion, even if it is accepted without the necessary controls, suggests at best that glutathione is of secondary and nonspecific import.

It is difficult for some to believe that a generalized defect in energy metabolism—a process so fundamental to every cell in the body—could be responsible for the highly specialized features of schizophrenia. On the other hand, a moderate lack of oxygen, an essential requirement of practically every tissue, produces highly selective manifestations involving especially the higher mental functions and as suggestive of schizophrenia as manifestations produced by many of the more popular hallucinogens. It may not, therefore, be completely appropriate that, in a search for biochemical factors etiologically related to schizophrenic psychoses, the center of interest today appears to have shifted to other, more specialized aspects of metabolism.

Amino Acids and Amines

The well-controlled studies of the Gjessings (1938, 1939, 1958) on nitrogen metabolism in periodic catatonia arouse considerable interest in that they suggest the possibility of a relationship between intermediary protein metabolism and schizophrenia, although earlier workers had postulated defects in amino acid metabolism in this disease (Buscaino, 1958). The hallucinogenic properties of some compounds related directly or indirectly to biological amines reawakened this interest, and the techniques of paper chromatography offered new and almost unlimited opportunity for studying the subject.

The first group to report chromatographic studies of the urine of schizophrenic and control groups found certain differences in the amino acid pattern and, in addition, the presence of certain unidentified imidazoles in the urine of schizophrenics (Young, Berry, Beerstecher, 1951). Although a normal group of comparable age was used for comparison, there is no indication of the extent to which dietary and other variables were controlled, and the authors were properly cautious in their conclusions. In a more extensive series of studies, another group has reported a significantly higher than normal concentration of aromatic compounds in the urine of schizophrenic patients (McGeer, McNair, McGeer, Gibson, 1957) and has suggested that there are certain qualitative differences in the excretion of such compounds (McGeer, Brown,

McGeer, 1957). Others have reported the abnormal presence of un-identified amines (Georgi, Honegger, Jordan, Rieder, Rottenberg, 1956) or indoles (Riegelhaupt, 1956), and one group has reported the absence of a normally occurring indole (Cafruny & Domino, 1958) in the urine of schizophrenic patients. In some of these studies there appears to have been no control relative to possible drug therapy or to volume or concentration of urine, and in few of them was there control of it. There are numerous mechanisms whereby vitamin deficiencies may cause substantial changes in the complex patterns of the intermediary metabolism of amino acids. In addition, the fact that a large number of aromatic compounds in the urine have recently been shown to be of dietary origin (Armstrong & Shaw, 1956; Armstrong & Shaw, 1958; Armstrong, Wall, & Parker, 1956; Booth, Emerson, Jones, & Deeds, 1957; Waalkes, Sjoerdsma, Creveling, Weissbach, Undenfriend, 1958) suggests the need for considerably more caution than has usually been employed in drawing conclusions with regard to this variable. Another point which has not been emphasized sufficiently is that chromatographic procedures which make possible the simultaneous determination of scores of substances, many of them unknown, re-quire statistical analyses somewhat different from those which were developed for the testing of single, well-determined hy-potheses. It is merely a restatement of statistical theory to point out that in a determination of 100 different compounds carried out simultaneously on two samples of the *same* population, we would be expected to show a difference significant at the 0.05 level! It is interesting to note that a more recent study was able to demon-strate considerably fewer differences between the urines of normal and schizophrenic populations and drew very limited and guarded conclusions (Acheson, Paul, Tomlinson, 1958). In our own labora-tory, Mann and LaBrosse (in press) undertook a search for urinary phenolic acids, in terms of quantity excreted in a standard time interval rather than in terms of concentration, which dis-closed significantly higher levels of four compounds in the urine of schizophrenics than in that of the normal test subjects. These compounds were found to be known metabolites of substances in coffee, and their presence in the urine was, in fact, better corre-lated with the ingestion of this beverage than with schizophrenia.

The hypothesis that a disordered amino acid metabolism is a fundamental component of some forms of schizophrenia remains an attractive though fairly general one, chromatography as a means of searching for supporting evidence is convenient and valuable, and preliminary indications of differences are certainly provocative. Proof that any of these differences are characteristic of even a segment of the disease rather than artifactual or incidental has not yet been obtained.

The Epinephrine Hypothesis

The theory which relates the pathogenesis of schizophrenia to faulty metabolism of epinephrine (Osmond, 1955; Osmond & Smythies, 1952; Hoffer, 1957; Hoffer, Osmond & Smythies, 1954) is imaginative, ingenious, and plausible. It postulates that the symptoms of the disease are caused by the action of abnormal, hallucinogenic derivatives of epinephrine, presumably adrenochrome or adrenolutin. By including the concept of an enzymatic, possibly genetic, defect with another factor, epinephrine release, which may be activated by stressful life situations (Szara, Axelrod, & Perlin, 1958), it encompasses the evidence for sociological as well as constitutional factors in the etiology of the schizophrenias.

The possibility that some of the oxidation products of epinephrine are psychotomimetic received support from anecdotal reports of psychological disturbances associated with the therapeutic use of the compound, especially when it was discolored (Osmond, 1955), and from some early experiments in which the administration of adrenochrome or adrenolutin in appreciable dosage was followed by certain unusual mental manifestations (Hoffer, Osmond, & Smythies, 1954). A number of investigators failed to demonstrate any hallucinogenic properties in adrenochrome (Rinkel & Solomon, 1957), and the original authors were not always able to confirm their earlier results.

Meanwhile, reports were emerging from the group at Tulane University, suggesting a gross disturbance in epinephrine metabolism in schizophrenic patients. Five years previously, Holmberg and Laurell (1951) had demonstrated a more rapid oxidation of epinephrine in vitro in the presence of pregnancy serum than with serum from the umbilical cord and had suggested that this was due to higher concentrations of ceruloplasmin in the former. There had also been a few reports of an increase in levels of this protein in the blood of schizophrenics. Leach and Heath (1956) reported a striking acceleration in the vitro oxidation of epinephrine in the presence of plasma from schizophrenic patients as compared with that from normal subjects and shortly thereafter implicated ceruloplasmin or some variant of ceruloplasmin as the oxidizing substance (Leach, Cohen, Heath, Martens, 1956). Hoffer and Kenyon (1957) promptly reported evidence that the substance formed from epinephrine by blood serum in vitro was adrenolutin and pointed out how this strengthened the epinephrine hypothesis.

All of the evidence does not, however, support the epinephrine theory. In the past few years the major metabolites of epinephrine have been identified: 3-methoxy-4-hydroxymandelic acid, by Armstrong and his associates (Armstrong, McMillan, & Shaw, 1957), and its precursor, metanephrine, by Axelrod and his coworkers of this laboratory (Axelrod, Tomchick, 1958), where, in addition, the principal pathways of epinephrine metabolism in animals (Axelrod, Kety, 1958) have been demonstrated. The metabolites of C^{14}-labeled epinephrine in the urine of schizophrenic patients (Resnick, Wolfe, Freemen, Elmadjian, 1958) and in normal man (Kirshner, Goodall, Rosen, 1958) have been studied independently by others. No evidence has been found for the oxidation of epinephrine via adrenochrome and adrenolutin in any of these populations. Although it has been reported that there are appreciable amounts of adrenochrome in the blood of normal subjects and that these amounts increase considerably following administration of lysergic acid diethylamide (Hoffer, 1958), Szara, Axelrod, and Perlin, using techniques of high sensitivity, have been unable to detect adrenochrome in the blood of normal test subjects or in that of acute or chronic schizophrenic patients (1958). In a recent ingenious study of the rate of destruction of epinephrine in vivo, no difference between normal subjects and schizophrenic patients was found in this regard (Holland, Cohen, Goldenberg, Sha, Leifer, 1958). Finally, it has been shown, by McDonald (1958) in our laboratory and by members of the Tulane group themselves (Angel, Leach, Martens, Cohen, Heath, 1957), that the low level of ascorbic acid in the blood is an important and uncontrolled variable in the rapid in vitro oxidation of epinephrine by plasma from schizophrenic patients. The fact that McDonald has been able to produce wide fluctuations in the epinephrine oxidation phenomenon, from normal to highly abnormal rates, in both normal subjects and schizophrenics merely by altering the level of ascorbic acid in the blood by dietary means, and that this has had no effect on the mental processes of either group, is quite convincing evidence of the dietary and secondary nature of the phenomenon.

It should be pointed out that none of this negative evidence invalidates the theory that some abnormal product of epinephrine metabolism, existing somewhere in the body, produces the major symptoms of schizophrenia; it does, however, considerably weaken the evidence which has been used to support the theory. In addition, there is the bothersome observation of numerous workers (Lindemann, 1935; Heath, Leach, Byers, Martens, Feigley, 1958; Dynes & Tod, 1940) that the administration of epinephrine to schizophrenics, which, according to the theory, should aggravate the psychotic symptoms, is not accompanied by appreciably greater mental disturbance than occurs in normal subjects.

Quite recently a new report on inconstant psychotomimetic effects of epinephrine oxidation products in a small number of subjects has appeared (Taubmann & Jantz, 1957), with evidence suggesting that the psychotic substance is neither adrenochrome nor adrenolutin, that it is active in microgram quantities, and that it is highly labile. This report, like the previous ones which described the psychotomimetic effects of epinephrine products, is highly subjective and incompletely controlled. Even if these conclusions are accepted, the relevance of such hallucinogens to, or their presence in, schizophrenia remains to be demonstrated.

REFERENCES

Acheson, R. M., Paul, R. M., & Tomlinson, R. V. *Can. J. Biochem. Physiol.*, 1958, **36**, 295.

Altschule, M. D., Henneman, D. H., Holliday, P., & Goncz, R. M. *A.M.A. Arch. Internal Med.*, 1956, **98**, 35.

Altschule, M. D., Henneman, D. H., Holliday, P. D., & Goncz, R. M. *A.M.A. Arch. Internal Med.*, 1957, **99**, 22.

Angel, C., Leach, B. E., Martens, S., Cohen, M., & Heath, R. G. *A.M.A. Arch. Neurol. Psychiat.*, 1957, **78**, 500.

Aprison, M. H. & Grosz, H. J. *A.M.A. Arch. Neurol. Psychiat.*, 1958, **79**, 575.

Armstrong, M. D., McMillan, A., & Shaw, K. N. F. *Biochem. et Biophys.*, 1957, Acta 25, 422.

Armstrong, M. D., & Shaw, K. N. F. *J. Biol. Chem.*, 1956, **225**, 269.

Armstrong, M. D., Shaw, K. N. F., Gortatowski, M. J., & Singer, H. *J. Biol. Chem.*, 1958, **223**, 17.

Armstrong, M. D., Wall, P. E., & Parker, V. J. *J. Biol. Chem.*, 1956, **218**, 921.

Axelrod, J., Senoh, S., & Witkop, B. *J. Biol. Chem.*, 1958, **233**, 697.

Axelrod, J., & Tomchick, R. *J. Biol. Chem.*, 1958, **233**, 702.

Barak, A. J., Fumoller, F. L., & Stevens, J. D. *A.M.A. Arch. Neurol. Psychiat.*, 1958, **80**, 237.

Benjamin, J. D. *Psychosom. Med.*, 1958, **20**, 427.

Board, F., Persky, H., & Hamburg, D. A. *Psychosom. Med.*, 1956, **18**, 324.

Booth, A. N., Emerson, O. H., Hones, F. T., & Deeds, F. *J. Biol. Chem.*, 1957, **229**, 51.

Boszormenyi-Nagy, I., & Gerty, F. J. *J. Nervous Mental Disease*, 1955, **121**, 53.

Boszormenyi-Nagy, I., Gerty, F. J., & Kueber, J. *J. Nervous Mental Disease*, 1956, **124**, 413.

Buscaino, V. M. *Acta Neurol.* (Naples), 1958, **13**, 1.

Cafruny, E. J., & Domino, E. F. *A.M.A. Arch. Neurol. Psychiat.*, 1958, **79**, 336.

Dastur, D. K. *A.M.A. Arch. Neurol. Psychiat.*, 1959, **81**, 601.

David, G. B. The pathological anatomy of the schizophrenias. In *Schizophrenia: Somatic Aspects.* London: Pergamon, 1957. Pp. 93-130.

Dynes, J. B., & Tod, H. *J. Neurol. Psychiat.*, 1940, **3**, 1.

Elmadjian, R., Hope, J. M., & Lamson, E. T. *J. Clin. Endocrinol. and Metabolism*, 1957, **17**, 608.

Evarts, E. V. *Psychiat. Research Repts.*, 1958, **9**, 52.

Fischer, R., Georgi, R., Weber, R., & Piaget, R. M. *Schweiz. med. Wochschr.*, 1950, **80**, 129.

Freedman, D. A. *Diseases of Nervous System*, 1958, **19**, 108.

Georgi, F., Honegger, C. G., Jordan, D., Rieder, H. P., & Rottenberg, M. *Klin. Wochschr.*, 1956, **34**, 799.

Gjessing, L., Bernhardsen, A., & Froshaug, H. *J. Mental Sci.*, 1958, **104**, 188.

Gjessing, R. *J. Mental Sci.*, 1938, **84**, 608.

Gjessing, R. *Arch. Psychiat. Nervenkrankh*, 1939, **106**, 525.

Gordan, G. S., Estess, F. M., Adams, J. E., Bowman, K. M., & Simon, A. *A.M.A. Arch. Neurol. Psychiat.*, 1955, **73**, 544.

Harris, M. M. *A.M.A. Arch. Neurol. Psychiat.*, 1942, **48**, 761.

Heath, R. G., Leach, B. E., Byers, L. W., Martens, S., & Feigley, C. A. *Am. J. Psychiat.*, 1958, **114**, 683.

Hoffer, A. *J. Clin. Exptl. Psychopathol.*, 1957, **18**, 27.

Hoffer, A. *Am. J. Psychiat.*, 1958, **114**, 752.

Hoffer, A., & Kenyon, M. *A.M.A. Arch. Neurol. Psychiat.*, 1957, **77**, 437.

Hoffer, A., Osmond, H., & Smythies, J. *J. Mental Sci.*, 1954, **100**, 29.

Holland, B., Cohen, G., Goldenberg, M., Sha, J., & Leifer, L. *Federation Proc.*, 1958, **17**, 378.

Holmberg, C. G., & Laurell, C. B. *Scand. J. Clin. & Lab. Invest.*, 1951, **3**, 103.

Horwitt, M. K. Report of Elgin Project No. 3 with emphasis on liver dysfunction. *Nutrition Symposium Ser. No. 7.* New York: National Vitamin Foundation, 1953. Pp. 67-83.

Horwitt, M. K. *Science*, 1956, **124**, 429.

Horwitt, M. K., Liebert, E., Kreisler, O., & Wittman, P. *Bull. Natl. Research Council* (U.S.), 1948, 116.

Kelsey, F. O., Gullock, A. H., & Kelsey, F. E. *A.M.A. Arch. Neurol. Psychiat.*, 1957, **77**, 543.

Kety, S. S., Woodford, R. B., Harmel, M. H., Freyhan, F. A., Appel, K. E., & Schmidt, C. F. *Am. J. Psychiat.*, 1948, **104**, 765.

Keup, W. *Monatsschr. Psychiat. Neurol.*, 1954, **128**, 56.

Kirshner, N., Goodall, McC., & Rosen, L. *Proc. Soc. Exptl. Biol.*, 1958, **98**, 627.

Kopin, I. J. *Science*, 1959, **129**, 835.

Kornetsky, C. Personal communication.

Labrosse, E. H., Axelrod, J., & Kety, S. S. *Science*, 1958, **128**, 593.

Leach, B. E., Cohen, M., Heath, R. G., & Martens, S. *A.M.A. Arch. Neurol. Psychiat.* 1956, **76**, 635.

Leach, B. E., & Heath, R. G. *A.M.A. Arch. Neurol. Psychiat.*, 1956, **76**, 444.

Lindemann, E. *Am. J. Psychiat.*, 1935, **91**, 983.

Longo, V., Buscaino, G. A., D'Andrea, F., Uras, A., Ferrari, E., Rinaldi, F., & Pasolini, F. *Acta Neurol.* (Naples), 1953, Quad. III, 21.

Lovett Doust, J. W. *J. Mental Sci.*, 1952, **93**, 143.

Mann, J. D., & Labrosse, E. H. *A.M.A. Arch. Genl. Psychiat.*, in press.

Martens, S., Leach, B. E., Heath, R. G., & Cohen, M. *A.M.A. Arch. Neurol. Psychiat.*, 1956, **76**, 630.

McDonald, R. K. Plasma ceruloplasmin and ascorbic acid levels in schizophrenia. Paper presented at the annual meeting of the American Psychiatric Association, Chicago, Ill., 1957.

McDonald, R. K. *J. Chronic Diseases*, 1958, 8, 366.

McFarland, R. A., & Goldstein, H. *Am. J. Psychiat.*, 1938, **95**, 509.

McGeer, E. G., Brown, W. T., & McGeer, P. L. *J. Nervous Mental Disease*, 1957, **125**, 176.

McGeer, P. L., McNair, F. E., McGeer, E. G., & Gibson, W. C. *J. Nervous Mental Disease*, 1957, **125**, 166.

Meduna, L. J., Gerty, F. J., & Urse, V. G. *A.M.A. Arch. Neurol. Psychiat.*, 1942, 47, 38.

Morgan, M. S., & Pilgrim, F. J. *Proc. Soc. Exptl. Biol. Med.*, 1952, **79**, 106.

Moya, F., Dewar, J., MacIntosh, M., Hirsch, S., & Townsend, R. *Can. J. Biochem. and Physiol.*, 1958, **36**, 505.

Moya, F., Szerb, J. C., & MacIntosh, M. *Can. J. Biochem. and Physiol.*, 1956, **34**, 563.

Osmond, H. *Diseases of Nervous System*, 1955, **16**, 101.

Osmond, H., & Smythies, J. *J. Mental Sci.*, 1952, **98**, 309.

Perlin, S., & Lee, A. R. *Am. J. Psychiat.*, in press.

Peters, G. Dementia praecox. In *Handbuch der Speziellen Pathologischen Anatomie und Histologie*. Lubarsch, Henke, & Rossle (Eds.), Berlin: Springer, 1956, vol. 13, pt. 4. Pp. 1-52.

Resnick, O., Wolfe, J. M., Freeman, H., & Elmadjian, F. *Science*, 1958, **127**, 1116.

Richter, D. Biochemical aspects of schizophrenia. In *Schizophrenia: Somatic Aspects*. London: Pergamon, 1957. Pp. 53-75.

Riegelhaupt, L. M. *J. Nervous Mental Disease*, 1956, **123**, 383.

Rinkel, M., & Solomon, H. C. *J. Clin. Exptl. Psychopathol.*, 1957, **18**, 323.

Schottstaedt, W. W., Grace, W. J., & Wolff, H. G. *J. Psychosom. Research*, 1956, **1**, 147.

Schottstaedt, W. W., Grace, W. J., & Wolff, H. G. *J. Psychosom. Research*, 1956, **1**, 292.

Sokoloff, L., Perlin, S., Kornetsky, C., & Kety, S. S. *Ann. N.Y. Acad. Sci.*, 1957, **66**, 468.

Surikov, M. P., Ushakov, G. K., Il'ina, B. N., Verbliunskaia, A. A., & Khokh-
    lov, L. K.   *Zhur. Nevropatol.*, 1957, **57**, 237.
Szara, S., Axelrod, J., & Perlin, S.   *Am. J. Psychiat.*, 1958, **115**, 162.
Taubmann, G., & Jantz, H.   *Nervenarzi*, 1957, **28**, 485.
Thudichum, J. W. L.   *A treatise on the chemical constitution of the brain.*
    London: Balliere, Tindall, & Cox, 1884.
Vestergaard, P., Abbott, M. T., Kline, N. S., & Stanley, A. M.   *J. Clin. Exptl.
    Psychopathol.*, 1958, **19**, 44.
Waalkes, T. P., Sjoerdsma, A., Creveling, C. R., Weissbach, H., & Udenfriend,
    S.   *Science*, 1958, **127**, 648.
Wilson, W. P., Schieve, J. F., & Scheinberg, P.   *A.M.A. Arch. Neurol. Psy-
    chiat.*, 1952, **68**, 651.
Young, H. K., Berry, H. K., & Beerstecher, E.   *University Texas Publ. No.
    5109*, 1951. Pp. 189-197.

PART II

In Part I of this article an attempt was made to discuss the possible sources of error peculiar to biological research in schizophrenia, including the possible heterogeneity of that symptom complex and the presence of certain biological features—such as adventitious disease, nutritional deficiencies, disturbances associated with abnormal motor or emotional states, and changes brought about by treatment, all of which may be said to result from the disease or from its current management rather than to be factors in its genesis. The difficulty of avoiding subjective bias was emphasized. Some of the hypotheses relating to oxygen, carbohydrate, and energy metabolism, to amino acid metabolism, and to epinephrine were presented, and the existing evidence relevant to them was discussed. Among the recent or current concepts there remain to be discussed those concerned with ceruloplasmin, with serotonin, and with the general genetic aspects of schizophrenic disorders.

Ceruloplasmin and Taraxein

The rise and fall of interest in ceruloplasmin as a biochemical factor significantly related to schizophrenia is one of the briefest, if not one of the most enlightening, chapters in the history of biological psychiatry. The upsurge of interest can be ascribed to a report that a young Swedish biochemist had discovered a new test for schizophrenia. The test depended upon the oxidation of N, N-dimethyl-*p*-phenylenediamine by ceruloplasmin (Akerfeldt, 1957;

Gibbs, 1957). It is difficult to understand the exaggerated interest which this report aroused, since Holmberg and Laurell (1951) had demonstrated previously that ceruloplasmin was capable of oxidizing a number of substances, including phenylenediamine and epinephrine, and Leach and Heath (1956) had already published a procedure based on epinephrine oxidation which was equally valid as a means of distinguishing schizophrenics from normal subjects and had identified the oxidizing substance as ceruloplasmin (Leach, Cohen, Heath, Martens, 1956). All of these observations were compatible with earlier reports in the German literature (Keup, 1954) of an increase in serum copper in schizophrenia and with the demonstration that practically all of the serum copper was in the form of ceruloplasmin and that the levels of this compound in blood were elevated during pregnancy and in a large number of diseases (Holmberg & Laurell, 1948; Markowitz, Gubler, Mahoney, Cartwright, Wintrobe, 1955). There had even been preliminary observations of an increase in blood ceruloplasmin in schizophrenia (Markowitz, Gubler, Mahoney, Cartwright, Wintrobe, 1955). Following the announcement of the Akerfeldt test, however, interest in copper and ceruloplasmin rose, and very soon a number of investigators reported this reaction, or some modification of it, to be positive in a high percentage of schizophrenics (Gibbs, 1957; Abood, Gibbs, & Gibbs, 1957), although as a diagnostic test the Akerfeldt procedure was discredited because of the large number of diseases, besides schizophrenia, in which the results were positive. Both Akerfeldt and Heath recognized that ascorbic acid could inhibit the oxidation of phenylenediamine and of epinephrine, respectively, but neither felt that this was crucial to his findings, since each had satisfied himself that the feeding of large doses of ascorbic acid to the patients had not influenced the respective reactions (Gibbs, 1957). In addition, Abood (1957), who used a modification of the Akerfeldt procedure which was not affected by ascorbic acid, was able to obtain a positive reaction indicating abnormally high ceruloplasmin levels in two-thirds of the more than 250 schizophrenics he had examined.

In the past 18 months there has been a remarkable decline in the interest in, and the reported levels of, ceruloplasmin in schizophrenia. In May of 1957, McDonald (1957) reported his findings on three groups of schizophrenics, one group from the wards of the National Institute of Mental Health, where the patients had been maintained on a more than adequate diet, and two groups from state hospitals. He performed the Akerfeldt test and the

Abood modification of it, as well as independent tests to measure ascorbic acid and copper, on these groups and on three groups of controls. In none of the schizophrenic groups was there an increase in ceruloplasmin. In the state-hospital patients and one group of controls, however, ascorbic acid levels were low and the results of Akerfeldt test were positive, whereas in schizophrenic patients from the National Institute of Mental Health, levels of ascorbic acid were normal and the results of Akerfeldt tests were negative. It was clear that a high ceruloplasmin level was not characteristic of schizophrenia and that a positive response to the Akerfeldt test, where it occurred, could be completely explained by a dietary insufficiency of ascorbic acid.

In findings of the Tulane group, the mean values for serum copper in schizophrenia have decreased from a high of 216 micrograms per 100 milliliters in 1956 (Leach, Cohen, Heath, & Martens, 1956) to 145 micrograms per 100 milliliters at the end of 1957 (Leach & Heath, 1956), mean normal values having remained at 122 and 124 micrograms per 100 milliliters during the same period. Other groups have found slight differences or no differences at all with respect to blood levels of ceruloplasmin or copper between schizophrenic and normal subjects (Scheinberg, Morell, Harris, Berger, 1957; Horwitt, Meyer, Harvey, Haffron, 1957; Frohman, Goodman, Luby, Beckett, Senf, 1958; Aprison & Grosz, 1958) and no support for the theory that the Akerfeldt test is a means of distinguishing between schizophrenic and nonschizophrenic patients (Aprison & Drew, 1958). It is not clear why some schizophrenics apparently show an elevated level of ceruloplasmin in the blood; among suggested explanations are dietary factors, hepatic damage, chronic infection, or the possibility that excitement tends to raise the level of ceruloplasmin in the blood, as preliminary experiments appear to indicate (Ostfeld, Abood, Marcus, 1958).

Quite early in their studies, members of the Tulane group recognized that the potent oxidant effects of the serum of schizophrenics on epinephrine in vitro could not be satisfactorily explained by the ceruloplasmin levels alone (Leach, Cohen, Heath, & Martens, 1956). Before they recognized the importance to this reaction of ascorbic acid deficiency (Angel, Leach, Martens, Cohen, & Heath, 1958), they had postulated the presence in the blood of schizophrenics of a qualitatively different form of ceruloplasmin (Leach, Cohen, Heath, & Martens, 1956), which they proceeded to isolate and to test in monkey and man, and to which they have given the name *taraxein* (from the Greek root *tarassein*, meaning "to disturb"). They have reported that when certain batches of this material were tested in monkeys, marked behavior and electroencephalographic changes occurred. When samples of these active batches were injected intravenously at a rapid rate into carefully selected prisoner volunteers, all of the subjects developed symptoms which have been described as characteristic of schizophrenia —disorganization and fragmentation of thought, autism, feelings of depersonalization, paranoid ideas, auditory hallucinations, and catatonic behavior (Heath, Martens, Leach, Cohen, Feigley, 1958; Heath, Martens, Leach, Cohen, & Angel, 1957).

Demonstration of toxic materials in the blood and in the body fluids of schizophrenic patients is not new. The voluminous and inconclusive work of earlier investigators was well reviewed by Keup in 1954. Since that time, many new reports have appeared, although there has been no extensive substantiation of any of them. The results of one, on the toxicity of serum and urine of schizophrenic patients for the larvae of *Xenopus laevis* (Fischer, 1953), were disputed by the laboratory in which the work was done (Georgi, Rieder, & Weber, 1954). Edisen (1956) was unable to demonstrate toxicity of such serum for the species of tadpole previously used, or for other species and other genera. A report that serum from schizophrenic patients is toxic to cells in tissue culture (Fedoroff, 1955) lost some of its significance when 1 year later the same laboratory reported that the sera of surgical patients (Fedoroff & Moffer, 1956) was of camparable toxicity. Reports that injection of certain extracts of the urine of schizophrenic patients induces electroencephalographic and behavioral changes in rats (Wada, 1957) or disturbances in web construction in spiders (Rieder, 1957) have not yet received confirmation in the scientific literature. Such urine, however, has been reported to have no effect on the Siamese fighting fish, which is remarkably sensitive to certain hallucinogens (Smith & Moody, 1956). Contrary to earlier findings, a recent attempt to demonstrate behavioral changes in rats following the injection of cerebrospinal fluid from catatonic patients was unsuccessful (Shapiro, 1956). A highly significant decrease in rope-climbing speed in rats injected with sera from psychotic patients as opposed to sera from nonpsychotic controls has been reported by Winter and Flataker (1957). Their later finding (1958) that the phenomenon occurs with sera of patients with a wide variety of mental disorders, including mental retardation and alcoholism, and that there is a considerable variation in this index between similar groups at different hospitals, coupled with the inability of at least one other investigator (Kornetsky, personal communication; Ghent & Freedman, 1958) to demonstrate this phenomenon in the small group of schizophrenic patients under investigation in this laboratory, suggests that the quite real and statistically significant phenomenon originally observed may be related to variables other than those specific for, or fundamental to, schizophrenia. More recently, Ghent and Freedman (1958) have reported their inability to confirm the observations of Winter and Flataker.

It has been reported that rabbits pretreated with serum from schizophrenics do not exhibit a pressor response following the local application of an epinephrine solution to the cerebral cortex (Minz & Walaszek, 1957). No difference between the action of sera from normal subjects and that from schizophrenics was demonstrated by means of this procedure in tests of sera from a small number of individuals on our wards.

The significance of all of these studies in animals, whether the studies are successful or unsuccessful in demonstrating a toxic factor in schizophrenia, is quite irrelevant to, and considerably dwarfed by, the implications of the taraxein studies. It is because of the tremendous implications which these results could have in the etiology and rational therapy of this important disorder that a reviewer must evaluate them with even more than the usual care.

In the first place, the important biochemical phenomena originally reported in schizophrenia—lowered blood levels of glutathoine and rapid oxidation of epinephrine in vitro—which prompted the search for taraxein and directed work on its isolation toward the ceruloplasmin fraction of serum (Heath, Martens, Leach, Cohen, & Feigley, 1958; Heath, Leach, Byers, Martens, & Feigley, 1958; Heath, Martens, Leach, Cohen, & Angel, 1957), have since been controverted by data reported by the same group as well as by others and have been regarded by most workers as spurious or at least unrelated in any direct way to the schizophrenic process (Angel, Leach, Martens, Cohen, & Heath, 1957; McDonald, 1958; Barak, Humoller, & Stevens, 1958). This, in itself, does not preclude the possible validity of the taraxeien phenomenon, since bona fide discoveries have occasionally been made on the basis of erroneous leads; it does, however, reduce the probability of its occurrence from that involved in a logical interrelationship of sequential proven steps to the extremely small chance of selecting this particular and heretofore unknown substance from the thousands of substances which occur in blood and which might have been chosen.

One attempt by Robins, Smith, and Lowe (1957) to confirm the Tulane findings, in tests in which they used comparable numbers and types of subjects and at least equally rigorous controls, was quite unsuccessful. In 20 subjects who at different times received saline or extracts of blood from normal or schizophrenic donors, prepared according to the method for preparing taraxein, there were only five instances of mental or behavioral disturbance resembling those cited in the original report on taraxein, and these occurred with equal frequency following the administration of saline, extracts of normal plasma, or taraxein. It is easy to dismiss the negative findings with taraxein on the basis of the difficulty of reproducing exactly the 29 steps described in its preparation; it is considerably more difficult to dismiss the observation that a few subjects who received only saline or normal blood extract developed psychotic manifestations similar to those reported with taraxein.

During the preliminary investigations it was stated, on the basis of unpublished studies (Leach, Cohen, Heath, & Martens, 1956), that taraxein was qualitatively different from ceruloplasmin. A physicochemical or other objective characterization of taraxein would do much to dispel some of the confusion regarding its nature. Is it possible, for example, that taraxein is, in fact, ceruloplasmin but ceruloplasmin that derives its special properties from the psychosocial characteristics of the situation in which it has been tested? This question was raised more than a year ago (Kety, 1957), and since then additional evidence has become available which tends to support it. This is a detailed report from a psychoanalyst at Tulane of the experience of one of his patients who received taraxein (Lief, 1957). Even though a "double blind" procedure was said to have been used, there are enough possibilities for the operation of unconscious bias in this one case, if it is at all typical of the means used to demonstrate the psychotomimetic properties of taraxein, to raise some doubts concerning the validity of these properties. The subject, a psychiatric resident, knew before the injection that he was to get either saline or a potent sample of taraxein which had made a monkey catatonic for several hours. Immediately following the injection he noted venous distension, tachycardia, a swollen feeling of the head, and flushing of the head and face, which, a footnote explains, was probably a reaction to the ammonium sulfate in the taraxein solution. Following these symptoms, which the subject could hardly have attributed to saline, there ensued a period of introspective cogitation, with occasional mild mental disturbances quite compatible with the anxiety-producing nature of the situation, with the preparation and cues which the subject had received, and with his anticipation of marked psychotic reactions and not necessarily symptomatic of a chemical toxin at all. The changes were not qualitatively dissimilar to those which Robins and his associates had on a few occasions obtained with their control solutions (Robins, Smith, & Lowe, 1957). The report of the observer who injected the material was longer and mentioned more numerous and more bizarre subjective feelings than the subject himself reported. The observer's summary of the subject's reactions as blocking of thought processes, autism, bodily estrangement, and suspiciousness seems incompletely supported by the subject's retrospective report.

The possibility, remote as it may be, that the reported effects of taraxein are the result of a combination of suggestion, nonspecific toxic reactions from ammonium sulfate or other contaminants, and reinforcement of these cues by the unconscious biases of subject and observer through the device of an unstructured interview, is one which has not been ruled out. Hypotheses related to the mechanism of action of this material have moved from concern with abnormalities in the blood to concern with abnormalities in the blood-brain barrier; but the question of whether taraxein acts as a biological cause or as a mediator of some of the symptoms of schizophrenia is by no means resolved. I have already mentioned the only attempt of which I am aware on the part of an independent group to confirm the original results in a controlled series of significant size, and that attempt was unsuccessful.

Serotonin

Serotonin, an important derivative of tryptophan, was first shown to exist in the brain in high concentration by Amin, Crawford, and Gaddum (1954). Interest in its possible function in the central nervous system and speculation that it might even be related to schizophrenia were inspired by the finding that certain hallucinogens, notably lysergic acid diethylamide, could, in extremely low concentration, block the effects of serotonin on smooth muscle. Thus, Woolley and Shaw in 1954 wrote: "The demonstrated ability of such agents to antagonize the action of serotonin in smooth muscle and the finding of serotonin in the brain suggest that the mental changes caused by the drugs are the result of a serotonin-deficiency which they induce in the brain. If this be true, then the naturally occurring mental disorders—for example, schizophrenia—which are mimicked by these drugs, may be pictured as being the result of a cerebral serotonin deficiency arising from a metabolic failure. . . ." Simultaneously, in England, Gaddum (1954) was speculating, "it is possible that the HT in our brains plays an essential part in keeping us sane and that the effect of LSD is due to its inhibitory action on the HT in the brain." Since that time additional evidence has appeared to strengthen these hypotheses.

Levels of serotonin have been found to be considerably higher in the limbic system and other areas of the brain which appear to be associated with emotional states (Bogdanski, Weissbach, & Udenfriend, 1957; Paasonen, MacLean, & Giarman, 1957) than elsewhere. Bulotenin, or dimethyl serotonin, extracted from a hallucinogenic snuff of West Indian tribes, was found to have some properties similar to those of lysergic acid diethylamide (Evarts, 1956; Fabing & Hawkins, 1956). A major discovery was the finding that the ataractic agent, reserpine, causes a profound and persistent fall in the level of serotonin in the brain (Shore, Pletscher, Tomich, Carlsson, Kuntzman, & Brodie, 1957), a process which more closely parallels the mentals effects of reserpine than does its own concentration in the brain. By administration of the precursor, 5-hydroxytryptophan, the levels of serotonin can be markedly elevated in the brain, with behavioral effects described as resembling those of lysergic acid diethylamide (Udenfriend, Weissbach, Bogdanski, 1957)—a finding quite at odds with the original hypotheses. On the other hand, administration of this precursor to mental patients, along with a benzyl analog of serotonin to block the peripheral effects of the amine, has been reported, in preliminary trials, to suppress the disease (Woolley, 1957), while confusion is compounded by the report that the benzyl analog alone is an effective tranquilizing drug in chronically psychotic patients (Rudy, Costa, Rinaldi, & Himwich, 1958).

Still another bit of evidence supporting the hypotheses of a central function for serotonin was the accidental discovery of toxic psychoses in a certain fraction of tuberculous patients treated with iproniazid (Crane, 1956; Pleasure, 1954), which has led to the therapeutic use of this drug in psychic depression. It is known that iproniazid inhibits the action of monoamine oxidase, an enzyme which destroys serotonin, and it has been shown that iproniazid increases the levels of this amine in the brain (Udenfriend, Weissbach, & Bogdanski, 1957).

There are certain inconsistencies in the data cited above to support the serotonin hypotheses, and no single theory has been found to explain all of the findings, even though full use is made of the concept of "free" and "bound" forms and of the common pharmacological principle of stimulant and depressant effects from the same drug under different circumstances. Moreover, certain weaknesses have appeared in each of the main supporting hypotheses, and these should be noted.

Although the ability of the hallucinogen lysergic acid diethylamide to block effects of serotonin on smooth muscle prompted the development of the hypotheses relating serotonin to mental function or disease, a number of lysergic acid derivatives have since been studied, and the correlation between mental effects and antiserotonin activity in the series as a whole is quite poor (Rothlin, 1957). One of these compounds is 2-bromo-lysergic acid diethylamide; this has 1.5 times the antiserotonin activity of lysergic acid diethylamide, and through this property, its presence in the brain, after systemic administration, can be demonstrated, but in doses more than 15 times as great it produces none of the mental effects of lysergic acid diethylamide (Rothlin, 1957). A recent report that, at least in one preparation, lysergic acid diethylamide in low concentration behaves like serotonin and does not antagonize it (Welsh & McCoy, 1957) seems to reconcile some of the empirical inconsistencies in the field, although it is quite at odds with the original hypotheses based on the antagonistic action of lysergic acid diethylamide.

Levels of norepinephrine as well as serotonin are markedly lowered in the brain following administration of reserpine (Holzbauer & Vogt, 1956; Vogt, 1957). In fact, the brain concentrations of these two amines follow each other so closely in their response to reserpine as to suggest some mechanism common to both and perhaps obtaining as well for other active amines in the brain. In one study, 3,4-dihydroxyphenylalanine, a precursor of norepinephrine, was capable of counteracting the behavioral effects of reserpine, whereas the precursor of serotonin was ineffective (Carlsson, Lindqvist, & Magnusson, 1957). Moreover, the effects of iproniazid are not limited to brain serotonin; a comparable effect on norepinephrine has been reported (Spector, Prockop, Shore, & Brodie, 1958), and it is possible that other amines or substances still to be discovered in the brain may be affected by what may be a nonspecific inhibitor of a relatively nonspecific enzyme. Of great interest in this connection are recent studies of Olds and Olds (1958) indicating a positive behavioral response for iproniazid injected into the hypothalamus but not for serotonin or norepinephrine.

Chlorpromazine, which has the same therapeutic efficacy as reserpine in disturbed behavior, is apparently able to achieve this action without any known effect on serotonin. In addition, the provocative observation that iproniazid, which elevates serotonin levels in the brain, can cause a toxic psychosis loses some of its impact when one realizes that isoniazid, which does not inhibit monoamine oxidase and can hardly raise the brain serotonin concentration, produces a similar psychosis (Pleasure, 1954; Jackson, 1957).

It seems reasonable to conclude that the serotonin as well as the norepinephrine in the brain have some important functions there, and the evidence in general supports this thesis, even though it also suggests that their roles still remain to be defined.

If the picture of the role which serotonin plays in central nervous function is blurred, the direct evidence to support the early speculations that it is involved in mental illness is meager and contradictory. From all of the evidence cited above, one could find a basis for predicting that in schizophrenia the serotonin levels in the brain, if they are altered at all, should be quite low or quite high. Results confirming both predictions have been reported.

The urinary excretion of 5-hydroxyin-doleacetic acid has been used as an indicator of the portion of ingested tryptophan which is metabolized through serotonin to form that end product. Although excretion of 5-hydroxyindoleacetic acid is normal in schizophrenic patients under ordinary circumstances (Buscaino, Stefanachi, 1958; Feldstein, Hoagland, & Freeman, 1958), it may be altered by challenging the metabolic systems with large doses of tryptophan. Zeller and his associates have reported a failure on the part of schizophrenics, under these circumstances, to increase their output of 5-hydroxyindoleacetic acid, while nonpsychotic controls double theirs (Zeller, Bernsohn, Inskip, Lauer, 1957; Lauer, Inskip, Bernsohn, & Zeller, 1958). Banerjee and Agarwal, on the other hand, have reported exactly the opposite results; in their study it was the schizophrenics who doubled their output of the serotonin end product, while the output of the controls remain unchanged (1958).

Kopin, of our laboratory, has had the opportunity to perform a similar study on schizophrenics and normal controls maintained on a good and reasonably controlled diet and given no drugs. In each group there was a slightly greater than twofold increase in output of 5-hydroxyindoleacetic acid following a tryptophan load, and there was no significant deviation from this pattern in any single case (Kopin, 1959).

That the heuristic speculations of Woolley and Shaw, and of Gaddum, have not yet been established does not mean that they are invalid. The widespread experimental activity which they stimulated has broadened and deepened our knowledge of the metabolism and pharmacology of serotonin and of its effects on behavior and may lead the way to definitive evaluation of its possible role in normal and pathological states.

Genetics and Schizophrenic Disorders

Many of the current hypotheses concerning the schizophrenia complex are original and attractive even though, up to this time, evidence directly implicating any one of them in the disease itself is hardly compelling. There is, nevertheless, cogent evidence that is responsible to a large extent for the present reawakening of the long dormant biochemical thinking in this area and sufficiently convincing to promote its continued development. Genetic studies have recently assumed such a role, and it appears worth while briefly to review them in the present context.

In earlier studies on large populations, a remarkable correlation was reported between the incidence of schizophrenia and the degree of consanguinity in relatives of known schizophrenics (Kallman, 1946). These findings were not conclusive, however, since the influence of socioenvironmental factors was not controlled. Better evidence is obtained from the examination of the co-twins and siblings of schizophrenics; a number of such studies have been completed and are summarized in Table 1. (Kallmann, 1946; Luxenburger, 1928; Rosanoff, Handy, Plesset, & Brush, 1934; Slater, 1953). The concordance rate for schizophrenia is extremely high for monozygotic twins in all the studies, while that for dizygotic twins is low and not significantly different from that in siblings, to which, of course, dizygotic twins are quite comparable genetically. Even these studies, however, are not completely free from possible sources of error, and this makes it difficult to arrive at a definitive conclusion regarding the role of genetic factors in this disease. One cannot assume that environmental similarities and mutual interactions in identical twins, who are always of the same sex and whose striking physical congruence is often accentuated by parental attitudes, play an insignificant role in the high concordance rate of schizophrenia in this group. This factor could be controlled by a study of twins separated at birth (of such twins no statistically valid series has yet been compiled) or by a comparison of the concordance rates in monozygotic twins and in dizygotic twins whose zygosity had been mistakenly evaluated by the twins themselves and by their parents and associates. Another possible means of better controlling the environmental variables would be to make a careful study of schizophrenia in adopted children, with comparison of the incidence in blood relatives and in foster relatives. Perhaps only a survey on a national scale would provide the requisite number of cases for any of these studies.

TABLE 1
CONCORDANCE RATES FOR SCHIZOPHRENIA FOUND IN STUDIES OF TWINS

Investigator	Number of pairs		Concordance rate* (%)	
	Dizygotic	Monozygotic	Dizygotic	Monozygotic
Luxenburger (1928)	48	17	2	59 (67)
Rosanoff et al. (1934)	101	41	10	61
Kallmann (1946)	517	174	10 (15)	69 (86)
Slater (1953)	115	41	11 (14)	68 (76)

* Figures in parentheses indicate rate after correction for the chance that a co-twin, normal at the time of observation, may develop the disease later.

A less satisfactory resolution of this problem can be obtained by an appraisal of environmental similarities in normal fraternal and identical twins. Such a study, on over 100 specific aspects of the environment, has been made (Wilson, 1934), and I have assembled the results into a rough index of environmental similarity (Table 2). Although a difference is apparent, in the crude measurement of environmental congruence, between identical and fraternal twins of like sex, it is not statistically significant and can account for only a small fraction of the large difference in concordance with respect to schizophrenia between these types of twins. On the other hand, there is a highly significant difference in environmental similarity between fraternal twins of like and unlike sex which is sufficient to account for the difference in concordance with respect to schizophrenic psychosis between them, for which, of course, there is no tenable genetic explanation.

TABLE 2

ENVIRONMENTAL FACTORS IN STUDIES OF SCHIZOPHRENIA IN TWINS

Sex	Environmental similarity in normal twins* (%)	Number of pairs	Concordance with respect to schizophrenia† (%)	Number of pairs
		Identical twins		
Same	61	70	86	174
		Fraternal twins		
Same	53	69	18	296
Different	26	55	10	221
		Siblings		
Same			16	
Different			12	

* Estimated from data of P. T. Wilson (1934).
† From data of F. J. Kallmann (1946).

Two recent reports have been used, but by no means conclusively, in support of the position that too much significance has been attached to environmental factors as determining causes in this disease group. Chapman (1957), reporting a case of concordant early infantile autism in identical twins, points out that this disorder has never been reported as concordant in fraternal twins, whereas it has been described in three sets of identical twins. Since fraternal twins occur nearly three times as frequently as identical twins, the evidence cited is suggestive, in spite of the small numbers involved; furthermore, the disease may develop before the personal identifications and interactions peculiar to monozygotic twins have had much chance to operate. Another interesting finding in over 150 families with a single schizophrenic member is that no ordinal position in the family appears to carry specific vulnerability to schizophrenia (Grosz & Miller, 1958)—a finding completely compatible with genetic theory but more difficult to reconcile with theories of environmental etiology if the assumption is correct that different positions within the family are subject to varying degrees of stress. Of course one may argue quite properly that schizophrenogenic stress exists and can be evaluated only in terms of the reaction between each individual and his own environment, so that any position on a social, economic, occupational, or birth-order scale may be associated with greatly different degrees of stress for different individuals.

Another possible source of error in the twin studies which have been reported is the personal bias of the investigators who made the judgment of zygosity and the diagnosis of schizophrenia in the co-twins. Until a more definitive study is carried out in which these judgments are made independently, a rough evaluation is possible, at least for the diagnosis of schizophrenia, if not for zygosity, on the basis of diagnoses arrived at in the various hospitals to which the co-twins may have been admitted before or irrespective of their involvement in the study—diagnoses which are not likely to have been contaminated by knowledge about their zygosity. Kallmann has been kind enough to review the material collected in his 1946-49 survey from that point of view. Of 174 monozygotic co-twins of schizophrenic index cases, 103, or 59 percent, had been diagnosed schizophrenic by Kallmann, while 87, or 50 percent, had received a psychiatric hospital diagnosis of schizophrenia prior to any examination made by him. On the other hand, he had made the diagnosis of schizophrenia in 47, or 9.1 percent, of 517 dizygotic co-twins as compared to a hospital diagnosis in 31, or 6 percent. Although the concordance rates based only on hospital diagnoses are lower in both types of twins, for obvious reasons, the striking difference between the two concordance rates remains. Slater (1953) has published individual protocols of his cases from which I have made judgments of zygosity and schizophrenia. Of 21 pairs of twins who could be considered definitely uniovular, 15, or 75 percent, were concordant with respect to the simple criterion of admission to a mental hospital, whereas in only 12, or 10.3 percent, of 116 binovular or questionably binovular pairs was there a history of the co-twin's having been admitted to a mental hospital for any psychosis. On the basis of this analysis of the two most recent series, it seems that only a small component of the great difference in concordance rates reported for schizophrenia between uniovular and binovular twins can be attributed to the operation of personal bias in the diagnosis of the disease in the co-twin.

Even the most uncritical acceptance of all the genetic data, however, cannot lead to the conclusion that the schizophrenic illnesses are the result of genetic factors alone. In 14 to 30 percent of the cases in which schizophrenia occurs in one of a pair of monozygotic twins, the genetically identical partner is found to be free of the disorder (Table 1). Attention has already been called (Table 2) to the higher concordance with respect to schizophrenia and the greater environmental similarities in like-sexed fraternal twins or siblings than in those of unlike sex, and from the same source

(Kallmann, 1946) a difference in concordance is reported between monozygotic twins separated some years before the study (77.6 percent) as opposed to those not separated (91.5 percent). Neither of these observations is compatible with a purely genetic etiology of the disease, and both suggest the operation of environmental factors. Rosenthal (in press) and Jackson (in press) have pointed out the striking preponderance of female over male pairs concordant for schizophrenia in all of the reported series, whether they be monozygotic or dizygotic twins, siblings, or parent-child pairs. If sampling errors resulting from the greater mobility of males are excluded and the observations are taken as a reflection of the true incidence of this phenomenon, several explanations for it on the basis of social interaction can be given, but none based on a purely genetic grounds, unless sex linkage is invoked, for which there is no other evidence.

Clausen has critically reviewed the extensive literature supporting the importance of environmental factors in the etiology of schizophrenic disorders (1959). The evidence there seems quite as suggestive as the genetic evidence but by no means more conclusive, since few studies in either field have been completely objective or adequately controlled.

It is both interesting and important to note that even if the conclusions of both the genetic and the environmental approaches to the etiology of schizophrenic psychoses are accepted uncritically, they are not mutually exclusive. Both are compatible with the hypothesis that this group of diseases results from the operation of socio-environmental factors on some hereditary predisposition, or from an interaction of the two, each being necessary but neither alone sufficient. An excellent example of such a relationship is seen in tuberculosis, where the importance of the environmental microbial factor is undisputed and where, as Lurie (Lurie, Abramson, & Heppelston, 1952) has shown, genetic susceptibility is likewise important; a population sufficiently heterogeneous with respect to susceptibility and exposure to tuberculosis yields results in contingency and twin studies (Planansky & Allen, 1953) which, before the discovery of the tubercle bacillus, could easily have been used to prove a primary genetic cause—almost as convincingly as the results of similar studies have been used to prove such a cause in schizophrenia. Interestingly enough, studies of tuberculosis made from the socioenvironmental point of view would obviously provide data offering equally convincing proof that exogenous, social, and economic factors play a part. One hypothesis with respect to the schizophrenic psychoses which remains compatible with all the evidence from the genetic as well as the psycho-social disciplines is that these disorders, like tuberculosis, require the operation of environmental factors upon a genetically determined predisposition.

Résumé

Although the evidence for genetic and therefore biological factors as important and necessary components in the etiology of many or all of the schizophrenias is quite compelling, the sign-posts pointing the way to their discovery are at present quite blurred and, to me at least, illegible.

Genetic factors may operate through some ubiquitous enzyme system to effect general changes in one or another metabolic pathway—changes detectable through studies of blood or urine—and it is to be hoped that the currently active search in these areas will continue.

It is at least equally possible, however, that these genetic factors may operate only through enzymes or metabolic processes peculiar to or confined within the brain, or even within extremely localized areas of the brain. We are in need of new hypotheses such as those of Elkes (1956) and many already discussed. In this connection, gamma-amino-butyric acid appears to be just as interesting a substance about which to construct working hypotheses as are the catechols or the indoles. It has been isolated only from nervous tissue, and its metabolism in such tissue has been investigated in some detail (Roberts & Frankel, 1950; Roberts, Rothstein, & Baxter, 1958), while its neurophysiological properties appear to be better defined than are those of the other two groups (Purpura, Girardo, Grundfest, 1957; Iwama & Jasper, 1957); in addition, its inhibitory properties may have special relevance to diseases where a failure in central inhibition seems to be involved.

Amphetamine possesses remarkable psychotomimetic properties which should not be overlooked. Its ability to produce a clinical syndrome often indistinguishable from schizophrenia (Connell, 1957) and the possible relation of amphetamine to the naturally occurring catechol amines make it at least as interesting as lysergic acid diethylamide.

In addition to techniques at present available in neurochemistry, neurophysiology, and behavioral pharmacology, the development of new methods designed to yield information on processes occurring within the psychotic brain will be needed before our explorations in this field have been exhausted.

But the biochemist must not lose sight of the possibility, which is certainly as great as any of the others, that the genetic factors in schizophrenia operate to determine inappropriate interconnections or interaction between chemically normal components of the brain; if that should prove to be the case, the physiological psychologist, the neurophysiologist, or the anatomist is likely to find meaningful information long before the biochemist does. It would take many biochemists a long time to find a noisy circuit in a radio receiver if they restricted themselves to chemical techniques.

These possibilities are mentioned only to indicate how large is the haystack in which we are searching for the needle; one cannot avoid a feeling of humility when one realizes how slight the chance is that any one of us has already found it, or will find it in a relatively short time.

That is no cause for discouragement, however. It is not necessary that one be convinced of the truth of a particular hypothesis to justify devoting one's energies to testing it. It is enough that one regard it as worth testing, and that the tools be adequate. Modern biochemistry, with its wealth of new knowledge of intermediary metabolism and its array of new techniques for the separation and identification of compounds and the tracing of their metabolic pathways, has provided the biologist interested in mental illness with an armamentarium which his predecessor of only a generation ago could hardly have envisioned. If he chooses from among the approaches which may lead to a definition of the biological factors in schizophrenia those which will in any case lead to a better understanding of the nervous system and of thought processes and behavior, the present surge of enthusiasm will not have been misdirected.

REFERENCES

Abood, L. G., Gibbs, F. A., & Gibbs, E.   *A.M.A. Arch. Neurol. Psychiat.*, 1957, 17, 643.

Akerfeldt, S.   *Science*, 1957, 125, 117.

Amin, A. H., Crawford, T. B. B., & Gaddum, J. H.   *J. Physiol.* (London), 1954, 126, 596.

Angel, C., Leach, B. E., Martens, S., Cohen, M., & Heath, R. G.   *A.M.A. Arch. Neurol. Psychiat.*, 1957, 79, 500.

Aprison, M. H., & Drew, A. L.   *Science*, 1958, 127, 758.
   Arch. Neurol. Psychiat., 1957, 79, 500.

Aprison, M. H., & Grosz, H. J.   *A.M.A. Arch. Neurol. Psychiat.*, 1958, 79, 575.

Banerjee, S., & Agarwal, P. S.   *Proc. Soc. Exptl. Biol. Med.*, 1958, 97, 657.

Barak, A. J., Humoller, F. L., & Stevens, J. D. *A.M.A. Arch. Neurol. Psychiat.*, 1958, **80**, 237.

Bogdanski, D. F., Weisbach, H., & Udenfriend, S. *J. Neurochem.*, 1957, **1**, 272.

Buscaino, G. A., & Stefanachi, L. *A.M.A. Neurol. Psychiat.*, 1958, **80**, 78.

Carlsson, A., Lindqvist, M., & Magnusson, T. *Nature*, 1957, **180**, 1200.

Chapman, A. H. *A.M.A. Arch. Neurol. Psychiat.*, 1957, **78**, 621.

Clausen, J. A. *Sociology today.* Merton, Broom, & Cottrell (Eds.), New York: Basic Books, 1959.

Connell, P. H. *Biochem. J.*, 1957, **65**, 7p.

Crane, G. E. *J. Nervous Mental Disease*, 1956, **124**, 322.

Edisen, C. B. *Diseases of Nervous System*, 1956, **17**, 77.

Elkes, J. "Neuropharmacology." In *Trans. Josiah Macy, Jr. Foundation 3rd Conf.*, 1956.

Evarts, E. V. *A.M.A. Arch. Neurol. Psychiat.*, 1956, **75**, 49.

Fabing, H. D., & Hawkins, J. R. *Science*, 1956, **123**, 886.

Fedoroff, S. *Anat. Record*, 1955, **121**, 394.

Fedoroff, S., & Hoffer, A. *J. Nervous Mental Disease*, 1956, **124**, 396.

Feldstein, A., Hoagland, H., & Freeman, H. *Science*, 1958, **128**, 358.

Fischer, R. *Proc. Intern. Physiol. Congr.*, 1953. Pp. 350-351.

Frohman, C. E., Goodman, M., Luby, E. D., Beckett, P. G. S., & Senf, R. *A.M.A. Arch. Neurol. Psychiat.*, 1958, **79**, 730.

Gaddum, J. H. *Ciba Foundation Symposium on Hypertension.* Boston: Little, Brown, 1954.

Georgi, F., Rieder, H. P., & Weber, R. *Science*, 1954, **120**, 504.

Ghent, L., & Freedman, A. M. *Am. J. Psychiat.*, 1958, **115**, 465.

Gibbs, F. A. (Ed.). *Blood Tests in Mental Illness.* Chicago: Brain Research Foundation, 1957.

Grosz, H. J., & Miller, I. *Science*, 1958, **128**, 30.

Heath, R. G., Leach, B. E., Byers, L. W., Martens, S., & Feigley, C. A. *Am. J. Psychiat.* 1958, **114**, 683.

Heath, R. G., Martens, S., Leach, B. E., Cohen, M., & Angel, C. *Am. J. Psychiat.*, 1957, **114**, 14.

Heath, R. G., Martens, S., Leach, B. E., Cohen, M., & Feigley, C. A. *Am. J. Psychiat.*, 1958, **114**, 917.

Holmberg, C. G., & Laurell, C. B. *Acta Chem. Scand.*, 1948, **2**, 550.

Holmberg, C. G., & Laurell, C. B. *Scand. J. Clin. & Lab. Invest.*, 1951, **3**, 103.

Holzbauer, M., & Vogt, M. *J. Neurochem.*, 1956, **1**, 8.

Horwitt, M. K., Meyer, B. J., Meyer, A. C., Harvey, C. C., & Haffron, D. *A.M.A. Arch. Neurol. Psychiat.*, 1957, **78**, 275.

Iwama, K., & Jasper, H. H. *J. Physiol.* (London), 1957, **138**, 365.

Jackson, D. D. (Ed.). *The study of schizophrenia.* New York: Basic Books, in press.

Jackson, S. L. O. *Brit. Med. J.*, 1957, **2**, 743.

Kallmann, F. J. *Am. J. Psychiat.*, 1946, **103**, 309.

Kety, S. S. *Trans. Josiah Macy, Jr. Foundation, 4th Conf.*, 1957.

Keup, W. *Monatsschr. Psychiat. Neurol.*, 1954, **128**, 56.

Kopin, I. J. *Science*, 1959, **129**, 835.

Kornetsky, C. Personal communication.

Lauer, J. W., Inskip, W. M., Bernsohn, J., & Zeller, E. A. *A.M.A. Arch. Neurol. Psychiat.*, 1958, **80**, 122.

Leach, B. E., Cohen, M., Heath, R. C., & Martens, S. *A.M.A. Arch. Neurol. Psychiat.*, 1956, **76**, 635.

Leach, B. E., & Heath, R. G. *A.M.A. Arch. Neurol. Psychiat.*, 1956, **76**, 444.

Lief, H. I. *A.M.A. Arch. Neurol. Psychiat.*, 1957, **78**, 624.

Lurie, M. B., Abramson, S., & Heppelston, A. *J. Exptl. Med.*, 1952, **95**, 119.

Luxenburger, H. *Z. ges. Neurol. Psychiat.*, 1928, **116**, 297.

Markowitz, H., Gubler, C. J., Mahoney, J. P., Cartwright, G. E., & Wintrobe, M. M. *J. Clin. Invest.*, 1955, **34**, 1498.

McDonald, R. K. Plasma ceruloplasmin and ascorbic acid levels in schizophrenia. Paper presented at the annual meeting of the American Psychiatric Association, Chicago, Ill., 1957.

McDonald, R. K. *J. Chronic Diseases*, 1958, **8**, 366.

Minz, B., & Walaszek, E. J. *Compt. rend.*, 1957, **244**, 1974.

Olds, J., & Olds, M. E. *Science*, 1958, **127**, 1175.

Ostfeld, A. M., Abood, L. G., & Marcus, D. A. *A.M.A. Arch. Neurol. Psychiat.*, 1958, **79**, 317.

Paasonen, M. K., MacLean, P. D., & Giarman, N. J. *J. Neurochem.*, 1957, **1**, 326.

Planansky, K., & Allen, G. *Am. J. Human Genet.*, 1953, **5**, 322.

Pleasure, H. *A.M.A. Arch. Neurol. Psychiat.*, 1954, **72**, 313.

Purpura, D. P., Girardo, M., & Grundfest, H. *Science*, 1957, **125**, 1200.

Rieder, H. P. *Psychiat. et Neurol.*, 1957, **134**, 378.

Roberts, E., & Frankel, S. *J. Biol. Chem.*, 1950, **187**, 55.

Roberts, E., Rothstein, M., & Baxter, C. F. *Proc. Exptl. Biol. Med.*, 1958, **97**, 796.

Robins, E., Smith, K., & Lowe, I. P. Neuropharmacology. In *Trans. Josiah Macy, Jr. Foundation, 4th Conf.*, 1957.

Rosanoff, A. J., Handy, L. M., Plesset, I. R., & Brush, S. *Am. J. Psychiat.*, 1934, **91**, 247.

Rosenthal, D. *J. Nervous Mental Disease*, in press.

Rothlin, E. *Ann. N.Y. Acad. Sci.*, 1957, **66**, 668.

Rudy, L. H., Costa, E., Rinaldi, F., & Himwich, H. E. *J. Nervous Mental Disease*, 1958, **126**, 284.

Scheinberg, I. H., Morell, A. G., Harris, R. S., & Berger, A. *Science*, 1957, **126**, 925.

Shapiro, A. K. *J. Nervous Mental Disease*, 1956, **123**, 65.

Shore, P. A., Pletscher, A., Tomich, E. G., Carlsson, A., Kuntzman, R., & Brodie, B. B. *Ann. N.Y. Acad. Sci.*, 1957, **66**, 609.

Slater, E. Psychotic and neurotic illnesses in twins. *Medical Research Council Special Report No. 278.* London: H.M. Stationery Office, 1953.

Smith, K., & Moody, A. C. *Diseases of Nervous System*, 1956, **17**, 327.

Spector, S., Prockop, D., Shore, P. A., & Brodie, B. B. *Science*, 1958, **127**, 704.

Udenfriend, S., Weissbach, H., & Bogdanski, D. F.   *Ann. N.Y. Acad. Sci.*, 1957, **66**, 602.

Vogt, M.   In *Metabolism of the nervous system.* D. Richter (Ed.), London: Pergamon, 1957. Pp. 553-565.

Wada, J.   *Proc. Soc. Biol. Psychiatrists, 12th Ann. Conv.*, 1957.

Welsh, J. H., & McCoy, A. C.   *Science*, 1957, **125**, 348.

Wilson, P. T.   *Human biology*, 1934, **6**, 324.

Winter, C. A., & Flataker, L.   *A.M.A. Arch. Neurol. Psychiat.*, 1958, **80**, 441.

Winter, C. A., & Flataker, L.   *Proc. Soc. Biol. Psychiatrists, 12th Ann. Conv.*, 1957.

Woolley, D. W.   *Science*, 1957, **125**, 752.

Woolley, D. W., & Shaw, E.   *Science*, 1954, **119**, 587.

Zeller, E. A., Bernsohn, J., Inskip, W. M., & Lauer, J. W.   *Naturwissenschaften*, 1957, **44**, 427.

16

Psychotherapy as a Learning Process

INTRODUCTION

The following two articles differ from those presented earlier in that they are not concerned with pathology per se. Instead, they deal with some of the processes by which pathology can be eliminated, that is, with therapy.

An increased understanding of pathology may lead to an increase of the adequacy of our therapeutic approaches. On the other hand, a thorough understanding and careful evaluation of therapeutic approaches could be used to validate our understanding of pathology. The understanding of the different therapeutic approaches is important because their nature will reflect the different conceptions about the nature and causes of pathology. That is, any systematic attempt to eliminate pathology must be based, implicitly or explicitly, on some specific idea of the important aspects or causes of pathology. The evaluation of the differential effectiveness of the various approaches becomes important because the effectiveness of an approach should to a large extent reflect the adequacy of the conception of pathology on which the approach is based.

The types of therapeutic approaches reviewed and evaluated in the following articles are based on a learning theory approach to understanding pathology.[1] As was pointed out in earlier articles, the learning theory position suggests that pathology consists of maladaptive or inappropriate responses that have been acquired

[1] The student interested in an extensive review and discussion of the research on the more traditional approach to psychotherapy might read the article by H. J. Eysenck, "The effects of psychotherapy," which appeared in the *International Journal of Psychiatry*, 1965, 1, 99-142.

through learning. Wolpe (1961) defined neurotic behavior as "any persistent habit of unadaptive behavior acquired by learning in a physiologically normal organism," but the failure to learn an adaptive response has also been considered neurotic behavior.

It should be noted that the learning of pathological responses is governed by the same principles that guide all other learning. That is, it is not a different or pathological form of learning, but the learning of different or pathological responses by the same means by which normal responses are learned. This is important, because if the learning process is the same in both situations, all of our previously acquired knowledge concerning learning can be brought to bear on the problems of understanding behavior pathology and its development. To some extent this was illustrated by Wilson in his paper "On Behavior Pathology" and by Sandler in his paper "Masochism: An Empirical Analysis." With regard to treatment or therapy, the learning position suggests that the principles and techniques of learning should be used to replace pathological responses with adaptive, appropriate responses. As the reader will see in the following article by Albert Bandura, numerous principles of learning have been employed in eliminating pathological responses and in establishing the new responses (e.g., classical conditioning, instrumental conditioning, rewards, punishment, extinction, and massed and distributed practice). Because of the wide variety of principles available, the therapist has some freedom in picking the approach that is best suited to a particular problem of the patient rather than using a standard approach to all problems. Even though the approaches are very different from one another, they share one important factor: they are all based on the principles of learning that have been developed and validated in controlled laboratory research.

It might be helpful, before presenting Bandura's article, to review briefly the two major types of learning and their relation to therapy. *Classical conditioning* is, of course, the type of learning that was first identified by Pavlov when he discovered that if the sound of a bell was consistently presented to a dog along with food and if the food caused the dog to salivate, after a while the sound of the bell *alone* would elicit the salivation response. Classical conditioning is used in therapy primarily to associate new emotional responses with various stimuli. That is, if a particular emotional response is consistently paired with a stimulus, in time the stimulus will elicit the emotional response on its own. In counterconditioning an inappropriate neurotic emotional response, the therapist tries to classically condition a new emotional response to the stimulus or stimulus situation in which the subject is responding inappropriately. Once the relationship between the stimulus and the new appropriate response is stronger than the relationship between the stimulus and the old inappropriate response, the new response will replace the old response, thus inhibiting the neurotic behavior. In this way, for example, a response of relaxation could inhibit the giving of inappropriate fear (phobic) responses to various stimuli. The technique for doing this is discussed and illustrated by Bandura. The reverse can also be done; that is, the patient who is not anxious when it would be helpful to be anxious could have a fear response paired with a stimulus such that he would later become anxious in the presence of the stimulus. This is illustrated by Bandura in the treatment of alcoholics. An important point to remember with regard to the classical conditioning of responses, both in the development of pathology and in the therapeutic counterconditioning, is that the conditioned responses are not under voluntary control and therefore either the neurotic or a new appropriate response will be used automatically by the responding individual.

Operant or *instrumental conditioning* in the laboratory is best illustrated by the work of Skinner who showed how responses can be "shaped" or controlled by rewarding or punishing the individual after the response in question has been made. Unlike classically conditioned responses, operantly conditioned responses are under voluntary control. Whether or not the response is given, then, depends on whether or not giving it will result in the goal or reward that the individual is seeking. Often neurotic behavior is not as maladaptive as it appears on the surface, for it may lead to some reward. For example, frequent misbehavior by a schoolchild may lead to the reward that the child is seeking, that is, the teacher's attention. Here therapy would involve the rearrangement of the behavior-consequence contingencies so that only socially approved behavior would be rewarded.

It should be noted that the principles of learning that have been developed and validated in the laboratory are not used exclusively by the learning-theory-oriented therapists. On the contrary, a careful evaluation of traditional psychotherapeutic techniques reveals the implicit use of many of the principles of learning. It seems that, within the traditional framework, techniques consonant with the learning principles were developed over the years, probably because in trying different approaches those that we now know to be based on the principles of learning were empirically found to be effective and hence were retained. Because the learning-related techniques have been incorporated to some degree within the traditional therapeutic approaches, it has been suggested by some that the degree of success found in the use of traditional methods can be attributed to the effects of learning. With regard to this point it is interesting to note that whereas the effects of traditional therapy have often been explained in terms of learning, the effects of learning theory therapy have not been accounted for by the more traditional theories of therapy. Although some principles derivable from learning theory are used by both groups of therapists, the fact that the learning theory group makes explicit use of the underlying theory enables this group to make wider, more systematic, and more consistent use of the principles which, if the theory is correct, should result in greater effectiveness.

In reading the article by Bandura, the reader should note the different principles and combinations of principles of learning that are employed to meet and overcome different neurotic problems. At the same time the reader should be careful to note the implicit and explicit assumptions about the nature of pathology on which the therapeutic approaches are based (e.g., symptoms are merely learned responses and do not represent unconscious conflicts). These are the issues over which the learning theory therapists and the more traditional therapists are still in hot dispute.

Wolpe, J. The systematic desensitization treatment of neuroses. *Journal of Nervous and Mental Diseases*, 1961, **132**, 189-203.

16

PSYCHOTHERAPY AS A LEARNING PROCESS

ALBERT BANDURA

While it is customary to conceptualize psychotherapy as a learning process, few therapists accept the full implications of this position. Indeed, this is best illustrated by the writings of the learning theorists themselves. Most of our current methods of psychotherapy represent an accumulation of more or less uncontrolled clinical experiences and, in many instances, those who have written about psychotherapy in terms of learning theory have merely substituted a new language; the practice remains essentially unchanged (Dollard, Auld, & White, 1954; Dollard & Miller, 1950; Shoben, 1949).

If one seriously subscribes to the view that psychotherapy is a learning process, the methods of treatment should be derived from our knowledge of learning and motivation. Such an orientation is likely to yield new techniques of treatment which, in many respects, may differ markedly from the procedures currently in use.

Psychotherapy rests on a very simple but fundamental assumption, i.e., human behavior is modifiable through psychological procedures. When skeptics raise the question, "Does psychotherapy work?" they may be responding in part to the mysticism that has come to surround the term. Perhaps the more meaningful question, and one which avoids the surplus meanings associated with the term "psychotherapy," is as follows: Can human behavior be modified through psychological means and if so, what are the learning mechanisms that mediate behavior change?

In the sections that follow, some of these learning mechanisms will be discussed, and studies in which systematic attempts have been made to apply these principles of learning to the area of psychotherapy will be reviewed. Since learning theory itself is still somewhat incomplete, the list of psychological processes by which changes in behavior can occur should not be regarded as exhaustive, nor are they necessarily without overlap.

SOURCE. Reprinted with permission of the American Psychological Association and the author from the *Psychological Bulletin*, 1961, 58, 143-159.

515

Counterconditioning

Of the various treatment methods derived from learning theory, those based on the principle of counterconditioning have been elaborated in greatest detail. Wolpe (1954, 1958, 1959) gives a thorough account of this method, and additional examples of cases treated in this manner are provided by Jones (1956), Lazarus and Rachman (1957), Meyer (1957), and Rachman (1959). Briefly, the principle involved is as follows: if strong responses which are incompatible with anxiety reactions can be made to occur in the presence of anxiety evoking cues, the incompatible responses will become attached to these cues and thereby weaken or eliminate the anxiety responses.

The first systematic psychotherapeutic application of this method was reported by Jones (1924b) in the treatment of Peter, a boy who showed severe phobic reactions to animals, fur objects, cotton, hair, and mechanical toys. Counterconditioning was achieved by feeding the child in the presence of initially small but gradually increasing anxiety-arousing stimuli. A rabbit in a cage was placed in the room at some distance so as not to disturb the boy's eating. Each day the rabbit was brought nearer to the table and eventually removed from the cage. During the final stage of treatment, the rabbit was placed on the feeding table and even in Peter's lap. Tests of generalization revealed that the fear responses had been effectively eliminated, not only toward the rabbit, but toward the previously feared furry objects as well.

In this connection, it would be interesting to speculate on the diagnosis and treatment Peter would have received had he been seen by Melanie Klein (1949) rather than by Mary Cover Jones!

It is interesting to note that while both Shoben (1949) and Wolpe (1958) propose a therapy based on the principle of counter-conditioning, their treatment methods are radically different. According to Shoben, the patient discusses and thinks about stimulus situations that are anxiety provoking in the context of an inter-personal situation which simultaneously elicits positive affective responses from the patient. The therapeutic process consists in connecting the anxiety provoking stimuli, which are symbolically reproduced, with the comfort reaction made to the therapeutic relationship.

Shoben's paper represents primarily a counterconditioning in-terpretation of the behavior changes brought about through conventional forms of psychotherapy since, apart from highlighting the role of positive emotional reactions in the treatment process, no new techniques deliberately designed to facilitate relearning through counterconditioning are proposed.

This is not the case with Wolpe, who has made a radical departure from tradition. In his treatment, which he calls reciprocal inhibition, Wolpe makes systematic use of three types of responses which are antagonistic to, and therefore inhibitory of, anxiety. These are: assertive or approach responses, sexual responses, and relaxation responses.

On the basis of historical information, interview data, and psychological test responses, the therapist constructs an anxiety hierarchy, a ranked list of stimuli to which the patient reacts with anxiety. In the case of desensitization based on relaxation, the patient is hypnotized and given relaxation suggestions. He is then asked to imagine a scene representing the weakest item on the anxiety hierarchy and, if the relaxation is unimpaired, this is followed by having the patient imagine the next item on the list, and so on. Thus, the anxiety cues are gradually increased from session to session until the last phobic stimulus can be presented without impairing the relaxed state. Through this procedure, relaxation responses eventually come to be attached to the anxiety evoking stimuli.

Wolpe reports remarkable therapeutic success with a wide range of neurotic reactions treated on this counterconditioning principle. He also contends that the favorable outcomes achieved by the more conventional psychotherapeutic methods may result from the reciprocal inhibition of anxiety by strong positive responses evoked in the patient-therapist relationship.

Although the counterconditioning method has been employed most extensively in eliminating anxiety-motivated avoidance reactions and inhibitions, it has been used with some success in reducing maladaptive approach responses as well. In the latter case, the goal object is repeatedly associated with some form of aversive stimulus.

Raymond (1956), for example, used nausea as the aversion experience in the treatment of a patient who presented a fetish for handbags and perambulators which brought him into frequent contact with the law in that he repeatedly smeared mucus on ladies' handbags and destroyed perambulators by running into them with his motorcycle. Though the patient had undergone psychoanalytic treatment, and was fully aware of the origin and the sexual significance of his behavior, nevertheless, the fetish persisted.

The treatment consisted of showing the patient a collection of handbags, perambulators, and colored illustrations just before the onset of nausea produced by injections of apomorphine. The conditioning was repeated every 2 hours day and night for 1 week plus additional sessions 8 days and 6 months later.

Raymond reports that, not only was the fetish successfully eliminated, but also the patient showed a vast improvement in his social (and legal) relationships, was promoted to a more responsible position in his work, and no longer required the fetish fantasies to enable him to have sexual intercourse.

Nauseant drugs, especially emetine, have also been utilized as the unconditioned stimulus in the aversion treatment of alcoholism (Thirmann, 1949; Thompson & Bielinski, 1953; Voegtlen, 1940; Wallace, 1949). Usually 8 to 10 treatments in which the sight, smell, and taste of alcohol is associated with the onset of nausea is sufficient to produce abstinence. Of 1,000 or more cases on whom adequate follow-up data are reported, approximately 60% of the patients have been totally abstinent following the treatment. Voegtlen (1940) suggests that a few preventive treatments given at an interval of about 6 months may further improve the results yielded by this method.

Despite these encouraging findings, most psychotherapists are unlikely to be impressed since, in their opinion, the underlying causes for the alcoholism have in no way been modified by the conditioning procedure and, if anything, the mere removal of the alcoholism would tend to produce symptom substitution or other adverse effects. A full discussion of this issue will be presented later. In this particular context, however, several aspects of the Thompson and Bielinski (1953) data are worth noting. Among the alcoholic patients whom they treated, six "suffered from mental disorders not due to alcohol or associated deficiency states." It was planned, by the authors, to follow up the aversion treatment with psychotherapy for the underlying psychosis. This, however, proved unnecessary since all but one of the patients, a case of chronic mental deterioration, showed marked improvement and were in a state of remission.

Max (1935) employed a strong electric shock as the aversive stimulus in treating a patient who tended to display homosexual behavior following exposure to a fetishistic stimulus. Both the fetish and the homosexual behavior were removed through a series of avoidance conditioning sessions in which the patient was administered shock in the presence of the fetishistic object.

Wolpe (1958) has also reported favorable results with a similar procedure in the treatment of obsessions.

A further variation of the counterconditioning procedure has been developed by Mowrer and Mowrer (1938) for use with enuretic patients. The device consists of a wired bed pad which sets off a loud buzzer and awakens the child as soon as micturition begins. Bladder tension thus becomes a cue for waking up which, in turn, is followed by sphincter contraction. Once bladder pressure becomes a stimulus for the more remote sphincter control response, the child is able to remain dry for relatively long periods of time without wakening.

Mowrer and Mowrer (1938) report complete success with 30 children treated by this method; similarly, Davidson and Douglass (1950) achieved highly successful results with 20 chronic enuretic children (15 cured, 5 markedly improved) ; of 5 cases treated by Morgan and Witmer (1939), 4 of the children not only gained full sphincter control, but also made a significant improvement in their social behavior. The one child with whom the conditioning approach had failed was later found to have bladder difficulties which required medical attention.

Some additional evidence for the efficacy of this method is provided by Martin and Kubly (1955) who obtained follow-up information from 118 of 220 parents who had treated their children at home with this type of conditioning apparatus. In 74% of the cases, according to the parents' replies, the treatment was successful.

Extinction

"When a learned response is repeated without reinforcement the strength of the tendency to perform that response undergoes a progressive decrease" (Dollard & Miller, 1950). Extinction involves the development of inhibitory potential which is composed of two components. The evocation of any reaction generates reactive inhibition (I_r) which presumably dissipates with time. When reactive inhibition (fatigue, etc.) reaches a high point, the cessation of activity alleviates this negative motivational state and any stimuli associated with the cessation of the response become conditioned inhibitors ($_sI_r$).

One factor that has been shown to influence the rate of extinction of maladaptive and anxiety-motivated behavior is the interval between extinction trials. In general, there tends to be little diminution in the strength of fear-motivated behavior when extinction trials are widely distributed, whereas under massed trials, reactive inhibition builds up rapidly and consequently extinction is accelerated (Calvin, Clifford, Clifford, Bolden, & Harvey, 1956; Edmonson & Amsel, 1954).

An illustration of the application of this principle is provided by Yates (1958) in the treatment of tics. Yates demonstrated, in line with the findings from laboratory studies of extinction under massed and distributed practice, that massed sessions in which the patient performed tics voluntarily followed by prolonged rest to allow for the dissipation of reactive inhibition was the most effective procedure for extinguishing the tics.

It should be noted that the extinction procedure employed by Yates is very similar to Dunlap's method of negative practice, in which the subject reproduces the negative behaviors voluntarily without reinforcement (Dunlap, 1932; Lehner, 1954). This method has been applied most frequently, with varying degrees of success, to the treatment of speech disorders (Fishman, 1937; Meissner, 1946; Rutherford, 1940; Sheehan, 1951; Sheehan & Voas, 1957). If the effectiveness of this psychotherapeutic technique is due primarily to extinction, as suggested by Yates' study, the usual practice of terminating a treatment session before the subject becomes fatigued (Lehner, 1954), would have the effect of reducing the rate of extinction, and may in part account for the divergent results yielded by this method.

Additional examples of the therapeutic application of extinction procedures are provided by Jones (1955), and most recently by C. D. Williams (1959).

Most of the conventional forms of psychotherapy rely heavily on extinction effects although the therapist may not label these as such. For example, many therapists consider *permissiveness* to be a necessary condition of therapeutic change (Alexander, 1956; Dollard & Miller, 1950; Rogers, 1951). It is expected that when a patient expresses thoughts or feelings that provoke anxiety or guilt and the therapist does not disapprove, criticize, or withdraw interest, the fear or guilt will be gradually weakened or extinguished. The extinction effects are believed to generalize to thoughts concerning related topics that were originally inhibited, and to verbal and physical forms of behavior as well (Dollard & Miller, 1950).

Some evidence for the relationship between permissiveness and the extinction of anxiety is provided in two studies recently reported by Dittes (1957a, 1957b). In one study (1957b) involving an analysis of patient-therapist interaction sequences, Dittes found that permissive responses on the part of the therapist were followed by a corresponding decrease in the patient's anxiety (as measured by the GSR) and the occurrence of avoidance behaviors. A sequential analysis of the therapeutic sessions (Dittes, 1957a), revealed that, at the onset of treatment, sex expressions were accompanied by strong anxiety reactions; under the cumulative effects of permissiveness, the anxiety gradually extinguished.

In contrast to counterconditioning, extinction is likely to be a less effective and a more time consuming method for eliminating maladaptive behavior (Jones, 1924a; Dollard & Miller, 1950); in the case of conventional interview therapy, the relatively long intervals between interview sessions, and the ritualistic adherence to the 50-minute hour may further reduce the occurrence of extinction effects.

Discrimination Learning

Human functioning would be extremely difficult and inefficient if a person had to learn appropriate behavior for every specific situation he encountered. Fortunately, patterns of behavior learned in one situation will transfer or generalize to other similar situations. On the other hand, if a person overgeneralizes from one situation to another, or if the generalization is based on superficial or irrelevant cues, behavior becomes inappropriate and maladaptive.

In most theories of psychotherapy, therefore, discrimination learning, believed to be accomplished through the gaining of awareness or insight, receives emphasis (Dollard & Miller, 1950; Fenichel, 1941; Rogers, 1951; Sullivan, 1953). It is generally assumed that if a patient is aware of the cues producing his behavior, of the responses he is making, and of the reasons that he responds the way he does, his behavior will become more susceptible to verbally-mediated control. Voluntarily guided, discriminative behavior will replace the automatic, overgeneralized reactions.

While this view is widely accepted, as evidenced in the almost exclusive reliance on interview procedures and on interpretative or labeling techniques, a few therapists (Alexander & French, 1946) have questioned the importance attached to awareness in producing modifications in behavior. Whereas most psychoanalysts (Fenichel, 1941), as well as therapists representing other points of view

(Fromm-Reichmann, 1950; Sullivan, 1953) consider insight a pre-condition of behavior change, Alexander and French consider in-sight or awareness a result of change rather than its cause. That is, as the patient's anxieties are gradually reduced through the permissive conditions of treatment, formerly inhibited thoughts are gradually restored to awareness.

Evidence obtained through controlled laboratory studies con-cerning the value of awareness in increasing the precision of discrimination has so far been largely negative or at least equivocal (Adams, 1957; Erikson, 1958; Razran, 1949). A study by Lacy and Smith (1954), in which they found aware subjects generalized anxiety reactions less extensively than did subjects who were un-aware of the conditioned stimulus provides evidence that awareness may aid discrimination. However, other aspects of their findings (e.g., the magnitude of the anxiety reactions to the generalization stimuli were greater than they were to the conditioned stimulus itself) indicate the need for replication.

If future research continues to demonstrate that awareness exerts little influence on the acquisition, generalization, and modi-fication of behavior, such negative results would cast serious doubt on the value of currently popular psychotherapeutic procedures whose primary aim is the development of insight.

Methods of Reward

Most theories of psychotherapy are based on the assumption that the patient has a repertoire of previously learned positive habits available to him, but that these adaptive patterns are in-hibited or blocked by competing responses motivated by anxiety or guilt. The goal of therapy, then, is to reduce the severity of the internal inhibitory controls, thus allowing the healthy patterns of behavior to emerge. Hence, the role of the therapist is to create permissive conditions under which the patient's "normal growth potentialities" are set free (Rogers, 1951). The fact that most of our theories of personality and therapeutic procedures have been developed primarily through work with oversocialized, neurotic patients may account in part for the prevalence of this view.

There is a large class of disorders (the undersocialized, anti-social personalities whose behavior reflects a failure of the social-ization process) for whom this model of personality and accompanying techniques of treatment are quite inappropriate (Bandura & Walters, 1959; Schmideberg, 1959). Such antisocial personalities are likely to present *learning deficits*, consequently the goal of therapy is the acquisition of secondary motives and the development of internal restraint habits. That antisocial patients prove unresponsive to psychotherapeutic methods developed for the treatment of oversocialized neurotics has been demonstrated in a number of studies comparing patients who remain in treatment with those who terminate treatment prematurely (Rubenstein & Lorr, 1956). It is for this class of patients that the greatest departures from traditional treatment methods are needed.

While counterconditioning, extinction, and discrimination learning may be effective ways of removing neurotic inhibitions, these methods may be of relatively little value in developing new positive habits. Primary and secondary rewards in the form of the therapist's interest and approval may play an important, if not indispensable, role in the treatment process. Once the patient has learned to want the interest and approval of the therapist, these rewards may then be used to promote the acquisition of new patterns of behavior. For certain classes of patients such as schizophrenics (Atkinson, 1957; Peters, 1953; Robinson, 1957) and delinquents (Cairns, 1959), who are either unresponsive to, or fearful of, social rewards, the therapist may have to rely initially on primary rewards in the treatment process.

An ingenious study by Peters and Jenkins (1954) illustrates the application of this principle in the treatment of schizophrenic patients. Chronic patients from closed wards were administered subshock injections of insulin designed to induce the hunger drive. The patients were then encouraged to solve a series of graded problem tasks with fudge as the reward. This program was followed 5 days a week for 3 months.

Initially the tasks involved simple mazes and obstruction problems in which the patients obtained the food reward directly upon successful completion of the problem. Tasks of gradually increasing difficulty were then administered involving multiple-choice learning and verbal-reasoning problems in which the experimenter personally mediated the primary rewards. After several weeks of such problem solving activities the insulin injections were discontinued and social rewards, which by this time had become more effective, were used in solving interpersonal problems that the patients were likely to encounter in their daily activities both inside and outside the hospital setting.

Comparison of the treated group with control groups, designed to isolate the effects of insulin and special attention, revealed that the patients in the reward group improved significantly in their social relationships in the hospital, whereas the patients in the control groups showed no such change.

King and Armitage (1958) report a somewhat similar study in which severely withdrawn schizophrenic patients were treated with operant conditioning methods; candy and cigarettes served as the primary rewards for eliciting and maintaining increasingly complex forms of behavior, i.e., psychomotor, verbal, and interpersonal responses. Unlike the Peters and Jenkins study, no attempt was made to manipulate the level of primary motivation.

An interesting feature of the experimental design was the inclusion of a group of patients who were treated with conventional interview therapy, as well as a recreational therapy and a no-therapy control group. It was found that the operant group, in relation to similar patients in the three control groups, made significantly more clinical improvement.

Skinner (1956b) and Lindsley (1956) working with adult psychotics, and Ferster (1959) working with autistic children, have been successful in developing substantial amounts of reality-oriented behavior in their patients through the use of reward. So far their work has been concerned primarily with the effect of schedules of reinforcement on the rate of evocation of simple impersonal reactions. There is every indication, however, that by varying the contingency of the reward (e.g., the patient must respond in certain specified ways to the behavior of another individual in order to produce the reward) adaptive interpersonal behaviors can be developed as well (Azran & Lindsley, 1956).

The effectiveness of social reinforcers in modifying behavior has been demonstrated repeatedly in verbal conditioning experiments (Krasner, 1958; Salzinger, 1959). Encouraged by these findings, several therapists have begun to experiment with operant conditioning as a method of treatment in its own right (Tilton, 1956; Ullman, Krasner, & Collins, in press; R. I. Williams, 1959) ; the operant conditioning studies cited earlier are also illustrative of this trend.

So far the study of generalization and permanence of behavior changes brought about through operant conditioning methods has received relatively little attention and the scanty data available are equivocal (Rogers, 1960; Sarason, 1957; Weide, 1959). The lack of consistency in results is hardly surprising considering that the experimental manipulations in many of the conditioning studies are barely sufficient to demonstrate conditioning effects, let alone generalization of changes to new situations. On the other hand, investigators who have conducted more intensive reinforcement sessions, in an effort to test the efficacy of operant conditioning methods as a therapeutic technique, have found significant changes in patients' interpersonal behavior in extra-experimental situations (King & Armitage, 1958; Peters & Jenkins, 1954; Ullman et al., in press). These findings are particularly noteworthy since the response classes involved are similar to those psychotherapists are primarily concerned in modifying through interview forms of treatment. If the favorable results yielded by these studies are replicated in future investigations, it is likely that the next few years will witness an increasing reliance on conditioning forms of psychotherapy, particularly in the treatment of psychotic patients.

At this point it might also be noted that, consistent with the results from verbal conditioning experiments, content analyses of psychotherapeutic interviews (Bandura, Lipsher, & Miller, 1960; Murray, 1956) suggest that many of the changes observed in psychotherapy, at least insofar as the patients' verbal behavior is concerned, can be accounted for in terms of the therapists' direct, although usually unwitting, reward and punishment of the patients' expressions.

Punishment

While positive habits can be readily developed through reward, the elimination of socially disapproved habits, which becomes very much an issue in the treatment of antisocial personalities, poses a far more complex problem.

The elimination of socially disapproved behaviors can be accomplished in several ways. They may be consistently unrewarded and thus extinguished. However, antisocial behavior, particularly of an extreme form, cannot simply be ignored in the hope that it will gradually extinguish. Furthermore, since the successful execution of antisocial acts may bring substantial material rewards as well as the approval and admiration of associates, it is extremely unlikely that such behavior would ever extinguish.

Although punishment may lead to the rapid disappearance of socially disapproved behavior, its effects are far more complex (Estes, 1944; Solomon, Kamin, & Wynne, 1953). If a person is punished for some socially disapproved habit, the impulse to perform the act becomes, through its association with punishment, a stimulus for anxiety. This anxiety then motivates competing responses which, if sufficiently strong, prevent the occurrence of, or inhibit, the disapproved behavior. Inhibited responses may not, however, thereby lose their strength, and may reappear in situations where the threat of punishment is weaker. Punishment may, in fact, prevent the extinction of a habit; if a habit is completely inhibited, it cannot occur and therefore cannot go unrewarded.

Several other factors point to the futility of punishment as a means of correcting many antisocial patterns. The threat of punishment is very likely to elicit conformity; indeed, the patient may obligingly do whatever he is told to do in order to avoid immediate difficulties. This does not mean, however, that he has acquired a set of sanctions that will be of service to him once he is outside the treatment situation. In fact, rather than leading to the development of internal controls, such methods are likely only to increase the patient's reliance on external restraints. Moreover, under these conditions, the majority of patients will develop the attitude that they will do only what they are told to do—and then often only half-heartedly—and that they will do as they please once they are free from the therapist's supervision (Bandura & Walters, 1959).

In addition, punishment may serve only to intensify hostility and other negative motivations and thus may further instigate the antisocial person to display the very behaviors that the punishment was intended to bring under control.

Mild aversive stimuli have been utilized, of course, in the treatment of voluntary patients who express a desire to rid themselves of specific debilitating conditions.

Liversedge and Sylvester (1955), for example, successfully treated seven cases of writer's cramp by means of a retraining procedure involving electric shock. In order to remove tremors, one component of the motor disorder, the patients were required to insert a stylus into a series of progressively smaller holes; each time the stylus made contact with the side of the hole the patients received a mild shock. The removal of the spasm component of the disorder was obtained in two ways. First, the patients traced various line patterns (similar to the movements required in writing) on a metal plate with a stylus, and any deviation from the path produced a shock. Following training on the apparatus, the subjects then wrote with an electrified pen which delivered a shock whenever excessive thumb pressure was applied.

Liversedge and Sylvester report that following the retraining the patients were able to resume work; a follow-up several months later indicated that the improvement was being maintained.

The aversive forms of therapy, described earlier in the section on counterconditioning procedures, also make use of mild punishment.

Social Imitation

Although a certain amount of learning takes place through direct training and reward, a good deal of a person's behavior repertoire may be acquired through imitation of what he observes in others. If this is the case, social imitation may serve as an effective vehicle for the transmission of prosocial behavior patterns in the treatment of antisocial patients.

Merely providing a model for imitation is not, however, sufficient. Even though the therapist exhibits the kinds of behaviors that he wants the patient to learn, this is likely to have little influence on him if he rejects the therapist as a model. Affectional nurturance is believed to be an important precondition for imitative learning to occur, in that affectional rewards increase the secondary reinforcing properties of the model, and thus predispose the imitator to pattern his behavior after the rewarding person (Mowrer, 1950; Sears, 1957; Whiting, 1954). Some positive evidence for the influence of social rewards on imitation is provided by Bandura and Huston (in press) in a recent study of identification as a process of incidental imitation.

In this investigation preschool children performed an orienting task but, unlike most incidental learning studies, the experimenter performed the diverting task as well, and the extent to which the subjects patterned their behavior after that of the experimenter-model was measured.

A two-choice discrimination problem similar to the one employed by Miller and Dollard (1941) in their experiments of social imitation was used as the diverting task. On each trial, one of two boxes was loaded with two rewards (small multicolor pictures of animals) and the object of the game was to guess which box contained the stickers. The experimenter-model (M) always had her turn first and in each instance chose the reward box. During M's trial, the subject remained at the starting point where he could observe the M's behavior. On each discrimination trial M exhibited certain verbal, motor, and aggressive patterns of behavior that were totally irrelevant to the task to which the subject's attention was directed. At the starting point, for example, M made a verbal response and then marched slowly toward the box containing the stickers, repeating, "March, march, march." On the lid of each box was a rubber doll which *M* knocked off aggressively when she reached the designated box. She then paused briefly, remarked, "Open the box," removed one sticker, and pasted it on a pastoral scene which hung on the wall immediately behind the boxes. The subject then took his turn and the number of *M*'s behaviors performed by the subject was recorded.

A control group was included in order to, (*a*) provide a check on whether the subjects' performances reflected genuine imitative learning or merely the chance occurrence of behaviors high in the subjects' response hierarchies, and (*b*) to determine whether subjects would adopt certain aspects of *M*'s behavior which involved considerable delay in reward. With the controls, therefore, *M* walked to the box, choosing a highly circuitous route along the sides of the experimental room; instead of aggressing toward the doll, she lifted it gently off the container.

The results of this study indicate that, insofar as preschool children are concerned, a good deal of incidental imitation of the behaviors displayed by an adult model does occur. Of the subjects in the experimental group, 88% adopted the *M*'s aggressive behavior, 44% imitated the marching, and 28% reproduced *M*'s verbalizations. In contrast, none of the control subjects behaved aggressively, marched, or verbalized, while 75% of the controls imitated the circuitous route to the containers.

In order to test the hypothesis that children who experience a rewarding relationship with an adult model adopt more of the model's behavior than do children who experience a relatively distant and cold relationship, half the subjects in the experiment were assigned to a nurturant condition; the other half of the subjects to a nonnurturant condition. During the nurturant sessions, which preceded the incidental learning, *M* played with subject, she responded readily to the subject's bids for attention, and in other ways fostered a consistently warm and rewarding interaction with the child. In contrast, during the nonnurturant sessions, the subject played alone while *M* busied herself with paperwork at a desk in the far corner of the room.

Consistent with the hypothesis, it was found that subjects who experienced the rewarding interaction with *M* adopted significantly more of *M*'s behavior than did subjects who were in the nonnurturance condition.

A more crucial test of the transmission of behavior patterns through the process of social imitation involves the delayed generalization of imitative responses to new situations in which the model is absent. A study of this type just completed, provides strong evidence that observation of the cues produced by the behavior of others is an effective means of eliciting responses for which the original probability is very low (Bandura, Ross, & Ross, 1964).

Empirical studies of the correlates of strong and weak identification with parents, lend additional support to the theory that rewards promote imitative learning. Boys whose fathers are highly rewarding and affectionate have been found to adopt the father-role in doll-play activities (Sears, 1953), to show father-son similarity in response to items on a personality questionnaire (Payne & Mussen, 1956), and to display masculine behaviors (Mussen & Distler, 1956, 1960) to a greater extent than boys whose fathers are relatively cold and nonrewarding.

The treatment of older unsocialized delinquents is a difficult task, since they are relatively self-sufficient and do not readily seek involvement with a therapist. In many cases, socialization can be accomplished only through residential care and treatment. In the treatment home, the therapist can personally administer many of the primary rewards and mediate between the boys' needs and gratifications. Through the repeated association with rewarding experiences for the boy, many of the therapist's attitudes and actions will acquire secondary reward value, and thus the patient will be motivated to reproduce these attitudes and actions in himself. Once these attitudes and values have been thus accepted, the boy's inhibition of antisocial tendencies will function independently of the therapist.

While treatment through social imitation has been suggested as a method for modifying antisocial patterns, it can be an effective procedure for the treatment of other forms of disorders as well. Jones (1924a), for example, found that the social example of children reacting normally to stimuli feared by another child was effective, in some instances, in eliminating such phobic reactions. In fact, next to counterconditioning, the method of social imitation proved to be most effective in eliminating inappropriate fears.

There is some suggestive evidence that by providing high prestige models and thus increasing the reinforcement value of the imitatee's behavior, the effectiveness of this method in promoting favorable adjustive patterns of behavior may be further increased (Jones, 1924a; Mausner, 1953, 1954; Miller & Dollard, 1941).

During the course of conventional psychotherapy, the patient is exposed to many incidental cues involving the therapist's values, attitudes, and patterns of behavior. They are incidental only because they are usually considered secondary or irrelevant to the task of resolving the patient's problems. Nevertheless, some of the changes observed in the patient's behavior may result, not so much from the intentional interaction between the patient and the therapist, but rather from active learning by the patient of the therapist's attitudes and values which the therapist never directly attempted to transmit. This is partially corroborated by Rosenthal (1955) who found that, in spite of the usual precautions taken by therapists to avoid imposing their values on their clients, the patients who were judged as showing the greatest improvement changed their moral values (in the areas of sex, aggression, and authority) in the direction of the values of their therapists, whereas patients who were unimproved became less like the therapist in values.

Factors Impeding Integration

In reviewing the literature on psychotherapy, it becomes clearly evident that learning theory and general psychology have exerted a remarkably minor influence on the practice of psychotherapy and, apart from the recent interest in Skinner's operant conditioning methods (Krasner, 1955; Skinner, 1953), most of the recent serious attempts to apply learning principles to clinical practice have been made by European psychotherapists (Jones, 1956; Lazarus & Rachman, 1957; Liversedge & Sylvester, 1955; Meyer, 1957; Rachman, 1959; Raymond, 1956; Wolpe, 1958; Yates, 1958). This isolation of the methods of treatment from our knowledge of learning and motivation will continue to exist for some time since there are several prevalent attitudes that impede adequate integration.

In the first place, the deliberate use of this principles of learning in the modification of human behavior implies, for most psychotherapists, manipulation and control of the patient, and control is seen by them as antihumanistic and, therefore, bad. Thus, advocates of a learning approach to psychotherapy are often charged with treating human beings as though they were rats or pigeons and of leading on the road to Orwell's *1984*.

This does not mean that psychotherapists do not influence and control their patients' behavior. On the contrary. In any interpersonal interaction, and psychotherapy is no exception, people influence and control one another (Frank, 1959; Skinner, 1956a). Although the patient's control of the therapist has not as yet been studied (such control is evident when patients subtly reward the therapist with interesting historical material and thereby avoid the discussion of their current interpersonal problems), there is considerable evidence that the therapist exercises personal control over his patients. A brief examination of interview protocols of patients treated by therapists representing differing theoretical orientations, clearly reveals that the patients have been thoroughly conditioned in their therapists' idiosyncratic languages. Client-centered patients, for example, tend to produce the client-centered terminology, theory, and goals, and their interview content shows little or no overlap with that of patients seen in psychoanalysis who, in turn, tend to speak the language of psychoanalytic theory (Heine, 1950). Even more direct evidence of the therapists' controlling influence is provided in studies of patient-therapist interactions (Bandura et al., 1960; Murray, 1956; Rogers, 1960). The results of these studies show that the therapist not only controls the patient by rewarding him with interest and approval when the patient behaves in a fashion the therapist desires, but that he also controls through punishment, in the form of mild disapproval and withdrawal of interest, when the patient behaves in ways that are threatening to the therapist or run counter to his goals.

One difficulty in understanding the changes that occur in the course of psychotherapy is that the independent variable, i.e., the therapist's behavior, is often vaguely or only partially defined. In an effort to minimize or to deny the therapist's directive influence on the patient, the therapist is typically depicted as a "catalyst" who, in some mysterious way, sets free positive adjustive patterns of behavior or similar outcomes usually described in very general and highly socially desirable terms.

It has been suggested, in the material presented in the preceding sections, that many of the changes that occur in psychotherapy derive from the unwitting application of well-known principles of learning. However, the occurrence of the necessary conditions for learning is more by accident than by intent and, perhaps, a more deliberate application of our knowledge of the learning process to psychotherapy would yield far more effective results.

The predominant approach in the development of psychotherapeutic procedures has been the "school" approach. A similar trend is noted in the treatment methods being derived from learning theory. Wolpe, for example, has selected the principle of counter-conditioning and built a "school" of psychotherapy around it; Dollard and Miller have focused on extinction and discrimination learning; and the followers of Skinner rely almost entirely on methods of reward. This stress on a few learning principles at the expense of neglecting other relevant ones will serve only to limit the effectiveness of psychotherapy.

A second factor that may account for the discontinuity between general psychology and psychotherapeutic practice is that the model of personality to which most therapists subscribe is somewhat dissonant with the currently developing principles of behavior.

In their formulations of personality functioning, psychotherapists are inclined to appeal to a variety of inner explanatory processes. In contrast, learning theorists view the organism as a far more mechanistic and simpler system, and consequently their formulations tend to be expressed for the most part in terms of antecedent-consequent relationships without reference to inner states.

Symptoms are learned S-R connections; once they are extinguished or deconditioned treatment is complete. Such treatment is based exclusively on present factors; like Lewin's theory, this one is a-historical. Nonverbal methods are favored over verbal ones, although a minor place is reserved for verbal methods of extinction and reconditioning. Concern is with *function*, not with *content*. The main difference between the two theories arises over the question of "symptomatic" treatment. According to orthodox theory, this is useless unless the underlying complexes are attacked. According to the present theory, there is no evidence for these putative complexes, and symptomatic treatment is all that is required (Eysenck, 1957, pp. 267-268). (Quoted by permission of Frederick A. Praeger, Inc.)

Changes in behavior brought about through such methods as counterconditioning are apt to be viewed by the "dynamically-oriented" therapist, as being not only superficial, "symptomatic" treatment, in that the basic underlying instigators of the behavior remain unchanged, but also potentially dangerous, since the direct elimination of a symptom may precipitate more seriously disturbed behavior.

This expectation receives little support from the generally favorable outcomes reported in the studies reviewed in this paper. In most cases where follow-up data were available to assess the long-term effects of the therapy, the patients, many of whom had been treated by conventional methods with little benefit, had evidently become considerably more effective in their social, vocational, and psychosexual adjustment. On the whole the evidence, while open to error, suggests that no matter what the origin of the maladaptive behavior may be, a change in behavior brought about through learning procedures may be all that is necessary for the alleviation of most forms of emotional disorders.

As Mowrer (1950) very aptly points out, the "symptom-underlying cause" formulation may represent inappropriate medical analogizing. Whether or not a given behavior will be considered normal or a symptom of an underlying disturbance will depend on whether or not somebody objects to the behavior. For example, aggressiveness on the part of children may be encouraged and considered a sign of healthy development by the parents, while the same behavior is viewed by school authorities and society as a symptom of a personality disorder (Bandura & Walters, 1959). Furthermore, behavior considered to be normal at one stage in development may be regarded as a "symptom of a personality disturbance" at a later period. In this connection it is very appropriate to repeat Mowrer's (1950) query: "And when does persisting behavior of this kind suddenly cease to be normal and become a symptom" (p. 474).

Thus, while a high fever is generally considered a sign of an underlying disease process regardless of when or where it occurs, whether a specific behavior will be viewed as normal or as a symptom of an underlying pathology is not independent of who makes the judgement, the social context in which the behavior occurs, the age of the person, as well as many other factors.

Another important difference between physical pathology and behavior pathology usually overlooked is that, in the case of most behavior disorders, it is not the underlying motivations that need to be altered or removed, but rather the ways in which the patient has learned to gratify his needs (Rotter, 1954). Thus, for example, if a patient displays deviant sexual behavior, the goal is not the removal of the underlying causes, i.e., sexual motivation, but rather the substitution of more socially approved instrumental and goal responses.

It might also be mentioned in passing, that, in the currently popular forms of psychotherapy, the role assumed by the therapist may bring him a good many direct or fantasied personal gratifications. In the course of treatment the patient may express considerable affection and admiration for the therapist, he may assign the therapist an omniscient status, and the reconstruction of the patient's history may be an intellectually stimulating activity. On the other hand, the methods derived from learning theory place the therapist in a less glamorous role, and this in itself may create some reluctance on the part of psychotherapists to part with the procedures currently in use.

Which of the two conceptual theories of personality—the psychodynamic or the social learning theory—is the more useful in generating effective procedures for the modification of human behavior remains to be demonstrated. While it is possible to present logical arguments and impressive clinical evidence for the efficiency of either approach, the best proving ground is the laboratory.

In evaluating psychotherapeutic methods, the common practice is to compare changes in a treated group with those of a nontreated control group. One drawback of this approach is that, while it answers the question as to whether or not a particular treatment is more effective than no intervention in producing changes along specific dimensions for certain classes of patients, it does not provide evidence concerning the relative effectiveness of alternative forms of psychotherapy.

It would be far more informative if, in future psychotherapy research, radically different forms of treatment were compared (King & Armitage, 1958; Rogers, 1959), since this approach would lead to a more rapid discarding of those of our cherished psychotherapeutic rituals that prove to be ineffective in, or even a handicap to, the successful treatment of emotional disorders.

REFERENCES

Adams, J. K.   Laboratory studies of behavior without awareness. *Psychological Bulletin*, 1957, 54, 393-405.

Alexander, F.   *Psychoanalysis and psychotherapy.* New York: Norton, 1956.

Alexander, F., & French, M. T.   *Psychoanalytic therapy.* New York: Ronald, 1946.

Atkinson, Rita L.   Paired-associate learning by schizophrenic and normal subjects under conditions of verbal reward and verbal punishment. Unpublished doctoral dissertation, Indiana University, 1957.

Azran, N. H., & Lindsley, O. R.   The reinforcement of cooperation between children. *Journal of Abnormal and Social Psychology*, 1956, 52, 100-102.

Bandura, A., & Houston, Aletha, C.   Identification as a process of incidental learning. *Journal of Abnormal and Social Psychology*, in press.

Bandura, A., Lipsher, D. H., & Miller, Paula, E.   Psychotherapists' approach-avoidance reactions to patients' expressions of hostility. *Journal of Consulting Psychology*, 1960, 24, 1-8.

Bandura, A., Ross, Dorothea, & Ross, Sheila, A.   Transmission of aggression through imitation of aggressive models. *Journal of Abnormal and Social Psychology*, 1964, **63**, 575-582.

Bandura, A., & Walters, R. H. *Adolescent aggression.* New York: Ronald, 1959.

Cairns, R. B. The influence of dependency-anxiety on the effectiveness of social reinforcers. Unpublished doctoral dissertation, Stanford University, 1959.

Calvin, A. D., Clifford, L. T., Clifford, B., Bolden, L., & Harvey, J. Experimental validation of conditioned inhibition. *Psychological Reports,* 1956, **2,** 51-56.

Davidson, J. R., & Douglass, E. Nocturnal enuresis: A special approach to treatment. *British Medical Journal,* 1950, **1,** 1345-1347.

Dittes, J. E. Extinction during psychotherapy of CSR accompanying "embarrassing" statements. *Journal of Abnormal and Social Psychology,* 1957, **54,** 187-191. (a)

Dittes, J. E. Galvanic skin responses as a measure of patient's reaction to therapist's permissiveness. *Journal of Abnormal and Social Psychology,* 1957, **55,** 295-303. (b)

Dollard, J., Auld, F., & White, A. M. *Steps in psychotherapy.* New York: Macmillan, 1954.

Dollard, J., & Miller, N. E. *Personality and psychotherapy.* New York: McGraw-Hill, 1950.

Dunlap, K. *Habits, their making and unmaking.* New York: Liveright, 1932.

Edmonson, B. W., & Amsel, A. The effects of massing and distribution of extinction trials on the persistence of a fear-motivated instrumental response. *Journal of Comparative and Physiological Psychology,* 1954, **47,** 117-123.

Erikson, C. W. Unconscious processes. In M. R. Jones (Ed.), *Nebraska symposium on motivation.* Lincoln: University of Nebraska Press, 1958.

Estes, W. K. An experimental study of punishment. *Psychological Monographs,* 1944, **57** (3, Whole No. 363).

Eysenck, H. J. *The dynamics of anxiety and hysteria.* New York: Praeger, 1957.

Fenichel, O. *Problems of psychoanalytic technique.* (Trans. by D. Brunswick) New York: Psychoanalytic Quarterly, 1941.

Ferster, C. B. Development of normal behavioral processes in autistic children. *Research Relating to Children,* 1959, No. 9, 30. (Abstract)

Fishman, H. C. A study of the efficiency of negative practice as a corrective for stammering. *Journal of Speech Disorders,* 1937, **2,** 67-72.

Frank, J. D. The dynamics of the psychotherapeutic relationship. *Psychiatry,* 1959, **22,** 17-39.

Fromm-Reichmann, Frieda. *Principle of intensive psychotherapy.* Chicago: University of Chicago Press, 1950.

Heine, R. W. An investigation of the relationship between change in personality from psychotherapy as reported by patients and the factors seen by patients as producing change. Unpublished doctoral dissertation, University of Chicago, 1950.

Jones, E. L.   Exploration of experimental extinction and spontaneous recovery in stuttering. In W. Johnson (Ed.), *Stuttering in children and adults*. Minneapolis: University of Minnesota Press, 1955.

Jones, H. G.   The application of conditioning and learning techniques to the treatment of a psychiatric patient. *Journal of Abnormal and Social Psychology*, 1956, 52, 414-419.

Jones, Mary C.   The elimination of childrens' fears. *Journal of Experimental Psychology*, 1924, 7, 290-382. (a)

Jones, Mary C.   A laboratory study of fear: The case of Peter. *Journal of Genetic Psychology*, 1924, 31, 308-315. (b)

King, G. F., & Armitage, S. G.   An operant-interpersonal therapeutic approach to schizophrenics of extreme pathology. *American Psychologist*, 1958, 13, 353. (Abstract)

Klein, Melanie. *The psycho-analysis of children*. London: Hogarth, 1959.

Krasner, L.   The use of generalized reinforcers in psychotherapy research. *Psychological Reports*, 1955, 1, 19-25.

Krasner, L.   Studies of the conditioning of verbal behavior. *Psychological Bulletin*, 1958, 55, 149-170.

Lacey, J. I., & Smith, R. I.   Conditioning and generalization of unconscious anxiety. *Science*, 1954, 120, 1-8.

Lazarus, A. A., & Rachman, S.   The use of systematic desensitization in psychotherapy. *South African Medical Journal*, 1957, 32, 934-937.

Lehner, G. F. J.   Negative practice as a psychotherapeutic technique. *Journal of General Psychology*, 1954, 51, 69-82.

Lindsley, O. R.   Operant conditioning methods applied to research in chronic schizophrenia. *Psychiatric Research Reports*, 1956, 5, 118-138.

Liversedge, L. A., & Sylvester, J. D.   Conditioning techniques in the treatment of writer's cramp. *Lancet*, 1955, 1, 1147-1149.

Martin, B., & Kubly, Delores.   Results of treatment of enuresis by a conditioned response method. *Journal of Consulting Psychology*, 1955, 19, 71-73.

Mausner, B.   Studies in social interaction: III. The effect of variation in one partner's prestige on the interaction of observer pairs. *Journal of Applied Psychology*, 1953, 37, 391-393.

Mausner, B.   The effect of one partner's success in a relevant task on the interaction of observer pairs. *Journal of Abnormal and Social Psychology*, 1954, 49, 557-560.

Max, L. W.   Breaking up a homosexual fixation by the conditioned reaction technique: A case study. *Psychological Bulletin*, 1935, 32, 734.

Meissner, J. H.   The relationship between voluntary nonfluency and stuttering. *Journal of Speech Disorders*, 1946, 11, 13-33.

Meyer, V.   The treatment of two phobit patients on the basis of learning principles: Case report. *Journal of Abnormal and Social Psychology*, 1957, 55, 261-266.

Miller, N. E., & Dollard, J.   *Social learning and imitation*. New Haven: Yale University Press, 1941.

Morgan, J. J. B., & Witmer, F. J.   The treatment of enuresis by the conditioned reaction technique. *Journal of Genetic Psychology*, 1939, 55, 59-65.

Mowrer, O. H.   *Learning theory and personality dynamics*. New York: Ronald, 1950.

Mowrer, O. H., & Mowrer, W. M.   Enuresis—a method for its study and treatment. *American Journal of Orthopsychiatry*, 1938, 8, 436-459.

Murray, E. J.   The content-analysis method of studying psychotherapy. *Psychological Monographs*, 1956, 70 (13, Whole No. 420).

Mussen, P., & Distler, L. M.   Masculinity, identification, and father-son relationships. *Journal of Abnormal and Social Psychology*, 1959, 59, 350-356.

Mussen, P., & Distler, L. M.   Child-rearing antecedents of masculine identification in kindergarten boys. *Child Development*, 1960, 31, 89-100.

Payne, D. E., & Mussen, P. H.   Parent-child relationships and father identification among adolescent boys. *Journal of Abnormal and Social Psychology*, 1956, 52, 358-362.

Peters, H. N.   Multiple choice learning in the chronic schizophrenic. *Journal of Clinical Psychology*, 1953, 9, 328-333.

Peters, H. N., & Jenkins, R. L.   Improvement of chronic schizophrenic patients with guided problem-solving motivated by hunger. *Psychiatric Quarterly Supplement*, 1954, 28, 84-101.

Rachman, S.   The treatment of anxiety and phobic reactions by systematic desensitization psychotherapy. *Journal of Abnormal and Social Psychology*, 1959, 58, 259-263.

Raymond, M. S.   Case of fetishism treated by aversion therapy. *British Medical Journal*, 1956, 2, 854-857.

Razran, G.   Stimulus generalization of conditioned responses. *Psychological Bulletin*, 1949, 46, 337-365.

Robinson, Nancy M.   Paired-associate learning by schizophrenic subjects under conditions of personal and impersonal reward and punishment. Unpublished doctoral dissertation, Stanford University, 1957.

Rogers, C. R.   *Client-centered therapy*. Boston: Houghton Mifflin, 1951.

Rogers, C. R.   Group discussion: Problems of controls. In E. H. Rubinstein & M. B. Parloff (Eds.), *Research in psychotherapy*. Washington, D. C.: American Psychological Association, 1959.

Rogers, J. M.   Operant conditioning in a quasi-therapy setting. *Journal of Abnormal and Social Psychology*, 1960, 60, 247-252.

Rosenthal, D.   Changes in some moral values following psychotherapy. *Journal of Consulting Psychology*, 1955, 19, 431-436.

Rotter, J. B.   *Social learning and clinical psychology*. Englewood Cliffs, N.J.: Prentice-Hall, 1954.

Rubenstein, E. A., & Lorr, M.   A comparison of terminators and remainers in outpatient psychotherapy. *Journal of Clinical Psychology*, 1956, 12, 345-349.

Rutherford, B. R.   The use of negative practice in speech therapy with children handicapped by cerebral palsy, athetoid type. *Journal of Speech Disorders*, 1940, 5, 259-264.

Salzinger, K. Experimental manipulation of verbal behavior: A review. *Journal of Genetic Psychology*, 1959, **61**, 65-94.

Sarason, Barbara R. The effects of verbally conditioned response classes on post-conditioning tasks. *Dissertation Abstract*, 1957, **12**, 679.

Schmidberg, Melitta. Psychotherapy of juvenile delinquents. *International Mental Health Research Newsletter*, 1959, **1**, 1-2.

Sears, Pauline S. Child-rearing factors related to playing of sex-typed roles. *American Psychologist*, 1953, **8**, 431. (Abstract)

Sears, R. R. Identification as a form of behavioral development. In D. B. Harris (Ed.), *The concept of development: An issue in the study of human behavior*. Minneapolis: University of Minnesota Press, 1957.

Sheehan, J. G. The modification of stuttering through non-reinforcement. *Journal of Abnormal and Social Psychology*, 1951, **46**, 51-63.

Sheehan, J. G., & Voas, R. B. Stuttering as conflict: I. Comparison of therapy techniques involving approach and avoidance. *Journal of Speech Disorders*, 1957, **22**, 714-723.

Shoben, E. J. Psychotherapy as a problem in learning theory. *Psychological Bulletin*, 1949, **46**, 366-392.

Skinner, B. F. *Science and human behavior*. New York: Macmillan, 1953.

Skinner, B. F. Some issues concerning the control of human behavior. *Science*, 1956, **124**, 1057-1066. (a)

Skinner, B. F. What is psychotic behavior? In *Theory and treatment of psychosis: Some newer aspects*. St. Louis: Washington University Studies, 1956. (b)

Solomon, R. L., Kamin, L. J., & Wynne, L. C. Traumatic avoidance learning: The outcomes of several extinction procedures with dogs. *Journal of Abnormal and Social Psychology*, 1953, **48**, 291-302.

Sullivan, H. S. *The interpersonal theory of psychiatry*. New York: Norton, 1953.

Thirmann, J. Conditioned-reflex treatment of alcoholism. *New England Journal of Medicine*, 1949, **241**, 368-370, 406-410.

Thompson, G. N., & Bielinski, B. Improvement in psychosis following conditioned reflex treatment in alcoholism. *Journal of Nervous and Mental Diseases*, 1953, **117**, 537-543.

Tilton, J. R. The use of instrumental motor and verbal learning techniques in the treatment of chronic schizophrenics. Unpublished doctoral dissertation, Michigan State University, 1956.

Ullman, L. P., Krasner, L., & Collins, Beverly J. Modification of behavior in group therapy associated with verbal conditioning. *Journal of Abnormal and Social Psychology*, in press.

Voegtlen, W. L. The treatment of alcoholism by establishing a conditioned reflex. *American Journal of Medical Science*, 1940, **119**, 802-810.

Wallace, J. A. The treatment of alcoholics by the conditioned reflex method. *Journal of the Tennessee Medical Association*, 1949, **42**, 125-128.

Weide, T. N. Conditioning and generalization of the use of affect-relevant words. Unpublished doctoral dissertation, Stanford University, 1959.

Whiting, J. W. M. The research program of the Laboratory of Human Development: The development of self-control. Cambridge: Harvard University Press, 1954. (Mimeo)

Williams, C. D. The elimination of tantrum behaviors by extinction procedures. *Journal of Abnormal and Social Psychology*, 1959, 59, 269.

Williams, R. I. Verbal conditioning in psychotherapy. *American Psychologist*, 1959, 14, 388. (Abstract)

Wolpe, J. Reciprocal inhibition as the main basis of psychotherapeutic effects. *American Medical Association Archives of Neurology and Psychiatry*, 1954, 72, 206-226.

Wolpe, J. *Psychotherapy by reciprocal inhibition.* Stanford: Stanford University Press, 1958.

Wolpe, J. Psychotherapy based on the principle of reciprocal inhibition. In A. Burton (Ed.), *Case studies in counseling and psychotherapy.* Englewood Cliffs, N. J.: Prentice-Hall, 1959.

Yates, A. J. The application of learning theory to the treatment of tics. *Journal of Abnormal and Social Psychology*, 1958, 56, 175-182.

17

Aversion Therapy for Sexual Deviations: A Critical Review

INTRODUCTION

In the following article M. Feldman describes and evaluates the application of therapy based on learning theory to the problems of sexual deviation. A number of things should be noted in reading this paper. First, it will quickly become apparent that even as applied to the limited area of sexual deviations learning theory generates numerous approaches and techniques for the modification of inappropriate behaviors. That is, radically different methods of treatment can be developed to meet different situations rather than using one basic approach for all. Second, and more importantly in terms of the aims of this book, the reader should note the model that is used for understanding sexual deviations. Rather than assuming that a deviation is the expression or result of some unresolved psychodynamic conflict, it is assumed the deviation is merely the result of the unfortunate learning of inappropriate responses. Since the problem results from learning rather than an unresolved conflict, treatment involves relearning rather than an attempt to bring to light and resolve the suspected conflict. Although for the most part this approach is ahistorical in that the therapist is not usually concerned with exactly how the inappropriate response was first learned, it does not necessarily suggest that it is fruitless to study the personal, biological, family, and cultural backgrounds of individuals who suffer from the learned symptoms. Some background factors may facilitate or predispose the individual to learn what might later be considered to be inappropriate responses.

Therapeutic practices based on learning theory have attracted increasing interest over the past few years, and there is now considerable evidence supporting the continued and expanded use of these techniques. This is not to say, however, that the theory and techniques are without their critics. On the contrary, some of the most active and affectively toned debates in psychology today are over the use of learning theory for the treatment of pathology. One of the problems often pointed to by the critics is that the applications of the techniques based on learning theory are somewhat limited. That is, although there now seems to be no doubt that the learning theory approach is very effective with certain behavior problems in which there are easily definable responses that can be manipulated, it has been suggested that the learning theory techniques offer very little for the "run-of-the-mill neurotic" who is just not as happy as he would like to be but who cannot point to specific behaviors or emotional reactions he would like altered. Some critics have gone as far as to suggest that a therapeutic approach built on principles derived from research on lower animals cannot deal with complex covert processes such as thinking. These critics suggest that learning theory must be limited to simple overt behavior or conditioned emotional responses. This is not a necessary limitation, however, and the possibility of manipulating covert responses should not be rejected merely because the learning-based techniques were developed on easily observable overt responses. The fact that persons tend to suppress thinking about unpleasant things and spend time thinking of pleasant events can be taken as support for the position that the performance of cognitive covert responses is subject to manipulation through negative and positive consequences in the same way that more overt and easily observable behaviors are subject to manipulation. It should be clear that the therapists who base their approach on learning theory consider cognitive responses as behavior just as they consider muscular movements as behavior. When the use of the term "behavior" is understood in its larger sense, it is clear that in calling themselves "behavior therapists" the learning theory therapists are not suggesting that their techniques can be applied only to overt responses.

In considering the problem of manipulating covert responses, which is probably more difficult than manipulating overt responses, it must be recalled that the learning theory approach is still relatively new and that each year innovations in techniques extend the realm of applications. As we become concerned with problems in which the undesired responses are less well defined, more creativity and ingenuity will be required to devise workable techniques. Naturally, it is entirely possible that at some point the difficulty will be greater than our ingenuity. At the present time, however, we have not yet reached that point.

In reading the following article the reader should note how some researchers have attempted to alter the cognitive elements as well as the specific motor elements of the disorders. The success or failure of these attempts have important implications for the adequacy of the learning-based model of psychopathology. Before reading the article, it should be noted that the traditional methods of psychotherapy or psychoanalysis have a very poor record in the treatment of sexual deviates. Since the inappropriate responses of these patients have been found difficult, if not impossible, to eliminate by the traditional approaches, it would seem that the application of learning theory therapy to sexual deviates would provide a stringent test for this approach to therapy.

AVERSION THERAPY FOR SEXUAL DEVIATIONS:
A CRITICAL REVIEW

M. P. FELDMAN

Prior to the 1950s, there appears to be only one reference (Max, 1935) to the treatment of sexual deviations by aversion therapy. Max required a homosexual patient to fantasize the attractive sexual stimulus in conjunction with electric shock, hence employing a classical conditioning approach. He found it necessary to use a shock higher than that usual in laboratory studies, to cause a "diminution of the emotional value of the sexual stimulus." This lasted for several days after each experimental period, and over 3 months the effect was cumulative. Max reports that 4 months after the end of treatment, the patient said: "The terrible neurosis has lost the battle, not completely but 95 per cent of the way." No further details are given of the long-term effect of this pioneering piece of work.

In the last few years, the great stimulus given to behavior therapy approaches by the work of Wolpe (1958), for the most part concentrated on the treatment of disorders such as phobias and obsessions, has also had an effect in the field of sexual deviations. A previous review of learning approaches to the treatment of sexual deviations has been given by Rachman (1961). No doubt more concerned to make a case for the clinical usefulness of these approaches, Rachman made little attempt to assess them critically. The present paper will describe aversion therapy techniques used to date, and also offer both specific and general criticisms of the methods employed.

There are two main arguments in favor of applying learning-theory techniques to the treatment of sexual deviations. Firstly, the outcome of treatment by various psychotherapeutic techniques, despite the optimism expressed by one or two authors, for example, Allen (1956) and Ellis (1956), is rather poor, Curran and Parr

SOURCE. Reprinted with permission of the American Psychological Association and the author from the *Psychological Bulletin*, 1966, **65**, 65-79.

(1957) found the rate of improvement to be no greater in 25 of their cases treated by psychotherapy than in 25 others who received little or no treatment. Woodward (1958) has reported a series of homosexual patients referred by the courts and treated at the London Institute for the Study and Treatment of Delinquency. Out of 113 referred for treatment, data are reported for only 64 who either completed treatment or left for some good reason. Only seven patients had no homosexual impulse and an increased heterosexual interest at the conclusion of their psychotherapy. Of these seven, all were bisexual at the onset of treatment, three having a Kinsey rating of 1 or 2 (Kinsey, Pomeroy, & Martin, 1948). Attempts made to obtain follow-up data were somewhat sketchy and inconclusive. With respect to psychoanalytic claims, Rubinstein (1958) was cautious: "Psycho-analysis can help to a certain extent and for a fair number. Some improve well beyond the original expectation." This recalls Freud's (1938) statement quoted in Jones (1964): "In a certain number of cases we succeed . . . in the majority of cases it is no longer possible . . . the result of our treatment cannot be predicted [p. 624]." A large-scale psychoanalytic study has been reported by Bieber et al. (1963). Out of 100 homosexual patients treated by full-scale psychoanalysis, 27% were solely heterosexual at the close of treatment. Those patients who did improve had all had heterosexual experience up to intercourse at some stage prior to treatment. Moreover, the authors report their results only at the close of treatment and give no follow-up data.

It is of interest that the major effort in the behavior-therapy field to date has been applied to such problems as phobias and obsessions in which the record of psychotherapy by no means supports an attitude of therapeutic pessimism. Indeed, in a controlled, albeit retrospective, comparison between behavior therapy and psychotherapy (Marks & Gelder, 1965; Cooper, Gelder, & Marks, 1965) the outcome was only slightly, if at all, in favor of behavior therapy.

The second argument concerns the intrinsic interest of applying learning-theory principles, derived in the laboratory, to a field in which the problem is one of real-life behavior. Sexual behavior may be described as consisting of two components, an intrinsic mediational component and an extrinsic behavioral component. The possibility of directly manipulating the latter and hence of influencing the former is theoretically, at any rate, quite evident. Clearly, most of the operant responses involved in homosexual behavior cannot be reproduced in a laboratory setting and are not, therefore, available for manipulation. However, homosexual behavior can be considered as being frequently initiated by the visual response of looking at an attractive sexual object. At least one sexual response is thus available for laboratory manipulation, and is utilized in almost all the techniques to be described in the present paper. The great majority of aversion therapists have used classical conditioning, that is, the attempt is made to associate anxiety or fear with the previously attractive homosexual stimulus. Only a small minority have used instrumental conditioning, in which the avoidance or escape from the punishing stimulus is contingent on the performance of a specific operant response—generally the avoidance of the previously attractive stimulus. Irrespective of the conditioning technique used, the underlying aim (although this is frequently not specifically stated) is to suppress the visual response of looking —in reality or fantasy—at an attractive but inappropriate sexual stimulus. It is hoped that this effect will generalize over the whole range of homosexual responses. In the case of other deviations such as transvestism and fetishism, responses such as looking at or wearing the fetish objects are readily available for laboratory manipulation. Once again, in the treatment of these deviations, most workers have used a classical conditioning technique.

Aversion Therapy Techniques Applied to Sexual Deviations

A list of reports on the application of aversion therapy to homosexuality is given in Table 1A, and a list of those concerning other sexual deviations appears in Table 1B. Each of these is summarized in Tables 1A and 1B, together with any criticisms which are specific to the particular report. Criticisms applicable to several reports, together with suggestions for improvement, appear later in the paper.

Homosexuality. The report of Max (1935) has been described earlier, and in view of its very brief nature, no further discussion will be given. An important contribution has been made by Freund (1960). He administered his patients a mixture of caffeine and apomorphine in a number of treatment sessions never exceeding 24. When the emetic mixture became effective, slides of dressed and undressed men were shown to the patient. During a second phase of treatment, the patient was shown films of nude or semi-nude women 7 hours after he had been administered testosterone propionate. Sixty-seven patients are reported on in the paper; treatment was refused to none. Out of 20 court referrals, only 3 achieved any kind of heterosexual adaptation, and in no case did this last for more than a few weeks. The first follow-up was carried out after 3 years. Out of the 47 patients who presented other than due to court referral, 12 had shown some long-term heterosexual adaptation. A second follow-up 2 years later traced the histories of these 12. At that time none of them could claim complete absence of homosexual desires, and only six could claim complete absence of homosexual behavior. Three of the group were, in fact, practicing homosexuality fairly frequently. Ten of them had heterosexual intercourse at least once every two weeks, but only three found females other than their wives sexually desirable. Moreover, even before treatment, two patients had become adapted to heterosexual intercourse. Clearly these results do not encourage an attitude of optimism either to the use of chemical aversion or to a classical conditioning approach. Freund's series is, however, the only one in the field which includes a satisfactorily long follow-up and in this respect, therefore, is a a model of its kind.

James (1962) used apomorphine in the treatment of a 40-year-old homosexual with a Kinsey rating of 6. The treatment was rather more rigorous than that of Freund, being carried out at 2-hour intervals. As soon as nausea occurred, a strong light was shone onto a large piece of cardboard on which were pasted several photographs of nude or semi-nude men. The patient was asked to select an attractive one, and to recreate the experiences he had with his current homosexual partner. This fantasy was verbally reinforced by the therapist on the first two or three occasions; thereafter a tape recording was played twice every 2 hours during the period of nausea. This consisted of an explanation of his homosexual behavior, together with the effect of this on him, such terms as "sickening" and "nauseating" being attached to the social consequences. The treatment was carried out for a period of 30 hours, and 24 hours later was repeated for 32 hours more. The following night the patient was awakened every 2 hours and was played a tape recording which optimistically explained the future consequences of his no longer being homosexual. During the 3 days following aversion treatment, photographs of sexually attractive young females were placed in his room, and each morning he received an injection of testosterone propionate and was told to retire to his room whenever he felt any sexual excitement.

The reader may feel somewhat bewildered by the mixture of techniques involved in this treatment. However, the outcome was highly satisfactory in that there was a complete change from

TABLE 1

ATTEMPTS TO APPLY AVERSION THERAPY TO SEXUAL DEVIATIONS

Author/s	Conditioning technique	Sexual stimulus (CS)	Aversive stimulus (UCS)	Relief stimulus	Number of completed cases
A. Homosexuality					
Max (1935)	Classical (100% reinforcement)	Fantasy	Electrical	None	1
Freund (1960)	Classical (100% reinforcement)	Male photographs	Chemical	Testosterone propionate; several hours later female photographs shown	47
James (1962)	Classical (100% reinforcement)	Male photographs	Chemical plus tape recording	Tape recording of delights of hetero-sexuality plus testosterone propionate and photographs of females	1
Thorpe, Schmidt, and Castell (1963)	Classical (VR/ VI; 15% reinforcement)	Male photographs	Electrical	Female pictures intro-duced during patient's masturbation	1
Thorpe and Schmidt (1964)	Classical (VR/ VI; 35% reinforcement)	Male photographs	Electrical	None	1

TABLE 1 (*Continued*)

Author/s	Conditioning technique	Sexual stimulus (CC)	Aversive stimulus (UCS)	Relief stimulus	Number of completed cases
A. Homosexuality					
Thorpe, Schmidt, Brown, and Castell (1964)	Classical, plus punishment for avoidance of male stimulus (100% reinforcement)	Tachistoscopically presented sexually attractive words, e.g., "homosexual"	Electrical	Tachistoscopically presented "female" words at the end of the learning series	3
McGuire and Vallance (1964)	Classical (100% reinforcement)	Fantasy	Electrical (mainly self-administered)	None	6
Feldman and MacCulloch (1964 and 1965)	Instrumental (anticipatory avoidance, VI/VR, ⅓ reinforced, ⅓ delay, and ⅓ nonreinforced trials)	Male photographs projected onto a screen	Electrical	Female photographs at offset of the male photographs	26 (to July, 1965)

TABLE 1 (*Continued*)

B. Other sexual deviations

Author/s	Problem	Conditioning technique	Sexual stimulus (CS)	Aversive stimulus (UCS)	Relief stimulus	Number of completed cases
Raymond (1956)	Fetishism (perambulators and handbags)	Classical (100% reinforcement)	Pictures of prams and handbags, plus the objects themselves	Chemical	None	1
Oswald (1962)	Fetishism (rubber mackintoshes)	Classical (100% reinforcement)	Rubber mackintoshes (objects)	Chemical	None	1
Cooper (1963)	Fetishism (female clothes)	Classical (100% reinforcement)	Dressing in female clothes	Chemical plus tape recording	Tape-recorded suggestions of the pleasures of ceasing the behavior	1
Clark (1963)	Fetishism (female clothes)	Classical (100% reinforcement)	Dressing in female clothes	Chemical	None	1
Barker (1965)	Transvestism Patient 1	Classical (100% reinforcement)	Photograph of the patient in female clothing	Chemical	None	1
	Patient 2	Instrumental escape (VI/VR; 50% reinforcement)	Dressing in female clothes	Electrical	Cessation of shock when clothes removed	1

TABLE 1 (*Continued*)

Author/s	Problem	Conditioning technique	Sexual stimulus (CS)	Aversive stimulus (UCS)	Relief stimulus	Number of completed cases
			B. Other sexual deviations			
Morgenstern, Pearce, and Rees (1965)	Tranvestism	Classical (100% reinforcement)	Dressing in female clothes	Chemical	None	19
MacCulloch, Feldman, and Mac-Culloch[a]	Various: transvestism, sadism, and compulsive masturbation	Instrumental (anticipatory avoidance, VI/VR; $\frac{1}{3}$ reinforced, $\frac{1}{3}$ delay, and $\frac{1}{3}$ nonreinforced trials)	Photographs of the patient in female clothes, or photographs of the sexual objects	Electrical	Photographs of wives or of the therapeutically desirable sexual object introduced at the offset of the CS	6
McGuire and Vallance (1964)	Various: including transvestism and compulsive masturbation	Classical (100% reinforcement)	Fantasy	Electrical (self-administered)	None	8
Thorpe, Schmidt, Brown, and Castell (1964)	Transvestism ($N=1$) Fetishism (motorcycles) ($N=1$)	Classical, plus punishment for avoidance of sexually attractive male stimulus (100% reinforcement)	Tachistoscopically presented sexually attractive words	Electrical	Tachistoscopically presented "female" words at the end of the learning series	2

[a] In preparation. See Footnote 1.

homosexual to heterosexual behavior, although the follow-up was only 5 months. The poor long-term results obtained by Freund in his large series should caution against placing too much weight on the outcome of James's single case.

We now have three papers from Thorpe and his colleagues. They tried three separate techniques for their first patient (Thorpe, Schmidt, & Castell, 1963). In the first of these, the patient was placed in a small room in front of a picture of a female which was visible only when illuminated by the psychologist. The patient was instructed to masturbate, using whatever fantasy he wished. He was told to report when orgasm was being reached. At this point the female picture was illuminated until the patient reported he had finished ejaculation. After 11 such trials, there was no change in the patient's masturbatory fantasy, which remained homosexual. The authors concluded that they may have been attempting backward conditioning by presenting the picture after reinforcement had commenced. They therefore tried a second technique, in which the female picture was illuminated for 1 second at random intervals during masturbation. The number of illuminations was increased until in the later trials the picture was more under illumination than in darkness. This method was also unsuccessful, and was therefore dropped. A third technique was then introduced, and was carried out in a room with a floor area of 9 square feet, which was completely covered by an electrical grid. This technique consisted of a combination of positive and negative conditioning trials conducted separately. The former were those described in connection with the second technique and 38 trials were given. The negative trials were carried out by illuminating one of the patient's own photograps of a nude male (we are not told for how long) and at the same time delivering a strong electric shock through the grid to his bare feet. The shock was turned on ½ to 1 second after the picture had been illuminated. A variable interval/variable ratio schedule of reinforcement (VI/VR) was used in conjunction with a classical conditioning technique. Within each trial, the picture was illuminated 40 times. On nine of these occasions, randomly selected, the patient was shocked. Usually, five trials were given per session, although on occasion this was increased to 10 trials. Each trial took 10 minutes, and 100 trials were given in all. It can be estimated that the patient was receiving between 200 and 400 illuminations of the male slide in each session. This large number of stimulus presentations introduces, in the event of a successful outcome of treatment, the possibility of stimulus satiation providing the explanatory factor in addition to the hypothesized classical conditioning. Follow-up contact appears to have been by letter. The patient reported utilizing heterosexual fantasy, and stated that he had had one attempt at heterosexual intercourse. Occasional homosexual patterns of behavior had occurred, but the patient was not unduly worried about these, which he regarded as a safety valve. Whereas, before treatment, he had only considered young men and boys, he now considered persons of both sexes. The authors admit that many would consider this patient to have technically relapsed. However, they predict a satisfactory heterosexual adjustment for him, and they therefore consider his treatment to have been successful.

Thorpe and Schmidt (1963) next report a case which they describe as a therapeutic faliure. The patient was required to stand in the same small room as used for the previous patient. A male picture was illuminated for 1 second, 84 times in 15 minutes at random intervals, and in 30 of these, randomly interspersed, the illumination was accompanied by a shock to the feet which began ½ second after the picture had appeared; that is, they again used classical conditioning and a VI/VR schedule. Kimble (1961) reports evidence that partial reinforcement hinders response acquisition by classical conditioning. In view of this fact, Thorpe's use of partial reinforcement is rather surprising. A further criticism concerns the very short stimulus exposure time. This hardly seems sufficient for the patient both to light adapt and to perceive the content of the stimulus. The patient received three sessions of treatment over a period of 2 days, after which he refused further treatment. It is by no means clear why a patient who received only a very few sessions should be described as a therapeutic failure, while one who received a much larger number of sessions of somewhat similar treatment should be described as a success despite "a technical relapse."

The third paper contributed by Thorpe and his colleagues (Thorpe, Schmidt, Brown, & Castell, 1964) describes a technique termed "Aversion relief therapy: A new method for general application." The range of usefulness for which they hope is illustrated by its application to three homosexuals, one transvestite, one motorcycle fetishist, one phobic, one obsessional and one compulsive overeater. The authors argue that verbal representations of behavior can be substituted for actual behavior with no loss of effectiveness, citing as support Wolpe's symbolic method of systematic desensitization (Wolpe, 1958). They also argue for the necessity of terminating aversive conditioning by a relief stimulus, which should in some way be associated with the behavior desired by the patient as a substitute for his socially unacceptable behavior. They prepared for each patient a disc which had up to 24 appropriate words typed on it, for example "homosexual" and its synonyms, the last word being a different one in each case. For instance, for the homosexual patient, a "relief" word such as "heterosexual" was used, and was never associated with shock. The patient was told to read the word aloud as it appeared in an illuminated aperture for about 2½ seconds, about 10 seconds being allowed between each word. As he did so, he received a shock. If he failed to do so, he received a more intense shock. In each session there were five such trials, each having a different number and order of words, but always terminated by a relief word. Each trial was separated by 5 minutes, and about one session per day was administered. The rationale behind shocking the patient as he reads a word clearly involves classical conditioning. That behind shocking him when he fails to do so is somewhat less clear. It could be argued in criticism that he is shocked for *avoiding* the previously attractive stimulus, the avoidance response having been set up by the classical conditioning procedure. An analogy would be the work of Solomon and Wynne (1953), who used an instrumental technique to set up an anticipatory avoidance response in dogs. They found that in order to extinguish this response, they had to resort to special procedures, described in Solomon, Kamin and Wynne (1953). One of these involved shocking the dog for carrying out the avoidance response. The method of Thorpe and his colleagues appears to involve the risk of doing this. At the very least, the situation appears less than clear-cut. Of the three homosexual patients described in this paper, all of whom responded well and who received between 14 and 30 sessions of treatment, only one appears to merit a Kinsey rating of more than 2. The majority of patients appearing for treatment for homosexuality at psychiatric clinics have a Kinsey rating of at least 4, so that the value of the technique requires much more supporting evidence. In addition, the maximum follow-up for any of the three was 4 weeks.

McGuire and Vallance (1964) describe what they state to be a classical conditioning technique. The patient is required to signal to the therapist when the image of his usual fantasy is clear. When he does so, a shock is administered. The procedure is repeated throughout a 20 to 30 minute session which is held up to six times per day. McGuire has designed a small and completely portable electrical apparatus used in the treatment, and this is usually handed over to the patient so that he can treat himself in his own home. He is told to use the apparatus whenever he is tempted to indulge in the fantasy concerned. One doubt concerning this technique lies in the interpretation of the term "clear." If this means that the patient has achieved a complete representation of his usual fantasy, the point is raised that at best the authors may be carrying out a variety of punishment learning (Estes, 1944). In this paradigm, the noxious stimulus occurs following the completion of the undesirable response. Estes showed extinction of a newly acquired avoidance response to be particularly rapid with this technique.

It is, of course, left to the patient himself to set the level of the shock, and this raises an additional and even more serious criticism. Sandler (1964) has provided a most useful discussion of the concept of masochism, defined as the situation in which a noxious stimulus does not result in the subject receiving it displaying avoidance behavior. Conversely, the noxious stimulus appears to be not only tolerated but even sought after. He provides a large number of experimental analogues to various clinical forms of masochistic behavior, so that in the most dramatic examples organisms have been found actually working for punishing results. In one variety of masochistic behavior, relevant in the present context, aversive stimuli might be paired with the reinforcer which follows a given activity. The end result may be that "the aversive stimulus becomes positively reinforcing in the same process [Skinner, 1953, p. 367]." This view is in accordance with analytic thinking. For instance, Fenichel (1945) states: "Certain experiences may have so firmly established the conviction that sexual pleasure must be associated with pain, that suffering has become the prerequisite for sexual pleasure [p. 357]." It might well be that self-treating patients will use a fairly low level of shock. This level then becomes associated with a very well-reinforced event, so that it serves as a positive reinforcer. Thus, far from the electrical shock being averting, it might become part of the normal fantasy situation.

McGuire and Vallance (1964) present treatment results for six homosexual patients of whom three discontinued treatment and three showed an improvement which could have been either mild, good, or symptom removed; it cannot be concluded which from their description. They state that the follow-up time in most cases was 1 month; a much longer one is clearly required. In a later paper (McGuire, Carlisle, & Young, 1965) these workers claim "at least as good results as the more elaborate mimes and cues provided by other aversion therapists [p. 187]." Unfortunately they provide no data to support their claim.

Solomon and Wynne (1953) and Turner and Solomon (1962), using both dog and human subjects and a neutral CS, demonstrated that the technique of anticipatory avoidance learning set up avoidance responses which were very highly resistant to extinction. Solomon (cited by Eysenck, 1964), using dogs as his subjects, and Aronfreed and Reber (1965), using children, have also shown the effectiveness of the technique in setting up highly stable avoidance responses to an attractive CS—a point particularly relevant in the present context. Feldman and MacCulloch (1964, 1965) have adapted the anticipatory avoidance technique to the clinical situation in the following way: The homosexual patient views a male slide which is back-projected onto a screen. He is instructed to leave the picture on for as long as he finds it attractive. After the slide has been on the screen for 8 seconds, the patient receives a shock if he has not by then removed it by means of a switch with which he is provided. If he does switch off within the 8-second period, he avoids the shock. Once the patient is avoiding regularly, he is placed on a standardized reinforcement schedule which consists of three types of trials, randomly interspersed. The first type consists of reinforced trials (the patient's attempt to switch off succeeds immediately). The second consists of delay trials (the patient's attempt to switch off is held up for varying intervals of time within the 8-second period. He does, however, eventually succeed in avoiding.) Finally, one-third of all trials are nonreinforced (the patient does receive a shock irrespective of his attempts to switch off). In addition, on two-fifths of the trials, selected at random, a female slide is projected onto the screen contiguous with the offset of the male slide, and is left on for about 10 seconds. This is then removed by the therapist and the patient can, if he wishes, request that it be returned. However, his request is met in an entirely random manner. A further feature is the use of hierarchies of male and female slides. The patient places the slides in their order of attractiveness for him so that treatment starts with the least attractive male slide being paired with the most attractive female slide; the two hierarchies then being moved along simultaneously. The interstimulus interval varies between 15 and 35 seconds randomly, and about 25 stimulus presentations (trials) are given per session, which lasts for about 20 minutes. This is a VI/VR reinforcement schedule, but in the context of an instrumental conditioning technique.

In a paper prepared for publication in September 1964, Feldman and MacCulloch (1965) reported that of their 16 patients who had at that time completed treatment, 10 had shown a complete absence of homosexual practice, together with a complete or almost complete absence of homosexual fantasy. In addition, these 10 were either actively practicing heterosexually or had strong heterosexual fantasies. The authors propose a change of this nature as a reasonable criterion of improvement. At that time, the follow-up period varied between 1 and 14 months. Twenty-six patients have completed treatment at the present time (July, 1965) and have been followed up for at least 3 months—the maximum follow-up is now 2 years. Eighteen patients have shown the kind of improvement which is defined above. Eight patients are wholly or largely unchanged. Ten further patients are either under treatment at the present time or have recently completed treatment but have been followed up for less than 3 months. Of this total sample, two-thirds had a pretreatment Kinsey rating of 5 or 6. All of the remaining patients had a Kinsey rating of at least 3. It is planned to extend the present series until it numbers approximately 40, and then to set up and carry out a fully controlled prospective trial.

One major criticism which can be made of this technique is that the reinforcement schedule is somewhat rigid (one-third of all trials are nonreinforced). It would probably be more satisfactory to gradually reduce the proportion of shock trials so as to increasingly approximate real-life conditions.

Other deviations. Raymond (1956) and Oswald (1962), treating respectively a perambulator fetishist and a rubber mackintosh fetishist, used substantially the same techniques. The description provided by Raymond will serve for both papers. His patient was shown a collection of handbags, perambulators, and colored illustrations immediately after receiving an injection of apomorphine and just before nausea was produced. The treatment was given every 2 hours, day and night. No food was allowed, and at night amphetamine was used to keep him awake. After a week of this regime, he spent 8 days at home. He then had several further days of the same type of treatment. He remained well for 3 years, at which time he began to find control more difficult, and received a further course of treatment. At the time of the last follow-up, 2 years later, he was still doing well (follow-up data in Coates, 1964). Oswald (1965) has reported a similarly long-term (54 months) follow-up of his fetishist patient. Cooper (1963) used emetine as the aversive stimulus and, as in the cases of Raymond and Oswald, employed classical conditioning with a 100%-reinforcement schedule in the treatment of a female clothes fetishist. In this case, the patient was actually required to carry out his fetishistic acts. With the onset of nausea and vomiting, the patient was returned to bed and received intensive moral suggestion. During the whole of the day he was not allowed to discard his female clothes, but was instructed to look at his reflection in the mirror and to reenact in his mind every detail of his "disgusting perversion." The patient was kept awake at night by means of amphetamine, and a tape recording was played every 2 hours for 20 minutes. The patient finally broke down after 7 days of this regime, having neither eaten nor slept for 6 days. Three days after treatment, a right ventricular stress was noted and this was considered to be due to a toxic myocarditis produced by emetine. Nine months after treatment he was still not practicing his fetishism, and was having normal intercourse with his wife. A very similar technique was used by Clark (1963), again with a female clothes fetishist. The emphasis on disgust placed by some therapists is shown by the following phrase from Clark: "At one session, by a particularly happy chance, one of his favourite pictures fell into the vomit in the basin so that the patient had to see it every time he puked [p. 405]." The follow-up was over a 3-month period, at the end of which the patient was still doing well.

Thus far, we have only single case studies, from which conclusions are notoriously difficult to draw. Barker (1965) reports the treatment of two patients. His first patient was treated with the use of apomorphine as the aversive stimulus, and slides of the patient in his female clothing were used as conditional stimuli. Reinforcement was 100%, and 68 treatment trials were given every 2 hours for 6 days and nights. The patient went abroad so that follow-up was difficult, but Barker states that as far as he knew the patient had remained symptom free for 18 months. Despite the apparent therapeutic effectiveness of chemical aversion for this patient, Barker found its disadvantages to be so substantial as to outweigh its advantages, and some of the criticisms he made will be listed in a later section. Barker's second patient was treated with the use of electrical aversive stimulation (as described by Thorpe, Schmidt, and Castell, 1963) and his wearing female clothes as the conditional stimulus. Treatment sessions, each consisting of five trials, were administered every $\frac{1}{2}$ hour, with 1 minute between each trial. Four hundred trials were given in all, over a 6-day period. The patient began to dress at the beginning of each trial and continued to do so until signalled to undress, either by shock from the grid or by a buzzer, randomly interspersed over the 400 trials. The signal recurred at intervals of 5, 10, or 15 seconds, randomly interspersed, until he was undressed, and the interval between commencement of dressing and signal onset was randomized at between 1 and 3 minutes. For the last 75 trials, no difference in rates of undressing between shock and nonshock trials were observed. No data, however, are given for the first 325 trials. Except for one isolated relapse, the patient is described as being symptom free for 14 months after treatment. Barker considered that a classical conditioning paradigm could not account for his successful result, and that the instrumental act of undressing associated with shock escape carried out on a 50% reinforcement schedule suggested that instrumental conditioning was playing an important part in symptom relief.

This argument is strengthened by a series of 19 transvestist patients reported by Morgenstern, Pearce, and Rees (1965). Of these patients, six refused treatment, six relapsed after completing treatment but practised much less frequently than prior to treatment, and seven ceased to cross-dress altogether. The 13 patients who completed treatment received 39 sessions, given three times per day. Apomorphine was used as the aversive stimulus, and injections were graded so that the peak effect of nausea and vomiting coincided with the completion of the cross-dressing ritual. The authors report on the relationship of battery of tests to the treatment outcome, the most significant relationship being that between outcome and a verbal conditioning (instrumental) procedure, whereas eye-blink conditioning (classical) showed no relationship with outcome. Only the cured patients showed evidence of verbal conditioning. Morgenstern, Pearce, and Rees conclude that an instrumental form of conditioning is involved in aversion therapy.

MacCulloch, Feldman, and MacCulloch,[1] using the same instrumental anticipatory avoidance technique as described above for the treatment of homosexuality, treated a group of six patients displaying various types of sexual deviation other than homosexuality. In the case of two transvestists, the sexual stimulus (CS) used was a photograph of the patient in his female clothing, and in the case of the other patients, the CS was the preferred sexual object. Relief stimuli were used for four of these patients; in three cases these were photographs of the patients' wives. Four of the six pa-

[1] A detailed report of treatment methods and patients' case histories is in preparation and will be given when a somewhat longer follow-up time has elapsed.

tients ceased their sexually deviant behavior; the present follow-up varying from 2 to 18 months.

McGuire and Vallance (1964) reported eight varied cases of sexual deviation treated by associating fantasy with self-administered electric shock. All eight were stated to have improved. In no case did the follow-up exceed 1 month.

Finally, Thorpe, Schmidt, Brown, and Castell (1964) using the technique applied by them to homosexuality and described earlier, treated one transvestist (with success) and one motorcycle fetishist. The former had been followed up for 2 weeks and the latter was still in treatment at the time of the report.

Discussion

Derivation from Experimental Findings

Very few of the techniques described above have been derived in any logical way from the general body of the experimental psychology of learning. Most of the papers quoted contain little or no discussion of the kind of predictions for treatment which learning theory would be expected to make. Eysenck (1965) has severely criticized this deficiency in the following terms: "For all the attention that is being paid to them by practitioners in the field, the theoretical and experimental advances in learning and conditioning methodology might just as well not have taken place [p. 12]." It would be unfortunate if behavior therapy were to part from the general body of experimental psychology and become an entirely separate field.

The Choice of Learning Paradigm

In contrast to the follow-up reports on phobic patients, (Cooper, Gelder, & Marks, 1965) which indicated a substantial rate of post-treatment spontaneous remission, sexual deviations appear rather to tend to relapse following treatment (cf. Freund, 1960). It is therefore mandatory to adopt the learning technique which is likely to be most resistant to extinction, as has been pointed out by Eysenck (1963). It is rather surprising that so many of the authors cited in Tables 1A and IB should have chosen to use classical conditioning, the effects of which are rather poorly resistant to extinction (Solomon & Brush, 1956). These authors report that instrumental avoidance learning techniques—such as anticipatory avoidance—appear to be by far the most highly resistant to extinction. It was pointed out earlier in the present paper that sexual behavior appears to have a very strong operant component, and the comments and results of Morgenstern, Pearce, and Rees (1965) and Barker (1965) support the case for an instrumental rather than a classical technique. Turner and Solomon (1962) have shown that within the context of an instrumental technique the subject should perform an operant response, rather than a reflexive one, for the greatest resistance to extinction.

It is desirable to incorporate into the training situation those variables which have been shown to further increase resistance to extinction. As listed by Feldman and MacCulloch (1965), some of these are as follows:

1. Learning trials should be distributed rather than massed.

2. Contiguity of stimulus and response, particularly at offset, should be maintained throughout.

3. Shock should be introduced at whatever level has been found to be unpleasant for the patient rather than gradually increased, thus possibly enabling the patient to habituate.

4. Partial reinforcement should be used in conjunction with instrumental techniques.

5. Reinforcement should be variable rather than fixed, both in ratio and in interval schedules.

6. There is a good deal of data which suggest that delaying a proportion of the patient's attempts to avoid should lead to greater resistance to extinction than immediate reinforcement.

7. In general, the greater the variation in the conditions of training the more will these approximate to the real life situation, thus avoiding, as far as possible, generalization decrement, probably the most potent source of rapidity of extinction.

Choice of the Aversive Stimulus: Chemical or Electrical

Both Rachman (1965) and Barker (1965) point out that chemical aversion is highly unpleasant, not only for the patient but also for the therapist and the nursing staff; there is also some evidence that it brings about increased aggressiveness on the part of the patient. Several other advantages of electrical aversion, as listed by Rachman, are as follows: precision of control, manipulability of variables, the possibility of using partial reinforcement, and the possibility of more accurate measurements of the progress of treatment. In connection with this last point, MacCulloch, Feldman, and Pinschof (1965) report data on the measurement of avoidance response latencies and pulse-rate changes during the treatment of

homosexual patients by electrical aversion. It will be recalled that
Barker (1965), in comparing the use of chemical and electrical
aversive techniques, used only two patients. As Raymond (1965)
points out, this sample is somewhat small. Raymond argues, without however presenting any more evidence than the subjective
report of one patient, for the use of chemical rather than electrical
aversion. It certainly seems reasonable to point out, in view of its
much more harmful side effects and the much greater pressure on
time of staff, that unless chemical aversion produces a better outcome than electrical aversion, there is no case for its use.

The Choice of the Conditional Stimulus

The patient may not always be able to reproduce his fantasy, and
merely handing him pictures to look at may not be sufficient to
hold his attention in face of the distractions of the treatment room.
A mechanically projected picture has the advantages of clarity of
reproduction and ease of control. With respect to the treatment of
transvestists and fetishists, the choice appears to be between the
patient wearing or handling his fetishistic stimuli, and of having
pictures of them presented by some mechanical means. Once again,
the argument concerning ease of control supports the use of slides
of the fetishistic stimulus. However, in those cases in which tactile
stimulation forms the central element of the fetish, the use of
slides is clearly inadequate. Wherever possible, the patient should
provide his own photographs of satisfying real-life stimuli to reduce the problem of generalization decrement.

The Introduction of an Alternative Response

A major problem is to substitute for the deviant sexual behavior
a form of sexual outlet that is both desired by the patient and is
socially possible. This will involve heterosexual fantasy and, ideally,
overt heterosexual behavior. Several techniques, particularly those
involving chemical aversion, make little or no attempt to carry out
this substitution. The more refined experimental control enabled
by the use of electrical aversion makes it readily possible. For
most homosexual patients, female sexual stimuli are either neutral
or unpleasant, and therefore evoke avoidance rather than approach
responses. The fact that patients feel relief (hence the term "relief" stimulus) when the male stimulus is removed, suggests a
method of changing these responses to female stimuli. In the
techniques of Feldman and MacCulloch (1965) and Thorpe,

Schmidt, Brown, and Castell (1964) this is achieved by introducing the female stimulus contiguous with the removal of the male stimulus. Kimble (1961) has summed up the experimental data on the use of relief stimuli as follows: "Stimuli associated with the cessation of shock are secondary reinforcers. Looking at it another way, they take on a value seemingly opposite of that acquired by stimuli which accompany shock onset [p. 176]." That is, the fact that the female slide is associated with the cessation of pain increases the likelihood that it will acquire positive reinforcing properties. It has been found helpful (Feldman & MacCulloch, 1965) to use photographs of wives or girlfriends as part of the hierarchy of female pictures wherever possible. This, of course, helps to reduce generalization decrement. The use made of a relief stimulus by Thorpe, Schmidt, Brown, and Castell (1964) can be criticized on the grounds of its predictability—it always appeared on the last stimulus presentation, indicating the end of the session, rather than the avoidance or cessation of pain. Moreover, the fact that a verbal stimulus is used makes the situation not particularly realistic.

McGuire, Carlyle, and Young (1965) instructed their patients that whatever the initial stimulus to masturbation, the fantasy in the 5 seconds just prior to orgasm must be of normal sexual intercourse. Thorpe, Schmidt, and Castell (1963) criticize their own somewhat similar technique on the grounds that its failure probably involved backward conditioning. A further objection can be made—several of the patients treated at Crumpsall Hospital have of their own accord attempted to fantasize females late in the masturbatory sequence. A frequent consequence has been detumescence, thus adding a further increment of strength to the habit of not approaching females.

It is suggested that the most effective combination is to introduce female photographs as relief stimuli in order to initiate approach responses to females, and then to gradually shape these in the manner described by Ferster (1965). He argues that it is desirable to start with a response which is relatively likely to be reinforced, such as simply speaking to females, and then to proceed up the hierarchy of responses which are increasingly less likely to be reinforced, not proceeding to the next one in the hierarchy until the preceding one has been very well established. The experience of the author and his colleagues is that it may take as long as 6 months before sexual approach responses to females are really well established, particularly in those patients who have either never had any sexual attraction to females or have not had such attraction for very long periods of time, say, 10 years or more.

The Use of Stimulus Hierarchies

For the purposes of the present discussion we shall confine our attention to homosexual patients, but the argument which follows applies equally to those displaying other sexual deviations. The great majority of techniques described in the present paper introduce male or female stimuli quite unsystematically, without regard to their relative degree of attractiveness or repulsion to the patient. At the onset of treatment the dominant sexual response is a homosexual one, the heterosexual response being nondominant. The problem is to design the treatment so as to reverse this situation. It is suggested that the order of presentation of conditional stimuli is a variable of considerable importance. In Wolpe's (1958) desensitization technique, principally applied to problems of approach learning such as phobias, the patient begins his treatment by exposure to a situation which is only slightly anxiety provoking, moving on to a more difficult situation when the previous step in the hierarchy is no longer evoking anxiety. Applying this principle to avoidance learning in the treatment of homosexuality, it seems logical to begin with a male stimulus which is only mildly attractive and to which an avoidance response may be set up with relative ease. It follows that if a female stimulus is introduced contiguous with the offset of the male stimulus, it should be as attractive to the patient as possible. This further increases the ease of setting up an avoidance response to the male stimulus (Kimble, 1961) as well as increasing the strength of approach to the female stimulus. Once the avoidance response to the first male stimulus and the approach response to the first female stimulus are well established, the patient can be taken along hierarchies of ascending attractiveness of male stimuli and descending attractiveness of female stimuli. The principles underlying the use of stimulus hierarchies are so well established in experimental psychology that their neglect by aversion therapists is rather surprising.

Clinical Factors

Some of the reports described above are marked by a rather moralistic overtone. This is particularly clear in the papers by Cooper (1963) and Clark (1963), in both of which the authors used tape recordings which stressed the "disgusting and unpleasant" nature of the patient's sexual deviation. Apart from the fact that this, particularly when used together with chemical aversion, might render the whole situation so unpleasant as to force the patient into a "flight into health," a further factor should also be mentioned. This is the unsuitability of the therapist expressing strong opinions concerning the patient's practices, particularly in the absence of evidence that such a degree of hectoring condemnation is essential to the effective outcome of treatment.

Westwood (1960) has pointed out that therapists tend to see an atypical sample of homosexuals. It is possible that this atypicality resides in the marked incidence of psychiatric disturbance displayed by homosexuals presenting themselves at psychiatric clinics. In many of the reports which are reviewed above, there is an inadequate psychiatric description of the patients concerned. No fewer than 18 of the 26 homosexual patients in Feldman and MacCulloch's series (see Table 1A) who have completed aversion therapy treatment to date have displayed psychopathology, ranging from a depressive psychosis to acute or chronic personality disorders. It is extremely important, therefore, that there be full psychiatric participation in aversion therapy treatment to enable the diagnosis of coexisting psychopathology, and the treatment of this where necessary and possible. None of the patients in the Feldman and MacCulloch series have received treatment in addition to avoidance learning other than adjuvant drug therapy and supportive psychotherapy of a superficial kind. No patients have received either drug therapy or psychotherapy as the sole or even major portion of their treatment.

A full description of the mental state at the onset of treatment makes it possible to set up predictive relationships between personality factors and the outcome of treatment. MacCulloch and Feldman[2] have found that those patients displaying self-insecure personality traits (Schneider, 1959) not only have a better motivation for treatment but show a better response to treatment than do those who show attention-seeking personality traits (Schneider, 1959).

All too often, the details of follow-up and outcome are extremely scanty. For instance, McGuire and Vallance (1964) state that most of their patients were followed up for 1 month. Thorpe's various patients (Thorpe & Schmidt, 1964; Thorpe, Schmidt, Brown, & Castell, 1964; Thorpe, Schmidt, & Castell, 1963) appear to have

---

[2] A report of this work is currently under editorial consideration.

been followed up for about the same length of time. Not only does it appear inappropriate and perhaps misleading to publish successful single cases, (therapists are, on the average, less likely to report unsuccessful single cases), it is also desirable that follow-up should be of at least several months' duration. Such longer follow-ups may well provide a very necessary correction of early optimism, particularly as most aversion therapists have used classical conditioning which shows a rather poor resistance to extinction. An apparently successful outcome may therefore resist relapse for the few weeks of a short-term follow-up, but may not survive a longer and correspondingly more searching assessment.

Pre- and Posttreatment Assessment

There is a very strong necessity for an objective evaluation of the direction of sexual interests before and after treatment which is independent of clinical data, and which will employ indices different from those involved in the treatment situation itself. Brown (1964) has described a technique in which the number of times a subject operates a shutter to reveal a picture is used to index the relative intensities of sexual interest. This technique has been criticized by Koenig (1965). A recent, and very promising, objective approach which involves eye-pupil responses to sexual stimuli is that of Hess, Seltzer, and Shlien (1965). Feldman, MacCulloch, Mellor, and Pinschof[3] are developing a sexual approach-avoidance scale which combines features of the semantic differential technique (Osgood, Succi, & Tannenbaum, 1957) and the personal questionnaire technique of Shapiro (1961), and is used to assess the relative levels of homo- and heteroerotic interest prior to and following treatment.

Conclusion

It cannot yet be said that there is an overwhelming case for the efficacy of any single aversion therapy technique in the treatment of any single sexual deviation, although the results obtained to date suggest that instrumental techniques are both theoretically more likely to be successful than those based on classical conditioning,

---

[3] Principal components analyses show the scale to be unifactorial both for homosexual patients and for heterosexual controls. The scale discriminates without overlap between controls and pretreatment patients, while improved patients, but not unimproved ones, show a considerable overlap with controls. One month test-retest reliability in controls is 0.8, and preliminary results indicate little change in homosexual patients over a pretreatment interval averaging 2 months. A report on this work is in preparation.

and have also achieved a reasonable measure of practical success. A major purpose of the present paper is to argue the need to derive any aversion therapy treatment logically from the general body of learning theory, rather than to construct ad hoc and undigested mixtures of often inappropriate and mutually contradictory variables. If, having carefully derived the treatment technique, it then fails, the reason for failure will lie in the unsuitability of the technique to the problem concerned, particularly if a large series of patients has been used so as to overcome the bias inherent in the single-case method. Should the treatment technique succeed, it can then be developed so as to maximize its effectiveness. Finally, it is argued most strongly that the future value of aversion therapy techniques depends upon therapists maintaining their links with, on the one hand, general experimental psychology, and on the other, with general clinical psychiatry.

REFERENCES

Allan, C. The treatment of homosexuality. *Medical Press*, 1956, **235**, 141.

Aronfreed, J., & Reber, A. Internalised behavioural suppression and the timing of social punishment. *Journal of Personality and Social Psychology*, 1965, **1**, 3-16.

Barker, J. C. Behaviour therapy for transvestism: A comparison of pharmacological and electrical aversion techniques. *British Journal of Psychiatry*, 1965, **111**, 268-276.

Bieber, B., Bieber, I., Dain, H. J., Dince, P. R., Drellich, M. G., Grand, H. G., Grundlach, R. H., Kremer, Malvina W., Wilbur, Cornelia B., & Bieber, T. B. *Homosexuality*. New York: Basic Books, 1963.

Brown, P. T. On the differentiation of homo- or hetero-erotic interest in the male: An operant technique illustrated in the case of a motorcycle fetishist. *Behaviour Research and Therapy*, 1964, **2**, 31-37.

Clark, D. F. Fetishism treated by negative conditioning. *British Journal of Psychiatry*, 1963, **109**, 404-408.

Coates, S. Clinical psychology in sexual deviation. In I. Rosen (Ed.), *The pathology and treatment of sexual deviation*. London: Oxford Univer. Press, 1964. Pp. 381-419.

Cooper, A. J. A case of fetishism and impotence treated by behaviour therapy. *British Journal of Psychiatry*, 1963, **109**, 649-652.

Cooper, J. E., Gelder, M. G., & Marks, I. M. Result of behaviour therapy in 77 psychiatric patients. *British Medical Journal*, 1965, **1**, 1222-1225.

Curran, D., & Parr, D. Homosexuality: An analysis of 100 male cases seen in private practice. *British Medical Journal*, 1957, **1**, 797-801.

Ellis, A. The effectiveness of psychotherapy with individuals who have severe homosexual problems. *Journal of Consulting Psychology*, 1956, **20**, 58-60.

Estes, W. K. An experimental study of punishment. *Psychological Monographs*, 1944, 57(3 Whole No. 263).

Eysenck, H. J. Behaviour therapy: Extinction and relapse in neurosis. *British Journal of Psychiatry*, 1963, 109, 12-19.

Eysenck, H. J. *Crime and personality*. London: Methuen, 1964.

Eysenck, H. J. (Ed.). *Experiments in behaviour therapy*. London: Pergamon, 1965.

Feldman, M. P., & MacCulloch, M. J. A systematic approach to the treatment of homosexuality by conditioned aversion. Preliminary report. *American Journal of Psychiatry*, 1964, 121, 167-172.

Feldman, M. P., & MacCulloch, M. J. The application of anticipatory avoidance learning to the treatment of homosexuality. I. Theory, technique and preliminary results. *Behaviour Research and Therapy*, 1965, 2, 165-183.

Fenichel, O. *The psychoanalytic theory of neurosis*. New York: Norton, 1945.

Ferster, C. B. Reinforcement and punishment in the control of homosexual behaviour by social agencies. In H. J. Eysenck (Ed.), *Experiments in behaviour therapy*. London: Pergamon, 1965. Pp. 189-207.

Freund, K. Some problems in the treatment of homosexuality. In H. J. Eysenck (Ed.), *Behaviour therapy and the neuroses*. London: Pergamon, 1960. Pp. 312-326.

Hess, E. H., Seltzer, A. L., & Shlien, J. M. Pupil response of hetero- and homosexual males to pictures of men and women: A pilot study. *Journal of Abnormal Psychology*, 1965, 70, 165-168.

James, B. Case of homosexuality treated by aversion therapy. *British Medical Journal*, 1962, 1, 768-770.

Jones, E. *The life and work of Sigmund Freud*. London: Pelican Books, 1964.

Kimble, G. *Conditioning and learning*. London: Methuen, 1961.

Kinsey, A. C., Pomeroy, W. B., & Martin, C. E. *Sexual behaviour in the human male*. Philadelphia: Saunders, 1948.

Koenig, Karl P. The differentiation of hetero- or homo-erotic interests in the male: Some comments on articles by Brown and Freund. *Behaviour Research and Therapy*, 1965, 2, 305-307.

MacCulloch, M. J., Feldman, M. P., & Pinschof, J. M. The application of anticipatory avoidance learning to the treatment of homosexuality. II. Response latencies and pulse rate changes. *Behaviour Research and Therapy*, 1965, 3, 21-44.

Marks, I. M., & Gelder, M. G. Behaviour therapy. *British Journal of Psychiatry*, 1965, 111, 561-573.

Max, L. W. Breaking up a homosexual fixation by the conditional reaction technique: A case study. *Psychological Bulletin*, 1935, 32, 734.

McGuire, R. J., Carlisle, J. M., & Young, B. G. Sexual deviations as conditioned behaviour: A hypothesis. *Behaviour Research and Therapy*, 1965, 2, 185-190.

McGuire, R. J., & Vallance, M. Aversion therapy by electric shock: A simple technique. *British Medical Journal*, 1964, 1, 151-153.

Morgenstern, F. S., Pearce, J. F., & Rees, L. W. Predicting the outcome of behaviour therapy by psychological tests. *Behaviour Research and Therapy*, 1965, **2**, 191-200.

Osgood, C. E., Succi, G. J., & Tannenbaum, P. *The measurement of meaning.* Urbana: Univer. Illinois Press, 1957.

Oswald, I. Induction of illusory and hallucinatory voices with consideration of behaviour therapy. *Journal of Mental Science*, 1962, **108**, 195-212.

Oswald, I. (Letter) *British Journal of Psychiatry*, 1965, **111**, 470.

Rachman, S. Sexual disorders and behaviour therapy. *American Journal of Psychiatry*, 1961, **118**, 235-240.

Rachman, S. Aversion therapy: Chemical or electrical? *Behaviour Research and Therapy*, 1965, **2**, 289-299.

Raymond, M. J. Case of fetishism treated by aversion therapy. *British Medical Journal*, 1956, **2**, 854-857.

Raymond, M. J. Behaviour therapy for transvestism. *British Journal of Psychiatry*, 1965, **111**, 552-553.

Rubenstein, C. N. Psychotherapeutic aspects of male homosexuality. *British Journal of Medical Psychology*, 1958, **31**, 14-18.

Sandler, J. Masochism: An empirical analysis. *Psychological Bulletin*, 1964, **62**, 197-205.

Schneider, K. *Psychopathic personalities.* London: Cassell, 1959.

Shapiro, M. B. *Manual of the personal questionnaire.* London: Institute of Psychiatry, 1961.

Skinner, R. B. F. *Science and human behaviour.* New York: Macmillan, 1953.

Solomon, R. L., & Brush, E. S. Experimentally derived conceptions of anxiety and aversion. In M. R. Jones (Ed.), *Nebraska Symposium on Motivation: 1956.* Lincoln: Univer. Nebraska Press, 1956. Pp. 212-305.

Solomon, R. L., Kamin, L. J., & Wynne, L. C. Traumatic avoidance learning: The outcomes of several extinction procedures with dogs. *Journal of Abnormal and Social Psychology*, 1953, **48**, 291-302.

Solomon, R. C., & Wynne, L. C. Traumatic avoidance learning: Acquisition in normal dogs. *Psychological Monographs*, 1953, **67**(4 Whole No. 354).

Thorpe, J. G., & Schmidt, E. Therapeutic failure in a case of aversion therapy. *Behaviour Research and Therapy*, 1964, **1**, 293-296.

Thorpe, J. G., Schmidt, E., Brown, P. T., & Castell, D. Aversion-relief therapy: A new method for general application. *Behaviour Research and Therapy*, 1964, **2**, 71-82.

Thorpe, J. G., Schmidt, E., & Castell, D. A comparison of positive and negative (aversive) conditioning in the treatment of homosexuality. *Behaviour Research and Therapy*, 1963, **1**, 357-362.

Turner, Lucille H., & Solomon, R. C. Human traumatic avoidance learning: Theory and experiments on the operant-respondent distinction and failures to learn. *Psychological Monographs*, 1962, **76**(40 Whole No. 559).

Westwood, G. *A minority: Homosexuality in Great Britain.* London: Longmans, 1960.

Wolpe, J.   *Psychotherapy by reciprocal inhibition.* Stanford: Stanford Univer. Press, 1958.

Woodward, Mary.   The diagnosis and treatment of homosexual offenders. *British Journal of Delinquency,* 1958, 9, 44-59.

Index